D0225957

# AMERICAN
# IMMIGRATION
# & ETHNICITY

*A 20-Volume Series of Distinguished Essays*

EDITED BY
George E. Pozzetta

A Garland Series

# TITLES IN THE SERIES

VOLUME 4

# IMMIGRANTS ON THE LAND

*Agriculture, Rural Life, and Small Towns*

EDITED BY
George E. Pozzetta

GARLAND PUBLISHING, INC.
New York & London
1991

HN 57
I 45
1991

Introduction Copyright © 1991 by George E. Pozzetta
All Rights Reserved

Library of Congress Cataloging-in-Publication Data

Immigrants on the land: agriculture, rural life, and small towns/ edited by George E. Pozzetta
p. cm.—(American immigration and ethnicity; v. 4)
Includes bibliographical references.
ISBN 0-8240-7404-1 (alk. paper)
1. United States—Rural conditions. 2. Immigrants—United States.
3. Agriculture—Social aspects—United States. 4. United States—
Ethnic relations. I. Pozzetta, George E. II. Series.
HN57.I45 1991
307.72—dc20          90-49262

Printed on acid-free, 250-year-life paper
Manufactured in the United States of America

# INTRODUCTION

*Once I thought to write a history of the
immigrants in America. Then I discovered
that the immigrants were American history.*

Oscar Handlin,
The Uprooted (1951)

When it first appeared forty years ago, Oscar Handlin's startling observation
occasioned disbelieving reactions; today, changes in historical scholarship have
moved immigrants much closer to the central position posited by Handlin than
perhaps even he ever considered possible. Once relegated to the fringes of historical
investigation, immigrants now speak to the main themes of American history with
an eloquence that belies the lack of attention they received earlier. In large part this
is true because of what has happened to the field of immigration studies. Drawing
from the momentum of the new social history, with its perspective "from the bottom
up" and its insistence on exploring the experiences of ordinary people, the scholarly
inquiry into immigration and ethnicity has produced an astounding outpouring of
books and articles over the past several decades.

This rich and complex historical literature has drawn heavily from the methodologies and insights of the other social sciences and humanities, and the wider
investigation into immigration has criss-crossed disciplinary boundaries at a rapid
pace. The major journals of History, Political Science, Anthropology, Sociology,
and Geography, for example, regularly carry essays dealing with the immigrant
experience, and hundreds of articles appear in the more specialized local, regional,
and topical publications of each discipline. Simply finding the relevant essays on any
given topic within the general field has become a substantial challenge to researchers.
This collection, therefore, represents an effort to bring together a selected cross
section of the most significant articles on immigration and ethnicity. It is not
definitive, no compilation treating with such broad-ranging and dynamic topics can
ever be, but it is indicative of the scholarship that has shaped—and continues to
shape—these important subjects. The major themes and issues of the field are
discussed below, and each volume contains an individualized listing of supplemental
readings for additional guidance. Taken together the collected essays contained

*v*

APR 8 1991

within these volumes explore the manifold ways in which "immigrants were American history."

The liberation of immigration studies from its previously marginalized position has flowed from a number of critical interpretive and conceptual advances. One of the most important of these has been the effort to place immigration to America in the context of broader patterns of movement. Alerted by Frank Thistlethwaite's pioneering work, which showed how European migration to America was only part of a much larger transatlantic population and technological exchange, researchers now realize that an American-centered perspective is too restrictive to comprehend the full dimensions of migration. Immigrants from all quarters of the globe often envisioned America as only one destination among many, and then not necessarily a permanent one. Outmoded conceptions of "America fever" and exclusive one-way movement have given way to more complex understandings of the various manners by which America attracted and retained immigrants. The best works have taken into account the ability of multinational labor markets, economic cycles, transportation networks, as well as individual familial strategies, to propel immigrants outward in multi-step journeys.

At the same time as Thistlethwaite called for attention to large scale movements, he also urged that scholars be sensitive to the highly particularized nature of small scale migrations. Instead of studying "an undifferentiated mass movement" of individuals from loosely defined nation states, he insisted that immigrants be seen as emanating from "innumerable particular cells, districts, villages, towns, each with an individual reaction or lack of it to the pull of migration." This perspective necessarily involved linking the homeland with the new land in very precise ways, accounting for the specific influences of such factors as chain migration, kinship networks, travel agents, steamship companies, and repatriation flows, as well as the highly individualized economies of local regions.

Rudolph J. Vecoli's seminal work on Italian peasants in Chicago has pushed the study of premigration backgrounds in new directions. By pointing out that old world cultures survived the ocean crossing and significantly influenced adaptations in America, Vecoli stimulated a broad-based inquiry into the various ways in which immigrant traditions articulated with new world realities. The resulting scholarship has shifted the emphasis of investigation away from attention to the forces of assimilation and cultural break-down to those of cultural persistence and ethnic continuity. Immigrants did not succumb passively to pressures for conformity, but rather followed patterns of resistance and accommodation to the new land by which they turned themselves into something new—ethnic Americans. The ethnic culture that they created has proved to be a dynamic quality that has had influence into the third and fourth generation and beyond.

Such a viewpoint has led to different conceptions of assimilation and acculturation. Less often have scholars viewed these processes as easy, straight-line movements from "foreign" to "American." Nor have they continued to be captivated by
images of a vast "Melting Pot" at work that has thoroughly erased differences.
Rather, newer studies have posited a syncretic outcome in which both immigrants
and the mainstream society have been changed, and the overall process of immigrant
integration has emerged as more contingent and unpredictable than previously
imagined. Attempts to preserve immigrant languages, value structures, and tradition, for example, could not, and did not, result in the exact replication of old-world
ways. In a process of "invention" and "negotiation," immigrants adapted their
ethnic cultures to meet changing historical circumstances and to resolve the
problems of duality inherent in their straddling of Old and New Worlds. At the same
time, the host society was changing, or "reinventing," its own cultural traditions, in
part because of the need to accommodate the presence of diverse clusters of
immigrants.

Much of the most stimulating new research carried out along these lines has
adopted the urban immigrant community as its setting. Community studies have
not only examined the institutional structures of settlements, but have also typically
attempted to penetrate into the "interior worlds" of newcomers to discover the
mentalities, values, and life strategies that shaped immigrant destinies. Such
inquiries have probed deeply into the families, kin groups, and neighborhoods that
formed the core of immigrant districts. Their conclusions have revised older
conceptions of immigrant neighborhoods that emphasized the social pathology of
family breakdown, crime, and deviant behavior. Immigrant communities emerge as
remarkably vibrant and complex entities that provided effective cushions between
the often strange and harsh dominant society and newly arrived residents. They also
were far from the homogenous bodies so often envisioned by outsiders, but rather
were replete with various "subethnic" divisions based upon distinctions of class,
religion, ideology, and local culture. The process of immigrant adaptation to
America, therefore, was as often marked by tension and conflict *within* ethnic
concentrations as it was by friction between the group and the receiving society.

Internal divisions were also features of immigrant communities in rural and
small town locations. However, the distinctive physical and cultural contexts
encountered in such settings meant that immigrants usually experienced different
adjustment patterns from those of their urban-dwelling cousins. More isolated from
mainstream contact and better able to establish a local hegemony, immigrant
settlements in these settings often maintained traditional languages and folkways for
longer periods of time and with less change than was possible in city neighborhoods.
The ethnic culture that rural immigrants crafted correspondingly reflected these
particular conditions.

Eschewing a reliance on sources generated by the host society and utilizing a broad range of foreign language materials, researchers have demonstrated the existence of a remarkable range of civic, labor, religious, recreational, cultural, and fraternal organizations created by immigrants. Each of these played important roles in mediating the difficult adjustment to new-world conditions, and the presence of these institutions points to the need of recognizing immigrants as active agents in determining their own futures. To be sure, they were often circumscribed in their actions by poverty, nativism, discrimination, and limited skills, but they typically responded with imaginative adaptations within the limits imposed upon them. Many formal immigration institutions such as labor unions and mutual aid societies, for example, employed collective strategies to overcome the constraints restricting immigrant lives. Informal familial and kin networks often assisted these initiatives with adjustments of their own to ease the process of insertion into America.

The most fundamental institution of all, the immigrant family, reveals these patterns clearly. Families did not disintegrate under the pressures of immigration, urbanization, and industrialization, but rather proved to be remarkably flexible and resilent. Family structures and values responded to the multiple challenges imposed by migration—both in urban centers and rural spaces—by expanding their roles to accommodate a variety of new demands. Immigrant women, in their capacities as mothers and daughters, played critical functions in these transformations. Recent work, however, has attempted to move the study of immigrant women beyond the family context and to view women as historical actors who were able to influence the larger society in many different ways. The broader challenge has been to reveal how women confronted the multiple dilemmas posed by migration, and, more generally, to insert the issue of gender into the wider interpretations of the immigrant experience.

Since most immigrants entered America in quest of work, and after the 1860s usually industrial work, their relationship to the labor performed assumed a special importance. The vast majority arrived with preindustrial cultural values and confronted a complex urban-industrial economy. This encounter was a crucial factor not only in understanding the patterns of immigrant assimilation and social mobility, but also in comprehending the nature of American industrialization and the processes by which an American working class came into being. Through their collective labor as workers, their actions as union members, and their varied responses to exploitation and insecurity, immigrants were critical elements in the shaping of a modern American economy and labor force. Researchers are continuing to explore the exact nature of this dialectical relationship as they attempt to link immigrant values and expectations with the demands of the workplace.

Just as scholars have pursued the immigrant into the factory, home, and mutual aid society, so too have they entered the doors of immigrant churches in their investigations. The denominational pluralism that has characterized American society is a direct outgrowth of the nation's ethnic pluralism. Older works concentrated on examining the institutional histories of different immigrant religions and on the conflict engendered by such issues as parochial education and the formation of national parishes. More recently scholars have moved the study of America's religious tapestry out of church buildings and diocesan boardrooms and into the streets and neighborhoods. By examining the "popular piety" of immigrants, researchers hope to understand more clearly the ways in which new arrivals integrated the actual practice of religion into their everyday lives.

Investigators have already learned much about the relationships between ethnicity and political behavior. Indeed, one of the most surprising findings of the "new political history" was the discovery that ethnocultural considerations—often in the form of religious indentifications—were critical influences in shaping American voting patterns. Election outcomes in many parts of the nation often hinged on such factors. Indeed, perhaps no aspect of the American political arena has been immune to the force of ethnicity. Currently, researchers have been interested in determining how immigrants shaped a political culture of their own as they adapted to the American environment. Arriving from dissimilar backgrounds and frequently containing within their ranks followers of many different political ideologies, immigrants cannot be neatly classified into simple categories. Whether as supporters of urban machines, leftist critics of American capitalism, or as second and third generation politicians pushing group demands, immigrants and their progeny have been essential ingredients in the American political equation.

The American educational system similarly underwent profound transformation due to the immigrant presence. Many newcomers approached this powerful institution with ambivalent feelings since education in America offered both an opportunity for future progress and a danger to valued traditions. For their part, schools and school officials were forced to cope with unprecedented problems of space, curriculum, rules of discipline, attendance, and staffing. Immigrants ultimately found it necessary to judge the worth of education defined in new-world terms, both in relation to themselves and their children. They reacted in various ways, ranging from the formation of separate educational initiatives that sought to maintain cherished values to the avoidance of formal educational institutions altogether. One thing was certain: both sides of the equation were changed by the contact.

America responded to the immigrant presence in varied ways. During periods of crisis, the host society often reacted by promoting rigid programs of Americanization that sought to strip away foreign customs and values. Research has shown that even programs of assistance and outreach, such as those offered by settlement houses and philanthropic agencies, often contained strong doses of social control. Immigrants were not unaware of these elements and frequently reacted to these

and such programs as bilingual education and affirmative action have engendered sharp public division. The present collection of essays, therefore, should be seen as providing the first installment of an important research agenda that needs to be open-ended in scope, responsive to new methodologies and interpretations, and cognizant of its relevance to contemporary American society.

The editor wishes to thank Leonard Dinnerstein, Victor Greene, Robert Singerman, Jeffrey Adler, Robert Zieger, and especially Rudolph Vecoli and Donna Gabaccia, for their helpful advice on this project.

GEORGE E. POZZETTA

# SUPPLEMENTAL READING

Tomas Almaguer, "Racial Discrimination and Class Conflict in Capitalist Agriculture: The Oxnard Sugar Beet Worker's Strike of 1903," *Labor History*, 25 (Summer 1984), 325–350.

Mie Liang Bickner, "The Forgotten Minority: Asian American Women," *Amerasia Journal*, 11 (Spring 1974), 1–17.

Melvin Dubofsky, "Organized Labor and the Immigrant in New York City, 1900–1918," *Labor History*, 2 (1961), 182–201.

Melvin Dubofsky, "Success and Failure of Socialism in New York City, 1900–1918," *Labor History*, 9 (Fall 1968), 361–375.

Charlotte Erickson, "Emigration from the British Isles to the U.S.A. in 1831," *Population Studies*, 35 (1981), 175–197.

Frances H. Early, "The French Canadian Family Economy and Standard-of-Living in Lowell, Massachusetts, 1870," *Journal of Family History*, 7 (Summer 1982), 180–199.

Howard M. Gitelman, "No Irish Need Apply: Patterns of and Response to Ethnic Discrimination in the Labor Market," *Labor History*, 14 (1973), 56–68.

Philip Gleason, "Confusion Compounded: The Melting Pot in the 1960s and 1970s," *Ethnicity*, 6 (1979), 10–20.

Philip Gleason, "The Melting Pot: Symbol of Fusion or Confusion?" *American Quarterly* SVI (Spring 1974), 20–46.

Bruce C. Levine, "Immigrant Workers, 'Equal Rights,' and Antislavery: The Germans of Newark, New Jersey," *Labor History*, 25 (Winter 1984), 26–52.

Hubert Perrier, "The Socialists and the Working Class in New York, 1890–1896," *Labor History*, 22, No. 4 (Fall 1981), 485–511.

Thaddeus Radzialowski, "Immigrant Nationalism and Feminism: Glos Polek and the Polish Women's Alliance in America, 1898–1980," *Review Journal of Philosophy and Social Science*, 2 (1972), 183–203.

Robert Swierenga, "Dutch Immigrant Demography, 1820–1880," *Journal of Family History*, 5 (Winter 1980), 390–405.

Peter Temin, "Labor Scarcity in America," *Journal of Interdisciplinary History*, 1 (Winter 1971), 251–264.

# CONTENTS

# The End of Immigration to the Cotton Fields

### By Robert L. Brandfon

In the pre-Civil War period few immigrants to the United States settled in the South. Post-Reconstruction leaders urged the promotion of immigration, which they considered essential, if the southern states were to match northern industrial achievement.[1] But these attempts to attract a larger share of the immigrant tide in the latter part of the nineteenth and early years of the twentieth centuries are well-known chronicles of failure,[2] reflecting an inability to rise above the South's dominant agriculturism. As a result, the South remained a second-class section, geared to the decisions of northeastern capitalism.

Xenophobia has been given as the chief reason for the defeat of southern efforts to attract immigrants.[3] Though playing its part, this reason alone is contradictory: why should the South, with an insignificant minority of foreigners echo the sentiments of northern immigration restrictionists? More fundamental reasons for the

[1] See *Proceedings of the Southern Interstate Immigration Convention, convened in Montgomery, Alabama, December 12-13, 1888* (Dallas, 1888); *Proceedings of the First Annual Session of the Southern Immigration Association of America* (Nashville, 1884); John C. C. Newton, *The New South* (Baltimore, 1887), pamphlet, Widener Library, Harvard University; Atticus G. Haygood, *The New South: Gratitude, Amendment, Hope* (Oxford, Ga., 1880), pamphlet, *ibid.*; John C. Reed, *The Old and New South* (New York, 1876), pamphlet, *ibid.*; Paul H. Buck, *The Road to Reunion* (Boston, 1937), 151-52.

[2] Walter L. Fleming, "Immigration to the Southern States," *Political Science Quarterly* (New York), XX (June, 1905), 276-97; Bert J. Lowenberg, "Efforts of the South to Encourage Immigration, 1865-1900," *South Atlantic Quarterly* (Durham), XXXIII (October, 1934), 363-85; Rowland T. Berthoff, "Southern Attitudes Toward Immigration, 1865-1914," *Journal of Southern History* (Baton Rouge), XVII (August, 1951), 328-60; C. Vann Woodward, *Origins of the New South, 1877-1913* (Baton Rouge, 1951), 297-99.

[3] John Higham, *Strangers in the Land: Patterns of American Nativism, 1860-1925* (New Brunswick, 1955), 169-71; Berthoff, "Southern Attitudes Toward Immigration," *Journal of Southern History*, XVII, 360.

defeat of southern efforts lay in confusion over ends. Post-Reconstruction leadership based its calls for increased immigration to the South on the illusory belief that factories would follow labor. By the dawn of the twentieth century, however, the South was far from becoming an industrial section. Compared with the northeast, the number of factories in the South was negligible. There was no real need for an industrial labor force. The remaining avenue for immigration, one closer to the agrarian nature of the southern economy, was farming. There was, however, little room for an influx of immigrant yeoman farmers. On the contrary, the southern economy already suffered from an over-abundance of yeomen increasingly sinking into tenancy on overcropped soils. Immigration, therefore, might be advantageous only if it could be used as a cheap agricultural labor force. This involved the channelling of white immigrants not to their own plots of land as yeomen but as laborers to the large and fertile plantations already flooded with the older source of southern labor—the Negro.

By the end of the nineteenth century, the Yazoo-Mississippi Delta, lying in the center of the rich flood plain of the lower Mississippi Valley, was a leading plantation area where the introduction of immigrant labor would further benefit its cotton-dominated economy. The extraordinarily rich soils of this area, reclaimed as a result of the post-Civil War leveeing of the Mississippi River, had created a new planter class specializing in the large-scale production of cotton, possessing a highly developed and nationally integrated rail network, and utilizing the highest concentration of Negro labor in the nation. The ambitions of the Yazoo area planters encompassed the full cultivation of the Delta's four million acres, of which fully two thirds remained in virgin wilderness in 1900.[4] Latent desires to expand their operations were brought to life by the rising

[4] A study of tenant systems of farming in the Yazoo-Mississippi Delta in 1913 (where 92 per cent of all farming was done by tenants and where 95.4 per cent of the tenants were Negro) revealed that the landlord was assured of a 6 to 7 per cent return on his investment when his land was operated by cash renters. Where the land was operated by share croppers the landlord sometimes received more than 21 per cent—the average return on share-cropped land was 13.6 per cent. Ernest A. Boeger and Emanuel A. Goldenweiser, *A Study of the Tenant Systems of Farming in the Yazoo-Mississippi Delta* (U.S. Department of Agriculture, Bulletin No. 337, Washington, 1916), 1-3, 7; Lee J. Langley, "Italians in the Cotton Fields," *Manufacturers' Record* (Baltimore), XLV (April 7, 1904), 250; Allen Gray to C. B. Phipard, June 29, 1904, Stuyvesant Fish Letters (Illinois Central Railroad Archives, Newberry Library, Chicago); Charles Scott to Stuyvesant Fish, April 5, 1902, *ibid.*; Edmondo Mayor des Planches, *Attraverso Gli Stati Uniti* (Torino, 1913), 134.

trend of cotton prices beginning in 1899, when a revived demand for more raw cotton to feed the world's burgeoning numbers of spindles lifted cotton prices out of a decade of depression.[5]

According to the planters, only the insufficiency of labor stood in the way of capitalizing fully on their opportunities.[6] The demands for more Negro labor for the Delta's cotton fields were meeting stiff competition from other areas of the South's economy. Cotton mills, phosphate mines, double tracking of railroads, cotton oil mills, saw mills, and the increased building of roads and levees were drawing heavily upon the available labor supply and retarding the normal flow of Negro labor westward from the worn-out lands of the seaboard states.[7] The new values placed upon Negro labor led these older areas to enforce laws preventing Delta labor agents from "kidnapping" their Negroes.[8] To make matters worse, James K. Vardaman's demagogic campaign for the governorship of Mississippi during the summer of 1903 inflamed the delicate state of racial tensions. The resultant intimidation put Delta Negroes in fear for their very lives. They were thus particularly susceptible to inducements that might be made to them by labor agents from the western South —Texas, Indian Territory (Oklahoma), Arkansas, and Missouri.[9]

Greater than the complaints over inadequate numbers was planter frustration and disgust with Negro labor in general. Despite the confining characteristics of tenant forms and the relatively high agricultural day wages (as much as seventy-five cents),[10] planters were unable to maintain a stable Negro agricultural labor force. Why, they asked, were Delta Negroes so poverty-stricken and in a

[5] New York Cotton Exchange, *Market Reports, 1879-1927*; James L. Watkins, *Production and Price of Cotton for One Hundred Years* (U.S. Department of Agriculture, Miscellaneous Series Bulletin No. 9, Washington, 1895), 18-20; *Lea's Cotton Book and Statistical History of the American Cotton Crop* (New Orleans, 1914), 33; *Manufacturers' Record*, XLIV (July 23, 1903), 2; XLV (May 12, 1904), 363-66, 370-73.
[6] Langley, "Italians in the Cotton Fields," *Manufacturers' Record*, XLV, 250; Scott to Fish, December 3, 1903, Fish Letters.
[7] *Manufacturers' Record*, XLV (June 2, 1904), 437; Woodward, *Origins of the New South*, 117-40; Berthoff, "Southern Attitudes Toward Immigration," *Journal of Southern History*, XVII, 329, 335.
[8] Edward P. Skene to J. C. Welling, December 17, 1904, Fish Letters.
[9] Edward Atkinson to Fish, September 23, 1903, *ibid.*; Albert D. Kirwan, *Revolt of the Rednecks* (Lexington, 1951), 145-48; Woodward, *Origins of the New South*, 351.
[10] E. L. Langsford and B. H. Thibodeaux, *Plantation Organization and Operation in the Yazoo-Mississippi Delta Area* (U.S. Department of Agriculture, Technical Bulletin 682, Washington, 1939), 5; Allen Gray to C. B. Phipard, June 29, 1904, Fish Letters.

3

state of peonage while working the most fertile soil in America? The tenant system, they argued, offered the unskilled generous opportunities. During his apprenticeship as a cropper, it protected him from the winds of destitution, hard times, and occasional crop failures. With the exercise of thrift and the application of skills employed on bounteous soils, planters reasoned, a man could easily rise on the graduated scale from cropper to renter to outright landowner. But, as Alfred H. Stone of Greenville explained, the Negro's innate laziness, inefficiency, and lack of thrift had squandered the advantages offered to him. Stone and other Delta planters complained bitterly of the Negro's reaction to growing indebtedness. He literally walked away from it, shiftlessly drifting from one plantation to another or to new adventures in one of the Delta towns.[11]

The alternative to Negro labor was the large-scale utilization of immigrants pouring into the United States at the end of the nineteenth century and continuing in increasing numbers during the first decade of the twentieth century. This new supply of cheap labor had its source in southern and eastern Europe, especially in Italy. In 1898-1899, the number of Italians entering the United States totalled 77,419. The following year this figure had increased to 100,135, and the year after that it reached a high of 135,996.[12] Deprived of the large quantities of Negroes they wished for and thoroughly dissatisfied with the Negro labor they already possessed, the Delta planters indulged in wild hopes of tapping this rich source of immigrant white labor.

Years before this great human flood made its way to the United States, a tiny trickle of Italian immigrant labor appeared in the Yazoo Delta. In the early 1880's *padrones* had been active in bringing laborers from northern cities to work on the Mississippi levees.[13] Some of these laborers might have formed the nucleus of the Delta's first Italian agricultural settlement at Friar's Point (Coahoma County) in 1885.

[11] Alfred H. Stone, *Studies in the American Race Problem* (New York, 1908), 102, 115-23; David L. Cohn, *Where I Was Born and Raised* (Boston, 1948), 121-41; William A. Percy, *Lanterns on the Levee* (New York, 1941), 282-84; Ray S. Baker, *Following the Color Line* (New York, 1908), 57-58, 77; clipping from Memphis *Commercial* (n.d.) enclosed in letter from W. G. Yerger to Fish, December 2, 1893, Fish Letters; Scott to Fish, January 6, 1905, *ibid.*; Scott to John C. Burrus, January 29, 1906, Burrus Papers (Mississippi Department of Archives and History, Jackson); Langley, "Italians in the Cotton Fields," *Manufacturers' Record*, XLV, 250.

[12] U.S. Commissioner-General of Immigration, *Annual Reports*, 1889-1901.

[13] New York *Tribune*, January 2, 1884.

The successful use of these Italians at Friar's Point stimulated planter dissatisfaction with Negro labor. Planters were now able to contrast the efficiency and value of the two types. The facts of comparison, the planters believed, were self-evident, and were published by Alfred H. Stone in 1893. The Italians at Friar's Point, he maintained, had made full use of the opportunities presented to them by the tenancy labor system. Quickly and without indebtedness they had risen from mere agricultural laborers to self-sufficient renters. "Contrast this," he added, "with the appearance of indolence, squalor, thriftlessness and decay which characterizes the house of the average negro tenant. . . . The secret of the difference in favor of the Italian lay in the fact that he had laid away from the previous year everything he needed, while, as he always had done and will do, the negro raised nothing, but relied on the planter to support him. The one did as much work as was possible, the other did only what constant watching compelled him to do."[14]

Addressing the American Economic Association in 1905 Stone, himself a leading Delta planter by that time, returned to his earlier theme. The southern Negro as a cotton laborer and renter was a failure, he emphatically declared, especially when competing with white labor. Large-scale Italian immigration into the Delta, he predicted, would result in the eventual displacement of the Negro by the white in the cotton fields. He inferred that this was a revolutionary belief, for it had always been taken as an article of faith that the Negro was both supreme and essential in cotton growing.[15]

By 1905, Stone's beliefs had gained widespread support among Delta planters. This was due to the good fortune (after a faltering start) of the Italian colony of Sunnyside, Arkansas. In 1895, Austin Corbin, New York banker, railroad organizer, and speculator in southern lands, embarked upon a scheme to settle his vast Arkansas estates with one hundred Italian families. In this endeavor, he had the support of Prince Ruspoli, the mayor of Rome. Lying on the western bank of the Mississippi River opposite Greenville, Corbin's lands were, for the most part, low-lying, undrained swamps, reeking of yellow fever and malaria. These unfavorable conditions, combined with the depressed cotton prices of 1895, defeated the efforts

[14] Clipping from Memphis *Commercial* (n.d.), enclosed in letter from W. G. Yerger to Fish, December 2, 1893, Fish Letters; U.S. Immigration Commission Reports, *Immigrants in Industries, Senate Docs.,* 61 Cong., 2 Sess., No. 633, Part 24, *Recent Immigrants in Agriculture,* Vol. I (Serial 5682), 308.
[15] Stone, *Studies in the American Race Problem,* 188-208.

of the Italian colonists, who were inexperienced in cotton growing and alien to the dangers of the Mississippi's alluvial lands. In 1897, many of them, under the valiant leadership of their priest, Father Pietro Bandini, moved in a band to the western part of Arkansas to found the village of Tontitown.

These disastrous beginnings, however, did not reflect the final outcome of Corbin's enterprise. In the first two years a good portion of the lands had been cleared and drained. Upon Corbin's death in 1897, the executors of his estate leased the Sunnyside lands to O. B. Crittenden and Company of Greenville, Mississippi. Crittenden and his partner, Leroy Percy, had long experience in the precarious operation of cotton growing. Their skills in plantation organization and management proved decisive in the eventual success of the Italian colony. The remaining Italians were encouraged to stay at Sunnyside and urged to send for their relatives and friends in Italy. Experienced Negro tenants were introduced on a segregated basis among Italian tenants. Despite the disappointment of rock bottom cotton prices in 1898,[16] the experiment survived. In following years higher cotton prices and the introduction of efficient methods of production and sale transformed the Sunnyside plantation into a model colony for Italian agricultural labor.[17]

Under Percy-Crittenden management a simple crop rent system was adopted. Each tenant was charged an annual seven-dollar-an-acre rental. Household supplies as well as doctor's care were furnished by the plantation store and charged to the tenant's account. When the crop was harvested, Percy and Crittenden bought the entire crop, deducting rents and amounts owed to the company. The difference went to the tenant whose margin of profit was determined by his ability to reduce costs to a minimum. In this, the Italians were very successful, devoting as much land as possible to cotton but cultivat-

[16] On October 15, 1898, cotton on the New York Cotton Exchange hit the lowest point in its history, dropping to 4 and 15/16 (middling inch). That year marked the absolute low point in the history of American cotton prices. U.S. Department of Commerce and Labor, Bureau of Census Bulletin 134, *Cotton Production and Distribution* (Washington, 1916), 51.

[17] For the Sunnyside operation see: "Reports of the Immigration Commission," Part 24, Vol. I, 319-37; Langley, "Italians in the Cotton Fields," *Manufacturers' Record*, XLV, 250; Alfred H. Stone, "Italian Cotton-Growers in Arkansas," *Review of Reviews* (New York), XXXV (February, 1907), 209-13; Stone, *Studies in the American Race Problem*, Chs. 3-5 and *passim*; *Review of Reviews*, XXXIV (September, 1906), 361-62; Mayor des Planches, *Attraverso Gli Stati Uniti*, 137-45; Robert F. Foerster, *The Italian Emigration of Our Times* (Cambridge, 1919), 368; Fleming, "Immigration to the Southern States," *Political Science Quarterly*, XX, 293.

ing small truck gardens to cut down purchases at the plantation store. This practice was in accord with their Old World backgrounds. Italians were at home in the Delta's share crop or share tenant system. These and other variations of tenancy had existed for centuries in the ungenerous lands of central and southern Italy. Absentee landlordism and the intense cultivation of minute plots of land by an agricultural proletariat characterized Italian farming. To every peasant in Italy each foot of earth was precious; to extract the most from it meant survival in life's precarious struggle. These values were transferred and applied to the fertile and vast acreages of the lower Mississippi Valley.[18] The result was an illusory belief on the part of the planters in the innate superiority of the Italian because he possessed what the Negro lacked—frugality and zealousness.

Italian tenants contrasted sharply with Negro tenants on the same plantation. In 1903, there were fifty-two Italian families on the Sunnyside plantation. Percy and Crittenden claimed to have paid them a total of $32,000 over and above their rents and expenses. In other years, Italian families were reported to have saved from $350 to $1,400 a year. As far as plantation finances were concerned, Percy estimated that for every dollar a Negro made on a crop the Italian made five. Investigating the 4,000-acre Sunnyside plantation in 1909, the Federal Immigration Commission substantiated planter beliefs about the inferiority of the Negro when placed in direct competition with white labor. Under almost identical conditions, the commissioners reported, the Italians raised nearly forty per cent more cotton per working hand than the Negro. In value produced per working hand, the Italian exceeded the Negro by eighty-five per cent. The Commission concluded, "Every comparison that can be drawn points clearly to the superiority of the Italian."[19]

The experience at Sunnyside convinced the planters that Italian immigration would eventually relieve their reliance upon the Negro. "If the immigration of these people is encouraged," declared Leroy Percy in 1904, "they will gradually take the place of the negro without there being any such violent change as to paralyze for a gener-

[18] Joseph E. Haven and Alan T. Hurd, "'Share' System in Italian Agriculture," *Monthly Labor Review* (Washington), XXVII (July, 1928), 31-32; Carl T. Schmidt, *The Plough and the Sword* (New York, 1938), 7-13; Foerster, *The Italian Emigration of Our Times*, 51-105.
[19] *Recent Immigrants in Agriculture*, I, 326; James F. Merry to J. M. Dickinson, March 28, 1905, Fish Letters; Langley, "Italians in the Cotton Fields," *Manufacturers' Record*, XLV, 250; Foerster, *The Italian Emigration of Our Times*, 368.

ation the prosperity of the country."[20] The replacement of the Negro in the cotton fields by a more efficient labor force would do more for the planters than increase their profits. It would alleviate their anxieties of having such a heavy concentration of Negroes surrounding them. Apprehensions for "the conservation of our institutions" echoed earlier fears voiced during the 1880's when the Delta was becoming the nation's blackest belt.[21]

At the turn of the century both racial and economic solutions seemed possible. In the 1880's planter appeals for white immigration had fallen on the skeptical ears of Mississippi's legislators. During the latter part of that decade and thereafter, the political situation had turned skepticism into hostility toward both the planters and their schemes for mixing the blood of Mississippi with foreign immigrants. The planters had then turned to securing the powerful support of the Illinois Central Railroad whose own best interests, it was thought, favored the promotion of immigration into the Delta.

During the 1870's the Illinois Central Railroad had gambled its future upon the revival of the southern economy,[22] in particular the port of New Orleans. Taking advantage of depression conditions following 1873, railroad officials succeeded in purchasing the bankrupt remains of disconnected north-south lines in central Mississippi, western Tennessee, and Kentucky. By this action they completed the first through line from New Orleans to Chicago. Profits from the southern trade exceeded all expectations. Thereafter, the overriding policy of the Illinois Central was to maintain its pre-empted monopoly of the north-south trade routes to and from New Orleans as the "Main Line of Mid-America." In accordance with this policy, and under the urging of its vigorous young president, Stuyvesant Fish, the Illinois Central purchased the competing Louisville, New

[20] Langley, "Italians in the Cotton Fields," *Manufacturers' Record*, XLV, 250.
[21] Statement by William L. Nugent of Jackson, Mississippi, in "Joint Committee to Investigate Public Offices," *Mississippi House Journal, 1886* (Jackson, 1886), 576.
[22] Certain aspects of the Illinois Central Railroad's history have been written: e.g., Paul W. Gates, *The Illinois Central Railroad and its Colonization Work* (Cambridge, 1934); Edwin S. S. Sunderland, *Illinois Central Railroad, Main Line of Mid-America; The Simplification of its Debt Structure, 1938-1952* (New York, 1952). A general account from 1851-1950 is Carlton J. Corliss, *Main Line of Mid-America, the Story of the Illinois Central* (New York, 1950). The most satisfactory account, however, of the Illinois Central Railroad's activities in the South can only be derived from its vast archives (from 1851-1906) deposited in the Newberry Library, Chicago. All statements concerning the Illinois Central's activities have been derived wholly from these sources.

Orleans and Texas Railroad in 1892. This addition to the strength of the Illinois Central's hold upon the trade of the lower Mississippi Valley had as its termini the cities of Memphis and New Orleans and ran through the length of the rich bottom lands of the Yazoo Delta. Becoming a major division of the Illinois Central it was more appropriately renamed the Yazoo and Mississippi Valley Railroad.

Included in the purchase of the Louisville, New Orleans and Texas Railroad were 546,628 acres of valuable Delta real estate. Following a pattern of land sales used successfully for its huge body of Illinois lands during the 1850's, the Illinois Central embarked upon a vain if energetic attempt to sell these lands to colonies of northern European immigrants and discontented northern farmers. Delta planters and Illinois Central railroad officials clashed, however, over the ulterior ends of immigration policy. The railroad's objective was to fill the Delta lands with yeoman farmers with a view to increasing freight volume. The planters, on the other hand, sought immigration as a source of cheap labor, not as a means of creating more landowners. Appeals to Stuyvesant Fish for his support of the planters' position first met with a polite but negative reply. "Without pretending to any familiarity with the subject," wrote the president of the Illinois Central in 1893, "the pressing need seems to me to be to encourage the black labor which you have, to habits of frugality and thrift, and to protect them from the 'sharks' of one kind and another who prey upon their simplicity and childlike appetites for sweets and gewgaws."[23]

Disappointment arising from the failure of the railroad to achieve the ends of its land sale policy did not dim increasing satisfaction over the value of the Delta's freight and passenger earnings. Yazoo Delta trade took on added importance in the railroad's balance sheet. The passing years thus drew tighter the common economic bonds between railroad and planter and eroded some of the hard-shelled self-interest of railroad officialdom. In addition, the winning charm of leading Delta planters supplemented economic bonds with personal class ties. The conscious ideals of the Delta's new gentleman planter class—wealth, honesty, paternalism, and moral integrity—were shared by higher officials of the railroad and were a refreshing relief to the base personalities of "bottom rail" southern politicians. Charles Scott of Rosedale, owner of 30,000 acres,

[23] Fish to W. G. Yerger, November 16, 1893, Fish Letters.

was a leading figure of this new Delta planter society. An eminent Delta lawyer, banker, railroad promoter, cotton planter, sportsman, philanthropist, and personal friend of important public figures, Scott skillfully combined the appeals of the southern romantic past with the successful business virtues of the twentieth century.[24] For this he was rewarded with the sufferance of northern high society.

Scott's friendship with the president of the Illinois Central Railroad allowed for a more intimate presentation of the planters' labor problem. Writing to Fish at the end of 1903, Scott suggested a personal conference between them. In the meantime, he reminded Fish that a large part of the Delta was still in forest, and the best interest of both railroad and planters was to bring this valuable land under the plow. "At present," he claimed, "we are without sufficient labor to work that which is already cleared. The fact is that on many of the larger plantations a considerable quantity of land lies fallow each year for the want of labor sufficient to work it. These conditions grow more and more acute each year, and as we can no longer bring negroes from Georgia, Alabama and the Carolines, [sic] we must turn elsewhere for a new supply of farm laborers." He concluded by asking the railroad's help in securing Negroes from Puerto Rico, or white laborers from Portugal and Italy.[25]

By the time of Scott's request, a number of circumstances had modified the railroad's earlier policy of getting more Delta lands under the plow. Virtually all of the railroad's Delta lands had been sold. Moreover, the Illinois Central monopolized the Delta's rail network. Yazoo and Mississippi Valley Railroad gross profits were very satisfactory, but operating costs were increasing yearly. Further expenses incurred by promoting immigration would eat up the margin of net profit.

All these considerations boiled down to the question of whether an increase in cotton freight would warrant additional expenditures by the railroad. In his reply to his friend Charles Scott, Fish gently tried to make this clear:

What I want to present to you, in all candor, is that the success of the railroad is no longer dependent upon bringing in increased acreage, from year to year, under the plow, however much we might like to see this happen. What I want you to understand is that it is hardly the function of

[24] The National Cyclopaedia of American Biography (New York), XVII (1920), 231; Wirt A. Williams (ed.), History of Bolivar County, Mississippi (Jackson, 1948), 507-11 and passim.
[25] Scott to Fish, December 3, 1903, Fish Letters.

the railroad to furnish agricultural labor to till the fields in the country through which it runs, and in the management of a railroad we must be selfish to a certain extent.[26]

He hastened to assure Scott and other Delta planters that the Illinois Central had not abandoned them. Rather, the railroad's interest "was necessarily less than it had been. . . ." Agricultural products, he explained, no longer formed a very large percentage of railroad freight. The Illinois Central was profiting greatly from a vigorously developing southern lumber trade. Lumber and coal had replaced cotton as the chief item of freight. Cotton freight on the Illinois Central and Yazoo and Mississippi Valley railroads did not yield "anything like one-half as much gross revenue as coal . . . and barely one-third as much as lumber. Add to this that there has been in recent years a very large increase in the revenue from passengers, and a greater increase in the revenue from that source than in the revenue from freight, and you will see why it is we have not at this moment the same motive of direct self-interest to import labor into the Delta that we had when offering lands for sale, and when the Y&MV co. was dependent almost entirely upon cotton for revenue."[27]

Within six months Fish had changed his mind. Repeated counterarguments from Scott denying the belief that coal and lumber-freight could be isolated from the economy of the Delta were supported by other high officials of the Illinois Central. Edward P. Skene of the land department and James F. Merry, assistant general passenger agent, both tried to convince Fish that the introduction of immigrant labor, particularly Italians, would in the long run prove beneficial to the railroad. Philanthropy joined in the pressure. The noted New England economist Edward Atkinson, another personal friend and adviser, thought it urgent that the railroad help to move Italians from Boston's deplorable slums to the railroad's southern lands in the Yazoo Delta.[28]

The most influential source of pressure, however, came from southern business circles. For them, 1903 was more than just another boom year. The South, they believed, was at last on the threshold of a prolonged era of happy prosperity. The cotton situation

[26] Fish to Scott, December 9, 1903, *ibid.*
[27] Fish to Scott, December 21, 1903, *ibid.*
[28] Scott to Fish, December 17 and 30, 1903; Skene to Welling, December 17, 1904, *ibid.* James F. Merry sent numerous articles to Fish about Italians in the Delta. Merry to Fish, April 13, 1904, Fish Letters; Fish to Merry, April 14, 1904, *ibid.*; Edward Atkinson to Fish, December 17, 1903; Fish to Atkinson, December 21, 1903, *ibid.*

was especially encouraging. A short supply was riding a rising demand curve. The resultant rise in prices would provide the opportunity to expand cotton cultivation. In turn, the opening up of new agricultural areas would mean an enlarged market for consumer goods and would lead to increased demands for new southern industries and manufactures. In the expansion of the cotton fields, so reasoned southern businessmen, lay the South's hope for keeping pace with the advancing industrialization of the rest of the nation. In this manner was "King Cotton" resurrected.

The editor of the *Manufacturers' Record*, speaking on behalf of southern business circles, challenged the railroads to support the planters' vital search for more labor:

> Are the railroad people interested in the development of the South and Southwest equal to such an occasion? Are they broad enough to grasp the opportunity? These are the questions which they must meet. If they let this opportunity pass because of any pretense of financial inability to carry out this work on a scale many times larger than they have ever considered theretofore, they will fail to utilize the one great chance—in fact, the only great chance which has come to the South in a century—for attracting a heavy movement of population southward.[29]

Once committed, Fish responded with characteristic decisiveness. He directed James F. Merry to entertain suggestions from the Delta's three leading planters, Leroy Percy, John M. Parker, and Charles Scott. Assuring Scott of his personal support in securing Italian labor for the Delta, Fish promised to "leave no stone unturned in that direction." And to Frank P. Sargent, United States Commissioner General of Immigration, he wrote, "If at any time you have good farm laborers coming in at Ellis Island, whom you do not know what to do with, I would be very glad to take the matter up with you, not only to supply Mr. Scott's wants, but those of others."[30]

His efforts culminated in the visit of the Italian ambassador to the lower Mississippi Valley as guest of the Illinois Central and other railroads. In the winter of 1904-1905, Baron Edmondo Mayor des Planches was invited to inspect personally the numerous Italian col-

---

[29] *Manufacturers' Record*, XLV (June 2, 1904), 438.
[30] Fish to Frank P. Sargent, January 3, 1905; Fish to Scott, January 3, 1905; Fish to Merry, May 5, 1904, Fish Letters. Scott was also interested in getting Chinese and Japanese labor. Scott to Fish, January 6, 1905; Fish to J. A. Harahan, January 10, 1905; Scott to Dickinson, February 1, 1905, *ibid.*

onies scattered throughout the South. By this method, planters and southern industrial interests hoped to assure the ambassador that his countrymen were receiving favorable treatment. The end result of the visit, it was hoped, would be Mayor des Planches' decisive support in influencing the immigration of Italians to the southern states.[31]

Mayor des Planches had already acquainted himself with the condition of Italian immigrants in other parts of the United States. In the summer of 1904, he had been authorized by his government to make a coast to coast inspection tour of Italian immigrant communities. This first trip took him through the cities of San Francisco, Los Angeles, El Paso, San Antonio, Houston, and New Orleans. His second trip, to be taken in the spring of 1905, would provide him with an intensive examination of conditions in agricultural communities of Texas, Louisiana, Mississippi, and Arkansas.

As a guest of the Southern Railroad in April, 1905, Mayor des Planches travelled westward across the breadth of the Yazoo Delta from Greenwood to Greenville, where he crossed the Mississippi to make a hasty inspection of Crittenden and Percy's Sunnyside plantation. After visiting numerous settlements on the western side of the Mississippi River, the ambassador was transported to St. Louis where he was greeted by several officials of the Illinois Central Railroad. From St. Louis he was conducted southward on the Illinois Central line to Memphis, and was transferred to the Yazoo and Mississippi Valley Railroad.

Upon his arrival in the Yazoo Delta, he was never lacking for company. His official host was Jacob M. Dickinson, former assistant attorney general of the United States and then general counsel for the Illinois Central Railroad. But others joined and left him throughout the trip. From Clarksdale to Rosedale the ambassador was accompanied by Charles Scott, eager to make Mayor des Planches' acquaintance before setting sail for Italy where he hoped to interest Italian emigration officials in channelling Italian peasants to his own Delta plantations. At Greenville, the ambassador was joined by Leroy Percy and William R. Campbell. Leaving the Delta, he was escorted to Jackson and introduced to Governor James K. Vardaman,

[31] Fish to Dickinson, April 10, 1905; Dickinson to Fish, April 10, 1905, *ibid.*; Frederick B. Stevenson, "Italian Colonies in the United States; A New Solution for the Immigration Problem," *Public Opinion* (New York), XXXIX (September 30, 1906), 456.

Thomas C. Catchings, and other influential lawyers and politicians.[32]

For the moment, at least, the ambassador's trip seemed to justify the railroad's invitation. Dickinson, instrumental in urging the undertaking upon Stuyvesant Fish, was particularly satisfied. "He made a delightful impression upon everyone he met." wrote Dickinson to his superiors. "I believe that the Company acted wisely in inaugurating and carrying out this trip, and that it will bear substantial results."[33] The ambassador had done his part well by urging the Italians living along the Illinois Central rail line to become American citizens, property owners, and home builders. Moreover, he had reported favorably on conditions in Mississippi and Louisiana to the Italian Bureau of Emigration in Rome.[34]

Optimism was short-lived. Even as Mayor des Planches was visiting New Orleans in May, 1905, yellow fever was appearing in the Crescent City and was in full rage by August. The cause of this disease had been isolated a few years earlier, and after strenuous and cooperative efforts on the part of its citizenry, New Orleans was enabled to contain it by the fall of 1905. For the first time in its long history this disastrous plague had not been allowed to run its deadly course. For Delta planters, however, New Orleans' triumph had been a pyrrhic victory: Italian immigration was discouraged. Once again, the Delta, though relatively untouched by this latest epidemic, was haunted by its age-old reputation as an unhealthy disease-ridden swamp.[35] All the efforts devoted to the successful visit of the Italian ambassador had been undone.

In Rome, Charles Scott was a discouraged witness to the fears engendered among Italian emigration officials. During the early summer of 1905, Scott, armed with introductions from Mayor des Planches, visited the Italian commissioner general of emigration in Rome. He believed he had convinced the commissioner of the wisdom of settling Italians on southern farms and away from the

[32] Mayor des Planches, *Attraverso Gli Stati Uniti*, 129-36, 250-56; Dickinson to Signor E. Mayor des Planches, March 28, 1905, Fish Letters; Fish to Dickinson, April 25, 1905; Fish to Henry White, August 14, 1905, *ibid*. Mayor des Planches wrote several letters of introduction for Scott to leading Italian emigration officials. Mayor des Planches to Dickinson, July 19, 1905, *ibid*.
[33] Dickinson to Fish and Harahan, May 24, 1905, Fish Letters.
[34] Mayor des Planches to Dickinson, July 10, 1905, *ibid*.
[35] Eleanor McMain, "Behind the Yellow Fever in Little Palermo," *Charities* (New York), XV (November 4, 1905), 152-59; Samuel H. Adams, "Yellow Fever: A Problem Solved," *McClure's Magazine* (New York), XXVII (June, 1906), 178-92; Fish to Harahan, July 26, 1905, Fish Letters.

wretched life of the cities. No sooner had his interview ended than news of the outbreak of yellow fever in New Orleans alarmed the emigration officials. Thereafter, Scott complained, Italian officials turned their attention to settling emigrants in Texas.[36]

More subtle factors defeated southern hopes for a significant share of cheap Italian labor. Foremost among these were the powerful reasons every Italian had for leaving his past behind him. In the late nineteenth century, Italy was for the first time undergoing the strains of modern industrialization, setting loose the inevitable movement of population from farm to city. This was accentuated in southern Italy and Sicily by disenchantment with unification and declining agricultural prices. Dispossessed, a great flood of drifting farm labor sought escape in the higher wages of factory life and crowded into cities unprepared to absorb them. In this sense, the flood tide of Italian immigration to the United States was an international projection of similar population movements occurring within Italy.

Everywhere, this movement was looked upon as temporary. The sole object was to save some money and return to the native land. This motive guided the actions of great numbers of Italian farm laborers who sought high wages in the industrial cities of the United States.[37] A mere perusal of wages offered by industry in the northern and north central states during 1903 reveal their marked superiority to the forty to seventy-five cents per day offered to farm laborers by Yazoo Delta planters.[38] The long period needed to accumulate significant savings as an agricultural tenant offered little more.

In addition, the plantation-tenant system itself tended to repel the uprooted immigrant farming classes. Why, they asked, undertake the expense and hazards of a 5,000-mile journey to exchange one type of tenancy for another? Although planters widely claimed that a laborer could rise from tenancy to outright ownership, neither Scott nor the owners of Sunnyside would allow tenants to purchase any of their plantation lands.[39] Sound reasoning supported this policy. The plantation was a business system representing the in-

[36] Scott to Fish, October 30, 1905, Fish Letters.
[37] Foerster, *The Italian Emigration of Our Times*, 342-62, 416-30.
[38] "Nineteenth Annual Report of the Commissioner of Labor, 1904," *House Docs.*, 58 Cong., 3 Sess., No. 428 (Serial 4861), 233-434; James H. Blodgett, *Wages of Farm Labor in the United States. Results of Twelve Statistical Investigations, 1866-1902* (U.S. Department of Agriculture, Bureau of Statistics, Miscellaneous Series Bulletin No. 26, Washington, 1903), 18-19.
[39] Mayor des Planches, *Attraverso Gli Stati Uniti*, 138, 253.

tegrated sum of all its parts—lands, gins, houses, stores, barns, tools, equipment, warehouses. Naturally enough, the piecemeal sale of any of these parts, especially the lands, meant an end to the plantation. This situation thus reveals the incongruities of planter claims about tenant opportunities. Having once entered the plantation system, the tenant was more an employee of a coordinated business enterprise than an apprentice who, by thrift and hard work, could some day own the land he worked. For the tenant, the plantation could only be a manner of living. It could not possibly be a means to economic independence or social mobility.

For the Italian, this type of enforced tenancy was entirely unsatisfactory. Coming from a land where property ownership, however small, meant great social prestige, he was not destined to remain a mere agricultural worker or tenant for long. The Immigration Commission predicted in 1910 that "where land is cheap and where opportunities for economic and social advancement are many the Italian rural laborer for wages will not outlast the first generation. . . . The Italian seems destined to become a property owner, rather than an agricultural laborer."[40] Neither cheap land nor opportunities for economic and social advancement were available for Italians in the Yazoo Delta.

The isolation of the plantation from other economic outlets also inhibited Italian tenancy in the Delta. In theory, the tenant was free to sell his cotton to whomever he wished. In fact, however, he had no choice but to sell to the plantation company. The company owned the nearest practicable gin, compress, and warehouse. It had the factoring connections with the outside world. For the tenant to transport his products to competitors would raise his operating costs, something he could not afford to do. Isolation also brought on tenant suspicions about the good faith of the plantation company store. Immigrants overheard by the Italian ambassador at Sunnyside grumbled about the company store selling its goods for higher prices than the shops in Greenville.[41]

Lastly, a haphazard immigration system led to inevitable charges of peonage, exploitation, and mistreatment. For example, in the Yazoo Delta at a place called Marathon, the Italian ambassador was met by an angry crowd of Italians claiming betrayal. Enticed by

---

[40] *Recent Immigrants in Agriculture,* I, 244.
[41] Mayor des Planches, *Attraverso Gli Stati Uniti,* 143-44.

glowing pictures of a southern paradise, they were discouraged by impure water and unhealthful living conditions. Already, they complained, the fever had carried off a dozen of their number. Moreover, they had been assured before going to Marathon that work was available. But upon their arrival they learned that the harvest had already taken place. They were thus left to drift for themelves in a primitive country and among a hostile people whose language they could not understand.[42]

Mayor des Planches continually emphasized the necessity for orderly and planned immigration. Spontaneous migration had the virtues of individualism but led to the exploitation of immigrants by *padrones*. The most satisfactory migration, the ambassador believed, was by groups. The movement of whole colonies would necessarily require planning, coordination, and agreement among all the parties concerned. Climate, pure water, nutritious food, proximity to transportation, and the stability of the immigrants would have to be accounted for in advance. Above all, clear contracts were essential. These would outline the specific rights and duties of both planter and immigrants. "Under these conditions," the ambassador declared, "Italian migration can come and will come to the South. Otherwise, no."[43]

No one was more willing to meet these requirements than the Delta planter. Bringing in whole colonies was for him the most efficient and economical way of making tenant contracts. By happy coincidence it satisfied the immigrants too. Homogeneous ethnic groupings eased the burden of being alone among completely foreign surroundings. In their desire to contract entire colonies the planters had the support of the Italian emigration office in Rome. American cities were believed detrimental to the physical and moral health of the immigrants. Despite the outbreak of yellow fever, officials in the emigration office were still willing to direct Italian emigres to the southern states, if it could be done in an orderly, clearly defined way.[44]

But it could not be done. Neither the apparent need for orderly

[42] *Ibid.*, 253-56.
[43] *Ibid.*, 256.
[44] *Ibid.*, 279, 284; Scott to Fish, October 30, 1905, Fish Letters; G. E. Di Palma-Castiglione, "Italian Immigration into the United States, 1901-1904," *American Journal of Sociology* (Chicago), XI (September, 1905), 202-206; Frank P. Sargent to Fish, January 10, 1905, Fish Letters.

group migration nor the planter willingness to bring it about had any effect on loosening the tight restrictions of the American anti-contract labor laws. These strictly forbade the advance contracting of labor in a foreign country, even by mere advertisement. By the beginning of the twentieth century, American immigration officials were attempting to give these laws greater enforcement. In its efforts to safeguard their nationals from exploitation by planning for their employment in advance, the Italian government found the American anti-contract labor laws "an almost insuperable obstacle."

To overcome these legal and other barriers, planters sought the aid of the Italian government in contracting whole groups of Italians upon their arrival in the United States. Support for this scheme was not forthcoming from officials of the Italian emigration office. Remembering the unfortunate experience at Marathon, they feared the uncertainties of these arrangements. Once in America, the immigrants were no longer under the protective and guiding care of the emigration office. The American ambassador to Italy, Henry White, explained the position of the Italian officials: "They cannot well assume the responsibility of advising their people to proceed to places at which the latter cannot be certain before leaving home of finding employment."[45]

One remaining factor provided the final blow to the declining hopes of the Delta planters. This was the resentment of the immigrants by native Americans. The Italian's inability to adjust to familiar patterns of behavior marked him as un-American. "Sin" played its part. Southern evangelicalism was particularly disturbed over the strange Catholicism, the incomprehensible language, and the Babylonian wine drinking, music, and dancing. Worst of all, the Italian's exclusiveness and the mystery of his ways were too reminiscent of the Negro.

A distinction was made among southern Italians (including Sicilians) and northern Italians. The latter, it was generally believed, were capable of being assimilated into American society and were thus the more desirable. Southerners had their doubts about the others. Representative Adam Byrd of Philadelphia, Mississippi, echoed these beliefs in Congress:

[45] White to Fish, October 14, 1905, Fish Letters. Apparently, the Foran Anti-Contract Labor Law of 1885 did have an effect upon Italian emigration officials even though, as Charlotte Erickson points out—*American Industry and the European Immigrant, 1860-1885* (Cambridge, 1957), 170-76—it was easily evaded by American labor agents.

I have witnessed the degradation of certain of this foreign element in my own section, who prefer a hut to a home, who believe not in the American idea of home comforts, who prefer a monkey and an organ to a piano, who pack their children away like sardines in their crowed huts. In other words, most of them live a life of utter degradation, and I am not one to make the honest yeomanry of my section labor in competition with such people.

Byrd claimed not to be against those Italians who made efforts to be Americans. He himself had supported ex-Governor Andrew H. Longino who was of Italian descent. But Longino was of north Italian extraction; the "dagoes" of south Italy Byrd believed would never assimilate. "Hundreds of them," he exclaimed, "may be seen in New Orleans today, three generations from Italy, still pushing carts, yelling 'Banans,' 'Banans,' 'Banans'!!"[46]

Discrimination was accompanied by lynchings and threats of violence. The gruesome record began in 1891 when eleven Sicilians, being held for trial on charges of murdering the New Orleans police chief, were taken from prison and hanged by a mob. The following year, six Italians, charged with murder at Hahnsville, Louisiana, were taken from the parish jail by an unidentified mob and three of the prisoners were hanged. In 1899, five Italians were lynched in Tallulah, Louisiana, in a dispute over the wounding of a native American physician. In the summer of 1901, Vincerrzo Serio and his father were shot and killed at Erwin, Mississippi, not far from Greenville. And in 1907, Frank Scaglioni, a crippled shoemaker and leader of the Italian colony at Sumrall, Mississippi, was severely beaten and threatened with hanging if he persisted in his efforts to protect his fellow Italians from discrimination. Official protests by the Italian government against these offenses went unheeded. Local sentiment against Italians made it impossible to prosecute the offenders.[47]

The Italian immigrants failed to see the reason for these attacks. Language and customs notwithstanding, they had proved themselves reliable, efficient, and thrifty workers. Were not these virtues

[46] *Cong. Record,* 60 Cong., 1 Sess., 884-85 (January 20, 1908); *Recent Immigrants in Agriculture,* I, 244; Merry to Fish, July 5, 1904, Fish Letters.

[47] Senator Augusto Pierantoni, "Italian Feeling on American Lynching," *The Independent* (New York), LV (August 27, 1903), 2040-42; Mayor des Planches, *Attraverso Gli Stati Uniti,* 255; *The Outlook* (New York), LXII (August 5, 1899), 735; LXXXVII (November 16, 1907), 556-58; Berthoff, "Southern Attitudes Toward Immigration," *Journal of Southern History,* XVII, 343-44.

in the very best of yeoman farmer traditions and what the planters themselves desired in their tenants? The planters' insistence upon bunching all the Italians into isolated colonies retarded the immigrants' assimilation into the rest of society. Their seclusion on the plantation meant that little or no provision was made for the American education of their children, and violence served only to pull the immigrants even closer together for security.

The planters were admittedly not interested in the assimilation of their Italian tenants. Washing their hands of personal relationships, the question of immigrant labor was for them "purely one of abstract economics."[48] Planter attitudes left the white Italian isolated within white society and not fully accepted by it. The result was his categorization with the non-white labor groups—Chinese, Mexicans, Indians, and Negroes. This treatment seemed more offensive to Italian officials than the beatings and lynchings. The Italian was being considered by the planter and railroad magnate as nothing more than a more efficient replacement for the Negro. "The company," commented Mayor des Planches on the Sunnyside operation, "is a company of speculation. From the settler it tries to draw the greatest profit without caring about his well-being. The Italian at Sunnyside is a human machine of production. Better than the Negro, a more perfect machine [than the Negro] but beside him a machine nevertheless."[49]

The identification with non-white labor, especially the Negro, robbed the Italian of his status as a white man. This status decline was reinforced by the servility associated with working on the plantation. In the Delta, no self-respecting white man labored on the huge cotton plantations. This was Negro's work. It was the badge of his inferiority. By replacing the Negro in the same type of work and under the same conditions, the Italians assumed the status of Negroes. One blended into the other, and southern thinking made no effort to distinguish between them.[50]

[48] Stone, *Studies in the American Race Problem*, 198.
[49] Mayor des Planches, *Attraverso Gli Stati Uniti*, 145, 287.
[50] *Ibid.*, 138. The unwillingness of the white man to do what was considered Negro's work was, in the opinion of the Illinois Central Railroad's industrial commissioner, the chief reason for the failure to develop cotton spinning mills in the Yazoo Delta. "The average white citizen of Vicksburg," said the industrial commissioner, "would look upon it as an insult to be requested to work in a cotton mill. This is the situation in the larger cities in the Delta. In the country the white men will not work in the field and all the work is done by the negro." George C. Power to Fish, February 26, 1900, Fish Letters. See also, Paul S. Taylor, *Mexican Labor in the United States, Demmit County, Winter Garden District, South Texas* (Berkeley, 1930).

Italian emigration officials were aware of the motives behind planter designs to bring more of their citizens to the South. The Italian ambassador understood why he had been treated with such courtesy by all the rich planters, eminent politicians, and railroad magnates—those groups were convinced that white immigrant labor would bring the southern economy into the twentieth century and somehow rid the South of its race problem. But unless the Italian immigrant received the recognition of a white man in a white man's society, these theories would never be tested.

The conditions of labor under the plantation system and the patterns of racial identification combined and interacted to frustrate the sanguine hopes for new sources of non-Negro labor. Significant numbers of Italians never made their way to the lower South. The high water mark of Italian immigrants into the Delta was reached in 1910 when their number made up a mere 2.3 per cent of the small total white population.[51] Thereafter, their numbers declined and the concentrations of Italians in Washington and Bolivar counties were scattered throughout the rest of the Delta. The Negro remained, as ever, the sole source of plantation labor.

In 1907, the boll weevil first entered the state of Mississippi in the area around Natchez, causing havoc among a Negro labor force already impoverished by deteriorated soils. Delta planters made the most of this opportunity. Laying aside their ideas for Italian labor, planters brought the forsaken Negroes into the Delta by the wagon load.[52] This action, taken when hopes of immigrant labor were dimming, symbolized the planter's final surrender to the Negro. Predictions foretelling of his eventual displacement had come to nothing. The Delta's cotton fields, for better or worse, were left in the hands of the Negro tenant, and the earlier declaration of Frederick Douglass that the dependence of planters, landowners, and the old master class upon the Negro "is nearly complete and perfect"[53] rang true with greater authority.

[51] U.S. Census Office, *Thirteenth Census*, II, *Population* (Washington, 1913), 1044-62; *Fourteenth Census*, III, *Population* (Washington, 1922), 543. In 1910, foreign born in Texas, Arkansas, Louisiana, and Mississippi represented an average of 2.7 per cent of the total population of those states. Texas and Louisiana showed the highest percentages, 6.2 and 3.2, respectively. Of the 8,924,493 people in those four states, only 31,259 were Italian-born and two thirds of these lived in Louisiana, primarily in New Orleans. U.S. Census Office, *Thirteenth Census*, II, *Population*, 113, 773, 799, 1039.

[52] Alfred H. Stone and Julian Fort, *The Truth about the Boll Weevil* (Greenville, Miss., 1911), pamphlet, Widener Library, Harvard University.

[53] Frederick Douglass, *Life and Times* (Hartford, 1881), 438.

# Chinese Livelihood in Rural California: The Impact of Economic Change, 1860–1880

Sucheng Chan

*The author is a member of the history department in the University of California, Santa Cruz.*

T HE HISTORICAL literature on Chinese Americans is quite uneven in the topics covered, in the geographic focus of the studies, and in scholarly quality. Since American reaction to Chinese immigration was negative, much scholarly effort has been devoted to explaining the causes of the anti-Chinese movement, which culminated in Chinese exclusion in 1882. Major monographs by Mary Roberts Coolidge, Elmer Clarence Sandmeyer, Gunther Barth, Stuart Creighton Miller, Robert McClellan, and Alexander Saxton have offered different explanations for the anti-Chinese movement.[1] Delber L. McKee investigated how the federal government implemented the exclusionary legislation and

I thank Gunther Barth, Roger Daniels, and Alexander Saxton for helpful comments on an earlier version of this paper presented at the 1981 meeting of the American Historical Association.

[1]Mary Roberts Coolidge, *Chinese Immigration* (New York, 1909), shows how the fragile balance in the political strength of the Democratic and Republican parties in the post-Civil War period — in California as well as in the nation — led politicians to appeal to anti-Chinese sentiment to win votes, with lower class whites participating most actively in anti-Chinese activities. Elmer Clarence Sandmeyer, *The Anti-Chinese Movement in California* (Urbana, 1939), states that the anti-Chinese movement had multiple causes, but singles out racial antagonism and the fear of economic competition as the most important. Gunther Barth, *Bitter Strength: A History of the Chinese in the United States, 1850–1870* (Cambridge, Mass., 1964), argues that as sojourners, the Chinese had only a limited goal in coming to the United States — to earn money — so they were viewed as unassimilable by Americans who considered their presence to be a "threat to the realization of the Califor-

*Pacific Historical Review*

© 1984, by the Pacific Coast Branch American Historical Association

the reaction of China and Chinese Americans to it, while Fred W. Riggs traced the political process which led to the repeal of the various exclusion laws in 1943.[2] These works necessarily focus on those whom Roger Daniels has called the "excluders" rather than on the "excluded," so even though they illuminate the temper of the times, they provide little insight into the attitudes of the Chinese themselves — why they came, how they perceived the United States, and what their communities were like.

Available studies of Chinese immigrant communities fall into two categories: those that treat Chinatowns as a special type of community with features distinct from Anglo-American ones and those that describe facets of particular communities. In both instances, communities are analyzed mainly in terms of their institutional structure. The works of Rose Hum Lee, Stanford M. Lyman, S. W. Kung, Betty Lee Sung, Francis L. K. Hsu, and Jack Chen — though differing vastly in scholarly sophistication and tone — share the common characteristic of being general surveys of Chinese American life.[3] Chinatowns are treated as a distinct

nia vision" — the belief that the most perfect form of American civilization was "destined to culminate on the shore of the Pacific." Stuart Creighton Miller, *The Unwelcome Immigrant: The American Image of the Chinese, 1785–1882* (Berkeley and Los Angeles, 1969), challenges the thesis that the anti-Chinese movement was a peculiarly California phenomenon by demonstrating that Americans in other parts of the country had held negative stereotypes of the Chinese long before any Chinese immigrants set foot on American soil. Robert McClellan, *The Heathen Chinee: A Study of American Attitudes toward China, 1890–1905* (Athens, Ohio, 1971), also discusses the negative images of the Chinese in American literature, showing how Americans based their evaluations of the Chinese on "private needs and not upon the realities of Chinese life." Alexander Saxton, *The Indispensable Enemy: Labor and the Anti-Chinese Movement in California* (Berkeley and Los Angeles, 1971), traces the "ideological baggage" of the anti-Chinese movement to different strands of thought which shaped the Democratic and Republican parties, as well as the labor movement. By emphasizing the white workingmen's sense of displacement and deprivation in the latter half of the nineteenth century, Saxton chronicles how the anti-Chinese movement aided the skilled-crafts component of the labor movement to consolidate its own position, on the one hand, while uniting skilled and unskilled workers in a common anti-Chinese cause, on the other hand. The Chinese were perceived to be tools of monopolists, so hostility against Chinese was in part displaced hostility against those with money and power.

[2]Delber W. McKee, *Chinese Exclusion versus the Open Door Policy, 1900–1906: Clashes over China Policy in the Roosevelt Era* (Detroit, 1977); and Fred W. Riggs, *Pressures on Congress: A Study of the Repeal of Chinese Exclusion* (New York, 1950).

[3]Rose Hum Lee, *The Chinese in the U.S.A.* (Hong Kong, 1960); Stanford M. Lyman, "The Structure of Chinese Society in Nineteenth-Century America" (Ph.D. dissertation, University of California, Berkeley, 1961); Stanford M. Lyman, *Chinese Americans* (New York, 1974); S. W. Kung, *Chinese in American Life: Some Aspects of Their History, Status, Problems, and Contributions* (Seattle, 1962); Betty Lee Sung, *Mountain of Gold: The Story of the Chinese in*

type of community, so that regardless of where a Chinatown is located, its social structure is implied to be similar to that of any other Chinatown. Studies of individual Chinatowns, in contrast, have greater temporal and geographic specificity. Some of the early writings portrayed the more exotic or lurid aspects of San Francisco's Chinatown.[4] More recent studies describe either San Francisco's Chinatown or analyze certain aspects of New York's Chinatown.[5] Two exceptions to the typological approach and the heavy emphasis on San Francisco or New York are James W. Loewen's investigation of the Chinese in the Mississippi Delta and Melford Weiss's analysis of the Chinese in "Valley City," California.[6] Loewen's work is unique because, unlike other authors who elucidate the social structure of Chinese American communities in terms of institutional patterns brought over from China, he considers the pattern of racial segregation peculiar to the South to be a more important influence than Chinese cultural and social heritage on the Delta Chinese community.

The reliance on San Francisco data by so many authors has created a false impression that all Chinese communities in America are merely smaller replicas of the one in San Francisco and that the Chinese American historical experience is quite homogeneous. Although the importance of San Francisco as the cultural, social, political, and economic center of "Chinese America"

---

*America* (New York, 1967); Francis L. K. Hsu, *The Challenge of the American Dream: The Chinese in the United States* (Belmont, Calif, 1971); and Jack Chen, *The Chinese of America* (San Francisco, 1980).

[4] Among the more respectable nineteenth-century eyewitness accounts of San Francisco's Chinatown are William W. Bode, *Lights and Shadows of Chinatown* (San Francisco, 1896); Iza Duffis Hardy, *Through Cities and Prairie Land: Sketches of an American Tour* (Chicago, 1882); William H. Irwin, *Pictures of Old Chinatown by Arnold Genthe* (New York, 1908); Benjamin E. Lloyd, *Lights and Shades in San Francisco* (San Francisco, 1876); and Helen H. Jackson, *Bits of Travel at Home* (Boston, 1878). Later accounts of nineteenth-century Chinese life include Alexander McLeod, *Pigtails and Gold Dust: A Panorama of Chinese Life in Early California* (Caldwell, 1947); and Charles Morley, "The Chinese in California, as Reported by Henryk Sienkiewicz," *California Historical Society Quarterly,* XXXIV (1955), 301–316.

[5] Victor G. and Brett de Bary Nee, *Longtime Californ': A Documentary Study of an American Chinatown* (New York, 1972); Chia-ling Kuo, *Social and Political Change in New York's Chinatown: The Role of Voluntary Associations* (New York, 1977); Peter Kwong, *Chinatown, New York: Labor and Politics, 1930–1950* (New York, 1979); and Bernard Wong, *Chinatown: Economic Adaptations and Ethnic Identity of the Chinese* (New York, 1982).

[6] James W. Loewen, *The Mississippi Chinese: Between Black and White* (Cambridge, Mass., 1971); and Melford S. Weiss, *Valley City: A Chinese Community in America* (Cambridge, Mass., 1974).

is beyond dispute, the city and county of San Francisco never contained the majority of the Chinese-ancestry population in California, much less in the United States. Throughout the second half of the nineteenth century, the largest proportion of Chinese immigrants lived in the rural counties of California. During the first two decades of Chinese immigration, an overwhelming proportion of the Chinese population located in the mining counties, first in the southern mines, and after the mid-1860s in the northern mines. From the 1870s through the 1890s, quite a large contingent worked in the Trinity and Klamath mining regions. (See Table 1.)

As a settlement center, San Francisco achieved genuine demographic preeminence only in the 1880s and 1890s when two factors fostered the city's emergence as the premier city of "Chinese America": 1) the development of manufacturing industries, which provided employment for Chinese, and 2) the anti-Chinese movement, which caused many Chinese to flock to the city's segregated Chinatown in search of security. Even in 1880 and 1890, only 20.6 percent and 24.0 percent, respectively, of the total Chinese population in the United States lived in San Francisco, while 50.6 percent and 43.4 percent, respectively, lived in California outside of San Francisco.[7] For that reason, a balanced view of the Chinese American historical experience cannot overlook the rural segment of the Chinese immigrant population.

Although more Chinese lived in rural California than in any other part of the country throughout the nineteenth century, there has been no overall study of the Chinese in rural America. Glimpses of rural life are available only in traveller's accounts[8] and in a few studies of Chinese labor, such as those by George Seward and Ping Chiu.[9] The paucity of primary sources is one

---

[7] The word "lived" is used only for convenience. Since the Chinese population in the American West in the nineteenth century was a highly mobile one, given the nature of the work they did, census counts of the Chinese population represent the demographic distribution only at particular points in time.

[8] Glimpses of the Chinese in rural California may be found in several kinds of travellers' accounts: articles written by reporters sent out by eastern newspapers that appeared in serial form, sections on the Chinese in books written by contemporary observers, and occasional references to the Chinese in unpublished diaries and reminiscences. There is also scattered mention of the Chinese in local histories.

[9] George F. Seward, *Chinese Immigration: Its Social and Economic Aspects* (New York, 1881); and Ping Chiu, *Chinese Labor in California, 1850–1880: An Economic Study* (Madison, 1967).

reason for the lack of studies of the Chinese in rural America. Newspapers published in the rural counties seldom mentioned the Chinese, and when they did, the news was of the sensational sort or dealt with the pros and cons of continued Chinese immigration.[10] Some documents in Chinese have been salvaged but these provide only episodic evidence on Chinese economic and social life in rural California, and it is difficult to judge how representative the individual cases may be.[11] The dearth of written sources cannot be remedied by the use of oral history interviews, since no persons who could tell us something about life in the nineteenth century are still alive.

For systematic information, the two most useful archival sources are the U.S. manuscript population census and the county archival documents, which are available in the office of the county recorder in every county in California.[12] These sources provide information on the demographic composition and occupational structure of Chinese communities in rural California, even though they tell nothing about the subjective aspects of the Chinese experience. This study of the Chinese occupational structure in three rural California counties is based on such census and county archival records.

Sacramento, Yuba, and San Joaquin counties were chosen for study because they contained three of the most important Chinatowns outside of San Francisco in the nineteenth century — Sacramento, Marysville, and Stockton. Only the Chinatown in Oroville, Butte County, was of equal importance. However, since

---

[10] In the four scrapbooks of newspaper clippings on the Chinese collected by Hubert Howe Bancroft's assistants, only a dozen or so items out of several thousand are nonjudgmental in tone. See *Bancroft Scraps*, vols. 6–9, Bancroft Library, University of California, Berkeley.

[11] Among the most complete runs of manuscripts in Chinese are the business records of Chung Tai, a general merchandise firm in North San Juan, Nevada County; the business records of Wing On Wo, a firm in Dutch Flat, Placer County; and disinterment lists from the Chinese cemetery at Fiddletown, Amador County. The first two items — and less complete records of other Chinese stores and several gambling houses in rural California — are at the Bancroft Library, University of California, Berkeley, while the third item is in the Chinese American History Archives, Asian American Studies Library, University of California, Berkeley.

[12] For a discussion of the value of county archival documents for researching Chinese American economic and social history, see Sucheng Chan, "Using California County Archives for Research in Chinese American History," *Annals of the Chinese Historical Society of the Pacific Northwest*, I (1983), 49–55.

conditions in Butte and Yuba counties were quite similar, the inclusion of Butte County in this study would have been redundant.[13] In looking at Sacramento, Yuba, and San Joaquin counties, it is possible to shed new light on the Chinese clustered in the larger rural Chinatowns as well as those scattered throughout the countryside.

The historical importance of Sacramento and Marysville has been imprinted upon the collective memory of Chinese Americans through the language they use. To this day, Chinese Americans call San Francisco "Dai Fou" (Big City), Sacramento "Yee Fou" (Second City), and Marysville "Sam Fou" (Third City). Stockton has not been deemed significant enough for inclusion in this terminological ranking, but it and San Joaquin County are part of this study because initial large-scale Chinese entry there was due to the development of agriculture, and not to mining and trading as in Sacramento and Yuba counties. An examination of developments in San Joaquin County makes it possible to determine whether the original economic magnet attracting Chinese to a locality had any impact on the subsequent development of the pattern of Chinese livelihood there.

The years 1860–1880 have been chosen for analysis because they represent a period of significant change and development for the Chinese population in California. In the first two decades of Chinese immigration, the majority of the Chinese in rural California worked as independent miners and entrepreneurs. Only from the late 1860s onwards did an increasing number begin to earn their living as wage laborers. This fact is worth emphasizing because the Chinese have been depicted all too frequently as "cheap labor" and little more. Such a depiction distorts historical reality. The Chinese in rural California initially engaged in a wide range of occupations, many of which did not involve wage labor. Changing socioeconomic conditions in the American West, along with racial discrimination — rather than Chinese "willingness" to be cheap labor — were responsible for proletarianizing the Chinese population.

In this study, occupations have been grouped under four cate-

---

[13] Besides, a study of the Chinese in Butte County has already been published: Susan W. Book, *The Chinese in Butte County, California, 1860–1920* (San Francisco, 1976).

gories on the basis of function: primary extraction and production, which includes farming, fishing, and mining; manual labor, which includes agricultural as well as nonagricultural labor; personal service, which includes employment as servants, cooks, and prostitutes; and entrepreneurs, professionals and artisans, which includes all persons earning a living through the sale of merchandise or the practice of a trade or profession.

Between 1860 and 1880, tenant farming, paid farm labor, nonagricultural labor, and personal services replaced gold mining and independent entrepreneurship as the foundation of economic life for the Chinese in rural California. In the process, more and more Chinese became dependent on white employers for their livelihood, both in the towns and in the rural areas. Chart I provides an overview of the changes in the Chinese occupational structure between 1860 and 1880. In 1860, artisans, professionals and entrepreneurs made up the largest proportion of the Chinese population in the rural Chinatowns, while miners — who comprised almost all of the persons in the category "primary extraction and production" — were numerically dominant in the hinterland. A decade later, the absolute number as well as relative percentage of persons engaged in primary extraction and production had declined due to the exodus from the mines, while the number in nonagricultural labor and personal services had increased greatly. The number of artisans, professionals, and entrepreneurs remained about the same. In 1880, though mining occupied even fewer persons, an increasing number of Chinese farmers account for the rise in the absolute number of persons in primary extraction and production, particularly in Sacramento County. The number of persons in agricultural and nonagricultural labor increased, while the number in personal services and in independent enterprises remained about the same.

These longitudinal changes show that the Chinese communities were able to support a fairly consistent number of entrepreneurs throughout this period, but the economic opportunities open to the rest of the Chinese population depended on changes in the larger economy. Discriminatory actions and legislation also increasingly restricted the range of Chinese economic activities, as a hierarchical division of labor along racial lines became firmly institutionalized on the Pacific Coast. Unlike the American South, where the line of cleavage was drawn between black and white, in California the dichotomy was between Chinese and white. As the nineteenth century progressed, Chinese were relegated in increasing numbers to menial, low-paid, and low-status jobs.

## OCCUPATIONAL STRUCTURE, 1860

The gold rush had a greater impact on the Chinese population in California than it did on other ethnic groups in the state. Throughout the mining era, a larger proportion of the Chinese engaged in mining than did their counterparts among other ethnic groups. In 1860, 70.4 percent of all gainfully employed Chinese above the age of fifteen were miners, compared to 31.6 percent among non-Chinese gainfully employed persons.[14] Moreover, the Chinese remained in mining longer than the non-Chinese population. White miners had begun their exodus from the mines by the mid-1850s, but Chinese miners began to drift out only after 1863.[15] As late as 1900, small clusters of aging Chinese miners were still listed in the manuscript population census.

Chinese miners worked mainly placer claims, so they were found primarily along streams and rivers. An analysis of the locational distribution of Chinese miners in Yuba County indicates that in 1860, Chinese miners were concentrated most heavily along the Yuba River and its tributaries. The number of Chinese miners was largest in Long Bar, North-east, Foster Bar, and Slate Range townships — townships through which the Yuba, Middle Yuba, and North Yuba rivers flow. In contrast, few Chinese miners were found in Rose Bar, Parks Bar, and New York townships, where a range of mountains is located. There were gold deposits in these latter townships, however, for the number of white miners in them was large.[16] In these mountainous areas, the gold de-

---

[14] The 1860 census counted 34,933 Chinese, of whom 433 were below age fifteen. I am making the assumption that the 34,500 Chinese above age fifteen were gainfully employed. Of these, 24,282 were miners. There were 58,291 non-Chinese miners among 184,692 gainfully employed non-Chinese adults. U.S. Bureau of the Census, *Eighth Census of the United States: Population, 1860* (Washington, D.C., 1864), 26 and 35.

[15] Chiu, *Chinese Labor in California*, 25–26.

[16] Based on my tally of miners in Yuba County, the townships with relatively large numbers of Chinese miners were Long Bar Township with 494 Chinese and 250 non-Chinese miners, North-east Township with 161 Chinese and 226 non-Chinese miners, Foster Bar

posits were in hardrock quartz claims, and Chinese miners did not have the capital to purchase the necessary heavy equipment to work such deposits, nor did they feel secure enough to invest in expensive machinery that they might be forced to abandon.

In the 1860s, most of the Chinese miners along the Yuba River and its tributaries were independent prospectors and not laborers for mining companies. They frequently formed their own companies consisting of up to forty partners.[17] Many Chinese miners in Yuba County obtained their claims through preemption rather than through purchase. Preemption claims did not have to be bought; the claimants only had to file the necessary documents in the county recorder's office and put up markers to show the boundaries of their claims. The ability of Chinese miners to file preemption claims is worth noting, for it has been commonly assumed that due to anti-Chinese sentiment in the mines, Chinese immigrants had to resort to buying worked-over claims abandoned by white miners.[18]

The earliest Chinese preemption claims appeared in Yuba County records in 1856. Ah Louie and Company claimed 240 feet at Buckeye Bar along the Yuba River, while Sham Kee claimed 4,200 feet eight miles outside of Marysville City, also along the Yuba River.[19] Records of prices paid by Chinese miners for claims they purchased indicate the approximate amount of money that they saved when they were able to obtain claims through preemption. In 1856, Ah Chung and Company purchased two claims of sixty feet each from Frederick Antenheimer

---

Township with 271 Chinese and 245 non-Chinese miners, and Slate Range Township with 272 Chinese and 538 non-Chinese miners. The townships with few Chinese were Rose Bar Township with 13 Chinese and 568 non-Chinese miners, Parks Bar Township with 27 Chinese and 196 non-Chinese miners, and New York Township with 64 Chinese and 407 non-Chinese miners. U.S. Bureau of the Census, "Eighth Census of the United States: Population, 1860" (Manuscript census for Yuba County, California).

[17]The figure is based on the maximum size of Chinese miners' households enumerated in the 1860 manuscript population census, and on the number of partners listed in a random sample of records of mining claims and leases of mining grounds in California's mining counties.

[18]Saxton, *The Indispensable Enemy*, 53.

[19]Yuba County, California, "Preemptions" (Marysville, 1856–1865), 1: 349 and 353. (All citations from county archival records will give the first page of the document only. All Chinese names are spelled as they appear in the county records. No consistent transliteration is used because it is not possible to do so without knowing what the Chinese characters are.)

(the Yuba County tax collector) and John Lawrence for $620. The purchase price included two wheelbarrows and running planks.[20] In the following year, Antenheimer and Ferdinand Furning sold two claims measuring ninety feet each to Ah Locke and Thin Shue for $695, and threw into the bargain two frame houses, two pumps, and miscellaneous mining tools.[21] Those Chinese who were able to obtain claims through preemption therefore saved hundreds and perhaps even thousands of dollars.

Contrary to the situation in some counties where Chinese miners were driven away from good claims that they had located, quite a number of Chinese miners along the Yuba River in both Yuba and Sierra counties were allowed to work the same locations year after year. In January 1869, four different Chinese companies filed multiple preemption claims at Missouri Bar on the Yuba River. Hong Fook Kong and Company, with ten partners, filed ten claims of 100 feet each, which they renewed annually between 1870 and 1874. Then they disappeared from the county records until March 1878, when they filed thirty-two claims with thirty-two partners. By 1879, however, the larger group had splintered, and Hong Fook Kong and Company was once again composed of ten partners filing ten claims. These claims were renewed in 1880 and 1881.[22]

Three other groups also worked the same stretch of the Yuba River during the twelve-year period between 1869 and 1881. In Key and Company, with six partners, filed six claims contiguous to Hong Fook Kong and Company's claims, stretching upriver for 600 feet.[23] Jim and Company, with four partners, filed four claims upriver from In Key and Company's claims.[24] Both companies followed the same pattern of claims renewal as Hong Fook Kong and Company. The fourth group, Ah King and Company, had six partners who filed claims which were not contiguous to the other three companies during the same period of time. Perhaps that is why in 1878, when they filed thirty-two claims with thirty-two partners (a

[20] *Ibid.*, unnumbered pages.
[21] *Ibid.*
[22] Yuba County, California, "Preemptions" (Marysville, 1865–1881), 2: 198, 204, 217, 224, 231, 236, 307, 329, 352 and 384.
[23] *Ibid.*, 2: 198, 204, 217, 224, 230, 235, 352 and 383.
[24] *Ibid.*, 2: 198, 205, 216, 224, 231, 236, 328, 351 and 384.

different group of persons from the thirty-two in the Hong Fook Kong Company), three of the partners were not individuals but corporate entities: Hong Fook Kong and Company, In Key and Company, and a fifth group called Ah Kong and Company.[25] It may be surmised that certain Chinese miners were buying shares in other people's claims in different localities. This second example of a company enlarging its membership also showed that such larger groupings had a tendency to splinte: for by 1879, Ah King and Company was back to six partners.

Mining was an extremely important source of livelihood for the Chinese-in Yuba County. Almost eighty percent of the Chinese there in 1860 were miners, whereas only 21.4 percent of the non-Chinese population were miners. The Chinese constituted 35.9 percent of all the miners in the county, but they made up only 13 percent of the total population. In California as a whole, 29.4 percent of all miners in 1860 were Chinese, while 9.2 percent of the total population were Chinese.

The economic and social importance of gold mining in 1860 led to a bifurcated social structure in rural Chinese immigrant communities. There was a large number of miners who did not grow their own food except for fresh produce cultivated in some corner of their mining grounds. To supply the needs of these miners for food and personal services, there appeared a small group of Chinese entrepreneurs, most of whom lived in the towns in the mining counties, or in cities such as Sacramento, Marysville, and Stockton — the three major supply posts and transportation nodes of the entire mining region.

The occupational structure of the Chinese population in the three cities differed sharply from that found among the Chinese in the hinterlands. In each of the three cities, persons engaged in merchandising and various trades made up the largest portion of the Chinese population. Sacramento City, being the largest of the three with a Chinese population of 980, had the greatest range of occupations, with artisans, professionals, and entrepreneurs comprising 49.4 percent of the city's Chinese population. Marysville, second in importance as an urban center in the Sacramento Valley with a Chinese population of 227, had 34.8 percent of its Chinese

---

[25]*Ibid.*, 2: 199, 204, 217, 225, 232, 237 and 306.

population earning a living as merchants, professionals, and artisans. Stockton, located at the northern end of the San Joaquin Valley, being relatively farther away from the center of activities in the southern mines, was less crucial as a supply post and consequently, had the least differentiated occupational structure, the bulk of its Chinese population of 115 persons being laundrymen.[26]

Next in importance to the urban entrepreneurs, artisans, and professionals were persons engaged in personal service, which included cooks, servants, waiters and dishwashers, and prostitutes.[27] So employed were 20.8 percent of the Chinese population in Sacramento, 41.4 percent in Marysville, and 29.6 percent in Stockton. By far the largest number of persons in this grouping were prostitutes, with 113 in Sacramento, 75 in Marysville, and 18 in Stockton. In 1860, there were as yet few Chinese servants.

The remaining occupational categories were relatively unimportant. Individuals engaged in mining, truck gardening, and fishing ranged from 8.7 percent of the Chinese population in Stockton to 11.9 percent in Marysville and 16.3 percent in Sacramento. Manual laborers ranged from half a percent in Stockton to 5 percent in Sacramento. Finally, approximately 10 percent of the Chinese population in each city was unemployed in 1860.[28]

Chinese living outside city limits in Sacramento and Yuba counties were almost all miners. (There were only nine Chinese living outside of Stockton in San Joaquin County in 1860.) Chinese farm laborers had not yet become an important element in the rural landscape in 1860. Varden Fuller and Carey McWilliams have stated that Chinese had entered the harvest labor market to work as migratory farm laborers in significant num-

---

[26] My tally and computation are from U.S. Bureau of the Census, "Eighth Census of the United States: Population, 1860" (Manuscript census for Sacramento, Yuba, and San Joaquin counties, California). It should be noted that my tallies do not always coincide with the figures given in the published census; after discovering numerous computation errors in the published census, I decided to trust my own counts.

[27] Prostitutes have been included in the "personal services" category because their function is to satisfy the personal, sexual needs of their customers. Others may disagree with my reasoning, and choose to list them either as "laborers," since their work provides profits for pimps and brothel owners, or as "professionals" — prostitution being referred to as the "oldest profession."

[28] My tally and computation are from U.S. Bureau of the Census, "Eighth Census of the United States: Population, 1860" (Manuscript census for Sacramento, Yuba, and San Joaquin counties, California).

bers by the late 1850s,[29] but census data do not support their assertions. Even though the 1860 census was taken between June and August, and both Sacramento and San Joaquin counties, in particular, had thriving wheat-growing areas, no Chinese farm laborers were enumerated in the census of the three counties. Census data indicate that the Chinese who first worked on farms were cooks, with 18 in Sacramento County, 35 in Yuba County, and 8 in San Joaquin County.

In terms of the integration of the Chinese immigrant population into the larger society, the miners were certainly very much a part of the mining economy, although contemporaneous accounts indicate that, for the most part, the Chinese miners kept to themselves for the sake of safety.[30] Other than miners, the only Chinese who interacted with whites were cooks, servants, and laundrymen, because they were dependent on white employers for their livelihood. Some prostitutes also served white customers, but it is not known how many did so.[31] Mining and personal service, then, were the two main avenues for sporadic social interaction between Chinese and whites in the 1860s.

## OCCUPATIONAL STRUCTURE, 1870

In the decade between 1860 and 1870, four significant developments in the larger California economy influenced the occupa-

---

[29] Varden Fuller, "The Supply of Agricultural Labor as a Factor in the Evolution of Farm Organization in California," in U.S. Senate Committee on Education and Labor, *Hearings Pursuant to Senate Resolution 266*, 76 Cong., 3 sess., Part 54, Exhibit A (1940), 19777–19898; and Carey McWilliams, *Factories in the Field: The Story of Migratory Farm Labor in California* (Boston, 1939).

[30] Accounts of acts of violence against Chinese miners—some resulting in death—as reported in local newspapers were sometimes reprinted in the San Francisco press. For example, the *San Francisco Bulletin* (Dec. 18, 1856) reprinted an item from the *Shasta Republican* stating that "hundreds of Chinese" had been "slaughtered in cold blood" during the last five years by "desperados," and that Francis Blair was the first white man ever to be hanged for murdering Chinese. The *San Francisco Bulletin* (May 19, 1857) reprinted an item from the Auburn *Placer Press* reporting that Chinese miners at Kelly's Bar had been robbed by men with double-barreled guns; the writer noted that though the Chinese recognized the robbers as men who had previously robbed them at Dutch Ravine, they could not hope for justice since Chinese testimony was not accepted in court.

[31] Lucie Cheng Hirata, "Free, Indentured, Enslaved: Chinese Prostitutes in Nineteenth-century America," *Signs: Journal of Women in Culture and Society*, V (1979), 13, states that the "higher-class" prostitutes served only Chinese customers, while the "lower-class" ones served a mixed clientele of Chinese and whites. Hirata based her assertion on undocu-

tional structure of the rural Chinese immigrant population: the decline of mining, the emergence of San Francisco as a manufacturing center, the growth of intensive agriculture, and the completion of the transcontinental railroad. Through immigration, the Chinese population had increased during the decade. Mining absorbed a far smaller absolute number as well as percentage of the Chinese population, but other opportunities for earning a living in light manufacturing, agriculture, and common labor became available.

Gold mining declined enormously in importance as a source of livelihood for the rural Chinese population in California between 1860 and 1870. In 1860, there had been 24,282 Chinese among a total of 82,573 miners in the state, but by 1870, of the some 43,000 miners left in California, about 16,000 were Chinese. Compared to a decade earlier when miners made up over seventy percent of the Chinese population in California, they now constituted only about a third.[32]

A significant divergence had developed between the economy of San Francisco and the rest of the state by 1870. Such a trend was clearly observable as it affected the Chinese immigrant population. In San Francisco, 27.2 percent of the gainfully employed Chinese worked in light manufacturing. Four industries — cigar and tobacco manufacturing, the boot and shoe industry, woolen mills

---

mented and somewhat casual remarks in Charles Caldwell Dobie, *San Francisco's China-town* (New York, 1936), 195, 242–243.

[32]There are problems with figures for the 1870 census. Chinese are listed discretely in U.S. Bureau of the Census, *Ninth Census of the United States: Population, 1870* (Washington, D.C., 1872), 722, Table XXX, column 19, but the figures there do not match those tallied either by Ping Chiu or me. Ping Chiu, who cited the same page from the same source, stated that there were 30,330 miners in 1870, of whom 17,363 were Chinese. He probably misread the published figure of 36,339 as 30,330, but there is no indication how he arrived at the figure of 17,363 since the published number was 9,087. (Chiu, *Chinese Labor in California*, 27.) According to my own count, there were 15,283 Chinese miners in the following sixteen counties: Del Norte, Klamath, Siskiyou, Trinity, and Shasta (in the Trinity-Klamath mining region), Plumas, Butte, Sierra, Yuba, Nevada, and Placer (in the northern mining region), El Dorado, Amador, Calaveras, Tuolumne, and Mariposa (in the southern mining region), and Sacramento. There were doubtless scattered clusters of Chinese miners in other counties which were not investigated; therefore, 16,000 Chinese miners is a reasonable estimate. I have used an estimated total of 43,000 miners because the number of non-Chinese miners of listed nationalities was 25,734 (sum of the nationalities listed in columns 8–18 of Table XXX cited above), the unlisted residue was 1,518, and the number of Chinese miners I counted was about 16,000. This total is about 7,000 more than the published figure of 36,339.

and the sewing trades — employed over 2,300 Chinese workers. In contrast, in all of rural California, only 174 persons, or only 0.7 percent of the gainfully employed Chinese adults, worked in light manufacturing, 96 of whom were in the shoe industry, 48 were in the cigar industry, 28 were in the sewing trades, with 1 each in a woolen mill and in an iron foundry, respectively.[33] Fifteen of the shoemakers lived in Sacramento City, 6 in Marysville, and 1 in Stockton. Of the cigar makers, 35 worked in Sacramento City and 3 in Marysville. Eleven of the individuals engaged in the sewing trades lived in Sacramento, while 8 lived in Yuba County.[34] Thus, although Sacramento and Marysville also had nascent light manufacturing industries, the number of Chinese employed in this sector was miniscule compared to San Francisco.

After manufacturing, independent businesses and various professions absorbed the largest number of Chinese in San Francisco. These trades provided a livelihood to 25.8 percent of the gainfully employed Chinese in the city. Nonagricultural manual laborers made up 24.8 percent of the gainfully employed, while those in personal service constituted 14.8 percent. Only 6 percent of the San Francisco Chinese population were in primary extraction and production, and over three-fifths of them were miners visiting the city. The only important resident group in primary production was 145 fishermen.[35]

In rural California, on the other hand, over 17,000 of the 37,000 Chinese remained in primary extraction and production — a sector that supported forty-six percent of them. Miners numbered some 16,000; truck gardeners and farmers some 1,000; while 151 fishermen made up the rest of this group. Next in numerical importance were almost 6,000 nonagricultural laborers; slightly over 3,000 providers of personal service; and almost

---

[33] My computation has been adapted from U.S. Bureau of the Census, *Ninth Census of the United States: Population, 1870*, 722, 799. Those who use figures from the 1870 published census should realize that the subtotals given for each economic sector do not coincide with the sum of the individual occupational categories because residual categories — each containing only a small number of individuals — were not included.

[34] My tally is from U.S. Bureau of the Census, "Ninth Census of the United States: Population, 1870" (Manuscript census for Sacramento, Yuba, and San Joaquin counties, California).

[35] My computation is based on U.S. Bureau of the Census, *Ninth Census of the United States: Population, 1870*, 799.

3,000 artisans, professionals, and entrepreneurs. Even though labor-intensive agriculture was developing, in 1870 only a little over 2,000 Chinese in rural California as a whole worked as agricultural laborers.[36]

The three counties in this study differ from rural California seen as a whole: a much larger percentage of their Chinese population had entered agriculture by 1870. Sacramento County led the state in the transformation of its agriculture from extensive grain cultivation to intensive fruit and hop growing. In 1870, Sacramento County ranked first in the state in the value of its orchard products, and fifth in the value of its market garden products. Truck gardening had been an important means of livelihood for the Sacramento Chinese as far back as the 1850s. By 1870, although truck gardening continued to be important, Chinese agriculturalists had begun to move out of small-scale truck gardening inside the city of Sacramento into large-scale tenant farming in the Sacramento Delta. While 35 Chinese truck gardeners and 4 farmers resided within city limits (compared to 110 truck gardeners cultivating plots within city limits a decade earlier), 37 truck gardeners and 26 farmers now tilled the soil in the Sacramento Delta.

The presence of Chinese farmers in the Sacramento Delta was first documented narratively in a newspaper account in 1869, and statistically in the 1870 manuscript agriculture census.[37] In 1873, the first lease was officially recorded between two Chinese tenants, Chou Ying and Wee Ying, and George D. Roberts, president of the Tide Land Reclamation Company which had employed many Chinese to drain the peat islands of the delta. Chou Ying and Wee Ying leased 551 acres in three tracts on a mixed cash-rent and share-crop basis. On one tract, they paid eight dollars per acre, while on the other two tracts, they were to give the

---

[36]*Ibid.*

[37]The *Sacramento Bee* (Nov. 11, 1869) noted the presence of a "Chinese colony" whose members were successfully "cultivating the ground on a cooperative plan" on land leased from J. V. Simmons. The reporter stated that there were two white women married to two of the Chinese farmers in this group. U.S. Bureau of the Census, "Ninth Census of the United States: Productions of Agriculture, 1870" (Manuscript census for California) lists fourteen Chinese farmers—three in Franklin Township and nine in Georgiana Township, Sacramento County, and two in Merritt Township, Yolo County. These farmers grew Irish and sweet potatoes as well as vegetables on farms ranging from 25 to 340 acres in size.

landlord a fourth of the crops. However, the lease stipulated that if the tenants chose to grow Chinese vegetables, then the landlord did not wish to have any of the crops; instead, a cash rent of ten dollars per acre would be paid.[38]

In the late 1870s, other Chinese tenants leased plots ranging from 160 acres to 200 acres for rents ranging from fifteen dollars per acre for unimproved land to eighty dollars per acre for land with growing orchards. Most of these leased farms were in the so-called backswamps of the peat islands, where the danger of floods was much greater. White owner-operators usually retained farms along the elevated natural levees for their own cultivation.[39] It is difficult to compare the rent paid by Chinese tenants to that paid by white tenants, for the former usually leased farms on a cash rental basis, while almost all the latter leased them on a share-cropping basis.

Chinese had also begun to work as farm laborers by 1870, but they were found in significant numbers only in Sacramento and San Joaquin counties, with 567 and 224 persons, respectively. The largest concentration of Chinese farm laborers in Sacramento County was in Sutter, Franklin, and Georgiana townships — the three townships along the Sacramento River in the delta portion of the county. The only other cluster of Chinese farmworkers was in the hopfields of American and Center townships, along the American River. In these areas, approximately a third of them lived in the households of white farmers, while the remainder lived in their own households. Since the number of Chinese farmers was still relatively small, it can be assumed that almost all the Chinese agricultural laborers worked for white farmers in 1870.[40] In San Joaquin County, the Chinese farm laborers were also in the delta region. No Chinese farm laborers

---

[38]Sacramento County, California, "Leases" (Sacramento, 1853–1923), B: 95.

[39]The tenure status of farmers was given in U.S. Bureau of the Census, "Tenth Census of the United States: Productions of Agriculture, 1880" (Manuscript census). By matching the names of owner-operators against plat maps of Sacramento County in the California State Archives, it is possible to determine the locations of owner-operated farms — almost all of which were found on the natural levees along the rims of the delta's islands and mainland tracts.

[40]My tally and computation are from U.S. Bureau of the Census, "Ninth Census of the United States: Population, 1870" (Manuscript census for Sacramento County, California).

were enumerated in Yuba County, but Marysville had sixty Chinese truck gardeners.[41]

The completion of the transcontinental railroad in 1869 disgorged thousands of Chinese workers into the labor market all over the western states. Many of these discharged workers returned to California where most of them sought work as nonagricultural common laborers. Their presence was especially noticeable in Marysville and Stockton. In the former city, common laborers made up 45.6 percent of the Chinese population, while in the latter, the figure was 44.3 percent.[42] Levee building and maintenance, road-building, and other hard construction work probably engaged most of these persons. If this was indeed the case, then Chinese laborers were responsible for building many of the roads, ditches, levees, and bridges in these areas.

By 1870, a tripartite division of labor had emerged within the Chinese immigrant population: independent miners and agriculturalists, independent urban entrepreneurs earning their living largely within ethnic enclaves, and a numerically growing group of wage-earners who depended on employment from the larger society for their livelihood.

The number of persons in primary extraction and production varied according to locality. This group comprised less than 5 percent of the total Chinese population in the three cities. In the countryside, there were no Chinese miners or farmers in San Joaquin County, while in Sacramento County outside of Sacramento City, miners, farmers, truck gardeners and fishermen made up 43.7 percent of the Chinese population, and in Yuba County outside of Marysville, 64.8 percent of the Chinese were in agriculture or mining.

Proportionately (but not in absolute numbers), artisans, professionals, and entrepreneurs had declined in importance in the three cities by 1870. Moreover, within this grouping, some subtle but significant changes had occurred during the 1860–1870 decade. Practitioners of certain skilled trades, such as bakers, cabinetmakers, and carpenters, had all but disappeared, most probably because better organization by whites had driven the

---

[41] *Ibid.*, (Manuscript census for San Joaquin and Yuba counties).
[42] *Ibid.*

handful of Chinese in these occupations in the 1860s out of them. On the other hand, occupations requiring a small amount of capital investment had grown in importance. The number of boardinghouse keepers increased, reflecting the emergence of Sacramento, Marysville, and Stockton as important stopping places for transient Chinese migrant laborers. The number of professional gamblers had also increased dramatically, perhaps indicating that some individuals had discovered a profitable way to earn a living by exploiting their fellowmen's need for recreation. Chinese had also carved a niche for themselves as vegetable vendors manning stationary stalls (in contrast to peripatetic Chinese vegetable peddlers, long a familiar sight on the California scene). Lastly, Chinese appeared for the first time in 1870 in a number of semiskilled trades, such as brick, barrel, and candle making.

Persons dependent on white employers for their livelihood had increased greatly in number. They included farm laborers, nonagricultural common laborers, wage-earners in light manufacturing, and a growing number of persons providing personal service.[43] Together with laundrymen whose customers were mainly white, this group embraced the majority of the Chinese population in all three cities and in rural Sacramento County. In rural Yuba County, they made up a third of the Chinese population, while in rural San Joaquin County, they included almost the entire Chinese population.

If employment by whites is viewed as a channel for interaction with the larger society, then the Chinese population in rural California in 1870 was in more frequent interaction with the white population than a decade earlier. Although such interaction was

---

[43] As indicated in the manuscript census, Chinese servants and cooks in rural California almost invariably lived either in the households of white families or in their own households. For that reason, I think I am justified in assuming that almost all of them worked for white employers. Kwong, *Chinatown, New York;* 38, made a statement which is puzzling: "They had little capital, yet wanted work that would avoid dependence on either white employers or workers. Service jobs — as laundrymen, domestic servants, workers in Chinese restaurants — fitted these requirements." In my view, domestic servants cannot be lumped together with laundrymen and restaurant workers because a very large portion of Chinese servants worked for white employers. The situation in San Francisco and New York may have differed from rural California due to a smaller percentage of live-in servants. Not having analyzed the San Francisco and New York manuscript census data, I cannot say if this was in fact the case. If it was, then such urban day-servants would indeed have interacted with their white masters less since they did not live in their employers' households.

mainly in the form of employer-employee relations, and even though such social relations were hardly a good basis for providing genuine understanding between the two groups, it nonetheless cannot be said that the Chinese lived only in their own segregated world by the beginning of their third decade of settlement in California.

## OCCUPATIONAL STRUCTURE, 1880

Between 1870 and 1880, two major trends and one minor one can be detected in the evolution of the occupational structure of Chinese communities in rural California. First, while the relative percentage of persons engaged in primary extraction and production remained about the same as ten years earlier, the composition of this group changed. The absolute number of miners in Sacramento and Yuba counties remained more or less constant, but because the overall Chinese population had increased considerably, the percentage of miners in the total population declined. An increasing number of farmers, particularly in Sacramento and San Joaquin counties, compensated for the decrease in the number of miners. Agriculture had become a very important source of livelihood as well as a channel for upward social mobility for the rural Chinese population.

Second, both the absolute number as well as the percentage of common laborers fell significantly in Marysville and Stockton. This was probably because a large number of the discharged railroad workers had by now found employment in other lines of work. Some no doubt had returned to China, while others had become farm laborers.

Third, a small number of Chinese had begun to work in factories in Sacramento, Yuba, and San Joaquin counties. The majority of them worked in woolen mills in the cities of Sacramento, Marysville, and Stockton. In the latter city, a handful of Chinese also worked in a paper mill. But these numbers are so small that it cannot be argued that a trend was developing. Sacramento City was the only place in rural California where Chinese entry into manufacturing and factory production was clearly visible — there, thirty-four Chinese cigar makers and twenty-eight woolen mill workers resided. There were also forty-four persons engaged in the sewing trades, but it is not clear how many worked as independent artisans and how many worked in sewing factories.[44]

By 1880, Chinese immigrants were working in agriculture as owner-operators, small-scale tenants, large-scale tenants, farm laborers, fruit and vegetable peddlers, commission merchants, and farm cooks. (The small-scale tenants are differentiated from the large-scale ones because the *scale* of operations made a great difference in the *mode* of operation: the former usually cultivated vegetables and berries, employing few, if any, hired hands, while the latter most commonly grew potatoes, onions, beans, and deciduous fruit, employing large numbers of seasonal laborers.) In the 1880s, tenant farmers and farm laborers became the two most numerous groups of Chinese immigrant agriculturalists.

The Sacramento-San Joaquin Delta and the bottomlands along the Sacramento and Feather rivers were the two regions where Chinese settlers first farmed in California on a large scale. The patterns of agriculture undertaken in these two areas contrast strikingly with each other. In the Sacramento-San Joaquin Delta, Chinese tenant farmers cultivated both Irish and sweet potatoes, onions and beans. (Asparagus, the crop which made the delta world famous, did not become important commercially until the turn of the century.) These crops were grown because they were most suitable for the soil and climatic conditions of the delta and not because they required a lot of hand labor. Thus, it was the availability of fertile land, and *not* because the Chinese were allegedly willing to provide "cheap labor," which drew Chinese immigrants into agriculture in the delta. In 1880, there were 537 Chinese farmers in that part of the delta which lies within the boundaries of Sacramento and San Joaquin counties. A smaller number was found in the section of the delta located in Contra Costa, Yolo, and Solano counties. They had been drawn there because the peat soil was so fertile that three crops could be grown each year. In short, the delta was a popular area because the potential profit to be made was great, but it was also a high-risk area because of periodic floods.[45] Chinese who were willing to take

---

[44] My tally and computation are from U.S. Bureau of the Census, "Tenth Census of the United States: Population, 1880" (Manuscript census for Sacramento, Yuba, and San Joaquin counties).

[45] "Slickens" (sediment) from hydraulic mining in the 1860s through 1880s raised river-

those risks were entrepreneurs in the true sense of the word.

Along the bottomlands of the middle stretch of the Sacramento River and along the Feather River, a different pattern of agriculture evolved with Chinese participation. There, labor-intensive fruit growing was undertaken alongside the cultivation of vegetables on a field (rather than market garden) scale. White landowners had already planted orchards in the area around Marysville prior to the Chinese entry into agriculture. However, many new orchards were planted with Chinese labor beginning in the mid-1870s.

The Chinese developed a symbiotic relationship with the landowners. Those Chinese who planted orchards for their landlords were employed not as farm laborers but as tenant farmers. Landowners leased several hundred acres at a time to Chinese tenants who were then required to prepare the ground for planting, and sometimes even to supply the saplings needed. These tenants, in turn, had responsibility for recruiting the requisite labor supply during the planting, thinning, weeding, and harvesting seasons. While the orchards were growing, the Chinese de facto were renting the land between the growing saplings for their own use. They grew berries and vegetables between the rows of trees. In some instances, a graduated rental payment calibrated to the life cycle of the fruit trees was set up. When the trees were young, and their roots had not yet spread, the tenants paid a relatively high rent for use of the land between the trees. Then by the third and fourth years, when the trees' roots had spread out far enough to be injured if the land in between were plowed for other crops, the rent would be decreased because the land could no longer be used for other crops. At the same time the trees had not yet begun to bear fruit so no income could be obtained from the land. By the fifth and sixth years, when the trees began to bear and the Chinese tenants could sell the fruit, their rent increased again. In

---

beds and greatly increased the probability of floods, while simultaneously ruining the topsoil of the flooded areas. The Sacramento-San Joaquin Delta is an inverted delta which provides the only outlet to the sea for both the Sacramento and San Joaquin rivers. The peat islands and tracts of the delta were constantly subjected to flooding. When natural or man-made levees broke, the centers of the islands, known as the backswamps, would flood first since they were lower than the surrounding levees, and they sometimes took years to drain. Crop losses during certain years were total.

this manner, the Chinese acted simultaneously as tenants who leased land to grow crops of their own and as caretakers for the growing orchards.[46]

By 1880, agriculture had become economically important to the state and to the rural Chinese immigrant communities. In rural Sacramento County, 1,123 out of a population of 3,278 Chinese (over a third of the population) depended on agriculture for their livelihood. The only other occupations of almost equal numerical importance were mining, with 1,070 persons, and nonagricultural manual labor, with 711 persons. In rural San Joaquin County, 723 persons (three-fifths of the total population) depended on agriculture for a living.[47]

Chinese involvement in California agriculture in both the Sacramento-San Joaquin Delta and the bottomlands along the Sacramento and Feather rivers was also important in the 1880s because the nature of Chinese tenancy helped to determine the pattern of Chinese interaction with the larger society. Chinese large-scale tenants always needed seasonal help, which they recruited from the rural Chinatowns. The white landowners usually had no direct dealing with these seasonal laborers. The tenants made the decision on how many workers to hire, how much to pay them, and how long to keep them. In other words, the tenants assumed all the managerial responsibility for cultivating the land. In some instances, landlords continued to live on their farms, while in other cases, they were absentee. The tenant farmers acted as middlemen who funneled jobs to their compatriots, on the one hand, and labor and managerial expertise to white landowners, on the other hand. County archival records indicate that many of these Chinese tenants operated hundreds and sometimes even thousands of acres[48] — a scale of agriculture undreamed of in the Pearl River Delta of Kwangtung Province from which most of them had emigrated. Agriculture was one of the most important channels

---

[46]This information has been drawn from numerous leases in Yuba, Sutter, and Tehama counties.

[47]My tally is from U.S. Bureau of the Census, "Tenth Census of the United States: Population, 1880" (Manuscript census for Sacramento and San Joaquin counties).

[48]In the Sutter-Yuba basin, the average size of farms leased by Chinese tenants ranged from 94 acres in 1881 to 842 acres in 1875. The Chinese tenant who operated on a larger scale for a longer period of time than any of his compatriots was Chin Lung, who farmed the San Joaquin Delta from the 1890s until the end of World War I.

for upward social mobility among rural Chinese immigrants in nineteenth-century California.

The tenant farmers were not the only ones to use their position for upward social mobility. Those who worked for them also hoped that their association with the tenants would eventually give them a share of the agricultural dividends. The mechanism for accomplishing this was the partnership system used by Chinese immigrants in urban enterprises as well as in agriculture. County archival records provide the names of many agricultural companies known as "yuen" (garden) in Chinese. Individuals' names were frequently listed alongside the companies' names, so that we know the number of partners in each outfit. Each partner signed his own name in Chinese characters on the county documents. The manuscript population census provides corroborating evidence on the emerging practice of forming partnerships: in the 1870 census, the majority of Chinese farm laborers lived in their own households, but by 1880 in the two areas under examination, the majority of Chinese farmworkers lived in the households of Chinese tenant farmers, where some members were explicitly listed as partners, while others were designated laborers. The farm laborers were taken into the tenant farmers' households not only as workers, but also as potential partners. The practice was still discernible in the 1900 manuscript census.[49]

Next to agriculture in attracting Chinese came nonagricultural common labor, followed by personal service occupations. In the three cities, entrepreneurs, artisans, and professionals were still important, ranging from 26.4 percent of the Chinese population in Marysville to 36 percent of the population in Sacramento.[50]

In terms of interaction with white employers, a portion of the farm laborers, all the nonagricultural common laborers, most of

---

[49] In 1880, 60 percent of the Chinese farm laborers in Sacramento County and 30 percent of those in San Joaquin County lived in the households of Chinese farmers; in 1900, the percentages were 52 and 82, respectively. (These percentages are based on my tally and computation from U.S. Bureau of the Census, "Tenth Census of the United States: Population, 1880" and "Twelfth Census of the United States: Population, 1900" (Manuscript census for Sacramento and San Joaquin counties). No tally can be done for 1890 since the 1890 manuscript census was destroyed in a fire in the U.S. Department of Commerce building in 1921.

[50] My tally and computation are from U.S. Bureau of the Census, "Tenth Census of the United States: Population. 1880" (Manuscript Census for Sacramento, Yuba, and San Joaquin counties).

those in personal service, factory workers, and laundrymen were the most important groups. In Sacramento City in 1880, 70 percent of the Chinese were dependent on white employers for their livelihood. In the rest of Sacramento County, the proportion was 44 percent. In Marysville, 67 percent of the total Chinese population depended on white employment, while 31 percent did so in the rest of Yuba County. In Stockton and the rest of San Joaquin County, the proportions were 29 percent and 78 percent, respectively. Thus, by 1880, the rural Chinese population was highly dependent on the economy outside their own ethnic communities for subsistence. Moreover, they had made a full transition from being independent producers to wage-earners.

*        *        *

By way of conclusion, a number of propositions may be advanced. Generally speaking, structural changes within the California economy were the major determinants of change in the occupational structure of the Chinese population in rural California. Although racism also had a great effect because it restricted the range of occupations open to the Chinese, its impact is more difficult to measure. At a more refined level of analysis, regional variations are discernible. By comparing San Francisco with interior cities such as Sacramento and Marysville on the one hand, and with the rural hinterland on the other hand, it appears that the degree and pattern of integration of the Chinese labor force into the overall economy depended on several factors: a region's initial economic base, its degree of urbanization, and its degree of industrialization. One pattern emerged in localities where the initial economy was based on mining but which soon turned to agriculture: in the countryside, few Chinese became wage-earners until the 1870s, while in the towns, as time passed, the larger and more urban the setting, the greater was the number of Chinese dependent on white employment. A second pattern was found in localities such as San Joaquin County where there had been no mining. There, the rural Chinese depended almost entirely on white landowners and other employers for their livelihood from the beginning of their settlement in the region. San Francisco showed yet another pattern of development.

In this city, the industrial center of the state, small-scale Chinese manufacturers competed with whites to employ the community's Chinese residents.

Finally, it is clear that at no time in the 1860–1880 period was the Chinese population completely segregated into ethnic enclaves, but neither was it fully integrated into the larger economy and society. Consequently, the Chinese fitted into two social stratification systems, which overlapped but were not coincidental with each other. However, given the nature of the data presented here, it is not possible to specify exactly how these two systems affected each other because occupational divisions and rankings represent only one aspect of society. A full understanding of any society's social structure must take into account the perceptions, attitudes, and patterns of noneconomic social interaction of many different persons and groups. Thus, to provide a broader understanding of the historical evolution of race relations in rural California, theories about the process of labor differentiation during different stages of economic development must be combined with theories about how human consciousness is molded.

**Table 1**
**Distribution of Chinese in California by Region and Year, 1860 – 1900**

|  | 1860 | 1870[a] | 1880 | 1890 | 1900 |
|---|---|---|---|---|---|
| Southern Mines[b] | 14,792 | 7,236 | 5,120 | 1,602 | 767 |
| Northern Mines[c] | 11,104 | 11,177 | 13,255 | 5,781 | 3,614 |
| Klamath/Trinity Mines[d] | 3,476 | 3,911 | 5,531 | 2,100 | 1,233 |
| Sacramento Valley[e] | 1,866 | 5,683 | 8,503 | 8,640 | 5,959 |
| San Joaquin Valley[f] | 653 | 2,790 | 4,869 | 7,657 | 6,165 |
| San Francisco | 2,719 | 12,022 | 21,745 | 25,833 | 13,954 |
| Other Bay Area[g] | 295 | 5,240 | 11,445 | 9,882 | 6,511 |
| Los Angeles | 11 | 234 | 1,169 | 4,424 | 3,209 |
| Other California[h] | 17 | 984 | 3,495 | 6,553 | 4,341 |
| TOTAL CALIFORNIA | 34,933 | 49,277 | 75,132 | 72,472 | 45,753 |
| (Total U.S.) | (34,933) | (63,199) | (105,465) | (107,488) | (89,863) |

Notes:

[a]The 1870 published census figures included 33 Japanese. In this table, these 33 persons have been subtracted from the published combined total of 49,310.

[b]Includes El Dorado, Amador, Calaveras, Tuolumne, and Mariposa counties.

[c]Includes Plumas, Butte, Sierra, Yuba, Nevada, and Placer counties.

[d]Includes Del Norte, Humboldt, Klamath (dissolved as a county in 1874), Siskiyou, Trinity, and Shasta counties.

[e]Includes Tehama, Glenn (after 1891), Colusa, Sutter, Yolo, Solano, and Sacramento counties. (The western portions of Butte, Yuba, and Placer counties are also part of the Sacramento Valley.)

[f]Includes San Joaquin, Stanislaus, Merced, Madera (after 1893), Fresno, Kings (after 1893), Tulare, and Kern (after 1866) counties.

[g]Includes Marin, Sonoma, Napa, Contra Costa, Alameda, Santa Clara, and San Mateo counties. (Solano County, included as part of the Sacramento Valley above, can also be counted as one of the Bay Area counties.)

[h]Includes Modoc (after 1874), Lassen (after 1864), Alpine (after 1864), Mono (after 1861), Inyo (after 1866), San Bernardino, Riverside (after 1893), San Diego, Orange (after 1889), Ventura (after 1873), Santa Barbara, San Luis Obispo, Monterey, San Benito (after 1874), Santa Cruz, Lake (after 1861), and Mendocino counties. Imperial County was not established until 1907.

*Sources*: The regional figures are computed from numbers for individual counties given in U.S Bureau of the Census, *Ninth Census of the United States: Population, 1870* (Washington, D.C., 1872), 15; and *Twelfth Census of the United States: Population, 1900* (Washington, D.C., 1902), 565.

**Table 2**

**Occupational Structure of the Chinese Population in Sacramento City and County, Marysville City and Yuba County, and Stockton City and San Joaquin County, California, 1860**

| Occupational Category | Sacramento City | Rest of Sacramento County | Marysville City | Rest of Yuba County | Stockton City | Rest of San Joaquin County |
|---|---|---|---|---|---|---|
| **PRIMARY EXTRACTION AND PRODUCTION** | | | | | | |
| Miners | 23 | 633 | 5 | 1,418 | 0 | 0 |
| Truck gardeners | 70 | 15 | 20 | 14 | 0 | 0 |
| Farmers | 0 | 3 | 0 | 0 | 0 | 0 |
| Fishermen | 67 | 0 | 2 | 0 | 10 | 0 |
| **MANUAL LABOR— AGRICULTURAL** | | | | | | |
| Farm laborers | 0 | 0 | 0 | 0 | 0 | 1 |
| Woodmen | 9 | 0 | 0 | 0 | 0 | 0 |
| **MANUAL LABOR— NONAGRICULTURAL** | | | | | | |
| Common laborers | 41 | 11 | 7 | 7 | 6 | 0 |
| **PERSONAL SERVICE** | | | | | | |
| Cooks | 27 | 18 | 12 | 35 | 10 | 8 |
| Servants | 63 | 10 | 6 | 5 | 0 | 0 |
| Waiters/dishwashers | 1 | 0 | 1 | 0 | 6 | 0 |
| Prostitutes (specified) | 105 | 0 | 0 | 0 | 18 | 0 |
| Prostitutes (probable) | 8 | 5 | 75 | 2 | 0 | 0 |
| **ARTISANS, PROFESSIONALS, AND ENTREPRENEURS** | | | | | | |
| Bakers | 19 | 0 | 0 | 0 | 0 | 0 |
| Barbers | 9 | 0 | 3 | 1 | 0 | 0 |
| Boarding house keepers | 2 | 0 | 6 | 0 | 2 | 0 |
| Butchers/fish sellers | 20 | 1 | 3 | 1 | 3 | 0 |
| Cabinet makers | 7 | 0 | 0 | 0 | 0 | 0 |

| | | | | | | |
|---|---|---|---|---|---|---|
| Carpenters | 9 | 0 | 0 | 1 | 0 | 0 |
| Clerks | 3 | 0 | 0 | 1 | 1 | 0 |
| Fortune tellers | 2 | 0 | 0 | 0 | 0 | 0 |
| Gamblers | 0 | 0 | 0 | 1 | 0 | 0 |
| Labor contractors | 5 | 0 | 0 | 0 | 0 | 0 |
| Laundrymen/laundresses | 272 | 3 | 53 | 12 | 37 | 0 |
| Medical practitioners | 27 | 2 | 4 | 4 | 0 | 0 |
| Merchants/storekeepers/ grocers | 50 | 37 | 8 | 22 | 4 | 0 |
| Musicians | 16 | 0 | 0 | 0 | 0 | 0 |
| Peddlers | 7 | 0 | 1 | 0 | 0 | 0 |
| Poultry dealers | 3 | 0 | 0 | 0 | 0 | 0 |
| Silversmith | 2 | 0 | 0 | 0 | 0 | 0 |
| Tailors | 21 | 1 | 1 | 0 | 0 | 0 |
| Teamsters | 10 | 0 | 0 | 0 | 4 | 0 |
| WIVES AND CHILDREN | 64 | 0 | 3 | 0 | 2 | 0 |
| INMATES | 3 | 0 | 7 | 0 | 10 | 0 |
| MEN WITH NO OCCUPATIONS | 15 | 0 | 10 | 0 | 2 | 0 |
| TOTAL | 980 | 739 | 227 | 1,524 | 115 | 9 |
| Percent in primary extraction and production | 16.3% | 88.1% | 11.9% | 94.0% | 8.7% | 0 |
| Percent in manual labor | 5.1% | 1.5% | 3.1% | 0.5% | 5.2% | 11.1% |
| Percent in personal service | 20.8% | 4.5% | 41.4% | 2.8% | 29.6% | 88.9% |
| Percent artisans, professionals and entrepreneurs | 49.4% | 6.0% | 34.8% | 2.8% | 44.4% | 0 |
| Percent with no occupation | 8.4% | 0 | 8.8% | 0 | 12.2% | 0 |

*Source:* Based on my tallies from U.S. Bureau of the Census, "Eighth Census of the United States: Population, 1860" (Manuscript census for Sacramento, Yuba, and San Joaquin counties).

### Table 3
Occupational Structure of the Chinese Population in Sacramento City and County, Marysville City and Yuba County, and Stockton City and San Joaquin County, California, 1870

| Occupational Category | Sacramento City | Rest of Sacramento County | Marysville City | Rest of Yuba County | Stockton City | Rest of San Joaquin County |
|---|---|---|---|---|---|---|
| PRIMARY EXTRACTION AND PRODUCTION | | | | | | |
| Miners | 4 | 875 | 0 | 588 | 13 | 0 |
| Truck gardeners | 35 | 37 | 60 | 6 | 0 | 0 |
| Farmers | 4 | 26 | 0 | 0 | 0 | 0 |
| Fishermen | 3 | 0 | 0 | 0 | 100 | 1 |
| MANUAL LABOR— AGRICULTURAL | | | | | | |
| Farm laborers and hop pickers | 0 | 567 | 0 | 22 | 4 | 224 |
| Woodmen | 2 | 23 | 5 | 4 | 0 | 0 |
| MANUAL LABOR— NONAGRICULTURAL | | | | | | |
| Common laborers | 264 | 224 | 650 | 165 | 473 | 49 |
| Levee builders | 0 | 250 | 0 | 0 | 0 | 0 |
| Factory workers | 23 | 0 | 0 | 0 | 0 | 0 |
| Railroad workers | 8 | 0 | 0 | 6 | 0 | 169 |
| PERSONAL SERVICE | | | | | | |
| Cooks | 70 | 42 | 188 | 63 | 132 | 88 |
| Servants | 122 | 0 | 23 | 14 | 78 | 5 |
| Waiters/dishwashers | 4 | 0 | 0 | 4 | 4 | 0 |
| Prostitutes (specified) | 0 | 44 | 117 | 15 | 36 | 0 |
| Prostitutes (probable) | 169 | 0 | 12 | 5 | 2 | 0 |
| ARTISANS, PROFESSIONALS, AND ENTREPRENEURS | | | | | | |
| Bakers | 1 | 0 | 1 | 0 | 0 | 0 |
| Barbers | 18 | 0 | 10 | 0 | 0 | 0 |
| Barrel makers | 6 | 0 | 0 | 0 | 0 | 0 |
| Boarding house keepers | 16 | 0 | 18 | 0 | 26 | 0 |
| Boot/shoe makers | 15 | 0 | 6 | 1 | 1 | 0 |
| Brick makers | 0 | 41 | 0 | 0 | 0 | 0 |
| Butchers/fish sellers | 22 | 3 | 20 | 0 | 0 | 0 |

| | | | | | | |
|---|---|---|---|---|---|---|
| Candle makers | 2 | 0 | 0 | 0 | 0 | 0 |
| Cigar makers | 35 | 0 | 3 | 0 | 0 | 0 |
| Clerks | 28 | 0 | 3 | 5 | 13 | 0 |
| Gamblers | 40 | 8 | 29 | 0 | 40 | 0 |
| Jewelers | 0 | 0 | 1 | 0 | 0 | 0 |
| Labor contractors | 1 | 0 | 1 | 0 | 0 | 0 |
| Laundrymen/laundresses | 246 | 1 | 154 | 6 | 89 | 7 |
| Medical practitioners | 15 | 0 | 17 | 4 | 2 | 0 |
| Merchants/storekeepers | 28 | 4 | 60 | 6 | 10 | 0 |
| Musicians | 0 | 0 | 4 | 0 | 0 | 0 |
| Opium dealers | 0 | 0 | 1 | 0 | 2 | 0 |
| Peddlers | 6 | 0 | 0 | 0 | 14 | 5 |
| Pickle makers | 3 | 0 | 0 | 0 | 0 | 0 |
| Potters | 0 | 1 | 0 | 0 | 0 | 0 |
| Restaurant keepers | 2 | 0 | 9 | 0 | 2 | 0 |
| Tailors/seamstresses | 11 | 0 | 6 | 2 | 0 | 0 |
| Tea merchants | 2 | 0 | 0 | 0 | 0 | 0 |
| Teachers | 0 | 0 | 2 | 0 | 0 | 0 |
| Teamsters/mule packers | 9 | 0 | 0 | 3 | 4 | 0 |
| Tinsmiths | 3 | 0 | 0 | 0 | 0 | 0 |
| Vegetable/fruit vendors | 18 | 0 | 0 | 0 | 1 | 0 |
| WIVES AND CHILDREN | 74 | 0 | 0 | 0 | 2 | 0 |
| INMATES | 0 | 0 | 5 | 0 | 5 | 0 |
| MEN WITH NO OCCUPATIONS | 22 | 1 | 10 | 2 | 15 | 1 |
| TOTAL | 1,331 | 2,147 | 1,415 | 917 | 1,069 | 549 |
| Percent in primary extraction and production | 3.5% | 43.7% | 4.2% | 64.8% | 10.7% | 0.2% |
| Percent in manual labor | 22.3% | 49.6% | 46.3% | 21.5% | 44.6% | 80.5% |
| Percent in personal service | 27.4% | 4.0% | 24.0% | 10.6% | 23.6% | 16.9% |
| Percent artisans, professionals and entrepreneurs | 39.6% | 2.7% | 24.4% | 2.9% | 19.1% | 2.2% |
| Percent with no occupation | 7.2% | 0 | 1.1% | 0.2% | 2.1% | 0.2% |

*Source:* Based on my tallies from U.S. Bureau of the Census, "Ninth Census of the United States: Population, 1870" (Manuscript census for Sacramento, Yuba, and San Joaquin counties).

53

## Table 4

### Occupational Structure of the Chinese Population in Sacramento City and County, Marysville City and Yuba County, and Stockton City and San Joaquin County, California, 1880

| Occupational Category | Sacramento City | Rest of Sacramento County | Marysville City | Rest of Yuba County | Stockton City | Rest of San Joaquin County |
|---|---|---|---|---|---|---|
| **PRIMARY EXTRACTION AND PRODUCTION** | | | | | | |
| Miners | 0 | 1,070 | 4 | 559 | 0 | 3 |
| Truck gardeners | 95 | 94 | 47 | 45 | 1 | 93 |
| Farmers | 0 | 438 | 0 | 0 | 1 | 99 |
| Fishermen | 0 | 9 | 1 | 0 | 91 | 3 |
| **MANUAL LABOR—AGRICULTURAL** | | | | | | |
| Farm laborers | 3 | 534 | 98 | 53 | 0 | 449 |
| Woodmen | 0 | 23 | 1 | 3 | 3 | 82 |
| Fish factory workers | 0 | 33 | 0 | 0 | 0 | 0 |
| **MANUAL LABOR—NONAGRICULTURAL** | | | | | | |
| Common laborers | 450 | 705 | 246 | 123 | 17 | 113 |
| Reclamation laborers | 0 | 0 | 0 | 0 | 0 | 41 |
| Railroad workers | 0 | 6 | 0 | 12 | 0 | 79 |
| **PERSONAL SERVICE** | | | | | | |
| Cooks | 104 | 87 | 191 | 76 | 117 | 151 |
| Servants | 229 | 15 | 1 | 1 | 25 | 22 |
| Waiters/dishwashers | 26 | 0 | 0 | 1 | 4 | 0 |
| Bootblacks | 0 | 0 | 2 | 0 | 0 | 0 |
| Prostitutes (specified) | 2 | 2 | 40 | 18 | 22 | 0 |
| Prostitutes (probable) | 63 | 32 | 10 | 2 | 14 | 0 |
| **INDUSTRIAL FACTORY WORKERS** | | | | | | |
| Mill workers | 28 | 0 | 46 | 0 | 31 | 0 |

| ARTISANS, PROFESSIONALS, AND ENTREPRENEURS | | | | | | |
|---|---|---|---|---|---|---|
| Bakers | 0 | 0 | 1 | 0 | 0 | 0 |
| Barbers | 13 | 7 | 14 | 0 | 9 | 1 |
| Boarding house keepers | 0 | 0 | 1 | 0 | 6 | 0 |
| Boot/shoe makers | 3 | 4 | 0 | 0 | 2 | 1 |
| Brick makers | 9 | 0 | 0 | 0 | 0 | 24 |
| Broom makers | 2 | 0 | 0 | 0 | 0 | 0 |
| Brothel owners | 0 | 0 | 1 | 0 | 0 | 0 |
| Bucket makers | 9 | 7 | 8 | 0 | 0 | 0 |
| Butchers/fish sellers | 26 | 0 | 0 | 0 | 1 | 2 |
| Candy makers | 1 | 1 | 8 | 0 | 0 | 0 |
| Carpenters | 0 | 0 | 0 | 0 | 1 | 1 |
| Chair makers | 7 | 0 | 0 | 0 | 0 | 0 |
| Cheese makers | 6 | 0 | 0 | 0 | 0 | 0 |
| Cigar makers | 34 | 9 | 2 | 0 | 1 | 0 |
| Clerks/bookkeepers | 5 | 0 | 14 | 0 | 7 | 2 |
| Fortune tellers | 1 | 0 | 0 | 0 | 0 | 0 |
| Furniture dealers | 0 | 0 | 2 | 0 | 0 | 0 |
| Gamblers | 60 | 8 | 24 | 8 | 0 | 0 |
| Interpreters | 0 | 0 | 0 | 1 | 2 | 0 |
| Jewelers | 1 | 0 | 2 | 0 | 0 | 0 |
| Labor contractors | 305 | 0 | 0 | 0 | 3 | 2 |
| Laundrymen/laundresses | 0 | 41 | 81 | 15 | 62 | 60 |
| Medical practitioners | 38 | 0 | 4 | 1 | 4 | 3 |
| Merchants/storekeepers | 0 | 56 | 39 | 9 | 26 | 6 |
| Musicians/actors | 6 | 0 | 58 | 0 | 0 | 0 |
| Opium dealers | 6 | 8 | 2 | 0 | 9 | 0 |
| Peddlers/scavengers | 0 | 2 | 0 | 1 | 6 | 0 |
| Religious personnel | 11 | 3 | 2 | 0 | 0 | 0 |
| Restaurant keepers | 0 | 0 | 1 | 0 | 6 | 2 |
| Solicitors | 0 | 0 | 0 | 0 | 0 | 1 |
| Tailors/seamstresses | 44 | 4 | 6 | 0 | 8 | 0 |
| Vegetable/fruit vendors | 16 | 0 | 0 | 0 | 8 | 1 |
| Wood carvers | 0 | 0 | 1 | 0 | 0 | 0 |

## Table 4 (Continued)
### Occupational Structure of the Chinese Population in Sacramento City and County, Marysville City and Yuba County, and Stockton City and San Joaquin County, California, 1880

| Occupational Category | Sacramento City | Rest of Sacramento County | Marysville City | Rest of Yuba County | Stockton City | Rest of San Joaquin County |
|---|---|---|---|---|---|---|
| WIVES AND CHILDREN | 28 | 20 | 36 | 8 | 17 | 4 |
| INMATES | 0 | 0 | 8 | 0 | 36 | 8 |
| MEN WITH NO OCCUPATIONS | 43 | 60 | 2 | 7 | 34 | 12 |
| OCCUPATIONS UNDECIPHERABLE | 0 | 0 | 24 | 0 | 0 | 0 |
| TOTAL | 1,674 | 3,278 | 1,028 | 943 | 574 | 1,263 |
| Percent in primary extraction and production | 5.7% | 49.2% | 5.1% | 64.1% | 16.2% | 15.7% |
| Percent in manual labor | 27.1% | 39.7% | 33.6% | 20.3% | 3.5% | 60.5% |
| Percent in personal service | 25.3% | 4.2% | 23.7% | 10.4% | 31.7% | 13.7% |
| Percent in factory work | 1.7% | 0 | 4.5% | 0 | 5.4% | 0 |
| Percent artisans, professionals and entrepreneurs | 36.0% | 4.6% | 26.4% | 3.7% | 28.1% | 8.2% |
| Percent with no occupation | 4.3% | 2.4% | 6.8% | 1.6% | 15.2% | 2.0% |

Source: Based on tallies from U.S. Bureau of the Census, "Tenth Census of the United States: Population, 1880" (Manuscript census for Sacramento, Yuba, and San Joaquin counties).

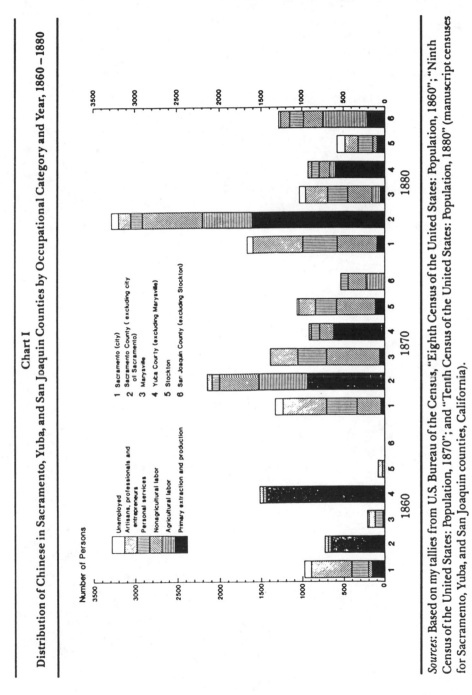

Chart I

Distribution of Chinese in Sacramento, Yuba, and San Joaquin Counties by Occupational Category and Year, 1860 – 1880

Unemployed
Artisans, professionals and entrepreneurs
Personal services
Nonagricultural labor
Agricultural labor
Primary extraction and production

1 Sacramento (city)
2 Sacramento County ( excluding city of Sacramento)
3 Marysville
4 Yuba County (excluding Marysville)
5 Stockton
6 San Joaquin County (excluding Stockton)

Number of Persons

*Sources:* Based on my tallies from U.S. Bureau of the Census, "Eighth Census of the United States: Population, 1860"; "Ninth Census of the United States: Population, 1870"; and "Tenth Census of the United States: Population, 1880" (manuscript censuses for Sacramento, Yuba, and San Joaquin counties, California).

# Landless by Law: Japanese Immigrants in California Agriculture to 1941

*Besides racial prejudice against them, the Japanese are not allowed the privilege of becoming full citizens of the United States, thus being prevented from developing along many lines. Among these, the most noteworthy is the California Alien Land Law and the consequent laws which prohibit Japanese from possessing land unless they are citizens. Under these circumstances, can it justly and fairly be claimed that the Japanese are non-assimilable?*

Kiichi Kanzaki, *California and the Japanese*, 1921

THE Japanese occupy a unique place in the history of America's immigrants. They were denied the privilege of naturalization (until 1952), forbidden to purchase or lease farm land (in California, 1913-1956), driven from their homes by the wartime evacuation and confined in concentration camps (1942-1945). Yet the Japanese are now one of the most successful of all ethnic groups in America. The narrative of this remarkable experience has been written often and well, and detailed studies of its political, legal, and social aspects have been made. Economic historians, however, have done relatively little to analyze and learn from the Japanese-American experience.

My paper, which attempts to fill this gap, offers a brief sketch of the involvement of the Japanese in California agriculture during the half century before the Second World War. I then consider two related issues in the economic history of discrimination against the Japanese in America: first, the discrimination against them in the agricultural labor and land rental markets; second, the legal discrimination against them required by the alien land laws of California. A concluding section takes a broad view of and offers some generalizations about this historical experience.

## IMMIGRATION AND EMPLOYMENT

Substantial numbers of Japanese immigrants arrived for the first time in the mainland United States during the 1890s. The volume of

*Journal of Economic History*, Vol. XXXVIII, No. 1 (March 1978). Copyright © The Economic History Association. All rights reserved.

I have received valuable advice and bibliographical assistance from Tetsuden Kashima and Frank Miyamoto at the University of Washington; through correspondence, Masakazu Iwata (Biola College) and Harry H. L. Kitano (UCLA) were helpful. To all of them, my sincere gratitude.

205

arrivals increased sharply at the turn of the century, and the period 1900-1908 witnessed the greatest influx. The United States census of 1910 counted more than 72,000 Japanese in the continental United States, but this enumeration was especially defective and the actual number was perhaps as much as 20,000 larger.[1] After the Gentlemen's Agreement went into effect in 1908, Japanese immigration declined and included a much larger proportion of women. Although the United States census of 1920 showed a total increase of almost 39,000 Japanese during the preceding decade, the increase was less than 14,000 for foreign-born males, and much of that apparent increase was probably spurious, reflecting only the greater completeness of the 1920 count. With the new immigration law in effect after 1924, Japanese immigration became negligible. Although natural increase pushed the resident population up, a considerable net emigration pulled it down, and by 1940 the Japanese population, including both the native- and the foreign-born, numbered only 127,000.[2]

The first Japanese immigrants found a wide variety of jobs, scattered throughout the western states. Railroads, logging and lumbering camps, mines, canneries, and domestic service provided a large part of their employment during the 1890s. After 1900, however, the immigrant workers, predominantly young unmarried males, tended to migrate away from such jobs to find employment in agriculture; increasingly they concentrated in California, especially in the areas where the acreage of labor-intensive crops was being expanded in the Central Valley and near Los Angeles. The Immigration Commission estimated that California agriculture provided employment for 30,000 Japanese during the summer months of 1909.[3] According to the records of the Japanese associations in California, two-thirds of those gainfully occupied in 1910 worked in agriculture.[4] From this peak, the relative importance of agricultural employment declined somewhat, and the absolute number of Japanese involved also fell. Still, as

[1] U.S. Bureau of the Census, *Chinese and Japanese in the United States, 1910*, Bulletin no. 127 (Washington, 1914), p. 7; H. A. Millis, "Some of the Economic Aspects of Japanese Immigration," *American Economic Review*, 5 (Dec. 1915), 789.

[2] U.S., Congress, House, Tolan Committee, *National Defense Migration*, 77th Cong., 2d sess., 1942, no. 2124, p. 94; Dorothy Swaine Thomas, "Some Social Aspects of Japanese-American Demography," *Proceedings of the American Philosophical Society*, 94 (Oct. 19, 1950), 459-62; William Petersen, "A Note on Statistics," in his *Japanese Americans: Oppression and Success* (New York, 1971), pp. 14-19.

[3] U.S., Immigration Commission, *Reports*, XXIII (Washington, 1911), p. 61.

[4] *Japanese American Yearbook* of 1911, cited in Edward K. Strong, *The Second-Generation Japanese Problem* (Stanford, 1934), p. 216. H. A. Millis, *The Japanese Problem in the United States* (New York, 1915), p. 103, cites similar estimates by the California Commissioner of Labor.

late as 1940, more than 17,000 found employment in California agriculture, and just over half of the Japanese males employed in the state remained in farming. In the production of vegetables, berries, fruit, and grapes, they exerted themselves prodigiously. In 1941 they accounted for an estimated 30-35 percent of the value of all commercial truck crops grown in California.[5]

During the period 1900-1920 many Japanese in California agriculture left work as wage laborers and became farm tenants and, less frequently, owner operators. The federal census of agriculture in 1920 enumerated more than 5,000 Japanese farm operators, nine-tenths of them tenants, in the state.[6] Skilled farmers, working intensely for long hours in a hot climate, often in a backbreaking stooped position, they proved formidable competitors in the land rental markets. As such they gained both the respect of the large white landlords and the enmity of the small white tenant farmers. Partly because of their success as independent farmers, they became the target of hostile land laws, enacted first in 1913 and strengthened by amendments in 1920, 1923, and 1927. On paper these laws left the Japanese immigrants no legal position in agriculture except that of wage laborer, but in practice, as we shall see, the laws became dead letters.[7]

### MARKET DISCRIMINATION

During the earliest period of their employment in California agriculture, the Japanese generally worked for wages, and they received lower wages than whites for similar work. Although this racial difference tended to narrow after the turn of the century, two extensive surveys reveal that it remained substantial as late as 1909.

In that year the California Commissioner of Labor undertook, at the special request of the state legislature, a study of California's Japanese population. The agricultural portion of the inquiry involved visits to 4,102 farms scattered over 36 counties; of the farms investigated, 1,733 were operated by Japanese owners or tenants, 2,369 by white operators equally divided between those employing only white laborers and those employing racially mixed labor forces.[8] Some findings of the study with respect to wages appear in Table 1.

[5] *House Reports* [Tolan Committee], pp. 105, 117-18.

[6] U.S. Census, *Agriculture, 1920*, V (Washington, 1922), p. 312.

[7] For a much longer and more detailed survey of the subjects discussed in this section, see Masakazu Iwata, "The Japanese Immigrants in California Agriculture," *Agricultural History*, 36 (Jan. 1962), 25-37.

[8] [J. D. Mackenzie], "A Summary by Labor Commissioner J. D. Mackenzie of the Report of the 'Special State Investigation of 1909' of the Japanese in California. Given to the Press May 30,

TABLE 1

DAILY WAGE RATES (WITHOUT BOARD) PAID BY WHITE EMPLOYERS
TO WHITE AND JAPANESE LABORERS, SELECTED FARM
OCCUPATIONS, CALIFORNIA, 1909

| Occupation | Whites | | Japanese | |
|---|---|---|---|---|
| | Number reporting | Average wage | Number reporting | Average wage |
| Berry pickers | 9 | $1.86 | 59 | $1.63 |
| Celery cutters | 20 | 1.50 | 101 | 1.50 |
| Cultivators | 141 | 1.69 | 127 | 1.34 |
| Farm hands | 1,187 | 1.70 | 2,026 | 1.47 |
| Fruit pickers | 1,424 | 1.73 | 3,186 | 1.58 |
| Grape pickers | 147 | 2.00 | 929 | 1.75 |
| Hoers | 273 | 1.88 | 274 | 1.69 |
| Laborers | 186 | 1.84 | 1,067 | 1.45 |
| Packers | 165 | 1.78 | 440 | 1.55 |
| Pruners | 225 | 1.36 | 1,408 | 1.39 |
| Teamsters | 454 | 2.05 | 59 | 1.74 |
| Total | 5,189 | 1.80 | 10,676 | 1.54 |

Source: California Commissioner of Labor, *Fourteenth Biennial Report*, insert, p. 270, as
reproduced in H. A. Millis, *The Japanese Problem in the United States* (New York,
1915), p. 120.

The table shows that the average wage rate of Japanese workers
hired by white employers fell 26 cents per day, or 14 percent, below
that of white workers, although wage rates were about the same in
two occupations, pruning and celery cutting. The Commissioner's
report cautioned, however, that $1.54 per day "cannot be taken as the
average earnings of the Japanese, for 49.2 per cent of the entire
number employed were working by contract or piecework, under
which condition the earnings of the japanese are much larger than
those of the whites." The report also noted that Japanese farm
operators hired 17,784 workers, of whom 96 percent were Japanese,
and paid an average wage of $1.65 per day without board, "showing
that the Japanese were better paid by their own countrymen than by
the white farmer."[9]

Also in 1909, agents of the U.S. Immigration Commission collected
information from 5,793 wage laborers in California agriculture, and
their findings closely paralleled those of the Labor Commissioner. The
Immigration Commission's report observed that wages varied considerably among districts, but in most places "there is a discrimination of

1910," printed in Sidney L. Gulick, *The American Japanese Problem* (New York, 1914), pp.
316-23.
    [9] Ibid., pp. 317-18.

about 25 cents per day in favor of white men as against Japanese and other Asiatics engaged in the same work." In a few places, daily wages for seasonal work were reported to be the same for both races. Most seasonal workers, however, received piece-rate wages, and on this basis the Japanese made "from 10 to 100 per cent larger average earnings per day than at day rates," the earnings of some individual workers reaching $6 or more per day. The Japanese earned more than whites on the piece-rate system because they worked "longer hours and with closer application to their work, for piece rates are now usually the same for all races."[10] The report also confirmed that Japanese workers received higher wages when hired by Japanese employers, and it noted, insightfully, that "the higher wages paid by the Japanese farmers have . . . tended to compel white farmers to pay more to their Japanese employees."[11]

This competitive pressure increased rapidly after 1909, and within a few years racial discrimination against the Japanese in the farm l.bor market had virtually disappeared. Millis reported in 1915 that "lower payment of Japanese than of white men engaged in the same occupations is almost entirely a matter of the past." In addition, piece rates remained uniform for white and Japanese laborers.[12] After the Gentlemen's Agreement went into effect in 1908, the influx of Japanese laborers fell dramatically. Resident alien workers increasingly moved into positions as tenants or, less frequently, as owner operators. This shift reduced the ranks of potential victims of discrimination and swelled the number of nondiscriminating employers in the wage labor market. More and more the Japanese wage laborers found jobs with Japanese employers. In 1920 the State Board of Control averred that "there are probably more white laborers working for Oriental farmers than there are Oriental laborers working for American farmers," and some observers adduced evidence that in 1919-1920 the Japanese actually received higher wages than whites, the premium being compensation for superior work and the performance of particularly onerous tasks.[13]

While the transition from wage labor to tenancy played a central role in eliminating racial wage discrimination, the newly-established tenants immediately encountered another form of discrimination in

[10] U.S., Immigration Commission, *Reports*, XXIII, pp. 66-67; see also pp. 61-67.
[11] Ibid., XXIV, p. 40; see also pp. 33-43.
[12] Millis, *The Japanese Problem*, p. 124; idem, "Economic Aspects," p. 796.
[13] State Board of Control of California, *California and the Oriental: Japanese, Chinese, and Hindus*, rev. ed. (Sacramento, 1922), pp. 58, 60, 115, 229, 239-40.

the land rental market. All sources agree that the Japanese paid higher rental rates than white tenants. The Immigration Commission concluded in 1909 that "the offer of comparatively high rents, though not universal, is fairly general." Six years later Millis observed that the racial difference in rental rates had probably diminished but had not yet disappeared. Then, noting that the higher rents paid by the Japanese had never been a matter of dispute, he abruptly dropped the subject, remarking that "further detail need not be added."[14]

Further detail would have been illuminating, however, for neither the reports of the Immigration Commission nor the later observations by Millis established the magnitude of the discrimination faced by Japanese tenants in the land rental market. Table 2 sheds some light on this matter. The data shown there were originally collected in the federal agricultural census of 1920 but were neither compiled nor published by the Census Bureau. Early in the 1920s Clyde Chambers, a USDA economist, obtained permission to draw a sample of the data, and the evidence in Table 2 is taken from his study.[15] The 1,901 Japanese tenant farms that were sampled were located in eight different counties, and they provide a reliable basis for judgment; the 1,745 white tenant farms that were sampled furnish a substantial comparative standard.

The table supports several conclusions. First, the Japanese tenants invariably occupied more valuable land than their white neighbors; in some places, such as Alameda, Orange, Sacramento, and Solano Counties, much more valuable land. Second, the Japanese invariably paid higher rent per acre than their white counterparts. (Neither of these related racial differences, of course, implies anything about racial discrimination.) Third, and most importantly, the Japanese generally paid higher rents relative to land values than did their white counterparts, the only exceptions being the longer-term tenants in Alameda and Orange Counties. In some cases the racial differences in the ratio of rent to value were small and would probably fall short of standard significance levels in a statistical test (which cannot be performed in the absence of the individual observations from which the averages were computed). In many cases, however, the racial differences were large and almost certainly significant: in four cases the Japanese ratio exceeded the white by three percentage points or

[14] U.S., Immigration Commission, *Reports*, XXIII, p. 82; Millis, *The Japanese Problem*, pp. 142-43.
[15] Clyde R. Chambers, *Relation of Land Income to Land Value*, USDA Bulletin no. 1224 (Washington, June 11, 1924).

## TABLE 2
### AVERAGE RENT, AVERAGE VALUE, AND RATIO OF RENT TO VALUE FOR FARMS CLASSIFIED BY RACE OF TENANT AND PERIOD OF OCCUPANCY, SELECTED COUNTIES, CALIFORNIA, 1920[a]

| County and period of occupancy of farm | Whites | | | | Japanese | | | |
|---|---|---|---|---|---|---|---|---|
| | Number of farms | Ave. cash rent/acre | Ave. value/acre | Ratio | Number of farms | Ave. cash rent/acre | Ave. value/acre | Ratio |
| **Alameda** | | | | | | | | |
| Total | 194 | $5.19 | $152 | 3.4 | 88 | $27.00 | $913 | 3.0 |
| 1 year | 50 | 11.66 | 338 | 3.5 | 25 | 31.76 | 562 | 5.7 |
| 2 or More | 144 | 4.50 | 132 | 3.4 | 63 | 25.97 | 969 | 2.6 |
| **Imperial** | | | | | | | | |
| Total | 509 | 19.96 | 176 | 11.3 | 272 | 27.08 | 209 | 13.0 |
| 1 Year | 343 | 20.96 | 176 | 11.9 | 178 | 29.58 | 216 | 13.7 |
| 2 or More | 166 | 18.24 | 178 | 10.3 | 94 | 23.68 | 200 | 11.9 |
| **Los Angeles** | | | | | | | | |
| Total | 442 | 12.88 | 506 | 2.5 | 996 | 23.06 | 743 | 3.1 |
| 1 Year | 223 | 15.34 | 505 | 3.0 | 358 | 23.55 | 738 | 3.2 |
| 2 or More | 219 | 11.50 | 507 | 2.3 | 638 | 22.81 | 745 | 3.1 |
| **Orange** | | | | | | | | |
| Total | 30 | 8.15 | 292 | 2.8 | 41 | 23.11 | 699 | 3.3 |
| 1 Year | 12 | 7.69 | 411 | 1.9 | 12 | 24.23 | 494 | 4.9 |
| 2 or More | 18 | 8.44 | 218 | 3.9 | 29 | 22.79 | 757 | 3.0 |
| **Sacramento** | | | | | | | | |
| Total | 141 | 5.96 | 128 | 4.6 | 259 | 24.45 | 380 | 6.4 |
| 1 Year | 61 | 7.89 | 125 | 6.3 | 60 | 25.82 | 353 | 7.3 |
| 2 or More | 80 | 5.24 | 129 | 4.0 | 199 | 24.03 | 388 | 6.2 |
| **San Joaquin** | | | | | | | | |
| Total | 210 | $12.53 | $250 | 5.0 | 119 | $23.67 | $314 | 7.5 |
| 1 Year | 101 | 13.46 | 233 | 5.8 | 58 | 24.57 | 324 | 7.6 |
| 2 or More | 109 | 11.79 | 264 | 4.5 | 61 | 22.53 | 301 | 7.5 |

211

### TABLE 2 (CONTINUED)
### AVERAGE RENT, AVERAGE VALUE, AND RATIO OF RENT TO VALUE FOR FARMS CLASSIFIED BY RACE OF TENANT AND PERIOD OF OCCUPANCY, SELECTED COUNTIES, CALIFORNIA, 1920[a]

| County and period of occupancy of farm | Japanese | | | | Whites | | | |
|---|---|---|---|---|---|---|---|---|
| | Number of farms | Ave. cash rent/acre | Ave. value/acre. | Ratio | Number of farms | Ave. cash rent/acre | Ave. value/acre | Ratio |
| Santa Clara | | | | | | | | |
| Total | 106 | 8.95 | 290 | 3.1 | 83 | 23.29 | 537 | 4.3 |
| 1 Year | 35 | 12.32 | 310 | 4.0 | 22 | 22.06 | 442 | 5.0 |
| 2 or More | 71 | 7.99 | 285 | 2.8 | 61 | 23.68 | 568 | 4.2 |
| Solano | | | | | | | | |
| Total | 113 | 6.57 | 113 | 5.8 | 43 | 29.65 | 301 | 9.9 |
| 1 Year | 45 | 5.51 | 96 | 5.7 | 9 | 71.12 | 683 | 10.4 |
| 2 or More | 68 | 7.00 | 119 | 5.9 | 34 | 26.46 | 272 | 9.7 |

[a] Data apply only to tenants unrelated by kinship to landlords and to farms of 10 acres or more.
Source: Clyde R. Chambers, *Relation of Land Income to Land Value*, USDA Bulletin no. 1224 (Washington, June 11, 1924), pp. 74-76.

more (first-year tenants in Orange and Solano, longer-term tenants in San Joaquin and Solano Counties). Given that the cash rents were accurately reported and that the average land values were unbiased estimates, the conclusion is inescapable that landlords, as late as 1920, effectively discriminated against the Japanese in the land rental market. The average Japanese tenant probably paid a rental premium equal to one or two percent of the land's estimated value.

I shall not stop to judge whether this premium was "large" or "small." A more intriguing question is why it existed at all. Contemporaries adduced plausible reasons why the Japanese were willing or able to pay higher rents than whites: more ambition; greater willingness to bear risk; the ability to work harder, longer, and more efficiently; more unpaid family labor; lower standards of living; fewer alternative opportunities—all were advanced to account for the willingness of the Japanese to outbid white tenants.[16] There the matter was allowed to rest, the question of why the Japanese tenants found it *necessary* to pay a rental premium never having been raised. Tc my knowledge, only one contemporary recognized the inadequacy of explanations referring exclusively to the tenants' side of the market. Anticipating Gary Becker's model of the economics of discrimination by more than 30 years, Chambers wrote: "Japanese tenants can and will pay considerably more for the use of the land than the white tenants. *Since the landowners prefer to rent to white tenants without this rent premium,* the Japanese have to pay this premium in order to get the use of the land." Chambers, however, was too good an economist to stop there, and he added, insightfully:

The fact alone, that the Japanese have to pay higher rents than the white tenants in order to get the use of the land does not explain why the Japanese rents are higher relative to the value of the land. If the Japanese were found grouped in large communities which the buyers and sellers of land regarded as stable, and if the Japanese could not become owners of this land, as is the case, then the buyers and sellers of land in these communities would base their values on the income the farms would earn when leased to Japanese tenants. Then the ratios of rent to value in these communities would be the same as the ratios in communities of white tenants, although the rents would probably be higher. The fact that the Japanese were paying relatively higher rents than the white tenants would not alter the situation, for the values would be directly based upon those rents, regardless of the factors determining them. The percentage of Japanese tenants, however, is small and the permanent value of the land is based upon what white operators can make it earn.[17]

[16] Ibid., p. 58; U.S., Immigration Commission, *Reports*, XXIII, p. 82; Millis, *The Japanese Problem*, pp. 141-44; idem, "Economic Aspects," p. 800.
[17] Chambers, "Relation of Land Income," pp. 58-59 (italics added).

This is excellent economic analysis, and Chambers' model offers a coherent explanation of the prevailing discrimination against the Japanese in the land rental market, *provided one accepts his assertion that the landowners (all of them?) preferred white tenants unless the Japanese paid a rental premium.*

My uneasiness with this explanation arises from my skepticism about the realism of its pivotal assumption. If a substantial number of landlords preferred wealth to the pleasures of discriminating against the Japanese, then competition among landlords would have tended to reduce the prevailing racial difference in rental rates. In fact, the Japanese in California were not without friends, chief among whom were the large landlords raising labor-intensive crops and operating their ranches with tenant labor.[18] Such landlords could have had a profound impact on the market, especially after 1920, when the rapid rise in the number of Japanese tenants halted and then reversed itself. My conjecture is that the existence of a racial rental premium in 1920 represented a disequilibrium situation: competitive forces had yet to overcome the discrimination exerted during the years 1900-1920 when the Japanese were rushing headlong into the rental markets of a few districts. This conjecture suggests that the discriminatory rental premium should have disappeared during the period 1920-1940. Unfortunately, I have been unable to find any systematically compiled data on the rents paid by tenants of the two races during these years. I greatly regret the lack of such evidence, for without it one cannot conduct a clearcut test of whether competition or racial discrimination ultimately triumphed in this important market.

## LEGAL DISCRIMINATION

The Japanese, in the eyes of the California whites, were indistinguishable from the Chinese, and hence the whites' longstanding anti-Chinese hostilities inevitably descended on the newcomers from the Orient. Although they seldom suffered from the mob violence that had often plagued the Chinese of California in the nineteenth century, the Japanese became a similar target for legal discrimination and exclusion. Pure racism supplied the main impetus for the whites' desire to discriminate, but the success of the Japanese in agriculture

[18] Millis, *The Japanese Problem*, pp. 204, 223-24; T. Iyenaga and Kenoske Sato, *Japan and the California Problem* (New York, 1921), pp. 123-24; C. McWilliams, "Once again the 'Yellow Peril,'" *Nation*, 140 (June 26, 1935), 736; Roger Daniels, *The Politics of Prejudice* (Berkeley, 1962), p. 48.

certainly heightened preexisting hostilities. By concentrating in a few districts, the Japanese farmers made their accomplishments more conspicuous, and their gains in land tenure and crop production were easily exaggerated by those who despised them on racial grounds or feared them as economic competitors. Seldom have so few innocuous people inspired so much irrational hatred and apprehension.

In these circumstances some form of legal discrimination against the Japanese was highly probable, and after several years of agitation by politicians and organizations representing a variety of labor, agricultural, and civic interests the state legislature passed the Alien Land Law of 1913.[19] Its authors openly designed the law to make life unpleasant for the state's Oriental aliens. In the words of the law's co-author, State Attorney General U. S. Webb, the objective was "to limit their presence by curtailing their privileges which they may enjoy here; for they will not come in large numbers and long abide with us if they may not acquire land."[20]

Still, in a feeble attempt to disguise the affront to Japan, the law was written without any mention of the Japanese. On its face it appeared only to define certain property rights of "all aliens eligible to citizenship under the laws of the United States." It provided, however, that "all aliens other than those" could enjoy only such property rights as "prescribed by any treaty now existing between the government of the United States and the nation or country of which such alien is a citizen or subject"; the single exception was that aliens ineligible for citizenship could "lease lands in this state for agricultural purposes for a term not exceeding three years." As the Japanese were legally ineligible for naturalization, and as the treaty of 1911 between Japan and the United States gave the Japanese no explicit rights to own or lease agricultural land in the United States, and as the Chinese had long been denied the privilege of immigration, the act in effect applied only to the Japanese. To plug a potential loophole, the restrictions of the act were also placed upon corporations of which a majority of the members were aliens ineligible to citizenship or which had issued a majority of their stock to such aliens. The state attorney general was empowered to institute escheat proceedings against property acquired in violation of the act.

[19] Cal. Stats., Ch. 113, 1913 (May 19, 1913) took effect Aug. 10, 1913. On the political machinations that surrounded the passage of this law, see Daniels, *Politics of Prejudice*, pp. 46-64.

[20] Speech before the Commonwealth Club of San Francisco, Aug. 9, 1913, cited in Frank F. Chuman, *The Bamboo People: The Law and Japanese-Americans* (Del Mar, Calif., 1976), p. 48.

Under the Alien Land Law of 1913, the only interest in agricultural land that a Japanese alien could legally acquire was a leasehold for a term not exceeding three years. But the law was immediately, openly, and widely evaded, and the Japanese continued to acquire ownership rights and unrestricted leaseholds. Three evasive devices played important roles during the years 1913-1920.

Probably the most significant was the purchase of land in the names of native-born (citizen) sons and daughters. As almost all the offspring were then minors, such purchases required the appointment of a legal guardian or properly qualified trustee. Usually the alien parent of the citizen child applied for and was granted guardianship, and few objections to this practice arose until after the First World War. In 1919 and 1920, with the renewal of widespread agitation against the Japanese, some courts adopted a hostile stance, refusing to grant such guardianships or rescinding those already granted. The character of the presiding judges became decisive. "If the man was liberal-minded," observed Jean Pajus, "the harried litigants who appeared before him were treated leniently; if he happened to be rabidly contra-alien, his victims did not have the ghost of a chance." In a guardianship case brought before him in 1920, a judge in Santa Clara County remarked: "I will deal with it . . . just as I do with white children; there is no distinction . . . . We can't sit here and punish people according to our notions." Only a year earlier, however, a judge in Tulare County had ruled quite differently. Not content to deny the application for guardianship of a Japanese mother who had earlier purchased an orchard in her daughter's name, the judge used the occasion to rail against "this contract . . . made purely as an evasion of the law to prevent Japanese from buying property in this state"; he reproachfully advised that "the attorneys of this state should refrain, as far as possible, from handling any such proposition as this."[21]

Japanese purchasers of land could avoid the potential difficulties of guardianships by "borrowing the name" of an American citizen of legal age. Sometimes Hawaiian-born Japanese, who were generally older than those born on the mainland, supplied their names for this purpose. Hawaiian-born Kazuo Miyamoto tells in his autobiography how distant relatives approached him during his senior year at Stan-

---

[21] Jean Pajus, *The Real Japanese California* (Berkeley, 1937), pp. 131-34; see also pp. 135-36; and U.S., Congress, House, Committee on Immigration and Naturalization, *Japanese Immigration: Hearings*, 66th Cong., 2d sess., 1921, pp. 404, 873-76.

ford University to present this proposition: "The whole crux of the arrangement is in the getting of a trustworthy citizen who will not betray the Japanese farmers. Since you are twenty-one years old, you can lease these farms for us. What do you think? In return Mr. Tanaka will guarantee the expense to put you through medical school." For financially straitened Miyamoto, "nobody could have planned anything more convenient at such an opportune time."[22] Sympathetic white citizens also provided names, often as trustees. L. M. Landsborough, of the Florin district, near Sacramento, testified before a House Committee in 1920 that he had purchased six different parcels, containing over 100 acres, for Japanese farmers, taking the deeds in his name. Paid only for the clerical work involved, he acquired no substantive interest in the properties and later transferred the deeds to native-born Japanese children when payment for the land had been completed. By steadfastly refusing to admit any wrongdoing to his inquisitors, Landsborough provoked Congressman John Raker to say that "on the face of the record, here is the Japanese who has no title to or who is not entitled to own the land; he is running it, farming it, controlling it, just the same as though he owned it, but using you and your name, and, through you, is violating the law; isn't that right?" Momentarily intimidated, Landsborough confessed, "Well, I think it is."[23]

The third major device employed to evade the Alien Land Law of 1913 was the formation of "dummy" corporations. Provided that American citizens constituted a majority of the stockholders and held a majority of the issued stock, a corporation did not violate the law. Such a corporation could be easily formed by a Japanese couple with two native-born children, assisted by a cooperative American attorney. Each person could be a stockowner, three citizens and two aliens making citizens a majority of the members; and enough of the stock owned by the children could be issued to the attorney, acting as their trustee, to give the citizens a majority ownership of the issued stock. A handful of lawyers specialized in this exotic branch of corporate law: of 30 Japanese farming corporations in Merced County in 1920, 23 issued large blocks of stock to trustees Albert H. Elliot and Guy C. Calden, who served as attorneys for the Japanese Association of America.[24] An official of the State Board of Control in 1920 compiled a

[22] Kazuo Miyamoto, *Hawaii: End of the Rainbow* (Rutland, Vt., 1964), pp. 237-39.
[23] House Committee, *Japanese Immigration*, p. 263. For Landsborough's full testimony, see pp. 244-74. See also Dorothy Swaine Thomas, *The Salvage* (Berkeley, 1952), p. 181.
[24] House Committee, *Japanese Immigration*, pp. 428-34; see also pp. 215-20, 325-26, 503-8,

list of 302 Japanese farming corporations owning almost 48,000 acres.[25] In his unpublished research, Masakazu Iwata has identified 416 companies formed before 1921 ("370 were organized to operate farms and the remainder formed for the specific purpose of land purchase and floricultural operations") which held almost 66,000 acres.[26] Concerned about this practice, the State Board of Control complained: "It is a source of deep regret that there are attorneys in the state who despite their oath to support the constitution and the laws of this state, nevertheless sell their legal talent in aiding this breach of the spirit and purpose of the Alien Land Law."[27]

The Alien Land Law of 1913 simply did not accomplish what its proponents had intended. Through its wide loopholes, multitudes of Japanese farmers adroitly passed. With the end of the war and the onset of renewed agitation against the Japanese, the dogs of racism howled for an amended law. Political feuds prevented passage of new legislation in 1919. The next year the legislature did not convene, but the anti-Japanese forces managed to place an initiative proposal before the electorate at the general election. In this way they secured, by a margin of three-to-one, passage of the Alien Land Law of 1920.[28]

This law sought to close all the loopholes of the 1913 act. In effect, it denied Japanese aliens all rights of ownership *and* leasehold over agricultural land, forbade them to become members of or acquire shares in any corporation entitled to hold agricultural land, and prohibited them from acting as guardians for minors owning or leasing land. The law provided for escheat proceedings to be brought by the attorney general or any district attorney against illegally held interests in land. It defined several *prima facie* presumptions of intent to evade the law, including the taking of an interest in real estate in the name of a citizen when consideration was paid by an ineligible alien. Criminal penalties were established (up to two years imprisonment and five thousand dollars fine) for those who conspired to violate the law. The final section of the act, a clear confession of legal insecurity, declared: "If any section, subsection, sentence, clause or phrase of this act is for any reason held to be unconstitutional, such decision shall not affect the validity of the remaining portions of this act."

---

841-42, 900 for additional evidence on the services of attorneys for Japanese farming corporations.

[25] Ibid., pp. 420-24.

[26] Personal correspondence, Masakazu Iwata to the author, June 22, 1977 and Aug. 5, 1977.

[27] State Board of Control, *California and the Oriental*, p. 69.

[28] Cal. Stats., 1921, Initiative Act of 1920, p. lxxxiii (approved Nov. 2, 1920; became effective Dec. 9, 1920). On the political machinations that surrounded the passage of this law, see Daniels, *Politics of Prejudice*, pp. 79-91.

In general, the courts upheld the constitutionality of the Initiative Act and its subsequent amendments.[29] In several cases decided in 1923 the U. S. Supreme Court held that the act was not arbitrary and unreasonable in its discrimination against aliens ineligible to citizenship and that it did not deny them due process of law.[30] Said Justice Butler: "The allegiance of the farmers to the state directly affects its strength and safety. We think it within the power of the state to deny to ineligible aliens the privilege to use agricultural lands within its borders."[31] Exactly how the operation of a few thousand small vegetable and fruit farms by the Japanese threatened the strength and safety of California was not explained by the learned Justice.

While these cases were still moving through the federal courts, however, the Supreme Court of California decided a separate case of far-reaching importance. In *Estate of Tetsubumi Yano*,[32] the court concluded that "the provisions of the Initiative Act of 1920 forbidding the appointment of an alien resident, ineligible to citizenship, as guardian of the farming land of his native-born child, and authorizing the removal of such parent, if previously appointed as such guardian, are invalid," being denials of equal protection of the law. This decision opened a crack in the law through which many Japanese farmers would subsequently squeeze by making "gifts" of land to their minor children, for whom they acted as legal guardians and farm managers.[33]

The Japanese also employed other devices to circumvent the alien land laws after 1920. Probably the most common were collusive, unwritten arrangements whereby the alien leased a farm *de facto* while acting only as a salaried manager *de jure*. By 1928 Eliot Mears perceived that "over the state there is a general lack of enforcement" of the alien land laws. Edward K. Strong, after directing a survey (10 percent sample) of the California Japanese in 1930, observed that "on many occasions men reported that they were managers or foremen,

[29] The most important amendments were: 45 Cal. Stats. 1020 (June 20, 1923), declaring sharecropping agreements to constitute an interest in real property; and Cal. Stats., 1927, Ch. 528, Sec. 9a and 9b, placing the burden of proof on the alleged ineligible alien in cases of contested citizenship.

[30] *Porterfield v. Webb*, 263 U.S. 225 (Nov. 12, 1923); *Webb v. O'Brien*, 263 U.S. 313 (Nov. 19, 1923); *Frick v. Webb*, 263 U.S. 326 (Nov. 19, 1923).

[31] The best treatments of the legal and constitutional aspects of the alien land laws are Chuman, *Bamboo People*, passim, and Dudley O. McGovney, "The Anti-Japanese Land Laws of California and Ten Other States," *California Law Review*, 35 (Mar. 1947), 7-60.

[32] 188 Cal. 645 (May 1, 1922).

[33] Pajus, *The Real Japanese California*, pp. 136-41; Chuman, *Bamboo People*, p. 119; McGovney, "Anti-Japanese Land Laws," pp. 28-30. The *Yano* doctrine was later sustained in *People v. Fujita*, 215 Cal. 166 (1932) and in *Kiyoko Nishi v. Downing*, 21 C.A. 2d 1 (May 11, 1937).

only to admit later that they were renting or had purchased the land. As far as could be discovered by our interviewers, the land law is non-operative in many sections of the state if not in all parts." One large landowner told Strong that he had never heard of the alien land laws and that many white landowners in his district rented to Japanese tenants.[34] A decision by the U. S. Supreme Court in 1934 made it virtually impossible for the state to invoke the criminal sanctions of the alien land laws by proving that a conspiracy had transpired.[35] In 1935 Carey McWilliams declared the law a dead letter: "It is no longer enforced," he said, "nor is there any sentiment for its enforcement."[36]

White landlords and Japanese farmers evaded the law because both parties gained wealth by doing so. Many contemporary observers noted that strict enforcement of the law would have severely damaged the interests of large landowning whites, and "when it is to the advantage of the whites to lease their land to Japanese, they find a way to do it."[37] Local district attorneys, acting with self-serving circumspection, rarely brought escheat proceedings against violators of the law.[38] In some districts landlords and tenants simply ignored the law without resorting to any evasive devices whatever.[39] Finally, as more and more native-born Japanese came of age in the 1930s, evasion became unnecessary, land titles and leaseholds being taken in the names of adult citizen members of Japanese families.

Under the alien land laws, as amended in 1923, aliens ineligible to citizenship could not legally "acquire, possess, enjoy, use, cultivate,

[34] Eliot Grinnell Mears, *Resident Orientals on the Pacific Coast: Their Legal and Economic Status* (Chicago, 1928), p. 253; Strong, *Second-Generation Japanese Problem*, pp. 211-12; Thomas, *The Salvage*, p. 182.

[35] *Morrison v. California*, 291 U.S. 82 (Jan. 8, 1934).

[36] McWilliams, "Once again the 'Yellow Peril,' " p. 736. See also Grace Cable Keroher, "California's Anti-Orientalism," in Clarence A. Peters, comp., *The Immigration Problem* (New York, 1948), p. 183.

[37] Strong, *Second-Generation Japanese Problem*, pp. 45, 212. See also McWilliams, "Once again the 'Yellow Peril,' " p. 736; Edwin E. Ferguson, "The California Alien Land Law and the 14th Amendment," *California Law Review*, 35 (Mar. 1947), 72; Thomas, *The Salvage*, p. 24.

[38] Mears, *Resident Orientals*, p. 254. Chuman (*Bamboo People*, pp. 117-18) finds 16 reported escheat cases between 1920 and 1940. Undoubtedly others took place in the superior courts but were not appealed and hence not reported.

[39] "My own father who was a farmer seemed to have little difficulty in southern California in renting land without resorting to devious means to get around the law. The law was possibly not enforced with rigidity here" (personal correspondence, Masakazu Iwata to the author, June 22, 1977). "[I]n the 1920's it may have been necessary for father to rely on one of his Caucasian friends, a banker in San Fernando by the name of Walker, to sign lease papers. But as far as my own recollection goes, in the latter 1920's and the 1930's he acquired land simply on an oral promise. There seemed not to be any hassle regarding this as far as he was concerned" (idem, Aug. 5, 1977).

occupy, and transfer real property." As Justice Butler correctly observed, "the Act as a whole evidences legislative intention that ineligible aliens shall not be permitted to have or enjoy any privileges in respect to the use or the benefit of land for agricultural purposes."[40] But these sweeping intentions were never realized, nor were they even approximated. We have seen how the Japanese, in cooperation with white landowners and a handful of resourceful lawyers, devised means of circumventing the obstacles erected by the state legislature. It remains to examine the quantitative record of Japanese involvement in California agriculture as a final test of the laws' effects.

Clearly, the alien land laws did not drive the Japanese out of agriculture. A majority of the employed males still found employment in farming as late as 1940. Nor were they reduced to wage laborers. Table 3 shows that the number of self-declared owners rose continuously. The number of tenants probably reached a peak in 1920, as the table indicates, but the apparently precipitous drop from 1920 to 1930 was largely spurious. Much of this decline was offset by the greatly increased number describing themselves as "managers," a common ruse to evade the alien land laws. By 1940 the number declaring themselves managers had shrunk drastically, which is consistent with the evidence already marshalled on the changing modes of evasion and nonenforcement of the laws. The total number of Japanese farm operators in 1940 was virtually the same as it had been 20 years earlier. In this light, the alien land laws appear to have failed utterly.

Table 4 brings together scattered data on the acreage owned and leased by Japanese farmers. For all years except 1942, the data originated in surveys made by the Japanese Association of America. Although not completely accurate, these are the most reliable data available on acreage operated. (The federal census data, by comparison, are substantially smaller, for obvious reasons.) Total acreage reached a peak in 1920, fell abruptly during the next two years, then declined slowly for the duration of the period. Anticipating the new restrictions imminent in 1920, the Japanese simply bit off more than they could chew. Overextended, they almost certainly had to reduce their acreage sometime afterwards; the collapse of farm prices in 1921 must have hastened the day. Perhaps the Initiative Act of 1920 also contributed in those first dark days when many farmers were confused and uncertain about whether the new legal restrictions could be circumvented. Between 1932 and 1942 the owned acreage increased

---

[40] 45 Cal. Stats. 1020 (June 20, 1923); *Webb v. O'Brien*, 263 U.S. 313 (Nov. 19, 1923).

TABLE 3
U.S. CENSUS AND WRA ENUMERATIONS OF JAPANESE FARMS,
BY TENURE STATUS OF OPERATORS,
CALIFORNIA, 1910-1942

| Date | Owners | Tenants | Managers | Total |
|------|--------|---------|----------|-------|
| 1910 | 233 | 1,547 | 36 | 1,816 |
| 1920 | 506 | 4,533 | 113 | 5,152 |
| 1930 | 560 | 1,580 | 1,616 | 3,756 |
| 1940 | 1,290 | 3,596 | 249 | 5,135 |
| 1942 | 1,703 | 3,195 | 10 | 4,908 |

Sources: For 1910 and 1920, U.S. Census, *Agriculture, 1920*, V (1922), p. 312; for 1930 and 1940, U.S. Census, *Agriculture, 1940*, III (1943), p. 224; for 1942, War Relocation Authority evacuee property records, cited in Adon Poli and Warren M. Engstrand, "Japanese Agriculture on the Pacific Coast," *Journal of Land and Public Utility Economics*, 21 (Nov. 1945), 355.

considerably, while the rented acreage continued to decline. This difference suggests that something other than the land laws was at work. Evidently, a plethora of obstacles notwithstanding, Japanese farmers continued to climb upward on the "tenure ladder."

A final important element, neglected in most assessments of the effects of the land laws, was demographic change. The virtual cessation of immigration and substantial emigration after 1924, along with normal mortality, caused the population of alien adult males to decline steadily from about 32,000 in 1920 to only about 21,000 in 1940,

TABLE 4
FARM ACREAGE OPERATED BY JAPANESE OWNERS AND TENANTS,
CALIFORNIA, 1905-1942

| Date | Acres owned (in 1,000's) | Acres rented or worked under annual labor contract (in 1,000's) | Total |
|------|--------------------------|-----------------------------------------------------------------|-------|
| 1905 | 2 | 60 | 62 |
| 1913 | 27 | 255 | 282 |
| 1920 | 75 | 383 | 458 |
| 1922 | 51 | 280 | 330[a] |
| 1925 | 42 | 266 | 308 |
| 1932 | 38 | 250 | 288 |
| 1942 | 69 | 163 | 232 |

[a] Discrepancy due to rounding.
Sources: Except for 1942, the original authority for all years is the Japanese Association of America, as cited by Kiichi Kanzaki, *California and the Japanese* (San Francisco, 1921), p. 55; Yamato Ichihashi, *Japanese in the United States* (Stanford, 1932), p. 193; Edward K. Strong, Jr., *Japanese in California* (Stanford, 1933), p. 138. For 1942, the original authority is the War Relocation Authority evacuee property records, cited in Adon Poli and Warren M. Engstrand, "Japanese Agriculture on the Pacific Coast," *Journal of Land and Public Utility Economics*, 21 (Nov. 1945), 355.

a decline of approximately one-third.[41] In 1920 the census counted a total of 5,039 Japanese farm owners and tenants, virtually all of whom can be assumed to have been alien adult males. In 1940 there were 3,911 alien Japanese males who admitted that they were farmers or farm managers.[42] Inasmuch as the true manager component was negligible, the implication is that during the period of the most stringent land laws, 1920-1940, the number of *alien* Japanese farmers declined by about 22 percent, or *much less than the corresponding population*. In 1920 one of every 6.4 male adult aliens was a farm operator; in 1940 one of every 5.4. As the number of *rural* adult aliens had probably declined even more rapidly than the total,[43] the conclusion applies *a fortiori:* the Japanese immigrants substantially improved their tenure status in California agriculture during the two decades after the passage of the harsh Initiative Act of 1920.

### MELTING POT BE DAMNED

One can write much of the economic history of the Japanese immigrants by employing the theme of discriminatory challenge and market response. Confronted by wage discrimination and limited opportunities for advancement in the farm labor market, the Japanese responded by going into business for themselves, mainly as tenants. Encountering discrimination in the land rental market, a growing number responded by acquiring ownership of farm land. In the face of highly restrictive land laws, they devised the means to continue operating their farms and, after a transitory reversal in the early 1920s, steadily advanced up the tenure ladder. On every occasion when attempts to discriminate against them took place, market counterpressures—the lure of wealth awaiting the nondiscriminators—worked to free them from discriminatory restraints. On the eve of the Second World War, the immigrant generation had attained an economic position of solid middle class dimensions. With a high rate of self-employment, considerable ownership of land and other property, and a comfortable standard of living, the Japanese of rural California could look back with well justified pride. They had, it appeared, triumphed over racial discrimination in both the market and the law.

Of course, there was another, less cheerful side to the story. To an

---

[41] U.S. Census, *Population, 1920*, III (1922), p. 128; U.S. Census, *Population, 1940: Characteristics of the Nonwhite Population by Race* (1943), p. 98.

[42] Table 3 above; and *House Reports* [Tolan Committee], p. 105.

[43] The alien rural Japanese population of all ages fell from 18,479 in 1920 to 8,915 in 1940, a decline of over half. See U.S. Census, *Population, 1940*, II (1943), p. 518.

important extent, the alien land laws had fallen into desuetude because they had been, in the minds of many of their initial supporters, no more than means to an end. That end was Oriental exclusion, and after its attainment in the immigration act of 1924, only a few felt threatened by the dwindling numbers of resident alien Japanese and their well-behaved children.[44] The Japanese and the large white landowners became, as Carey McWilliams expressed it in the mid-thirties, "partners in an unholy and highly profitable conspiracy." But, suspecting that the racists might only be sleeping, McWilliams sensed the imminence of new dangers and wondered: "Will their economic alliances protect them?"[45] We know now, of course, that their alliances did not protect them when the storm came, and in the hysteria of 1942-1945 the immigrant generation lost practically everything it had so arduously accumulated. Emerging from the concentration camps in 1945, the aging immigrants were too old to start anew. Their children, much younger and more vigorous, with excellent educations, would make extraordinary economic progress in the postwar era. But their great gains should blind no one to the vast losses of their parents, losses for which only token restitution was ever made.[46]

There was a time, especially in the early 1920s, when the question of Japanese immigrant assimilation provoked vigorous debate. The exclusionists adamantly maintained that the Japanese were unassimilable, hence undesirable, and ought not to be admitted to the country at all. More honest white spokesmen put the matter bluntly: "It is not a question of whether the Jap is assimilable or not," said an official of the Los Angeles Chamber of Commerce; "we do not want to assimilate him."[47] Kiichi Kanzaki, General Secretary of the Japanese Association of America, knew that assimilation was a phony issue and that the real issue was white racism. "If," he said,

after establishing all sorts of barriers on the way of assimilation, it [is] always contended that the Japanese are nonassimilable, this is nothing but another way of stating that the whites are nonassimilable. . . . In other words, they want to assimilate others but they do not want to be assimilated by others. Their assumption is their racial superiority, and unless this is adjusted no question of assimilation can be permanently settled.[48]

[44] Mears, *Resident Orientals*, p. 178; *House Reports* [Tolan Committee], pp. 85-86; McGovney, "The Anti-Japanese Land Laws," pp. 51-52; Ferguson, "The California Alien Land Law," p. 72; Strong, *Second-Generation Japanese Problem*, p. 46.
[45] McWilliams, "Once again the 'Yellow Peril,' " p. 736.
[46] Petersen, *Japanese Americans*, pp. 104-8.
[47] Statement of Dr. George P. Clements, manager of the agricultural department, Los Angeles Chamber of Commerce, printed in House Committee, *Japanese Immigration*, p. 1008.
[48] Testimony of K. Kanzaki, ibid., p. 655.

The Japanese were quite willing to go more than half way in accommodating themselves to white culture, but white racism reared its head at every turn. "I know America is the melting pot," said Yo Suzuki of Stockton, ". . . and we are ready to melt, but some American people hate us; hate us by appearance, color of skin, and so on; and they say the Japanese can not be assimilated. I think that is wrong."[49] Most whites now would probably agree with Suzuki. But the white Americans' change of heart—if it really is that—came too late to save the immigrant victims of California's longstanding anti-Oriental racism.

ROBERT HIGGS, *University of Washington*

[49] Testimony of Yo Suzuki, president of Stockton Growers' Exchange, ibid., p. 516.

# MIGRATION TO AN AMERICAN FRONTIER*

## JOHN C. HUDSON

ABSTRACT. A sample of one thousand autobiographies written by North Dakota pioneers during the late 1930s reveals a complex pattern of migration and earning a living on the western frontier from 1875 to 1915. North Dakota was settled by eastern Canadians as part of the general westward trend of settlement across the prairies. German, German Russian, and Scandinavian-born settlers moved within discrete information-migration networks which were strengthened by a strong tendency toward marriage within the group that was preserved in the migration process. American stock settlers came from diverse origins and often worked at a succession of farm and nonfarm jobs as they moved westward. Population turnover and labor mobility resulted from the rapid growth of a specialized economic system which offered many opportunities. Seasonal labor migration was common in the early years before transition to a more stable system. The cultural geography of the northern plains emerged from diverse ethnic origins and a common orientation to the market economy.

IN a recent book, George Wilson Pierson purports to find in the "M-factor" (for migration) a key to the American experience.[1] To Pierson, a critic of the frontier thesis, "Americanization by Motion" is a worthy replacement for Turner's ideas about American institutions. Recent historical studies have shown that massive population mobility is nothing new; Americans were a "restless, migratory people" well back into the nineteenth century.[2] The current situation, in which an average of one in four or five Americans moves each year, differs only in degree from that prevailing in earlier generations.

According to Stephan Thernstrom, late nineteenth century urban dwellers who did not find upward mobility "were tossed helplessly about from city to city, from state to state, alienated but invisible and impotent."[3] Discovery of this large population turnover, which ran from the frontier to the metropolis, has naturally stimulated thought on the effects of migration on social institutions, especially those of the working class for whom migration and upward mobility were often not synonymous. Since rural to urban migration began well before the frontier of population had completed its sweep across the continent, the processes shaping the nation's settlement pattern today have their origins in the earliest of these movements. "It might be argued that most fundamentally the historical geography of North America is a study of the forces that cause men to move, starting with the transatlantic migration itself and carrying on through the wanderings over the continent the migrants reached."[4]

Juxtaposition of these ideas against those of migration modelers, who seek rational motivation for population movements based on notions of expected satisfaction, the friction of dis-

Dr. Hudson is Associate Professor of Geography at Northwestern University in Evanston, IL 60201.

* The support of National Science Foundation Grant GS-42844 is gratefully acknowledged.

[1] G. W. Pierson, *The Moving American* (New York: Alfred A. Knopf, 1972). A similar theme with a more contemporary focus is developed in V. Packard, *A Nation of Strangers* (New York: David McKay, 1972).

[2] S. Thernstrom and P. R. Knights, "Men in Motion: Some Data and Speculations about Urban Population Mobility in Nineteenth Century America," in T. K. Hareven, ed., *Anonymous Americans: Explorations in Nineteenth-Century Social History* (Englewood Cliffs, NJ: Prentice-Hall, Inc., 1971), pp. 17–47.

[3] S. Thernstrom, "Urbanization, Migration, and Social Mobility in Late Nineteenth-Century America," in B. J. Bernstein, ed., *Towards a New Past: Dissenting Essays in American History* (New York: Pantheon Books, 1968), pp. 158–75.

[4] J. E. Vance, Jr., "California and the Search for the Ideal," *Annals*, Association of American Geographers, Vol. 62 (1972), p. 194.

ANNALS OF THE ASSOCIATION OF AMERICAN GEOGRAPHERS Vol. 66, No. 2, June 1976
© 1976 by the Association of American Geographers. Printed in U.S.A.

tance, and other venerated concepts, makes it hard to believe that the same phenomenon is being described. Rootless individuals living in a constantly changing environment with little sense of community sounds more like particles in Brownian motion than like the pushes and pulls to overcome inertia and distance friction which are discussed in contemporary models of migration. At the very least it is clear that migration may be conceptualized in many different ways, that it is nearly as difficult to predict as to understand, and that its consequences go deeply into nearly all facets of human geography.[5] The admission that circulation may be a more significant starting point than location rapidly diminishes the stock of concepts that might be brought to bear by a discipline accustomed to studying things in place; what initially appears as an "inherently geographical" phenomenon even becomes difficult to map on closer examination.

## MIGRATION STUDIES

Whether migration is a way of life or merely a series of responses to economic stimuli does not alter its significance. Focussing on areal units and recording migrations between them may obscure many aspects of the process, but areal unit data remain the principal source and the concepts developed as a result constitute the bulk of available generalizations.

The study of past migrations has relied heavily on comparing manuscript censuses for various decades and computing population turnover rates. Studies of nineteenth century frontier populations by Malin in Kansas and Curti in Wisconsin established that the frontier was not a stable zone where agriculturalists moved once and for all to occupy the land; the frontier was, instead, a zone of considerable in and out movement.[6] Urban historians have documented similar high rates of population mobility for nineteenth century American cities.[7] Studies

revealing low mobility rates in the past one hundred years would be truly exceptional, so widespread and constant was the circulation of individuals. Surely there were place-to-place as well as class variations in these rates of turnover, though as yet there seems to be little systematic study of their geography.

Turnover studies reveal nothing about individuals after they leave a given study location, or before they arrive. Changing jobs is a prime reason for moving, so studies confined to a single place are essentially useless for a study of interregional migration and associated occupational mobility. The strong evidence for massive population turnover on the farm and in the city and the lack of any data connecting individual moves into life histories fosters the Brownian motion view of migration—a chaotic movement in which many individuals are "tossed helplessly about."

When other kinds of data, such as life histories, are available they are almost always seized upon by migration researchers looking for a more detailed view of the process. During 1938 and 1939 the State Historical Society of North Dakota and the Works Progress Administration undertook an ambitious "Historical Data Project," collecting questionnaires and autobiographies from several thousand pioneer settlers in the state. White occupance of the region was so comparatively recent that many people living in the late 1930s remembered the early days and were able to respond to the survey. This paper is an analysis of approximately one thousand of these completed records. It is an effort to place frontier migration in the broader perspective of interregional and international migration, to examine several hypotheses about migration and mobility in American life, and to examine some of the influences on the way of life in the northern plains, one of the remaining lacunae on the map of American culture areas.

## DAKOTA SETTLEMENTS

The first massive influx of settlers into Dakota Territory occurred in the 1880s. The westward push beyond the subhumid Middle West took place during an era of liberal land policy and coincided with the arrival of thousands of north-

---

[5] An up-to-date review of migration literature is in R. P. Shaw, *Migration Theory and Fact* (Philadelphia: Regional Science Research Institute, 1975).

[6] J. C. Malin, "The Turnover of Farm Population in Kansas," *Kansas Historical Quarterly*, Vol. 4 (1935), pp. 339–72; and M. Curti et al., *The Making of an American Community* (Stanford: Stanford University Press, 1959).

[7] Thernstrom and Knights, op. cit., footnote 2. A critical review of recent historical studies on mobility and migration is S. L. Engerman, "Up or Out: Social and Geographic Mobility in the United States," *Journal of Interdisciplinary History*, Vol. 3 (1975), pp. 469–89.

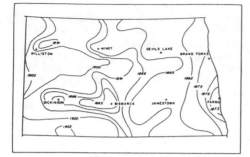

FIG. 1. Spread of frontier settlement in North Dakota. Isochrones based on median date of first dwellings in blocks of sixteen townships. Source for this and following figures: Historical Data Project files (sample).

ern European immigrants. Dakota Territory became the new home of landless Middle Westerners, Norwegians, Germans, Swedes, Canadians, and other groups who came in smaller numbers. The two Dakotas achieved separate statehood in 1889, preceding a decade of diminished growth caused by a sharp downturn in transatlantic migration and a period of contraction in American agriculture. At the beginning of the twentieth century these trends were reversed and a second, although smaller, "boom" drew the frontier westward across the Missouri River and into central Montana (Fig. 1).

Since North Dakota was settled around the magic date of 1890, which supposedly marked the closing of the frontier, it offers a particularly valuable comparison with earlier frontiers and with the emerging urban society. Conditions for settlement during this brief period toward the end of westward expansion and during the rise of an urban-industrial economy are reflected in migration patterns. European immigrants, especially, were filtered through the Northeast and Middle West on their way to the plains frontier, a fact reflected in numerous shifts of occupation by the immigrants in their westward movement through the increasingly diverse regional economies.

The underlying motives for each individual's decision to join in this migration are not available, though it must be supposed in each case that some combination of a conscious desire to better one's lot plus the magical appeal of the frontier was responsible. Much can be made of the perceived versus real opportunities open to those who moved toward the Great Plains—

whether there was deception in the process of luring people to the west (there was), and whether many who joined in should have done so. A less pathological view is suggested by the data presented here. What is most striking is not the lack of information possessed by pioneers wandering into the unknown grasslands, but rather the apparently well-used information networks specific to ethnic groups which formed a bond between the widely scattered enclaves, and the usefulness of these informal networks in spreading information about economic opportunities when and where they arose. It is appropriate to begin the analysis of these migrations with a description of the various groups and to thus build up an overall picture of the process.

### ONTARIO SETTLERS

Ontario natives were most numerous among the Canadian-born who settled northern Dakota. Their migration to the American west was often no more than one generation removed from a transatlantic crossing by their ancestors (Fig. 2). Three-fourths of the Ontario-born Dakota pioneers had foreign-born parents, with Scotch, Irish, and English ancestry predominating.

One or two generations before the migration to North Dakota, the Canada Company was vigorously promoting settlement by these groups in the Huron Tract north of London, Ontario.[8] Their offspring, in turn, moved to Dakota in large numbers between 1875 and 1880, as did several organized groups from Glengarry County, east of Ottawa. The Glengarry colony itself had resulted from the resettlement of a disbanded group of Scottish Highlanders early in the nineteenth century. Those from the Ontario Glengarry settled near Pembina, where the Red River of the North crosses the international boundary.

A third source area within Ontario illustrates the rapid turnover of population in the westward movement in North America. Bruce and Grey counties, between Lake Huron and Georgian Bay, had just begun to be settled in 1851; the population increased tenfold by 1861, and more than doubled again by 1881. The popula-

[8] R. L. Gentilcore, "Settlement," in R. L. Gentilcore, ed., *Ontario: Studies in Canadian Geography* (Toronto: University of Toronto Press, 1972), pp. 23–44.

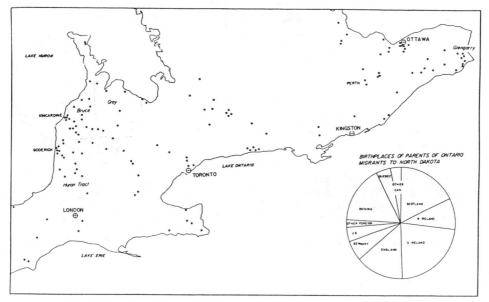

FIG. 2.    Birthplaces of Ontario migrants to North Dakota.

tion of 65,000 in these two counties in 1881 represented a density as great or greater than that in the more agriculturally favorable counties to the south and east, making them likely source areas for subsequent frontiers.

Nearly all Ontarians who migrated to North Dakota did so directly, with no intervening place of residence. They generally moved by rail or water to the western end of the Great Lakes and then via St. Paul to Winnipeg, where settlement fanned out to the south and west. Most of them took land in Manitoba, but thousands were induced to cross the border between Pembina and the Turtle Mountains (Fig. 3).[9]

This southward movement was begun by the Métis around 1820; it was repeated half a century later by the Ontario settlers and by those from Quebec and Nova Scotia. The French Canadians stuck close to the forested areas, but those of Scotch, Irish, and English ancestry eventually moved out onto the prairies. The international boundary west of the Turtle Mountains eventually saw a net movement in the opposite direction; between 1907 and 1909 alone more than 100,000 Americans moved north to Saskatchewan and Alberta, responding to the Laurier government's policy of active solicitation of farmers in the upper Middle West.[10]

### GERMAN RUSSIANS

In contrast to the Ontario natives who traveled the least distance of any of the foreign-born groups, the German Russians who settled the

[9] The Ross family from Bruce County, Ontario, came to the United States because "Canada gave reservations for Indians, half breeds and Mennonites. This was the best land and British subjects had to take what land was left. Uncle Sam said if they came to Dakota Territory they could have the best land available and he would take care of them." Some of those who came via Winnipeg had planned to settle in Manitoba. Mary McGinnis' family from Dungannon, Ontario, intended to settle near Brandon, but did not like the country. The Northern Pacific railroad had an advertising map for Dakota lands in the hotel lobby at Brandon where they stayed; another advertisement boomed the Okanagan valley of British Columbia, but they chose Dakota. A detailed study of southern and

western Manitoba settlement is J. L. Tyman, *By Section, Township and Range* (Brandon, Manitoba: Assiniboine Historical Society, 1972).
[10] K. D. Bicha, *The American Farmer and the Canadian West* (Lawrence, Kansas: Coronado Press, 1968); and H. Troper, *Only Farmers Need Apply: Official Canadian Government Encouragement of Immigration from the United States, 1896–1911* (Toronto: Griffin House, 1972).

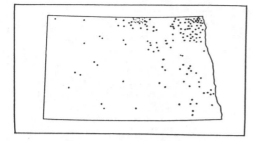

FIG. 3.   First Dakota residences of Ontario group.

Dakotas in large numbers during the late 1880s made a long and often difficult journey from their adopted homelands in south Russia. German Russians moved almost exclusively within a network of colonies established by their predecessors and by immigration agents who were eager to lure these sturdy farmers to the North American Great Plains.[11]

The movement of large colonies to America followed approximately one hundred years after Catherine the Great had attracted German peasants to southern Russia. There they had lived in agricultural villages of a few hundred inhabitants each, usually founded either as wholly Catholic or wholly Protestant communities. Most of those in this sample who eventually moved to North Dakota were living north of the Danube delta in Bessarabia and traced their ancestry to Baden, Bavaria, or Württemberg. Some emigrated via Odessa, but most chose to retrace their ancestors' steps and left for New York via Hamburg or Bremen.

The climate in the Dakotas almost exactly matched that to which they had grown accustomed in south Russia.[12] By the time the settlers had dispersed to their homesteads they were agricultural innovators. Though an oversimplification, they are often credited with bringing wheat culture to the semiarid North American grasslands. Certainly they were the only settlers in the region preadapted to this way of life.

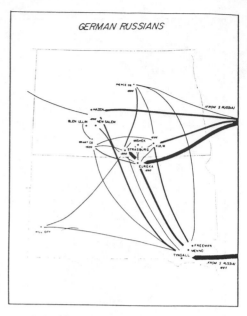

FIG. 4.   German Russian migrations to North Dakota. Median dates of arrival in the various colonies are shown in italics.

After the first group of settlers chose lands near Yankton, South Dakota, German Russian Catholics, Mennonites, and Hutterites established separate settlements around Tyndall, Menno, and Freeman, which served as a staging area for later expansion northward in the Dakotas and finally into Canada (Fig. 4). The peasant agricultural village from south Russia did not fit the American land system, though the Hutterites retained and even strengthened their communal settlement pattern. Small, agriculturally based towns did proliferate, however, and the spread of German Russians across Dakota saw the creation of dozens of village-centered rural communities; many hamlets were identified as either "Katholisch," "Evangelisch," or "Mennoniten." Noncolony Hutterites generally settled in Mennonite communities.[13]

The first and largest North Dakota German Russian enclaves were along the southern border of the state, around Kulm, Wishek, and Strasburg (Fig. 5). Later, groups from this area and directly from south Russia were settled by

---

[11] They were not unaware that they were being sought and that immigration agents tended to exaggerate. Andrew and Valzurika Wentz from Rudolph, South Russia, recalled talking with other immigrants on the voyage to New York: "we were willing to discount the stories fifty percent and still be well-satisfied."

[12] North American climatic analogs for USSR crop regions are shown in *USSR Agriculture Atlas* (Washington, D.C.: Central Intelligence Agency, 1974) p. 6.

[13] J. A. Hostetler, *Hutterite Society* (Baltimore: Johns Hopkins University Press, 1974), pp. 121–22.

FIG. 5. Combined house and barn of a German Russian settler on the Missouri Coteau four miles northwest of Kulm, North Dakota, 1894. The size and shape of the building is very similar to those occupied by German peasants in the agricultural villages of south Russia, where the house portion was next to the street but fenced off with a solid stone wall running the length of the village. Edwin Mueller collection; State Historical Society of North Dakota.

railroad immigration officials west of the Missouri River near New Salem and Glen Ullin, and farther north in Pierce and McHenry counties. It was not uncommon to find individuals in these later colonies who had lived in all of the previously established Dakota settlement areas, and nearly everyone had relatives in each one. The channels of migration and social communication were well established but, like the communities themselves, they were practically closed to outsiders. The economic life of the German Russian settlements was not closed, however; these settlements established themselves early as major grain shipping points.[14]

GERMANS

German-born and German American pioneers in northern Dakota had language and often religion in common with the German Russians, but there were few other similarities. By 1880 the large German population in North America was widely scattered in urban and rural concentrations. Such enclaves often attracted newer immigrants, but their kinship bonds and information feedbacks were neither as strong nor as exclusive as those of the German Russians. Those calling themselves Germans in this sample came from several parts of the German Empire, with a majority from the northern provinces, especially Pomerania and Brandenburg, or from Alsace-Lorraine. Of all the immigrant groups who came to North Da-

[14] A promotional bulletin of the day described Eureka: "You must not return," Gertrude added, "without a visit to Eureka, the northern terminus of the 'Milwaukee', in McPherson county. This county and those adjoining, is largely settled by German Russians, who came to the country from Russia but were originally from Württemberg, Germany, and are excellent farmers. This town has thirty-two elevators and warehouses in busy operation, and these will average loading during the season thirty-six cars every twenty-four hours, the largest amount of wheat received from first hands of any town in the world." S. H. Arnold, *South Dakota . . The Sunshine State* (Chicago: Chicago, Milwaukee and St. Paul Railroad, 1897), p. 9.

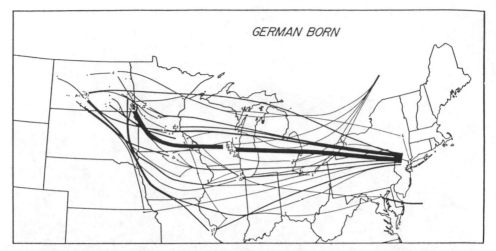

FIG. 6. Migration routes and previous occupations of German-born North Dakota settlers. "I" indicates work as a farm or nonfarm laborer; open triangle indicates employment as a skilled or clerical worker, merchant, or professional; a dot indicates farm owner or tenant. Occupations are not differentiated within North Dakota.

kota they were the least likely to have had prior agricultural experience in North America. On the northern plains they did not gain a reputation for being the best farmers.

Most of the Germans entered through New York, but some came up the St. Lawrence, and some entered at Baltimore (Fig. 6). They moved westward in a succession of usually blue-collar, nonfarm jobs in or around major industrial centers. Buffalo, Cleveland, Detroit, Chicago, St. Louis, and Milwaukee were to those from Prussia what Tyndall, Menno, Freeman, and Eureka were for their German-speaking counterparts from Bessarabia. As they moved toward the frontier the German-born turned to agriculture, usually as tenant farmers; nearly all took homesteads when they reached free land.

One large group of Germans that moved to southeastern North Dakota around 1875 had been iron miners in Dodge County, Wisconsin (Figs. 6 and 7). They were recruited for that work in their homeland, but when the mines declined they decided to leave Wisconsin. They settled in the Red River valley west of Wahpeton, raised wheat and oats for sale, worked as farm or railroad laborers, and generally improvised, making molasses from sugar beets, yeast from wild hops, coffee from milled baked peas and barley, and beer for weddings and the Fourth of July.

Another large German colonization was carried out by the Deutscher Evangelischer Colonizations Verein, with headquarters in Chicago.[15] New Salem, later a port of entry for the German Russians, was established by this society in 1882. The colony was advertised in the German language press and drew German settlers from a wide area in the United States and directly from Germany. This settlement was really a company town. The railroad not only sold settlers the land and the means of transportation but also sold them their food (potatoes cost $4 per bushel the first winter), and hired German and Cornish miners for the company coal mine nearby. Later the German population here turned to dairying.

### SCANDINAVIANS

The exodus of Norwegians and Swedes from overpopulated rural districts in those countries after 1850 was also engineered in part by railroad and public immigration groups in the United States. Those who sought the Scandinavians more or less succeeded in getting them where they wanted them—on the homesteads and railroad quarter sections of the Middle West. This immigration probably would not

---

15 E. B. Robinson, *History of North Dakota* (Lincoln: University of Nebraska Press, 1966), p. 195.

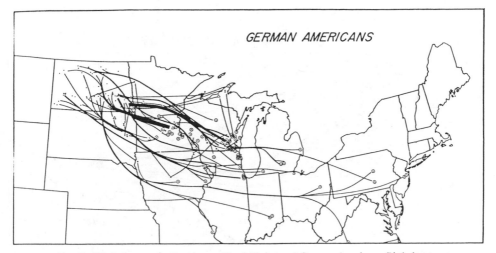

FIG. 7. Birthplaces and migration to North Dakota of German Americans. Birthplaces are indicated with circled dots. See caption for Figure 6.

have continued but for the volume of letters sent home by the early immigrants praising the new lands. These letters, in turn, would not have had such an impact if literacy had not been so widespread in the two countries.[16]

---

[16] A recent collection of immigrant letters is H. A. Barton, ed., *Letters from the Promised Land: Swedes in America, 1840–1914* (Minneapolis: University of Minnesota Press, 1975).

Swedes from Värmland, Dalsland, Småland, and other provinces settled northern Dakota in the 1880s. By 1910 there were nearly 30,000 Swedes in the state, and more than four times that many Norwegians. Before moving to the northern plains many Swedes worked in the lumber camps of northern Minnesota; others were farmers, especially in the heavily Swedish areas around Willmar and Alexandria in central Minnesota (Fig. 8). Later North Dakota set-

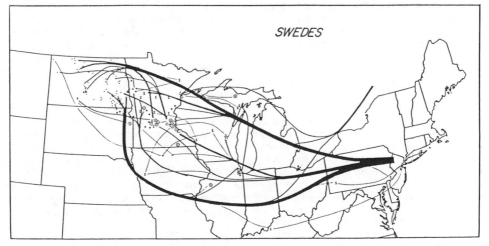

FIG. 8. Migration routes and occupations of Swedish and Swedish American pioneers in North Dakota. See captions for Figures 6 and 7.

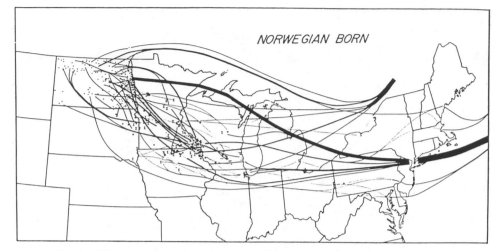

FIG. 9. Migration routes and previous occupations of Norwegian-born North Dakota pioneers. See caption for Figure 6.

tlers born to Swedish parents came from these enclaves and from Chicago and the Twin Cities.

Axel Johnson from Småland came to Renville County north of Minot in 1886 with his mother, two brothers, household goods, two cows, a wagon, an ox team, and a walking plow. They had lived briefly near Alexandria where Axel, Olander, and John had done farm work. Axel's first crop was potatoes; Olander, who homesteaded nearby, first tried flax; other Swedes from central Minnesota first planted wheat. Pioneer homes were just as experimental. Some built log houses from timber along the Mouse River, others frame structures, and some, especially on the uplands, used sod. They supplemented their income with farm work for others locally or with winter jobs in the Minnesota woods.

For Swedes and Norwegians in America, newspapers printed in their native languages served as information clearinghouses, carrying news from home and from their fellow countrymen who had moved west. A typical sequence of events began with an initial small group moving to a new location in response to advertising or traveler's accounts in a native language newspaper; then a trickle of migrants came to the new location from several previously established enclaves in response to personal or published correspondence encouraging others to follow. This sequence occurred over and over again as

small groups, many of only a few families each, took up land at progressively more distant locations.

Norwegian settlement of the northern Middle West was accomplished by this semipublic circulation of information.[17] Except for a few scattered communities within and around New York and several other small clusters around ports where Norwegian seamen were based, the Norwegians ignored the country east of Lake Michigan. Few of those who eventually settled North Dakota even sought work in the Northeast, unlike the Germans. Instead they moved directly to the Middle West and settled on farms as owners, tenants, or laborers depending on their means and when and where they arrived. When Iowa and southern Minnesota had been taken, they turned west to Dakota.

One single colony, Spring Grove in Houston and Fillmore counties, southeastern Minnesota, was the temporary home of many Norwegians who eventually settled North Dakota (Fig. 9); it was also the birthplace of many Norwegian Americans who settled in the state (Fig. 10). In 1875 there were 16,000 Norwegians in these two counties, far in excess of the agricultural capacity of this hilly area. Another important

---

[17] C. C. Qualey, *Norwegian Settlement in the United States* (Northfield, Minnesota: Norwegian-American Historical Association, 1938).

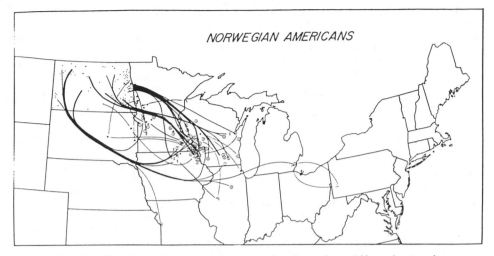

FIG. 10.  Birthplaces, migration routes, and previous occupations of Norwegian American pioneers in North Dakota. See captions for Figures 6 and 7.

source area was Mitchell and Worth counties, along the northern border of Iowa; St. Ansgar and Northwood there were founded by Norwegians from southern Wisconsin in 1853.[18] Migrants from these two communities later went to the Goose River valley in eastern North Dakota, founding another Northwood.

In April of 1888 more than a dozen families from Spring Grove moved to Wells County, northwest of Fargo. Andrew and Helmer Gilbertson hired an emigrant car (a glorified boxcar) and brought each family's goods, making three trips back and forth until all in the group were moved. The Anders Elken family brought two cows, two calves, a barrel of salt pork, a cook stove, 250 fence posts, a mower, a corn planter, a cultivator, and a breaking plow.[19]

[18] Qualey, op. cit., footnote 17, pp. 92–93.

[19] Their bill of lading illustrates that they were well aware of the scarcity of timber where they planned to settle and that they did not intend to specialize in wheat monoculture. The Elkens apparently intended to experiment, as did most others. First crops showed no systematic variation with national or regional origins. Flax was often tried on a newly broken piece of prairie land since it seemed to do better than most other crops; nearly all the German Russians started with some acreage in flax and the practice became common by the late 1890s. On the other hand, Joe Greffre, who had worked as a commercial fisherman out of Muscatine, Iowa, moved to Bowman County, North Dakota, in 1907 and planted his first acreage to muskmelons and corn; later he

The Elkens and their similarly well-equipped neighbors settled the north half of township 150-69, which they quickly named Norway Lake. They built frame shacks for shelter, broke ten or fifteen acres apiece which they sowed to wheat or flax, and built a school and a Lutheran church. Six miles to the south the same events were being enacted by a dozen German families from Wisconsin who called their community Hamburg—prudently changed to "Hamberg" in 1917—and also built their own school and Lutheran church.

The mosaic of rural communities was thus built up, with Norwegians either at hand or not far away over most of the state. Norwegian farmers took some of the best land, beginning in the Red River valley and then moving west to the spring wheat region of the glaciated Missouri plateau northwest of Williston. They were not agricultural innovators like the German Russians, but they were successful farmers, adapting quickly to grassland agriculture. Like the Germans and the Swedes, Norwegians supplemented their incomes from farm work or other sources. Many men were carpenters, teamsters, and railroad employees when work

came more in line with dryland farming preferences. The learning process involved is described in J. C. Malin, "The Adaptation of the Agricultural System to the Subhumid Environment," *Agricultural History*, Vol. 10 (1936), pp. 118–41.

did not keep them on the homestead. Single women, especially, worked as maids, cooks, and laundresses for the more affluent landowners in town, though "home" was always on the quarter sections homesteaded, preempted, or otherwise held by the family.

### OLDER AMERICAN STOCK

The geographic origins and backgrounds of the North Dakota pioneers with American-born parents were nearly as diverse as the degrees of success they enjoyed when they moved to the northern plains. Oliver Dalrymple, a lawyer turned farmer, managed more than fifty thousand acres of bonanza farms in the Red River valley for eastern investors and was shipping wheat to Lake Superior in trainloads by the early 1880s. The opposite extreme must have been reached by a group of ten families from Asbury Park, New Jersey, who rented farms amidst the stony hills and alkali sloughs of central North Dakota believing they could make a quick killing in wheat and flax. In between were the many who "made it" and then "lost it," such as Arthur C. Townley from Browns Valley, Minnesota, once proclaimed "Flax King of the Golden Valley" but later (after he lost it) a leader of the farmers' attack on big business.

"Land hunger," a term often used to describe the motivations of Europeans who took homesteads in North America, is seldom used in connection with the natives. Still, for thousands of Middle Western farmers, escaping tenancy must have been a prime reason for moving west to take a homestead. For the restless young bookkeeper in New York a Dakota homestead meant adventure; for the south Texas cowhand tired of the long drives to summer range on the Little Missouri, it meant settling down to a quieter life. For all, migration to the northern plains frontier meant finding a way of adapting their own skills to the region's resources.[20]

---

[20] The variations in migrants' accounts of the process defy categorization. Billy Humphrey, from Great Kanawha Falls, West Virginia, tried farming (unsuccessfully) four times moving west across the Kentucky hills, and then became a peddler, which took him north to Roberts, Illinois, where he opened a barbershop. Later he joined up with a group of local farmers who were moving to West End, Dakota Territory, where he opened another barbershop, kept bees, and filed on a homestead, to which he commuted on weekends. His neighbor in West End was George Bingham from Rochester, Minnesota, who had been a

The birthplaces of second or later generation American-born Dakota pioneers who were principally engaged in farming on the northern plains were scattered from Maine to the eastern edge of the Red River valley (Fig. 11). Few came from the south, the one exception being Anglo Texans who came north with cattle and decided to stay.

Many of those who came from the Northeast were single young men (as was typical of all groups migrating to the frontier) who worked at a succession of jobs before taking a homestead in Dakota. They worked in the Pennsylvania oil fields, looked for gold at Eureka, Nevada, read law, joined the U.S. Cavalry, worked as lumberjacks, farmhands, millhands, and laid rails. Some were farmers, but they were less likely to have been so engaged than were their Middle Western-born counterparts who also moved west. Their migration extended the more or less east-west stratification of population movements through the upper Mississippi valley and into the plains.

The mode of transportation chosen depended on the length of the journey. Short moves were often by wagon; wagon trains were assembled for the longer migrations, but they were loaded into emigrant cars at a central location for the remainder of the trip (Fig. 12). In 1883 Jeremiah Williams of Des Moines loaded fifty-five

---

farm machinery salesman in Aberdeen, but came to West End to homestead. His occupations were stage driver and road grader but he also sold "snake root" to "easterners" and operated a steam threshing rig. John Fowler, Chicago, operated a beer parlor in West End until the townsite folded. He then moved the beer parlor to his homestead, where he also raised wheat, and later he opened a pool hall in Minnewaukan.

James Coulter was born in Cleveland in 1854. By 1881, when he settled in Dawson, he had moved more than twenty times, working as a telegrapher, pharmacist, rancher, farmer, coal dealer, and pool hall operator. Also in Dawson lived Ben Woesner from Jonesville, Indiana, who had a homestead but made his living doing farm work, picking buffalo bones, and taking "the rich people from the cities hunting." Later he collected bounties, hunting coyotes from a Model "T". R. M. Argersinger from Johnstown, New York, worked in a sawmill in Duluth and built grain elevators in the northwest before filing a claim near Forman. To earn a living he got work with a carpenter building a hotel, then opened a saloon. When saloons were voted out he opened a drugstore, then ran a livery stable, sold it to buy a hotel, and later traded the hotel for a house and operated a taxi; he never did get around to farming.

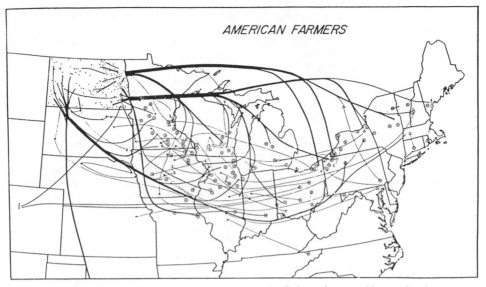

FIG. 11. Birthplaces and occupational changes for Dakota pioneers with American-born parents. Those who engaged mainly in farm work during their first five years in North Dakota are shown. See captions for Figures 6 and 7.

FIG. 12. Unloading an emigrant car at Richardton, North Dakota, 1910. The Middle Western family pictured took land thirty-five miles south in Hettinger County. William H. Brown collection; State Historical Society of North Dakota.

of his friends and neighbors and their belongings into nineteen Dakota-bound emigrant cars and started the settlement of Lake Williams, northeast of Bismarck; in the spring of 1884 an emigrant train of forty-four cars left Pike County, Missouri, for Devils Lake, where the group unloaded and sought homesteads.[21] In 1898 Wilfred Ruth, a West Virginian farming near Adel, Iowa, responded to the same Great Northern land advertisement his neighbors saw, and they hired emigrant cars for the trip to Minot; the same promotion enticed a group of Pennsylvania German farmers from Carroll City, Maryland, to settle in the next township. Not all who moved in emigrant cars were in large groups, nor did all such groups travel by rail, but it was the most common mode once a network of rail lines had been laid.

Many of the offspring of earlier generations of Americans sought a living in Dakota as farmers or ranchers, but the frontier also attracted merchants, craftsmen, and professional people who, although they often filed on a piece of land, clearly intended to make their living in town. The geographical origins of this group, as revealed in the sample, were widely scattered behind the frontier (Fig. 13). Some of the migrants were well connected back east; others were drifters who probably had no intention of settling in Dakota, but arrived there on a railroad labor gang or threshing crew and decided to remain. Louis Smith from Boston was an Amherst man, class of '79. After college, he worked in his uncle's hardware business at Windom and St. Paul, Minnesota. He and his brother came out to Dakota in 1882 looking for business sites and decided to open a hardware store at the new townsite of Hope, northwest of Fargo. Later he ran a coal and wood yard and acquired land. At the Hope House, where he boarded, he met Nellie Van Husen from St. Catherines, Ontario, who had come to Dakota as a dressmaker. They married, raised seven children, and remained in the community.

These men and women founded most of the central places in Dakota, opening up businesses on railroad townsites or, in many cases, erect-

ing a shack in the middle of nowhere to which they affixed a sign proclaiming it a town. When one business failed, they tried another. When their self-proclaimed town attracted neither merchants nor railroad lines they simply moved the shack elsewhere or sold it to a homesteader and started again. There was no orderly collection of "places" performing central functions into which the aspiring merchant could move with any certainty that the town would continue. A homesteader trekking his way to what he thought was the closest mercantile establishment might see another one on the way just opening for business; it was not an occasion for rejoicing since by the time he made the trip again the fellow might have moved it.

### SMALLER GROUPS

To these groups represented in largest numbers were added many others who sought a living on the Dakota frontier. Danes, Poles, Bohemians, Welsh, Dutch, and Luxembourgers all came in small bands of relatives and friends. In 1882, 200 Icelanders sailed from Scotland to Boston; from there they went by rail to Buffalo, then by boat to Duluth where the group split up, some settling in Wisconsin and Minnesota, others continuing west to Dakota. Their settlement near Pembina received another 400 from Iceland in 1887, via Quebec and Winnipeg. The Icelandic settlements were scattered within the area settled by Scots and Irish from Ontario. In 1883 Father Brunel from Quebec led seventy-five French Canadians into this parkland area near the international boundary east of Bottineau. In the same year, Charlie Cree and a group of French Chippewas from Fort Belknap Agency, Montana, took allotments nearby.

Martin Iron Bull was taught to be a medicine man in Montana; he and James All Yellow, who came from Aberdeen, got jobs with the Indian agency at Fort Yates, issuing rations and working as Indian policemen. In 1885 a New York company established seven Russian Jewish families in a colony north of Devils Lake. Later others were attracted to the settlement. When the homesteaders proved up in five years, the company bought back their claims for about $500 each, though some remained and started businesses in Devils Lake. Ellen Garvey from Richmond, Virginia, was "the only colored lady farmer in Ramsey County;" her mother had been a slave and her father was a Cavalry officer at Fort Totten near Devils Lake. Pictures of

---

[21] Early spring of each year saw a peak in the number of new arrivals. Since spring comes a month or two later (and then lasts for a day or so) on the northern plains, many homesteaders found themselves searching for land in a blizzard. The experience was enough to make some forget the whole venture then and there.

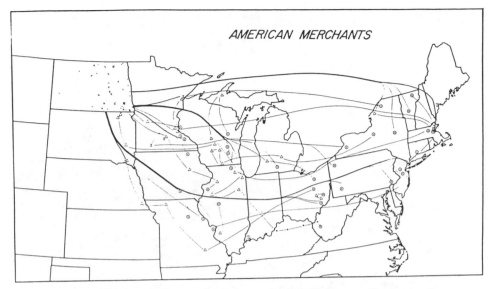

*AMERICAN MERCHANTS*

FIG. 13. Birthplaces and occupational changes for Dakota pioneers with American-born parents. Those who were principally self-employed in the trades during their first five years in North Dakota are shown. See captions for Figures 6 and 7.

Dakota harvests sometimes show Blacks working as harvest hands, though few were homesteaders.

### THE MIGRATION PROCESSS

It is traditional in accounts such as this to pause here and describe how, out of all these inputs to the frontier, a distinctly American (or, in this case, North Dakotan) population was forged from the sons and daughters of many lands. Since the old "melting pot" analogy has now been discredited by a nation intent on celebrating its plural state of existence, those who would update the analogy have been put at considerable pains to do so, speaking of lumps in the stew that will not cook away, and so on.[22] Apart from the inherent limitations of considering people and their habits as soup, this analogy ignores what seems obvious.

The people who settled the frontier were not passive; they were neither tugged out by the magnet of free land, pushed ahead by the glacially slow but sure advance of civilization into the wilderness, nor expelled like a cloud of

steam by the labor safety valve of the great eastern cities, to mention a few more dubious analogies. The frontier population was recruited by those who knew their business, and the frontier was sought by those who had heard, even vaguely, about the opportunities it offered (Fig. 14). Uncertainty was reduced and dreams were translated into action when a few pioneers moved west and reported favorably, not to the general population, but to relatives and friends at home. The information feedbacks were private (letters) or semipublic (foreign language newspapers) for the non-English speaking groups. The migrations thus encouraged were not secret, of course.[23] Oftentimes others joined in a group migration as "Dakota fever" spread through a Middle Western community, but the long-distance information networks remained discrete—just as discrete as the population subgroups internally linked but effectively cut off from one another as a result.

[22] W. Zelinsky, *The Cultural Geography of the United States* (Englewood Cliffs, NJ: Prentice-Hall, Inc., 1973), p. 32.

[23] The spread of migration-inducing information is discussed in John Hudson, "Two Dakota Homestead Frontiers," *Annals*, Association of American Geographers, Vol. 63 (1973), pp. 442–62.

FIG. 14. Publicity photo issued by the William H. Brown Company of Chicago which sold land near Flasher and Mott in southwestern North Dakota. The caption read "This is how they make the start on the prairie. There is a comfortable farm house now and a good big barn and it looks like an Eastern farm home after just three years of cultivation. The people are happy and contented. You can buy the same kind of land at $15.00 to $25.00 an acre." State Historical Society of North Dakota.

Those who had an overview of what was happening were in the Minneapolis headquarters of the railroad land companies, in the territorial immigration bureau at Yankton, but in few other places. They were the ones who ran newspaper advertisements, sent agents to Christiania and Hamburg as well as to New York and Quebec City, and set up booths displaying bountiful harvests of grain at county fairs from New York practically to the Dakota border, all in hopes of luring new settlers. As in any market, there were sellers and buyers, both active, and with their own network of operations, formal or informal. Add to this the fact that Dakota was not the only territory or state with its salesmen so deployed, and the fact that those receiving information about frontiers heard about Texas, California, and dozens of other places as well, then an idea of the magnitude of information flow emerges.

The maps of migration suggest that westward movement of the frontier population was accomplished through successive concentrations and scatterings of the foreign-born and first-generation groups and through what appears to have been a haphazard series of trial and error approaches by the native-born. They came in contact with one another at various points and all eventually took up land, many times in the same county of a single state. Did this experience produce social contact between groups of the kinship variety?

## Marriage

One of the most often used and certainly one of the simplest surrogate measures of the amount of social contact between ethnic groups out of their homelands is their degree of intermarriage. It is not perfect, especially because of two spatial-statistical problems. If a group lives in small, exclusive neighborhoods, urban or rural, endogamy is likely to be high because of the marriage-propinquity factor alone, regardless of the group's norms on intermarriage.

Table 1.—Proportion of Marriages within Ethnic or Residence Groups for North Dakota Pioneers Married in the United States or Canada

| | Married outside North Dakota | Married in North Dakota | Total |
|---|---|---|---|
| *Proportion of men marrying within group* | | | |
| Foreign-born | | | |
| German Russian | 1.000 | .970 | .975 |
| German | .857 | .750 | .785 |
| Swedish | .667 | .600 | .622 |
| Norwegian | .943 | .926 | .932 |
| Ontario[a] | .677 | .465 | .554 |
| First generation | | | |
| German American | .600 | .696 | .658 |
| Norwegian American | .714 | .933 | .863 |
| American stock born in | | | |
| Northeast[b] | .800 | .473 | .641 |
| Middle West | .686 | .420 | .554 |
| *Proportion of women marrying within group* | | | |
| Foreign-born | | | |
| German Russian | 1.000 | .865 | .889 |
| German | .900 | .843 | .865 |
| Swedish | .636 | .933 | .808 |
| Norwegian | .857 | .899 | .885 |
| Ontario[a] | .750 | .465 | .577 |
| First generation | | | |
| German American | .692 | .917 | .838 |
| Norwegian American | .923 | .814 | .855 |
| American stock born in | | | |
| Northeast[b] | .640 | .409 | .532 |
| Middle West | .660 | .344 | .491 |

[a] Marriages among those of Scots, Irish, or English descent.
[b] States east of Ohio.

Also, even if marriage partners were picked at random, Luxembourgers would be less likely to marry Luxembourgers than Italians would be to marry Italians simply because there are fewer Luxembourgers in the total population. The following data on marriages on the Dakota frontier should be interpreted with this fact in mind.

Marriage data were computed only for the groups represented in largest numbers (Table 1). Of 790 marriages which could be classified by place of occurrence, fifty-two took place in Europe, 286 in the United States outside of North Dakota, and 452 occurred within the state, reflecting the young age of the pioneers. All but one of the European marriages involved partners born in the same country. For the Ontario migrant group, marriages in Ontario are included, but no other foreign marriages are tabulated.

The proportion of within-group marriages shows no systematic difference between men and women. For most of the foreign-born, marriage outside the group became slightly more likely on the Dakota frontier than it was in their communities of residence farther south and east, but endogamy prevailed.[24] German Russians were the most endogamous, followed by Norwegians; their colonies were the most internally structured and they preserved this through successive moves into Dakota. The slight tendency toward exogamy on the frontier was not apparent for the first generation of the foreign-born, however; German and Norwegian Americans were no less likely to move within their "own" circles when they moved to a frontier community than were the young men and women of the same age born to parents who had not emigrated. The one exception is Norwegian American women.

Whether this degree of endogamy was high or low can be determined by comparing marriage data for Americans with native-born parents. For the older American stock, previous locality groupings had little effect on choosing a marriage partner on the Dakota frontier. Ohioans often had affinities for other Buckeyes, as did Hoosiers for other Hoosiers, living in a strange land hundreds of miles from home, but it apparently did not affect the institution of marriage. Ontarians of Scotch, Irish, and English descent were also likely to marry outside their group when they reached Dakota, most often taking American-born wives or husbands.

Assuming marriage data represent a reliable surrogate for a larger set of social relationships,

[24] The proportion of Norwegians marrying within the group was nearly the same in Dakota as it was on the Trempealeau County, Wisconsin frontier in 1880 (.938 for men, .831 for women in Trempealeau County); within-group marriage among Germans was slightly more common there (.885 for men, .955 for women) than in the Dakota sample; Curti, op. cit., footnote 6, p. 105. Among the German-born in the North Central states in 1970, the proportions are .241 for men and .286 for women over age forty-five (*U.S. Census of Population*, 1970). Intermediate in this range are data collected in Clay County in the Red River valley of Minnesota in the early 1940s; the proportions with spouses of the same nationality (including first and second generation as well as foreign-born) were German, .387; Norwegian, .467; and Swedish, .190; L. Nelson, "Intermarriage Among Nationality Groups in a Rural Area of Minnesota," *American Journal of Sociology*, Vol. 48 (1943), p. 589.

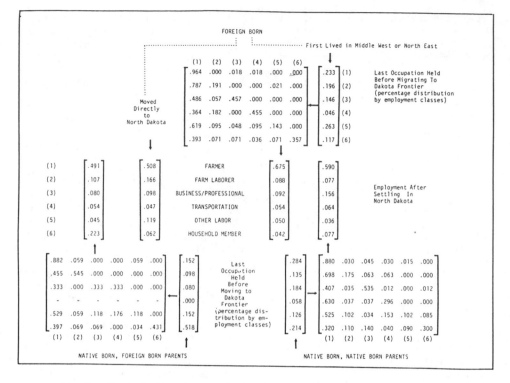

FIG. 15.  Occupational mobility and the frontier migration process (based on a sample of 1,013 migrant records). The *i*th element (i = 1, . . . 6) in each column represents the proportion employed in each category. The element $a_{ij}$ in each transition matrix represents the proportion of individuals moving from category *i* to category *j*. Thus, 19.6 percent of the Dakota-bound foreign-born who settled in states to the east began as farm laborers; when they moved to North Dakota, 78.7 percent of the farm laborers became farmers; 67.5 percent of the foreign-born first settling outside North Dakota began as farmers when they reached the state.

it appears that the frontier migration process consisted of a series of spatially overlapping but socially discrete patterns of movement. For the non-English speaking population, migration fostered endogamy which in turn preserved the group itself through successive moves into and out of the Middle West to the Dakota frontier of the 1880s and later. The groups coming the shortest distances intermarried most freely; those coming from farthest away were the most endogamous. The frontier did not break up these patterns any more than the cities did; if there was a Dakota melting pot, New Englanders, Scotch-Irish Canadians, and Iowa farm boys were in it, not the others.

*Migration and Mobility*

This impression of pluralism should not be taken to the extreme, to envision a patchwork of tiny communities whose inhabitants spoke only to one another. There were such social neighborhoods, but there were also other locality groupings, such as trade areas and journeys to work, in which economic motives took precedence and out of which a much larger set of interesting relationships between people and place evolved. To understand the role of migration in the economic life of the frontier it is instructive to examine the sequence of occupations pursued by four types of migrants as they moved west: foreign-born pioneers moving directly to northern Dakota, foreign-born who first settled in the Northeast or Middle West, first generation groups born outside Dakota, and native-born pioneers born to native parents (Fig. 15).

The proportion of farmers in each group increased dramatically when they reached the homestead frontier. Part of this increase was related to the youth of immigrants who had worked only on the family farm before coming to Dakota; the rest of the increase in the farmer category was caused largely by a decrease in the proportion employed as laborers, on farms and in other ways. Although farmer tenants and owners are not differentiated, it may be supposed that the transition to farming in Dakota, where free or cheap land abounded, at least initially, meant achieving owner status for those who had not been owners before.

Westward migration and mobility show a definite relationship for the foreign-born. For any pair of foreign-born pioneers who eventually settled in North Dakota, the one making a temporary home in the Northeast or Middle West was only half as likely to start farming immediately as was the one who settled on the Dakota frontier in the first place, but when the first of the pair finally moved to Dakota he was more likely to be a farmer than the immigrant who came directly. Nearly half of the Dakota-bound foreign-born worked as laborers initially, but when they arrived in Dakota two-thirds started as farmers. This change reflects the types of work available to an immigrant in the older part of the nation and the increased wealth of those who had worked first as laborers.

In comparison, the proportion in each group engaged in trade, or as craftsmen, managers, clerks, or professionals remained stable; it was highest for the native-born native-stock group and remained that way through migration. This proportion actually declined among the foreign-born who moved in stages; coopers, tinsmiths, and cobblers from the old country joined the rush into farming when they reached Dakota, though many returned to their trades when they saw the shortage of skilled labor on the frontier.

The categories used to describe these mobility data do not conform to the common practice among social scientists of labeling people by the color of their collars. The principal reason for these labels seems to be to determine if mobility is up or down, so a dichotomous classification is useful. Where farm and nonfarm

occupations are mixed it is nearly meaningless to discuss occupational mobility in terms of levels; is a person "climbing" or "skidding" when he quits his farm and opens a saloon? An analogous notion within agriculture is the concept of the "agricultural ladder," up which laborers climb to tenancy, then ownership, and finally to large-scale ownership.[25] The rungs on the ladder and the color of the collar pertain more to status than to income, and their relationship to the economic well-being of the people is somewhat tangential.

The laborer category was more commonly occupied by the foreign-born than by the native-born, but movement to the frontier tended to eradicate these differences in the best Turnerian tradition of equality of opportunity. The foreign-born and first generation made the transition from blue to white collar much less frequently than the native stock in late nineteenth century American cities.[26] Assuming that farm and nonfarm laborers are blue collar, and applying the ridiculous label "white collar" to farmers (owners and/or operators), then the agricultural ladder seems to have been working better for the foreign-born on the Dakota frontier than whatever ladder was available to their urban counterparts.

To conceive of occupational mobility as "up" or "down" and to classify migration as "in" or "out" is simplistic in the sense that it obscures the geography in addition to being a rather coarse level of analysis. Since scholars in various fields have their own special ways of looking at things, geographers should not claim that occupational mobility is outside their ken because it is "nonspatial"; mobility may appear that way because it is usually discussed by people who are content to speak of ladders or ele-

[25] S. Lee, "The Theory of the Agricultural Ladder," *Agricultural History*, Vol. 21 (1947), p. 56. Although tenancy may indicate an intermediate status and as such be "lower" than ownership on the mobility scale, renting a farm from a large landowner did not always produce the often alleged exploitation of human beings and land resources. An eastern North Dakota example of the benefits as well as the liabilities of tenancy is in A. G. Bogue, "Foreclosure Tenancy on the Northern Plains," *Agricultural History*, Vol. 39 (1965), pp. 3–16.

[26] S. Thernstrom, "Immigrants and WASPS: Ethnic Differences in Occupational Mobility in Boston, 1890–1940," in S. Thernstrom and R. Sennett, eds., *Nineteenth Century Cities, Essays in New Urban History* (New Haven: Yale University Press, 1969), pp. 125–64.

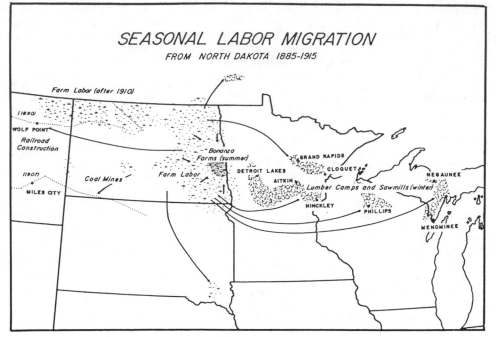

FIG. 16. Seasonal labor migration on the Dakota frontier. Dotted lines indicate principal transcontinental railroad activity. The general direction of seasonal movement was toward the east in winter and toward the west in summer. Coal mines in western North Dakota drew farmers from the southwestern corner of the state.

vators. Mobility is also a matter of changing occupations in order to survive, exploiting one set of resources in one area, then perhaps other resources in other areas. This is the nature of an intricate pattern of job changes that arose on the northern plains frontier during and after initial agricultural settlement (Fig. 16).

*Seasonal Migration*

It is well known that lumberjacks, millhands, and railroad laborers took up homesteads as the frontier moved west; it is not as well known that they worked at these occupations while they were farming. Men did not work off their farms because a 160-acre homestead was too small to support a family; in the early years, especially, even fewer acres were used effectively. Men worked off their farms because of the basic necessity for cash income in order to survive the transition to a more established economic life.

Forty percent of the homesteaders in my sample had worked off their farms at some time during the early years. Most common was farm labor within thirty miles from home. The arrangements varied little from place to place: they worked for wages far more often than they shared work in a cooperative arrangement. From the very beginning there were "custom farmers" who derived their income from breaking the prairie sod, and others made much of their living during harvest season with a steam-powered threshing rig. Those for whom they worked derived their income, in turn, from other sources. Within Dakota the bonanza farms of the Red River valley were large employers during the harvest. Many homesteaders in eastern North Dakota got their start on a cash basis working for Dalrymple, Cass-Cheney, Grandin Brothers, E. H. Steele, and other big operators (Fig. 17).

In addition to seasonal labor migration within Dakota, there was an annual winter exodus to the lumber camps in the Upper Lake states.

FIG. 17. Harvest hands working a separator on the 20,000 acre Dalrymple bonanza near Casselton, North Dakota, 1890. Theodore Mattson collection; State Historical Society of North Dakota.

Many waited until early spring when the sawmills opened. In summer it was either back to farm work or construction. Grading for hundreds of miles of railroad track and other labor took the Dakota farm population west with construction gangs, where some remained to work in lumber camps.

During their long absences, the women and children did the farm work, battled blizzards, and fought prairie fires. Some bachelor homesteaders returned to their claims infrequently. It was not uncommon for them to find their claim shacks missing because of fires or theft of that scarce commodity, lumber. Four or five years of seasonal labor was enough, one way or the other. Some settled down to full-time farming on their own lands, others turned to other occupations, and, of course, many decided their fortunes had best be sought elsewhere.

The territory supporting the frontier population was thus much larger than the individual's quarter-section. Movement to the frontier was followed by another kind of migration that involved the whole northern part of the country from the Great Lakes to the Pacific at one time or another. There was also a constant shifting of occupation from farm to town and from business to business as the regional economy began

to take shape. This occupational mobility was of a very different sort than in the city.

*Frontier Mobility*

Two separate images of American frontier life have the population either as rugged and self-sufficient or as willing helpmates for one another in barn raisings, housing bees, and so forth. To these characterizations must be added a third which seems most relevant for the late nineteenth century—the frontiersman as multiply employed. On the Dakota frontier a relatively fine division of labor began to appear as soon as settlers arrived. Turner's waves of settlement and accompanying stages of economic complexity were plainly impossible in a region where settlement was so rapid.

All of the major groups settling the northern plains, with perhaps the exception of the German Russians, came from highly structured societies where technological progress had created many specialized roles with a division of labor to match. Northwestern Europe and eastern North America were similar in this respect; when their people moved out to the Dakota grasslands they carried with them the common expectation that their individual skills would be marketable. There were no rules about who

FIG. 18.  Summer work on a grading crew at Mott, North Dakota. The grain elevators on the horizon were not built in the wrong place—the railroad line being graded was the second one to reach this thriving community. Brown collection; State Historical Society of North Dakota.

should perform what type of work, and many a person worked at a variety of specialized jobs simultaneously or in succession. With these relationships in a state of fluidity, shifting occupations did not indicate that the individual was searching for a stable niche in the system, but rather that there were many such niches, and many to fill them. A man who owned a team of horses could use them on the farm or, equally well, hire out on a railroad grading crew (Fig. 18). Rudimentary knowledge of carpentry was common, and many were able to participate in the construction boom that naturally accompanied the new settlement. The attraction was working for wages rather than sitting back on the homestead waiting to see if the crops would mature.[27]

At this point the information networks established in the migration process became relevant again. In the first years after taking a claim many individuals returned to their previous communities of residence for seasonal work. The German Russians settling in central Dakota thus were most apt to return to the southeastern Dakota colonies for farm work, especially in years when their own harvests were poor. Those who had worked in the woods before coming to Dakota similarly returned there in the winter, since they were aware of precisely the way in which they could get such jobs again (Fig. 19). Migration routes were often retraced in the pattern of seasonal work trips, which tended to stimulate more migration. When a homesteader-farm laborer from Dakota came back to his old community to marry or get temporary work (or both), or when a Dakota homesteader-lumberjack told others about his winter trip back to northern Minnesota, the established channels of communication were re-

[27] The division of labor could lead to a complete separation of the traditional frontier roles of homesteader-as-farmer. In 1886 a man named Larson was considered to be the biggest farmer in Benson County, Dakota Territory. Larson owned a cook shack, a barn, and a blacksmith shop (all portable), but not a single acre of farm land. He rented land on half-shares from settlers such as E. J. Rolle, who homesteaded a quarter in Benson County in 1885. Rolle lived in a sod house on his claim but did no farming, preferring to work at his trade, which was carpentry; most of his work was building houses for new settlers in town. The money he made in carpentry was invested in more land which he rented to Larson.

FIG. 19. Winter work for a North Dakota settler and his horses at a pole and tie camp in Minnesota. Mary Bishop collection; State Historical Society of North Dakota.

activated. The effect was to link farms and forests to the east with the western frontier, and to strengthen the bonds through inclusion of information about work opportunities.

A decade after initial settlement the population was still highly mobile, though longer-distance seasonal migrations had started to disappear. The railroads had been built, the "woods" became the "cutover," and centralized control of bonanza farms gradually broke up into share tenant parcels in a process resembling that which occurred on the southern plantation. The large frontier population lost those temporary individuals attracted by the boom as many moved west with the flurry of activity on successive frontiers.

The new migration patterns were internal (Fig. 20). Turnover on the farm drew in the offspring of the original settlers. Farm tenancy increased, especially in eastern North Dakota, because of mortgage foreclosures and because the original homesteaders retained their land when they moved to town; some returned briefly when World War I caused a shortage of farm labor, but the net movement was away from the farm, and it remained that way. A second-

ary occupational mobility caused by these new vacancies resembled the pattern in the Middle West a generation or two earlier. The frontier migration process thus ended by absorption into a more stabilized set of economic and social relationships whose course eventually saw the syndrome of rural depopulation and decline in the small towns.

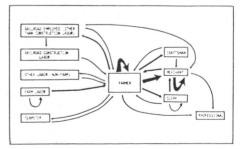

FIG. 20. Occupational mobility of the frontier population after settling in North Dakota (based on a sample of 856 job changes within the state, 1880–1910). Width of line is proportional to numbers making the transition. Farm to farm moves were most common, followed by farm to town moves as the early settlers shifted into nonagricultural occupations.

FIG. 21. Towns were ports of entry for the new settlers, and they vigorously competed with one another for the business the new arrivals brought. Bowman had been in existence for about a year when this scene was recorded in 1908. Bowman county collection; State Historical Society of North Dakota.

### FINAL SPECULATIONS

Migration accomplishes more than a mere rearrangement of population. Those thousands of people who managed to get to the Dakota frontier not only brought themselves and their possessions, but also their attitudes, habits, and their individual strategies for coping with new situations. These data, along with what else is known about northern plains life, offer grounds for some speculations about the emergent cultural geography of the region.

Had there been no foreign influences one might make a case for simple extension of a New England or Northern culture area north-westward across Minnesota into the Red River valley and then directly west. The experiences of most of the older American stock settlers in North Dakota had been north of a line running from central Ohio through southeastern Iowa and thence northwest to the Missouri River at the boundary between the two Dakotas. Linguistic studies indicate the difficulty of drawing such a boundary, however, because mixing with Midland influences began in the central Middle West.[28]

Such an interpretation would not be useful for two other reasons. Culture area models are weakest where they involve multiple origins, clearly an essential for understanding the northern plains. Any attempt to overcome this difficulty through including foreign-born groups as subcultural units would miss the role of economic activity in bringing the various groups together. Although social patterns could remain discrete in rural ethnic neighborhoods, trade areas nearly always encompassed a variety of such neighborhoods, drawing diverse groups together in the market places which, in turn, connected the population with the national economy (Fig. 21). The grain buyers, the millers, the railroad tycoons, and the politicians whom they often owned were all represented symbolically, if not in fact, in the trade center.

[28] H. B. Allen, *The Linguistic Atlas of the Upper Midwest*, Volume 1 (Minneapolis: University of Minnesota Press, 1973).

More than anything else, the way of earning a living was the way of life.

Earning a living often involved migration on a short or a long term basis in order to tap as many resources as possible, a factor especially apparent in the seasonal migration of labor. Agrarian socialism, which was probably more developed in North Dakota than in any other state, fit into a broader distribution of labor unrest during the first two decades of this century. There were strong socialist sentiments in mining, lumbering, and grain farming areas throughout the West. For the northern plains, the diffusion paths of radical politics might well have been established in the seasonal exchange of labor. Another hypothesis has it that Swedes and Norwegians brought political radicalism with them from Europe; this hypothesis may be true, but nowhere did radicalism find a more fertile ground than in the areas, first linked through migration and seasonal labor exchange, running from the mines and lumber camps around Lake Superior to the cash grain farms of western North Dakota.

The Dakota frontier was not a melting pot, nor did the cultural geography of this region emerge from the mosaic of rural ethnic enclaves because of an early and common orientation to the economic necessities of life controlled or mediated through the sphere of influence of the Twin Cities. The way of life on the northern plains was not the result, either, of the westward extension of a cultural complex from farther east, because the Northeast was only one of several important source areas. Labor mobility and a large turnover of population on the Dakota frontier was evidence of a wide rather than a narrow range of opportunities open to the population, contrasting this frontier with current interpretations of late nineteenth and early twentieth century American cities. The similarities and contrasts with previous frontiers and with simultaneous happenings in the city illustrate the unique circumstances of a particular time and place and at the same time highlight a familiar set of cultural geographic processes which interacted to produce such a unique result.

# A Century and a Half of Ethnic Change in Texas, 1836–1986

TERRY G. JORDAN*

IN THE CULTURAL AS IN THE ENVIRONMENTAL SENSE, TEXAS HAS ALWAYS been a borderland or even a shatterbelt. The Amerindian regional diversity of pre-Columbian times, based partially in climatic contrasts, was obliterated, only to be replaced by an even more complex human mosaic. Those who would understand Texas, now as well as 150 years ago, must once and for all discard the myth of the typical Texan, a chauvinistic notion that, on occasion, has even penetrated the scholarly community,[1] and accept the concept of a multiethnic society. Texas is a unit only in the functional political sense; culturally it is a balkanized zone entrapped in an artificial administrative framework.[2]

Texans, in short, inhabit a border province. The state, in common with eastern Canada, Belgium, Switzerland, Alsace-Lorraine, and South Tirol, lies astride a fundamental culturo-linguistic divide between Romance and Germanic civilizations, a divide lent heightened contrast here by the addition of a large non-European, Amerindian cultural component on the Latin side.

In such situations, when an artificial political framework is imposed upon a cultural borderland, ethnic groups are created. Ethnicity implies minority status in a larger society dominated numerically, and

---

*Terry G. Jordan, Walter Prescott Webb Professor at the University of Texas, Austin, has published many articles and books on cultural geography. His recent works include *Texas Log Buildings: A Folk Architecture* (1978), *Texas Graveyards: A Cultural Legacy* (1982), and *American Log Buildings: An Old World Heritage* (1985).

[1] Evon Z. Vogt, "American Subcultural Continua as Exemplified by the Mormons and Texans," *American Anthropologist*, LVII (1955), 1,163–1,172; Joseph Leach, *The Typical Texan: Biography of an American Myth* (Dallas, 1952).

[2] This is the theme of Terry G. Jordan, John L. Bean, Jr., and William M. Holmes, *Texas: A Geography* (Boulder, Colo., 1984). See also Terry G. Jordan, "Population Origin Groups in Rural Texas," Map Supplement No. 13, *Annals of the Association of American Geographers*, LX (June, 1970), 404–405, plus folded map; Terry G. Jordan, "Population Origins in Texas, 1850," *Geographical Review*, LIX (Jan., 1969), 83–103; and Donald W. Meinig, *Imperial Texas: An Interpretive Essay in Cultural Geography* (Austin, 1969).

usually socially, economically, and politically as well, by a host culture.[3] In Texas, the host/dominant group throughout the past century and a half has consisted of old-stock Anglo-Americans, here defined as whites of colonial eastern-seaboard ancestry.[4] More precisely, *southern* Anglos served as the host culture in Texas through most of that period. Even as early as 1830, a mere fifteen years or so after southern pioneers began settling Texas, they had acquired majority status (figure 1). The war of independence in 1836 formalized the host culture claim of southern Anglos by awarding them political, social, and economic overlordship.

Though basically British-derived, the host group was itself far from internally homogeneous. Southern Anglos numbered not just English, Scotch-Irish, and Welsh among their ancestors, but also Pennsylvania Germans, Hudson Valley Dutch, French Huguenots, Delaware Valley Finns and Swedes, and others. These diverse groups, far to the east of Texas, blended through intermarriage to form the southern Anglo population. The Texian victors of 1836 lived in Finnish log cabins, fought with German long rifles, drank Scottish whiskey, adhered to British dissenter Protestantism, and introduced the language and common law of the English. Walk among their tombstones in the graveyards of rural Texas and you will find the Scotch-Irish McLane and Ross, the Germans Snider and Buckner, the English Alsbury and Cooper, the Dutch De Witt and Kuykendall, the Welsh Williams and Jones, the Huguenots Lamar and Alley, the Swedes Swanson and Justice.

Even in colonial times, the Anglo host group had formed two distinct southern subcultures, one rooted in the coastal plain and based in the

---

[3] Wsevolod W. Isajiw, "Definitions of Ethnicity," *Ethnicity,* I (July, 1974), 111–124; Terry G. Jordan and Lester Rowntree, "Ethnic Geography," Chapter 9 in *The Human Mosaic: A Thematic Introduction to Cultural Geography* (4th ed.; New York, 1986), 271–304.

[4] Basic sources on the southern Anglo-Americans include Terry G. Jordan, "The Texan Appalachia," *Annals of the Association of American Geographers,* LX (Sept., 1970), 409–427; Henry Stuart Foote, *Texas and the Texans; or, Advance of the Anglo-Americans to the South-West* (2 vols.; Philadelphia, 1841); Rex W. Strickland, "Anglo-American Activities in Northeastern Texas, 1803–1845" (Ph.D. diss., University of Texas, 1937); Lester G. Bugbee, "The Old Three Hundred: A List of Settlers in Austin's First Colony," *Quarterly of the Texas State Historical Association,* I (Oct., 1897), 108–117 (this journal is cited hereafter as *QTSHA*); Mark E. Nackman, "Anglo-American Migrants to the West: Men of Broken Fortunes? The Case of Texas, 1821–1846," *Western Historical Quarterly,* V (Oct., 1974), 441–455; Barnes F. Lathrop, *Migration into East Texas, 1835–1860* (Austin, 1949); Seymour V. Connor, *The Peters Colony of Texas* (Austin, 1959); William W. White, "Migration into West Texas, 1845–1860" (M.A. thesis, University of Texas, 1948); Homer L. Kerr, "Migration into Texas, 1865–1880" (Ph.D. diss., University of Texas, 1953); R. Marsh Smith, "Migration of Georgians to Texas, 1821–1870," *Georgia Historical Quarterly,* XX (Dec., 1936), 307–325; Ethel Zively Rather, "De Witt's Colony," *QTSHA,* VIII (Oct., 1904), 95–192; and Eugene C. Barker, *The Life of Stephen F. Austin, Founder of Texas, 1793–1836: A Chapter in the Westward Movement of the Anglo-American People* (Nashville, 1925).

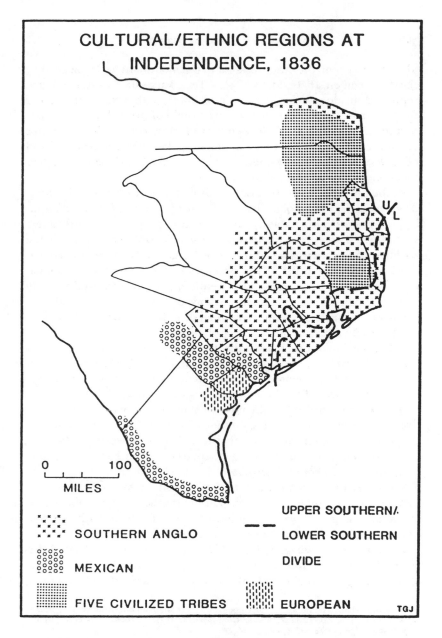

**CULTURAL/ETHNIC REGIONS AT INDEPENDENCE, 1836**

0     100

MILES

UPPER SOUTHERN/

— —

LOWER SOUTHERN

DIVIDE

SOUTHERN ANGLO

MEXICAN

FIVE CIVILIZED TRIBES

EUROPEAN

TGJ

Figure 1

At the time of the Texas Revolution, Anglo settlers, mainly of upper southern origin, were concentrated in the southeastern part of Texas, while an Irish-Mexican "barrier" had been set up in their coastal path. Cherokee Indians occupied much of northeastern Texas. (Source: Mexican censuses in the Nacogdoches Archives [Archives Division, Texas State Library, Austin] and Bexar Archives [Eugene C. Barker Texas History Center, University of Texas, Austin].)

plantation system, the other resident in the mountains and practiced by slaveless yeomen. In Texas, by 1850, a Texarkana–to–San Antonio line separated the domain of the planter, or lower southerner, to the east of the line, from the western interior stronghold of the yeoman, or upper southerner (figure 2).[5] While members of these two Anglo subgroups established distinctive rural economies, spoke different dialects, and often disagreed politically, they resembled each other closely enough to function as a single host culture in Texas.

At the time of the first federal census in Texas in 1850, the southern Anglo majority was absolute, but hardly, at 53 percent of the total population, overwhelming (table 1). As the century progressed, southerners strengthened somewhat their numerical hold on Texas, though the abolition of slavery weakened their overlordship. By 1887, they constituted nearly three-fifths of the population, the highest proportional level they were ever to reach. The twentieth century witnessed a steady deterioration and eventual disappearance of the host culture majority, for as we celebrate the sesquicentennial of independence, Anglos constitute less than half of the state population.

In fact, one might well argue that the Anglo host culture has ceased to be "southern." A western or southwestern self-image of Anglo-Texans developed, perhaps beginning as early as postbellum times, with the result that members of the host culture began thinking of themselves in nonsouthern terms.[6] When the novelist William Humphrey left his native Clarksville, it remained a southern town, but when he returned thirty-two years later, he found that it had become western.[7] Cotton, corn, overalls, and sharecropping disappeared from East Texas; stetsons, boots, and beef cattle replaced them. The South, whose military defeat never rested gently upon the self-confident Anglo-Texans, succumbed a second time, to the West. Let the cavaliers of Virginia, accustomed to losing civil wars, keep alive the Confederate faith. Texans would turn their eyes and hearts to the setting sun.

This shift of self-image from South to West, in turn, facilitated the absorption of numerous acculturated or assimilated Europeans and northern Anglos into the host culture. Even such a redefined, enlarged

---

[5] Terry G. Jordan, "The Imprint of the Upper and Lower South on Mid-Nineteenth-Century Texas," *Annals of the Association of American Geographers*, LVII (Dec., 1967), 667–690; Jordan, "Population Origins in Texas," 87–89.

[6] Wilbur Zelinsky, "North America's Vernacular Regions," *Annals of the Association of American Geographers*, LXX (Mar., 1980), 14.

[7] William Humphrey, *Farther Off from Heaven* (New York, 1977), 239. See also James W. Lee, "The Old South in Texas Literature," Don Graham, James W. Lee, and William T. Pilkington (eds.), *The Texas Literary Tradition: Fiction, Folklore, History* (Austin, 1983), 46, 48.

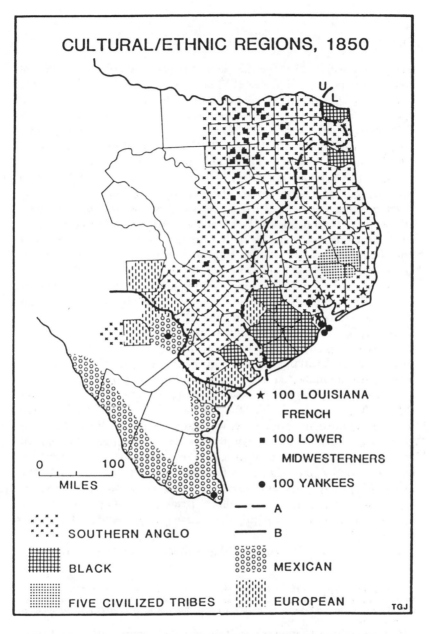

**CULTURAL/ETHNIC REGIONS, 1850**

★ 100 LOUISIANA
   FRENCH

▪ 100 LOWER
   MIDWESTERNERS

● 100 YANKEES

– – – A

——— B

SOUTHERN ANGLO

BLACK

FIVE CIVILIZED TRIBES

MEXICAN

EUROPEAN

TGJ

Figure 2

By mid-century, settlement had spread west to the Cross Timbers. *A* = upper southern/lower southern divide; *B* = north and east of this line, blacks outnumbered Hispanics. "Yankees" are natives of New England and New York; "Lower Midwesterners" are natives of Ohio, Indiana, and Illinois. Military personnel at frontier posts are not included in the count. (Source: United States census of 1850, including a hand count of the manuscript population schedules.)

group, however, cannot, on the basis of the census, claim a majority of the present population (table 2). This startling fact is revealed by the 1980 United States census, the first to include a question on remote ancestry. Even if the host culture is generously defined as those persons fully or even partially of British ancestry, the number accounts for only 45 percent of the total (table 1). This includes, for example, persons who responded that they were of English–French–German or American Indian–German–Irish ancestry, persons, in other words, who were less than half of British blood. Also included are 426,000 Texans reporting full or partial Scotch-Irish ancestry, amounting to only 4 percent of those responding. To be sure, many Anglos failed to respond to the census question, causing their numbers to be undercounted, but add the figures as you will, the total of persons claiming *any* English, Irish, Welsh, or Scotch blood falls well short of half the population.[8] Profound cultural shifts will surely accompany this loss of Anglo majority, this tipping of the ethnic balance in Texas. Increasingly, Anglo dominance retreats northward (figure 3).

As long as the Anglo host culture remained southern in character, northerners functioned much like an ethnic group in Texas. Walter Prescott Webb, recalling his youth in Stephens County, once told of a lone northern family that settled in his exclusively southern, Confederate-sympathizing neighborhood. Several quite pretty daughters graced the family, but, added Webb, "they never married, of course."[9] A segment of the northern population was Yankee—derived from New England, New York, and their daughter states of Michigan, Wisconsin, and Minnesota in the upper Midwest. Though only about 3,000 Yankees lived in Texas by 1850, they were far above average in wealth and education.[10] Typically, Yankees worked as merchants, artisans, or other professionals in the towns of antebellum Texas or as officers among soldiers on the frontier.[11] A highly distinctive group, distinguished from the bulk of southern Anglos by education, profession, place of residence, and wealth, Yankees wielded influence out of proportion to

---

[8] United States Census of Population and Housing, 1980, Summary Tape File 4, "Technical Documentation" (Washington, D.C., 1983); and United States Census of Population, "Public-Use Microdata Samples" (Washington, D.C., 1983). Both of these sources are unpublished computer tapes.

[9] Professor Webb told this anecdote in the classroom in the fall semester, 1960, at the University of Texas.

[10] Hand count of MSS free population schedules, United States census of 1850, including natives of New England, New York, Michigan, Wisconsin, and their Texas-born children.

[11] Arthur C. Burnett, *Yankees in the Republic of Texas: Some Notes on Their Origin and Impact* (Houston, 1952).

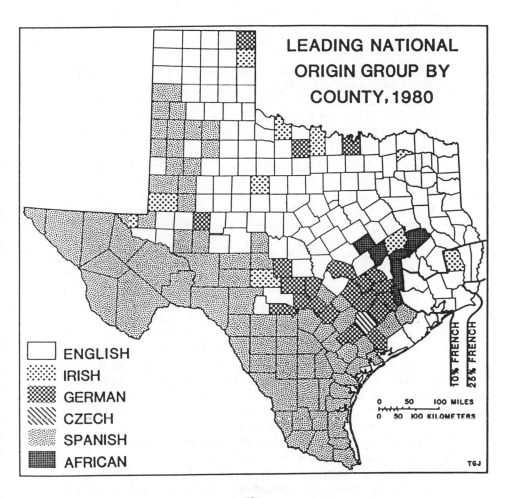

Figure 3

In each county, persons claiming full or partial ancestry from the group
indicated were more numerous than any other. Had persons of English, Irish, Scottish, and Welsh ancestry been combined, the resultant
"British" group would have claimed some counties shown as Spanish,
German, and African. The Irish, largely Protestant or Scotch-Irish, are
common wherever the English are, and the apparent islandlike character of their plurality is misleading. Loving County had precisely the
same numbers of Irish and Spanish. (Source: United States Census of
Population and Housing, 1980, Summary Tape File 4, "Technical Documentation" [Washington, D.C., 1983], unpublished computer tape.)

their numbers, as is suggested by the election of Connecticut native Elisha Pease as governor in 1853 and 1855.

In the period from 1865 to 1880, the Yankee states continued to provide about 2 percent of the white immigrants to Texas.[12] The leading contributing state of birth by 1890, as in 1850, was New York.[13] By the 1970s, Michigan had supplanted New York as the principal source state in an accelerating Yankee immigration. While these northerners are easily absorbed into the Anglo host culture today, their dialect remains distinctive.

Another component of the northern Anglo-American group, derived from the Ohio-to-Nebraska belt of lower midwestern states, made up 5 percent of the immigrant white population by 1850, and natives of Illinois outnumbered those from any other state in Dallas County.[14] Forty years later, Illini remained twice as numerous as natives of any other midwestern state, and the influx of lower midwesterners between 1865 and 1880 accounted for 8 percent of the whites coming to Texas in postbellum times.[15] Immigration from the Ohio-to-Nebraska belt has persisted to the present day, lending a midwestern flavor to the top two tiers of counties in the Panhandle, to the rural northern Blackland Prairie, and to parts of Dallas and Houston. Even the lower Rio Grande Valley and the Gulf Coast region display pockets of rural midwestern influence, as is suggested by town names like Buckeye in Matagorda County, Bloomington in Victoria County, Iowa Colony in Brazoria County, and Ohio in Cameron County.[16]

If the enlarged old-stock Anglo host culture accounts for roughly half of the Texas population, the other half is ethnic. Between 1940 and 1950, an ethnic event of pivotal importance to the cultural future of the state occurred, entirely unnoticed at the time. Perhaps in the year 1947 or 1948, persons of Hispanic ancestry surpassed blacks in number to become the largest ethnic minority in Texas (table 3). Since that time, the Hispanic element has continued to grow very rapidly and may well outnumber blacks two-to-one as we observe the sesquicentennial of

---

[12] Kerr, "Migration into Texas," 73–74.

[13] *The Seventh Census of the United States: 1850* (Washington, D.C., 1853), xxxvi–xxxvii; Eleventh Census of the United States, Vol. XI, Pt. 1, *Population of the United States, 1890* (Washington, D.C., 1894), 560–573.

[14] Hand count of MSS free population schedules, United States census of 1850; the midwestern total includes natives of Ohio, Indiana, Illinois, Iowa, Kansas, Nebraska, and their Texas-born children.

[15] Eleventh Census, Vol. XI, Pt. 1, 560–573; Kerr, "Migration into Texas," 73.

[16] Walter Prescott Webb, H. Bailey Carroll, and Eldon Stephen Branda (eds.), *The Handbook of Texas* (3 vols.; Austin, 1952, 1976), I, 176, 237, 891, II, 303.

the war that extinguished Hispanic rule. Today perhaps one-quarter of the Texas population is Hispanic in origin, and the massive continuing immigration from Mexico has the potential further to increase the proportion in future decades.[17] Texas, in 1980, had the second largest Hispanic population among the states, ranking behind California; and the cities of San Antonio, Houston, and El Paso were among the top eight American metropolitan areas in size of Hispanic population.

Ironically, during the century-and-a-half of Spanish and Mexican colonization and rule, from 1680 to 1836, no substantial Hispanic population accumulated in Texas, while the 150 years of Anglo control produced a Spanish surnamed group of over three million. When Mexican political authority ended at San Jacinto, no more than 7,000 or 8,000 Spaniards, Christianized Indians, and mestizos resided in Texas, already for a decade a minority group in their own homeland. The 1850 census schedules suggest an Hispanic population of only about 14,000, less than 7 percent of the Texas total (tables 1, 3). Nor, in the following four decades, did the growth of the Hispanic population by natural increase and immigration keep pace with Anglos, blacks, and Europeans. In the 1850s, a mere 2.3 percent of Texas white immigrants came from Mexico, a proportion that becomes much smaller if the sizable black immigration of that decade is considered.[18] Between 1860 and 1880, Latin American countries, led by Mexico, accounted for 6.5 percent of the total immigration to Texas, falling from 10 percent in

---

[17] Basic sources on Hispanic-Texans include Paul S. Taylor, *An American-Mexican Frontier: Nueces County, Texas* (Chapel Hill, N.C., 1934); Richard L. Nostrand, "The Hispanic-American Borderland: Delimitation of an American Culture Region," *Annals of the Association of American Geographers*, LX (Dec., 1970), 638–661; Richard L. Nostrand, "Mexican Americans circa 1850," ibid., LXV (Sept., 1975), 378–390 [a colored map serving as a companion to this article appeared in *Historical Geography Newsletter*, V (Fall, 1975), following p. 30]; Ozzie G. Simmons, "Anglo-Americans and Mexican Americans in South Texas" (Ph.D. diss., Harvard University, 1952); Pauline R. Kibbe, *Latin Americans in Texas* (Albuquerque, 1946); M. S. Handman, "The Mexican Immigrant in Texas," *Southwestern Political and Social Science Quarterly*, VII (June, 1926), 33–41; Herbert E. Bolton, *Texas in the Middle Eighteenth Century* (Berkeley, 1915); I. J. Cox, "The Early Settlers of San Fernando," *QTSHA*, V (Oct., 1901), 142–160; James A. Wilson, *Tejanos, Chicanos, and Mexicanos: A Partially Annotated, Historical Bibliography* (San Marcos, Texas, 1974); William Madsen, *The Mexican-Americans of South Texas* (2nd ed.; New York, 1973); Mary Ellen Goodman et al., *The Mexican-American Population of Houston: A Survey in the Field, 1965–1970*, Rice University Studies, LVII, No. 3 (Houston, 1971); Arnoldo De León, *The Tejano Community, 1836–1900* (Albuquerque, 1982); Arnoldo De León, *They Called Them Greasers: Anglo Attitudes toward Mexicans in Texas, 1821–1900* (Austin, 1983); Mario T. García, *Desert Immigrants: The Mexicans of El Paso, 1880–1920* (New Haven, Conn., 1981); Gilberto Hinojosa, *A Borderlands Town in Transition: Laredo, 1755–1870* (College Station, Tex., 1983).

[18] White, "Migration into West Texas," 13, 20; Barnes F. Lathrop, "Migration into East Texas, 1835–1860," *Southwestern Historical Quarterly*, LII (July, 1948), 31 (the *Quarterly* is cited hereafter as *SHQ*). The total achieved by adding White's and Lathrop's samples is 7,260 immigrant families, of whom 169 were from Mexico.

the 1863–1866 period to only 4.9 percent between 1875 and 1878.[19] By the time of the state census in 1887, Hispanics numbered 83,000 and formed only 4 percent of the Texas population (table 1). The Anglicization of the state seemed within reach; demographically the host culture enjoyed its finest hour.

Hispanics, outnumbered in 1887 fourteen-to-one by southern Anglos, five-to-one by blacks, almost three-to-one by Europeans, and even by Germans alone, appeared on their way to ethnic eclipse in Texas, though they continued to form majorities in thirteen counties of the border area (figures 4, 5). An observer at the beginning of the last decade of the nineteenth century could hardly have imagined what was to come.

Most observers believe the mass immigration from Mexico began about 1910, coinciding with a revolution there and the spread of railroads, which brought commercial agriculture into South Texas. In reality, however, the major influx of Mexicans began in the 1890s. The number of Mexican-born rose from 52,000 to 71,000 between 1890 and 1900; the increase in immigration alone equaled the percentage growth of the Texas population at large. By 1910, Mexican-born totaled 125,000, and an additional 108,000 native Texans reported one or both parents born in Mexico.[20] The generation 1890–1910, then, witnessed an immigration of perhaps 100,000 from Mexico, more than doubling the Hispanic population of 1887. If the old-stock Mexican group were added to the 1910 figure for first and second generation "foreign white stock," an Hispanic element of at least 300,000 would likely result. Clearly, the ethnic winds had shifted in that twenty-year span, allowing the Mexican population to grow threefold while the total number of Texas inhabitants increased by only 75 percent.

Since 1910, a tenfold growth of the Hispanic group has occurred (table 3). Key factors in the twentieth-century immigration have been the steady industrialization of Texas and an explosive birth rate in Mexico. Much of the immigration has been illegal, a situation rich in irony. In the early 1830s, harassed Mexican border troops proved incapable of halting a large-scale influx of illegal Anglo aliens ("wetnecks"?) crossing the Sabine and Red rivers; in the 1980s, the pattern is re-

---

[19] Kerr, "Migration into Texas," 74, 75, 135, 137.

[20] Eleventh Census, Vol. XI, Pt. 1, p. 606; United States, Bureau of the Census, *Abstract of the Twelfth Census of the United States, 1900* (Washington, D.C., 1904), 61; Thirteenth Census of the United States Taken in the Year 1910, Vol. III, *Population, 1910* (Washington, D.C., 1913), 799.

versed. Latin American countries beyond Mexico, such as El Salvador, have begun sending substantial numbers of illegal migrants.

So lengthy and sizable an immigration is bound to be a diverse one. As a result, the Hispanic population is internally the most complex ethnic group in Texas. It consists of many different national origin groups, though Mexicans dominate; joins Castilian Spaniard, Amerindian, and African; overlaps a complete socioeconomic range; and derives from assorted periods of migration. Not even the basic traditional defining traits—Spanish tongue and Catholic faith—suffice any longer to encompass this group. English has made inroads, as is suggested by the fact that 6 percent of the Texas Hispanic population did not list Spanish as the language of household use in 1980.[21] Protestantism, too, has spread among the Hispanics. As of 1984, various major Protestant denominations had won a total of about 140,000 Latin American converts in Texas, led by the Southern Baptists, who account for half the total.[22] By this measure, Protestantism now claims 5 percent of the Texas Hispanics. The derisive label *agringado* is applied by some of their ethnic kin to such acculturated persons.

One of the major internal divisions within the Hispanic group is based upon time of immigration. On school playgrounds, year of arrival helps determine status. Greatest prestige belongs to the Tejanos, descendants of the colonial population. In San Antonio, Canary Islander ancestry is of some social consequence, since that group constituted the first civilian settlers of Spanish Texas. Often descended from land-grant families, Tejanos tend to be wealthier than the norm, highly acculturated, and, in many cases, intermarried with Anglos. Lowest on the socio-economic scale are recently arrived laborers, many of whom live in urban slums or in rural *colonias* in the lower Rio Grande Valley.

---

[21] 1980 Census of Population, Vol. I, Characteristics of the Population, Chapter C, *General Social and Economic Characteristics*, Pt. 45, Texas, Sec. 1 (Washington, D.C., 1983), 110, 141. The figures are based on the Spanish-origin population five years or more of age. Of 2,632,758 such persons, 2,484,188 reported using Spanish at home.

[22] The following 1984 figures for Hispanic members were provided by church officials: Southern Baptist Convention, 70,000; Assembly of God, 38,046; United Methodist, 16,000; Presbyterian Church, 5,300; Seventh-Day Adventist, 4,000; American Lutheran Church, 2,500; Lutheran Church—Missouri Synod, 1,947; Disciples of Christ (Christian Church), 580; Lutheran Church in America, 500. See also: Andrew J. Weigert, William V. D'Antonio, and Arthur J. Rubel, "Protestantism and Assimilation among Mexican Americans," *Journal for the Scientific Study of Religion*, X (Fall, 1971), 219–232; Martha C. M. Remy, "Protestant Churches and Mexican-Americans in South Texas" (Ph.D. diss., University of Texas, Austin, 1970); Jose Galindo-Alvirez, "Latin American Methodism in the Southwest: A History of the Rio Grande Conference" (M.A. thesis, Lamar University, 1962); and James C. Thrash, "Spanish-Speaking Presbyterians in South Texas" (M.A. thesis, Texas A&I University, 1969).

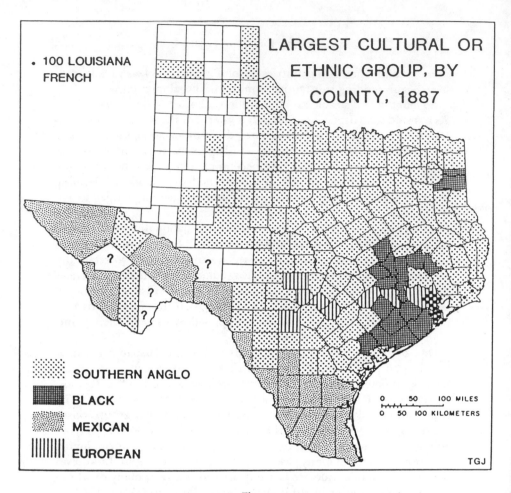

At the golden jubilee of Texas independence, the Anglo host culture enjoyed, proportionately and areally, its finest hour. Louisiana French were interpreted to be persons of French ancestry living in the far southeastern counties. (Source: Texas State Census of 1887, published in L. L. Foster (ed.), *First Annual Report of the Agricultural Bureau of the Department of Agriculture, Insurance, Statistics, and History, 1887–88* [Austin, 1889], 1–249. Adjustments were made for missing data for Encinal County and for flawed data for Gillespie County on the basis of manuscript population schedules of the 1880 U.S. census and the published 1890 U.S. census, *Population of the United States, 1890* [Washington, D.C., 1894].)

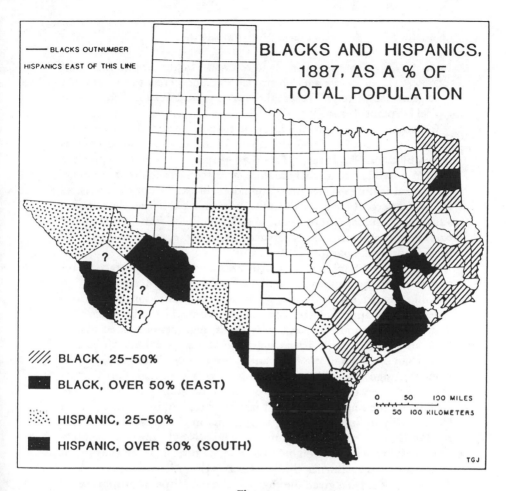

Figure 5

The spatial segregation between blacks and Hispanics is evident, and the dividing line remained much as it had been in 1850. The missing Encinal County figures were estimated, based upon a hand count of the 1880 census manuscript population schedules. (Source: Texas State Census of 1887, in Foster [ed.], *First Annual Report*, 1–249.)

In 1976, sixty-five *colonias* in Cameron and Hidalgo counties housed 32,000 persons, mostly agricultural laborers, 80 percent of whom had immigrated since 1960.[23] Just as there is no typical Texan, so there is no typical Hispanic-Texan.

In geographical terms, the internal Hispanic contrasts are best described by a Pecos River boundary. West of that stream, and best exemplified by the El Paso area, is found an Hispanic subculture with close links to New Mexico and Chihuahua, as is seen in such traditional architectural features as flat roofs and adobe brick. East of the Pecos, by contrast, a second Hispanic subculture prevails, exhibiting closer ties to adjacent Coahuila, Nuevo León, and Tamaulipas. Stone, caliche, and *palisado* (picket) construction replaces adobe there, and a favored roof form features the parapet gable.

These two Hispanic-Texan subcultures have been reinforced in recent years by the pattern of immigration flow from Mexico. The San Antonio district of the Immigration and Naturalization Service collected data on apprehended illegal aliens, from which it becomes clear that, as of the middle 1970s, South Texas migrants emanated mainly from an adjacent northeastern region in Mexico. Coahuila alone sent more than one-fifth of the total, and other sizable contingents arrived from Durango, Tamaulipas, San Luis Potosí, Zacatecas, and Guanajuato. Closeness to South Texas appears to be an important factor in channeling the migration. The Trans-Pecos region, by contrast, draws most heavily upon neighboring Chihuahua in the present migration, reinforcing the traditional regionalism. Surprisingly, the western Mesa Central of Mexico, centered in Jalisco and Michoacán, sends the bulk of its emigrants to California, though Texas is closer.[24]

One might expect, given the sharp rise in the Hispanic proportion of the Texas population in the last century, accompanied by the huge numerical increase, that the geographical area with a Mexican-American majority would have increased greatly. This has not been the case (figures 5, 6, 7). Indeed, the trend between 1880 and 1930 was for Mexican majorities to weaken or even be lost in South Texas. Among the river-front counties, Cameron declined from 88 percent Mexican in 1880 to 50 percent in 1930, Hidalgo from 98 to 54 percent, Zapata from 99 to 51, and Webb-Encinal from 92 to 70. Duval County, where

---

[23] *The Colonias of the Lower Rio Grande Valley of South Texas: A Policy Perspective*, Lyndon B. Johnson School of Public Affairs, Policy Research Project Report No. 18 (Austin, 1977).

[24] Richard C. Jones, "Undocumented Migration from Mexico: Some Geographical Questions," *Annals of the Association of American Geographers*, LXXII (Mar., 1982), 83–84.

nine of every ten persons was Mexican in 1880, was less than one-third Hispanic fifty years later.[25] Aided by a net Anglo emigration from South Texas since 1960, Mexicans have decisively reversed this trend. More notably, the past fifty years have also witnessed a significant northward movement of Hispanic people within the state, as can be seen in the significant enlargement of the area in which they form between a quarter and a half of the total population, as well as in the northward and eastward shift in the boundary of the district housing more Mexicans than blacks (figures 5, 6, 7). Four counties that had black *majorities* as recently as 1900—Brazoria, Fort Bend, Matagorda, and Wharton—housed more Hispanics than blacks by 1980.[26]

Denton County, in North Texas, provides a good example of the spread of the Mexican population into new areas. Only 14 persons of Hispanic ethnicity lived in Denton County in 1887, contrasted with 905 blacks; and by 1930 the Mexican total had risen to 254, still less than one-eighth the number of Afro-Americans.[27] Some had come as railroad workers, while others labored on farms and ranches in the county. Many Anglo cemeteries in rural Denton County contain a few, spatially segregated, Mexican graves dating from the early part of the century. The Menchaca family operated a Mexican-food cafe as early as 1916 on the east side of the Denton courthouse square. Even so, Spanish-surnamed counts revealed only 242 such persons in the county in 1950 and 885 in 1960. Beginning in the 1960s, an upswing in immigration occurred, with South Texas as the leading source, and in the following decade Hispanics surpassed blacks to become the largest Denton County minority. The 1980 census enumerated 6,286 Hispanic persons, or 4.5 percent of the county population, surpassing the black total of 6,135.[28]

Until fairly recently, a rather orderly steplike geographical progression was evident in the northward intrastate migration of Hispanics.

---

[25] Robert C. Spillman, "A Historical Geography of Mexican American Population Patterns in the South Texas Hispanic Borderland: 1850–1970" (M.A. thesis, University of Southern Mississippi, 1977), 38, 61, based upon his hand count of the MSS population schedules of the 1880 United States census; see also Mattie L. Wooten, "Racial, National, and Nativity Trends in Texas, 1870–1930," *Southwestern Social Science Quarterly*, XIV (June, 1933), 62–69.

[26] Thirteenth Census, Vol. III, *Population, 1910*, pp. 805–851.

[27] L. L. Foster (ed.), *First Annual Report of the Agricultural Bureau of the Department of Agriculture, Insurance, Statistics, and History, 1887–88* (Austin, 1889), 55; Fifteenth Census of the United States: 1930, *Population*, Vol. III, Pt. 2 (Washington, D.C., 1932), 978, 1,014.

[28] Terry G. Jordan, "County Bicentennial Affair Rich in Spanish History," Denton *Record-Chronicle*, Feb. 11, 1976; 1980 Census of Population, Vol. I, Chapter C, Pt. 45, Texas, Sec. 1, pp. 51, 79, 101; United States Census of Population: 1950, *Persons of Spanish Surname*, Special Report (Washington, D.C., 1953), p. 3C–45; United States Census of Population: 1960, Subject Reports, PC(2)-1B, *Persons of Spanish Surname* (Washington, D.C., 1963).

The newly arrived immigrant could be expected to settle in one of the rural *colonias*, near the Rio Grande in South Texas. As acculturation progressed, the people moved farther north and up the socioeconomic ladder. In this manner, certain West Texas counties derived much or most of their Hispanic population from South Texas.[29] Today, however, sophisticated networks funnel illegal aliens far north of the border, often well beyond Texas.

The Hispanic immigration has differed from that of other ethnic minorities in some fundamental ways. Mexicans entering Texas find a familiar place. The rivers they cross, the towns and counties they settle in, even the streets they live on often bear Spanish names. Radio and television stations, newspapers, and church services employing their mother tongue await them. The century and a half of Hispanic rule is the basis of much of the sense of familiarity, providing not just toponyms and a venerable population base upon which to build, but also the unexpressed or even subconscious belief that "this land is rightfully ours." In immigration, no ocean is crossed, and the ancestral homeland remains adjacent, permitting close cultural ties. Too, the volume and duration of Mexican immigration are unrivaled by other ethnic groups and provide continual cultural reinforcement. For all these reasons, Hispanic ethnicity remains vital and acculturation is retarded.

The rapid numerical and proportional growth of the Spanish-surnamed population, coupled with the enhanced viability of Mexican ethnicity, together constitute the most significant ethnic development in Texas at the Sesquicentennial. As the Mexican element translates numbers and proportions into political power and social clout, Texas becomes increasingly Hispanicized, or better, re-Hispanicized.

Afro-Americans, forming the second largest ethnic group, have been present in Texas from Spanish times, and eighteenth-century censuses clearly acknowledge their presence, both as pure Africans and in an array of mixtures with Indians and Spaniards, in places such as San Antonio and Nacogdoches.[30] Indeed, nearly 16,000 Texas blacks claimed Hispanic ancestry in the census of 1980.[31]

Still, relatively few blacks lived in Texas prior to 1836. Anglos introduced only modest numbers of Afro-Americans prior to indepen-

---

[29] Ronald C. Sheck, "Mexican-American Migration to Selected Texas Panhandle Urban Places" (Discussion Paper No. 20, Dept. of Geography, Ohio State University, 1971).

[30] See, for example, W. H. Timmons, "The Population of the El Paso Area—A Census of 1784," *New Mexico Historical Review*, LII (Oct., 1977), 314.

[31] 1980 Census of Population, Vol. I, Chapter C, Pt. 45, Texas, Sec. 1, p. 59.

dence, both because the status of slaves was uncertain under Mexican law and because the large majority of early Anglo settlers came from southern mountain states, where slavery was uncommon.[32] According to the Mexican census taken in 1835, all of East Texas, which was later to become the focus of black settlement, had only 588 slaves in its population, or about 12 percent of the total. The municipality (county) of San Augustine had the highest proportion, at 23 percent, while neighboring Tenaha (present Shelby County) was lowest with only 3 percent. The largest black population at that time, numbering 243, lived in adjacent Sabine Municipality.[33] In Texas as a whole by 1836, the time of independence, no more than one-tenth of the inhabitants were black.

A dramatic increase in slave immigration occurred in the late 1830s, accompanying the first large influx of white planters from southern coastal states. The Republic legalized slavery almost at once, removing the major bar to planter immigration, and by 1840 Texans payed taxes on over twelve thousand black slaves, a total that should be adjusted upward to about 15,000 because of missing tax lists for several counties.[34] Roughly one-fifth of the total population was black in that year. The large-scale introduction of slaves accelerated still more after Texas joined the Union, and by the time of the Civil War nearly 200,000 blacks, forming almost one-third of the total population, lived in the state.[35] Texas seemed well on its way to following the coastal southern model of black majority.

The Civil War and emancipation effectively halted the Africanization of Texas. The influx of blacks largely ended in 1865, and in the following fifteen years only 6 percent of the immigrants to the state were

---

[32] Basic sources on Afro-Texans include Alwyn Barr, *Black Texans: A History of Negroes in Texas, 1528–1971* (Austin, 1973); Eugene C. Barker, "The Influence of Slavery in the Colonization of Texas," *SHQ*, XXVIII (July, 1924), 1–33; Lester G. Bugbee, "Slavery in Early Texas," *Political Science Quarterly*, XIII (Sept., 1898), 389–412, (Dec.), 648–668; Bruce A. Glasrud, "Black Texans, 1900–1930: A History" (Ph.D. diss., Texas Tech University, 1969); Lawrence D. Rice, "The Negro in Texas, 1874–1900" (Ph.D. diss., Texas Tech University, 1967); Neil G. Sapper, "A Survey of the History of the Black People of Texas, 1930–1954" (Ph.D. diss., Texas Tech University, 1972); Harold Schoen, "The Free Negro in the Republic of Texas," *SHQ* XXXIX (Apr., 1936), 292–308; ibid., XL (July, 1936), 26–34, (Oct.), 85–113, (Jan., 1937), 169–199, (Apr.), 267–289; ibid., XLI (July, 1937), 83–108; Ronnie C. Tyler and Lawrence R. Murphy (eds.), *The Slave Narratives of Texas* (Austin, 1974).

[33] MSS censuses for the municipalities of Bevil, Nacogdoches, Sabine, San Augustine, and Tenaha, 1835, in the Nacogdoches Archives (Archives Division, Texas State Library, Austin), and published in Marion D. Mullins, *First Census of Texas, 1829–1836* (Washington, D.C., 1959).

[34] Gifford E. White (ed.), *The 1840 Census of the Republic of Texas* (Austin, 1966). The 1840 distribution of slaves in Texas is mapped in Stanley A. Arbingast et al., *Atlas of Texas* (5th ed.; Austin, 1976), 52 (maps compiled by Terry G. Jordan).

[35] *Population of the United States in 1860, Compiled from the Original Returns of the Eighth Census* (Washington, D.C., 1864), 479, 483, 486.

black, a proportion that fell even lower in later decades.[36] Indicative of the virtual cessation of black immigration is the fact that by 1880 nearly three-quarters of all Afro-Americans in the state were of Texas birth, as opposed to less than half the whites.[37] As a consequence, the proportion of blacks in the total population steadily dwindled after 1865, falling to only 12 percent at present. Actual numbers have risen modestly through natural increase, in spite of a large emigration of Texas blacks to the North and to California in the first half of the twentieth century.

The black settlement of Texas, then, occurred largely between 1836 and 1865. The major contributing states included Alabama, where nearly one-fifth of all Texas slaves were born, Virginia (13 percent), Georgia (12 percent), and Mississippi (11 percent).[38] Virginia ranked proportionately much higher as a birthplace of blacks than of Anglo-Texans, primarily because of the lively export of excess slaves from the worn-out tobacco districts of the Chesapeake Tidewater. Some Texas blacks arrived directly from Africa in an illegal trade lasting from the 1820s to the Civil War, and the census of 1880 revealed that, in number of African-born, Texas ranked highest among all the states.[39]

The region settled by blacks lay east of the Texarkana–to–San Antonio line, coinciding with the domain of the lower southern whites. Thirteen counties in that area had black majorities by 1860, led by Wharton County, where over four-fifths of the population was slave. More exactly, blacks were concentrated along the major rivers of eastern and southeastern Texas, especially the lower Brazos, Colorado, and Trinity. The Red River and some of its right-bank tributaries, most notably Cypress Bayou, also formed a major plantation district. After emancipation, black freedmen remained in these same areas, where they retained majorities in twelve counties as late as 1887.[40] Throughout the nineteenth century, there was almost no spatial overlap of blacks and Hispanics in Texas, and a clearly defined dividing line between the two groups followed the axis of the San Antonio River, com-

[36] Kerr, "Migration into Texas," 73–75.

[37] Tenth Census, 1880, *Statistics of the Population of the United States at the Tenth Census* (Washington, D.C., 1883), 484–492.

[38] Ninth Census, 1870, Vol. I, *The Statistics of the Population of the United States* (Washington, D.C., 1872), 328–342; *Statistics of the Population at the Tenth Census*, 488–492.

[39] *Statistics of Population at the Tenth Census*, 492. See also Eugene C. Barker, "The African Slave Trade in Texas," *QTSHA*, VI (Oct., 1902), 145–158; and Fred Robbins, "The Origin and Development of the African Slave Trade in Galveston, Texas, and Surrounding Areas from 1816 to 1836," *East Texas Historical Journal*, IX (Oct., 1971), 153–161.

[40] Foster, *First Annual Report*, 1–249.

Portrait of a young black man in Austin, Texas, 1880. Courtesy Eugene
Barker Texas History Center, University of Texas, Austin.

ing to the Gulf along the border separating San Patricio and Refugio counties (figure 5).

The twentieth century has witnessed a severe weakening of the black rural stronghold in East Texas (table 4). Migration to Houston, Dallas, and other cities, as well as the flight to northern and western states, left only four black-majority counties by 1930 (figure 6).[41] The subsequent demise of the sharecropper system and conversion of East Texas to pasture and pine plantation undercut the remaining rural communities. At the Sesquicentennial, no Texas county has a black majority, and in only nine do Afro-Americans constitute more than one-fourth of the population (figure 7). Rural black hamlets and neighborhoods can still be found in East Texas, but they are dwindling.

Today, black population and culture are dominantly urban. Afro-Texans traded the rural river valleys for the city ghettoes. The largest concentrations are found in Houston, Dallas, and Fort Worth. Beaumont, among cities of more than 100,000 inhabitants, had the highest proportion of blacks in the total population in 1980 with 37 percent, and the other such cities in which blacks formed proportions greater than their statewide percentage were Dallas (29 percent), Houston (28), Fort Worth (23), and Waco (22).[42] In the urban setting, blacks remain highly segregated from Hispanics. Unique to the twentieth-century city, however, is the residential segregation of Anglos and blacks. Two peoples who had for several centuries shared rural and town neighborhoods as master and servant parted residential company as Texas became urbanized. While this segregation imposed many burdens and indignities upon the blacks, it permitted ethnic rejuvenation and strengthened their sense of identity. By concentrating in urban ghettoes, Texas blacks were better able to survive culturally in the century 1860 to 1960, which witnessed their fall from one-third to one-eighth of the total population.

To a great extent, the proportional decline of the Texas black population coincided with the rise of the Hispanic element (table 3). Since 1887, blacks have increased only fourfold in number while Hispanics have grown thirty-sixfold. The cultural implications of this shift are profound. Indeed, the widely held self-image of Anglo-Texans as westerners rather than southerners may be linked in part to the displacement of blacks by Mexicans as the largest ethnic minority.

---

[41] Fifteenth Census, 1930, *Population*, Vol. III, Pt. 2, pp. 975–990.

[42] 1980 Census of Population, Vol. I, Chapter C, Part 45, Texas, Sec. 1, pp. 34–49.

Anglos, Hispanics, and blacks all represent old-stock American populations; that is, they are descended in part or whole from immigrants who entered North America in colonial times. One other major Texas ethnic group shares old-stock status—the Louisiana French (table 1).[43] Persons of French ancestry form the largest national-origin group in Louisiana and dominate a southern triangular area in that state, with apexes at the mouth of the Mississippi, Alexandria, and Lake Charles. Though this area is adjacent to Texas, notable migration across the Sabine by Louisiana French began relatively late and remained rather modest in scale.

Cajuns, or *acadiens*, who form the largest and most viable of the several Louisiana French subcultures, began entering Texas in small numbers in the 1820s, and they have from that time constituted the most sizable and important French ethnic group in the state. Most of the thousand or so ethnic French in Texas by 1850 lived in the far southeastern counties and bore typically Cajun surnames, though a small contingent of Louisiana Creole French settled in the town of Liberty about that time (figure 2).[44] Most of the early Cajun settlers engaged in cattle ranching on the Coastal Prairie, and one, Taylor White (born Leblanc), owned the largest herds in that area during the 1820s and 1830s.[45] By 1887, the French element in Southeast Texas had increased very modestly to about 2,300 (table 1) (figure 4).

Following the temporal pattern of Mexican immigration, Cajuns began their major influx about the turn of the century. The trigger was the discovery of oil at Spindletop, followed by the industrialization of the Houston area and the Golden Triangle. Port Arthur bears perhaps the deepest Cajun imprint, but telephone directories for nearly every town and city from the lower Sabine westward to Houston and Gal-

---

[43] Sources on the Louisiana French in Texas include Mary M. Withers, "The Acadians of Jefferson County, Texas," *Texas Gulf Historical and Biographical Record*, VII (Nov., 1971), 42–48; M. LeRoy Ellis, "La culture acadienne dans le sud-est du Texas," *Revue de Louisiane/Louisiana Review*, II (Summer, 1973), 99–101; Miriam Partlow, "Immigration of the Creoles," Chapter 17 in her book *Liberty, Liberty County, and the Atascosito District* (Austin, 1974); Dean R. Louder and Michael J. Leblanc, "Les Cadjins de l'Est du Texas," Dean R. Louder and Eric Waddell (eds.), *Du continent perdu à l'archipel retrouvé: le Québec et l'Amérique française*, Travaux du Département de Géographie de l'Université Laval, No. 6 (Québec, 1983), 259–271; Peveril Meigs, "An Ethno-Telephonic Survey of French Louisiana," *Annals of the Association of American Geographers*, XXXI (Dec., 1941), 243–250.

[44] Seventh Census, 1850, MSS free population schedules, Galveston, Harris, Jefferson, and Liberty counties, Texas; Partlow, "Immigration of Creoles," 189–192.

[45] Ruth G. Francis, "The Coastal Cow Country—The Saga of James Taylor White, First," *Coastal Cattleman*, VI (Sept., 1940), 21–23; Terry G. Jordan, *Trails to Texas: Southern Roots of Western Cattle Ranching* (Lincoln, Neb., 1981), 79, 80.

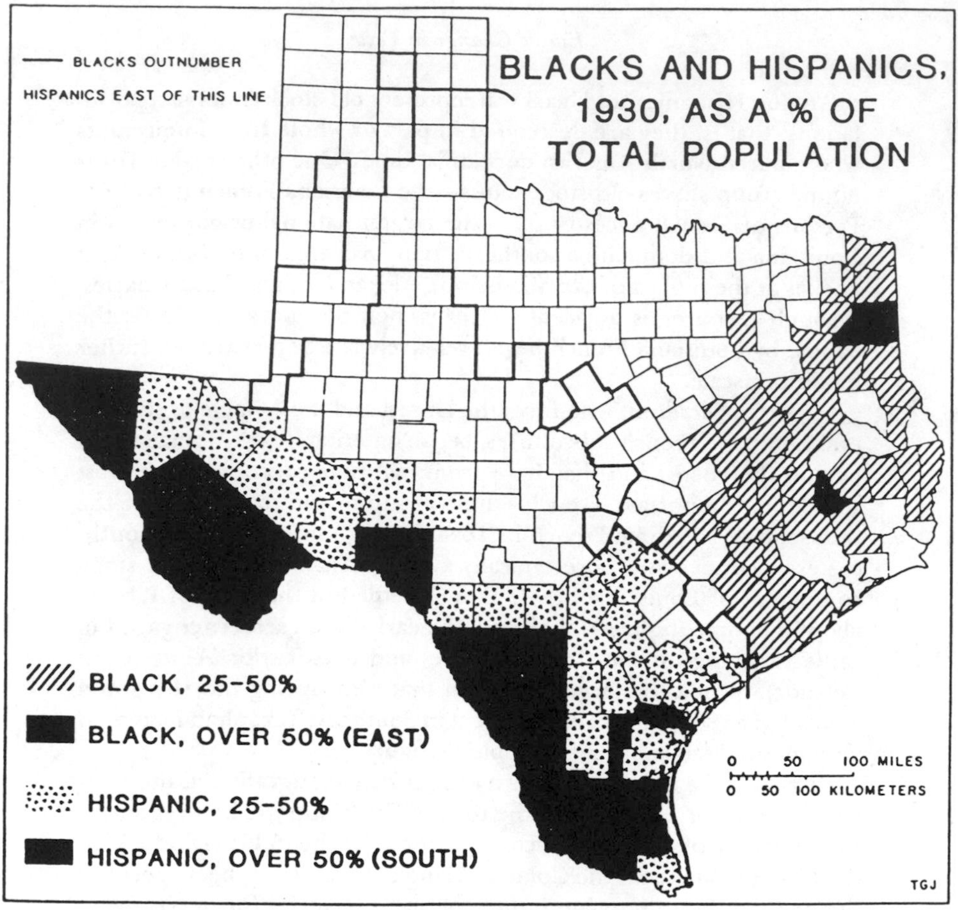
BLACKS OUTNUMBER
HISPANICS EAST OF THIS LINE
BLACKS AND HISPANICS, 1930, AS A % OF TOTAL POPULATION
BLACK, 25-50%
BLACK, OVER 50% (EAST)
HISPANIC, 25-50%
HISPANIC, OVER 50% (SOUTH)
0 50 100 MILES
0 50 100 KILOMETERS
TGJ

Figure 6

Note the weakening of the black areas since 1887 and the eastward shift of the Hispanic/black border. (Source: Fifteenth Census of the United States: 1930, *Population*, Vol. III, Pt. 2 [Washington, D.C., 1932], 975–990, 1,014–1,015.)

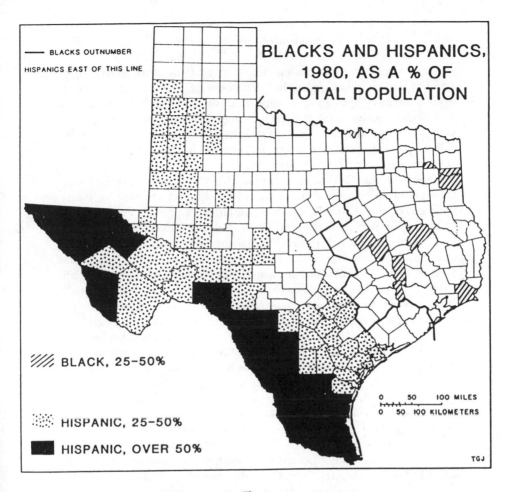

Figure 7

At the Sesquicentennial, the East Texas black stronghold has virtually
vanished and the Hispanic/black border lies much farther east than in
1930. The advancing geographical Hispanicization of Texas in the last
century is evident by comparing figures 5 and 7. (Source: 1980 Census
of Population, Vol. I, Characteristics of the Population, Chapter C, *General Social and Economic Characteristics*, Pt. 45, Texas, Sec. 1 [Washington,
D.C., 1983], 49–58, 77–86.)

veston list numerous Cajun entries, such as Broussard, Boudreaux, Landry, Hebert, and Guedry. In 1980, about 375,000 persons claiming French ancestry lived in southeastern Texas, but nowhere do Cajuns approach majority status (table 1). Orange County is the most purely Gallic in Texas, with 26 percent of its inhabitants claiming in 1980 to be fully or partially French in origin, followed by Jefferson and Chambers counties, each at 21 percent (figure 3).

Though Texas Cajuns, in common with Mexicans, live adjacent to their ancestral homeland, unhindered even by an intervening international border, their ethnicity is at present endangered. This vulnerability stems in part from the gradual decay of the Cajun culture in Louisiana itself, where acculturation has made deep inroads, but the greater cause is likely the ease with which Cajuns can mesh into local non-French groups. Most Cajuns are white, though many have some Indian blood, and no barriers block their joining the Anglo host culture.[46] Black Cajuns, similarly, are easily absorbed into the English-speaking Afro-American population of Southeast Texas urban ghettoes. Thus, in 1970 some 91,000 Texans reported French as the mother tongue spoken during their childhood, while only 48,000 responded in 1980 that they presently use French while at home.[47] Linguistically, at least, the Louisiana French are succumbing in Southeast Texas.

Immigration directly from Europe played an important role in the peopling of Texas during the past century and a half. Persons involved in this migration and their Texas-born children formed about one-tenth of the state population by the turn of the century (table 5). While the 1980 census does not permit separation of old-stock persons of colonial European ancestry from those descended from the nineteenth- and twentieth-century immigration, perhaps a fair approximation can be derived by adding the total of all persons listing full-blood ancestry from non-British Europe. If enumerated in this manner, the European ethnic population of Texas in 1980 was 1,366,000, or 12 percent of those responding.[48]

The model and precedent for European immigration was established by Catholic Irish who came in the late 1820s and early 1830s,

[46] William F. Rushton, *The Cajuns, from Acadia to Louisiana* (New York, 1979), 5, 7, 9.

[47] United States Bureau of the Census, 1970 Census of Population, Vol. I, *Characteristics of the Population*, Pt. 45, Texas (Washington, D.C., 1973), Sec. 2, p. 1,291; 1980 Census of Population, Vol. I, Chapter C, Pt. 45, Texas, Sec. 1, p. 110.

[48] 1980 Census of Population, *Ancestry of the Population by State: 1980*, Supplementary Report, PC80-S1-10 (Washington, D.C., 1983), 38, 50.

when Texas was still under Mexican rule.[49] Two Coastal Bend colonies, San Patricio and Refugio, resulted from these empresario projects, and Irish continued to dominate the counties bearing those names for at least a generation. The settlement zone, probably by design, lay between the southern Anglo and Hispanic population clusters, and the Mexican government likely sought thereby to impose a Catholic-European barrier in the path of the westward-surging Anglos. When tied to the Mexican empresario colony at Victoria and the much older mestizo-Spanish concentration in the upper San Antonio River Valley, the two Irish colonies did, indeed, by 1835 take on the appearance of links in a Celto-Romance Catholic barrier stretched thinly from Matagorda Bay to the Balcones Escarpment (figure 1).

Subsequent nineteenth-century European immigrants, though largely continental rather than British in origin, sought out the same seam between Anglo and Hispanic culture areas, causing south-central Texas to take on a balkanized ethnic character (figures 2, 4). The first groups to follow the Irish, and eventually to account for fully half the European immigration, were the Germans (table 5).[50] Forming a "German belt," ten traditionally rural counties in South-Central Texas—Austin, Colorado, Comal, De Witt, Fayette, Gillespie, Guadalupe, Kendall, Medina, and Washington—housed the principal Teutonic concentration. Additional strength was added by early, major urban clusters of Germans at San Antonio, Houston, and Galveston. By 1880 these cities, as well as some smaller towns, such as Victoria, were one-fifth to one-third German in population. Europeans were much more likely than southern Anglos, blacks, or Hispanics to settle in the cities and towns of nineteenth-century Texas, and one should look to the urban scene for some of the deepest continental cultural imprints. Those who would understand, for example, the evolution of San Antonio as one of the ten largest American cities must consider the fact that Germans formed

---

[49] Sources on the Catholic Irish include William H. Oberste, *Texas Irish Empresarios and Their Colonies* (Austin, 1953); Rachel B. Hébert, *The Forgotten Colony: San Patricio de Hibernia* (Burnet, Tex., 1981); Bernadine Rice, "The Irish in Texas," *Journal of the American Irish Historical Society*, XXX (1932), 60–70.

[50] For the ethnic balkanization of Central Texas, see Jean T. Hannaford, "The Cultural Impact of European Settlement in Central Texas" (M.A. thesis, University of Texas, Austin, 1970), and Oscar Lewis, *On the Edge of the Black Waxy: A Cultural Survey of Bell County, Texas*, Washington University Studies, New Series, Social and Philosophical Sciences, No. 7 (St. Louis, 1948). Basic sources on the Germans include Terry G. Jordan, "The German Element in Texas: An Overview," *Rice University Studies*, LXIII (Summer, 1977), 1–11; Rudolph L. Biesele, *The History of the German Settlements in Texas, 1831–1861* (Austin, 1930); Terry G. Jordan, *German Seed in Texas Soil: Immigrant Farmers in Nineteenth-Century Texas* (Austin, 1966); Glen E. Lich and Dona B. Reeves (eds.), *German Culture in Texas* (Boston, 1980); Glen E. Lich, *The German Texans* (San Antonio, 1981).

one-third of its population as late as 1880. Regrettably, we lack in-depth ethnic studies of preindustrial towns and cities in Texas.[51]

Most parts of Germany, except the Catholic South, contributed significantly to the Texas migration, as did ethnic German areas in Alsace, Switzerland, and Russia. The largest groups consisted of Hessians and lower Saxons. Immigration began in the 1830s and was directed initially to lands lying between the lower Brazos and Colorado rivers, where an original colonist, a low-German Oldenburger named Friedrich Dirks (alias Ernst) had settled in 1831.[52]

German immigration followed a pattern that became typical for the European groups and depended upon a "dominant personality," a forceful, influential leader to trigger the movement. A key device often employed was the "America letter," an exaggerated, highly favorable description of the new homeland designed to encourage friends and relatives to follow.[53] Dirks's America letter, dated 1832, survives. In it, he described a land with a winterless Italian climate, abundant game and fish, immense free land grants, gold and silver to be had nearby, low taxes, and huge privately owned herds of livestock, a land where only three months' labor was necessary each year to make a living.[54]

The migration set afoot in this manner was drawn from confined districts within the mother country and can thus best be described as "cluster migration." Texas European groups, then, typically came from certain small areas and were atypical of the countries at large. Within Texas, migration was initially directed to a "mother colony." The village of Industry in Austin County, laid out on Dirks's property in the 1830s, served this function for the early German immigrants. Newly arrived settlers typically came to the mother colony, lived there while acquiring capital and experience, and then moved out to form daughter colonies nearby.

The Germans attracted through Dirks's influence caused Texas to become widely known in Germany. The publicity in turn helped guide an organized colonization effort led by the Adelsverein, or Society of

---

[51] See, however, Ralph A. Wooster, "Foreigners in the Principal Towns of Ante-Bellum Texas," *SHQ*, LXVI (Oct., 1962), 208–220; and Fred R. von der Mehden (ed.), *The Ethnic Groups of Houston*, Rice University Studies, New Series, No. 3 (Houston, 1984).

[52] Terry G. Jordan, "The Pattern of Origins of the Adelsverein German Colonists," *Texana*, VI (Fall, 1968), 245–257; Elsie Montgomery and Austin H. Montgomery, Jr., "The Other Germans," *Texana*, IX, No. 3 (1971), 230–248.

[53] These concepts are discussed in Jordan, "German Element in Texas," 1, 3–4.

[54] The Dirks/Ernst letter appears in Detlef Dunt, *Reise nach Texas, nebst Nachrichten von diesem Lande, für Deutsche, welche nach Amerika zu gehen beabsichtigen* (Bremen, 1834), 4–16.

Nobles, a group of investors drawn from the petty nobility of western Germany. This society introduced more than 7,000 Hessians and Saxons in the 1840s, mainly into the Hill Country between and including New Braunfels and Fredericksburg.[55] In a similar project, in the same decade, empresario Henri Castro brought several thousand settlers, mainly Alsatians, and founded a string of colonies in Medina County.[56]

German immigration, briefly interrupted by the Civil War, resumed at an even greater volume between 1865 and 1890, after which the Teutonic influx subsided.[57] Toward the close of the major period of immigration, in 1887, the 130,000 Germans in Texas constituted the second largest ethnic group in the state, after the blacks, and made up well over half of the European element.[58] A century later, over 750,000 Texans claimed to be wholly of German origin, a figure that perhaps accurately reflects the size of the ethnic segment of the German-descended population. An additional almost one-and-one-half million persons listed partial German ancestry, but these no doubt included many old-stock Americans descended from the colonial Pennsylvania "Dutch" and who should not be regarded as ethnics (table 2).

In the 1850s, three parallel and strikingly similar Slavic migrations to Texas began, involving Czechs, Silesian Poles, and Wends (Sorbs) (table 5). Each was prompted or led by a church figure, emanated from a confined source area, and was directed to the south-central part of Texas. Czech immigration began about 1850, spurred by the America letter of Protestant minister Ernst Bergmann (Arnost Horák); drew most heavily upon northeastern Moravia; and funneled through the mother colony of Fayetteville, near La Grange. The influx continued until 1914 and ultimately produced the largest rural Czech population of any state.[59] From a nucleus on the Fayette Prairie, Czechs spread to form scores of colonies in the black-soiled grasslands of Texas, rarely venturing into adjacent, sandy-oak lands. This rich environmental base helped them become highly successful farmers. In 1980 nearly 180,000

---

[55] See Hubert G. H. Wilhelm, "Organized German Settlement and Its Effects on the Frontier of South-Central Texas" (Ph.D. diss., Louisiana State University, 1968).

[56] Bobby D. Weaver, *Castro's Colony: Empresario Development in Texas, 1842–1865* (College Station, Tex., 1985).

[57] Terry G. Jordan, "The German Settlement of Texas after 1865," *SHQ*, LXXIII (Oct., 1969), 193–212.

[58] Foster (ed.), *First Annual Report*, xlvi.

[59] The only satisfactory sources on the Czechs, though largely descriptive, are Henry R. Maresh and Estelle Hudson, *Czech Pioneers of the Southwest* (Dallas, 1934); Henry R. Maresh, "The Czechs in Texas," *SHQ*, L (Oct., 1946), 236–240, plus map; Mollie E. Stasney, "The Czechs in Texas" (M.A. thesis, University of Texas, 1938); and Clinton Machann and James W. Mendl, *Krásná Amerika: A Study of the Texas Czechs, 1851–1939* (Austin, 1983).

persons claimed full or partial Czech ancestry, placing Texas second among the states (table 2).

Wendish immigration, guided by Lutheran pastor Jan Kilian, drew upon a tiny homeland in the southeastern corner of the present German Democratic Republic.[60] Serbin, or "place where the Wends live," became the mother colony in the sandy-oak forests of Lee County in the middle 1850s, and Wends later spread out to dominate the greater part of the county and to establish daughter colonies as far afield as the Corpus Christi and Vernon areas. No other Wendish settlements exist in the Americas.

The oldest Polish colony in the United States, Panna Maria in Karnes County, was founded in 1854 by Silesians led by the Franciscan priest Leopold Moczygemba.[61] These Poles eventually founded a chain of daughter colonies along the axis of the San Antonio River, scattered among the north-bank tributaries of that stream. In postbellum times, they were joined by Galician Poles, who established colonies on old plantation lands in the Brazos and San Jacinto river valleys, most notably at Bremond. The only other rural Slavic colony was established by a small group of Lutheran Slovaks at Pakan in Wheeler County, in the Panhandle region, in 1903.[62]

Texas houses the southernmost Scandinavian rural settlements in the United States (tables 2, 5). While small in size, these colonies offer the unusual situation of Norwegians, Swedes, and Danes living in a subtropical setting. Norwegians, initially under the leadership of the liberal newspaper editor Johan Reinert Reiersen, established a mother colony, Four Mile Prairie, on the border of Kaufman and Van Zandt counties in the middle 1840s, only to see the settlement largely abandoned a decade later, when a second leader, Cleng Peerson, led the Norwegians to the hill lands of Bosque County.[63] The earliest immi-

---

[60]The best source on Wends remains George E. Engerrand, *The So-Called Wends of Germany and Their Colonies in Texas and in Australia* (Austin, 1934), but also recommended are Anne Blasig, *The Wends of Texas* (San Antonio, 1954) and Sylvia A. Grider, *The Wendish Texans* (San Antonio, 1982).

[61]The definitive work on the Silesians is T. Lindsay Baker, *The First Polish Americans: Silesian Settlements in Texas* (College Station, Tex., 1979). See also Maria Starczewska, "The Historical Geography of the Oldest Polish Settlement in the United States," *Polish Review*, XII (Spring, 1967), 11–39; and [T. Lindsay Baker], "Poles in Texas," Southwest Educational Development Laboratory, Ethnic Heritage Studies Program, Texas Heritage Unit (Poles), Resource Guide, Developmental Edition (Austin, 1975).

[62]The Pakan Slovaks remain unstudied. My remarks are based upon a visit to the settlement and informal interviews with several residents in March, 1979.

[63]On the Norwegians, see Oris E. Pierson, "Norwegian Settlements in Bosque County, Texas" (M.A. thesis, University of Texas, 1947); Axel Arneson, "Norwegian Settlements

grants came from hill hamlets in Aust-Agder province in southern Norway, a region bearing a startling terrain resemblance to the Bosque area. A second, and larger, contingent departed the fertile eastern shores of Lake Mjösa in Hedmark province, north of Oslo, to join the Bosque settlement.

Swedish immigration, derived very largely from the county of Jönköping in Småland province, interior southern Sweden, was drawn to Texas through the promotional and philanthropic efforts of S. M. Swenson, a native of the county who had come to Texas in the 1830s.[64] Headquartered in Austin, Swenson brought the Smålanders to that city, and many later founded farming colonies, such as New Sweden, on the adjacent Blackland Prairie of eastern Travis and Williamson counties. The world's southernmost Danish colony was established in 1894 on the table-flat coastal prairie at Danevang, "level place where the Danes live," in Wharton County.[65] This settlement is noteworthy for the success of its farmers, based in an Old World tradition of mutual aid.

Italians, who in 1887 ranked only ninth among the European immigrant groups, rose to fifth position a generation later (table 5).[66] The bulk of the Italians came to the cities and mining towns of Texas, though agricultural colonies were established by Piemontese at Montague and by Sicilians in the Brazos Valley. Thurber, a coal-mining town in Erath County, had a notable Italian concentration. Utopian liberals from France founded La Réunion in Dallas County in the 1850s, and, though this colony soon failed, its residue of craftsmen and intellectuals perhaps played a formative role in making the infant city of Dallas something more than a typical North Texas county seat.[67] Dutch founded Nederland and several other Southeast Texas communities,

in Texas," *SHQ*, XLV (Oct., 1941), 125–135; Darwin Payne, "Early Norwegians in Northeast Texas," *SHQ*, LXV (Oct., 1961), 196–203; Peter L. Petersen, "A New Oslo on the Plains: The Anders L. Mordt Land Company and Norwegian Migration to the Texas Panhandle," *Panhandle-Plains Historical Review*, XLIX (1976), 25–54; and Odd Magnar Syversen and Derwood Johnson, *Norge i Texas* (Stange, Norway, 1982).

[64] The best study of the Swedes remains Ernest Severin, *Svenskarne i Texas i ord och bild* (2 vols.; n.p., 1919). Without acknowledging his source, Carl M. Rosenquist borrowed heavily from Severin to produce "The Swedes of Texas" (Ph.D. diss., University of Chicago, 1930). See also Mary W. Clark, *The Swenson Saga and the S M S Ranches* (Austin, 1976); and James Zambus, "Ericksdahl, a Swedish Community in Jones County, Texas," *West Texas Historical Association Year Book*, XLIX (1973), 59–68.

[65] Grace C. Grantham, "The Danes in Wharton County" (M.A. thesis, Texas A&I University, 1947); Thomas P. Christensen, "Danevang, Texas," *SHQ*, XXXII (July, 1928), 67–73.

[66] Valentine J. Belfiglio, *The Italian Experience in Texas* (Austin, 1983).

[67] William J. Hammond and Margaret F. Hammond, *La Réunion, a French Settlement in Texas* (Dallas, 1958); Ermance V. Rejebian, "La Reunion: The French Colony in Dallas County," *SHQ*, XLIII (Apr., 1940), 472–478.

while Greeks developed ethnic neighborhoods in several cities and settled as fishermen in certain port towns.[68]

Jewish migration began as a modest Sephardic influx as early as the period of Spanish and Mexican rule. They were followed, especially after 1865, by Ashkenazic Germans and still later, between 1890 and 1920, by Ashkenazic Poles and Russians. Over 2,000 Jews immigrated through the port of Galveston during the 1907–1914 period alone.[69] Today, the Jewish population is concentrated in Houston and Dallas, but synagogues in such small towns as Brenham, Corsicana, and Schulenburg serve as reminders that the Jewish presence in Texas is widespread.

The Oriental element in Texas is also of long standing, though the bulk of the influx has occurred since the middle 1960s, when highly unfavorable immigration laws were modified. Chinese were the first to come, mainly as railroad workers in the 1870s, leaving as a heritage almost exclusively male groups at El Paso and in Robertson County.[70] In the latter instance, wives were found among the Brazos Valley black population, producing the fascinating, but unstudied, "black Chinese" of Calvert. The El Paso group remained bachelors and consequently died out. Harassed Chinese from Mexico accompanied General John Pershing's return from a military foray across the border in the teens. Japanese farmers from Hawaii and the West Coast founded a number of market gardening colonies in Southeast Texas, most notably at Webster and Terry.[71]

These efforts remained small and inconsequential. The total Oriental population in 1910 stood at only 943, and by 1930 had risen to but 1,576, including 703 Chinese, 519 Japanese, 288 Filipinos, 49 "Hindus," and 17 Koreans.[72] The 1980 total, by contrast, stood at about 120,000,

[68]W. T. Block, "Tulip Transplants to East Texas: The Dutch Migration to Nederland, Port Arthur, and Winnie," *East Texas Historical Journal,* XIII (Fall, 1975), 36–50.

[69]Henry Cohen, *One Hundred Years of Jewry in Texas* (Dallas, 1936); Betty J. Maynard, *The Dallas Jewish Community Study* (Dallas, 1974); Elaine H. Maas, "The Jews of Houston: An Ethnographic Study" (Ph.D. diss., Rice University, 1973); Ronald A. Axelrod, "Rabbi Henry Cohen and the Galveston Immigration Movement, 1907–1914," *East Texas Historical Journal,* XV ([Spring], 1977), 24–37.

[70]Nancy Farrar, *The Chinese in El Paso* (El Paso, 1972); Edward J. M. Rhoads, "The Chinese in Texas," *SHQ,* LXXXI (July, 1977), 1–36.

[71]Lillie Mae Tomlinson, "The Japanese Colony in Orange County," *University of Texas Bulletin,* No. 2746 (Dec., 1927) [*The History Teachers' Bulletin,* XIV (1927), 141–145]; Gwendolyn Wingate, "The Kishi Colony," in F. E. Abernethy (ed.), *The Folklore of Texan Cultures* (Austin, 1974), 327–337; Webb, Carroll, and Branda (eds.), *Handbook of Texas,* II, 875.

[72]Thirteenth Census, Vol. III, *Population, 1910,* 799; Fifteenth Census, 1930, *Population,* Vol. III, Pt. 2, p. 941.

reflecting the changed laws and the aftermath of the Korean and Viet-namese wars.[73] While many poor refugees were among these Orientals, the group as a whole is far above average in education and wealth. In-cluded are many workers in the professions and in high-technology industries.

In the traditional view, the Amerindian population of Texas perished in epidemics and warfare or was driven across the border into Okla-homa and Mexico. All that remains, supposedly, are a few shards of tribes that immigrated from New Mexico and the southeastern states, in particular the Alabama-Coushatta of the Big Thicket; the Tigua, liv-ing in the *barrio indio* of El Paso's Ysleta community; and the Kickapoo, who seasonally come to Eagle Pass from northern Mexico.[74] Most cen-suses support the notion of Amerindian elimination from the state (table 4), for only 702 were enumerated in 1910, 1,001 in 1930, and 5,750 in 1960.[75]

Several facts combine to undermine this traditional view. First, sub-stantial Amerindian immigration has occurred recently, drawn mainly from eastern Oklahoma and the Four Corners region of the Southwest. Navajos and Choctaws are the largest groups, and Dallas has become their principal goal. Several Amerindian ethnic neighborhoods have formed in that city, though not based upon specific tribal identity.

Second, the 1980 census delivered the startling news that 631,000 Texans claimed some measure of Amerindian ancestry (table 2). This very substantial figure did not include partially Indian persons in the Hispanic and Cajun groups, requiring the addition of perhaps another three million to the total of Texans who are partially of Amerindian an-cestry. If correct, this figure suggests that one-quarter or more of the Texas white population has some measure of Indian blood. Nor does it end there. The recent upsurge in interest in Afro-American genealogy has revealed that many blacks also have Indian blood. Some such ex-

---

[73] 1980 Census, *Ancestry of the Population*, 44, 62.

[74] J. W. Fewkes, "The Pueblo Settlements Near El Paso," *American Anthropologist*, LV (Jan./Mar., 1902), 57–72; Alan H. Minter, "The Tigua Indians of the Pueblo de Ysleta del Sur, El Paso County, Texas," *West Texas Historical Association Year Book*, XLV (1969), 30–44; Tom Dia-mond, *The Tigua Indians of El Paso* (Denver, 1966); John H. Bounds, "The Alabama-Coushatta-Indians of Texas," *Journal of Geography*, LXX (Mar., 1971), 175–182; Rotha M. Berry, "The Alabama and Coushatta Indians of Texas," *Texas Geographic Magazine*, XII (Fall, 1948), 19–23; Harriet Smither, "The Alabama Indians of Texas," *SHQ*, XXXVI (Oct., 1932), 83–108; Randy E. Grothe, "The Kickapoo: Strangers in Their Own Land," Dallas *Morning News*, May 8, 1977. See also William W. Newcomb, Jr., *The Indians of Texas* (Austin, 1961).

[75] Thirteenth Census, Vol. III, *Population, 1910*, 799; Fifteenth Census, 1930, *Population*, Vol. III, Pt. 2, p. 1,014; Eighteenth Census of the United States, *Census of Population: 1960*, Vol. I, Characteristics of the Population, Pt. 45, Texas (Washington, D.C., 1961), 64.

amples are well documented, including the "redbone" Ashworth family of Southeast Texas and the "Seminole Negroes" of Brackettville.[76]

Clearly, the notion of Indian elimination must be discarded, and it is time to seek the cultural imprint that so massive a genetic contribution implies. Genealogists know that a great many southern Anglo families have some Indian progenitors, and such mixing seems to have been common on the southern frontier (table 4). Could it even be that some measure of the cultural distinctiveness of the South, of Anglo-Texas, is based in partial Amerindian ancestry? A recent study of traditional funerary material culture suggests as much.[77]

Of course, the number of *ethnic* Amerindians in Texas, as defined by the Census Bureau, is much smaller, though rapidly growing. The total rose from 18,000 in 1970 to over 50,000 in 1980.[78] Curiously, more than twice that many Texans claimed pure Amerindian ancestry (table 2).

In ethnic terms, then, Texas at the Sesquicentennial remains what it has always been—a borderland, a zone of contact and friction between very different cultures (figure 3). The ethnic mosaic has shifted, kaleidoscope-like, during those 150 years, but the underlying diversity has proven durable. Such contact zones can be pleasant and exciting places to dwell, where multiple heritages enrich daily life. Perhaps we glimpse the future at the little Karnes County Catholic town of Cestohowa, where Poles and Mexicans now share the same parish. A glassed-in shrine in front of the church there contains, side-by-side, images of both Our Lady of Guadalupe and the Black Virgin of Czestochowa.

Borderlands can also become scenes of bigotry and conflict. Very soon, Texans of all cultural and ethnic backgrounds will have to decide whether their border province, in the coming century, will resemble troubled Belgium, where Dutch and French went separate ways, or whether it will be like Switzerland, where a long tradition of mutual respect has permitted a Teutonic majority to coexist peacefully in political union with Romance minorities.[79]

---

[76] Kenneth Wiggins Porter, "The Seminole Negro-Indian Scouts, 1870–1881," *SHQ*, LV (Jan., 1952), 358–377; Andrew F. Muir, "The Free Negro in Jefferson and Orange Counties, Texas," *Journal of Negro History*, XXXV (Apr., 1950), 183–206; Kenneth W. Porter, "Negroes and Indians on the Texas Frontier, 1834–1874," *SHQ*, LIII (Oct., 1949), 151–163.

[77] William A. Owens, *This Stubborn Soil* (New York, 1966), 80–85; Terry G. Jordan, *Texas Graveyards: A Cultural Legacy* (Austin, 1982), 17, 34–40.

[78] 1970 Census of Population, Vol. 1, Pt. 45, Sec. 2, p. 1,269; 1980 Census of Population, Vol. I, Chapter C, Pt. 45, Texas, Sec. 1, p. 31.

[79] On the problems in Belgium, see Glen V. Stephenson, "Cultural Regionalism and the Unitary State Idea in Belgium," *Geographical Review*, LXII (Oct., 1972), 501–523.

One might even wish for a hybridized culture whose practitioners value all its diverse roots, a culture produced by a lively exchange between Anglo and Latin civilizations. France, drawing from both its Germanic north and its Mediterranean south, would be a splendid model, but it required a millennium to fashion. Indeed, regardless of how Texans respond to the cultural challenge facing them, fundamental ethnic contrasts such as those in our state do not fade easily or quickly. Intrastate ethnic-based regionalism will persist for generations to come. At best, it will provide cross-cultural stimulation; at worst, it could lead to violence and even partition.

The immense popularity of the Institute of Texan Cultures museum in San Antonio and of its associated annual Texas Folklife Festival, where the state's many different ethnic minorities and the Anglo host culture are afforded due, even exaggerated and saccharine, respect, might indicate that, at the Sesquicentennial, Texans are ready to assume the needed attitude of tolerance, are ready to acknowledge their border province status. If, however, we make the wrong decisions, bleeding Ireland might even become our model. Texans should be reminded that the English, using an effective educational system, successfully destroyed the Irish Celtic language, only to find that the resultant English-speaking Irish Catholics hated them even more than before and went on to pursue political separation. Ethnicity and its baggage of prejudice often survive the demise of the associated language, and memories of ethnic oppression are well-nigh indelible.

Table 1

Cultural/Ethnic/National Origin Groups in Texas, 1850–1980

| Group | 1850[a] | 1887[b] | 1980[c] |
|---|---|---|---|
| Old-Stock Southern Anglo-Americans | 114,500 (53%) | 1,156,000 (57%) | 5,100,000 (45%) |
| Old-Stock Northern Anglo-Americans | 10,000 (4½%) | 148,000 (7%) | |
| Mexicans | 14,000 (6½%) | 83,000 (4%) | 2,495,000 (22%) |
| Blacks (African) | 58,600 (27%) | 396,000 (20%) | 1,368,000 (12%) |
| Louisiana French | 600 (<1%) | 2,300 (<1%) | 375,000 (3%) |
| Europeans | 16,000 (7½%) | 225,000 (11%) | 1,315,000 (12%) |
| Orientals | 0 (–) | 800 (<1%) | 120,000 (1%) |
| Amerindians | ? (–) | 800 (<1%) | 117,000 (1%) |
| Other or unknown | 2,000 (<1%) | 2,900 (<1%) | 520,000 (4%) |
| Total Population | 215,700 (100%) | 2,015,000 (100%) | 11,412,781 (100%) |

SOURCES:

[a] Hand count of the manuscript free population schedules of the 1850 United States census, including an estimate for the El Paso area, which was not enumerated. The Louisiana French total is represented by the French surnamed population of Harris, Galveston, Jefferson, and Liberty counties. The black total is from *The Seventh Census of the United States: 1850* (Washington, D.C., 1853), 504.

[b] L. L. Foster (ed.), *First Annual Report of the Agricultural Bureau of the Department of Agriculture, Insurance, Statistics, and History, 1887–88* (Austin, 1889), xlvi, 1–249. The Anglo-American population was subdivided into northern and southern groups on the basis of the United States census of 1890 (Vol. II, Pt. 1, pp. 568–571) figures for state of nativity for "native whites of native parents," with the Texas-born held neutral. For the adjustment of the Hispanic population, see Terry G. Jordan, "The 1887 Census of Texas' Hispanic Population," *Aztlan*, XII (Autumn, 1981), 274–275. The fragmentary total for American Indians was adjusted upward on the basis of the 1890 U.S. census, as was the total for Orientals, which in the state census included only Chinese (U.S. census of 1890, Vol. XI, Pt. 1, p. 609). The Louisiana French total is based on the "French" population of Galveston, Hardin, Harris, Jefferson, Liberty, and Orange counties; this total was subtracted from the European total. See Foster (ed.), *First Annual Report*, 35, 80, 95, 96, 118, 139, 173.

[c] Based upon the response to question 14 in the long form of the 1980 census: "What is this person's ancestry?" The results are available in the 1980 Census of Population and Housing, more exactly in (1) *Ancestry of the Population by State: 1980*, Supplementary Report PC80-S1-10 (Washington, D.C., 1983), 20, 38, 44, 50, 56, 62, 68; (2) "Public-Use Microdata Samples," unpublished computer tape (Washington, D.C., 1983); and (3) "Technical Documentation," Summary Tape File 4, unpublished computer tape (Washington, D.C., 1983). Only 11,412,781 of 14,229,191 Texans gave usable responses. The "Old-Stock Anglo-American" figure is the total of persons reporting full or partial

English, Irish, Welsh, or Scottish ancestry, with adjustments for internal redundancies such as "Scotch-Irish." The "Louisiana French" total is based on the "French" and "partially French" population of Chambers, Galveston, Hardin, Harris, Jefferson, Liberty, and Orange counties. The "European" total represents only those persons reporting *pure continental* European ancestry, minus the estimate for pure-blood Louisiana French and plus the total for British-born. The Amerindian total includes those persons reporting only Amerindian ancestry, and the same is true for Orientals. "Mexicans" include all persons reporting full or partial ancestral ties to Mexico and excludes all other Hispanics. The black total includes persons reporting full or partial ancestry in sub-Saharan Africa, excluding the Republic of South Africa.

## Table 2

### Selected Origin Groups in Texas, 1980

| Group | Number of Persons Wholly of this Origin | Number of Persons Partially of this Origin | Total | Total as a Percentage of Respondents |
|---|---|---|---|---|
| British[a] | 2,280,336 | | | |
| English | 1,639,322 | 1,444,001 | 3,083,323 | 27% |
| Irish | 572,815 | 1,847,752 | 2,420,567 | 21% |
| Scottish | 55,711 | 601,181 | 656,892 | 6% |
| German[b] | 814,152 | | | |
| Germany | 754,388 | 1,414,559 | 2,168,947 | 19% |
| Dutch | 45,838 | 251,513 | 297,351 | 2½% |
| Scandinavian[c] | 70,461 | | | |
| Swedish | 34,687 | 86,588 | 121,275 | 1% |
| Norwegian | 20,875 | 44,460 | 65,335 | <1% |
| Slavic[d] | 191,189 | | | |
| Czech | 91,495 | 87,437 | 178,932 | 1½% |
| Polish | 70,688 | 96,777 | 167,465 | 1½% |
| Southern European[e] | 100,728 | | | |
| Italian | 78,592 | 111,207 | 189,799 | 1½% |
| Greek | 13,759 | 10,561 | 24,320 | <1% |
| French[f] | 162,846 | | | |
| France | 152,072 | 521,605 | 673,677 | 6% |
| Europe, total[g] | 3,646,602 | | | |
| Mexican | 2,385,793 | 109,242 | 2,495,035 | 22% |
| Sub-Saharan African[h] | 1,342,915 | 24,819 | 1,367,734 | 12% |
| Asian[i] | 119,100 | 17,692 | 136,792 | 1% |
| Amerindian | 117,496 | 513,781 | 631,277 | 6% |
| Total | 7,859,393 | | | |

ªBritish includes English, Irish, Scottish, Northern Irish, Welsh, and Manx.

ᵇGerman includes also Alsatian, Austrian, Dutch, Luxembourger, 70 percent of the Swiss total, and 60 percent of the Belgian total. Many or most who responded "Dutch" are probably actually German.

ᶜScandinavian includes Danish, Norwegian, Swedish, Icelandic, and "Scandinavian."

ᵈSlavic includes Belorussians, Bulgarians, Croatians, Czechs, "Eastern Europeans," Polish, Russians, Ruthenians, Serbians, "Slavic," Slovaks, Slovenes, Ukrainians, and Yugoslavians. Wends were not enumerated.

ᵉSouthern European includes Albanians, Basques, Cypriots, Greeks, Italians, Maltese, Portuguese, and Spaniards.

ᶠFrench also includes French-Canadian, one-fifth of the Swiss total, and 40 percent of the Belgians.

ᵍThe European total also includes full-blood Estonians, Finns, Gypsies, Hungarians, Latvians, Lithuanians, Romanians, and "other Europeans."

ʰExcludes South Africa, Cape Verde Islands.

ⁱExcludes Middle Easterners, includes Pakistanis.

SOURCE:

1980 Census of Population, *Ancestry of the Population by State: 1980*, Supplementary Report, PC80-S1-10 (Washington, D.C., 1983), 20, 38, 44, 50, 56, 62, 68.

Table 3

The Hispanic-Black Population Shift in Texas

| Year | Number of Hispanics | Number of Blacks |
|------|---------------------|------------------|
| | (% of total state population in parentheses) | |
| 1850ª | 13,712 (6%) | 58,558 (27%) |
| 1887ᵇ | 83,433 (4%) | 395,576 (20%) |
| 1930ᶜ | 683,681 (12%) | 854,964 (15%) |
| 1940ᵈ | 738,440 (12%) | 924,391 (14%) |
| 1950ᵉ | 1,027,455 (13%) | 977,458 (13%) |
| 1960ᶠ | 1,417,810 (15%) | 1,187,125 (12%) |
| 1970ᵍ | 2,059,671 (18%) | 1,399,005 (12%) |
| 1980ʰ | 2,982,583 (21%) | 1,704,741 (12%) |

NOTES AND SOURCES:

ªSpanish-surnamed, based upon a hand count of the 1850 manuscript U.S. census schedules, with an estimate of 2,500 added for the El Paso area, which was not enumerated. *The Seventh Census of the United States: 1850* (Washington, D.C., 1853), 504.

ᵇL. L. Foster (ed.), *First Annual Report of the Agricultural Bureau of the Department of Agriculture, Insurance, Statistics, and History, 1887–88* (Austin, 1889), xlvi. A refinement of the Hispanic total is based upon Terry G. Jordan, "The 1887 Census of Texas' Hispanic Population," *Aztlan*, XII (Autumn, 1981), 275.

<sup></sup>ᶜHispanic is defined as "Mexican race." Fifteenth Census of the United States: 1930, *Population*, Vol. III, Pt. 2 (Washington, D.C., 1932), 975, 1,014.

ᵈSixteenth Census of the United States: 1940, *Population*, Vol. II, Pt. 1 (Washington, D.C., 1943), 52. Hispanics are represented by "Spanish mother tongue."

ᵉUnited States Census of Population: 1950, Vol. II, *Characteristics of the Population*, Pt. 43, Texas (Washington, D.C., 1952), 63; and Special Report, *Persons of Spanish Surname* (Washington, D.C., 1953), p. 3C-6, which lists the Hispanic figures for 1930, 1940, and 1950.

ᶠEighteenth Census of the United States, *Census of Population: 1960*, Vol. I, Pt. 45, Texas (Washington, D.C., 1961), 64; and Subject Reports, No. PC(2)-1B, *Persons of Spanish Surname* (Washington, D.C., 1963).

ᵍUnited States, Bureau of the Census, 1970 Census of Population, Vol. I, *Characteristics of the Population*, Pt. 45, Texas (Washington, D.C., 1973), Sec. 1, p. 103, and Sec. 2, pp. 1,269, 1,270.

ʰ1980 Census of Population, Vol. I, Characteristics of the Population, Chapter C, *General Social and Economic Characteristics*, Pt. 45, Texas, Sec. 1 (Washington, D.C., 1983), 31, 59.

## Table 4

## Ethnic Evolution of a Texas County, 1835–1980: Shelby County, East Texas

| Group | | 1835 | 1850 | 1887 | 1930 | 1980 |
|---|---|---|---|---|---|---|
| Old-Stock Anglos | Southern | 74% | 73% | 84% | 74% | 73% |
| | Northern | | 3% | | | |
| Afro-Americans | | 3% | 23% | 15% | 25% | 21% |
| Europeans | | 0% | 1% | <1% | <1% | 5% |
| Hispanics | | 0% | 0% | 0% | <1% | <1% |
| Amerindians | | 23% | 0% | 0% | <1% | <1% |

SOURCES:

MSS Mexican census of the Municipality of Tenaha, 1835, in the Nacogdoches Archives (Archives Division, Texas State Library, Austin); hand count of the MSS free population schedules, United States Census of 1850; *The Seventh Census of the United States: 1850* (Washington, D.C., 1853), 504; L. L. Foster (ed.), *First Annual Report of the Agricultural Bureau of the Department of Agriculture, Insurance, Statistics, and History, 1887–88* (Austin, 1889), 202–203; Fifteenth Census of the United States: 1930, *Population*, Vol. III, Pt. 2 (Washington, D.C., 1932), 988, 1,015, 1,018, 1,022; for 1980, black, Amerindian, and Hispanic percentages are based on 1980 Census of Population, Characteristics of the Population, Chapter C, *General Social and Economic Characteristics*, Pt. 45, Texas, Sec. 1 (Washington, D.C., 1983), 57, 85; and the Old-Stock Anglo and European figures are based upon United States Census of Population and Housing, 1980, Summary Tape File 4, "Technical Documentation" (Washington, D.C., 1983), unpublished computer tape.

Table 5

European White Stock in Texas, 1910

| Country | Persons of European Birth plus American-Born with at Least One European-Born Parent | As a Percentage of European White Stock |
|---|---|---|
| Germany [a] | 171,776 | 50% |
| Austria [b] | 53,100 | 16% |
| England | 26,260 | 8% |
| Ireland | 22,914 | 7% |
| Italy | 14,013 | 4% |
| Sweden | 11,598 | 3% |
| Russia [c] | 10,615 | 3% |
| Scotland | 6,835 | 2% |
| France [d] | 5,805 | 2% |
| Switzerland [e] | 4,616 | 1% |
| Other Europe | 13,893 | 4% |
| Total | 341,425 | 100% |
| Total Texas population | 3,896,542 | |

[a] Includes Wends, Silesian Poles, and many Jews.
[b] Mainly Czechs; includes also Galician Poles.
[c] Mainly Ashkenazic Jews.
[d] Includes many German Alsatians.
[e] Mainly ethnic Germans.

SOURCE:
Thirteenth Census of the United States, 1910, Vol. III, *Population, 1910,* 799.

# Religious Schism and the Development of
# Rural Immigrant Communities:
# Norwegian Lutherans in Western Wisconsin, 1880-1905

*Ann M. Legreid and David Ward*

As thousands of European immigrants settled on the American frontier during the last century, they rapidly developed that network of associations described as community. Among these associations, the church was frequently predominant. "To men reared in an age of faith," writes Timothy Smith, "they took it for granted that the church congregation must be the nucleus of all their new associations," and they turned to the church as much "in search for a long lost community," as "a testimony of [their] new-found grace."[1] Religious life took on these new dimensions in frontier settings where the role of the church as a social focus was greatly enhanced. Sunday morning worship evolved as a time for community announcements, death notices, the exchange of neighborhood news, and the sale or barter of goods and services between parishioners. Church activities promoted the development of a strong sense of solidarity that carried over into purely secular activities. In part because of these well-developed social functions, the church was as involved in the establishment of some degree of social order and group consciousness as it was in doctrine and sacraments. As the provider of the parochial social, economic and religious needs of frontier families, the church became a missionary body, and because of its adherence to the language, customs and social practices of the immigrant, a direct link between the New World and the Old.[2]

This congregational link also reflected the subnational or local loyalties upon which frontier ethnic communities were based. Once established, small homogeneous settlements became the primary sources of information for potential emigrants. Consequently, recruitment was highly selective of neighbors, friends and relatives in the Old World. Among Norwegians the **bygd** or locality usually defined the sources of immigrant communities so that local sentiments and dialect variations persisted in the New World. "A remarkable aspect of the tendency of the Norwegian migrants to flock together" notes Theodore Blegen, "was that it was not enough for them to seek fellow Norwegians. They went further and associated themselves with people who had come out of the very valley, the very **bygd**, from which they themselves hailed in the old country."[3] To many emigrants, migration was

a means to preserve group solidarity and cooperation, and once established in the New World they attempted to retain Old World patterns of life. To be sure, immigrants from different **bygds** settled near to each other on the frontier and the unavoidable intermingling of different local sub-cultures eased mutual suspicions inherited from the motherland. Nevertheless, this weakening of exclusionary sentiments was relatively slow and each local group retained a strong sense of identity. Certainly intermarriage between **bygd** groups was frowned upon and initially relatively rare.

Among Norwegians, ethnic community was firmly based upon local congregationalism. While the church reinforced and served the local community, religious affiliations were subject to frequent schisms. In some communities, doctrinal debates provoked secessions and the frontier church was at times an arena of conflict. Despite their formal adherence to Lutheranism, Norwegians brought a diversity of religious opinion to the Midwest. Elements of Reformation piety and anti-clericalism thrived alongside the strictly conservative and state church loyalties. This religious diversity was unchecked on the frontier where the heavy hand of the state church no longer prevailed. The principles of voluntary membership and competitive denominationalism were rapidly established and, consequently, secession from established congregations created a complex pattern of overlapping ideologically defined parishes. In Norwegian communities schism and secession were frequent enough to question the assumption that the immigrant church was a primary source of community cohesion. On the other hand, doctrinal debate provoked social interaction, and periodic conflicts may have reinforced the cohesiveness of the disputants. Moreover, the doctrinal sources of schism may have been rooted in overt and latent tensions transferred from homeland parish life which, during the early years of settlement, were overshadowed by the need for security and companionship. New patterns of occupational stratification and the emergence of an American-born generation may also have compounded these transplanted differences in social backgrounds, local origins, and sectarian ideologies. While the growth of the immigrant population alone necessitated the formation of daughter congregations with churches more conveniently located with respect to the changing extent of Norwegian settlement, the rate at which new congregations were formed also recorded the effects of frequent schisms.

Ann M. Legreid is a doctoral student at the University of Wisconsin-Madison. David Ward, co-editor of **The Journal of Historical Geography** from 1976-1982, is professor of Geography at the University of Wisconsin-Madison.

13

This process of secession has been documented among Norwegian Lutherans in three valleys which extended across several townships on the border of Trempealeau and Jackson counties in west central Wisconsin from the period of initial settlement in the 1850s to about 1905 (Figs. 1 & 2). While Yankees predominated in the first influx of settlers, Norwegians from the Solør district of eastern Norway, who had originally settled in southeast Wisconsin, were among the pioneers in the Trempealeau Valley. The first Norwegians who settled in the valley of North Beaver Creek in 1857 were also offshoots of older settlements but most later settlers came directly from the Hardanger Fjord county of Vestlandet in the west of Norway.[4] Norwegian settlement in the valley of South Beaver Creek was established in 1860 when Norwegian settlers came directly and largely from Solør, eastern Norway, and the parishes of Biri, Faaberg, and Ringsaker in east-central Norway.[5]

The old American element had acquired much of the choice land following passage of the Graduation Act, particularly the lush, much desired prairies of southern Trempealeau County and choice lands along the Trempealeau River and lower Beaver Creek.[6] The Norwegians who eventually became the predominant group in the region came too late to acquire the choicest tracts. Some of them purchased land from speculators, generally at modest markups, but most immigrants obtained their farms directly from the land offices. In general, the Norwegians preferred the hills and coulees over the open, fertile prairies lying to the southwest. "Large tracts of land previously considered valuable only for timber," noted editor Luce in 1867, "were taken for homesteads by the Norwegians, who formerly accustomed to a severe climate and ungenerous soil, counted the rich hillsides and coolies of Wisconsin a most desirable acquisition."[7] For Norwegians arriving in the mid-50s, there was a reasonable supply of this land. Only small pieces of the hill country were held as "scrip" lands by old American settlers and land speculators, and a few sections had been reserved under the Swamp Lands and Improvement Acts.

After 1862 most land was acquired as homesteads, and the post-Civil War period witnessed a tremendous surge in Norwegian settlement. Homesteading continued as the major means of procurement throughout the 1870s and 1880s, but railroad lands also became a prime source after 1872 when the first line penetrated the area. Very early the West Wisconsin Railroad organized immigration promotion activity and appointed propagandist ticket agents among the local Norwegian population. The prior settlement of many Norwegian farmers in the townships, coupled with the warm reception they were offered by the Yankee population and press, greatly facilitated the colonization efforts of the rail company.[8]

The penetration of Norwegians into the townships converged with that of a number of other nationality groups including the German, Irish, Swedish, Danish, Scotch, English and Polish. With the exception of the

Germans in North Bend Township and the Irish in Ettrick, however, their numbers were proportionately small.[9] By 1880, Norwegians predominated in North Beaver Creek, especially in Ettrick Township, and to a lesser extent in Trempealeau Valley, where other foreign and native born groups were present (Fig. 3). The South Beaver Creek Norwegians were also well established, but they were clustered in two distinct sections of Ettrick and Melrose townships. Twenty-five years later, the Norwegians not only had retained their initial land holdings but also had expanded their territory to accommodate the flow of newcomers from Norway (Fig. 3). By 1905, the Norwegian settlements clearly represented the largest single foreign-born element in the population of these townships. This consolidation of ethnically homogeneous communities was achieved both by purchases from non-Norwegian landowners and the settlement of leftover forties deliberately reserved by pioneers for subsequent arrivals. These immigrants came almost without exception directly from Norway and had, therefore, encountered few Americanizing influences which may have modified their reactions to this new environment.

Until 1880, the three predominantly Norwegian communities were served by three "mother" congregations, each an "open country" establishment, centrally located in the communities they serviced. By 1905, the secession of pietistic and Anti-Missouri elements had spawned several additional congregations in the North Beaver Creek and Trempealeau Valley settlements. In contrast, the congregation in South Beaver Creek withstood these disruptive confrontations and remained the only church in the valley. This paper attempts to relate these contrasting responses to schismatic movements to the effects of occupational patterns, generational differences, and the degree of Norwegian predominance within the local population.

### The Religious Background of Schism

Most schisms were derived from pietistic confrontations with Lutheran orthodoxy which had profoundly affected the Church in Norway both before and during the period of greatest emigration. Far removed from a state church, these same confrontations produced a succession of schisms and shifting synodical affiliations among Norwegian Lutherans in America. The American cohort of the Church of Norway or the Norwegian Synod was formally organized at Koshkonong in 1853 as a response to the weakly structured congregations of lay preachers who had predominated in many immigrant settlements. Indeed, as early as 1846, revivalists under the lay leadership of Elling Eielsen had organized their own synod (Table 1). Eielsen and his followers were extreme in their pietistic views, and lay preachers were not typical of the larger Haugean pietistic movement flourishing in Norway. Many Haugean lay people had initially joined congregations affiliated with the Norwegian Synod rather than associate with Eielsen's following and in 1876 formed their own Haugean Synod. Even with the organiza-

14

## SYNODS OF NORWEGIAN-AMERICAN LUTHERANISM
### 1846-1900

| Date of Organization | | Synod |
|---|---|---|
| 1846 | | Eielsen's (revivalist) |
| 1848 | | The New York |
| 1851 | | Northern Illinois (primarily Norwegian, also some American-born) |
| 1851 | | The Norwegian Evangelical Lutheran Church in America |
| 1853 | | The Norwegian |
| 1860 | | Scandinavian-Augustana (included Danes and Swedes) |
| 1870 | "The Middle Way" | Norwegian-Augustana (primarily Norwegian, some Swedes) |
| 1870 | | Norwegian-Danish Conference |
| 1876 | Hauge's (revivalist) | |
| 1887 | | The Anti-Missourian Brotherhood |
| 1890 | | The United Norwegian Lutheran Church in America (UNLCA) |
| 1893 | | The Friends of Augsburg |
| 1897 | | The Lutheran Free Church |
| 1900 | | The Lutheran Brotherhood |

tion of the Haugean body, Eielsen retained many supporters who differed from Hauge and his lay disciples on certain theological issues.[10] With the veritable flood of immigrants to the Midwest, substantial numbers of pastors and lay people were also drawn to the "middle way" or "broad church" in an effort to avoid the orthodoxy of the Norwegian Synod and the emotional pietism of Hauge and Eielsen (Table 1). By 1870, a well-defined "middle way" had surfaced in the form of three new ecclesiastical bodies: the Norwegian Augustana Synod, the Norwegian-Danish Conference, and the Scandinavian Augustana Synod. All in all, by 1900 Norwegian Lutherans had formally organized at least fourteen different synodical units, with only the "middle way" extending noticeably across ethnic boundaries.[11] The German Missourians were undeniably the largest and most influential Lutheran group in America in the mid-nineteenth century, and the Norwegian Synod turned to them, almost instinctively, for assistance in the training of their clergy and in the founding of congregations among Norwegian settlers. Beginning in 1859, the Norwegian Synod sent its prospective clergymen to the German theological seminary in St. Louis and thereafter turned to them repeatedly for advice and support in their controversies with other Norwegian Lutheran synods.[12] In 1872, the synod formalized its association with the German Missourians by uniting with them and the Wisconsin Synod to form the Synodical Conference (Table 1). The close relationship of the synod leadership with the Missourians greatly displeased the mass of Norwegian immigrants since the Missourians advocated views with which they disagreed. Among the controversial issues were slavery, the common school, and especially,

the question of predestination. Involvement in the predestination debate prompted the Synod, in 1883, to cut off its fellowship with the Missourians (Table 1). The years of bitter debate culminated in the withdrawal of the Missouri leader, F. A. Schmidt, and about one-third of the synod membership in 1887, thus initiating the Anti-Missourian Brotherhood.[13]

As sentiments concerning the election doctrine began to crystallize, and tensions mounted, religious realignments were spurred among the member congregations of the synod. These realignments assumed two forms. The most widespread form was reaffiliation which involved the secession of dissenters from the original congregation in order to join the existing Anti-Missourian Brotherhood. The second form of realignment was schism which occurred when dissenters from existing congregations could not reach a compromise with other affiliations and divided to create an additional religious body. Locally, these antipathies were reflected in fierce competition between congregations for membership, charges and countercharges of transgression of parish boundaries, in addition to the formation of dissenting congregations and shifting synodical affiliations. By 1880, the effects of schism were clearly evident in the congregational structure of Norwegian Lutherans in Trempealeau and Jackson counties (Fig. 4). Churches of different synods were located close to each other and by 1905, this process of secession had intensified (Fig. 5).

### Congregational Organization in the Study Area
Since the Norwegian Synod was determined to provide formal, ordained leadership to meet the needs of immigrant communities, it is not surprising that the

15

145

three congregations founded to serve the Trempealeau Valley and Beaver Creek communities were established by a ministry affiliated at the outset with the conservative synod. The growth of congregations among the Norwegians of western Wisconsin paralleled the development of the communities themselves. In 1857, only three years after the first group of Norwegian immigrants entered the Trempealeau Valley, the Rev. H. A. Stub organized its first congregation, which was to be the parent body of numerous congregations sprouting later.

. The Trempealeau Valley congregation was destined to undergo three major divisions between 1868 and 1879. The first of these divisions spawned the Eielsen congregation (Fig. 6). In 1876, the secessionists themselves split into the Eielsen and Hauge factions. The Conference people seceded from the parent church in 1870, worshipping alone until 1890 when they were joined by the Anti-Missourians, creating one congregation in nearby Blair. A large number had also seceded from the original church in 1879 to create another congregation of the synod and, subsequently, they split internally in 1889 over the election controversy. A group of Anti-Missourians also partitioned from the "mother" congregation in 1889 over the election issue and joined the Anti-Missourians and the Conference people in Blair in 1890 to form the Norwegian Evangelical Congregation. In short, by 1916 the "mother" body in Trempealeau Valley had generated six additional congregations. Three of these were affiliated with the Haugean Synod and one each with the Norwegian, Eielsen, and the United Norwegian Lutheran Church in America (UNLCA) synods.

The North Beaver Creek congregation (Figure 7) was organized and its constitution adopted in the fall of 1859. The "mother" congregation left the Norwegian Synod in 1888 over the election doctrine, affiliating first with the Anti-Missourians and then with the newly formed United Norwegian Lutheran Church in America in 1890. Some members, however, retained their Missouri orientation and their affiliation with the Norwegian Synod.[14] The South Beaver Creek "mother" congregation was organized in 1867 (Fig. 7). Up to that point, the valley's pioneers had worshipped with the congregation in North Beaver Creek. Because of long distances for travel, the Valley's residents voted to construct a church of their own, a cooperative effort between two spatially distinct subcommunities.[15] Mill Creek Valley was occupied almost completely by immigrants from Solør, eastern Norway, whereas the South Beaver Creek Valley housed a more diverse local population which originated in Biri, Ringsaker, and Faaberg parishes.

## Membership Patterns: 1880-1905

The spatial patterns of each religious affiliation in 1880 were quite extensive, but each of the three "mother" congregations occupied mutually exclusive territories (Fig. 8).[16] The parish areas suggest that the community church served clusters of settlers who formed spatially well-defined congregations. These membership patterns were also uncomplicated by the existence of competing congregations. There were no other Lutheran churches, German or otherwise, within the range of the "mother" congregations in 1880, but other denominations, chiefly Presbyterian, were represented in Melrose and North Bend.[17] Norwegian settlers, scattered beyond lands held by other national groups, were also served by these churches. The Trempealeau Valley and South Beaver Creek community churches both extended across other ethnic areas in Curran and Melrose townships respectively to serve sizable outliers of Norwegians. Since all three churches were affiliated with the same synod, the boundaries of their membership fields also responded to the alternative attraction of neighboring congregations. The Trempealeau Valley parish area was truncated on its western fringes by the presence of a young, though thriving, congregation in Blair. Similarly, the range of the South Beaver Creek parish was restricted by the Hardies Creek parish lying in Gale Township to the southwest.

The membership patterns of the "mother" congregations in 1880, like trade or banking hinterlands, exhibited a certain degree of locational continuity over time. With the expansion and consolidation of rural service centers, it might be argued that church-centered communities would grow increasingly cohesive and exclusive over time and new congregations would emerge in response to the growth of smaller outlying settlements. Because of frequent schisms this rational assignment of congregational territories was disrupted and by 1905, there had been a striking transformation of the ecclesiastical map. Exclusive control by the "mother" congregations was supplanted by shared control among several overlapping congregations. Membership patterns became more complex and fragmented with the emergence of at least four additional, competing congregations (Fig. 9).

The fragmentation of membership patterns in the Trempealeau Valley and North Beaver Creek communities left both "mother" congregations numerically weakened, but they were still dominant both numerically and spatially. The North Beaver Creek congregation lost its pastor and 161 members or about one-third of its contingent to the Missouri side but retained a majority of 432 Anti-Missourian followers.[18] The Trempealeau Valley congregation lost 65 of its 250-300 members to the Anti-Missourian cause, and it had already lost larger segments with the secession of the Eielsen and Haugean elements.[19] These groups included the members of the newly organized Upper Beaver Creek congregation.

As a result of this schismatic activity, the Trempealeau Valley community remained predominantly Missourian in its view and the Beaver Creek predominantly Anti-Missourian. The Rev. B. Hovde, an uncompromising Missourian pastor, had served both communities during the election debate. In the Beaver Creek Valley he led a minority following of Missourians out of the "mother" church and founded a new affiliate

16

Table 2:

## OCCUPATION, BY CONGREGATION
### Norwegian Heads of Household
### 1905

| Occupation | North Beaver Creek (Ns) | North Beaver Creek (UNLCA) | Tremp. Valley (Ns) | Upper Beaver Creek (Hs) | Taylor (Ns) | South BC (Ns) |
|---|---|---|---|---|---|---|
| Farming |  |  |  |  |  |  |
| Farmer-Owner | 39 | 49 | 84 | 29 | 46 | 37 |
| Farmer-Renter |  | 2 | 2 | 1 | 1 | 1 |
| Laborer |  |  | 2 | 1 | 4 |  |
| Retired | 2 | 1 |  |  | 2 |  |
| Crafts |  |  |  |  |  |  |
| Carpenter | 1 |  | 1 |  | 1 |  |
| Painter |  |  | 1 |  |  |  |
| Livery |  |  | 1 |  |  |  |
| Merchant-Clerk |  |  |  |  | 2 |  |
| Professional |  |  |  |  |  |  |
| Preacher |  |  | 1 |  | 1 |  |
| Miscellaneous |  | 1 |  |  | 1 | 1 |
| Total # Household Heads | 42 | 53 | 92 | 31 | 58 | 39 |
| % Farmers of Total | 92.8 | 96.2 | 93.5 | 96.8 | 81.0 | 94.9 |

of the Norwegian Synod farther up the valley. On the other hand, in Trempealeau Valley, Hovde and his Missourian majority were for awhile denied the privilege of worshipping in the "mother" church. When the Anti-Missourians left the valley to join their counterparts in Blair, Hovde and his following were able to resume use of the original structure.[20]

In contrast, the membership patterns of the South Beaver Creek settlements reveal no obvious response to the theological issues that had rocked both the Trempealeau and North Beaver Creek communities. These issues may, of course, have been debated, but continued affiliation with the Norwegian Synod throughout the span of twenty-five years suggests that this congregation accepted the Missourians' stance on election and other issues. There may have been members with Anti-Missourian views, but they apparently decided against secession.

The South Beaverites may have been conscious of German Lutherans whose settlement both surrounded and partitioned their parish. Just how influential the Germans may have been or how strong they were in their Missourian views is unknown. It is, however, plausible that the presence of other ethnic groups, including both the Germans and Irish, may have encouraged the Norwegians to retain a unified congre-

gation. It is also possible that neither faction considered themselves numerically strong enough to secede from the "mother" church and create a viable, lasting congregation. Finally, the cultural bonds of this community from a specific Norwegian locality may have been so tight that doctrinal disputation was too muted to provoke secession.

The generalized map of membership patterns for 1905 indicates the more pronounced effects of adjacent congregations on the Trempealeau Valley (Fig. 9). Here the range of membership was most noticeably reduced in Preston and Curran townships where at least two new congregations had been established. Non-Norwegian members were rare despite the inclusion of their lands within the territories of the Norwegian churches. By 1905, the membership configurations of schismatic and nonschismatic communities were quite distinct. Communities which experienced schism showed a complex pattern of overlapping congregations indicating that theology rather than convenience stimulated the multiplication of churches. Only in ethnically plural South Beaver Creek were compact and exclusive territories maintained. Elsewhere the realignment of memberships and synodical associations revealed the divisive impact of the immigrant church in some frontier communities.

17

Table 3:

## MEAN AGE, BY CONGREGATION
### Norwegian Heads of Household
### 1880 and 1905

| Year | North Beaver Creek (Ns) | North Beaver Creek (UNLCA) | Trempealeau Valley (Ns) |
|---|---|---|---|
| 1880 | | 42.8* | 44.0* |
| 1905 | 46.4 | 47.1 | 49.0 |

| Year | Upper Beaver Creek (Hs) | Taylor (Ns) | South Beaver Creek (Ns) |
|---|---|---|---|
| 1880 | —— | —— | 43.8 |
| 1905 | 41.7 | 50.2 | 44.0 |

\* Indicates mean age before division.
—— Congregation not yet organized.

### Social Sources of Schism

These spiritual fissures, however, may express occupational, generational, and ethnic sources of community discord. While occupational differentiation was weakly developed among pioneering settlers who came to the Midwest to establish farms, subsequent generations may have moved into the service sector. Upwardly mobile or non-farm elements of the community may have been a source of new values and attitudes which threatened established traditions and thereby contributed to the process of secession.

While foreign-born settlers in Trempealeau County found a range of occupational opportunities,[21] the memberships of these few local congregations were not representative of this diversity. They all displayed very little variety in their occupational profiles and of the total number of heads of household for the six congregations, the percentage of farmers ranged from a low of 81.0 percent for the Taylor congregation to a high 96.8 percent for Upper Beaver Creek (Table 2). Norwegians maintained the occupational commitments of the immigrant generation, and changes in the economic structure of the counties as a whole were unlikely to have been a direct source of community discord and schism among them.

Despite the persistence of occupational patterns, it is possible that a growing, native-born generation may have resisted the continuation of traditional patterns of life and worship. If religious differences were indeed related to generational tensions then the dissenting configurations would display the lower mean ages of the native-born children of the immigrant generation. There were not, however, any striking differences in the mean age of householders who remained loyal to the "mother" churches and those who seceded (Table 3).

Since the one congregation which withstood secession was also in an area where Norwegians were not

as predominant, it is possible that interethnic differences were of greater consequence than intraethnic cleavages. Whenever Norwegian communities were extensive, it was possible for bygd loyalties to assume a greater salience. These local attachments based on long established Old World communities may have affected reactions to doctrinal debates, and schismatic loyalties may record the continuing effect of bygd origins. Whenever Norwegians were a minority, these local loyalties may have been subdued; but whenever they predominated, local rather than national loyalties prevailed. Alternatively, smaller clusters of Norwegians were more likely to be derived from one, or at the most two, neighboring bygder, and these local loyalties would have reinforced their sense of difference from adjacent national groups.

This case study has uncovered no decisive factor in religious schism, but the process of secession itself did resemble the denominational and congregational developments observed in other protestant immigrant churches. During the initial phase of denominational competition, according to H. Richard Niebuhr, the immigrant churches tended to differentiate themselves as cultural organizations, emphasizing their uniqueness on cultural rather than doctrinal grounds.[22] In the first years, a desire for security and companionship may have overshadowed very subtle differences of religious opinion, and the emergence of "daughter" congregations may simply have resulted from community growth and redefinition which required new churches to serve larger and more highly differentiated settlements. The frequency of schism, however, attested to the contribution of religious discord to the creation of new congregations especially when rivalry arose between culturally similar groups. While doctrinal differences were a potent influence in schisms these divisions were probably related to latent tensions transferred from homeland parish life. Like other Scandinavian societies,

18

the Norwegian populace was divided hierarchically into classes of nobility, family farmers holding land, tenant farmers, and agricultural laborers without land. Conventional class distinctions aside, there were additional, more subtle, distinctions which marked one peasant farmer off from another. Just as the landholding peasant enjoyed greater prestige than did his nonlandholding counterpart, the well-to-do peasant of the rich eastern valleys was marked off from his struggling countrymen in the bleak mountain settlements of the west.

Varying intensities of religious enthusiasm were also characteristic of different parishes in Norway and in the New World; they were revealed in a wide range of religious doctrines and church-going habits. The religious patterns which emerged were not closely related to such factors as socio-economic conditions in this country or intergenerational differences but the presence of competing national groups did discourage schism. It is, of course, conceivable that the response of any congregation to a theological issue was heavily conditioned by the professional opinion, if not the personal whims, of its pastor. It was the Lutheran pastor, generally serving a "circuit" of congregations, who brought controversial doctrinal topics to the limelight in pioneer settlements. The depth of his feeling on any given issue, therefore, was probably registered directly in the discussions which followed.

Among Norwegian Lutherans conflict over the issue of predestination spurred a rash of splinterings and synodical reaffiliations amounting to a loss of one-third of the membership of the once-preeminent Norwegian Synod. This Synod had been the stronghold of traditionalism in faith and practice among the Norwegian-Americans. For thousands, despite its doctrinal strife, it was the closest point of contact with the motherland, and schism within its ranks did not seriously alter Norwegian group identity. The acceptance of American values and patterns of life continued to come through the prism of the immigrants' cultural experience, of which their religious life was but one part. In the long run, the scope and frequency of religious controversies did not reduce the communion of the Lutheran Church as a whole. The waves of doctrinal discord may, in fact, have garnered some unexpected benefits for the cause of Norwegian Lutheranism, particularly in the form of increased interest and participation in the debates.

Studies of immigrant settlements have commonly stressed the role of the church in group identification. As a community focus, it nurtured a sense of community by adherence to a common set of values and traditions. The spatial outcome of schism in this case study, however, suggests that within the larger immigrant community, the church acquired a divisive role in those communities where secessions occurred. While the division of communities by religious disagreement may have prompted the diminution or collapse of community interaction, the partitioning of the "mother" community may also have given rise to smaller communities that were more homogeneous and intense in terms of personal interaction than the original congregation. Schism might be more appropriately associated with community transformation or redefinition than with breakdown.

19

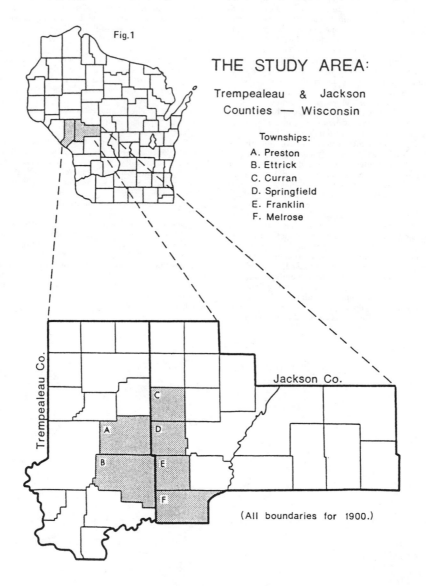

Fig.1

# THE STUDY AREA:

Trempealeau & Jackson
Counties — Wisconsin

Townships:
A. Preston
B. Ettrick
C. Curran
D. Springfield
E. Franklin
F. Melrose

Trempealeau Co.

Jackson Co.

(All boundaries for 1900.)

20

150

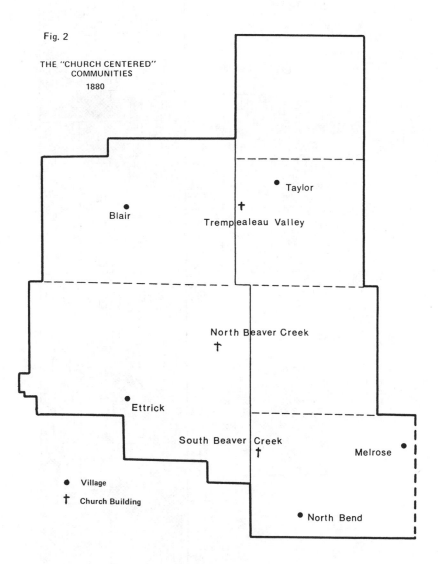

Fig. 2

THE "CHURCH CENTERED"
COMMUNITIES
1880

Taylor

Blair

Trempealeau Valley

North Beaver Creek

Ettrick

South Beaver Creek

Melrose

Village

Church Building

North Bend

21

151

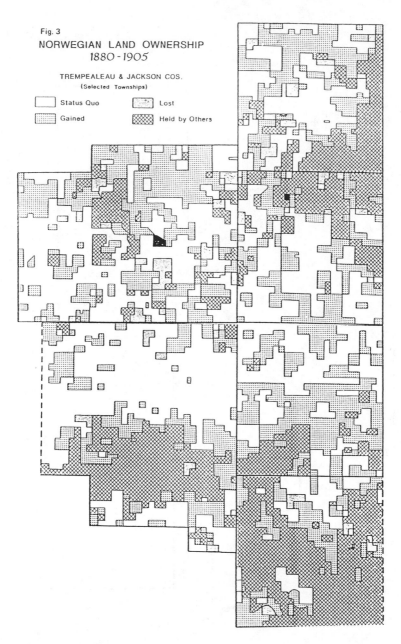

Fig. 3

NORWEGIAN LAND OWNERSHIP
1880 - 1905

TREMPEALEAU & JACKSON COS.
(Selected Townships)

Status Quo   Lost

Gained   Held by Others

22

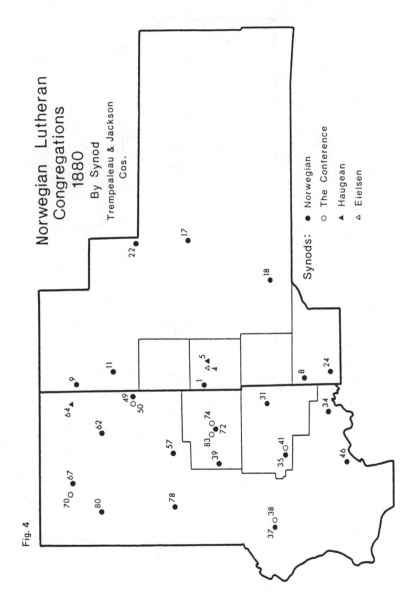

Fig. 4

Norwegian Lutheran
Congregations
1880
By Synod
Trempealeau & Jackson
Cos.

Synods: ● Norwegian
○ The Conference
▲ Haugean
△ Eielsen

23

153

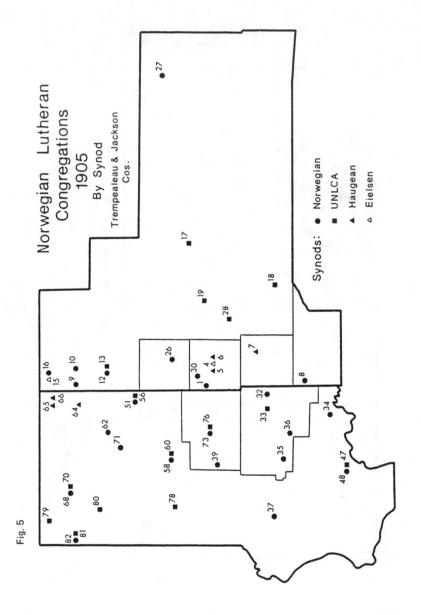

Fig. 5

Norwegian Lutheran
Congregations
1905
By Synod
Trempealeau & Jackson
Cos.

Synods:
● Norwegian
■ UNLCA
▲ Haugean
△ Eielsen

Fig. 6

TREMPEALEAU VALLEY CONGREGATIONS

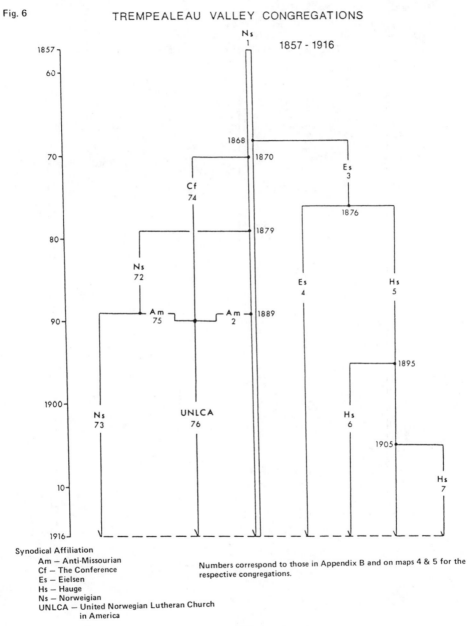

1857 - 1916

Synodical Affiliation
 Am — Anti-Missourian
 Cf — The Conference
 Es — Eielsen
 Hs — Hauge
 Ns — Norweigian
 UNLCA — United Norwegian Lutheran Church
           in America

Numbers correspond to those in Appendix B and on maps 4 & 5 for the
respective congregations.

25

Fig. 7

# THE BEAVER CREEK CONGREGATIONS

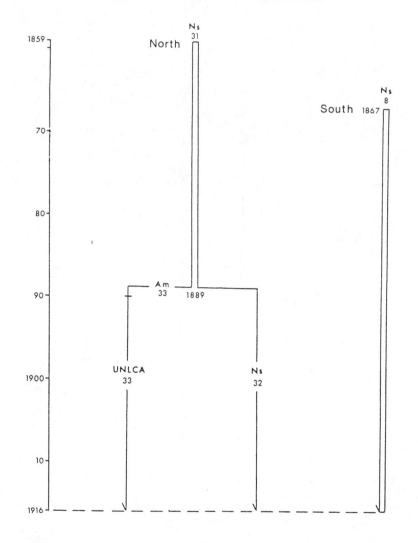

26

156

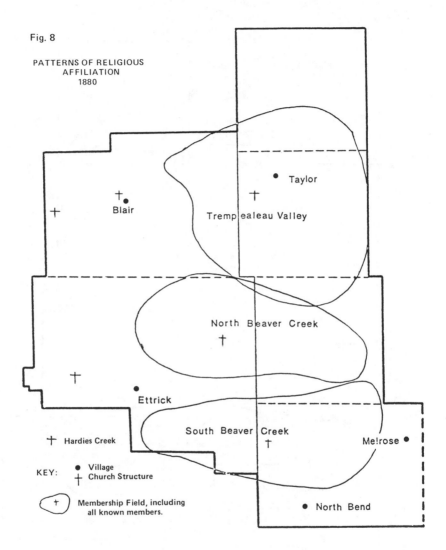

Fig. 8

PATTERNS OF RELIGIOUS
AFFILIATION
1880

● Taylor

✝
● Blair

✝

✝ Trempealeau Valley

North Beaver Creek
✝

✝

● Ettrick

South Beaver Creek
✝

● Melrose

✝ Hardies Creek

KEY:   ● Village
       ✝ Church Structure

● North Bend

   ✝   Membership Field, including
       all known members.

27

157

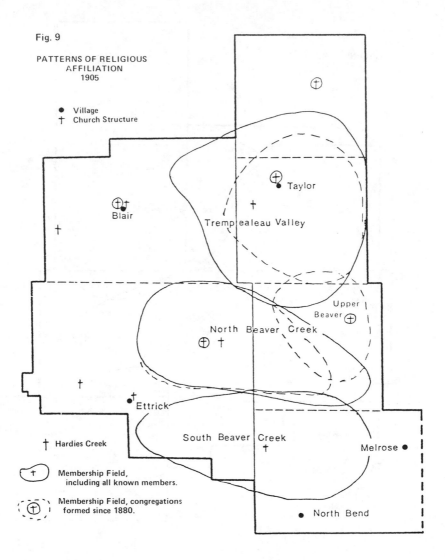

Fig. 9

PATTERNS OF RELIGIOUS
AFFILIATION
1905

● Village
✝ Church Structure

Taylor

Blair

Trempealeau Valley

Upper
Beaver

North Beaver Creek

Ettrick

Hardies Creek

South Beaver Creek

Melrose

Membership Field,
including all known members.

Membership Field, congregations
formed since 1880.

North Bend

28

158

# Notes

1. Timothy L. Smith, "Congregation, State, and Denomination: The Forming of the American Religious Structure," **William and Mary Quarterly,** 3d ser., XXV (April 1968), 160.
2. Robert C. Ostergren, "A Community Transplanted: The Formative Experience of a Swedish Immigrant Community in the Upper Middle West," **Journal of Historical Geography** 5 (April 1979), 189-212.
3. Theodore C. Blegen, **Norwegian Migration to America: The American Transition** (Northfield, 1940), 77.
4. **Our Heritage** (North Beaver Creek Lutheran Churches, 1959), 16-18.
5. Franklyn Curtiss-Wedge, **History of Trempealeau County** (Chicago and Winona, 1917), 831.
6. Merle Curti, **The Making of an American Community** (Stanford, 1959), 185.
7. **Galesville Transcript,** July 19, 1867.
8. **Whitehall Times,** March 31, 1881.
9. The ethnicity and religious affiliation of each household was derived from plat maps, census materials and church registries. These sources were not always available for identical years but despite some chronological gaps, landownership by ethnic origin was determined for 1880 and 1905. Each census recorded individuals in the order in which they were interviewed by the census enumerator. The order of the schedules, with certain exceptions, represents the route taken by the enumerator. By locating the first individual enumerated on the plat map, it is possible to reconstruct the path of the census marshall as he passed from that household to other households in the township. There were, of course, discontinuities in the route followed, and some uncertainty in the location of a few households but these gaps are rarely serious and the most probable course of the enumerator is self-evident. For a complete explication of this method see Michael Conzen's "Spatial Data from Nineteenth Century Manuscript Censuses: A Technique for Rural Settlement and Land Use Analysis," **Professional Geographer,** 21 (Sept. 1969), 337-43.
10. E. Clifford Nelson and Eugene L. Fevold, **The Lutheran Church Among Norwegian Americans** (Minneapolis, 1960), 126-33, 149-50.
11. **Ibid.,** 123-24.
12. **Ibid.,** 161-63.
13. **Ibid.,** 253-70.
14. **Our Heritage,** 16-18.
15. South Beaver Creek Lutheran Church, 100th Anniversary, 1867-1967, 12-13.
16. Patterns of religious affiliation were based on cross references between church registries and the census schedules. Since Norwegian clergymen recorded only official acts, the church registries were limited to lists of baptisms, confirmations, weddings, and funerals. The church records lacked a complete listing of church members and as a result, it was impossible to match names from the church books directly to names on the plat maps. Rather, it was necessary to trace the names of confirmands and baptized children from a ten year period (1875-1885 and 1900-1910) to the names of their parent or "head of household" listed in the census schedules. The heads of household were, in turn, plotted on township maps to show the location of church members in 1880 and again in 1905. The boundaries of these memberships were drawn by including all known church members of Norwegian ancestry. These generalized membership maps were constructed for both 1880 and 1905 to document changes in the spatial extent of church memberships over the period.
17. **Melrose Chronicle,** March 22, 1973.
18. D. M. Norlie, **Norwegian People in America** (Minneapolis, 1925), 219-20.
19. **Ibid.,** 189-90.
20. Centennial Committee, **This, Our Beloved Valley** (Blair-Preston, 1925), 10.
21. Curti, **American Community,** 57.
22. H. Richard Niebuhr, **The Social Sources of Denominationalism** (New York, 1929).

29

# Ethnic Group Settlement on the Great Plains

FREDERICK C. LUEBKE

The importance of foreign-born immigrants and their children for the settlement of the Great Plains has been largely overlooked by historians of the frontier and of the trans-Mississippi West. While an extensive literature exists treating Indian history and Indian-white relationships, white populations have usually been treated as homogeneous. In such a classic study as Walter Prescott Webb's *The Great Plains*, ethnic groups of European origin are scarcely mentioned. More recent interpretations of the region note differences between Indians, Chicanos, Orientals, and blacks, but fail to distinguish European ethnic groups, such as Norwegians, Germans, and Czechs from each other or from the native-born populations.[1]

Analysis of census data for the nineteenth century, however, reveals that the foreign-born and their children often constituted a majority of the frontier population of the Great Plains states. In 1870, when the fringe of settlement moved onto the eastern reaches of the Great Plains, 25 percent of the 123,000 persons in the newly created state of Nebraska were foreign-born. Together with the second generation, they accounted for 54 percent of all inhabitants, excluding Indians. Even as late as 1900, immigrants and natives of foreign parentage formed 47 percent of the state's

Frederick C. Luebke is professor of history at the University of Nebraska—Lincoln. This article was originally commissioned by the University of Mid-America, a consortium of midwestern universities for the development of non-traditional education, for inclusion in its textbook/reader as part of the UMA course, "The Great Plains Experience: A Cultural History." Printed by permission; rights retained by University of Mid-America.

[1] Walter P. Webb, *The Great Plains* (New York, 1931). As a recent example, see Arrell M. Gibson, *The West in the Life of the Nation* (Lexington, Massachusetts, 1976).

population, while in North Dakota the proportion reached 78 percent, the highest figure registered for any state in the union.[2]

The percentages of foreign-born persons were greater in states north of Nebraska and lower in those to the south. In 1870, Kansas registered 13 percent, about half the Nebraska proportion, while Oklahoma remained closed to white settlement and the Texas portion of the Great Plains remained mostly unoccupied. In Dakota Territory, however, the percentage of foreign-born persons in 1870 was startlingly high at 34 percent, while in the plains and mountain territories of Wyoming and Montana it spiraled to 39 percent.[3]

When data from the county level are examined, the importance of white ethnic groups for the settlement of the Great Plains becomes even more obvious. The foreign-born were often more numerous proportionately on the fringe of settlement than they were in the older or eastern parts of the Great Plains states. To illustrate with the example of Nebraska, the proportion of foreign-born persons in nearly all counties located on or near the Great Plains proper in 1870 exceeded the percentages recorded for the state as a whole. Figures of 50 percent and above were common, and the highest proportions were, as a rule, recorded in the westernmost counties. After 1870, however, when the frontier of settlement edged onto the High Plains, the concentration of the foreign-born was not sustained to the same extent, though significant ethnic settlements were not uncommon.

In order to understand the role of white ethnic groups in the history of the Great Plains, one must first relate it to the larger general patterns of emigration to America. During the first fifty years following the American Revolution, until approximately 1825, few Europeans emigrated to the United States. During those years the frontier of settlement moved steadily westward across the Appalachian Mountains into the vast interior. By 1820, Louisiana, Mississippi, Missouri, and Illinois had achieved statehood. Because there were few immigrants in the country, the process

[2] Unless otherwise noted, the quantitative data presented in this paper are taken from the several volumes on population produced by the U.S. Bureau of the Census from the Eighth Census (1860) through the Thirteenth Census (1910). See also *Statistical Review of Immigration 1820–1910—Distribution of Immigrants 1850–1900*, vol. 3 of *Reports of the* [Dillingham] *Immigration Commission* (Washington. 1911).

[3] Cf. J. Neale Carman, *Foreign-Language Units of Kansas*, vol. 1, *Historical Atlas and Statistics* (Lawrence, 1962), 33–37.

of settlement was achieved by Anglo-Americans. This fact is the basis for
the myth that immigrants were unable to cope with the frontier environment.[4] By the 1840s, however, immense numbers of Irish, Germans, and
English entered the country and many went to the frontier territories of
that time—Michigan, Wisconsin, Iowa, and Texas. Following a dip in
immigration during the Civil War, a new and greater flood of humanity
inundated the United States, climaxing in the 1880s, the precise years when
the Great Plains states were being settled. The vast majority of these people came from Germany, the Scandinavian countries, Great Britain, Ireland, and, to a lesser extent, from Bohemia and Russia. Following a reduc-
tion during the 1890s, the flow of immigration into the United States
increased steadily and reached its largest annual total in 1907. By this time,
however, when the major sources of emigrants to the United States had
shifted to southern and eastern European countries, the Great Plains
region had been settled. Although some twentieth-century immigrants
found homes in eastern Montana, western parts of the Dakotas, and in
other areas where some land was still available for homesteading, relatively
few of them came to the Great Plains.

Most immigrants who were attracted to the region were farmers or
persons who hoped to succeed by taking up some form of agriculture.
Although they could be found in the towns and villages of the plains, they
were proportionately more numerous in the rural areas. A large though
undetermined proportion of the immigrants lived in eastern states before
migrating to the plains. They frequently had pursued urban-type occupations there in order to accumulate sufficient capital to start a new life
on a western farm.

Most European immigrants came to the Great Plains in family units,
with relatives and neighbors following later. Formal colonization was
important for some ethnic groups, and in some cases large numbers of
persons came as the result of highly organized programs. Some European
groups would have preferred to recreate the peasant village setting they
were accustomed to, but ordinarily this was not possible because of government land policies. Moreover, government grants of land to the railroads were made in checkerboard patterns, a practice that effectively

---

[4] John A. Hawgood, *The Tragedy of German-America* (New York, [1940] 1970),
22–23, provides the classic statement of this idea.

prevented immigrants from massing large tracts in the solid or contiguous blocks necessary for the European pattern.[5]

The most important single cause that impelled people to leave Europe was economic. For example, poverty and famine in Ireland were overpowering in the 1840s and 1850s. The inability of preindustrial Germany, especially its southwestern provinces, to support its exploding population in the nineteenth century is unquestioned; and in England the enclosure movement sent vast numbers of unemployed persons to the cities and from thence to America. But each country had it own array of expelling forces that were also political, religious, social, and psychological. To illustrate, the revolutions of 1848 sent many thousands of political refugees to the United States; later, in the 1880s, countless young German men fled to escape service in Bismarck's army; many thousands of Russian Jews were driven out by pogroms after 1881; Swedes were especially resentful of the social and political privileges of the upper classes. Whole communities were sometimes flushed with "America fever" as the departure of one person or family stimulated the imaginations of friends and relatives, all eager to escape poverty and oppression. Visions were further enlarged as "America letters" were received from those who had gone before. Each country presents a different pattern of causes that changed with the passage of time. In any case, decisions to emigrate were made individually, and each person's motives were complex, not readily unraveled or subject to easy classification.[6]

Scholars have produced an extensive and sophisticated literature during recent decades that connects emigration from Europe to fluctuations in the economic cycles of Europe and the United States. Earlier studies concluded that the volume of emigration was governed primarily by economic conditions within the United States, but subsequent analyses, more subtle and comprehensive, demonstrated that the flow of emigration was related to European capital investment in the United States. When, for example, British investments were halted in the 1870s because of a

---

[5] For a model survey of immigrant groups in one state see Douglas Hale, "European Immigrants in Oklahoma: A Survey," *Chronicles of Oklahoma*, 53 (Summer 1975), 179–203.

[6] The best recent summary of causes of European emigration is in Philip Taylor, *The Distant Magnet* (New York, 1971), chapters 1–5.

glut of capital in America, a panic and economic depression followed with immigration decreasing accordingly.[7]

Even though European immigration dropped sharply after the devastating Panic of 1873 (the total in 1878 was only one-fourth that of 1873), settlers continued to move onto the Great Plains at approximately the same rate as before. Moreover, immigrants continued to be numerically important, attracted as they were by the land made available by the Homestead Act of 1862, by the advertisements of railroad companies, the efforts of colonization societies, and the blandishments of state boards of immigration.

The Homestead Act opened millions of acres for settlement. In order to obtain a farm of 160 acres virtually without cost, an applicant was required to reside upon his claim for not less than five years and to improve it through cultivation. To qualify for a claim, a homesteader had to be a citizen or to have taken out his first papers for naturalization. During the 1870s and 1880s many thousands of immigrants acquired farms by this means from the Oklahoma border north through Kansas and Nebraska to the Dakota and Montana territories.

The attraction of land ownership was overpowering for many Europeans. News of the Homestead Act spurred uncountable numbers of immigrants to the Great Plains. Land ownership had great symbolic value for the typical newcomer. In Europe, where society was more highly structured, respect and honor were paid to landowners—the larger the tract, the greater the prestige. To the typical European peasant, caught in a land squeeze, 160 acres seemed an immense tract. Moreover, the security afforded by land ownership compensated for the intense feelings of confusion, anxiety, and rootlessness that afflicted many immigrants as they adjusted to life in a strange and alien environment. By contrast, the typical native-born American tended to view land ownership as a means to wealth rather than as an end in itself. When increased population in a given area forced up the value of land, the American farmer frequently sold out for a profit and started out again farther west. Not encumbered with a sentimental attachment to the soil, the old-stock American might exploit it, abuse it, and leave it without regret.

---

[7] The most important single volume to probe economic factors is Brinley Thomas, *Migration and Economic Growth: A Study in Great Britain and the Atlantic Economy* (Cambridge: Cambridge University Press, 1954). For a convenient summary of this literature see Kristian Hvidt, *Flight to America: The Social Background of 300,000 Danish Emigrants* (New York, 1975), 29–36.

Much of the best land on the Great Plains was not available for homesteading. The federal government had granted it to great railroad companies in order to subsidize the construction of lines into uninhabited territories. Holding alternate square miles of land ten miles on both sides of their rights-of-way, the Union Pacific, the Santa Fe, the Burlington, and the Northern Pacific railroads, among others, conducted systematic efforts to attract buyers to the veritable Eden they often claimed the Great Plains to be. European immigrants bought much of this railroad land, often in response to circulars distributed throughout England, Germany, and the Scandinavian countries by agents dispatched to Europe by the companies. Sometimes these agents organized whole colonies of emigrants, varying in size from ten to a hundred families, on vast tracts of railroad land sold at bargain rates. The railroad companies knew that if a colony were successful its population would subsequently be swelled by friends and relatives who would come later of their own accord. The railroad would prosper correspondingly.[8]

Not all colonization efforts were connected with railroads. Some were organized by ethnoreligious societies, such as the Irish Catholic Colonization Society, the Swedish Agricultural Company, the Hebrew Union Agricultural Society, and the Welsh Land and Emigrant Society of America. Most of these societies were eager to get their countrymen out of the congested cities of the eastern United States to the rich lands of the West where, they believed, the immigrant would have a better chance to prosper and to retain his religion, language, and culture. Such societies often worked closely with the railroads, steamship companies, and state boards of immigration.[9]

[8] Richard C. Overton, *Burlington West: A Colonization History of the Burlington Railroad* (Cambridge: Harvard University Press, 1941); James B. Hedges, "The Colonization Work of the Northern Pacific Railroad," *Mississippi Valley Historical Review*, 13 (December 1926), 311–42; John D. Unruh, Jr., "The Burlington and Missouri River Railroad Brings the Mennonites to Nebraska, 1873–1878," *Nebraska History*, 45 (March and June 1964), 3–30, 177–206; Morris N. Spencer, "The Union Pacific's Utilization of Its Land Grant with Emphasis on Its Colonization Program" (Ph.D. diss., University of Nebraska, 1950); Barry Combs, "The Union Pacific Railroad and the Early Settlement of Nebraska, 1868–1880," *Nebraska History*, 50 (Spring 1969), 1–26.

[9] James P. Shannon, *Catholic Colonization on the Western Frontier* (New Haven, 1957); M. Evangela Henthorne, *The Irish Catholic Colonization Association of the United States* (Champaign, 1932); Henry W. Casper, *History of the Catholic Church in Nebraska*, vol. 3, *Catholic Chapters in Nebraska Immigration, 1870–1900* (3 v., Milwaukee, 1960–66), 35–54; Ruth Billdt, *Pioneer Swedish-American Culture in Central Kansas* (Lindsborg, Kansas, 1965).

During the 1860s and early 1870s most of the state and territorial governments of the Great Plains region established boards of immigration designed to stimulate settlement in their respective lands. While the quality and extent of these bureaucratic efforts varied greatly from state to state, most were curtailed or ended by the depression and grasshopper plagues of the 1870s, when few legislators were willing to fund such ventures. They left immigration work in private hands. In Dakota Territory, however, an immigration commission was revived in 1885.[10]

Among the private agencies it is difficult to overestimate the importance of the churches in the settlement of the Great Plains. Lutherans, Catholics, Mennonites, Evangelicals—all depended for support upon the gathering of immigrants in a given area and hence had an institutional interest in maintaining a steady flow of new arrivals. The efforts of clergymen to induce immigration were ordinarily unsystematic and informal, but nonetheless effective. Migrants would be exhorted to settle in a place where a congregation of their own faith had already been established. The immigrants in turn relied heavily on the church to provide social intercourse with others who shared their language, customs, and beliefs. Of all immigrant institutions, the church was the easiest to establish, the most effective in its mission, and hence the most long-lived. Unlike most ethnic institutions, the church survived the transition to an English-speaking society.[11]

By far the most numerous immigrant people to settle in the Great Plains states were the Germans. They were most heavily concentrated in Nebraska, where in 1900, persons of German stock (first and second

[10] Helen M. Anderson, "The Influence of Railway Advertising upon the Settlement of Nebraska" (M.A. thesis, University of Nebraska, 1926), 47–50; Herbert Schell, "Official Immigration Activities of Dakota Territory," *North Dakota Historical Quarterly*, 7 (October 1932), 5–24; Ralph E. Blodgett, "The Colorado Territorial Board of Immigration," *Colorado Magazine*, 46 (Summer 1969), 245–56. For a later period, see Warren A. Henke, "Imagery, Immigration and the Myth of North Dakota, 1890–1933," *North Dakota History*, 38 (Fall 1971), 412–91.

[11] Denominational histories constitute a rich source for the history of ethnic groups. One of the most comprehensive is the three-volume work by Henry W. Casper, n. 9, above. For other examples, see Paul C. Nyholm, *The Americanization of the Danish Lutheran Church in America* (Minneapolis, 1963); George M. Stephenson, *Religious Aspects of Swedish Immigration* (Minneapolis, 1932); George Eisenach, *A History of the German Congregational Churches in the United States* (Yankton, S.D., 1938); C. Henry Smith, *The Story of the Mennonites* (4th ed., rev., Newton, Kansas, 1957). In addition there are many graduate theses and dissertations treating immigrant church history on state and local levels.

generation, or the immigrants and their children) accounted for 18 percent of the total population. In Kansas, they constituted a significantly smaller proportion of the population (9 percent). Much less numerous in the sparsely populated Dakotas, they nevertheless formed 14 percent in South Dakota and 10 percent in North Dakota. Even in Oklahoma, which was not opened to settlement until the 1890s, the Germans were by far the most numerous single ethnic group.[12]

Although they formed heavy concentrations in certain specific areas, the Germans were widely distributed, and at least a few could be found in nearly every county on the plains. The proportion of farmers among them was very high, and consequently they were more numerous in the humid, eastern counties of Nebraska, Kansas, and the Dakotas than in counties solidly within the Great Plains region. Similarly, they tended to be more numerous in the countryside than in the towns. Occupationally, the town Germans were especially successful as merchants and craftsmen, serving their countrymen from the surrounding farms.

The Germans were unusually heterogeneous. Germany itself emerged as a unified country only in 1871; hence, provincial identities were unusually strong among the Germans. These were bolstered by strong religious feeling. Lutheran Germans and Catholic Germans would have remarkably little to do with each other, and neither group felt a bond of affection for more secular-minded, unchurched, or freethinking fellow Germans.[13]

German emigration in the post-Civil War period was especially strong in northern and northeastern areas of Germany, where Protestantism dominated. Consequently, a smaller proportion of Catholic Germans settled in the Great Plains states than had earlier emigrated to Wisconsin, Minnesota, Iowa, Illinois, Indiana, and Ohio. In the eastern states the Germans were sufficiently numerous to erect a complex of ethnic institutions that functioned to ease their adjustment to American life and

[12] Considering their numbers, the Germans of the Great Plains states have received little scholarly attention. My *Immigrants and Politics: The Germans of Nebraska, 1880–1900* (Lincoln, 1969) contains chapters on patterns of German settlement and assimilation. See also Hildegard Binder Johnson, "The Location of German Immigrants in the Middle West," *Annals of the Association of American Geographers,* 41 (March 1951), 1–41. J. C. Ruppenthal, "The German Element in Central Kansas," *Kansas Historical Collections,* 13 (1913–14), 513–33, and Harley J. Stuckey, "The German Element in Kansas," in John Bright, ed., *Kansas: The First Century* (New York, 1956), 329–54, both emphasize Germans from Russia.

[13] See my *Bonds of Loyalty: German Americans and World War I* (DeKalb, Illinois, 1974), chapter 2.

to perpetuate immigrant culture. On the Great Plains, churches were the most common German institutions; however, in some towns, especially on the eastern fringes of the plains, the Germans were also able to establish German-language newspapers, social organizations of various kinds, business ventures such as banks and insurance companies, plus restaurants, butcher shops, and taverns.

The census data can be somewhat misleading because the Germans were first of all a culture group rather than a people to be identified with a particular country. Thus, most Swiss, Alsatians, and Austrians who came to the Great Plains states were also Germans in language and culture, and almost all persons registered in the census of the Great Plains states as having been born in Russia were actually Germans whose families had migrated 50 to 100 years earlier to Russia, settling in Bessarabia, the area north of the Black Sea, and the Volga River region. There, at the invitation of Russian rulers, they lived in exclusively German communities. Having been granted significant cultural and political autonomy when they came, these Germans learned in 1871, to their great dismay, that their special privileges had been withdrawn. Faced with programs of Russification and conscription into the imperial army, substantial numbers of these Germans decided to emigrate. Beginning in 1873, the flow continued until World War I.[14]

The Russian Germans went to many lands, but the United States attracted most of them. Oriented to an agricultural way of life, they naturally sought out the cheap lands of the Great Plains. In contrast to the Germans from Germany, the Russian Germans retained a remarkable sense of cohesion and formed tightly knit communities, highly integrated on the basis of their religion and their origin in Russia. Most who came to Nebraska, Kansas, and Oklahoma emigrated from the Volga region, while the Dakotas received those from the region north of the Black Sea. Similarly, Catholics among them settled in specific communities in North Dakota and Kansas, but are almost entirely absent from Nebraska. Mennonites founded large communities in Kansas, Oklahoma, and South Dakota, but they are less common in North Dakota, Colorado, and Nebraska. Meanwhile, Lutheran and Congregational com-

[14] Hattie Plum Williams, *The Czar's Germans* (Lincoln: American Historical Society of Germans from Russia, 1975); Adam Giesinger, *From Catharine to Khrushchev: The Story of Russia's Germans* (Winnipeg, 1974); Adolph Schock, *In Quest of Free Land* (San Jose: San Jose State College, 1964); Gustav E. Reimer and G. R. Gaeddert, *Exiled by the Czar* (Newton, Kansas: Mennonite Publications Office, 1956).

munities of Russian Germans are numerous in Nebraska, Colorado, and the Dakotas.[15]

Russian Germans are most significant, both proportionately and in raw numbers, in North Dakota, where they dominate the central and south central part of the state. This area extends southward into South Dakota between the Missouri and the James rivers. Another South Dakota area of concentration lies in the southeastern part of the state on the fringe of the Great Plains. In Nebraska, Russian Germans are especially numerous in Lincoln and west along the Burlington Railroad. Another important district is centered in the North Platte Valley around Scottsbluff. A similar concentration is located in the South Platte Valley stretching west and southwest to Denver in Colorado. Kansas has two main enclaves—the Mennonite area north of Wichita and the Catholic communities of Ellis County near Hays. In Oklahoma, the Russian-Germans are found solidly within the Great Plains west and northwest of Oklahoma City.[16]

The Russian Germans are especially important in the development of the Great Plains area. They revolutionized wheat production in the southern plains through the introduction of Turkey Red wheat, a hard winter wheat especially suited to the Great Plains environment. Unusually thrifty, hardworking, and persistent, the Russian Germans succeeded agriculturally where others faltered. They provided a substantial reservoir of labor for the construction and maintenance of railroads in the West, and in the early twentieth century, their labor, organized chiefly on a family basis, made sugar beet culture a success in Nebraska and Colorado.[17]

[15] Richard Sallet, trans. by LaVern J. Rippley and Armand Bauer, *Russian-German Settlements in the United States* (Fargo, North Dakota, [1931] 1974).

[16] Hattie Plum Williams, *A Social Study of the Russian German* (Lincoln, 1916); Mary Eloise Johannes, *A Study of the Russian-German Settlements in Ellis County, Kansas* (Washington, 1946); Francis S. Laing, "German-Russian Settlements in Ellis County, Kansas," *Kansas State Historical Collections*, 11 (1909–10), 489–528; Alberta Pantle, "Settlement of the Krimmer Mennonite Brethren at Gnadenau, Marion County," *Kansas Historical Quarterly*, 13 (February 1945), 259–85; James R. Griess, *The German-Russians: Those Who Came to Sutton* (Hastings, Nebraska, 1968); Albert J. Petersen, Jr., "German-Russian Catholic Colonization in Western Kansas: A Settlement Geography" (Ph.D. diss., Louisiana State University, 1970); Norman E. Saul, "The Migration of the Russian-Germans to Kansas," *Kansas Historical Quarterly*, 40 (Spring 1974), 38–62.

[17] Roger Welsch, "Germans from Russia: A Place to Call Home," in *Broken Hoops and Plains People* ([Lincoln] University of Nebraska Curriculum Development Center, 1976), 193–235.

Their descendants remain on the plains today and constitute a major element contributing to contemporary Great Plains conservatism.

Other German-speaking immigrants on the plains were the Swiss, Austrians, and Alsatians. These groups were rarely numerous enough to form strong colonies of their own. Consequently, the Swiss Germans usually merged with Germans from Germany, although identifiable colonies developed in Platte County, Nebraska, and near New Basel, Bern, and Gridley, in Kansas.[18] Austrians are usually difficult to identify. While some were clearly German-speaking people from various parts of the Austrian Empire, others were actually Polish, Slovenian, or other non-German groups. Although Alsace became part of Germany in 1871, Alsatians often indicated France as the country of their birth. Finally, it should be noted that some of the persons classified as English-speaking Canadians in the census data were actually the children of German emigrants who lived in Canada for some years before moving on to the United States.

The second largest group of immigrants on the Great Plains is formed by a combination of English, Scottish, Welsh, Irish, and English Canadians. The most numerous group of English-speaking people were the Irish. Inveterate haters of the English, they continued to stream to America in the decades after the devastating famines of the mid-nineteenth century. Desperately poor and lacking education and craft skills, the Irish did not ordinarily possess the means to establish themselves on farms. Hence, they tended to congregate in the towns, where they worked as common laborers and as railroad workers. Nevertheless, Irish farm colonies were not unknown on the Great Plains. Perhaps the best known is O'Neill, Nebraska, and the several communities founded by the Irish Catholic Colonization Society during the 1870s in Greeley County, Nebraska.[19] An undetermined number of persons listed as Irish-born in the census manuscripts were Scotch-Irish Protestants from northern Ireland.

The English were spread with remarkable evenness across the Great Plains states, although they clearly preferred the towns to the countryside. Not handicapped by their language, religion, or culture, they were able to

---

[18] Carman, *Foreign-Language Units of Kansas*, 70.

[19] There are almost no studies of Irish immigrants on the Great Plains. They must therefore be approached through colonization histories, e.g. Henthorne or Shannon, church histories, e.g. Casper (see above), or local histories, such as the centennial history of O'Neill, Nebraska: Burns E. McCulloh, *A Piece of Emerald* (O'Neill: Miles Publishing Co., 1974). The best treatment of Irish colonization in Nebraska is in Casper's third volume, *Catholic Chapters in Nebraska Immigration*, 3–97.

fit into American society with relative ease, even though many were poor farm laborers, with little education, who had been victimized by technological changes in Britain. Other English immigrants prospered as craftsmen, merchants, and professionals; hence, proportionately fewer pursued farming, compared to the Germans or Scandinavians.

A few English colonies were founded on the Great Plains. Runnymede in Kansas was intended by its founder in 1887 to be a place to convert the second sons of English gentry into sober, industrious farmers. But the young men were more interested in gambling, racing, hunting, drinking, and wenching than in farming, and they abandoned the place when their remittances from home were cut off. Victoria, Kansas, was only slightly more successful. Also intended for young British gentlemen, this venture was established by a Scotsman who introduced Aberdeen Angus cattle to the Great Plains.[20]

The experiences of Scots on the Great Plains very closely duplicate those of the English. A few colonies developed here and there, but the Scots rarely congregated in identifiable groups. By contrast, the Welsh were somewhat more inclined to cluster together. Most numerous in Kansas, they settled in substantial numbers in Emporia. Most Welsh communities in Kansas, Nebraska, and South Dakota were organized around Presbyterian or Congregational churches, many of which offered services in the Welsh language. Limited by their small numbers, very few Welsh communities on the Great Plains survived to the end of the nineteenth century.[21]

---

[20] The causes and promotion of English emigration are treated by Oscar Winther in several articles: "English Migration to the American West," *Huntington Library Quarterly*, 27 (February 1964), 159–73; "The English in Nebraska, 1857–1880," *Nebraska History*, 48 (Autumn 1967), 209–24; and "The English and Kansas, 1865–1890," in John Clark, ed., *The Frontier Challenge: Responses to the Trans-Mississippi West* (Lawrence, 1971), 235–73. In the same vein is Ronald A. Wells, "Migration and the Image of Nebraska in England," *Nebraska History*, 54 (Fall 1973), 475–91. See also William J. Chapman, "The Wakefield Colony," *Transactions of the Kansas State Historical Society*, 10 (1907–8), 485–533; Nyle H. Miller, ed., "An English Runnymede in Kansas," *Kansas Historical Quarterly*, 41 (Spring and Summer 1975), 22–62 and 183–224; Blanche M. Taylor, "The English Colonies in Kansas, 1870–1895," *Historical Magazine of the Protestant Episcopal Church*, 41 (March 1972), 17–35.

[21] Richard L. Guenther, "A History of the Welsh Community of Carroll, Nebraska," *Nebraska History*, 46 (September 1965), 209–24; Carolyn B. Berneking, "The Welsh Settlers of Emporia: A Cultural History," *Kansas Historical Quarterly*, 37 (Autumn 1971), 269–80.

Of the Scandinavian people in the Great Plains states, the Norwegians are the most numerous. At least half settled in North Dakota, where they are by far the largest single ethnic group. Most common in the eastern counties of the Red River Valley, they are also numerous in the north and west, surrounding the Russian Germans who occupy the south central part of the state. They were predominantly farmers and have adhered strongly to Lutheranism. More homogeneous than their cultural cousins, the Germans, they were, nevertheless, often divided by disputes between pietists and the orthodox within their churches. Their immigrant culture, however, conditioned them to favor cooperative economic and political ventures. Thus, their attitudes help to explain the curious mixture of conservatism and radical progressivism that has been characteristic of North Dakota politics in the twentieth century.

In South Dakota, the Norwegians have been outnumbered only by the more widely distributed Germans. Concentrated in the eastern counties of the state, they have not been numerous on the Great Plains proper. A few are found in the northeastern part of Nebraska, but they are almost entirely absent from the southern plains states.[22]

The Swedes constitute the second largest Scandinavian group. Swedish settlers found Nebraska most to their liking. Already in the 1860s, they formed strong rural enclaves in the eastern part of the state, and by the 1880s, large colonies had been established on the plains, most notably in Polk and Phelps counties. Like the Norwegians, Swedes tended to cluster according to the province of their origin. Although they were more secular-minded than the Norwegians, the Swedes also tended to divide among the several churches, with the pietists favoring the Mission Covenant, Baptist, and Methodist churches, and the orthodox retaining their traditional adherence to the Lutheran church. In Kansas, the Swedes founded a very substantial colony in McPherson County on the eastern edge of the Great Plains, immediately northwest of the great Russian German Mennonite region. Buttressed by a full complement of ethnic institutions, including Bethany College of Lindsborg, the Swedes have been remarkably successful in politics, much like the Norwegians in North

[22] Carlton Qualey, *Norwegian Settlement in the United States* (New York, [1938] 1970) surveys settlement patterns and introduces pre-1938 bibliography. Since then little has been published, but see Aagot Raaen, *Grass of the Earth: Immigrant Life in the Dakota Country* (Northfield, Minnesota, 1950); D. Jerome Tweton, "Three Scandinavian Immigrants in the American West," *Nebraska History*, 45 (September 1964), 253–64; and church histories, such as Eugene C. Nelson, *The Lutheran Church among Norwegian Americans* (Minneapolis, 1960).

Dakota. In the Dakotas the Swedes have constituted a substantial minority, though dominated by the more numerous Norwegians.[23]

Like the Norwegians, the Danes have avoided the southern plains. They are most prominent in Nebraska, where at Blair on the Missouri River they established the only four-year Danish college in the United States. Their most substantial concentration on the Great Plains is located at Dannebrog in Howard County, Nebraska, and in rural Kearney County, Nebraska.[24]

Of the many Slavic ethnic groups, only two, the Czechs and the Poles, settled in significant numbers on the Great Plains. Although isolated individuals of both groups arrived before the Civil War, most Czechs and Poles entered the country after the Great Plains region was settled. Hence, in the United States, the Slavic ethnic peoples are preeminently urban. Yet some of them were led, chiefly through church agencies, to the West. Of the two groups, the Czechs (Bohemians) were much more numerous.

More Czechs settled in Nebraska than in all other states of the Great Plains combined. The majority of the Nebraska Czechs settled in five counties (Douglas, Saunders, Butler, Colfax, and Saline), all of which are located east of the Great Plains proper. Yet they formed substantial minorities in several counties farther west, notably Boyd, Howard, and Valley. Despite Old World antagonisms, Czechs frequently tended to settle in places where Germans had gone first; they often understood the German language and their way of life was similar. On the plains most Czechs engaged in agriculture.

Although Czechs were traditionally members of the Catholic church, they were unusual in that a large percentage were outspokenly rationalist,

---

[23] Helge Nelson, *The Swedes and Swedish Settlements in North America* (Lund, Sweden, 1943) emphasizes geographic distribution. O. Fritiof Ander, *The Cultural Heritage of the Swedish Immigration* (Rock Island, Illinois, 1956) offers a good bibliography. Kansas Swedes have received much attention. See the works of Emory Lindquist, *Smoky Valley People: A History of Lindsborg, Kansas* (1953); *Vision for a Valley* (1970); "The Swedish Immigrant and Life in Kansas," *Kansas Historical Quarterly*, 29 (Spring 1963), 1–24, and "Swedes in Kansas before the Civil War," ibid., 19 (August 1951), 254–68. Ruth Billdt, *Pioneer Swedish-American Culture in Central Kansas* is useful, but see J. Iverne Dowie, *Prairie Grass Dividing* (Rock Island, Illinois, 1959) and "Unge Man, Ga Westerhut," *Nebraska History*, 54 (Spring 1973), 47–63.

[24] William E. Christensen, *Saga of the Tower: A History of Dana College and Trinity Seminary* (Blair, Nebraska, 1959); Alfred C. Nielsen, *Life in an American Denmark* (Des Moines, 1962); Kenneth E. Miller, "Danish Socialism and the Kansas Prairie," *Kansas Historical Quarterly*, 38 (Summer 1972), 156–68.

freethinking, or agnostic. This anticlerical element revered the memory of the great pre-Reformation figure John Hus as the father of Czech nationalism. Such sentiments were transferred to America, where a system of fraternal lodges was developed that served many of the functions normally provided by the church, especially in rural settings. Czechs from Moravia were commonly more firmly attached to the Catholic church than those from Bohemia.[25]

The Poles were the only other Slavic people to settle in significant numbers on the Great Plains. Except for their much smaller numbers, Polish distribution and occupations were similar to those of the Czechs. While most Polish immigrants settled in the industrial cities of the East and Midwest, a few engaged in farming as far west as the Great Plains. As with the Czechs, the Nebraska Poles outnumbered those of all other Great Plains states combined, not including Texas. The majority were brought to Nebraska by a church-related colonization program during the 1880s that sought to remove Polish immigrants from the coal fields of Pennsylvania and other eastern centers of industrial activity to a rural society where, it was believed, they could more easily succeed in a material way and at the same time retain their ethnic language and customs. Except for the sizable colony in Omaha, most Nebraska Poles settled on farms in Platte County and on the eastern limits of the Sandhills in Howard and Sherman counties. Strongly Catholic in their religion, they settled close to Czechs, Germans, and Irish immigrants of the same faith. The Platte County Poles, who named their community Tarnov, were from Austrian Poland, while those in Howard and Sherman counties emigrated from German Poland.[26]

The Jews were one of the most distinctive, though numerically less significant, ethnoreligious groups to enter the Great Plains region, coming first from Germany and later from Russia. Two very different kinds of settlement occurred. The first consisted of isolated individuals, usually of

[25] F. J. Swehla, "Bohemians in Central Kansas," *Kansas Historical Collections,* 13 (1913–14), 469–512; Rose Rosický, *A History of the Czechs (Bohemians) in Nebraska* (Omaha, 1929); Robert I. Kutak, *The Story of a Bohemian-American Village* (New York, [1933] 1970) treats Milligan, Nebraska; Russell W. Lynch, "Czech Farmers in Oklahoma," *Department of Geography Bulletin,* 39 (Stillwater: Oklahoma A and M, 1942); Vladimir Kucera and Alfred Novacek, eds., *Czechs and Nebraska* (Ord, Nebraska, 1967); Joseph G. Svoboda, "Czechs: The Love of Liberty," in *Broken Hoops and Plains People,* 153–90.

[26] Poles are treated extensively in Casper, *Catholic Chapters in Nebraska Immigration,* 143–89; Meroe J. Owens, "John Barzynski, Land Agent," *Nebraska History,* 36 (June 1955), 81–91.

German origin, who served isolated rural settlers as itinerant merchants. Gradually, those who were successful in such ventures chose a town in which to reside permanently; there they often operated clothing stores and were rapidly assimilated into small-town society. If they retained strong Jewish religious values, they were likely to migrate later, when their children began to mature, to larger cities where they expected to find a community of persons who shared their beliefs.

The second type of Jewish settlement on the Great Plains occurred chiefly in the 1880s and 1890s when established German Jewish organizations sought to locate incoming Russian Jews, often impoverished and illiterate, in agricultural colonies in various parts of the country. Because much land was still available for purchase or homesteading on the Great Plains, the region inevitably attracted a dozen or so of these communal agricultural settlements, none of which lasted for more than a few years. The best known of these communities was Beersheba, located thirty-five miles northwest of Dodge City, Kansas. Sponsored by the Hebrew Union Agricultural Society of Cincinnati, this colony consisted of about twenty families. Although its failure may be attributed to drought, poor land, ignorance of farming methods, and inadequate financial support, most startling was the refusal of its sponsors to plan appropriately or to adjust to environmental conditions as they actually existed on the plains.[27]

Other similar colonies were established elsewhere in western Kansas and in the Dakotas. After several years the colonists in every instance drifted to larger cities. Omaha, for example, received several families that deserted the Painted Woods colony near Devils Lake, North Dakota. As late as 1908 another Jewish colony was founded, this one in the midst of the Sandhills in Cherry County, Nebraska, where fourteen young families homesteaded land under the terms of the Kinkaid Act of 1904, which permitted farms up to 640 acres instead of the inadequate 160 acres of the original Homestead Act. Most of these families engaged in stock raising and remained long enough (five years) to acquire title to the land. By 1915 all had departed.[28]

[27] For general historiographical purposes see Robert E. Levinson, "American Jews in the West," *Western Historical Quarterly*, V (July 1974), 285–94. See also Leo Shpall, "Jewish Agricultural Colonies in the United States," *Agricultural History*, 24 (July 1950), 120–46, and Elbert L. Sapinsley, "Jewish Agricultural Colonies in the West: The Kansas Example," *Western States Jewish Historical Quarterly*, 3 (April 1971); A. James Rudin, "Beersheba, Kansas: 'God's Pure Air on Government Land'," *Kansas Historical Quarterly*, 24 (Autumn 1968), 282–98.

[28] Ella Fleischman Auerbach, "A Record of the Jewish Settlement in Nebraska" (typescript, Nebraska State Historical Society, 1927); Carol Gendler, "The Jews of

Rural and small-town concentrations of French Canadians grew in several areas. The largest number settled in North Dakota south of the Canadian border. A cluster of more than a hundred persons also developed around Campbell, Nebraska. Most had come west after living a short time near Kankakee, Illinois. A similar, larger enclave of Canadians developed seventy-five miles southeast in Concordia, Kansas. All were firmly attached to the Catholic church.

Two basic elements may be distinguished among the Chicanos of the Great Plains. One major element of the population of New Mexico consists of persons sometimes called Hispanos—members of an ethnic group that has resulted from the intermarriage of Indians and Spanish since 1600. From Santa Fe, the center of the Hispano area, these people spread eastward and northward onto the Great Plains in the nineteenth century. By 1870 they occupied much of the upper reaches of both the Pecos and Canadian rivers and the area east of the Sangre de Cristo Mountains north to tributaries of the Arkansas. Today they constitute as much as 40 percent of the population of the counties in these parts of New Mexico and Colorado. Thus, Hispanos must be considered as among the original and numerically dominant people in this part of the southern Great Plains. When members of this group migrated to work in the fields of Kansas and Nebraska, they were in a relationship akin to that of the blacks who moved to the plains from another part of the country. On the other hand, most of the so-called Chicanos on the Great Plains have been Mexicans rather than New Mexicans. They must be classified as foreign-born persons; their status technically resembles that of Canadian immigrants.

Movement of settlers from Mexico onto the central and northern Great Plains areas is a phenomenon only of the past fifty years. Many persons were propelled northward by the suffering and confusion of the Mexican Revolution after 1910. After World War I, Chicanos or Mexican-Americans gradually replaced Russian Germans in the sugar beet fields as migrant workers. They have also worked extensively in meat packing and in railroad construction and maintenance. Inevitably, a few have remained as permanent residents of such communities as Scottsbluff and Grand Island, Nebraska, and Dodge City, Garden City, and

Omaha—The First Sixty Years," *Western States Jewish Historical Quarterly,* 5 (April and July 1973) and 6 (January, April, and July 1974); Lois Fields Schwartz, "Early Jewish Agricultural Colonies in North Dakota," *North Dakota History,* 32 (October 1965), 217–32.

Wichita, Kansas. Generally, the Mexican-Americans have been highly retentive of their language and culture, a trait intensified by decades of discrimination, poverty, and inadequate education.[29]

Although blacks have been found on the Great Plains from the earliest penetration of the region, they never constituted a numerically large element of the population in the nineteenth century. Before the Civil War, blacks were to be found among the Cherokee and Creek Indians of Oklahoma, and some were slaves. About seventy-five were counted in Nebraska Territory in 1860, of whom a half dozen were slaves of army officers stationed at Fort Kearny; the remainder lived along the Missouri River, east of the Great Plains. During the postwar period, blacks could often be found as drovers or cooks in the outfits that brought Texas cattle to Kansas and Nebraska railroads. It is commonly estimated that blacks accounted for about five thousand of the thirty-five thousand men engaged in driving cattle from Texas. While most of these men returned to the South, a few remained as ranch hands on the central and northern Great Plains. They suffered less discrimination in this occupation than in most that were available to blacks at that time, and while they could rise to the prestigious post of cook, they could never become foremen or trail bosses. Similarly, blacks were to be found as cooks and deckhands on the steamboats of the Upper Missouri River and later as porters on passenger trains crossing the plains. Generally, they were burdened with the most menial of tasks and were regularly denied any position of authority over white men. Black women also occasionally found employment in frontier plains communities as servants and laundresses. The circumstances of employment in each instance militated against family life and permanent residence. Blacks were usually exploited by the society rather than allowed to be an integral part of society, even on a segregated basis.[30]

[29] An extensive bibliography on Spanish-speaking groups in the United States has developed during the past decade. Like the classic accounts by Carey McWilliams, *North from Mexico: The Spanish-speaking People of the United States* (New York, [1949] 1968) and Manuel Gamio, *Mexican Immigration to the United States* (New York, [1930] 1971), recent studies treat the Great Plains region only incidentally. A useful guide to recent research is Juan Gómez-Quiñones and Luis Leobardo Arroyo, "On the State of Chicano History," *Western Historical Quarterly*, VII (April 1976), 155–85. It includes references to other historiographical and bibliographical materials. Ralph Grajeda, "Chicanos: The Mestizo Heritage," in *Broken Hoops and Plains People*, 47–98, surveys the Chicano presence in Nebraska.

[30] A full treatment is to be found in W. Sherman Savage, *Blacks in the West* (Westport, Connecticut, 1976), but see also Kenneth Porter, *The Negro on the American Frontier* (New York, 1970) and Philip Durham and Everett L. Jones, *The Negro*

So it was also with the famed "Buffalo soldiers" of the Ninth and Tenth Cavalry and the Twenty-fourth and Twenty-fifth Infantry divisions, which, throughout the last decades of the nineteenth century, were stationed at dreary, distant, isolated posts on the Great Plains and in the mountain and desert country of the Southwest. Bringing law and order to the frontier, they pursued Indians who left their reservations and guarded railroad construction crews, survey parties, and stagecoaches. Often not well treated by the army itself, these black soldiers frequently suffered from the hostility of the very people they protected. Indeed, they were stationed on the Great Plains frontier precisely because it was sparsely populated and hence instances of racial conflict could be kept at a minimum.[31]

The first substantial effort to provide blacks with a permanent place on the plains came in 1879, when many thousands of former slaves journeyed from the South to a new "promised land" in Kansas. Perhaps as many as 40,000 Exodusters, as they were called, made their way up the Mississippi and Missouri rivers or trekked across Oklahoma, but a much smaller number made it to the high plains of western Kansas. The most famous colony of black homesteaders was established at Nicodemus in Graham County, which reached a peak population of 595 in 1910. Most blacks found employment in the cities and towns of Kansas, while others, broken and discouraged, returned to the South. By 1900, the black population of Kansas exceeded 50,000. Farther north in Nebraska, where a few black homesteaders also survived, there were only 6,000 blacks, mostly concentrated in Omaha. In the Dakotas, blacks constituted less than one-tenth of one percent of the population at the end of the nineteenth century. Oklahoma Territory attracted large numbers of blacks fleeing oppression in southern states after it was opened to settlement about 1890. They found the same caste relationships there as existed in the South, however, and began to isolate themselves in all-black communities. Between 1890 and 1910, approximately twenty-five black communities, such as Langston and Boley, were formed, as Oklahoma's black population

---

*Cowboys* (New York, 1965). William L. Katz, *The Black West* (rev. ed., Garden City, New York, 1973) offers excellent pictures.

[31] William H. Leckie, *The Buffalo Soldiers: A Narrative of the Negro Cavalry in the West* (Norman, 1967); Arlen Fowler, *The Black Infantry in the West, 1869–1891* (Westport, Connecticut, 1971). Jack Foner, *Blacks in the Military in American History* (New York, 1974) places the buffalo soldier in a larger perspective.

increased to 137,000 persons. Most were located in the eastern half of the state.[32]

In some communities of the Great Plains, the highest black population was attained in 1890, a year that came at the end of a prosperity cycle. For wealthy families in prosperous cities on the plains, such as Hastings, Grand Island, or North Platte, the employment of Negro house servants had become a mode of ostentatious display. The subsequent depression of the 1890s rendered such status symbols too expensive, and large numbers of the blacks thereupon left for points east.

In order to succeed in American society it was necessary for the immigrants to conform to certain basic standards of behavior. Old World standards of conduct sometimes served poorly in the new environment. It was particularly distressing for the newcomer to find that his dress, speech, and mannerisms were often derided or ridiculed. He had to accommodate his behavior to dominant patterns and he had to learn enough English to get along. Many newcomers speedily learned to participate freely and fully on many levels of American life.[33]

Accommodation of American norms depended on a wide range of variables. The most important factor was personal adaptation. The speed with which a person adjusted reflected individual attitudes and psychological needs. For one person, the consolations of orthodox religion were paramount; for another, economic security could be primary. For one immigrant, living in the midst of an ethnic enclave could be a psychological necessity; for another, it could be a hindrance to economic success. In general the rate of assimilation, of being absorbed into American society, was related directly to the number and quality of interpersonal contacts the immigrant had with persons of the host culture. Thus, if a person lived in the midst of an isolated farming community of Czechs, for example, days and sometimes weeks could pass in which the immigrant would

---

[32] Nell Painter, *The Exodusters* (New York, 1976) treats chiefly the causes of the emigration. See also Glen Schwendemann, "Nicodemus: Negro Haven on the Solomon," *Kansas Historical Quarterly*, 24 (Spring 1968), 10–31, and Mozell C. Hill, "The All-Negro Communities of Oklahoma," *Journal of Negro History*, 21 (July 1946). For an example of a black pioneer who experienced notable success on the Great Plains, see Robert Anderson, *From Slavery to Affluence: Memoirs of Robert Anderson, Ex-Slave* (Hemingford, Nebraska, 1927).

[33] I have discussed the problem of assimilation more extensively in *Immigrants and Politics*, 33–52. See also my "German Immigrants and the Churches in Nebraska," *Mid-America*, 50 (April 1968), 116–30.

have no communication with persons outside his family or ethnic group. Often the larger the ethnic community was, the slower was the rate of assimilation of its members. The effectiveness of ethnic institutions was also important. The church may have been the only ethnic institution in a given immigrant settlement, but it could so dominate an immigrant's life that he had few meaningful contacts with members of the host society. For example, assimilation was usually very slow in Mennonite and especially in Hutterite colonies in Kansas, South Dakota, and Montana. Furthermore, residents of polyglot communities tended to assimilate more quickly than those who lived in distinctively ethnic communities. Lack of uniformity in language and customs hastened the adoption of dominant American patterns. Other variables include education and economic success. Prosperity, often accompanied by a good education, usually meant rapid assimilation. Rate of immigration into an area was also important. If a large number of immigrants entered a community within a short period of time, the likelihood of exciting nativist fears was increased. Finally, the more mobile an immigrant was, the more rapid was his accommodation to American standards.

If the above generalizations are correct, it is apparent that, in order to understand the importance of ethnic settlers on the Great Plains, the mobility and persistence of ethnic groups and their marriage and family patterns must be studied in comparison to members of the dominant, native-born society. Yet very few studies of this kind exist. Since the Great Plains has always been an area of very low population, the numbers of any immigrant group in a given locality on the plains have necessarily been small by comparison to ethnic enclaves in urban and rural places in the East. Moreover, their numbers have ordinarily been too small to create or sustain many ethnic institutions. Hence, one might assume that assimilation was comparatively rapid on the Great Plains, despite the isolation that was common to many immigrants. Ordinarily more numerous in the countryside than in the towns, individual ethnic groups rarely were in a position to dominate Great Plains cities. Swedish dominance of Lindsborg, Kansas, for example, was an exception not often matched on the plains.

It is clear also that ethnic groups have been less mobile than dominant elements of the population. While we know that there was an outmigration from rural ethnic enclaves on the Great Plains, it is apparent that other members of the same ethnic group took the places of those who left. If Norwegians were the first to settle in a certain locality, their descendants may be found there today. The same is true of Swedes, Danes, Germans, Czechs, and Poles. Persistence was less common, however, among the English-speaking immigrant groups, the Jews, and the blacks. This suggests that persistence, as a dimension of assimilation, is related to the degree of difference that exists between the immigrants' culture and that of the receiving society.

The behavior patterns and value systems brought to America by the English, Scottish, and Welsh differed only slightly from what had become characteristic of Americans by the time the Great Plains area was settled. Even their Protestantism corresponded closely to the pietism typical of American religion. So easily were they able to slip into the American social structure that the development of ethnic subsocieties was largely superfluous. Hence, their mobility patterns seem to have been much like those of old-stock Americans. The maintenance of ethnic institutions among them was more an exercise in sentimentality than in social necessity.

The Irish were often significantly different from other English-speaking immigrants. They had the great advantage of speaking English, but in other respects, especially in their adherence to Catholicism, they were distinctive. Ethnic awareness among the Irish was also the product of their centuries-long struggle against English dominance in their homeland. Like the English, they rarely formed colonies on the plains but instead filtered into the area as individuals or as families. Much more conscious of their ethnicity than the English, they remain a cultural force in communities such as O'Neill and Greeley, Nebraska, where they were dominant during the frontier period.

Of the non-English-speaking ethnic groups, the Scandinavians usually assimilated the most rapidly. Even though they often prized their ethnic culture, they learned English rapidly and adapted quickly to the standards of social and political behavior established by the so-called WASPs (White Anglo-Saxon Protestants). Although their Lutheranism was imported, its moralism resembled American pietism. The Scandinavians were perceived as especially desirable immigrants. They quickly gained entrée to economic and political structures and were admitted to more exclusive social groups as the second generation intermarried with members of the established society. Norwegians, in contrast to their Swedish and Danish cousins, were somewhat more retentive of their ethnic culture and often resisted language transition, even as they retained adherence to their Lutheran churches. While the Scandinavians ordinarily assimilated rapidly, they have remained remarkably persistent in those parts of the Great Plains where their fathers first settled in the nineteenth century.

The Germans were usually unable to sustain ethnic institutions other than their Lutheran, Catholic, Mennonite, and Evangelical churches because of their widespread distribution throughout most parts of the Great Plains. An exception to this could be found in cities where they were unusually numerous, such as Grand Island or Hastings, Nebraska. German Lutherans, who were orthodox and ritualistic rather than pietistic, systematically used ethnic culture as a means to bolster religious commitment. One-room Lutheran parochial schools, with the pastor as teacher, were not uncommon in German settlements on the plains by the 1890s. By contrast, purely German Catholic parishes were rare, except among the Russian Germans. German Mennonites consciously developed isolated communities as a means of retaining religious purity and thus they were the slowest of the German groups to assimilate.

While the Germans were often cultural chauvinists, believing that their culture was superior to all others, the Germans from Russia were more conscious of themselves as an ethnic group that differed noticeably from the rest of the population. Cut off from the sources of German culture during their long residence in Russia, they were accustomed to stubbornly retaining their ethnic ways in an alien environment. Their women continued to wear their long black dresses and their shawls, the men, their old-world caps and coats. They were derided as "Rooshans" by the "Americans," but they gathered strength from each other, knowing that full social acceptance by established society was distant, if not unattainable, within their lifetimes. Inevitably, Russian German determination, persistence, and single-minded stubbornness became legendary. It is not surprising, therefore, that today the Germans from Russia are the only German group on the Great Plains who actively and consciously cultivate their ethnic heritage.

The Czechs and Poles were much like the Germans from Russia in this respect. Significantly different from the host society in language, religion, folkways, and culture, they have retained a sense of ethnic identity that immigrant groups such as Germans and Scandinavians have lost. Like the Irish in their historic struggle against the English, the Czechs resisted Austrian and German political and cultural imperialism for five hundred years. Inevitably, this heritage has intensified their sense of ethnic nationalism. The Czechs managed to retain a high level of cohesion while participating in significant ways in the economic and political life of the larger society.

Of all the European ethnic groups that attempted to establish enclaves on the Great Plains, the Jews differed the most from the dominant Anglo-American Protestant culture. Hobbled by poverty and ignorance of farming methods, speaking a strange tongue, significantly different in custom and manner, non-Christian in religion, their ethnoreligious consciousness intensified by centuries of Christian persecution, the Russian Jewish colonists could have succeeded only if their numbers had been greatly augmented. Had they settled in groups large enough to establish and maintain the strong ethnic institutions their differentness required for survival, they would have evoked a hostility comparable perhaps to that suffered by the Mormons in Nauvoo, Illinois. At the same time, it is unlikely that the physical environment of the Great Plains would have permitted the requisite concentration of population necessary for ethnic survival.

Similarly, the blacks on the plains, except those in Oklahoma, could not achieve the "critical mass" necessary for the survival of their agricultural communities. Most blacks who remained on the plains found homes in urban places where small enclaves could be formed. Isolated individuals or families could be found here or there, and some were remarkably well integrated into white society. But they were exceptions to the usual pattern.

From the point of view of the host society, most European ethnic groups were eagerly welcomed to help populate the Great Plains states. Old-stock Americans who held positions of leadership were in most instances kind, helpful, and generous to the newcomers. Ethnic conflict and conscious acts of discrimination were rare on the plains, in contrast to the ethnic conflicts often afflicting industrial and mining communities in the East and parts of the mountainous West. Because cultural differences were ordinarily not great, tolerance was easy; the assimilation process was allowed to proceed at its own pace. Instances of ethnic-based friction and sometimes open conflict were usually glossed over or ignored. Yet there was no question that dominant elements in the society expected the immigrants ultimately to conform fully to Anglo-American standards of behavior and attitude.

Despite the general goodwill that prevailed, the typical old-stock American had scant appreciation of the problems experienced by the immigrants—the psychological toll exacted by moving from one cultural milieu to another, the sensitivity of the newcomer to ridicule, the internal conflicts that often divided ethnic communities, or the generational differences that frequently lacerated family relationships. Nor could the typical old-stock American understand how and why ethnic differences accounted for variations in political behavior.

Sharp differences existed in the voting patterns of ethnic groups on the plains. The English, Scots, and Welsh tended to vote Republican, as did Scandinavian groups. The Irish, Czechs, and Poles were just as likely to vote Democratic. The heterogeneous Germans were harder to classify. While German Catholics could be expected to return solid Democratic majorities, German Protestants were likely to prefer Republican candidates, unless they were German Lutherans, as many were. The attitudes of all groups were rooted in ethnic culture and religion, and startling variations distinguished the several groups and subgroups. Issues that touched immigrant interests usually related to ethnic culture, such as prohibition, woman suffrage, Sabbatarian legislation, and regulation of parochial schools. Ethnic defenders of the Democratic party perceived their organization as the champion of the largest measure of personal liberty consistent with law and order. The Republican party, described by its defenders as the political vehicle of progress and reform, was understood by its ethnic enemies as an agency of cultural imperialism designed to impose Anglo-American patterns upon unwilling immigrant peoples. Inevitably, ethnic groups whose cultural values and attitudes resembled those of the dominant Anglo-Americans preferred the Republican party, as did individual immigrants who were psychologically attuned to a rapid assimilation; other groups, more pluralistic in their attitudes, recognized parallels between their values and the ideals traditionally expressed by the Democrats.

By the end of the nineteenth century, the Great Plains had been largely settled. Uninhabited pockets remained in western parts of the Dakotas and in eastern areas in Montana and Wyoming. These were rapidly filled before World War I, and many of the settlers, as earlier, were European immigrants. Foreign languages continued to be used in almost all of the ethnic enclaves on the plains from Columbus, Nebraska, to Fort Collins, Colorado, and from Prague, Oklahoma, to Strassburg, North Dakota. Foreign-language newspapers and periodicals, especially church-related publications produced in eastern cities, continued to be read by large numbers of Germans, Swedes, Norwegians, and Czechs. Ethnic churches and sometimes schools flourished, and even a few ethnic colleges had been founded. Here and there, banks, insurance companies, restaurants, and shops catered to ethnic clienteles. Ethnic politics, though never really approved of by the old-stock Americans, was taken for granted in most quarters. In all parts of the Great Plains there were monuments ranging from transcontinental railroads to fields of winter wheat that testified to the industry, perseverance, and ingenuity of settlers from many lands.

# The Irish Experience in Ontario: Rural or Urban?

Murray W. Nicolson

*Résumé/Abstract*

*Ce texte constitue une réaction face à plusieurs interprétations nouvelles qui, si elles sont acceptées, risquent de modifier la perception historique du rôle joué par les centres urbains dans l'adaptation des Irlandais catholiques en Ontario au 19e siècle. Donald Akenson, un historien du monde rural, estime que l'expérience canadienne des immigrants irlandais diffère de l'expérience américaine. Il prétend que la prédominance des Protestants à l'intérieur du groupe national, de même que les bases rurales de la communauté irlandaise, empêchent la formation de ghettos urbains et permettent une relative liberté d'action en terme de mobilité sociale. Par comparaison les Irlando-Américains, majoritairement catholiques, sont concentrés dans les ghettos urbains. De surcroît, les nouveaux historiens du Travail affirment que la montée des Chevaliers du Travail suscite un rapprochement entre les Orangistes et les Irlandais catholiques de Toronto qui, en dépit de leur haine ancestrale, s'attachent à former une culture ouvrière commune. Cette interprétation présuppose que la culture irlandaise catholique constitue une valeur bien faible pour être rejetée si facilement.*

*L'auteur estime qu'aucune de ces interprétations n'est fondée. Dans les ghettos torontois, la fusion de la culture paysanne irlandaise avec un catholicisme traditionnel, produit un nouveau courant urbain ethno-religieux — le catholicisme irlandais d'obédience tridentine. Cette culture se propage de la ville vers l'arrière-pays et, grâce aux réseaux de la métropole, d'un bout à l'autre de l'Ontario. Une société irlandaise repliée sur elle même se constitue, résultant du "privatisme," ceux qui y naissent ne la quittent qu'à leur mort. Les Irlandais catholiques se sont effectivement impliqués dans les organisations ouvrières afin d'améliorer la condition et l'avenir de leurs familles, mais ils ne se sont jamais associés avec leurs ennemis de toujours, les Orangistes, pour développer une nouvelle culture ouvrière.*

*The purpose of this paper is to respond to several new theories which, if accepted, could alter the historical perception of the role played by urban centres in the adjustment of Irish Catholics in nineteenth century Ontario. Donald Akenson, a rural historian, believes that the Canadian experience of Irish immigrants is not comparable to the American one. Akenson contends that the numerical dominance of Protestants within the national group and the rural basis of the Irish community, negated the formation of urban ghettos and allowed for a relative ease in social mobility. In comparison the American Irish were dominantly Catholic urban dwelling and ghettoized. In addition the new labour historians believe that the rise of the Knights of Labor caused the Orange and Catholic Irish in Toronto to resolve their generational hatred and set about to form a common working-class culture. This theory must presume that Irish Catholic culture was of little value to be rejected with such ease.*

*The writer contends that neither theory is valid. In the ghettos of Toronto the fusion of an Irish peasant culture with traditional Catholicism produced a new, urban, ethno-religious vehicle — Irish Tridentine Catholism. This culture, spread from the city to the hinterland and, by means of metropolitan linkage, throughout Ontario. Privatism created a closed Irish society, one they were born into and left when they died. Irish Catholics co-operated in labour organizations for the sake of their family's future, but never shared in the development of a new working-class culture with their old Orange enemies.*

Recently, the importance of the role played by urban centres in the adjustment of Irish Catholics in nineteenth

*Urban History Review/Revue d'histoire urbaine,* Vol. XIV, No. 1 (June/juin 1985)

century Ontario has been questioned. Donald Akenson, the eminent rural historian, believes Ontario's Irish were rurally based and dominantly Protestant. He also suggests that the Catholic Irish were neither ghettoized, not even chiefly urbanized, nor pauperized and that upward mobility was commonplace.[1] The implication is that Oscar Handlin's

"Boston Model"[2] cannot be applied to Canadian urban centres. Why? Because the American Irish were predominantly Catholic, ghettoized urban-dwellers, whose poverty and lack of social mobility made adjustment difficult. In addition, the new labour historians[3] contend that Irish Protestant and Catholic labourers in Toronto merged their identity in the late nineteenth century to form a common, working-class culture.[4] In the United States, Irish Catholics retained their ethno-religious culture within the framework of American unions and often dominated labour organizations.[5] Therefore, it is the purpose of this paper to examine the validity of these new assumptions regarding the Canadian Irish experience and to determine how they compare to more traditional concepts.

Given the expansive literature on the American Irish, it is important to ascertain whether or not the Ontario Irish experience is comparable. There appears to be a general consensus among American historians that the Irish experience in the New World diaspora is closely related to the process known as urbanization.[6] Furthermore, there is little doubt that religion played a role in this particular process. Stephen Thernstrom has aptly stated:

Religion, ideology, cultural traditions — these affected human behaviour in the past and shaped the meaning of the demographic and economic patterns which can be neatly plotted on a map or graph.[7]

Because of the absolute numerical dominance of Catholics within the Irish national unit emigrating to the United States and the rapid assimilation of the Protestant sector into the general Protestant population, American historians traditionally have studied an urban-dwelling Irish peasantry within the definition of its religion — Catholicism. The studies are broad in scope, dealing with social adjustment, poverty, ghettoization and family life.[8] Canadian Irish immigrants were predominantly Protestant who, like their American counterparts, assimilated quickly but also gained a new identity — "Orange Irish." Yet, in Canada, it became traditional to study both Catholic and Protestant groups as an Irish unit. That approach tends to restrict any clear examination of religion as an element in ethnic formation,[9] and makes any attempt at comparison with American studies confusing. However, if the urban-dwelling Irish Catholics in Ontario are examined separately from the Protestant Irish, some similarities emerge with the American experience in urban adjustment, ethnic solidarity, and religious participation and focus. In that context, the "Boston Model" can be utilized as an historical tool. In J.P. Dolan's evaluation, comparative studies are valid; the border between Canada and the United States has made little difference in the overall Irish Catholic experience.[10]

Nevertheless, before any continental consensus for a New World Irish Catholic diaspora can be reached, the Canadian Irish historian must come to terms with the possibility of a dominant, rural-based Irish Catholic population whose cultural influence might well be more important than the ghetto experience of an urban minority. If the historian accepts the theory of "urban as process"[11] wherein the urban environment is not just an incidental factor but an independent variable affecting ethnic groups, then the Irish, as the product of urban adjustment, become a reality. By incorporating the communication linkage implied in the metropolitan theory,[12] which unites urban centres to hinterlands, and expanding this theory to include social, cultural and religious functions[13] as well as those of a commercial nature, then "urban as process" has an extended role in the rural milieu. In other words, if a specific ethnic culture formed in an urban centre, it could be transferred through established communication linkages to the hinterland areas.

Encouraged by Dr. Gilbert Stelter, this author began to construct an urban model for Irish Catholics in Canada, utilizing Toronto as the example of a metropolitan centre. The model was to serve as an alternative to a growing tendency to study the urban Irish as a unit, ignoring the salient differences in culture created by religious differences.[14] In pursuing this task, it seemed the generally accepted assimilationist theory which evolved from Israel Zangwill's play, "The Melting Pot,"[15] (written in 1908) and from Robert Redford's, "Folk Urban Continuum,"[16] was being applied too rigidly. Consequently, this left a negligible Irish contribution to Canadian character. In formulating this model, some concepts utilized were those developed in the field of American Irish studies, particularly by Dennis Clark, Jay P. Dolan and James Sanders.[17] In addition, the work of Kenneth Duncan,[18] (who, almost two decades ago, wrote a valuable article on the Famine Irish in which he described the persistence and reinterpretation of a peasant culture in urban settings) was expanded. And cognizant of the work of John Modell and Lynn H. Lees, my research regarding the Irish urban experience led me to a conclusion similar to theirs:

The annals of American and English cities alike hardly suggest that accommodation was always easy or pleasant for the Irish. And the path of change led them from easy contact with the traditional culture of their homeland. Such distancing was felt by those who migrated, and by those who did not. That an urban Irish culture grew beyond Ireland's borders made a difference to both.[19]

The particularistic culture was ethno-religious in nature, a syncretic vehicle, urban-born and restricted to the Catholic segment of the national group in the world diaspora. In fact, Irish Catholics were the bearers of a peasant culture developed in the rural areas of Ireland. There is some evidence that prior to migration to Canada the Irish peasantry had already begun to adapt its culture to urban living as a transient labour force in the cities of Ireland and England.[20] Transiency blurred the urban or rural reality to the Irish peasant, for it was observed: "In 1834 the Royal Commission on the Poor Laws estimated that there were 2,385,000

38

beggars (including dependents) on the roads of Ireland at least part of the year."[21] There is no estimate of the inter-urban or rural-urban transiency that occurred in Irish or English cities. By the Famine, it would be difficult to ascertain what in Irish peasant culture was not affected by some form of urban process.

Despite what occurred in the Old World, peasant culture in the New World Irish diaspora was reinterpreted in urban settings and fused with traditional Catholicism to produce a new vehicle which sustained the urban survival of a distinctive ethnic group.[22] The new culture became standard in Canadian cities and was transferred through a series of communication linkages to the rural hinterland. In this social process, Irish Catholics blurred the borders of what was clearly urban or rural in Eastern Canada, particularly in Ontario. The Irish participated in the same culture, whether they lived in Cabbagetown, the Albion Hills or Kingston. In other words, ethnic persistence coupled with an urban-based religious institution can reinterpret a specific culture to allow for the emergence of a new, ethno-religious identity. This specific entity can appropriately be labelled "Irish Tridentine Catholicism."[23]

The Irish Catholics who entered Toronto and other Ontario cities during and after the Famine years of 1846-1848 were the bearers of a partially urbanized peasant culture. This peasantry was poverty-stricken, disease-ridden, uneducated, untrained, superstitious and detached from its Church. Nonetheless, it broke the Protestant consensus in Toronto and other Ontario cities. The Irish were regarded as an alien population and were restricted to the worst areas of the city, areas which remained Irish ghettos for decades. Being socially deprived and Catholic, they encountered differential treatment from the charter population in the workplace, public institutions and the courts of law. They received little financial assistance from the city and were perpetually assailed with the cry "a bowl of soup if ye'll change."[24] The use of souperism as a proselytizing tactic for assimilation persisted for decades.[25] Having relied on transiency in Ireland as a means for survival, the immigrants rapidly became a transient labour class of inter-urban, urban-rural nomads. Social mobility was slow; it took generations for any sizeable middle class to form, and when it did, it operated within the confines of a specific Irish society.

Granted, both the city and the Catholic Church, a weak institution in Toronto, were ill-prepared to deal with the social problems introduced by the sudden influx of Famine Irish immigrants in 1847. But in the face of rejection and the pressures exerted by an unsympathetic urban majority, the nominally Catholic Irish turned to what had been their central cultural focus — their Church. By 1851, the Irish Catholics formed one-quarter of Toronto's population and the Church organized quickly to meet the needs of its people. Over a short period of time, there developed a unity of purpose between the institutional church and its Irish laity. The

Irish family was the vehicle through which a religious counter-culture was transmitted. Through the establishment of a number of social institutions and agencies, the Church satisfied the basic needs of its people and gradually began to remodel the Irish community and to assist with the reinterpretation of culture. To counteract the differential treatment and proselytizing tactics the Irish were subjected to, the Church duplicated every public institution in the city, whether it was a home for the aged, poor house, hospital, refuge, training school, orphanage or children's aid society. It also introduced libraries, a savings bank and a burial society to direct the Irish towards means of self-help.[26] Newspapers, benevolent societies and religious organizations helped to create a self-sufficient ethnic community. The separate schools, originally staffed by members of religious orders from France, became Irish schools, perpetuating Irish identity to the extent they were the nurseries for Irish Catholic culture.[27]

As the areas of Irish concentration in the city increased in size and number, the church expanded similarly. Beginning with a single church in Cabbagetown and the Cathedral established before the arrival of the Famine immigrants, there were over a dozen by 1900. And it was from these parish nuclei that priests, religious orders, the St. Vincent de Paul Society and its female cognates went out to aid the poor, sick and aged. The Church stood as the arbitrator of the Irish future in the city; the steeples marked the beginning and end of the journey to work and to school, and the Irishman's last journey in this world. Surrounding the churches were rectories, schools, convents, halls, shabeens, book stores, grocery and dry goods stores — the visible signs of an Irish community. And within those enclaves, the Irish family developed a "Dearcadh," a particularistic viewpoint through which the Irish looked upon themselves, their community, and their relationship with the city and their God.[28]

As the Church became the central focus in Irish family life, the developing system of parishes, social institutions and societies attached to it united the Irish in the city into a cohesive unit. From the constant interaction between the Irish family and the Church, a distinctive culture emerged. Born in Cabbagetown, the water front, Claretown, Irish town and the Junction, it blossomed. And under the ecclesiastical shadow of Toronto, similar parish structures were organized and a communication linkage developed. A common Irish culture was transmitted through the Church's metropolitan system which integrated urban and rural parishes into a common network.[29]

The growth and spread of this particular culture was assisted by the various religious orders of women who established convents in the city and branch houses in rural areas. Postulants for the orders were drawn from both rural and urban areas. The nuns taught in the city's separate schools and founded convent schools which attracted the daughters of the more successful rural dwellers. Many of their students

39

became teachers in the countryside. There was a constant interaction between the laity and members of the religious orders when the sisters travelled into the hinterland to beg for food and supplies to meet the needs of the occupants of their agencies. Similarly, the priests and brothers ran schools in the city to educate teachers and leaders for both rural and urban areas. Country youths came to the city to be trained for the priesthood and returned as pastors of rural churches. Mission, a period of intense religious reflection, was a yearly occurrence in all parishes, and these were under the guidance of specifically trained priests from the city.[30]

There were other important components in the transmission of that culture. The Irish newspapers, printed in the city, were circulated to rural areas and passed from hand-to-hand, with the literate reading to the illiterate. Irish libraries were set up in the city and books were dispersed throughout the hinterland areas. The St. Vincent de Paul Society, whose primary purpose was to serve the poor, established councils in rural parishes which reported to the central council in Toronto. Through its membership, placement was found in Toronto's Catholic social institutions for the orphaned, aged, sick or destitute in the diocese. A whole interlocking set of kinship patterns developed, with relatives in both urban and rural areas. Families and friends gathered together for social events like the important rites of passage, picnics, bazaars and excursions.[31] Within a generation, the urban-born culture was identical in both urban and rural settings and it became an Irish fact in Ontario's history.

Irish Catholic families were alienated in Victorian Toronto's society because of their ethnicity and religion. Therefore it seems plausible to consider ethnicity, religion and family life as variables in any urban society. The new labour history professes to be cultural, but its concept of culture appears narrow and restrictive, and of an empirical Marxist nature. It tends to exclude the value of religion, ethnicity or family as constituting factors in the study of working-class history. Its authors seem to look upon those components as epiphenomenons of underlying class conflicts to be excluded from the study of workers.[32] Why? Could it be that their inclusion might fragment the concept of a unified working-class culture, leaving the dialetic without much substance?

Gregory Kealey and Bryan Palmer suggest that, with the rise of the Knights of Labor, the Orange and Catholic Irish in Toronto resolved their intense religious hatred and set about to formulate a common working-class culture.[33] That assumption implies that Irish Catholics abandoned their peculiar culture, developed in Toronto's ghettos in preference for a new cultural vehicle. At the turn of the century, Abraham Cahon observed that the socialist intellectuals "have underestimated the value of religion to the workers,"[34] a trend which seems current among new labour historians. In John Bodnar's evaluation, "the threat to families and enclaves of abject poverty provided the impetus for

mass labor organizations,"[35] and Tamara Hareven concluded that the family role was active and ongoing in the adaption to industrial society.[36] Yet the new labour historians apparently fail to notice the importance of family in the workers' lives. Considering the poverty and lack of job opportunities among Toronto's Irish Catholics, it seems the responsibility for family protection and survival was a major reason for their entry into the Knights of Labor. Most certainly, they were not in quest of a new culture.

The Orange and Catholic Irish had been antagonists for at least sixty-years in Toronto (and other areas of Ontario). The antagonism culminated in the Jubilee Riots of 1875 when eight thousand of them fought a pitched battle in the city's streets, and was followed by another riot in 1878 when the Irish nationalist, O'Donovan Rossa, came to Toronto on a speaking engagement. Yet Kealey suggests that shortly thereafter peace descended upon "Toronto the Good" through the Knights of Labor wherein "the old sectarian quarrels were gone."[37] It is difficult to believe that, in the early 1880s, Irish Catholics would "Kiss the Orange Sash" to unite with those who had been instrumental in locking them out of jobs, preferment or politics in the city.[38] If there was a common philosophy among working men, why did a mixed audience of workers in the 1890s enthusiastically receive an address by Daniel O'Donoghue, the Irish Catholic father of the Canadian labour movement, until it was discovered his philosophy was based on the Papal Encylical, Rerum Novarum, and the Orange element turned away in disgust? And if there was unity in the labour force between the Orange and Catholic Irish in Toronto, why had it not occurred in Ireland where the Orange Order divided the work force, excluding Catholics, and sought temporary accommodation when it suited their own purposes?[39]

The proponents of a unified working class culture are vague when describing the nature of that new, social vehicle, admitting:

We know next to nothing about their religious sentiments, about the songs they sang, the pubs they drank in, the popular theatre they attended, or the books they read.[40]

Yet, through research, this writer knows that Catholic workers were guided by religious principles, what songs they sang, the shabeens in which they drank, the concerts, picnics, excursions and soirees they attended, the books and papers they read, and the sports they played. Irish Catholic workers participated in their own culture and ethno-religious privatism excluded others. One did not join Irish Catholic society — one was born into it; and abandonment of religion meant denial of ethnicity. It is difficult to imagine that Irish Catholics, with such a strong sense of cultural identity, formed part of a unified working-class in Victorian Toronto.

40

190

In commenting on Donald Akenson's work, entitled "Ontario: Whatever Happened to the Irish?" Bryan Palmer stated: "The history of the Irish will never look the same after the devastating assaults mounted in this article."[41] In Akenson's opinion, the Irish in Ontario were rurally based and dominantly Protestant. However, what Akenson implies about the urban-dwelling Irish Catholics is open to question. He denies any urban ghetto existence or oral tradition, and stipulates that the Irish were not poverty-stricken and had adjusted easily to urban living with an accompanying social mobility.[42] Akenson's approach places limitations on the value of urban existence as a factor in cultural retention and reformation.

The historian can have little quarrel with the statement that there were more Protestant Irish than Catholic in Ontario. A. Gordon Darroch and Michael Ornstein gave a figure of 38% Catholic to 62% Protestant in an article written for the *Canadian Historical Review* in 1980.[43] In 1976, this author had determined that the Irish Catholics had declined from 48% of the national group to 38% between 1880 and 1900 in the city of Toronto alone.[44] But the belief that the Irish were domiciled in rural rather than urban centres is less certain. The Catholic Irish were the ghettoized element in the general Irish population and, therefore, it is interesting to examine their urban-rural ratio. Darroch and Ornstein stated that, in Ontario, 48.1% of Irish Catholics were farmers in 1871,[45] while Akenson gives a figure of 66.3% for rural-dwelling Irish Catholics.[46] One might conclude that the 18.2% difference is made up on non-farming, rural-dwellers in villages. However, were the village-dwellers a rural proletariat or did they represent urban commercial interests in the countryside, tied economically or socially to a central place through various forms of metropolitan linkage?

Quite clearly, a number of questions will have to be answered concerning the Irish Catholic population. What proportion of the farming population was farm owners, rentors or labourers? What was the duration of Irish Catholic rural occupancy and what proportion of the farm labourers supported families in urban centres by remittances? Considering the poverty and transiency of Irish labourers, were those counted as rural-dwellers in one year gone with the fairies the next? Even in well established, old Irish Catholic farming settlements, in families of twelve children, ten had departed for Canadian or American cities in two decades.[47] Furthermore, where did the Irish immigrants after 1848 find available land? Leo Johnson proposed that in the Home District most of it had been taken up by 1850.[48] As well, David Gagnon and Herbert Mays have intimated that Irish rural occupancy was declining in Peel County, and most likely all over Ontario, by the 1870s.[49] What about the structure of rural villages? Were they rural foci or metropolitan adjuncts for the transfer of goods, ideas and urban culture to the countryside?

Bryan Palmer notices that, by 1870, four out of ten city dwellers in Ontario were of Irish descent.[50] And J.L. Little observed:

Akenson himself demonstrates that in 1851 and 1861 an Irishman was twice as likely as any other Upper Canadian to find himself in the city . . . he provides no evidence for his suggestion that there was a steady progression from urban to rural place.[51]

Obviously there is a controversy over Irish urban-rural residential dominance that will have to be dealt with. It is most likely that the majority of Famine emigrants to Canada entered the cities where about forty per cent remained. A number of them had left for American centres and the rest sought work as spalpeens in rural areas. When this group of migratory workers is included with the established pre-Famine Irish population, it is possible a larger, but temporary, rural occupancy was realized. But considering that this transient population did not have the funds to purchase farms and, furthermore, was not acquainted with farming on the scale needed to be economically feasible in Ontario, most gradually returned to the cities to find work. Over a period of several decades, therefore, the urban-rural ratio was reversed.

Regardless of urban-rural ratios, Akenson contends that, unlike the American Irish, Irish Catholics in Canada did not go through the ghetto experience. That conclusion seems to have been based on an article by D.S. Shea.[52] Irish ghettos were common in most Canadian cities. George de Zwaan located an Irish Town or Paddy Town in Newmarket between 1850 and 1880,[53] while it was still a village. Peter Pineo noticed one in Hamilton in the same period.[54] In 1834, the municipal officials in York lamented about "the growing Shanty Town, consisting of the meanest sort of buildings."[55] Yet, when the pre-Famine Irish were pushed out of that area, they just recreated their ghettos on the Don Flats and eventually re-entered the city. H. Perkins Bull mentioned a number of Irish towns in the Humber Valley, on the other side of the city, quite similar to those in the Don Flats.[56] In his study of Toronto between 1850 and 1900, Peter Goheen shows persistent Irish ghettoization. He noticed that in 1870 there was "a fairly rigorous segregation at least of Roman Catholics within the city." He added: "Religious exclusion operated in the selective way we now attribute to ethnic exclusiveness in the city."[57] Goheen identified the existence of three major clusters of Irish concentration by 1899 — west of the mouth of the Don River or the old Cabbage Town area, the Bathurst and King Street area or Claretown, and the Toronto Junction area in the west end. In addition, the lightly inhabited eastern section of the city was predominantly Irish.[58]

Through research, this writer was able to locate at least a dozen minor areas of Irish concentration in Toronto. The areas of concentration began in the 1830s and were ghettos

41

by the 1850s. As time progressed, they became ethnically mixed, working Irish ghettos in America, Jo Ellen Vinyard observed:

Where work and housing necessitated that these families settle far from the church, schools or stores that served their nationality, new ones were built. By reaching out to the similar pocket on the next block and then the next, each group webbed its own together, breaking off when of sufficient size to be self sustaining.[62]

And similarly in Toronto, in a dozen concentrations or in numerous isolated family units, a culture formed and was retained and transmitted. The parish church was central to all activities and ruled in the social, political and economic realm of each unit.

In addition to stating there was little ghettoization, Akenson implies that the Irish Catholics were not poverty-stricken. In his opinion, Irish peasants "were well above the poverty line."[63] That illusionary belief might be dissipated if one refers to the Irish or secular newspapers of the era. The record books of the St. Vincent de Paul Society, the House of Providence and other social agencies, Catholic, Protestant and secular, show how severe the poverty was and that it became almost generational. Terry Crowley suggested that perhaps more of the Irish poor came to Canada than to the United States because passage was obtained on lumber ships that might otherwise have returned empty.[64]

Since Akenson believes the Irish Catholics were not pauperized, it follows logically that he would also believe they had an easy verticle mobility and adapted quickly to life in the city. That premise is difficult to accept when one learns that, generally, the population of Toronto looked upon the Irish as vermin or, at best, an obsolete people.[65] Confronted with that attitude, the Irish saw the city beyond their own community as a hollow town,[66] because they were locked out. As late as 1897, out of 656 municipal positions, Irish Catholics held 41; in a police force of 271 there were 16 Irish Catholics — and none in the law courts.[67] Michael Katz found that fifty-nine per cent of the Irish were labourers and twenty per cent were in the skilled trades,[68] which made them predominantly working class. In Katz's opinion the term "nigger" could be applied to the urban Irish in Canada[69] and he concluded that "being an Irish Catholic more than limited opportunity, it meant near pauperization."[70] Similarly, from documentary evidence, Harvey B. Graff believed that being Irish, particularly Catholic, in Toronto meant receiving differential treatment in both the work place and court of law.[71] The persistent vilification of the Irish by George Brown, Egerton Ryerson and the Orange Lodge culminated in the fact that those who bore Irish names or lived on a particular street in an Irish neighbourhood were almost automatically charged and convicted in the urban justice system. By the 1890s, during the reign of the Protestant Protective Association in Ontario, Irish Catholics were last hired, first fired, and were not even waited on in some Toronto stores. William Baker has cited Timothy Anglin who observed that Irish Catholics were never accepted socially in Toronto — even if successful they were ostracized in the Protestant city.[72]

In an apparent attempt to isolate the history of the Canadian Irish from the American experience, Akenson embellishes his work with an unproven assumption that the Canadian Irish Catholics had no oral memory of the Irish Famine or British oppression.[73] In urban centres, the Church, the schools, Irish societies and press kept the memory of the famine alive. An examination of Toronto's Irish newspapers' articles, the Bishops' letters and circulars, or the surviving student essays, as well as interviews with octogenarian descendents of Famine Irish immigrants, will verify there was little deficiency in Irish memory,[74] a memory which perpetuated a hatred towards Britain that is still expressed in our own age. Paul Blanchard, hardly a lover of the Irish or the Catholic Church, stated:

In the eighteenth and nineteenth centuries English Protestants taught Irish Catholics to hate and to fear because they used Protestantism as an auxilliary weapon of oppression.[75]

That hatred was carried to the New World. The souperism[76] employed by Protestants on the wharves in Quebec, Montreal, Kingston and Toronto did little to allay it. Those memories were entrenched in the Irish psyche and, as John F. Stock observed, "an Irish sub culture channelled ethnic hostilities through a number of code words"[77] — like Protestant, Orange and English.

Because Thomas Gallagher, in his book, *Paddy's Lament*,[78] described the vitality of those memories among the Irish in the United States, Akenson, in reviewing the work, labelled it as evil in the context that the book perpetuated hatred. Nonetheless, Gallagher presents an accurate account of the origins of Irish hatred for the British. But Gallagher is not the only author attacked. Kenneth Duncan, H. Clare Pentland and Michael Cross have been called subconsciously racist for their descriptions of the conditions of the famine immigrants.[79] Duncan has empathetically and analytically recorded the process underlying the Irish peasants' attempts to save their culture and other elements from a peasant past. Irish residential distinctiveness, violence, transiency, drunkenness and superstition were historical traits. Some were of peasant origin, others were defence mechanisms against the brutal methods of an alien English conqueror. An examination of primary sources shows Irish ghetto existence in Toronto was actually far worse than what Duncan described. One begins to wonder what Akenson considers acceptable regarding Irish adjustment. Would he consider William Shannon and Andrew Greeley erroneous for stating that puritanism was an element in Irish culture? In Shannon's view, Irish puritanism exalted purity, dis-

42

trusted natural human instincts, but "kept peasant values internalized in the home and family, sacrificing individuality for conformity."[80] Greeley implied that puritanism tended to make the Irish sexually naive.[81]

Among the Famine Irish immigrants, the love of dancing, singing and fighting, keeping livestock in their homes, and distaste for laws or a legal process to which they could not avail themselves are fact. That their peasant religion showed little distinction between natural or supernatural, living or dead, which produced wake customs that shocked the charter population, is historical. Andrew Greeley observed: "If one lives very close to the forces of life and death, maybe laughing at them is one way to survive."[82] Certainly drinking poteen in shabeens was almost endemic, and drunkenness, with its accompanying social malaise, a consequence. Greeley, an Irish American, in a humorous fashion admitted: "The Irish are only half sober when they start drinking."[83] A 'drop of the creature' was just one of many Irish defence methods or mechanisms to nullify to effects of an harsh environment or to serve as an escape from a brutal life bequeathed by the English. However, it was the reinterpretation of peasant cultural elements with the Catholicism of the age that created a viable vehicle to sustain the Irish in the ghettos of Toronto and other Canadian cities.

Within Akenson's writing there seems to be a veiled anti-Catholic and pro-British bias, a bias that is partially reflected in his, as yet, not fully formed model of a Protestant, rural Ontario Irishman. John Boyle noticed this British bias when he reviewed Akenson's work on education in Ireland. Akenson wrote: "the schools now inculcate Irish patriotism instead of British Hisotry."[84] In Boyle's opinion, the extinction of Irish history in Northern Ireland has resulted in "no addition to the public good."[85] Why does Akenson think that a free Ireland should study the history of an oppressor rather than that of its own people? Astonishingly, Akenson believes the causes of the Famine lay with the Irish peasants for adopting a monoculture and for procreating themselves to death. Actually, Britain relegated the Irish Catholic peasants to the most infertile lands which caused the adoption of the potato as a staple. The peasants grew other crops, but were expected to use them for rent payment to the English landlords. Akenson's statement of Irish peasant fecundity shows a lack of understanding of peasant populations generally. The Irish birth rate was no higher than most peasant societies of that period. At any rate, the amount of food that Britain shipped out of Ireland during the Famine years was more than sufficient to have aborted the clamity.[86]

One principal problem that Akenson must face in his search for a rural Irish Protestant model is a definition of the Orange, Ulster Protestant. The Ulster Irish were drawn from Scotland and England and brought their own peculiar culture with them to Ireland. They did not assimilate; they remained Scots or English. Akenson disclaims Orangism as

the Canadian identity of Ulster immigrants,[87] — but beyond that identity there is little else to set them apart. They dispersed among Methodist, Anglican and Presbyterian Churches and assimilated rapidly into the general Protestant population as they did in the United States. The difference in Ontario was the fact that their culture became a central element within Protestant culture. William Baker offers an explanation:

. . . Orangism grew and spread because its tenets were shared by the bulk of the Protestant population. Might it be, however, that non-Irish Protestants became increasingly Orange Irish in perspective and outlook?[88]

Actually, Irish Protestant identity was born in the urban lodges of Ontario, and through the expanding Orange network a new Irish Protestant culture was transferred to the hinterland.[89] In Toronto, the Protestant Irish had a single ethnic press, The Irish Protestant, that lasted for one year only,[90] whereas the Catholic Irish had a half dozen papers over a seventy year period. The Orange Sentinel served them adequately. As a group, Irish Protestants refused association with Irish Catholics. In the 1870s they developed a benevolent society through which they provided aid only to Protestant immigrants.[91] In view of the negative Irish stereotype that prevailed, the Protestant Irish abandoned the designation "Irish" and bequeathed their culture to Protestant Ontario. Therefore, it seems accurate to conclude that the Irish, regardless of religious background or rural-urban ratios, developed urban cultures and transferred them to the countryside of eastern Canada.

## NOTES

1. Donald H. Akenson, "Ontario: Whatever Happened to the Irish?", D.H. Akenson, ed., Canadian Papers in Rural History (Gananoque: Langdale Press, 1982), pp. 204-56.
2. Oscar Handlin, Boston's Immigrants (New York: Atheneum, 1976).
3. See: Gregory S. Kealey, Peter Warrian, eds., Essays In Canadian Working Class History (Toronto: McClelland and Stewart, 1976), pp. 7-12, passim.
4. Gregory S. Kealey, Bryan D. Palmer, "The Bonds of Unity: The Knights of Labor in Ontario, 1880-1900", Histoire sociale/Social History vol. XIV, no. 28 (November 1981), pp. 369-95.
5. Marc Karson, "Catholic Anti-Socialism", John H.M. Laslett, Seymour Martin Lipset, eds., Failure of a Dream? Essays in the History of American Socialism (New York: Anchor Press/Doubleday, 1974), pp. 164-200.
6. Theodore Hershberg, "The New Urban History: Towards an Interdisciplinary History of the City", Theodore Hershberg, ed., Philadelphia: Work, Space, Family, and Group Experience in the 19th Century (New York: Oxford University Press, 1981), pp. 3-35.
7. Stephen Thernstrom, "Reflections on the New Urban History", Daedalus, vol. 100 (Spring 1971), pp. 359-75, p. 374.
8. The literature on the American Irish is massive. See the Arno Series, "The Irish Americans".
9. Compare: Dennis Clarke, The Irish in Philadelphia: Ten Generations of Urban Experience (Philadelphia: Temple University Press, 1973) with D.S. Cross, "The Irish in Montreal 1867-1896", M.A. Thesis, McGill University, 1969.

43

193

10. From J.P. Dolan's remarks on M.W. Nicolson's paper, "Irish Catholic Education in Victorian Toronto: An Ethnic Response to Urban Conformity", presented for Canadian-American Urban Development: A Comparative Urban History Conference, University of Guelph, 1982.

11. Hershberg, "The New Urban History."

12. D.C. Masters, *The Rise of Toronto 1850-1890* (Toronto: University of Toronto Press, 1947), p. VIII.

13. Murray W. Nicolson, "Ecclesiastical Metropolitanism and the Evolution of the Catholic Archdiocese of Toronto", *Social History*, vol. XV, no. 29 ( May 1982), pp. 129-56.

14. Cross, "The Irish in Montreal"

15. Randall Miller, "Introduction", R. Miller, T.D. Marzik, eds., *Immigrants and Religion in Urban America* (Philadelphia: Temple University Press, 1977), pp. XI-XXII, p. XIII.

16. Robert Redford, "The Folk Society", *The American Journal of Sociology*, LII, 4 (1947), pp. 306-8.

17. Clark, *The Irish in Philadelphia*; Jay P. Dolan, *The Immigrant Church: New York's Irish and German Catholics 1815-1865* (Baltimore: John Hopkins University Press, 1975); James W. Sanders, *The Education of an Urban Minority: Catholics in Chicago 1833* (New York: Oxford University Press, 1977).

18. Kenneth Duncan, "Irish Famine Immigration and the Social Structure of Canada West", *Canadian Review of Sociology and Anthropology*, (1965), pp. 19-40.

19. John Modell, Lynn H. Lees, "The Irish Countryman Urbanized: A Comparative Perspective on the Famine Migration", *Journal of Urban History*, 3 (August 1977), pp. 391-408, p. 407.

20. Duncan, "Irish Famine Immigration".

21. Sharon Gmelch, Pat Langan, *Tinkers and Travellers* (Montreal: McGill-Queen's University Press, 1975) p. 10.

22. Murray W. Nicolson, "Irish Tridentine Catholicism in Victorian Toronto: Vessel for Ethno-Religious Persistence", paper presented at the Fiftieth Congress of the Canadian Catholic Historical Association, September 1983.

23. *Ibid.*

24. John McGonigal, "All the Big Irishmen are in the Ottawa Valley", Joan Finnigan, *Some of the Stories I Told You Were True* (Ottawa: Deneau Publishers, 1981), pp. 45-51, p. 51.

25. Murray W. Nicolson, "The Catholic Church and the Irish in Victorian Toronto", Ph.D. Thesis, University of Guelph, 1981.

26. Murray W. Nicolson, "The Irish Catholics and Social Action in Toronto 1850-1900", *Studies in History and Politics*, vol. 1, no. 1 (Fall 1980), pp. 30-55.

27. Nicolson, "Irish Catholic Education".

28. Murray W. Nicolson, "Peasants in an Urban Society: The Irish Catholics in Victorian Toronto", Robert Harney, ed., *The Meeting Place* (Toronto: to be published 1984).

29. Nicolson, "Ecclesiastical Metropolitanism".

30. Nicolson, "Irish Tridentine Catholicism".

31. Nicolson, "The Catholic Church and the Irish".

32. See: David Bercuson, "Through the Looking Glass of Culture: An Essay on the New Labour History and Working Class Culture in Recent Historical Writing", *Labour*, 7 (Spring 1981), pp. 95-112; Betsy Blackmar, "Class Conflicts in Canadian Cities", *Journal of Urban History*, vol. 10, no. 2 (February 1984), pp. 211-21; Murray W. Nicolson, "Six Days Shalt Thou Labour: The Catholic Church and the Irish Worker in Victorian Toronto", presented at the Canadian Historical Association Conference, June 1983.

33. Gregory S. Kealey and Bryan D. Palmer, "The Bonds of Unity"

34. Ronald Sanders, *The Downtown Jews. Portraits of an Immigrant Generation* (Scarborough: New American Library, 1977), caption on picture, "Preparing for the Sabbath", following p. 180.

35. Brian C. O'Connor, "Working-Class Kinship Networks: A Marriage of Methods", *Journal of Urban; History* vol. 10 (February 1984). pp. 187-194, p. 190.

36. *Ibid.*

37. Kealey and Palmer, "The Bonds of Unity", p. 395.

38. See particularly: *The Canadian Freeman* and the *Irish Canadian*, various issues 1850-1880.

39. The incident of audience response to O'Donoghue's address was supported by oral history collected from the son of an Irish Catholic witness. Andrew Boyd, *The Rise of the Irish Trade Unions* (Dublin: Anvil Books, 1972).

40. Kealey and Warrian, "Introduction", *Essays in Working Class History*, p. 11.

41. Bryan D. Palmer, "Town, Port, and Country: Speculations on the Capitalist Transformation of Canada", *Acadiensis*, vol. XII, no. 2 (Spring 1983), pp. 132-39, p. 133.

42. Akenson, "Ontario: Whatever Happened to the Irish?"

43. A. Gordon Darroch, Michael D. Ornstein, "Ethnicity and Occupational Structure in Canada in 1871: The Vertical Mosaic in Historical Perspective", *Canadian Historical Review*, LXI, 3 (1980). pp. 305-333, p. 311.

44. Nicolson, "The Catholic Church and the Irish".

45. Darroch and Ornstein, "Ethnicity and Occupational Structure", p. 326.

46. Akenson, "Ontario: Whatever Happened to the Irish?", p. 233.

47. Oral history collected for Ph.D. Thesis, 1978.

48. Leo Johnson, "Land Policy, Population Growth and Social Structure in the Home District", *Ontario Historical Society*, vol. LXIII (1971), pp. 139-55.

49. David Gagnon, Herbert Mays, "Historical Demography and Canadian Social History: Families and Land in Peel County Ontario", *Canadian Historical Society*, no. 1 (March 1973), pp. 28-47.

50. Palmer, "Town, Port and Country".

51. J.L. Little, review of D.H. Akenson, ed., *Canadian Papers in Rural History* in *Labour*, vol. 11, no. 11, (Spring 1983), pp. 218-21, p. 219.

52. D.S. Shea, "The Irish Immigrant Adjustment to Toronto: 1840-1860", *Canadian Catholic Historical Association Report, Study Sessions*, no. 39 (1972), pp. 53-60.

53. George de Zwaan, "Elite and Society: Newmarket, Ontario 1857-1880", M.A. Thesis, Queen's University, 1980; "Paddy Town was Newmarket's Little Ireland", The *Era*, 16 March 1983.

54. Peter C. Pinco, "Urban Analysis: Some Case Studies", N.H. Lithwick, Gilles Paquet, eds., *Urban Studies: A Canadian Perspective* (Toronto: Methuen, 1968), pp. 179-207, p. 188.

55. Rainer Baehre, "Pauper Emigration to Upper Canada in the 1830's, *Social History*, vol. XIV, no. 28 (November 1981) pp. 339-67, p. 356.

56. See: W. Perkins Bull, *From Macdonell to McGuigan: A History of the Growth of the Catholic Church in Upper Canada* (Toronto: The Perkins Bull Foundation, 1939).

57. Peter Goheen, *Victorian Toronto 1850-1900: Patterns and Processes of Growth* (Chicago: The University of Chicago Press, 1970), p. 151 and p. 154.

58. *Ibid.*, p. 186 and p. 213.

59. Nicolson, "The Catholic Church and the Irish".

60. Kathleen Neils-Conzen, "Immigrants, Immigrant Neighbourhoods, and Ethnic Identity: Historical Issues", *The Journal of American History*, vol. 66, no. 3 (December 1979), pp. 604-15.

61. David J. O'Brien, Mary Joan Roach, "Recent Developments in Urban Sociology" *Journal of Urban History*, vol. 10 (February 1984). pp. 145-170.

62. Jo Ellen Vinyard, *The Irish on the Urban Frontier, Nineteenth Century Detroit, 1850-1880* (New York: Arno Press, 1976), pp. 181-82.

63. Akenson, "Ontario: Whatever Happened to the Irish?", p. 225.

64. See: Institutional Records, Archdiocese of Toronto Archives, Conversation with Dr. Terry Crowley, University of Guelph, August 1983.

65. For the concept of ethnic obsolescence see: Samuel F. Yete, *The Choice: The Issue of Black Survival in America* (New York: Berkley Books, 1971), pp. 13-15.

66. For the concept of 'Hollow Town' see: Clifford Geertz, *The Social History of an Indonesian Town* (Cambridge: M.I.T. Press, 1965), p. 4.

67. *The Catholic Register*, 23 December 1897.

44

68. Michael Katz, *The People of Hamilton, Canada West* (Cambridge: Harvard University Press, 1975), Table 2.4.

69. Michael Katz, "Irish and Canadian Catholics: A Comparison", *The Social History Project*, Report no. 4 (1972-1973), pp. 35-36.

70. *Ibid.*, p. 67.

71. Harvey B. Graff, "The Reality and the Rhetoric: The Social and Economic Meaning of Literacy in Mid-Nineteenth Century: The Example of Literacy and Criminality", in Neil MacDonald, Alf Chaiton, eds., *Egerton Ryerson and His Times* (Toronto: MacMillan of Canada, 1978), pp. 187-220, p. 207.

72. William M. Baker, *Timothy Warren Anglin 1822-96: Irish Catholic Candian* (Toronto: University of Toronto Press, 1977), p. 243.

73. J. Moir, "The English-Speaking Catholic Church in Canada in the Nineteenth Century", *The Canadian Society of Church History Papers* (1970), pp. 1-19; T. Suttor, "Catholicism and Secular Culture: Australia and Canada Compared", *Culture*, XXX, no. 2 (June 1969), pp. 93-112.

74. Archdiocese of Toronto Archives, Bishops Charbonnel and Lynch Papers; St. Michael's College Archives, Student Papers.

75. Paul Blanchard, *The Irish and Catholic Power: An American Interpretation* (London: Derek Verschoyle, 1954), p. 35.

76. McGonigal, "All the Big Irishmen", p. 51.

77. John F. Stock, *International Conflict in an American City: Boston's Irish, Italians and Jews 1835-1944* (Westport: Greenwood Press, 1979), p. 71.

78. Thomas Gallagher, *Paddy's Lament: Ireland 1846-1847, Prelude to Hatred* (New York: Harcourt Brace Jovanovitch, 1982); Donald Akenson, "Review of Paddy's Lament", *Globe and Mail*, 7 August 1982.

72. Akenson, "Ontario: Whatever Happened to the Irish?", p. 224.

80. William Shannon, *the American Irish* (New York: The MacMillan Co., 1963), p. 22.

81. Andrew Greeley, *The Most Distressful Nation: The Taming of the American Irish* (Chicago: Quadrangle, 1972), p. 102.

82. *Ibid.*, p. 55.

83. Greeley, *The Most Distressful Nation*, p. 129.

84. Donald Akenson cited in review by John Boyle, "The Irish Education Experiment: The National System of Education in the Nineteenth Century", *History of Education Quarterly*, vol. XI, 2 (Summer 1971), pp. 195-203, p. 200.

85. *Ibid.*

86. Akenson, "Review of Paddy's Lament".

87. Akenson, "Ontario: Whatever Happened to the Irish?"

88. William Baker, "The Irish Connection", *Acadiensis*, vol. XII, no. 2 (Spring 1983), pp. 124-31, p. 131.

89. "Civic Officials, Clubs and Societies", in J.E. Middleton, *The Municipality of Toronto* (Toronto: The Dominion Publishing Co., 1923), pp. 773-89, p. 788 to 89; C.J. Houston, W.J. Smyth, *The Sash Canada Wore: A Historical Geography of the Orange Order in Canada* (Toronto: University of Toronto Press, 1980).

90. *The Irish Protestant*, 1896, listed in D. McLaren, *Ontario Ethno-Cultural Newspapers 1835-1972* (Toronto: University of Toronto Press, 1973), pp. 95-96, and p. 97.

91. The Records of the Irish Protestant Benevolent Society, Metropolitan Library, Toronto; J.G. Hodgins, *Irishmen in Canada: Their Union Not Inconsistent with the Development of Canadian National Feeling* (Toronto, 1875).

45

# European Settlement and Ethnicity Patterns on the Agricultural Frontiers of South Dakota

ROBERT C. OSTERGREN

The settlement of European immigrants on the agricultural frontiers of South Dakota largely took place in the years between the end of the Civil War and the turn of the century. According to the 1900 United States census, 401,570 people occupied South Dakota at the close of that settlement era. Of that number, the foreign-born and their children (foreign stock) accounted for 244,523, or over sixty percent of the total. This figure represented the highest proportion recorded in any census of the state, and by the standards of most states at that time, it was a very high proportion. Only a few states, mostly midwestern, could claim comparable foreign contributions to their populations. A major factor in the settlement of South Dakota was clearly the immigration of agricultural settlers of northwest European origins. In a large sense, the culture of the state owes much to their presence.

The aim of this study is to provide background information on the temporal and spatial patterns of ethnic settlement in South

Dakota and on the role played by ethnic groups in molding the state's distinctive agrarian society. For organizational purposes, the body of the essay is divided into three sections. The first discusses the general processes that brought all of South Dakota into the settled ecumene of the Upper Midwest, for the settlement patterns of South Dakota, or any other state, cannot be treated in isolation. The external forces that brought various groups to different parts of the state must be seen in the context of developments on midwestern frontiers in general. The second section describes the ethnic pattern that developed over time, focusing on the formation of communities and regional consciousness within the boundaries of the state. The last section deals with ethnic culture and its relationship to the agrarian society that emerged in South Dakota by the early part of the twentieth century.

### The Settlement Process

To be properly understood, the settlement of South Dakota must be seen in the context of the settlement of the larger region of which it is a part — the Upper Midwest. The states that make up this region (Wisconsin, Iowa, Minnesota, Nebraska, and the Dakotas) stand together in that they shared a common settlement experience. All of them were opened to white settlement through a succession of related Indian treaties. Much of their land was made available to potential settlers through federal land policies that sought to foster a certain type of agricultural settlement. All of them actively pursued recruitment strategies designed to lure northwestern Europeans to their agricultural frontiers. And, all of them ultimately fell under the economic control of the financial interests (banking, milling, railroads) of the regional emporia at Chicago, Milwaukee, and the Twin Cities, a situation that did much to shape their politics. Most importantly, the agricultural communities of the region were often linked to one another through a complex pattern of migration.

The advance of settlement in the Upper Midwest was in no way steady or relentless. On the contrary, it varied considerably in its efficiency and direction over time. Temporally, it responded to the boom and bust cycle of American economic conditions and, especially on the plains, to the cyclical pattern of climatic conditions. The frontier was known to retreat as well as advance. Spatially, the advance of settlement was influenced by a myriad of factors — environmental preference, Indian relations, the course of rivers and waterways, the colonization efforts of railroads and speculators, and so forth. A map of the settlement frontier at any point in time is a map of salients and backwaters, rarely a distinct line.

In spite of these complexities, one can generalize about the configuration of the frontier for the region as a whole, and to do so for 1860 — the approximate time when the midwestern frontier first impinged on the present-day boundaries of South Dakota — produces the following. Starting in Nebraska, the frontier followed the course of the Missouri River with the exception of a westward penetrating salient along the Platte River Valley. Farther north, the Missouri valley frontier took on a salient shape based on Sioux City, Iowa, and penetrated northwestward into Dakota Territory to a point just beyond Yankton. From the base of that salient, the frontier line swung sharply back into central Iowa, from where it swung gently northward to meet the Iowa-Minnesota border at roughly its midpoint. This rather abrupt retreat left all of northwestern Iowa and southwestern Minnesota well outside the settled ecumene. Farther north in Minnesota, the line formed another westward pointing salient, based this time on New Ulm and extending up the Minnesota valley toward Dakota Territory. A second Minnesota salient was located farther north. It followed the ecotone between the prairie and forest that extends in a broad arc from east-central Minnesota to the Red River Valley of the North. From the base of that salient, the frontier meandered in a easterly direction across Minnesota and Wisconsin to the shore of Green Bay on Lake Michigan.[1]

The configuration of the 1860 frontier has several implications for the settlement of South Dakota. In the first place, it marks a temporary lull in the frontier process in the Upper Midwest. The frontier was destined to hold this position or, in some cases, even retreat over the next half-dozen years as the nation fought the Civil War and as grasshoppers and marauding Indians buffeted the frontier zone. This lull in migration meant that the initial settlements (1850s) in the Missouri valley and the lower Big Sioux valley of Dakota Territory were more or less stillborn. Like all

1. *See* the Advance of Settlement maps in Robert C. Ostergren, "Geographic Perspectives on the History of Settlement in the Upper Middle West," *Upper Midwest History* 1 (1981): 30-31.

midwestern frontiers during this period, they were cut off by events from the life-giving commitment of capital and new settlers. Secondly, the tremendous lag in settlement advancement in northwestern Iowa and southwestern Minnesota, which was a reflection of the slow acceptance of open-prairie settlement in the preceding decades, meant that the bulk of what was to become eastern South Dakota was about as far from the advancing frontier as it could be, a distance that would not be covered until the beginning of the 1880s. Therefore, the early phases of settlement in Dakota Territory favored the Missouri valley and its tributaries on the one hand and the Red River Valley of the North, to which one of the Minnesota salients pointed, on the other. Much of eastern South Dakota was not destined to experience the initial settlement of the renewed waves of European immigrants that descended on the Midwest in the decade following the Civil War. It would instead experience the later waves of immigrants that arrived in the 1880s and the 1890s or the children of the earlier waves, who at that time began to move westward from the maturing communities on the older frontiers of Iowa, Minnesota, and Wisconsin.

In the 1890s, the broad pattern of settlement advance in the Upper Midwest would again directly affect the South Dakota experience. This time period witnessed another substantial slowing of the settlement process. The frontier, in fact, stalled roughly along the line of the Missouri River in the Dakotas and on the eastern margins of the Sand Hills in Nebraska. The only substantial settlement west of that line in 1890 was in Nebraska's Platte River Valley and in the Black Hills enclave of extreme western South Dakota. The halt was the result of a combination of factors, including the onset of drier, less hospitable environmental conditions on the western plains, the existence of large Indian reservations directly in the path of further settlement advance, and a marked slowdown in the rate of agricultural immigration to the United States, which was linked to a period of contraction in American agriculture.

By the beginning of the twentieth century, the situation changed and the advance of settlement resumed, taking the frontier across the western Dakotas and well into central Montana. The sources of agricultural pioneers had changed radically in the intervening years, however. Many of the settlers who settled the west-river counties were of Old-American stock. A considerable proportion entered from the south and were part of an American migration stream that had moved westward from the middle-

Atlantic states through the upper South and the Ohio valley to Missouri, Nebraska, Kansas, and Texas. The influx of this element into the western Dakotas is evidenced today by a marked northward bend to the linguistic boundary between middle-Atlantic and New England speech types that occurs along the Missouri valley in the Dakotas.[2] The halt of settlement along the Missouri and the shift in migration patterns that occurred once settlement resumed resulted in a fairly distinct western boundary of ethnic settlement in South Dakota. While many exceptions to the rule may be found, it is generally true that European settlement dominates the state east of the river, while a particular brand of Old-American culture prevails west of the river. This difference is an important factor in the tendency for South Dakotans to speak of "East River" and "West River" as separate regions or places.[3]

The progress of the settlement frontier in South Dakota is mapped in Figure 1, using data from the United States decennial censuses. The standard two-persons-per-square-mile census definition of settlement is used. The decennial isolines on the map reflect much of what has been suggested by the regional patterns discussed above. By 1870, the counties of Yankton, Clay, Union, and part of Lincoln were the only ones that could be called settled using the census definition. Much of the population had arrived during the years 1868-1873, a relatively prosperous period in American history that saw the reestablishment of the old Sioux-City-based frontier salient along the Missouri and its northward offshoot along the lower reaches of the Big Sioux River Valley.[4] The advance had been abruptly terminated in 1873 when the country plunged into a major economic depression. The depression was overtly precipitated by the financial collapse of the Northern Pacific railroad in 1873. Even before that time, however, a general uncertainty had manifested itself in congressional dissatisfaction with railroad finances and land management in frontier areas. This situation had a retarding effect on settlement

2. *See* the general dialect maps in Harold B. Allen, *The Linguistic Atlas of the Upper Middle West* (Minneapolis: University of Minnesota Press, 1973).

3. The east-river/west-river regionalism is based on more than ethnic differences. Significant differences in environment and economy also exist between the two halves of the state.

4. The early settlement of the salient, which had begun in 1858 following the treaty with the Yankton Sioux, had been almost entirely abandoned by 1862 in the face of repeated Indian attacks, grasshopper plagues, and drought. The area was in fact restored to the Indians for a short time after the Civil War.

**Figure 1.** Advance of Settlement

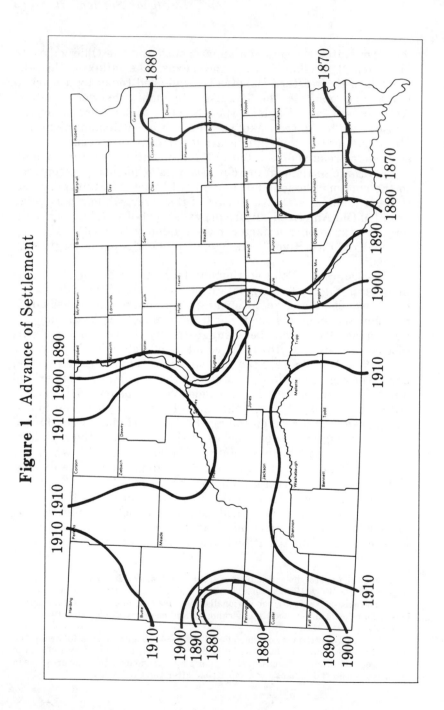

in South Dakota in that it helped to kill a bid to secure a land-grant railroad from Yankton to the north via the James River Valley. This failure not only deprived South Dakota of a land-grant railroad, it also eliminated the prospect of a rapid northward extension of settlement in the 1870s based on Yankton and forestalled railroad construction in general until the late 1870s.[5] Also retarding the advance of settlement in the mid-1870s was a period of intense drought and grasshopper infestation.

The bulk of the east-river country underwent settlement during the period 1879-1886, a period of national prosperity that coincided with the approach of railroad construction along the eastern boundary of South Dakota and settlement in northwestern Iowa and southwestern Minnesota. Known as the "Great Dakota Boom," the period is characterized by a very rapid east to west extension of the frontier, often spearheaded by the railroads, several of which were competitively laying a series of more or less parallel lines over the eastern half of the state. By 1887, the east-river rail network was complete. The towns of Eureka, Bowdle, Gettysburg, Pierre, and Chamberlain marked the western termini of the railroads and the temporary halt of the frontier along the Missouri River.[6] The only major areas east of the Missouri that were not settled by 1890 were reservations set aside for the Indians.

On the other side of the Missouri, most of the west-river country still belonged to the Indians at the end of the 1880s. All but a narrow strip along the western boundary of the present state was part of the Great Sioux Reservation. This narrow western strip included the Black Hills and the territory served by a number of north-south running railways and trails that had been established in conjunction with the range-cattle industry. The opening of the west-river country to white settlement began in 1889 with the extinguishment of Indian title to nine million acres of land on the Great Sioux Reservation. Relatively little agricultural settlement occurred before 1900, however, mainly due to the lack of railway connections in the west and the continued availability of good agricultural lands farther east. Instead, the initial opportunity went to the cattleman, and the west-river country remained largely his domain until around 1902, when homesteading began in earnest.

5. John C. Hudson, "Two Dakota Frontiers," *Annals of the Association of American Geographers* 63 (1973): 444-45.
6. Ibid., p. 451.

Between roughly 1902 and 1915, a second Dakota boom saw the systematic settlement of much of the so-called surplus lands of the western reservations. The map of settlement advance (Figure 1) accordingly shows a substantial movement of the frontier westward from the Missouri and eastward from the Black Hills during the period 1900-1910. By 1910, the range-cattle industry had largely disappeared from the most important zone of new settlement that stretched between Pierre and the Black Hills. It receded before the advance of dry-land agriculture and the new upsurge in railroad construction that linked the Black Hills with the old rail termini at Pierre and Chamberlain.

Thus, the agricultural settlement of South Dakota took place during three distinct boom periods—1868-1873, 1879-1886, and 1902-1915. Because of the differential timing of these periods, the pool of potential settlers was quite different in each of the boom periods. Each of the three corresponding settlement areas in South Dakota received a peculiar mix of immigrants determined by the location of potential source areas and the direction of existing migration streams at the time.

The southeastern corner of the state, which was settled during the earliest period, received a heavy proportion of Old-American

*Promotional efforts of the early twentieth century included post cards and flattering verses.*

stock. As much as one-half of the population in the southeastern counties during the early 1870s was reportedly "Yankee."[7] Many were veterans of the Union Army who had drifted to the frontier in the aftermath of the war. They were a naturally restless lot, and many did not remain in the area long. A smaller, but potentially more permanent, element of the population was immigrant and largely Scandinavian. The late 1860s and the early 1870s was a time of heavy emigration from the poorer agricultural districts of the Scandinavian countries. Much of it was motivated by depressingly poor harvests and, in some cases, terrible famine. As a consequence, this emigration predominantly consisted of family groups—a common characteristic of migration streams motivated by stressful circumstances. These immigrants came to the Midwest with the intention of locating areas where they could take land and settle permanently. In the southeastern counties of South Dakota, they rather quickly formed large and rather stable contiguous settlements, often displacing many of the earlier Yankee settlers.

Detailed study of the large Swedish settlement in Clay County, known as Dalesburg, found that most of its settlers were more or less direct immigrants from Europe.[8] These people were anything but haphazard in the manner in which they made their way to the Dakota frontier. They knew something of their destination before they left Sweden and, depending on their resources, mapped out a fairly direct route to their ultimate destination. In fact, strong routes of migration were established early. Emigrants who left provinces that had a long emigration history proceeded to Clay County via settlements in Wisconsin, Minnesota, or Iowa where they knew people who had emigrated in earlier years. Following some of these routes involved temporary stays with friends and relatives along the way. Some who proceeded in this fashion took several years to reach their ultimate destination. Others, who had no friends or relatives in America, accomplished the journey in a number of months. The important point is that most of the Scandinavian settlers of this area were recent

7. Douglas Chittick, "A Recipe for Nationality Stew," in *Dakota Panorama,* ed. J. Leonard Jennewein and Jane Boorman (n.p.: Dakota Territory Centennial Commission, 1961), p. 96.

8. Robert C. Ostergren, "Prairie Bound: Migration Patterns to a Swedish Settlement on the Dakota Frontier," in *Ethnicity on the Great Plains*, ed. Frederick C. Luebke (Lincoln: University of Nebraska Press for the Center for Great Plains Studies, 1980), pp. 73-91.

immigrants who had relatively little experience with American culture and economy. They made their way to the Dakota frontier quite directly or by way of acquaintances that shared their culture, and they settled down among people who had emigrated from the same agricultural regions of the homeland. The potential for cultural maintenance in these settlements was accordingly quite considerable.

In contrast to the counties settled during the 1868-1873 period, the east-river counties that were settled during the Great Dakota Boom of the 1880s drew their populations from more diverse sources. As in the southeastern counties, initial settlers were primarily Old-Americans, most of them from the old midwestern states of Illinois, Indiana, Michigan, Wisconsin, and Iowa, but also some from New York and parts of New England. Indeed, John C. Hudson found in his detailed study of Sanborn County that Iowa, Michigan, and New York State picnics were commonplace events during the county's frontier heyday.[9] The evidence suggests, however, that the initial preponderance of Old-Americans soon gave way to the foreign-born, who seemed to be more disposed to permanent settlement. In fact, Douglas Chittick claims that the severe drought of 1886-1887 effected a substantial exodus of Old-American stock from the east-river counties that was replaced by the continued arrival of European immigrants—thereby changing the composition of population in eastern South Dakota in the course of just a few years.[10]

Compared to the southeastern counties, the composition of the foreign-born in the Great Dakota Boom region was not only more diverse, but, in general, this foreign-born population had come to the Dakota frontier by less direct means. The earlier Scandinavians were soon joined by Germans, Bohemians, Dutch, Swiss, Finns, and German-Russians, as well as many other groups. A significant proportion of these new immigrants had resided for some time in the United States prior to their arrival on the Dakota frontier. Many who settled during this period were children who had accompanied parents to frontier settlements in Minnesota, Iowa, and Wisconsin twenty to thirty years earlier. As these older settlements matured in the 1880s, the pioneers' offspring often found insufficient opportunity. As this cohort of children reached maturity, married, and looked for a means of livelihood,

9. Hudson, "Two Dakota Frontiers," p. 448.
10. Chittick, "Recipe for Nationality Stew," p. 96.

they perceived that their best chances lay farther west on the Dakota frontier. Although they were foreign-born and were still inclined to marry and settle among their own kind, this generation also had more experience with American ways and the American agricultural economy than their parents. As a result, the potential for cultural maintenance in the new settlements was less. This is not to say that the foreign-born population of this region of South Dakota was entirely a product of midwestern "stepwise" migration. Many still came directly off the boat, especially among certain groups such as the German-Russians. On the whole, however, the proportion of long-term American residents was relatively high among the foreign-born who settled during the Great Dakota Boom.

The notion that midwestern migration to the frontier proceeded in a stepwise fashion from settlement to settlement is an old one. Studies have consistently demonstrated that each frontier gave up its youth to a new western frontier roughly one generation after its own settlement had been completed. In South Dakota's major east-river land boom, therefore, the major recruiting areas were found in southeastern Minnesota, western Wisconsin, and east-central Iowa — regions that were densely settled by German and Scandinavian immigrants in the decades before the Civil War. In fact, these areas were especially targeted for propaganda. Immigration officials, town agents, and railroad agents commonly gave speeches, distributed pamphlets printed in several languages, and set up exhibits at the agricultural fairs of these targeted regions throughout the late 1870s and the 1880s. Most territories competed in this way for settlers. The Dakotas were especially aggressive in this endeavor because they had to overcome a generally negative image of climatic extremes, grasshoppers, and Indians.[11]

In the case of the last Dakota boom (1902-1915), the migration fields were again quite different. This time, settlers were recruited from the southern plains states, to some extent from the older settlements in the east-river area, and, finally, from eastern

---

11. *See* John R. Milton, *South Dakota: A Bicentennial History* (New York: W. W. Norton & Co., 1977), pp. 82-85; Hudson, "Two Dakota Frontiers," p. 447; William H. Russell, "Promoters and Promotion Literature of Dakota Territory," *South Dakota Historical Collections* 26 (1952): 434-55; Herbert S. Schell, "Official Immigration Activities of Dakota Territory," *North Dakota Historical Quarterly* 7 (Oct. 1932): 5-24; and Kenneth M. Hammer, "Come to God's Country: Promotional Efforts in Dakota Territory, 1861-1889," *South Dakota History* 10 (Fall 1980): 291-309.

cities.[12] Much of this last surge was motivated by the propaganda of the so-called dry-farming movement, which promoted the idea that the semiarid western plains could be conquered agriculturally through the use of new dry-farming techniques such as deep plowing, cultivated fallow, and drought-resistant plant varieties. Many who came to the west-river area were disciples of the movement, but not experienced farmers. Recruitment was heavy among ranchers, tenants, and agricultural laborers on the southern plains and among urban dwellers in the East who were attracted to the possibility of possessing a farm on one of America's last frontiers. Many found dry-farming to be far more difficult and uncertain than they had anticipated and eventually left. The hardy ones that persisted became the core of the west-river agricultural population.[13] This population contained some foreign-born elements, but it was essentially very different from the population east of the Missouri River.

When considering the migrations that brought settlers to South Dakota's agricultural frontiers, it is important to keep in mind that timing and information flow were the two crucial factors that determined events. Timing meant that certain source areas, both in America and overseas, were "ripe" for migration to new frontiers at certain times. The flow of information was important in that people seldom left their homes for a new life in an unsettled land without first acquiring what they considered to be reasonably reliable information about their prospective destination. Pioneers did not wander blindly into the unknown grasslands. They apparently followed well-used information networks specific to their ethnic group. These networks linked widely scattered settlements and enclaves in Europe and the Midwest and served as an effective means of spreading information about economic opportunity wherever it arose. Once a few members of any group went to and settled in a new place, their success was reported in the older American settlements or in Europe and uncertainty was reduced. The flow of emigrants to the new frontier then proceeded with relative confidence because the information

12. For a recent discussion of the participation of the east-river settlements in the last Dakota boom, *see* Herbert S. Schell, "Widening Horizons at the Turn of the Century: The Last Dakota Land Boom," *South Dakota History* 12 (Summer/Fall 1982): 93-117.

13. The best treatment of the dry-farming movement and of the kind of settler attracted to it is found in Mary W. M. Hargreaves, *Dry Farming in the Northern Great Plains, 1900-1925* (Cambridge, Mass.: Harvard University Press, 1957).

feedbacks were private (letters and word of mouth) or, at worst, semipublic (foreign language newspapers) and were therefore trustworthy. While "Dakota Fever" may have been widespread, the information and migration flows that led to the frontier were discrete—as were the population subgroups that followed them and eventually occupied different parts of South Dakota.[14]

## The Ethnic Pattern

Accompanying this article is a series of maps (Figures 2-7) that depict the 1910 geographic distribution of the six most numerically significant ethnic groups in the state. The maps are based on data from the 1910 United States census, the timing of which is late enough to show both east- and west-river distributions. Each map imparts two pieces of information. The first is the number of people (circle size) residing in a county that belonged to a particular ethnic group or "stock." Inclusion requires that the individual either was born in the particular mother country or was the American-born child of someone born in that country. The second piece of information is that group's proportion of the total foreign stock residing in the county (shading). In other words, both the raw numbers and the relative importance of groups can be seen at the same time.[15]

A quick perusal of the maps will show that, even at the relatively gross scale of county data, a striking degree of localization or segregation of groups exists. To a large extent, ethnic groups tended to colonize particular areas of the state. This tendency is especially apparent in the eastern half of the state (one must bear in mind that the west-river patterns are difficult to interpret because the total foreign stock is usually a very small portion of the county population in the first place).[16] Further, when ethnic groups are mapped at the scale of the individual farm, the segregation is even more pronounced. With the aid of platbooks, ethnic

14. For an excellent treatment of the kind of information flows that brought settlers to the various Dakota frontiers, *see* John C. Hudson, "Migration to an American Frontier," *Annals of the Association of American Geographers* 66 (1976): 242-65. Swedish migration flows to Clay County are specifically treated in Ostergren, "Prairie Bound: Migration Patterns to a Swedish Settlement."

15. Similar maps are published for the entire Upper Midwest in Ostergren, "Geographic Perspectives on the History of Settlement," pp. 32-34.

16. In 1910, the foreign stock in South Dakota numbered 318,119 persons, or 54.4 percent of the total population of 583,888.

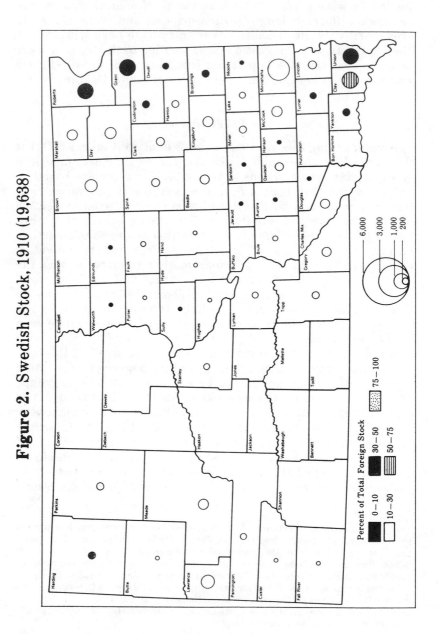

**Figure 2. Swedish Stock, 1910 (19,638)**

land-ownership maps can be constructed with some labor (the names of land owners must be cross-checked with names in the manuscript census in order to determine ethnicity) for any east-river county, and the result will be a "patchwork-quilt" pattern of ethnic clustering.[17] Thus, a basic geographic fact of ethnic settlement is the residential segregation that resulted from the natural desire to seek out one's own kind and from the ever-present influence of the information networks.

One of the first foreign groups to settle South Dakota in large numbers was the Swedes. The bulk of the Swedish settlement was in the eastern counties of the east-river area, with the strongest concentrations in the extreme southeastern and northeastern corners of the state. During the 1860s, the first settlements were established in Union, Clay, and Minnehaha counties. A substantial portion of these settlers were direct immigrants from areas of agricultural distress in Sweden. Others came from earlier established settlements in central Iowa and northern Illinois. During the Great Dakota Boom, the heaviest Swedish concentrations developed in Grant, Roberts, Marshall, Day, and Brown counties. Many of these settlers were second-generation migrants out of the large Swedish settlements of east-central Minnesota and extreme western Wisconsin. The evidence also suggests some westward movement from east-river settlements to selected west-river counties after the turn of the century.

The Norwegians, second only to the Germans, were one of the largest ethnic groups in South Dakota in 1910 (Figure 3). The Norwegian concentrations formed a more or less continuous band in the "row counties"—the easternmost tiers of counties along the border with Minnesota.[18] The general geographical configuration of Norwegian settlement in the Upper Midwest is that of a sweeping arc stretching from south-central Wisconsin through central Minnesota to the Red River Valley of the North. The clustering along South Dakota's eastern border is the westernmost extension of the central segment of this Norwegian "arc of settlement." The first Norwegian settlements were located in the south-

17. *See,* for example, D. R. Salonen, "Taking Hold: A Study of Land Acquisition, Land Ownership and Community Development in Northeast Brookings County, 1870-1916" (M.S. thesis, South Dakota State University, 1977). For an example from Minnesota, *see* John G. Rice, *Patterns of Ethnicity in a Minnesota County, 1880-1905,* University of Umeå, Geographical Reports, no. 4 (Umeå, Sweden, 1973).

18. Chittick, "Recipe for Nationality Stew," p. 135, uses the term "row counties" to describe the location of the heaviest Norwegian concentrations.

**Figure 3.** Norwegian Stock, 1910 (48,721)

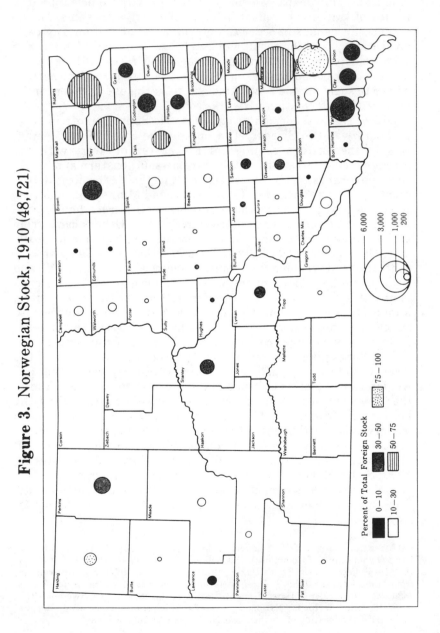

**Figure 4.** Danish Stock, 1910 (12,690)

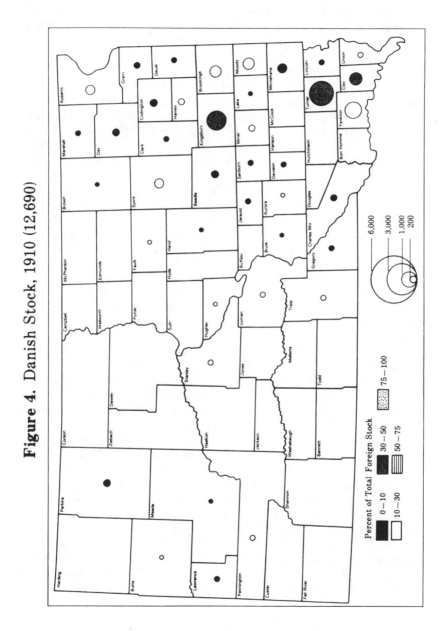

eastern counties of Union, Clay, and Yankton. As with the Swedes, these settlements received direct infusions of settlers from Norway, but linkages with older settlements in Iowa and Wisconsin were also important. In the Great Dakota Boom, Norwegian settlement spread along the Big Sioux and James valleys. In the majority of the row counties, the Norwegian share of the foreign stock exceeded fifty percent. In Lincoln County, it exceeded seventy-five percent. Many who settled these eastern counties came by way of the old Norwegian settlements in southeastern Minnesota and western Wisconsin, where considerable recruitment efforts were undertaken by the Dakota Territory Bureau of Immigration.[19]

The other Scandinavian group—the Danes—came via migration paths similar to those of the Norwegians. Their South Dakota settlements were essentially daughter settlements of older midwestern communities. The largest Danish settlement was in the vicinity of Viborg in Turner County, where the Danish stock accounted for nearly half of the foreign stock in 1910 (Figure 4). Major settlements were also established in Yankton, Clay, and Kingsbury counties. When the Danish distribution is added to the Swedish and Norwegian, the extent of the Scandinavian dominance all along the extreme eastern part of the state is apparent.

The Germans were the largest ethnic group, accounting for roughly one-fifth of the total foreign stock (Figure 5). If other German-speaking groups are included, such as the German-Russians, the Swiss, and the Austrians, the German element in the state probably exceeded one hundred thousand in number or one-third of the total. More so than any other group, the Germans developed settlements nearly everywhere in the state, including the west-river counties. The Germans were also less inclined to come in groups, migrating often as single families or individuals instead. They arrived in the state in a more or less continuous stream that spanned all settlement booms. Both Wisconsin and Illinois were important staging areas. Because of the great length of time that Germans had been arriving in the United States, many Dakota settlers were third generation. Many also came from blue-collar, nonfarm backgrounds in or around the industrial centers of Buffalo, Cleveland, Detroit, Saint Louis, Milwaukee, and Chicago. One researcher has suggested that of all groups, the

19. *See* Schell, "Official Immigration Activities," p. 19.

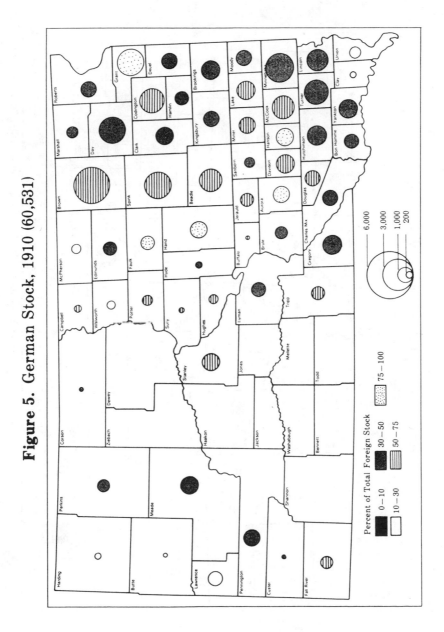

**Figure 5. German Stock, 1910 (60,531)**

## Figure 6. Russian* Stock, 1910 (30,678)

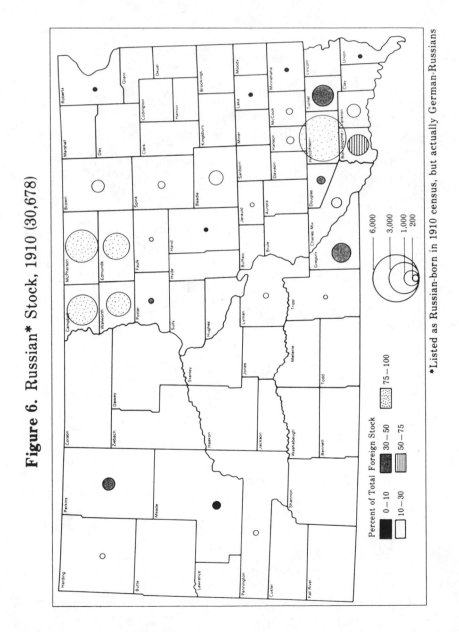

*Listed as Russian-born in 1910 census, but actually German-Russians

Germans, when taken as a whole, were the least likely to have had prior agricultural experience in America.[20]

One of the major and most cohesive ethnic groups was the German-Russians. The German-Russians were Russian-born, German-speaking people who emigrated from the large German agricultural colonies established in the south of Russia by Catherine II and Alexander I during the late eighteenth and early nineteenth centuries. The German colonies in Russia were concentrated in two areas—the Volga region and the region north of the Black Sea. These colonies had been settled by industrious peasants from various parts of Germany, Switzerland, and the low countries. Throughout the nineteenth century these colonies remained exceptionally close-knit. They preserved their German culture as well as their religious predilections. Most colonies were wholly Catholic or Protestant. Many belonged to rather exclusive Protestant movements, such as the Hutterites and the Mennonites.

The German-Russians arrived in South Dakota in considerable numbers during the late 1870s and developed an especially strong immigrant flow in the late 1880s. The geographic distribution of German-Russian stock (Figure 6) is a strongly segregated one, with two major east-river concentrations—one in the southern counties of Yankton, Bon Homme, Turner and Hutchinson; the other in the northern counties of Campbell, McPherson, Walworth, and Edmunds. Both concentrations have later extensions located in the west-river counties immediately to their west. The German-Russians made their way to South Dakota via extremely effective and discrete migration routes. They were lured to the region in part by railroad agents and immigration officials who prized the German-Russians for their exceptional reputation as agriculturalists. But they were also rather careful in the selection of settlement sites, commonly sending small groups ahead to locate and secure land before larger numbers arrived.[21] Thus, the German-Russians moved almost exclusively within a network of colonies established by their own kind and virtually closed to outsiders.[22] According to John C. Hudson, it was not uncommon in

20. Hudson, "Migration to an American Frontier," p. 248.
21. For a description of this practice, *see* G. August Bischoff, "A 1909 Report on Russian-German Settlements in Southern Dakota," trans. Anton H. Richter, *South Dakota History* 11 (Summer 1981): 186-89.
22. *See* the mapped migration routes of German-Russians in Hudson, "Migration to an American Frontier," p. 246. *See also* the discussion and maps of settlement patterns in Anton H. Richter, " 'Gebt ihr den Vorzug': The German-Lanuage Press of North and South Dakota," *South Dakota History* 10 (Summer 1980): 189-92.

*Wagonloads of sacked grain await shipment from Eureka, a German-Russian community in McPherson County and an important shipping point for wheat in the 1890s.*

the early part of this century to find individuals in the German-Russian settlements who had lived at one time or another in all of the established Dakota settlements. Nearly everyone had relatives in each settlement area.[23]

23. Hudson, "Migration to an American Frontier," p. 247.

*The main street of Eureka featured many German-named businesses such as this early drugstore.*

In South Dakota, most German-Russians came from the Black Sea colonies. The Volga group was more commonly found in the plains states located farther west and along the Pacific coast. Only a few of the Volga group settled in the state, primarily in the west-river counties of Perkins and Harding. The first German-Russian settlements were located near Yankton. Separate colonies were founded northwest of Yankton by Protestant and Catholic groups that arrived in the mid-1870s. Subsequent settlements were founded later in that decade around Tyndall, Menno, and Freeman. These clusters served as a staging area for later expansions during the 1880s to places farther west and into the counties along both sides of the border with North Dakota. Included among the German-Russians were colonies of Mennonites and Hutterites—highly cohesive Anabaptist groups, the latter of which organized its settlements on a communal model.

More than any other group, the German-Russians successfully transplanted the culture, social organization, and agricultural practices they had known in the homeland. While the American land-survey system discouraged the compact agricultural villages that they were accustomed to in Europe, they still founded numerous small agricultural hamlets that effectively served as focal points in their settlements. As in Russia, these hamlets were closely identified with certain regional and religious backgrounds. The economic life of the German-Russian settlements, however, was not completely closed. They are credited with bringing new forms of wheat culture to the semiarid grasslands. Their settlements became important centers for the diffusion of this culture and important shipping points for the early bountiful harvests of the new wheat varieties.

The other sizeable non-English-speaking group to settle in South Dakota was the Bohemians. Although listed in the 1910 United States census as Austrians, the Bohemians were the major representative of the Austro-Hungarian Empire to settle in the state (Figure 7). Theirs was a highly organized settlement process. The earliest contingents were organized in Chicago and proceeded westward to Knox County, Nebraska, and Bon Homme County in South Dakota. These early settlements were established in the late 1860s and early 1870s and were fairly direct migrations from the old world to the new. A large and compact settlement eventually developed around Tabor in Bon Homme County. Subsequent migration in the 1880s resulted in additional settlements in Charles Mix, Gregory, and Brule counties, with many

**Figure 7. Austrian\* Stock, 1910 (11,112)**

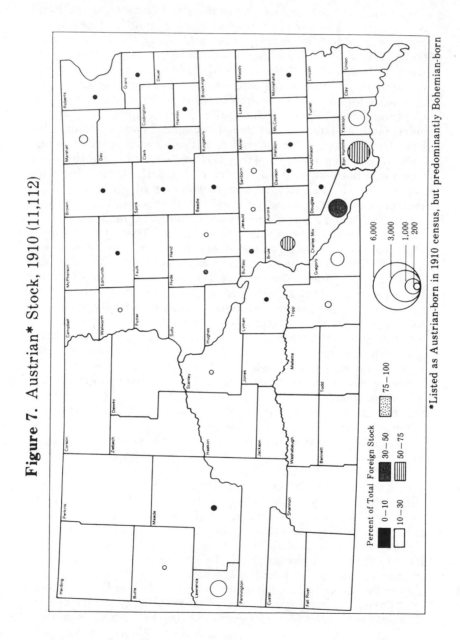

Percent of Total Foreign Stock

0 — 10
10 — 30
30 — 50
50 — 75
75 — 100

6,000
3,000
1,000
200

\*Listed as Austrian-born in 1910 census, but predominantly Bohemian-born

of the settlers coming from older settlements in Wisconsin and Iowa. The Bohemians were somewhat of an exception to the largely Protestant mix in South Dakota in that they were predominantly Roman Catholic.

One other major ethnic group with more than ten thousand stock in 1910 was represented in South Dakota—the Irish (11,422). It is difficult, however, to say anything remarkable about the distribution of this distinctive, but easily assimilated, English-speaking group. They were not known as agriculturalists in the Upper Midwest, and they seldom established close-knit homogeneous enclaves as other groups did. Rather, their distribution was ubiquitous (they represent roughly one to two percent of the foreign stock in virtually every county, both east and west river) and frequently oriented to local requirements for day labor and nonagricultural work in the towns.

Other groups of some size include the Dutch (5,285), who largely arrived as second-generation migrants from Dutch settlements in Michigan, Wisconsin, and Iowa. The first Dutch settlement was in Bon Homme County in 1873. Sizeable Dutch settlements were later established in Douglas and Charles Mix counties. Douglas County eventually contained the major concentration with the Dutch accounting for 19.2 percent of the foreign stock in that county in 1910. Also of local significance were the Finns (1,381). Finnish settlements of some size in the east-river counties were located at Lake Norden in Hamlin County and in Savo Township of Brown County. Like most Finnish agricultural communities in the Midwest, they were populated by Finns who had spent time in the industrial mining communities of Michigan, Wisconsin, and Minnesota. A third group of Finns took up residence in the northern Black Hills. Other small ethnic groups of less than one thousand persons occasionally supported a compact settlement or two, such as the Poles who had a settlement in the northern part of Day County, which was a daughter settlement of earlier communities in Minnesota and Wisconsin.

The ethnic pattern in South Dakota was a pattern of enclaves —a patchwork quilt—produced by the patterns of information flow and migration that brought settlers to the state.[24] The intriguing thing about the pattern is the realization that each of

24. For an idea of the pattern of ethnic enclaves, *see* the maps in Chittick, "Recipe for Nationality Stew," pp. 104-6, and in Richter, " 'Gebt ihr den Vorzug,' " p. 190.

*These Finnish immigrants settled in Savo Township in Brown County.*

these enclaves was a cultural and social entity, held together by the ties of kinship, culture, church, and linkage with other places. The nature of the environment, American social institutions, and the American economic system determined that the character of these immigrant agricultural communities would change over time. The general trend of that change and the difference between places in effecting that change is the essence of the impact of South Dakota's ethnic groups on its culture and economy.

### Ethnicity and Rural Life

The patchwork-quilt pattern of ethnic settlement in South Dakota was quickly institutionalized by the immigrant church. Indeed, one of the first undertakings in most immigrant settlements, beyond that of insuring survival, was the founding of a church. Organizational meetings commonly took place in a settler's home and were conducted by laymen because of the shortage of clergy in pioneer settlements. Usually, the new congregation's membership grew rapidly. A permanent building was soon erected and a call sent out for a permanent minister of the faith.

In a short time, most immigrant settlements supported at least one organized religious establishment.[25] Doctrinal differences and schism often fostered the establishment of more than one (especially among the Norwegians who seem to have been greatly inclined toward schismatic activity).

These churches and the spatial distribution of their membership, which normally coincided with the bounds of the ethnic settlement, defined a functional region with the church as the nodal point. At this time, no other institution on the frontier could serve this essential purpose of solidifying the ethnic settlement into a focused community. Townships, arbitrarily defined by the land survey, lacked the necessary social relevance. Towns in South Dakota were more often than not sited by the railroads and were intended to facilitate commerce, not social consciousness. Granges, cooperatives, and farmer's associations came much to late to provide social cohesiveness. Thus, depending on the cultural homogeneity of the local population, the membership field

25. For a good description of this process as it applied to German-Russian communities in southeastern South Dakota, *see* Bischoff, "1909 Report on Russian-German Settlements," pp. 193-98.

*A large Swedish settlement supported the Bloomingdale Swedish Baptist Church near Centerville, South Dakota.*

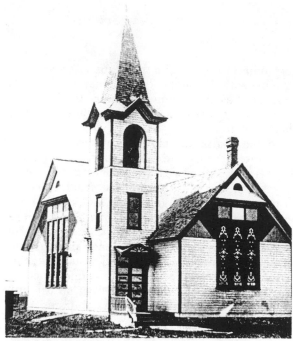

*The German Reform church in Chancellor, South Dakota, is one of many similar structures that dotted the plains. Below, the interior of a Scandinavian church in the Black Hills featured an altar painting in an elaborately carved wooden frame.*

of the rural church congregation often took on an exclusive character. Its well defined boundaries were a reflection of the ties of
kinship, culture, and linkage with other places that identified the
group that settled there.

In addition to this tendency to define "place" and "community,"
the church upheld values and preserved continuity with the cultural past. Services in rural immigrant churches were commonly
held in ethnic languages well into the early part of the twentieth
century. Church schools instructed the young in the old language,
and congregations postponed for as long as possible the inevitable need to begin keeping official records in English. Immigrant
churches observed the old holidays and preserved the traditional
music and customs. Women's organizations provided the opportunity to carry on folk crafts. From the pulpit, the clergy remon-
strated against the use of alcohol, loose morals, and casual association with outsiders. While the outside world could not be
avoided forever, the church functioned as the first, and in some
ways the only, defense against rapid change.[26]

As it performed these functions that were so basic to cultural
maintenance, the church also became a symbolic place and structure on the landscape. In South Dakota's open plains, the church
building was the dominant structure on the landscape, with the
possible exception of the grain elevator. With its white clapboard
siding and gleaming spire, it was visible for miles, as any traveler
of the backroads of the state can attest. Although most country
churches in South Dakota were quite similar in architectural
style, because building styles in the United States had become
more or less standardized by the latter half of the nineteenth century, there were considerable efforts on the part of immigrant settlers to add symbolic pieces of ornamentation to the outside.
These usually took the form of special kinds of crosses or carvings on the tower (much of which disappeared in a rush of remod-
eling that took place after World War II, but can still be seen in
old photographs or found discarded in church basements). More
so than the exteriors, the interiors of country churches were dec-
orated to resemble the cultural past. Carvings and decorative
woodwork modeled after some parish church in Europe, altar
paintings brought from the old country, and foreign-language in-
scriptions on ceilings and walls were commonplace features. In a

---

26. Robert C. Ostergren, "The Immigrant Church as a Symbol of Community and
Place in the Upper Midwest," *Great Plains Quarterly* 1 (Fall 1981): 228.

sense, one might even say that the contrast between the exteriors and the interiors of the immigrant churches symbolized what was happening to the immigrants themselves—they were becoming outwardly American and inwardly ethnic.[27]

In any case, the central role of the church as a conservative force that defended cultural continuity with the past cannot be overestimated. It was the key to cultural maintenance and local identity in all immigrant communities. Its relative strength was an important factor in determining the rate of cultural change. A measure of its local importance is the great number of country churches erected. By the turn of the century, many American church leaders lamented the fact that the American Midwest was simply "overchurched."[28] In recent decades, as people have left the countryside in increasing numbers and communities have been forced to merge, the abandonment of country churches is a stark reminder of the different social order that once existed.[29]

Without doubt, a strong ethnic, social, and cultural life, built around church and kinship, persisted well into this century in many parts of South Dakota. There was, of course, variation in the degree of persistence from group to group and from place to place, which is difficult to generalize about without an exhaustive study of the many communities. As suggested earlier, the variance was related to the background and migratory experience of each settlement in question. Cohesive groups that traveled exclusive paths to the Dakota frontier, such as the German-Russians, can be expected to have maintained their ethnic distinctiveness longer. At the other extreme, there were many German settlements, for example, in which the inhabitants had rather scattered origins and a lengthy experience with America. Another significant factor seems to be proximity to urban centers. The larger cities cast a shadow, so to speak, over the ability of a community to look inwardly on itself. On the other hand, this writer has no-

27. For a discussion of architectural style in rural church construction in the Upper Midwest, *see* ibid., pp. 229-30.

28. Ibid., p. 225.

29. South Dakota had 2,180 church organizations in 1916 with 199,017 members. Church membership in that year amounted to 28.5 percent of the total state population. It is generally thought that any "churched population" figure that approaches 30 percent is extremely high since most congregations report only adult communicant membership. For a complete statistical treatment of South Dakota religious bodies in 1890, 1906, 1916, and 1936, *see* Donald D. Parker, *Denominational Histories of South Dakota* ([Brookings]: South Dakota State University, [1964]), pp. 261-78.

ticed that although ethnic identity may fade in these old settlements, attachment to place and community persists. If one asks rural South Dakotans who they are, they will most likely give you the name of a place, not a group, and will express some affinity to that place. In many ways, the change that has occurred in this century has been a transferral of identity from ethnicity to place, which is really only a change of labels. The rediscovery of ethnicity today, which is so evident almost everywhere, is really quite plastic—it is a fashionably nostalgic label for localism.

Polemics aside, it is quite reasonable to describe most of South Dakota's early twentieth century rural immigrant society as socially and culturally ethnic, but economically American. At that time, most rural neighborhoods were still quite parochial and inward-looking socially. Interaction with other groups was generally difficult, mainly because of cultural values and prejudices. Most studies of ethnic intermarriage, for instance, find that it generally did not occur in rural areas until school consolidation in the twentieth century brought larger numbers of young people from different ethnic groups into contact with one another. Another inhibiting factor was that the church controlled the marriage process, and most immigrant churches had rather exclusive ideas about the whole subject of marriage outside the community. In his study of intermarriage among ethnic groups in North Dakota, John C. Hudson found that endogamy was the rule for all groups. In comparing groups, he found that the German-Russians were the most endogamous, followed by the Norwegians. The Old-Americans were the least endogamous.[30] While social contact across community and ethnic boundaries may not have been a widespread practice, social contact among the migration linkages between communities in various parts of the Midwest was common. Thus, marriages between young men who homesteaded in the Dakotas and young girls in older settlements in Minnesota, Wisconsin, or Iowa was an established pattern, as was the practice of taking a spouse in the old parish back in Europe. The major area of social contact between ethnic groups in South Dakota was the market town, which was basically a Yankee place and therefore neutral ground. This situation did not change until mass retirement among the settler generation caused large numbers of country folk to take up residence in town.

While a certain cultural identity and social aloofness was readily maintained, most immigrant farmers became Americanized

30. Hudson, "Migration to an American Frontier," pp. 256-58.

rapidly when it came to economic life. In part, it was the encounter with an alien environment that caused them to abandon the agricultural techniques and tools they had always known. With the exception of the German-Russians, few Dakota settlers had much experience with the open prairie or the semiarid plains. Nearly all dealt with the task of drawing a living from the new environment by engaging in experimentation and by borrowing ideas from others, especially the Americans. The prairie simply could not be conquered by equipment and agricultural practices known to people who had essentially farmed a woodland environment. A case in point, cited by Hudson, is the bill of lading for an "emigrant car" (box car) hired by a Norwegian farmer named Elkens when he moved his family to the Dakota frontier near Fargo in 1888. Elkens took two cows, two calves, a barrel of salt pork, a cook stove, 250 fence posts, a mower, a corn planter, a cultivator, a breaking plow, and miscellaneous items.[31] He obviously intended to experiment, as did most settlers. In fact, the first crops recorded all across the Dakotas exhibit no significant variation from national trends or between ethnic groups. Most studies have found that complete adaptation was the rule. The only evidence for ethnic preference comes in the form of what Terry G. Jordon calls "cultural rebound."[32] The idea here is that once economic stability was assured by successfully mastering the standard American crops and techniques, the immigrant was sometimes disposed to dabble in older practices and crops as a secondary endeavor, but never as his main effort to keep his family alive.

Economic adaptation was also encouraged by the fact that the immigrant farmer ultimately had to deal with the Americans in economic matters. The seed dealer, the implement dealer, the general merchant, the banker, the elevator operator, and, at least in the early days, even the elected officials in the trade town were all Americans. Business was conducted in town on American terms. Thus, we must take care not to go too far in our impressions of ethnic pluralism. The landscape may have been a patchwork quilt of tiny communities whose inhabitants spoke only to one another, but they all belonged to a larger economic community, which was the trade area of the local town. In this larger community, other considerations took precedence.

31. Ibid., p. 251.
32. Terry G. Jordan, *German Seed in Texas Soil: Immigrant Farmers in Nineteenth-Century Texas* (Austin: University of Texas Press, 1966), pp. 199-201.

One could say that the immigrant farmer lived simultaneously in two worlds — a social-cultural world based on kinship, religion, and continuity with the past and an economic world that was modern and alien, but absolutely essential. It was along the interface between these two worlds that change took place. Any activity that occupied the boundary zone between these worlds could be stressful to the first. A good example is land inheritance because land could be looked upon in two ways. It could be viewed entrepreneurially as a source of speculation or quick profit. In this sense, material advantage might outweigh communal and noneconomic goals. In another sense, land could be viewed as the giver of life — a symbol of familial accomplishment and identity in the community. Here, the ultimate goal would be its orderly inheritance in the interest of maintaining family and commu-

*The street signs in Tabor, South Dakota, illustrate a modern blend of cultures in an area heavily settled by Bohemians (Czechs).*

nity continuity. Issues such as this were crucial to what happened in ethnic communities across the state, and studies have shown that the response could be highly varied.[33]

## Conclusion

European immigrants played a significant role in the agricultural settlement of South Dakota and in the shaping of its rural culture. A major aim of this article, however, has been to point out that the role they played was as highly varied as their origins, the timing of their arrival, and the homogeneity of their settlements. To generalize too much about the propensity of any national group to maintain its culture in this new environment is an uncertain endeavor because every settlement was the product of discrete migration and information flows that linked it to other places in the Midwest and in Europe. Accordingly, its population had a particular past association with American culture and environments, with European culture and environments, and with the experience of migration under the conditions existing at a certain time. It is the great variety of these factors in South Dakota settlement history that makes its rural communities so distinctive and fascinating.

33. For a full discussion of land inheritance practice as a determinant of cultural maintenance in immigrant rural communities, *see* Robert C. Ostergren, "Land and Family in Rural Immigrant Communities," *Annals of the Association of American Geographers* 71 (1981): 400-411.

# LAND AND FAMILY IN RURAL IMMIGRANT COMMUNITIES

## ROBERT C. OSTERGREN

ABSTRACT. The maintenance of rural immigrant communities in the American Middle West depended upon the transmission of landed wealth within the family. An examination of land transfer practices in seven Swedish communities in Minnesota shows that there was variation in behavior between communities. These differences are related to the social and institutional character of the settlements and to land transfer patterns in migration-linked districts in Sweden.

IN recent years the experience of nineteenth century European migration to North America has been increasingly viewed as a trans-Atlantic phenomenon. Whereas in the past scholars tended to view European emigration and American immigration as distinct topics, each with its own set of problems, they are now more often viewed as a single experience that linked people and events on both sides of the Atlantic.[1] For the migrants themselves, the uprooting and subsequent resettlement provided both a continuity of experience and a divergence of experience with their European past. Continuity of experience generally was greatest in the area of social and cultural relationships where a degree of isolation could be maintained from American conditions. It was common, therefore, for Europeans to settle in cohesive neighborhoods where traditional ties with church, family, and homeland could be perpetuated, but at the same time they entered into occupations or tilled the soil in an economic environment where American organization prevailed. Here the experience was divergent—the traditions and customs of the past were abandoned almost immediately.

In the rural immigrant community an important interface between the divergent experience of economic life and the traditional experience of social and cultural life was the ownership and inheritance of land. In one sense, land could be viewed entrepreneurially as a source of specu-

lation or quick profit; material advantage might outweigh communal and noneconomic goals. In another sense, land could be viewed as the giver of life—a symbol of familial accomplishment and identity in the community. Here the ultimate goal would be its orderly inheritance in the interest of maintaining family and community continuity.[2] Studies of colonial society have shown the relationship between land and family to be a key variable in community development.[3] Yet we know relatively little about its role in the societies created by the westward expansion of the American agricultural frontier during the nineteenth century. The settlement of Middle Western frontiers, in particular, often involved direct migration between agricultural districts in Europe and "daughter settlements" in America. For these migration-linked communities there is a strong possibility, as Kathleen Conzen has suggested, that the maintenance of community in America and the maintenance of continuity with a European past revolved around this crucial relationship.[4]

---

Dr. Ostergren is Assistant Professor of Geography at the University of Wisconsin-Madison in Madison, WI 53706.

---

[1] An early statement of this perspective is Frank Thistlethwaite, "Migration from Europe Overseas in the Nineteenth and Twentieth Centuries," Xle Congres International des Sciences Historiques, Stockholm-Uppsala, Sweden: Almquist & Wiksell, 1960); a more recent overview may be found in Sune Åkerman, "From Stockholm to San Francisco," Annales Academaie Regiae Scientiarium Upsaliensis, Vol. 19 (1975).

[2] For background on this distinction see James A. Henretta, "Families and Farms: Mentalité in Pre-Industrial America," William and Mary Quarterly, 3rd series, Vol. 25 (1978), pp. 3–32 and the study on which Henretta's discussion is based: James T. Lemon, The Best Poor Man's Country: A Geographical Study of Early Southeastern Pennsylvania (Baltimore: Johns Hopkins University Press, 1972). See also, David P. Gagan, "The Indivisibility of Land: A Microanalysis of the System of Land Inheritance in Nineteenth Century Ontario," Journal of Economic History, Vol. 36 (1976), pp. 126–41.

[3] See for example, Philip J. Greven, Jr., Four Generations: Population, Land and Family in Colonial Andover, Massachusetts (Ithaca: Cornell University Press, 1970); Kenneth A. Lockridge, A New England Town, The First Hundred Years: Dedham, Massachusetts 1636–1736 (New York: Norton, 1970); and John Demos, A Little Commonwealth: Family Life in Plymouth Colony (New York, Oxford University Press, 1970).

[4] Kathleen N. Conzen, "Historical Approaches to the Study of Rural Ethnic Communities," in Frederick C. Luebke, ed., Ethnicity on the Great Plains (Lin-

ANNALS OF THE ASSOCIATION OF AMERICAN GEOGRAPHERS Vol. 71, No. 3, September 1981
© 1981 by the Association of American Geographers. Printed in U.S.A.

This is a study of the relationship between land and family in migration-linked rural communities in Sweden and America. The aim is to see how this relationship may have varied between immigrant communities and to assess the role of linkages with parent communities in Sweden in determining variation. The study is based on a group of Swedish settlements in east-central Minnesota and the origin areas in Sweden to which some of them were linked. These communities were chosen because of the high-quality data available for detailed work at the family level in Swedish and Swedish-American historical records and because the author had previous research experience with them.[5] The study focuses on the period 1885–1915 which was the post-migration era for these settlements and a period of consolidation and adjustment on both sides of the Atlantic. It was also a period in which the generation that had experienced the migrations reached old age and was succeeded by its children.

### Setting the Context:
### The Upper Rum Valley Settlements

The initial study area comprises the nine civil townships that form the immediate drainage basin of the great bend of the Rum River as it passes through Isanti County in east-central Minnesota (Fig. 1). Although opened to settlement in the 1850s, the serious occupation of the region took place during the two decades following the Civil War. During that period large numbers of Swedes, some Germans, and a sprinkling of New Englanders and New Yorkers arrived to take up homestead land and to purchase land

coln: University of Nebraska Press, 1980), pp. 9–13 and Kathleen N. Conzen, "Farm and Family: A German Settlement on the Minnesota Frontier," (paper presented at the American Historical Association Annual Meetings, Washington, D.C., December 1976). Others who have touched on this perspective in the American Midwest from a similar perspective include: Sonya Salamon, "Ethnic Differences in Farm Family Land Transfers," *Rural Sociology,* Vol. 45 (1980), pp. 290–308; Ingolf Vogeler, "Ethnicity, Religion and Farm Land Transfers in Western Wisconsin," *Ecumene,* Vol. 7 (1975), pp. 6–13; and Marianne Deininger and Douglas Marshall, "A Study of Land Ownership by Ethnic Groups from Frontier Times to the Present in a Marginal Farming Area of Minnesota," *Land Economics* (1955), pp. 351–60.

[5] Robert C. Ostergren, "A Community Transplanted: The Formative Experience of a Swedish Immigrant Community in the Upper Middle West," *Journal of Historical Geography,* Vol. 5 (1979), pp. 189–212.

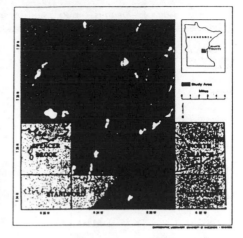

FIG. 1.    Isanti County and study area.

offered by the Lake Superior and Mississippi Railroad.[6] By 1885 the settlement frontier had passed over the region and by 1890 the best lands were largely gone, although substantial amounts of second-rate land remained in the hands of speculators or with the state government.

Dominating the settlement process were waves of Swedish immigrants, most of them arriving directly from Sweden. For the most part, they tended to come from certain provincial areas. Especially numerous were people from the provinces along the Bothnian coast of northern Sweden and the northwestern provinces of Dalarna, Jämtland and Värmland. Often particular districts and even parishes contributed heavily to the flow of new settlers. This specificity of origins resulted from strong axes of communication and migration that were developed between early settlers in the Rum Valley and their home districts. These axes served to channel additional migrants from the same districts to the valley resulting in a patchwork-quilt

[6] The Lake Superior and Mississippi Railroad held much of the land in the odd numbered sections throughout the eastern portions of Isanti County by virtue of its 1869 federal land grant. During the early 1870s the railroad put its land on the market and aggressively promoted its sale through agents in Sweden. See Lars Ljungmark, *For Sale Minnesota: Organized Promotion of Scandinavian Immigration, 1866-1873* (Chicago: Swedish Pioneer Historical Society, 1971).

TABLE 1.—ORIGINS AND RELIGIOUS AFFILIATION OF SWEDISH COMMUNITIES, 1885

| Community | House-holds 1885 | Dominant home district(s) (PROVINCE, parish) | No. | % | Church affiliation* | No. | % |
|---|---|---|---|---|---|---|---|
| Athens | 76 | DALARNA Rättvik, Orsa | 55 | 72.3 | Athens Luth, MC | 44 | 57.9 |
| Isanti | 126 | HÄLSINGLAND-MEDELPAD | 90 | 71.4 | Isanti Bapt | 70 | 56.3 |
| Cambridge East | 45 | VÄRMLAND-JÄMTLAND | 29 | 64.4 | Cambr. Luth east rotes | 24 | 53.3 |
| Cambridge West | 106 | DALARNA Rättvik | 82 | 77.4 | Cambr. Luth west rotes | 74 | 69.8 |
| Stanchfield | 159 | DALARNA Orsa | 134 | 84.3 | Stanchfield Bapt | 94 | 59.1 |
| Maple Ridge | 62 | VÄSTERGÖTLAND | 39 | 62.9 | Map. Rid. MC, Siloa Luth | 36 | 58.0 |
| Dalbo-Karmel | 127 | DALARNA Venjan | 86 | 67.7 | Dalbo Bapt Karmel MC Salem Luth | 69 | 54.3 |

* Abbreviations: MC = Mission Covenant, Bapt = Baptist, Luth = Lutheran.

pattern of "daughter settlements" representing different parts of Sweden.[7]

The study area was regionalized into communities to better identify these "daughter settlements" (Fig. 2). The communities shown on the map are delimited on the basis of common geographic origin in Sweden (or other origins in the case of German and Old American settlement) and common affiliation with a particular rural immigrant church(s).[8] The result is a fairly

---

[7] The importance of trans-Atlantic axes of migration and communication in the formation of immigrant communities is demonstrated for Swedes in Robert C. Ostergren, "Prairie Bound: Patterns of Migration to a Swedish Settlement on the Dakota Frontier," in Luebke, op. cit., footnote 4, pp. 73–91. See also, John G. Rice and Robert C. Ostergren, "The Decision to Emigrate: A Study in Diffusion," Geografiska Annaler, Vol. 60B (1978), pp. 1–15. For a larger treatment of the operation of migration flows in the Middle West see John C. Hudson, "Migration to an American Frontier," Annals, Association of American Geographers, Vol. 66 (1976), pp. 242–65.

[8] The importance of the rural immigrant church as the focal point of social and cultural organization in immigrant settlements is well documented. For a geographic perspective see: John G. Rice, Patterns of Ethnicity in a Minnesota County, 1880–1905 (Umeå, Sweden: Department of Geography, University of Umeå, Geographical Reports Nr 4, 1973), pp. 39–48; Robert C. Ostergren, "Cultural Homogeneity and Population Stability among Swedish Immigrants in Chisago County," Minnesota History, Vol. 47 (1973), pp. 255–69; and Jon Gjerde, "The Effect of Commu-

real approximation of the spatial structure of social interaction and cultural affinity in the valley. Most of these communities in 1885 could count at least two-thirds of their households as being homogeneous in terms of district or place of origin and most could claim a better than fifty percent membership in the local church (Table 1).[9]

While cultural and social life were differentiated from the beginning, early economic life was relatively uniform. The area was isolated from outside markets because of poor communications and although wheat was produced in modest quantities as a cash crop and rather la-

---

nity on Migration: Three Minnesota Townships 1885–1905," Journal of Historical Geography, Vol. 5 (1979), pp. 403–22.

[9] These figures represent households known to be from a particular origin area or members of a particular church. They are based on information gleaned from numerous sources, including federal and state census manuscripts, land ownership records, directories, church membership registers, and list compiled from church cemeteries. Such information, however, cannot be found for every household in the study area. The figures in Table 1, therefore, represent partial information. In actuality the proportion of households in each community hailing from specific origins or belonging to specific churches was probably somewhat higher. This is especially true of membership in the Baptist and Mission Covenant churches, where the absence of membership registers makes it necessary to rely on cemetery information to determine membership.

boriously hauled along forest trails to distant markets, most economic activity was directed towards local subsistence. While these conditions gradually improved, early economic life throughout the valley was more or less uniformly devoted to proving up the homestead, clearing additional land, and providing for the basics of life.[10]

It is the postsettlement period (1885–1915) that sees these conditions of economic life profoundly altered for the residents of the valley and it is this thirty year period that is the focus of this study. Early in the period the availability of unclaimed arable land declined drastically, closing off the opportunity for new settlement or the expansion of existing economic units without infringing on the property of others. It is also a time in which the pace of economic activity quickened. The brief era of the wheat frontier was closed for this part of Minnesota. Farmers had to clear additional land and diversify their operations. Potatoes became the staple crop in the area and a variety of other crops and animal husbandries were introduced. These changes occurred, in part, because the economic isolation of the formative years in these communities was broken in 1890 with the coming of the railroad branch line, which in turn led to the rise of local market towns, the principal one being the county seat at Cambridge. The intrusion of outside markets added enormously to the value of land and what was produced on it. Control of landed wealth became an important basis of success and integration with the American economy.

### Land and Family in the Postsettlement Period

The changing circumstances of the postsettlement period required by their nature that adjustments would have to be made in the relationship between people and resources. The aim of this section is to examine some of the general trends in this relationship for the study area as a whole in order to provide a base for the more detailed discussion of the response of individu-

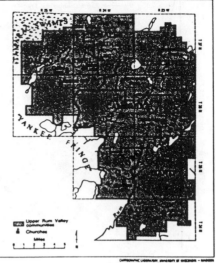

FIG. 2.   Upper Rum Valley communities.

als and communities that follows. Throughout this paper the basic unit of measurement is the *farm household* and the property it controls. The farm household is defined simply as the owner of an operating farm and those that live with him. It is not necessarily a nuclear family. Often it extended outward to include retired parents, married sons and daughters, relatives, and laborers. The degree of extension varied over time as families moved through the cycle of life.

The data base is the 1,460 farm households present in the study area between 1885 and 1915. Data were gathered on each household at five year intervals from federal and state manuscript censuses, county tax, probate, birth, death, and marriage records, directories and platbooks, church registers, cemetery lists, and, where possible, Swedish materials on their premigration history.

The number of households built to a peak level around 1905 and then declined (Table 2). The decline in the number of households after 1905 does not indicate a decline in total population. Actually the population continued to increase until sometime between 1915 and 1920. Average household size moved from just under five persons in 1885 to just over five in 1915; the increase stemmed largely from a greater degree of family extension towards the end of the pe-

---

[10] Information about economic life during the 1860s and 1870s is often found in "America letters" sent back to Sweden. See, for instance, Bjorn Hallerdt, ed. *Emigration från Dalarna* (Falun, Sweden: Dalarnas Museum, 1968), pp. 38–47. As late as 1880, the manuscripts of the federal agricultural census reveal that the average farmer in the area had managed to clear only eighteen acres for crops.

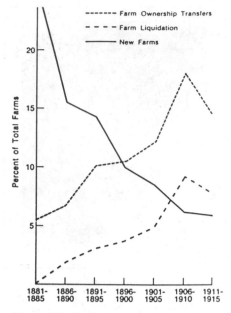

FIG. 3. New farms, farm ownership transfers, and farm liquidations as a percentage of total farms, 1881–1915.

real change in farm size. These values rose at a more or less steady rate with the exceptions of some slight decline in the late 1880s and a slower rate of increase in the late 1890s, both due to agricultural depression. The ownership of land remained throughout the period a most gainful means of wealth accumulation.

With respect to land acquisition and transfer two important trends may be seen (Fig. 3). First, the rate of new farm household establishment in the region dropped off drastically. During the settlement era it was common for as many as half of the households existing at the end of a five year period to have been newly established within that five year period. In the 1880s the rate fell precipitously from those high levels down to about fifteen percent and then declined gradually to just above five percent by 1915. This trend is a reflection of the closing of the settlement frontier. Good agricultural land was becoming scarce by the 1890s and new farms for inmigrants or the sons of local farmers could be established only from marginal land or through the purchase of land from existing units. A second trend is the steady increase in farm ownership transfer. The percentage of farms that were passed on to heirs or sold roughly tripled over the period 1881–1910, followed by a slight downturn after 1910. This trend reflects the aging of a pioneer population of more or less uniform age. Most settlers who took land in the 1860s and 1870s were in their late thirties and forties when they arrived. By the end of the 1890s and the first decade of the twentieth century they were in their late sixties and seventies and ready to relinquish their role as household head. The downturn in the rate of transfer after 1910 is indicative of the passing of this generation and the beginning of a new life cycle for the region.

riod. There was, however, a declining number of economic units on the land after 1905.

The period is also characterized by a very gradual increase in farm size. In 1885 the average farm had just over 100 acres; by 1915 the average had increased to nearly 110 acres. Although there was no great revolution in operating size, there was a substantial increase in landed wealth. The average value of a farm rose from $355 in 1885 to $1,469 in 1915 without any

TABLE 2.—FARM HOUSEHOLDS, 1885–1915

| Community | 1885 | 1890 | 1895 | 1900 | 1905 | 1910 | 1915 |
|---|---|---|---|---|---|---|---|
| Athens | 76 | 80 | 80 | 82 | 78 | 73 | 69 |
| Bradford | 24 | 30 | 30 | 30 | 32 | 30 | 25 |
| Cambridge East | 45 | 48 | 53 | 51 | 57 | 49 | 44 |
| Cambridge West | 106 | 124 | 141 | 145 | 145 | 128 | 119 |
| Dalbo-Karmel | 127 | 160 | 200 | 237 | 251 | 240 | 221 |
| Isanti | 126 | 138 | 153 | 151 | 160 | 149 | 136 |
| Maple Ridge | 62 | 84 | 105 | 124 | 132 | 116 | 106 |
| Stanchfield | 159 | 197 | 218 | 224 | 227 | 197 | 184 |
| Yankee fringe | 44 | 37 | 39 | 43 | 46 | 41 | 36 |
| Outside of communities | 88 | 105 | 122 | 129 | 148 | 132 | 113 |
| Totals | 858 | 1,003 | 1,141 | 1,216 | 1,276 | 1,155 | 1,053 |

TABLE 3.—MEAN SIZE OF LIQUIDATED AND INHERITED FARMS, 1881–1915

|  | 1881–1885 | 1886–1890 | 1891–1895 | 1896–1900 | 1901–1905 | 1906–1910 | 1911–1915 |
|---|---|---|---|---|---|---|---|
| No. of liquidated farms | — | 18 | 36 | 48 | 62 | 107 | 82 |
| Mean size (acres) of liquidated farms | — | 115.8 | 89.4 | 88.0 | 91.7 | 76.2 | 95.7 |
| No. of inherited farms | 46 | 60 | 80 | 78 | 83 | 102 | 70 |
| Mean size (acres) of inherited farms | 189.8 | 146.4 | 159.3 | 150.5 | 167.0 | 155.1 | 141.2 |

The transfer of farm ownership may be subdivided into two distinct types of activity. One is sale to an outside party. In this case the continuity of the family's relationship with the land is not preserved. The family farm is in fact liquidated. The other is sale or inheritance within the family. In this case continuity is maintained because some element of the family remains on the land. Throughout the postsettlement period the farm liquidation rate rose in parallel fashion to the rate of farm ownership transfer, which shows in-family inheritance or sale to have been a fairly constant factor (Fig. 3). In other words, the steady rise in transfers is largely explained by a rise in the liquidation rate rather than an increase in the rate of inheritance.[11] As farm proprietors reached retirement age and the opportunity to purchase new lands declined, there was increased incentive for some owners of existing units to sell out, usually to farmers that wished to pass landed wealth on to their heirs and needed to make additional land purchases in order that there be sufficient landed wealth to make the inheritance process viable. Under such circumstances the pressure for some farms to be liquidated was quite high.

It is quite clear that this pressure was greatest on the owners of smaller operations. Throughout the postsettlement period the average size of liquidated farms was substantially less than the average size of inherited farms (Table 3). There were very large farms that were liquidated and very small farms that were inherited, but on the whole there seems to have been a threshold for inheritance at 80 acres. Better than two-thirds of the inherited farms were 80 acres or more in size, while approximately two-thirds of the liquidated farms were 80 acres or less. In the

absence of a settlement frontier, land for new farms and inheritances was taken from the estates of smaller operators who, in turn, realized substantial financial gain in the high-priced land market.

For those farms that were passed on to heirs, there was differentiation in the inheritance procedure. This differentiation occurred in the timing of transfer, for which two systems were in operation. In one system inheritance occurred before the death or departure of the head of household. As heirs reached maturity, the head began to transfer wealth to them. In some cases the entire inheritance was passed on at once; the parents took on a secondary role to their son or sons in the control of the farm. In others, inheritance was transferred in piecemeal fashion: heirs received parcels at maturity but waited until their parent's retirement before the transfer was completed. In either case the transfer was generally completed before the death or departure of the head. In a second system inheritance occurred only after the death or departure of the household head. Here the inheritance was made through the instrument of a will that was enforced after death. Under this system the household head tended to control property much longer, often to the frustration of the heirs who faced the prospect of waiting almost indefinitely for the means of supporting themselves and a family. Of the two systems the former was the more efficient in affecting continuity of family ownership.

It is also common in land inheritance studies to distinguish between partible and impartible systems of inheritance. This distinction, however, seems to be relatively meaningless in the Rum Valley. Most of the transfers were partible in the sense that something was provided for all children. Although one or two sons might have been selected to acquire control of the farm, they usually did so with the understanding that the other children would be compensated. This

---

[11] A total of 872 transfers of farm ownership occurred over the thirty year period. Of these, 353 were liquidations and 519 were inheritances or in-family sales.

TABLE 4.—FARM LIQUIDATION AND TIMING OF LAND OWNERSHIP TRANSFERS BY COMMUNITY, 1885–1915

| Community | Liquidation rate[a] | Transfer after death/Transfer before death[b] |
|---|---|---|
| Dalbo | 29.1% | 0.91 |
| Cambridge West | 30.0 | 1.31 |
| Athens | 31.8 | 1.03 |
| Stanchfield | 37.5 | 1.63 |
| Bradford | 39.3 | 1.33 |
| Maple Ridge | 44.4 | 1.57 |
| Cambridge East | 47.4 | 2.17 |
| Isanti | 47.5 | 3.13 |
| Yankee fringe | 55.7 | 2.00 |
| Other Swedes | 60.0 | 3.44 |
| Total population | 41.0 | 1.63 |

[a] Percent of all land ownership transfers 1885–1915 resulting in liquidation.
[b] Ratio of land ownership transfers completed after death or departure of household head to those completed before death or departure (includes liquidations).

meant that the land was often mortgaged to provide compensatory payments to the others. In its intestacy laws the State of Minnesota provided equal inheritance for all children and although they were free to dispose of landed wealth in any way they wished, most landowners seemed to share this ideal.[12] The clearest measure of local differentiation in land inheritance, therefore, is in the timing.

### Land, Family, and Community

Given the fact that there was differentiation in land inheritance practice for the study area as a whole, the next step is to see if certain practices were more associated with some communities than others. It is quite natural in agricultural societies for families to adopt land inheritance strategies. Landed wealth was the symbol of the family's independence, past achievement, and future security. It was established at the cost of hard work and deprivation. Strategies for preserving it and passing it on to future generations were natural and important concerns. When strategies become associated with the community, however, they become more than an activity dictated by the economic needs and aspirations of the family. They become linked to the cultural and social needs of the community—its requirement for stability

and continuity with the past. It is at this point that the divergent experience of the economic world comes into contact with the need for continuity in the cultural and social world.

To determine the degree to which communities behaved differently, two measures—the rate of farm liquidation and the ratio of after death to before death timing in the transfer of property—were calculated for each community between 1885 and 1915 (Table 4). The communities may be divided into three groups in terms of the liquidation rate. The communities of Dalbo, Cambridge West, and Athens had very low rates. Only about thirty percent of all farms were liquidated in these communities over the thirty year period. A second group of five communities, including the German one (Bradford), had moderate rates. The Yankee population and the Swedish households that were outside community boundaries had the highest liquidation rates and constitute the third group. If the ratio of transfer timing is placed alongside the liquidation rates, the rank order and grouping of communities remains virtually unchanged. The proportion of after-death transfers is lowest in the group with the low liquidation rates. The highest proportions of after-death transfers are associated with the most unstable communities. Although there is no articulation of it in the historical record, there seems to have been an effort on the part of these communities to pursue certain strategies of land inheritance.[13]

A typical example of land inheritance strategy in one of the more stable communities is the experience of the immigrant Olof A. Wiklund and his family (Fig. 4). Wiklund emigrated with his wife and two children from Rättvik parish (Dalarna) in 1867 and settled in western Springvale township (Cambridge West community) in the same year. He was forty years old at the time. By 1885 he was fifty-nine and had a well established farm of 197 acres. His oldest son was twenty-seven and his American-born son was fifteen. In 1890 his daughter Anna married and the size of the farm declined to 168 acres. Whether the land was sold to provide cash for the marriage or because of hard times is not clear. In 1895 Olof A. purchased 42 acres for

---

[12] Kathleen Conzen arrived at similar conclusions in her study of German settlers in Minnesota, op. cit., footnote 4 (1976).

[13] To date the author has turned up no statement in diaries, wills, or other written documents that suggests any conscious strategy. The number of such sources is few, however, and there is no reason why such concerns would necessarily be recorded.

SWEDISH NAME AND FAMILY:   Stor Ollas Olof Andersson (born 1826)
Wife:   Margreta (born 1830)
Son:   Anders (born 1858)
Daughter:   Anna (born 1860)
SWEDISH PARISH AND VILLAGE:   Rättvik parish, Wikarbyn Village Number 70
EMIGRATED: 1867 at age 40
SETTLED: Springvale Township, Isanti County, Section 28, homestead.
AMERICAN BORN CHILDREN:   Son: Olof S. (born 1870)
AMERICAN NAME:   Olof A. Wiklund

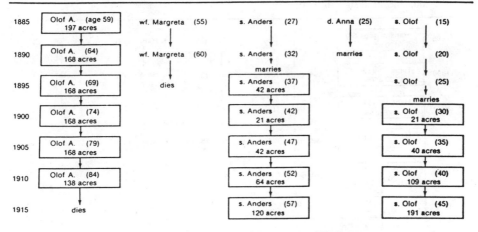

FIG. 4.   Before-death transfer property and life line.

oldest son Andrew (37 years) who married in that year. When his second son married three years later, Wiklund had one-half of Andrew's 42 acres transferred to the new couple. By 1905 the 42 acres had been restored to Andrew and young Olof had been assisted in the purchase of 40 acres of his own. By 1910 Olof A. reached seventy-nine years of age and began to reduce the size of his holdings while assisting the two sons in adding to theirs. He died in 1914 after transferring the remainder of his property to his sons. Throughout his lifetime both sons lived with their families under him in the same household; only after his death did they set up separate households and divide the farm into two operations.

For contrast, an example of an after death strategy in one of the less stable communities is the experience of Hans Peterson and his family (Fig. 5). Peterson emigrated from Torp parish (Medelpad) with his wife and three children at the age of thirty-five. He homesteaded in Isanti township (Isanti community) and operated a farm of 120 acres by 1885. Like Wiklund he had

two sons and a daughter on the farm, all in their twenties. Over the next ten years, however, Peterson retained complete control of the farm. During this time daughter Rebecca married and his two sons reached their middle and late thirties without being married. By 1900 Peterson was sixty-nine years old and still retained control of the land. The oldest son, Olof, had reached his forties and left for Cambridge village where he worked as a laborer for a few years and then disappeared. The second son, Hans, was still on the farm and unmarried at thirty-nine years of age. Five years later, Hans too gave up and left the farm for an unknown destination. In the next few years Peterson's wife died and the old man, living all alone except for hired help, began to sell off parcels of land to his neighbors and a purchaser from outside the community. He died in 1914 at the age of eighty-three and the farm was liquidated.

The experience of these two families was typical of their communities. Cambridge West families on the whole were very conservative—carefully laying out the transfer of property

SWEDISH NAME AND FAMILY:      Torp Henric Persson (born 1831)
                              Wife: Brita (born 1825)
                              Son: Olof (born 1856)
                              Son: Hans (born 1861)
                              Daughter: Rachel (born 1862)

SWEDISH PARISH AND VILLAGE:  Torp Parish, Hjeltanstorp Village

EMIGRATED:  1866, age 35

SETTLED:  Isanti Township, Isantic County, Section 24, homestead.

AMERICAN BORN CHILDREN:  None

AMERICAN NAME:  Hans Peterson

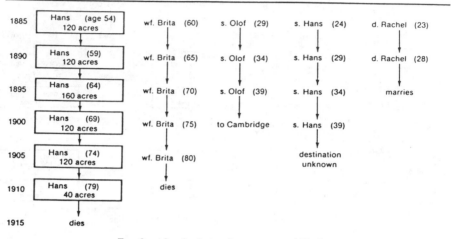

FIG. 5.   After-death transfer property and life line.

while the household head was alive and active. Even their after death transfers were more carefully planned and more successful than similar transfers in other communities. Most sons acquired land early and were able to start families. The pressure on land that this caused was eased through the purchase of land from owners in nearby communities and through the liquidation of smaller holdings that were often held by outsiders. In a territorial sense, the cumulative effect of these transfers was to sharpen the boundaries of the community over time, which could reflect a communal desire for a more closed or exclusive society.[14] Isanti families on the whole

exhibited very mixed behavior. Retention of sons in the community was low. The incidence of older and single land owners was high. There was frequent household turnover and land purchases within the community boundaries were frequently made by outsiders. On the other hand, there was a core of households that did quite effectively transfer land on to the new generation.

The question that quickly arises is whether the behavior isolated here really reflects family strategies or communal tendencies. Differential responses to salient economic opportunities might also be explained by noncultural restraints such as age composition, agricultural specialization, local differentiation in land values, distance from the local market town, or time of arrival. Undoubtedly these variables had an effect, but by all available evidence the effect was slight. Age composition and agricultural specialization

[14] Peter Munch has suggested that the change in the ecological structure of immigrant communities is a reflection of the "open" or "closed" nature of society. In both Athens and Cambridge West there was a noticeable consolidation of land holding. In the other conservative community, Dalbo, the land held by community members was compactly distributed from the beginning. See Peter A. Munch, "Segregation and Assimilation of Norwegian Settlements in Wiscon-

sin," *Norwegian-American Studies and Records*, Vol. 18 (1954), pp. 102–40.

varied little over the study area. The Germans and Yankees were inclined to emphasize cattle more than the Swedes, but the difference was a matter of degree. Land values did vary. The variation, however, was not between communities, but within communities. Land values were highest near the center of each community and were lowest around the peripheries, a pattern produced through the settlement process which featured the sequential taking of land in an outward direction from the respective community cores.[15] While this helps to explain the relative stability of core areas in the less stable communities it says little about differences between communities. Distance to market and time of arrival did certainly vary for all communities, but any correlation with land transfer leads to conflicting conclusions. Dalbo community, which was the furthest from market and the most recently settled, had the lowest liquidation rate and transfer ratio. On the other hand, Cambridge West, with exactly the opposite characteristics, had a liquidation rate and transfer ratio similar to Dalbo's.

A more plausible case can be made for cultural constraints. To an extent, observed behavior corresponds to the dominant cultural background of the community. All three conservative communities were dominated by emigrants of the Swedish province of Dalarna, while the less conservative communities were representative of other parts of Sweden. The one Dalarna community (Stanchfield) that had a high liquidation rate and transfer ratio was focused on a Baptist church, whereas the other Dalarna settlements were strongly Lutheran or Mission Covenant, which suggests that the institutional make-up of the community can also be a factor. The Augustana Lutheran Church, which was the American descendant of the State Church in Sweden, represented a very conservative approach to religion among Swedish-Americans. The Mission Covenant and, to a greater extent, the Swedish Baptist Church were pietistic reactions to the doctrinal conservatism of the Lutheran Church in Sweden and America. Although the precise causal mechanisms may be difficult to define, the fact remains that the conservative communities were Lutheran, those in the middle range

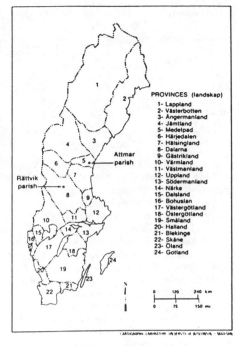

FIG. 6.  Swedish study areas.

were Baptist, and the Swedes with the highest liquidation rate lived outside community boundaries and were unchurched.

### The Trans-Atlantic Linkage

While land transfer strategies can be linked to the cultural background and institutional character of a community, they might also be linked to experience in another place. The communities that exhibited the most conservative land transfer behavior were linked by migration to the Swedish province of Dalarna—an area known for its self-contained parish communities, population stability, and strong freeholding traditions.[16] The other communities were representative of other areas of Sweden. These areas were less isolated from social and economic change in late nineteenth century Sweden. This

---

[15] Robert C. Ostergren, "Rättvik to Isanti: A Community Transplanted," unpublished doctoral dissertation, University of Minnesota, 1976, pp. 78–97 and 107–21.

[16] Two important examples of the Swedish literature on the distinctiveness of Dalarna are: Gustaf Näsström, *Dalarna som svenskt ideal* (Stockholm: Wahlstrand & Widstrand, 1937); and Olle Veirulf, ed., *Dalarna: ett vida berömt landskap* (Stockholm: AB Svensk Litteratur, 1951).

TABLE 5.—FARM LIQUIDATION AND TIMING OF LAND
OWNERSHIP TRANSFERS IN MIGRATION-LINKED
COMMUNITIES

| Community | Liquidation rate | Transfer after death/Transfer before death |
|---|---|---|
| Athens | 31.8% | 1.03 |
| Rättvik | 16.4% | 0.34 |
| Isanti | 47.5% | 3.13 |
| Attmar | 41.2% | 2.64 |
| (free hold only) | 26.9% | 1.60 |

was especially true of the areas in Hälsingland and Medelpad near the rapidly developing Bothnian Gulf coast. Through the latter part of the century there was a vigorous expansion of the timber industry in this region that caused dramatic changes in the social and economic system.[17] As a result, society there was more open, the population more mobile, economic opportunity more diverse, and the importance of the small freehold farm not as great as in Dalarna. Quite likely the experience with land was different and that difference was reflected in the behavior of emigrants in America. To test this, the contemporaneous land transfer practices of two migration-linked areas, one in Dalarna and the other in Medelpad, are examined (Fig. 6).

One is a five village area in the parish of Rättvik in Dalarna.[18] These five villages comprised the core of an administrative unit of the parish known as Gärdsjö fjärding. Located in the central part of the parish, the area was socially distinct from other parts of the parish and contained 236 farm households in 1885. Nearly all households owned the farms they worked. The nonagricultural population was small, consisting of a few professionals in the military and in the management of the forest land and small iron smelter operated by a large company in the area (Kopparbergs och Hofors bolag). A few laborers worked at the smelter, but most economic activity was traditional and tied to the land. During the period 1865–1885 these villages experienced fairly heavy emigration. The majority of the families that left went to Isanti County and set-

tled in the Athens community where they became the most numerous segment of the population.

The second area is a grouping of five villages in Attmar parish of Medelpad province.[19] The Attmar villages are also located in the central part of the parish, clustered above and below a mill site (Sörfors bruk) on a tributary of the Ljungan River. In contrast to Rättvik, there were two categories of land ownership. About forty percent of the 195 farm households in 1885 were freeholds. The remainder were *torpare*, an agricultural class that held some land but mainly relied on long-term contractual rights to land on the larger freehold farms, for a living. In addition there was a substantial number of landless households that were dependent on farm labor or the timber industry. Emigration was heavy in the area. Emigrants from Attmar and surrounding parishes were the strongest element of the Isanti community population.

The land transfer practices of these two Swedish districts are analyzed in the same manner as the Swedish-American communities to which they were linked. Over thirty years there were 175 land transfers in the Rättvik villages and 149 land transfers in the Attmar villages. This was proportionately fewer than had occurred in the American study area. The probable reason is that the age distribution of household heads was more even in the Swedish settlements. There was no clear generational cycle as there was in the newly settled Rum Valley. As in the American data, a clear differentiation can be seen in transfer timing. The importance of partible and impartible inheritance is unclear because probate records were not available for this study.[20]

An examination of liquidation rates and transfer ratios in these paired communities reveals a marked similarity of behavior (Table 5). Athens, which had one of the lowest American liquidation rates, mirrors the extremely low liquidation rate in Rättvik while Isanti, which had one of the highest American liquidation rates, is linked with a very similar rate in Attmar. The importance of after-death transfer was low in Athens.

---

[17] The classic work on economic development in this area is Filip Hjulström, Gunnar Arpi and Esse Lövgren, "Sundsvall-distriktet, 1850–1950," *Geographica*. Papers from the Geographical Institute, Uppsala University, Nr. 26 (1955).

[18] The five Rättvik villages are Övre Gärdsjö, Nedre Gärdsjö, Backa, Born, and Blecket.

[19] The six Attmar villages are Attmarby, Fjolsta, Söderlindsjö, Skedvik, Hamre, and Harv.

[20] The analysis is based on information extracted from parish registers (*husförhörslängd*) and tax registers (*mantalslängd* and *taxeringslängd*). The thirty year period used is 1885–1915 for Rättvik and somewhat earlier, 1875–1905, for Attmar because access to more recent data is difficult.

In Rättvik it was rare. Both Isanti and Attmar had high proportions of after death land ownership transfers.

There is circumstantial evidence, then, that differential experience in the home district was an important influence on what happened in America. Peasant farmers in Rättvik regarded land as an ancestral resource. Farms and property were handed down for generations and were central to the identification of families with their past and the community in a society that was just beginning to be touched by modernization in the late nineteenth century. In fact, individuals in this part of Sweden identified themselves through the use of a family farm name rather than the patronym. In Attmar, which literally was located at the center of nineteenth century industrialization along the Bothnian coast, the relationship between land and family was different. The timber milling industry had purchased vast tracts of land in order to secure access to timber, which in turn inflated the value of property and made it a speculative commodity. Industry also introduced wage earning into the economy and fostered the emergence of a working class. The railroads reached the area in the late 1870s, facilitating contact with the outside world (in contrast, the railroad reached Rättvik in 1890), and the population became increasingly mobile, moving away from traditional farm work in large numbers.[21] These two experiences appear to have imparted quite different responses to the economic situation in Minnesota's Rum River Valley.

Underlying this is the fact that land transfer experience in Attmar was differentiated by agricultural class. If the *torpare* class is removed from the analysis of Attmar, the liquidation rate and transfer ratio are substantially reduced. They are still high by Rättvik standards, but the behavior of the fully landed class in Attmar was clearly more conservative than that of the *torpare* class. Landed wealth was important to the *torp* as a stepping stone to economic independence, but the relationship often was not as permanent as it was for the freeholder. Land could be converted to capital that allowed one to take advantage of local, nonagricultural opportunity or to leave in search of opportunity elsewhere. Since a majority of the emigrants to the Isanti community were from this class, their liberal behavior towards land is explained, at least in part. They had relatively little experience in the long term management of landed wealth and a weak tradition of social ownership.

## Conclusion

This study contends that the inheritance of landed wealth was an important variable in the maintenance of family and community in rural immigrant settlements. The immigrant commonly participated in two societies simultaneously—a local society that was based on family, church, and tradition and a larger economic society that was competitive and individualistic. This dual participation was a natural adaptation to the new milieu. The accumulation and disposition of landed wealth, however, was an activity central to both experiences. Here the immigrant had to choose between an individualistic and a socially conscious response to material opportunity. In the case of the Swedish communities of Minnesota's Rum River Valley, the response was varied and influenced by social and institutional life in the community and an experiential linkage with a European past. Scholars have long been concerned with cohesiveness and maintenance of community in immigrant settlements and have often measured this in terms of population mobility. An understanding of the long-term relationship between land and family takes one a step closer in this concern, because it isolates the mechanism that underlies stability or turnover—the transmission of property.

This study also argues for the value of a grand sweep trans-Atlantic perspective in understanding structural and family change in immigrant communities. Although the material presented on migration-linked districts in Sweden is but a reconnaissance, the potential is clear. While migration and settlement in a new social and material environment altered the experience of the emigrant it did not erase his past. Seen from the perspective that change was occurring contemporaneously in Europe, a hypothesis worth testing might be that the experience of the emigrant was altered less, in some cases, than that of his neighbor who stayed behind.

---

[21] A recent and very good description of economic and social change in an area similar to Attmar is Mats Rolén, "Skogsbygd i omvandling: Studier kring befolkningsutveckling, omflyttning och social rörlighet i Revsunds tingslag 1820–1977," *Studia Historica Upsaliensia,* Nr. 107 (Uppsala, Sweden: University of Uppsala Historical Institution, 1979).

# FOREIGNERS IN FLORIDA:
## A STUDY OF IMMIGRATION PROMOTION, 1865-1910

*by* GEORGE E. POZZETTA\*

FOR MOST of the long American period, Floridians have been deeply concerned with the problem of attracting people to the borders of their state. Though the motivations behind the various efforts to induce migration into the state have changed, ranging from early desires simply to populate uninhabited lands to more modern concerns of tourism and development, the spirit has been remarkably consistent. Indeed, it has only been within the last few years that the "heresy" of imposing legal limits on population growth has been listened to with any degree of toleration. In no other period of Florida's past, however, have residents of the state attempted to entice settlers southward with a greater sense of urgency and need than in the decades following the Civil War.

At the close of hostilities in 1865 Floridians faced a massive task of rebuilding. Many farms and plantations lay abandoned, port areas had stagnated, and, perhaps most importantly, long standing relationships between blacks, the state's primary common labor pool, and white employers called for total reorganization and reconstitution. It called for no gift of prophesy to see that Florida would require the work of many hands to once again become a land of progress and prosperity.

Many Floridians reasoned that the key to renewed economic vitality was the rapid populating of the state's unused lands and the procurement of a stable labor force. The *Florida Agriculturist,* for many years the official organ of the Grange, consistently espoused this course of action as a means of alleviating the state's economic problems. "Unquestionably Florida's greatest need," the journal editorialized, "is immigration; next to immigration we need capital." "Some will undoubtedly place the last item first," it further explained, "but in so doing they make a mistake.

---

\*    Mr. Pozzetta is assistant professor of social sciences and history, University of Florida, Gainesville.

[164]

Capital is powerful but without the assistance of labor it is powerless."[1] Later in the century, when Henry W. Grady and other proponents of the "New South" heralded the region's industrialization, the call for settlers and workers grew louder and more insistent. A Jacksonville paper voiced the prevailing sentiment when it indicated that "the future of the state depends upon its success in drawing to it the population necessary to develop its resources."[2]

Superimposed over these basic concerns for settlers, however, was a strong and pervasive white discontent with the character of black labor within the state. Floridians were profoundly disturbed when large numbers of ex-slaves exercised their right to mobility and deserted the plantations and farms. In 1870 J. S. Adams, state Commissioner of Immigration, complained of "a scarcity of field labor in some parts of the State . . . on account of the strong disposition of the Freedmen . . . to gather together and in the immediate vicinity of the larger towns."[3] More than a decade later a resident of Orange County, Mrs. Leora B. Robinson, still found cause to have similar misgivings about black workers. Many blacks hired out on the railroads, she explained, but few remained in the county permanently, and "it is often difficult to find laborers for the ordinary work about the groves and farms."[4] If this siphoning off of workers continued, the future development of Florida would be placed in jeopardy.

Even more pronounced than the anxieties caused by Negro mobility was the dissatisfaction with the quality of those black laborers available within the state. Most whites believed that the freedmen were neither efficient nor dependable workers. As promoter Oliver M. Crosby indicated in his volume, *Florida*

---

1. "A Chapter on Immigration," *Florida Agriculturalist*, XVII (October 15, 1890), 584. For similar views see, "Immigrants Wanted," *Florida Agriculturalist*, XVIII (September 23, 1891), 514; "Immigration and our Resources," *Florida Agriculturalist*, III (January 19, 1881), 284; D. H. Jacques, *Florida as a Permanent Home* (Jacksonville, 1877), 31-32.
2. Jacksonville *Florida Times-Union*, February 4, 1897. See also, "Foreign Immigration to Florida," *Florida Agriculturalist*, I (October 31, 1874), 348; Jacksonville *Florida Times-Union*, March 7, 1882; *Gainesville Daily Sun*, February 26, 1905; "Wanted Immigrants," *Florida East Coast Homeseeker*, IX (October 1907), 334.
3. J. S. Adams, *Florida: Its Climate, Soil, and Productions* (New York, 1870), 66.
4. Leora B. Robinson, *Living in Florida* (Louisville, 1884), 70. For other concerns centered on black mobility, see, "The Negro Question Solving Itself," *Florida Agriculturalist*, VIII (July 29, 1885), 92.

*Facts,* "now that he [the black man] is free he has no idea of working more than is barely necessary to keep him in pork and grits.'' "[Newcomers to Florida] will be surprised to learn how utterly shiftless and devoid of all honor the average Southern darky is."[5] Others complained that blacks were only suited for the raising of cotton, that they could not be trusted to care for stock, that they were unable to use farm machinery, and that they could not give the care and attention necessary for diversified and intensive farming. Common opinion held, moreover, that any attempt to alter blacks was doomed to failure as they were considered "uneducatable." The *Florida Agriculturist* explained these deficiencies on the grounds that Negroes lacked "the mental ground work and its concomitant elements of industry, frugality, providentness and perseverance; their intellects have become dwarfed, their ambitions blunted."[6] Thus, in the latter decades of the nineteenth century, Floridians looked toward the future believing that they were saddled with a labor force that was inadequate to the tasks ahead in both quantity and quality.

Many citizens viewed the increasing tide of foreign immigration flowing into America as the state's great hope. If only a fraction of this folk movement could be diverted southward, Florida could replace its "improvident" work force and grow to its fullest potential. Fernandina's *Florida Mirror* put the matter succinctly: "[Blacks] will continue to multiply rapidly. . . . But the field of profitable employment of blacks will always be limited and never equal to the coming requirements of the South." The paper explained that an influx of immigrants was the answer to this quandry.[7] The fact that much of this immigration belonged to the white race made it seem all the more attractive. The central problem lay in finding an effective means of attracting these settlers.

---

5. Oliver Marvin Crosby, *Florida Facts Both Bright and Blue, A Guide Book* (New York, 1887), 21, 125. Additional adverse commentary on black labor is contained in, Jacksonville *Florida Dispatch*, February 22, 1886; "Intelligent Laborers Needed," *Florida Agriculturalist*, XX (May 24, 1893), 328; Jacksonville *Florida Dispatch*, August 9, 1886.
6. "The Negro of the South," *Florida Agriculturalist*, X (April 25, 1888), 404. See also, Jacksonville *Florida Dispatch*, July 6, 1885; Jacksonville *Florida Farmer and Fruit-Grower*, September 19, 1888.
7. Fernandina *Florida Mirror*, September 10, August 13, 1881.

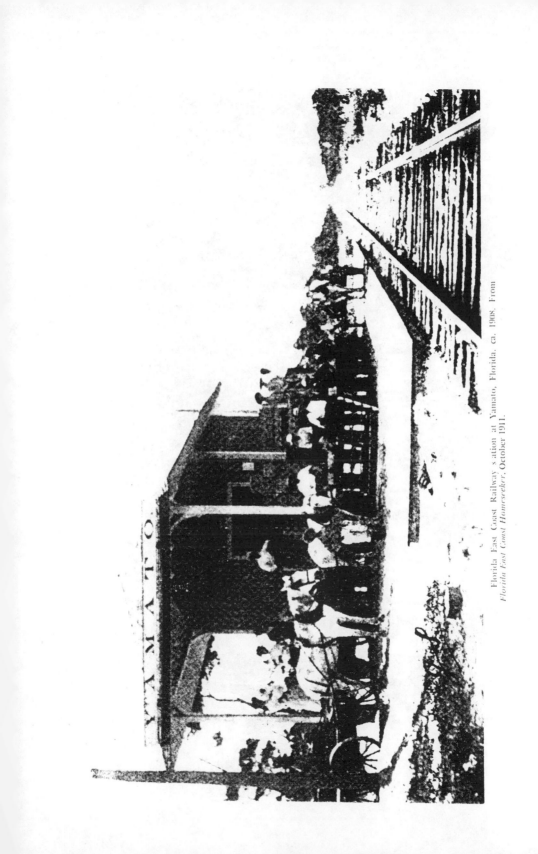

Florida East Coast Railway station at Yamato, Florida, ca. 1908. From *Florida East Coast Homeseeker*, October 1911.

Emigrants arriving in St. Johns County. *Florida East Coast Homeseeker,* XIII (July 1911), 266.

At first there was little disagreement among those groups and individuals actively interested in procuring immigrants as to the correct methods to be employed. Although occasionally agents and professional promoters were hired and sent to foreign countries to solicit immigrants, Floridians viewed the settlement effort primarily as an exercise in publicity and advertising. Dennis Eagan, Florida's Commissioner of Lands and Immigration in the early 1870s, typified this outlook when he argued that: "Perhaps the most effective means at our disposal for promoting immigration is the publication of pamphlets, essays, and articles treating on and describing our . . . resources, facilities for navigation, and opportunities for manufacturers."[8] Eagan and other immigration enthusiasts reasoned that a well-developed advertising campaign would produce two beneficial results. First, it would instruct uninformed foreigners as to the advantages of the state, and, since there were many, this would act as a powerful inducement to settle in Florida. Of equal importance, this publicity would counteract what Floridians believed to be a widespread and powerful information lobby working against state interests. In his first year of office Commissioner Eagan felt constrained to condemn vigorously the "Constant and injurious misrepresentation of the State . . . by parties North and in Europe, pecuniarily interested in the transportation of European emigrants to the Northern states."[9] Though the state's efforts to rebut this adverse publicity were untiring and widely supported, they met with only marginal success. As the *Florida Agriculturist* pointed out in its efforts to correct one out-of-state newspaper: "As we demolish one statement, it falls back on another to run down our State."[10]

8. Florida Commissioner of Lands and Immigration, *Report of the Commissioner of Lands and Immigration, January 1, 1874,* bound with Florida *House-Senate Journals,* 1874, 143. Copy in P. K. Yonge Library of Florida History, University of Florida, Gainesville. Support for this position was manifested in many parts of the state. See, "A Flood of Immigration," *Florida Agriculturalist,* I (January 24, 1874), 25; Jacksonville *Florida Dispatch,* April 24, 1878; Jacksonville *Florida Times-Union,* February 5, 1882; "To Induce Immigration," *Florida Agriculturalist,* X (October 19, 1887), 188.

9. Florida Commissioner of Lands and Immigration, *Report, 1874,* 141. Also note, Tallahassee *Florida Immigrant,* July 1877; "False Statements," *Florida Agriculturalist,* IV (September 7, 1881), 132; "Florida Condemned," *Florida Agriculturalist,* V (November 1, 1882), 196; Jacksonville *Florida Dispatch,* June 27, 1877.

10. "Our Detractors," *Florida Agriculturalist,* II (July 3, 1875), 212.

Prior to 1891 the major agency engaged in the advertising effort was the state Bureau of Immigration. Tracing its roots to a provision in the Constitution of 1868 calling for a "Commissioner of Immigration" and undergoing a number of administrative and legal alterations in its relatively short life, the bureau aggressively attempted to promote foreign settlement. Inadequate budgets, uninspired leadership, bitter factional disputes within the state government, and endless haggling over proper promotional methods combined to emasculate the bureau's effectiveness. The most significant outcome of its existence was the publication of a promotional pamphlet, *The Florida Settler*, which underwent several editions, a similar volume entitled *The Florida Colonist*, a short-lived newspaper called the *Florida Immigrant*, and the issuing of several thousand copies of a *Monthly Bulletin* (printed from 1889 to 1891).[11] Although it is impossible to determine precisely what effect these publishing ventures had upon settlement, contemporaries clearly viewed these efforts as failures and in 1891 the bureau was abolished.

Even during the bureau's tenure, however, there were other agencies within the state that had an active interest in immigration work. County and local governments, railroads, farm groups, real estate companies, wealthy land owners, mine operators, and industrialists had operated independently before the decade of the 1890s. Indeed, these disparate groups had directed an impressive volume of literature to almost every part of the world. By 1881, however, it was clear that some form of common action might easily avoid needless duplication of effort. Accordingly, on August 24, 1881, representatives from all parts of Florida met together in Jacksonville to discuss ways of coordinating promotional activities for the betterment of the state.[12] In attendance were sizable delegations from many of the counties as well as representatives from many local, state, and private agencies. Amidst a decided spirit of boosterism, the convention proclaimed

---

11. Florida Commissioner of Lands and Immigration, *Annual Report of the Commissioner of Lands and Immigration, January 1, 1877,* bound with Florida *Assembly Journal*, 1877, 48; Florida Commissioner of Agriculture, *Report of the Commissioner of Agriculture, January 1, 1891,* bound with Florida *Senate Journal*, 1891, 20-21; Florida Commissioner of Lands and Immigration, *Report, 1874,* 143.
12. Tampa *Sunland Tribune*, September 3, 17, 1881; Fernandina *Florida Mirror*, August 27, September 10, 1881.

that Florida had simply to devise methods of disseminating accurate and timely information about itself, and settlers would come flocking. After all, as one enthusiastic delegate explained, when God selected a home for man, He put him "in that zone which embraces Florida. . . . Florida should be the other Eden—the center of the world's glory!"[13] The assembly resolved that each county should establish immigration associations or committees to collect information and publish this material in pamphlet form. It further suggested that the state bureau of immigration should print descriptive volumes incorporating this information "in the different languages of European countries . . . and that said pamphlets be distributed among the masses of said European countries." Within the next few years, seven Florida counties heeded the first resolution and distributed their county journals as far as their limited budgets would allow.[14]

It is important to note that prior to 1900 these publishing ventures were directed toward immigrants of *all* types and nationalities. Although there were occasional references to the desirability of attracting only settlers who had resided for some time in the United States and hence were familiar with American institutions and values, in the main the welcome was open to *all*. Early in the 1870s, for example, the Commissioner of Lands and Immigration proclaimed his desire "to attract capital and population from other and less favored portions of the Union, from Europe, and especially from the south of France, south Germany, Italy, and other foreign countries."[15] A few years later the promotional magazine *Semi-Tropical Florida* mirrored these sentiments. "We want population from every State in the Union, and from every country in Europe," the volume urged,

---

13. Jacksonville *Florida Dispatch*, September 7, 1881.
14. "The Immigration Convention," *Florida Agriculturalist*, IV (September 7, 1881), 134. For a sampling of these pamphlets see the following, John W. Ashby, *Alachua, The Garden County of Florida, Its Resources and Advantages* (New York, 1888); Columbia County Immigration Association, *Columbia County, Florida: Description of her Climate, Soil, Health, and General Advantages* (Jacksonville, 1883); Duval County Commissioners, *Duval County, Florida: Showing its Statistics, Resources, Lands, Products, Climate and Population* (Jacksonville, 1885).
15. Florida Commissioner of Lands and Immigration, *Report, 1874,* 146. Consult also, "What Florida Needs," *Florida Agriculturalist*, XI (November 14, 1888), 220; Jacksonville *Florida Dispatch*, September 5, 1887, February 13, 1888; Jacksonville *Florida Farmer and Fruit Grower*, April 11, 1888.

"we have no prejudices to overcome."[16] In many sections of the state citizens expressed the belief that European farmers and farm laborers, with their knowledge of intensive farming methods, would assuredly prove to be a boon to Florida. Within this context, Floridians often indicated certain foreign groups as possessing special skills and characteristics which would make them particularly desirable as residents. Ironically, in many instances those immigrant groups singled out for special attention early in the period were precisely those peoples deemed most *undesirable* after the turn of the century.

Italian immigrants, for instance, attracted the favorable notice of Floridians soon after the Civil War. In 1872 citrus developer Henry S. Sanford labelled these newcomers "a most valuable class of immigrants" and explained that they were "intelligent and industrious, accustomed to orange and vine culture, and to a warm climate."[17] The prevalent perception of Florida as the "Italy of the South" only made the logic of Italian settlement seem more compelling.[18]

These favorable dispositions were considerably enhanced later in the century when reports of several productive Italian agricultural colonies in nearby states swept through the state. The successful experience of a colony of 500 Italians in Sunnyside, Arkansas, for example, received extensive coverage. Enthusiastic communications praised these old world farmers for their frugality and hardworking habits. The fact that stereotypes of blacks compared unfavorably with these reports, of course, received heavy stress. Moreover, Floridians took added reassurance from the alleged innate ability of Italians to excel in truck gardening, fruit culture, and intensive farming. As one optimistic commentator proclaimed, the Italian "can make the sandy soil of the pine land productive or reclaim the swamps and lowlands. He can give the southern planter his reliable thrifty labor to replace the erratic improvident negro, and can introduce and carry to

---

16. Seth French, *Semi-Tropical Florida; Its Climate, Soil and Productions, with a Sketch of Its History, Natural Features and Social Condition* (Chicago, 1879), 19, 20.
17. Tallahassee *Weekly Floridian*, January 14, 1873. See also, Cyrus L. Sulzberger, "What the United States Owes the Immigrant," *Charities*, XII (1904), 424; "Italians as Laborers," *Florida Agriculturalist*, XXXII (December 13, 1905), 802; Jacksonville *Florida Dispatch*, July 7, 1881.
18. Jacksonville *Florida Dispatch*, June 8, 1885; *Florida Tourist and Southern Investor's Guide* (Cedar Rapids, Iowa, 1898), 30.

perfection the vine growing and wine making which have made California famous."[19] The St. Cloud Sugar Plantation of Hamilton Disston, among other large employers of labor, utilized several hundred Italian workers.[20]

Existing concurrently with this desire for Italians, an equally strong expression of support for the importation of Chinese laborers became noticable. Shortly after the Civil War, various farm groups called attention to the industriousness and thriftiness of these workers and frequently commented that they outworked blacks.[21] Native farmers believed that the Chinese, like the Italians, possessed special talents for working on the soil. Thus, the supposed Chinese expertise in orchard tending, vine cultivation, and gardening were highly touted in Florida journals. By the turn of the century, however, as demands for labor reached unprecedented proportions, virtually all sections of the economy supported the call for these orientals. Indeed, one writer argued in 1904 that the quickest solution to Florida's labor problems was the wholesale importation of Chinese coolies. As the *Florida Times-Union* indicated, Chinese would be used to work the "South's mines, to till its fields, to pick its cotton, and to man its machinery in factories."[22]

Similar optimism attended the establishment in 1905 of Yamato, a colony of fifty Japanese families in Dade County. Initial reports concerning the settlement stressed the "great benefit to Florida" that would accrue from the "new methods of cultivation" and farming introduced by these immigrants.[23] Natives

19. Allan McLaughlin, "Italian and Other Latin Immigrants," *Popular Science Monthly*, LXV (1904), 346. See also, W. G. Leland, "Black vs. Italian Labor," *Nation*, LXXXII (February 1, 1906), 97; "Italians as Laborers," *Florida Agriculturalist*, XXXII (December 13, 1905), 802; "Italians as Immigrants," *Florida Agriculturalist*, XXXIV (July 3, 1907), 2.

20. Pat Dodson, "Hamilton Disston's St. Cloud Sugar Plantation, 1887-1901," *Florida Historical Quarterly*, XLIX (April 1971), 362.

21. "Chinese Cheap Labor," *Florida Agriculturalist*, I (January 24, 1874), 30; "Chinese Cheap Labor," *Florida Agriculturalist*, III (March 9, 1881), 337; "The Chinese and the Labor Problem," *Florida Agriculturalist*, XXXII (October 18, 1905), 664; "Chinese in Paradise," *Florida Agriculturalist*, XXXIII (July 18, 1906), 457.

22. Jacksonville *Florida Times-Union*, August 14, 1905. Also consult, "Would Chinese Labor Solve the Harvest Problem?" *Florida Agriculturalist*, XXXII (October 18, 1905), 664-65; "Farm Laborers," *Florida Agriculturalist*, XXXI (June 15, 1904), 376; "Chinese Labor," *Florida Agriculturalist*, XXXI (September 28, 1904), 616.

23. Jacksonville *Florida Times-Union*, January 9, 1904. In addition, see,

watched the colony's experiments with rice, tea, silk, tobacco, and various fruits with great attentiveness and predicted that much would be learned from their successes.

Records do not exist which show precisely how many immigrants came to Florida in response to the state's promotional activities. Florida was, however, one of the few southern states that increased its population during the period under question and assuredly a part of this growth was caused by migration. The 1890 census showed that Florida's white foreign stock population (foreign born or of foreign born parentage) stood at 33,698 (14.6 per cent of the whole) and its black foreign stock population at 6,912 (4.15 per cent of the whole). Hence, nearly twenty per cent of the state's population was of non-native stock. Given the critical need for workers and settlers, this segment was indeed considerable.[24] Moreover, census takers frequently missed entirely or returned sketchy reports on isolated labor and turpentine camps, railroad construction crews, and other transient job sites. It was precisely these employment areas which often possessed heavy foreign representation. Had these sources been more fully counted, the foreign presence would undoubtedly have been higher. By 1910, the total of foreign stock peoples had almost doubled; the major groups were Cubans (15,656), Germans (7,488), English (7,414), and Italians (7,413). This census report also included appreciable numbers of Finns, Turks, Chinese, Russians, and Greeks.[25]

The entrance of these immigrants into the native society was a process marred by considerable tension, distrust, and misunderstanding on the part of both foreigners and Floridians. Natives generally felt that newcomers should conform to the same social and economic arrangements then affecting blacks; they assumed that immigrants should be content to accept the bottom rung of society. The only difference, in native eyes, would be that these

---

"Yamato," *Florida East Coast Homeseeker*, X (July 1908), 225; Jacksonville *Florida Times-Union*, November 2, 1906; Walter L. Fleming, "Immigration to the Southern States," *Political Science Quarterly*, XX (June 1905), 285. The Yamato colony existed in the southern end of modern Palm Beach County, between present-day Delray Beach and Boca Raton.
24. U. S. Census Office, *Abstract of the Eleventh Census, 1890*, 2nd ed. (Washington, 1896), 54.
25. U. S. Bureau of the Census, *Thirteenth Census of the United States, 1910, Abstract with Supplement for Florida* (Washington, 1913), 585.

new arrivals would work more efficiently and dependably than the replaced Negroes. This was particularly true in respect to land ownership. Despite assertions proclaiming the ease with which settlers might obtain their own land, it often proved difficult for immigrants to do so. Unless they were supported by group-purchasing power, as in the case of the Japanese at Yamato, foreigners frequently found that they were unable to become independent property holders. Many land owners, particularly those possessing large acreages, hoped that the foreigners could merge smoothly into the tenant system and simply change places with Negro croppers.[26]

As early as 1873 the commissioner of immigration saw the need for a "disposition on the part of our planters to divide their plantations into small lots and lease or sell them to settlers."[27] Some Floridians argued that the prevalence of the tenant landholding system hindered efforts to attract newcomers to the state, but their words seemed to have had little effect. By the turn of the century the situation had barely changed. A 1901 United States Industrial Commission survey, intended to explore opportunities for distributing urban immigrants, found that a majority of counties continued to push for tenant-landholding arrangements. Columbia County, for instance, reported, "There are good opportunities to become a tenant farmer for a money rent or half the crops." Similarly, Gadsden County replied that: "Tenants have farm and outfit furnished them. Tenant furnishes the labor only and gets half the crop." Essentially the same replies were contained in the reports from Alachua, Calhoun, Walton, Madison, Volusia, Polk, Jackson, and Pasco counties.[28]

Land owners blamed the apparent failure of the tenant sys-

---

26. For information on land prices, wages, and tenancy see, Tallahassee *Weekly Floridian*, August 19, 1873; Dennis Eagan, *The Florida Settler, or Immigrant's Guide, Together with the Sixth Annual Report of the Commissioner of Lands and Immigration*, 2nd ed. (Tallahassee, 1874), 63; Florida, Department of Agriculture, *Florida: A Pamphlet Descriptive of Its History, Topography, Climate, Soil, Resources and Natural Advantages, In General and by Counties* (Tallahassee, 1904), 270-71; Jacksonville *Florida Dispatch*, September 5, 1887, June 7, 1886; Robert L. Brandfon, "The End of Immigration to the Cotton Fields," *Mississippi Valley Historical Review*, L (March 1964), 610.
27. Florida Commissioner of Lands and Immigration, *Report, 1874*, 146. Consult also, Jacksonville *Florida Dispatch*, May 24, 1886.
28. U. S. Industrial Commission, *Reports of the Industrial Commissioner, Immigration*, XV (Washington, 1901), 563-64.

tem to produce independent farmers on the laziness and inefficiency of blacks and defended tenancy as the best route to success for the unskilled and poor. Most immigrants knew better.
Many had left their home country because of such arrangements,
and had no desire to exchange one form of tenancy for another.
The attitude of Italian workers brought into the Sanford orange
groves was probably typical of other immigrants. "The Italians
w[oul]d have remained with you in Florida," wrote a correspondent to Henry Sanford in 1875, "if you had given them an
acre or two of land: that is their craving."[29]

Immigrants experienced other disappointments in Florida
when large·numbers, along with blacks, fell victim to peonage
exploitation. Plantations, turpentine camps, railroad construction projects, and naval stores farms all frequently counted peons
among their work forces. Immigrant labor agents from New York
and other cities, working in conjunction with Florida employers,
supplied sizable numbers of foreigners to these projects. One
typical case involved forty Greeks shipped to a railroad camp in
Punta Gorda. Employers held them in an isolated work camp,
patrolled them with armed guards and dogs, and forced them to
live under extremely harsh conditions. When workers attempted
to flee, they were pursued, beaten and/or shot, and returned to
the camp.[30] Unlike blacks, however, foreigners proved often able
to utilize the services of immigrant benevolent societies or con-
sular offices to dramatize their grievances and receive outside aid.
The adverse publicity generated by such news angered Floridians
anxious to preserve the "integrity" and "good name" of the state.

As more foreigners came to Florida and experienced difficulties in adjusting to conditions, native attitudes toward them began to change. Slowly in the 1890s, and then with increasing
vigor after the turn of the century, the state's earlier policy of
open welcome was replaced with a position of resistance to
foreign settlement. Sufficient hostility to immigrants had devel-

29.  ? to Henry S. Sanford, August 29, 1875, microfilm reel 28, Henry S.
     Sanford Papers, P. K. Yonge Library of Florida History. See also, Rob-
     ert Foerster, *The Italian Immigration of Our Times* (Cambridge, Mas-
     sachusetts, 1919), 369.
30.  Pete Daniel, *The Shadow of Slavery: Peonage in the South, 1901-1969*
     (Urbana, 1972), 40-41. Immigrants occasionally shared other undesirable
     fates with blacks. See Jacksonville *Florida Times-Union*, September 21,
     23, 26, 28, 30, 1910, for reports of the lynching of Italians in Tampa.

oped by 1895 to provoke reaction from the commissioner of agriculture. He argued that the prevailing sentiment of "Florida for Floridians" had adversely affected efforts to attract settlers and would ultimately prove damaging to Florida's attempts to progress.[31] His voice could not, however, stem the rising criticism.

Even previously-favored foreigners fell into disfavor as the new century wore on. The *Gainesville Sun*, which had once strongly encouraged the importation of Italian laborers, claimed in 1906 that, "the Italian is not a trustworthy, honest, nor faithful kind of laborer . . . [they] are given to making trouble wherever they go."[32] Chinese also came under attack for their heathen religion, their alleged immorality and criminality, and particularly for their racial differences. As one writer urged in 1906, "it would not be wise to add another race to the already disturbed conditions existing."[33] The agricultural commissioner's report for this same year indicated that a reversal of attitudes had taken place: "Let us see to it also that the doors are not opened too wide, that those people of undesirable classes of nationalities are not thrust upon us to become paupers and wards of the State . . . we believe . . . that the class of people Florida needs must, and can be, secured from adjoining States and from the Northern and Western states in large numbers. [These are the kind of people we want in Florida . . . we do not feel that it is wise to go after foreign peoples and leave the field just mentioned for others to exploit."

"There are those we do not want at any price, or for any purpose," the report continued. "In general, we do not want the people of Southern Europe, the Poles, the Hunns [sic] and the Italians from Southern Italy, etc. The classes of these people who emigrate are of the lowest order; socially, they are without recognition. Politically, they make up all the isms that afflict all

---

31. Florida Department of Agriculture, *Report of the Commissioner of Agriculture of the State of Florida, for the period beginning Jan. 1, 1895, and ending Dec. 31, 1896* (Tallahassee, 1896), 185.
32. *Gainesville Daily Sun,* July 15, 1906. Also see, "Italian Labor in the South," *Florida Agriculturalist,* XXXIII (February 14, 1906), 104; "The Labor Problem," *Florida Agriculturalist,* XXXIII (May 2, 1906), 280.
33. "The Labor Problem," *Florida Agriculturalist,* XXXIII (May 2, 1906), 280. Consult also, "Notes," *Florida Agriculturalist,* XXXI (September 28, 1904), 616; "The Chinese and the Labor Problem," *Florida Agriculturalist,* XXXII (October 18, 1905), 664; "Chinese Exclusion," *Florida Agriculturalist,* XXXVII (December 25, 1907), 8.

peoples and menace all governments; they are the breeders of socialism and anarchism, and are enemies of all forms of government control. . . . We are unequivocally opposed to the bringing into our midst such a people."[34]

The final gasp of the organized drive to attract foreigners came in 1908. Early in February of that year Governor Napoleon B. Broward issued a proclamation calling for a three-day immigration convention to be held in Tampa during the annual state fair. Broward personally invited each southern governor, and the Tampa Chamber of Commerce sent out more than 1,000 invitations to southern mayors, presidents of boards of trade and other commercial bodies, and to newspaper editors. Early responses seemed encouraging, and the *Tampa Morning Tribune* predicted that the conference would "doubtless result in a plan of magnificent proportions to induce settlers to enter the south."[35] Despite this boosterism, the convention was a failure.

Governor Broward proved to be the only governor in attendance, and he failed to return to the convention after his welcoming remarks at the opening session. Most of the afternoon of the first day's proceedings was taken up with reading telegrams of regret from non-attending delegates. C. Fred Thompson, secretary of the Tampa Chamber of Commerce, filled the remaining time with an emotional speech condemning reports of Florida peonage currently circulating in the country and abroad. The second day's work was disrupted early when three black delegations from local labor organizations were refused seats and asked to leave. Later, a misunderstanding as to meeting rooms resulted in approximately half of the delegates gathering in the ladies parlor. When these representatives discovered their error and found the correct location, they arrived "just in time to see the others marching out."[36]

34. Florida Department of Agriculture, *The Ninth Biennial Report of the Commissioner of Agriculture, State of Florida, for the period beginning January 1, 1905, and ending December 31, 1906* (Tallahassee, 1907), 37-38. Also see, "Foreign Immigration," *Florida Agriculturalist*, XXXIII (May 30, 1906), 244; Jacksonville *Florida Times-Union*, March 25, 1906.
35. *Tampa Morning Tribune*, January 3, 1908. Additional commentary is contained in, *Tampa Morning Tribune*, January 9, 11, 14, 23, February 7, 11, 1908; *Gainesville Daily Sun*, February 8, 1908; *Pensacola Journal*, February 7, 1908.
36. "No more Flowers," *Manufacturers' Record*, XVII (February 20, 1908), 42. See also, *Tampa Morning Tribune*, February 12, 13, 1908; *Miami*

The convention adjourned one day early and made no recommendations whatever regarding immigration except to declare that the national government should pass even more stringent laws against admission of foreigners. Throughout the sessions a strong undercurrent of sentiment against any kind of immigration was evident, and on one occasion several members supported a move to denounce the very purpose of the assembly. Thus, the convention called to promote immigration resolved itself into a vehement anti-immigration meeting.[37]

The reasons behind this reversal of attitudes are varied and complex. First, it is clear that considerations of religion profoundly worried many Floridians. Many immigrants—Italians, Poles, Spaniards, and Cubans—coming into the state, particularly after the 1880s, belonged to the Roman Catholic Church and they excited fears of papal influence and foreign domination. In 1891, the *Florida Times-Union* sounded the alarm over proposals to settle colonies of Italian Catholics within the state. Such groups, the paper explained, would have immigrants "gathered into communities and the children provided with teachers of their own race, so as to preserve their religious belief, native language and love of the lands of their nativity." Since these arrangements would preserve foreign religions and retard assimilation, the paper hoped that Floridians would "not tolerate" such plans.[38] The unfamiliar religious dogmas and theologies of oriental newcomers also caused concern in an area of the country that was primarily Protestant in faith and fundamentalist in outlook.

Other Floridians, who perhaps worried less over questions of religion, became agitated over considerations of radicalism. The increase in the Socialist vote within the state after 1900 and the popular identification of foreigners with this party resulted in native misgivings.[39] Italian Socialists, for instance, existed in suf-

*Metropolis*, February 13, 14, 1908; Jacksonville *Florida Times-Union*, February 14, 1908.

37. *Pensacola Journal*, February 15, 1908; Jacksonville *Florida Times-Union*, February 15, 1908.

38. Jacksonville *Florida Times-Union*, June 4, 1891. For added views see, Jacksonville *Florida Times-Union*, May 25, 1891; "Notes," *Florida Agriculturalist*, XXXI (September 28, 1904), 616.

39. Ray F. Robbins, "The Socialist Party in Florida 1900-1916" (M.A. thesis, Samford University, 1971), *passim; The World Almanac and Encyclopedia, 1910* (New York, 1910), 656.

ficient numbers in Tampa to form a separate Italian Socialist
Party complete with a brick meeting house. Recurrent strikes in
the tobacco and cigar industries, both heavily staffed by foreign
workers, gave rise to charges of anarchism and revolutionary influences. When Florida railroads and other businesses employing
large numbers of immigrants experienced similar work stoppages
after 1900, frequently accompanied by violence, it seemed that
the native population's worst fears concerning alien radicalism
had been confirmed.[40]

Issues centered on the problem of race engendered their own
brand of anxiety. In the late nineteenth century the South
gloried in the belief that it was the only distinctly "American"
section of the Union—a region where allegedly the pure American character could still be found. As R. E. Rose, the Florida
state chemist, explained in 1906, "the true American type . . . is
now found principally south of 'Mason and Dixon's Line' . . .
particularly in Florida, where most of our people can trace their
lineage, directly to the founders of the Republic, with little if
any admixture of foreign blood."[41] The thought of infusing alien
and allegedly inferior racial strains into this pure crucible of
Americanism horrified many natives. The rising national popularity of the eugenic movement, with its emphasis on the "superior Nordic races" and its condemnation of the supposedly degraded Latin or Mediterranean races, also served to turn Floridians against the immigrants.[42]

The social tensions produced by the introduction of the Jim
Crow system created additional problems for immigrant newcomers. At a time when Southerners were forging a new structure

40. Florida Department of Agriculture, *Florida: A Pamphlet*, 269, 276;
    U. S. Immigration Service, *Report of the Immigration Investigation
    Committee* (Washington, 1895), 133; Jacksonville *Florida Farmer and
    Fruit Grower*, May 19, 1894. For information concerning a railroad
    strike resulting in the deaths of four Italians and the wounding of
    many more see, Jacksonville *Florida Times-Union*, November 16, 1905.
41. R. E. Rose, "Florida Immigration—What Shall It Be?" *Proceedings of
    the Florida State Horticultural Society*, XIX (1906), 123. Consult also,
    "Florida Immigration—What Shall It Be?" *Florida Agriculturalist*,
    XXXIII (May 30, 1906), 338; Jacksonville *Florida Times-Union*, March
    25, 1906; "A Type of Immigrant," *Florida East Coast Homeseeker*, XI
    (June 1909), 192.
42. For a statement of the eugenic philosophy see, Thomas F. Gossett,
    *Race: The History of an Idea in America* (Dallas, 1963), 178, 308;
    Barbara M. Solomon, *Ancestors and Immigrants: A Changing New
    England Tradition* (Cambridge, Massachusetts, 1956), 141-51, 204-05.

of race relations with the establishment of segregation, immigrants frequently seemed to threaten the delicate balance. Foreigners often failed to share the racial biases of the native population and openly mixed with blacks. The experience of twenty-six Alsatian families brought to a plantation in Middle Florida is illustrative. Before one year was out, local residents observed that the new arrivals shared cottages with Negro tenants and that they "learned to talk the darky lingo a good deal quicker than they did United States."[43] This sort of behavior elicited hostile reactions from native whites. With the introduction of orientals and other "exotic" nationalities, moreover, many Floridians became concerned over the possibilities of new and potentially more dangerous race problems. Would the state have to establish accommodations and laws to cover white, black, *and* yellow?[44] To many it would be better to keep these strangers out entirely.

The widespread attack of the boll weevil in 1907 bankrupted many black farmers and caused an exodus of these workers into the labor market that did much to alleviate concerns of a labor shortage. The industrial recession beginning in that same year simultaneously served to reduce expectations for growth in manufacturing that would have called for increased labor needs. Hence, agricultural and industrial requirements for foreign workers lessened at precisely that juncture when these peoples began to be viewed increasingly in an unfavorable light.[45] By 1910, Floridians believed that if the state were to retain its racial integrity, to preserve its unique "American" character, and to protect its cherished institutions, it now had no room for those

---

43. Jacksonville *Florida Dispatch, Farmer & Fruit Grower*, August 14, 1890. Also see, Richard J. Amundson, "Henry S. Sanford and Labor Problems in the Florida Orange Industry," *Florida Historical Quarterly*, XLIII (January 1965), 239.

44. "The Labor Problem," *Florida Agriculturalist*, XXXIII (May 2, 1906), 280; "Notes," *Florida Agriculturalist*, XXXI (September 28, 1904), 616; Bert J. Lowenberg, "Efforts of the South to Encourage Immigration, 1865-1900," *South Atlantic Quarterly*, XXXIII (October 1934), 368. For early indications of these concerns see, Jacksonville *Florida Dispatch*, February 22, 1886.

45. See the following for comparative developments in other areas of the United States: Herbert E. Schell, "Official Immigration Activities of Dakota Territory," *North Dakota Historical Quarterly*, VII (1932-33), 5-24; Arthur J. Brown, "The Promotion of Immigration to Washington, 1854-1909," *Pacific Northwest Quarterly*, XXXVI (1945), 3-17; Edna Parker, "The Southern Pacific Railroad and Settlement in Southern California," *Pacific Historical Review*, VI (1937), 103-19; Brandfon, "End of Immigration," 591-611.

foreigners who had earlier received an open and enthusiastic welcome. Thus ended the campaign which began with such bright promise shortly after the Civil War.

*Journal of Historical Geography*, 3, 2 (1977) 155–175

# The role of culture and community in frontier prairie farming

John G. Rice

Frederick Jackson Turner described the American frontier as the great democratizer, a place where people from diverse backgrounds came together, shook off the shackles of their former cultures and blended into the American nation. Detailed study of nineteenth-century rural settlement in the Upper Middle West reveals a more complex picture. A marked spatial clustering of groups from the same country, province and even parish is readily observed. Often these groups were bound together in a close-knit community through the agency of a common church. This paper traces through four decades the farming behaviour and economic fortunes of several such groups who settled on the prairie of Kandiyohi County, Minnesota. The findings indicate that the ethnic community, especially where it consisted of people from a relatively restricted district in the old country, did help to make the frontier experience of its people rather different from that of their neighbours.

Rural settlement in the Upper Middle West during the nineteenth century was distinguished by a great number of different immigrant groups. Nowhere else in the United States was there such a variety of cultural backgrounds among the farming population. Many of the first settlers came directly from Europe. Others had spent short periods of time in places farther to the east.[1] Almost all had been farmers before they came, and each settler brought a set of values, attitudes and habits from his European homeland. For most of these immigrant farmers the land they came to was quite different from the land they left behind. There were woods and parklands, which might have recalled a little of home, but most of the land which lay waiting, especially beyond the Mississippi River, was prairie. This was an environment with which they had no experience. To the problems of adjusting to a strange society were added the difficulties of developing new strategies to cope with an unfamiliar and what often seemed even to be a hostile environment.[2]

The extent to which the varying cultural backgrounds of these settlers affected their farming practices and the degree of success which they achieved has been the subject of much comment in the literature. As Bogue points out, however, one finds all too frequently subjective generalizations rarely based on careful research.[3] One reason for the lack of research effort in this area may be the strong influence

---

[1] The source areas and migration routes of some one thousand North Dakota pioneers of different cultural backgrounds are discussed and mapped in J. C. Hudson, Migration to an American frontier, *Annals of the Association of American Geographers* 66 (1976) 242–65
[2] The reactions of Norwegian settlers to the prairie environment are well depicted by Ole Rolvaag in his novel *Giants in the earth* (New York and London 1927)
[3] A. G. Bogue, *From prairie to cornbelt* (Chicago and London 1963) 237

of the Turner thesis.[1] Frederick Jackson Turner saw the frontier as the crucible of democracy, a place filled with the spirit of individualism where Europeans could "... destroy the bonds of social caste that bound them in their older home ..." and "... hew out for themselves in a new country a destiny proportioned to the powers that God had given them".[2] For Turner the culture the settlers bore was unimportant because the frontier experience stripped them of their inheritance. It was the great leveller. It left men free from the encumbrances of their previous experience—as if they had been born again. In the words of George Pierson, "... it was the land these immigrants went to, rather than the traits they came with, that seemed to Turner *significant*".[3]

Despite the power which the Turner thesis has exerted over the mind of scholarship in America a curiosity has persisted, especially among non-academics, about the relationship between cultural background and farming patterns. Bogue identifies two propositions which may be found in accounts of midwestern agriculture.[4] One is that certain culture groups are responsible for introducing specific crops and farming techniques into American agriculture. The other is that some groups maintained over a considerable period of time distinctive farming practices which differed significantly from those being followed by others around them. He has no quarrel with the first of these, but he finds the second suspect, even though some work he himself has done in Iowa tends to lend it support.[5] Bogue is, however, equivocal about this issue. At one point we read, "We must remember, too, as we consider the decision-making of prairie farmers, that not all of them were alike in background or objectives and that their farming operations might differ considerably, even in the earliest days of settlement."[6] Later on, however, we read, "Perhaps cultural differences among western farmers were more apparent than real—most obvious in food ways, dress, and lingual traits, and less important when the farmer decided on his combination of major enterprises."[7] The problem seems to be that there are good *a priori* reasons for arguing both ways, and in the absence of detailed studies we can only continue to speculate.

In his study of settlement in a Wisconsin county Merle Curti sought to test the Turner thesis objectively by analysing a mountain of data on virtually all aspects of frontier life.[8] He is therefore more concerned with the relative success of the different culture groups than he is with what they chose to do. Looking at settlers who had come from the east as well as a number of immigrant groups he finds that, although the groups start out with roughly the same amount of farmland per household, measures of property value and value of implements, livestock and produce show the Americans and English-speaking foreign-born well ahead initially. As time passes, however, the poorer groups gain steadily and the differences are reduced. In the matter of economic status then, Curti finds Turner's ideas

[1] A good review and critical discussion of the Turner thesis is available in G. R. Taylor (Ed.), *The Turner thesis concerning the role of the frontier in American history* (Boston 1956)
[2] F. J. Turner, Contributions of the West to American democracy, pp. 19–33 of Taylor (Ed.) *op. cit.* 30
[3] G. W. Pierson, The frontier and American institutions: a criticism of the Turner thesis, pp. 47–65 of *ibid.* 365
[4] Bogue, *loc. cit.*
[5] Bogue, *op. cit.* 238
[6] Bogue, *op. cit.* 194
[7] Bogue, *op. cit.* 238
[8] M. Curti, *The making of an American community* (Stanford, Calif. 1959) 176–221

confirmed. He seems to be disturbed, however, by his discovery that the Norwegians in general make a poor showing and is forced to postulate that the environment in which they settled (hilly, wooded land) might be to blame.

There are two limitations in the kind of approach taken by Bogue and Curti. First, they have dealt exclusively with *national* groups. In working with large populations it would be unreasonable to expect the researcher to go beyond the census identification of country of birth. Yet we know that in rural areas of Europe during the nineteenth century culture varied considerably over short distances. Language, food, dress, building style and farming practices could be very different in two provinces of the same country, or even in two parishes of the same province. Second, the role of the local church-centred community in the development of rural society has not been fully appreciated. It commonly happened that immigrants settled in clusters and created church-centred communities that served to preserve cultural identity and even language through a number of generations. Where these communities were formed by people who had had close ties in the old country the stability of the population was especially strong.[1] In this situation one might reasonably expect the cultural background of the group to have more of an impact on the farming experience than in a situation where people came from disparate parts of the same country.

The task of realizing this kind of detail for an area larger than a few townships is formidable. Michael Conzen's work on Blooming Grove township near Madison, Wisconsin, demonstrates what can be achieved at this scale.[2] Conzen's main interest is in the effect of a nearby urban place on frontier farming, but he also looks at farming practices and the relative success of different culture groups. The problem with studying a single township, of course, is that the number of members in any class will probably be very small, making it difficult to generalize about the findings. The advantages of the micro-study probably far outweigh the disadvantages, however, and more work at this scale needs to be done.

In this study frontier farming will be examined within a six township area on the prairie of Kandiyohi County, Minnesota. It is part of a larger project in which a group of emigrants from a single parish in Sweden is being followed to North America in an effort to document fully the process of transplantation. Most of the settlers in the area were Swedes, though a large number of Norwegians and some families from Eastern North America and the British Isles also made their homes there. The Swedes came mainly from three provinces—Skåne, Småland and Dalarna—and almost all the people from Dalarna had left the parish of Gagnef or its chapelry of Mockfjärd. The Norwegians were more diverse in their origins, though the very early settlers tended to come from a few restricted districts. The area thus offers the possibility of comparing culture groups defined at the national, provincial and parochial levels. The three subnational Swedish culture groups were given further cohesion by the fact that each dominated one of the three major church communities. The primary aim of this study, then, is to look at the farming system which developed in the area and follow the fortunes of the culture groups through time in an effort to asses the role of culture and community in shaping these patterns. Attention will be directed specifically to the kinds of crops and livestock the farmers chose to emphasize and the economic status which they achieved.

[1] R. C. Ostergren, Cultural homogeneity and population stability among Swedish immigrants in Chicago County *Minnesota history* **43** (1973) 255–69 and J. G. Rice, *Patterns of ethnicity in a Minnesota county, 1880–1905* (Umeå, Sweden 1973) 64–91

[2] M. P. Conzen, *Frontier farming in an urban shadow* (Madison, Wis. 1971)

**Early settlement**

The study area is located about eighty-five miles due west of the Twin Cities (Fig. 1). The land is level to rolling prairie and contains a chain of lakes which are a source of the sluggish, eastward flowing Crow River.[1] In addition to these lakes there were before settlement a great number of prairie sloughs scattered over much of the area, and drainage was one of the major problems the early settlers had to face. Another was the scarcity of wood, the only trees being found in the groves of elm, ash and burr oak which fringed some of the lakes.

The land was surveyed in 1856 and placed on sole shortly afterward. The first settler to take land in the area filed a preemption claim in August of 1857, and within two years eighteen such claims had been entered.[2] Not surprisingly in a prairie environment all were located close to lakes. The first two settlers to break land were the from the East (Old Americans), but the rest were Swedes, mainly from the newly founded settlements at Chisago Lakes and New Scandia in the St Croix Valley. They learned of the region from a Swede, Jacob Fahlström, who had lived for many years among the Indians and was well acquainted with the region of the Kandiyohi lakes.

Claim taking went slowly in the late 1850s. Certainly the economic depression must have slowed activity, but more importantly the railroad had not reached Minnesota, and the trip by horse and wagon from St Paul took five or six days. Most settlers spent only brief periods of time in the summer on their claims—long enough to plough a small patch of land in the spring, sow some grain and harvest a crop in the fall. Winters were spent in the more established settlements to the east, the men taking work in the lumber camps of the Rum and St Croix valleys. Only six or seven families were staying in the area when, on 18th August 1862, news of the general Sioux uprising spread across the prairie. Packing what belongings they could, these settlers fled east at dawn the following day. For three years no one returned. The area lay within reach of Sioux raiding parties operating out of the Dakota Territory to the west and remained unsafe for settlement. By the spring of 1865 the line of military defence posts had been moved farther to the west, and in the autumn a few settlers began to filter back. Many had been soured by the experience, however, and altogether not more than half of the original claim filers returned.

In 1866 the pace of settlement picked up, and within two years the area was being inundated by a flood of new settlers. The great attraction was the free land now being offered under the Homestead Act passed in 1862. Virtually all of the land taken by settlers in the late 1860s was claimed under this act. As in the pre-uprising period the sites closest to the lakes were the first to be taken. From these early cores settlement spread quickly across the surrounding prairie (Fig. 2). By 1870 homesteaders had claimed almost 23,000 acres and most of the federal land was gone. What had not been granted to the state for railroads, education, internal

[1] The map of the environment was compiled from information extracted from the surveyors' field notes, plot maps in the county atlas of 1886 and a general soils map in the county atlas of 1972

[2] This study owes much to the wealth of information available in the Kandiyohi County history. Certainly one of the best of its kind ever published, this history contains, *inter alia*, lists of county, township and church officers, school board members, children who attended school in different years, as well as numerous biographies rich in detail. V. E. Lawson, *Illustrated history and descriptive and biographical review of Kandiyohi County, Minnesota* (Willmar, Minn. 1905)

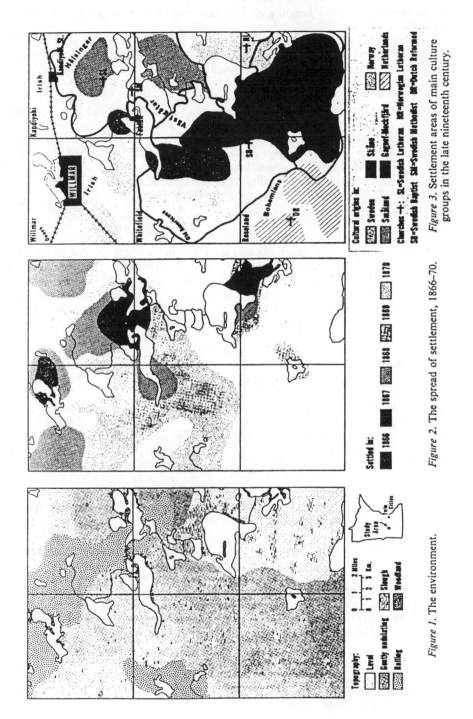

*Figure 3.* Settlement areas of main culture groups in the late nineteenth century.

*Figure 2.* The spread of settlement, 1866–70.

*Figure 1.* The environment.

improvements and the building of the state capital was in the hands of non-residents.

The availability of homestead land was not the only factor that promoted the rapid settlement of the area in the late 1860s. In 1864 the St Paul and Pacific Railroad Company had been granted a right-of-way through this area for its main line to the west. The line was surveyed in the summer of 1868 and the station villages of Willmar and Kandiyohi were plotted. Merchants were already setting up businesses in these places in 1869 although the tracks did not actually reach Willmar until the following year. By this time Kandiyohi, Willmar and Lake Lillian townships had been organized, the principal churches had been established and four schools were functioning. The federal census of 1870 returned a population of 1,150 in the study area, of whom 160 resided in Willmar and thirteen at Kandiyohi Station. A total of 276 families had now established themselves here—over one-third of all who would come during the first forty years.

### The settlers

Although for some purposes, notably the study of marriage ties and population persistence, the family is the most appropriate unit of study, in analysing economic activity a more useful entity is the household. The household may be composed of a single conjugal family or it may contain several, usually closely related. It may also include individuals who are not related to any of the families involved. The key feature of the household is that it comprises a group of people who live and work together.

In the early days of settlement the great majority of all households in this area held land. Tenancy was rare, and most of the landless people were young farm and railroad labourers, most of them single, a few with small families. Seldom do any of this group appear in two successive census rolls.[1] Their names are almost never inscribed in the church registers, and one searches in vain for mention of them in the county history. In only a few instances did labourers eventually acquire land and settle down as members of the community. Though few at first, their numbers increased with time and by 1905 probably twenty per cent of the area's rural population belonged to this restless group. It is an important and fascinating feature of frontier society, but a shortage of source material makes it difficult to study.

This study will deal exclusively with those households that held land. Figure 4 shows the relative sizes of the major culture groups over time, expressed in numbers of landholding households. The manuscript federal and state census rolls are the basic source for establishing the presence of a household. Since the last census which can be seen in manuscript form is the one taken by the state in 1905 the study could not be carried far beyond that date. By using real estate tax records, church membership lists and the Farmers' Atlas of 1915 it could be extended to 1910. The census has been used to establish the nationality of each household head. Church registers and material from the county history have permitted the identification of provincial and even parish origins for most of the Swedish population.

[1] For nineteenth-century Minnesota manuscripts of the federal census are available for 1860, 1870 and 1880. The 1890 census was destroyed in a fire and use of the one taken in 1900 is highly restricted. A census was also taken by the state at ten-year intervals from 1865 to 1905. All are open to public inspection

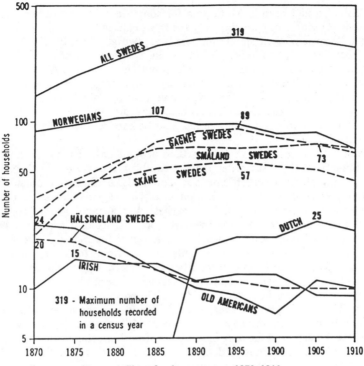

*Figure 4.* Size of culture groups, 1870–1910.

The total number of households in the area rose steadily to 1895 and then declined as farm size began to increase. Although the Old Americans, Irish and Norwegians were on the scene early, their relative importance diminished as time went by. As this happened the dominance of the Swedes increased until a large-scale colonization by Dutch settlers began in the southwest during the late 1880s. The distribution of these groups by the end of the nineteenth century can be seen in Fig. 3. Spatial clustering, not only of national but also of provincial groups, was pronounced.[1]

The groups varied in their farming backgrounds and in the paths they travelled on their way to the Kandiyohi prairie. Most of the Old Americans were Yankees with roots in New England. Many had been in Minnesota fifteen or twenty years before they arrived here. They were part of that vanguard of Yankee settlers who in the 1850s had dreamed of making Minnesota the New England of the West.

[1] The map provides a generalized picture of the distribution of the culture groups. In fact, of course, some intermixture was present. In an earlier study the author devised a measure of ethnic "segregation" based on ownership the of forty acre parcels of land (see Rice, *op. cit.* 49–56). The measure produces an index which varies from 1·000, representing complete segregation, to 0·000, representing complete integration. When this measure is applied to the entire county of Kindiyohi in 1905, the following results are obtained: Swedes 0·387, Norwegians 0·375, Dutch 0·525, Bohemians 0·285, Old Americans and Irish 0·288, Swedes from Gagnef–Mockfjärd 0·456, Småland 0·272. Skåne 0·327. Three random distributions of farm families and their land failed to produce an index higher than 0·081, indicating that the groups were segregated to a significant degree

The Irish also had been in Minnesota for some time. Most had been born in the Maritime Provinces of Canada; only the most elderly had come to America from Ireland. Because of their small numbers these two groups are dealt with together. This procedure is not entirely satisfactory since the Irish formed a distinct Catholic community, but the long experience which both had with the American system of commercial farming did set them apart from the more recent immigrant groups. They had tried their hands at farming in a number of places on their way to Kandiyohi and could be expected to have a better grasp of the full range of possibilities than the fresh immigrant. They might also be expected to have more capital to start out with.

The first Norwegians in the area settled around Lake Lillian in the southeast. They came from the Balsfjorden district south of Tromsø in North Norway and formed a spatially distinct settlement around the lake (much of it outside the study area to the east). By far the largest number of Norwegians, however, settled in the north around Willmar. Among the earliest was a small group from Vinje in Telemark and another from the western fjord district of Hardanger. No strong regionally based communities developed, however, as many of the first settlers moved away and other Norwegians with diverse origins took their place. Most of the Norwegians came from communities in western Wisconsin and had already gained ten or fifteen years of American farming experience before they arrived in Kandiyohi. They were, however, closer to their European past than the Old Americans or Irish. The farming system everywhere in Norway in the nineteenth century was based on the production of hay and livestock. Milk products from cows and goats dominated the diet, and the only bread grain of any importance was barley. For those settlers who came from Balsfjorden, Hardanger and other districts in the West and North fishing would have represented a secondary occupation probably as important as farming. In this fjord and mountain landscape the farms were necessarily very small, and the amount of meadow and pastureland was increased through the use of the high summer farm (seter). The settlers from Vinje and other parts of the eastern valleys may have enjoyed somewhat better farming, but there too subsidiary employment, perhaps the cutting and hauling of timber, was essential.

Unlike the Norwegians the Swedes developed several strong regionally based communities. The areas from which these groups came may be seen in Fig. 5. The most tightly-knit community was the one formed by the people from the Dalarna parish of Gagnef and its chapelry of Mockfjärd. The first families left this forest region in the spring of 1867, and by 1869 a large emigration was underway from the valley of Mockfjärd to the prairies of Kandiyohi. Of major importance in stimulating this movement were the crop failures of 1867–68, which brought distress to all of northern Europe, but the effect of the "American letters" cannot be overlooked. A note in the county history records that these letters were read and reread, passed from hand to hand until they themselves fell apart, whereupon several copies were often made to be circulated more widely. By 1873 eighty-seven people had left Mockfjärd for North America and all but seven had settled in Kandiyohi County. They had been joined by fifty-five emigrants from Gagnef and several families from neighbouring parishes. In the following years the direct emigration from Gagnef and Mockfjärd continued and their settlement came to occupy a large area.[1]

[1] Henceforth the distinction between Mockfjärd and Gagnef will not be maintained, and the name "Gagnef" will be used to cover both

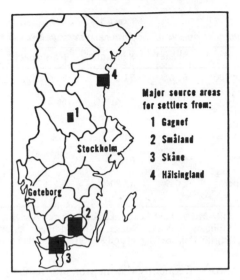

Major source areas for settlers from:

1 Gagnef
2 Småland
3 Skåne
4 Hälsingland

*Figure 5.* Source areas for Swedish settlers.

While the movement from Gagnef to Kandiyohi was direct, the other three groups considered here came via earlier established Swedish settlements in Illinois and eastern Minnesota. Most of the Småland settlers came from the region of Värend, one of the earliest parts of Sweden to experience "America fever", and therefore they often formed the largest element in the early settlements. These settlements continued to supply settlers for Kandiyohi, but many others arrived directly from Småland in response to letters sent home by friends and relatives. Though people from Värend remained most numerous many Småland families came from other parts of the province.

Skåne, the province to the south of Småland, also provided many of the first emigrants from Sweden. They came mainly from the plain of Kristianstad and forest region of Göinge to the north. Large numbers of these people had settled in Illinois in the 1850s, and it is from these communities that the first Skåne settlers in Kandiyohi seem to have come.

Although located in the North the province of Hälsingland also experienced an early emigration, largely because of the strength of the nonconformist movement there. Those who came to Kandiyohi had left the valleys of the northeast and made their way first to Illinois. Initially they were well represented among the settlers in the study area, but they failed to develop a major community here. They are included in the following analysis to provide a second northern group for comparative purposes.

Table 1 provides a rough comparison of the farming systems with which these four Swedish groups had been familiar.[1] Like the Norwegians the Gagnef settlers came from an area where arable land was confined to narrow valley bottoms and agriculture was based on livestock, especially cattle, and the use of the summer farm (*fäbod*). Here, too, the marginal nature of the environment forced the farmer

[1] The figures are based on information in G. Sundbärg, *Emigrationsutredningen* (Stockholm 1910). They describe the situation at the beginning of the twentieth century, but the regional differences they point up were of long standing

TABLE 1

*Some comparative aspects of the farming systems in Swedish source areas*

|  | Skåne* | Småland* | Hälsingland* | Gagnef* |
|---|---|---|---|---|
| Crofters per 100 farm units | 66·6 | 71·6 | 60·6 | 0·0 |
| Hectares cultivated per 100 inhabitants | 98·7 | 57·4 | 66·2 | 42·6 |
| Grain yields per inhabitant (kg) | 706 | 549 | 274 | 271 |
| Milk yield per inhabitant (kg) | 696 | 635 | 524 | 480 |
| Milk yield per cow (kg) | 2,069 | 1,790 | 1,516 | 1,545 |

* The following districts (*härader*) have been used for each provincial group: Skåne–Villands, Östra and Västra Göinge; Småland–Konga, Norrviddinge, Uppviddinge, Kinnevalds; Hälsingland–Forsa, Bergsjö, Delsbo; Gagnef and Mockfjärd together comprised a single district

to turn to part-time work, frequently the making and hauling of charcoal for the nearby iron industry. In contrast to much of the rest of Sweden the crofter (*torpare*) was absent in Gagnef. Much of Dalarna was traditionally a land of smallholders, although by the middle of the nineteenth century the cottager (*backstugusittare*) was a familiar figure. The emigration tended to be led by the land-holding families, however, and more than eighty per cent of the Gagnef settlers in Kandiyohi had owned their own farms. These farms were very small as the low grain and milk yields per inhabitant suggest. The effect of the short northern growing season is reflected in the low milk yield per cow.

In most ways the farming system in Hälsingland was similar to that in Gagnef. The main difference was that crofting was widespread there, and a number of the settlers in Kandiyohi came from this background. Crofters were also present among the immigrants from Skåne and Småland. The milk yield per cow suggests that Småland enjoyed a somewhat better environment than the northern areas. However, farming was unquestionably best in Skåne, especially on the plain of Kristianstad. Even the crofter here could be expected to have had a richer and more varied farming experience than the smallholder from Gagnef.

## The farming system

The basic source for studying nineteenth-century farming systems at the level of the household is the manuscript agricultural census. Since the files of those taken later than 1880 either have been destroyed or are not open to public inspection, an analysis of the impact of cultural background on farming practices could be carried out only for the early period. The census provides information about value of farm, implements, livestock and products, and about acreage and production of different crops and numbers of the various kinds of animals kept. Some of those who have used the census in the past have questioned its accuracy, and there are good reasons for doing so.[1] Most figures are estimates, as their well-rounded appearance clearly

[1] A critical discussion of the 1860 agricultural census may be found in H. B. Johnson, King wheat in southeastern Minnesota *Annals of the Association of American Geographers* 47 (1957) 350–62

testifies. Seldom do acreages for individual crops add up to the amount given for total area tilled. It is unclear how much of the land comprising each farm is owned by the operator and how much is rented. A comparison of the 1880 census reports with real estate tax records revealed that in only 64·1 per cent of the cases were the farm sizes reported in the two sources within ten acres of each other. Some of the discrepancy may be the result of land changing hands between the times the two reports were made, but probably much of it is due to renting. With all its problems, however, the agricultural census is the only source we have, and handled carefully it will probably yield a reasonably accurate picture of what farmers were doing.

The census rolls of both 1870 and 1880 show the grip which King wheat had on prairie agriculture in Minnesota at this time. In spite of the fact that the railroad did not reach Willmar until the summer of 1870 and no wheat was shipped out until the following spring, the 1870 census (reporting the situation in 1869) showed that the bulk of the sown area was devoted to this crop. In 1869 the St Paul and Pacific Railroad Company built grain elevators in both Willmar and Kandiyohi Station. By 1880 three additional elevators and a flour mill had been built in Willmar, and a second elevator had been added in Kandiyohi Station. In spite of the grasshopper plagues which had devastated the county in 1876–77 wheat was more dominant than ever, occupying seventy-five per cent of the total area tilled. The only other grain of any importance was oats. This was the most widely grown cereal crop in nineteenth-century Scandinavia, but an analysis of the wheat–oat ratio by culture group revealed that the Swedes and Norwegians were growing no more of it than the Old Americans and Irish. It mattered little that the Norwegian or the Swede from Gagnef or Hälsingland had had no experience with wheat at home. Faced with the realities of the market everybody grew it.

The raising of livestock was secondary to wheat farming. Animals were kept largely to supply needs of the family. A little butter, a few eggs and a fleece or two might be marketed each year, but most of the animal products were consumed at home. In this activity, without a market to dictate terms, people could afford to express their cultural preferences. Table 2 gives a comparative picture of the stock raising practices of the major culture groups in 1870 and 1880. It also shows what was happening in the home areas of the four Swedish groups in 1905.

Draught animals (columns 1 and 2) had more to do with the commercial than with the subsistence side of production, but even here there was opportunity to exercise choice. Both horses and oxen were used for draught in 1870, but oxen were far more numerous. Only among the Old American–Irish and Hälsingland groups were horses relatively important, yet all of the Swedish groups except the one from Småland had strong horse traditions. Between 1870 and 1880 the use of oxen declined dramatically. Cost appears to be the overriding determinant here. In the short run it was cheaper for the new settler to buy a pair of oxen to use while he got his farm started and accumulated a little capital. After a while he could afford to purchase a horse or two which, although individually more expensive, were more suited to the mowing and reaping machinery used at the time. All the groups were making the switch to horses in the 1870s. Oxen remained most important to the settlers from Gagnef, even though they were virtually unknown there, because a steady flow of new immigrants continued to arrive directly from that parish throughout the decade.

Column 3 in the table relates the number of non-draught animals to the total area cultivated and thus provides a measure of the relative importance of cropping and livestock raising. The three different kinds of animals have been reduced to a

TABLE 2

*Livestock raising*

|  | Draught | | | Non-draught | | |
|---|---|---|---|---|---|---|
|  | (1) | (2) | (3) | (4) | (5) | (6) |
|  | No. of animals/ 100 acres cultivated | % Oxen | No. of animal units/100 acres cultivated* | % Cattle | % Sheep | % Swine |
|  | *Kandiyohi*: 1870 | | | | | |
| Old Americans and Irish | 9·7 | 56·7 | 11·8 | 93·2 | 1·6 | 5·2 |
| Norwegians | 9·6 | 78·1 | 26·6 | 94·1 | 4·1 | 1·8 |
| Swedes from: | | | | | | |
| Skåne | 11·4 | 78·9 | 13·3 | 89·6 | 3·9 | 6·5 |
| Småland | 8·2 | 91·5 | 10·9 | 90·2 | 6·1 | 3·7 |
| Hälsingland | 13·0 | 46·9 | 20·7 | 88·5 | 6·8 | 4·7 |
| Gagnef | 10·4 | 83·7 | 21·1 | 95·0 | 4·9 | 3·1 |
|  | *Kandiyohi*: 1880 | | | | | |
| Old Americans and Irish | 4·9 | 6·1 | 10·3 | 91·0 | 2·6 | 6·4 |
| Norwegians | 6·4 | 23·4 | 18·0 | 90·7 | 6·8 | 2·5 |
| Swedes from: | | | | | | |
| Skåne | 5·1 | 2·0 | 16·2 | 89·0 | 8·1 | 2·9 |
| Småland | 6·4 | 25·0 | 18·6 | 88·1 | 7·4 | 4·5 |
| Hälsingland | 9·7 | 6·2 | 23·0 | 89·0 | 6·1 | 3·9 |
| Gagnef | 9·3 | 39·8 | 21·8 | 90·0 | 7·2 | 3·9 |
|  | *Sweden*: 1905† | | | | | |
| Swedes in: | | | | | | |
| Skåne | 8·4 | 5·4 | 32·4 | 69·7 | 2·9 | 27·4 |
| Småland | 14·5 | 68·1 | 50·4 | 87·0 | 5·6 | 7·4 |
| Hälsingland | 7·1 | 0·9 | 37·3 | 89·4 | 6·2 | 4·4 |
| Gagnef | 7·2 | 0·0 | 39·0 | 90·9 | 3·0 | 6·1 |

* Animal units have been calculated in the way used by the Swedish Bureau of Statistics (Statistika Centralbyrån) 1 cow = 10 sheep = 4 swine

† Data are from G. Sundbärg, *Emigrationsutredningen* (Stockholm 1910). The districts used for each provincial group are listed in the footnote to Table 1

common "animal unit" through the use of a standard formula (see footnote to table). The greater emphasis placed on livestock by the three North Scandinavian groups in 1870 agrees well with the farming backgrounds of these people. On the other hand the settlers from Småland have not preserved this trait. By 1880 the overall importance of animals has risen slightly and all the Scandinavian groups stand out strongly as livestock raisers in contrast to the Old Americans and Irish.

Columns 4–6 show the relative importance of cattle, sheep and swine for each group. Cattle were of overwhelming importance for all groups in both years. It is in the relative emphasis on sheep versus swine that one must look for cultural preferences to surface. Of all the groups the Swedes from Skåne had the greatest experience with swine. That experience is reflected, albeit weakly, in the 1870 pattern, but it has vanished in 1880. The groups from Hälsingland and Småland came from traditions in which sheep had been important, and again that shows up in the 1870 figures. The Norwegian preference for sheep over swine can also be linked easily to their previous experience. By 1880 all the Scandinavians once again stand together—this time as sheep raisers—in contrast to the Old Americans and Irish for whom swine were clearly more important.

The reasons why farmers chose particular activities may, of course, also be sought in the environment. The map in Fig. 6 shows that spatial pattern of farming practices in 1880. Livestock were considerably more important in the southeast while cropping dominated the north and west. A comparison with the map in Fig. 1 suggests good environmental reasons for this distribution. The southeastern part of the area is especially flat and until the turn of the century remained poorly drained. Land suitable for cultivation was therefore limited while meadow and rough pasture were in abundance. The high concentration of sheep here fits particularly well the picture of a marginal environment. Grain growing was more intensively practised no the better drained lands of the north and west, the greatest specialization in wheat occurring where these lands approached the rail line.[1]

It is difficult to determine to what extent location rather than cultural background influenced the choices a farmer made. A comparison of the map of culture groups in Fig. 3 with the one of farming practices shows, for example, that the Gagnef settlers were especially strongly concentrated within the poorly drained livestock region. In Table 2 we see that they, together with the people from Hälsingland, maintained the greatest emphasis on livestock in 1880. The latter, however, are living not in the wet lands but rather in the heart of the "wheat belt". Unfortunately the number of households is too small to test the reactions of members of the same culture group to different environmental conditions. One may fairly conclude, however, that an explanation of the farming pattern based on cultural background is no more satisfying than one involving environment and distance from market. This may be because we are looking at an area which had excellent agricultural potential and was tied quickly into the market system. In Chisago and Isanti Counties, where commercial wheat farming was not as well developed, there is stronger evidence for the preservation by Swedish settlers of traditional farming practices.[2]

Between 1880 and 1900 the farming system in Kandiyohi County began to change. The dominance of wheat slackened as farmers experimented with other crops and turned increasingly to livestock raising. In the first decade of the twentieth century the pace of change was dramatic. Wheat acreage fell from seventy-one per cent of the total area cultivated in 1900 to thirty-seven per cent in 1910. Substantial gains were made by corn, oats and barley. By 1910 there were twice as many cattle per farm as there had been in 1880. Butter production had increased by seventy per cent and most was now being marketed. With the expanding urban market in the Twin Cities area and the consequent increase in land values, the zone of extensive wheat production was moving quickly out of Minnesota and diversified farming was taking its place.

[1] Around Willmar wheat did not occupy a very high percentage of the total area tilled because much of this area seems to have remained unsown in 1879. This was a time in which the town was expanding rapidly, and the lack of cropping calls to mind Sinclair's argument that anticipation of urban encroachment reduces the intensity of agricultural land use. R. Sinclair, Von Thünen and urban sprawl *Annals of the Association of American Geographers* 57 (1967) 72–87. Conzen made the same observation on the urban fringe of nineteenth-century Madison. Conzen, *op. cit.* 96
[2] In her statistical analysis of frontier farming in these two counties Eva Hamberg found that cultural background was probably responsible for the emphasis placed by Swedes on the growing of oats and the keeping of sheep. E. Hamberg, *Studier i internationell migration* (Stockholm 1976) 92. Her findings are confirmed in R. C. Ostergren, Rättvik to Isanti: a community transplanted (unpubl. Ph.D. thesis, Univ. of Minnesota 1976)

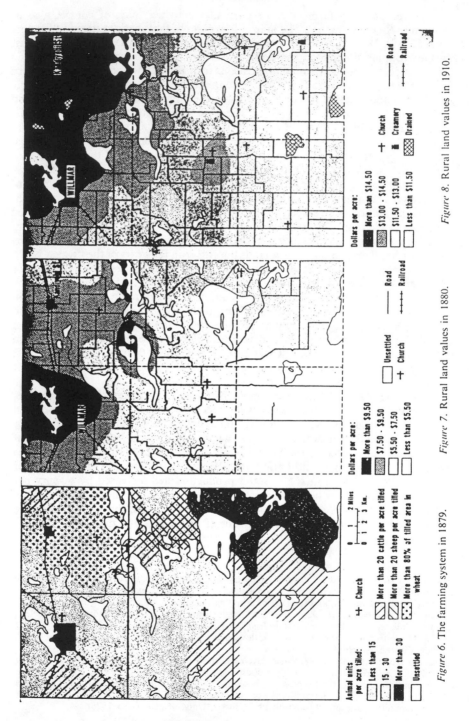

*Figure 8.* Rural land values in 1910.

*Figure 7.* Rural land values in 1880.

*Figure 6.* The farming system in 1879.

The trend in the study area was similar to that in the county as a whole. Co-operative creameries were established during the 1890s in Lake Lillian and White-field Townships and in Kandiyohi Station, and in 1905 in Willmar. Peter Lindquist, a settler from Gagnef, kept a record of the crops he sowed each year from 1871 to 1903.[1] His record shows the beginnings of the change.

TABLE 3

*Changing crop allocation on Peter Lindquist's farm*

| | Total acreage sown annually | Percentage sown to: | | | |
| | | wheat | oats | flax | corn |
| --- | --- | --- | --- | --- | --- |
| 1871–81 | 42·6 | 85·5 | 14·5 | 0·0 | 0·0 |
| 1882–92 | 111·3 | 74·8 | 21·0 | 4·2 | 0·0 |
| 1893–1903 | 323·2 | 70·2 | 11·7 | 14·9 | 3·2 |

If we could follow Lindquist's crop allocation to 1910 we would almost certainly witness the same dramatic drop in the relative importance of wheat that occurred in the country as a whole. We do not have the data to trace our culture groups through this agricultural revolution, but it seems fair to assume that they differed little in their responses to it.

## Economic status

In this study economic status has been measured in terms of wealth in real property. The source materials used are the real estate tax lists compiled each year and kept in the county courthouse. Because of the great amount of time required to extract data from these lists, only four years—1880, 1890, 1900 and 1910—were selected for study. The records show that the per acre value of farmland varied significantly across the area in all four years. The maps in Figs 7 and 8 show this variation in 1880 and 1910.

The tax assessors seemed to have had three criteria in mind as they made their judgements. One was certainly distance from Willmar and the rail line. Both maps show clearly the tendency for land values to decrease with increasing distance to market. The second was the quality of the land. A comparison with the map of the environment in Fig. 1 shows, for example, that the poorly drained level land in the southeast was still given a low value in 1910 even though it had been farmed thirty or forty years. The third criterion seems to have been intensity of land use. This is not readily apparent from the maps because of the way in which they have been constructed, but to test for it the value of homesteaded land was compared with the value of railroad land in Kandiyohi Township for both 1880 and 1910.[2] been constructed, but to test for it the value of homesteaded land was compared Since homestead land was found in even-numbered sections and railroad land in odd-numbered sections there could be no systematic difference between the two in either quality or distance from market. The only difference is that, since home-stead land was taken first, it had been cultivated for a longer period of time and was

[1] Lawson, *op. cit.* 348
[2] The maps were prepared by calculating the average value for moving four-square-mile cells. This technique was employed to smooth out the irregularities introduced by the checker-board pattern of land alienation

12

normally the site of the farm buildings. Railroad land was purchased later and added to the farm cores developed on the homestead land. The difference in land use intensity is reflected in the per acre values—$7.75 versus $7.20 in 1880, $16.55 versus $15.33 in 1910. In each case the value of railroad land is just under ninety-three per cent of homestead land.

A potential problem with using tax evaluation figures to estimate real wealth is the effect that distance from market had on these values. The problem would seem to be more severe for 1880 when land values around the village appear to be artificially elevated by the expectation of continued urban expansion.[1] Actually, farmers seem to have compensated both for this effect and for the effect of varying land quality by creating farms of different size. The properties lying at some distance from Willmar and especially in the poorer southeast tend to be considerably larger than those around Willmar. In fact, with one or two exceptions, the weathier landholders did not live close to Willmar or the rail line. The distance effect probably does not alter significantly the economic picture which the tax records paint, and these evaluations seem to be a good measure of wealth in real property.

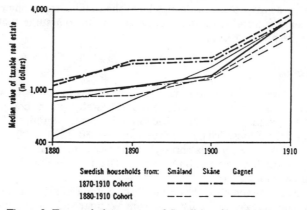

*Figure 9.* Economic betterment of Swedish cohorts, 1880–1910.

Others who have looked at the question of economic status have found it to be closely linked to persistence.[2] The longer a family stays in an area the wealthier it becomes, so that in a given year those who have been resident for the longest time should, *ceteris paribus*, be among the best off. Tables 4 and 5 show that this was

TABLE 4

*Median value of taxable real estate ($)*

|  | 1880 | 1890 | 1900 | 1910 |
|---|---|---|---|---|
| Old residents | 910 | 1,118 | 1,228 | 2,518 |
| Newcomers | 733 | 620 | 911 | 1,969 |

[1] Conzen points out another problem in this respect, namely that on the urban fringe the wealth of farmers may appear to be less than it actually is because they are liable to own property in town. Conzen, *op. cit.* 128

[2] See, for example, Curti, *op. cit.* 65–77 and Conzen, *op. cit.* 125–41

TABLE 5

*Median value of taxable real estate ($)*

|  | 1880*-90 | 1890*-1900 | 1900*-10 |
|---|---|---|---|
| Stayers | 881 | 963 | 1,167 |
| Leavers | 688 | 660 | 996 |

* Wealth at the beginning of the period

the case here. In Table 4, for each of the years studied, "newcomers", those who arrived during the previous decade, are compared with "old residents", those who had been in the area for more than ten years.

The higher property values of the established households are evident. Table 5 compares the real wealth of those households which persisted through each of the three decades between 1880 and 1910 with that of the ones which did not. Not only did one do better by staying longer, one also elected to stay longer if one was doing better.

Other studies have also pointed out that persistence may be related to community cohesion.[1] The social atmosphere produced in a rural church-centred community, particularly where the population derives largely from the same province in Europe, is conducive to putting down roots and inhibits rapid population turnover. This kind of "rural neighbourhood" is thus viewed as a community of a quasi "Gemeinschaft" type. To try to separate this effect on persistence from the effect of wealth the following analysis was performed. For each of the four observation years all landholding households were ranked by property value and then divided into five equal groups (quintiles). The persistence rates for the households in each quintile were then calculated for each of the three decades.[2] The results are shown in Table 6.

TABLE 6

*Decennial rates of persistence by quintile\**
*(percentage of households remaining)*

|  | 1 | 2 | 3 | 4 | 5 |
|---|---|---|---|---|---|
| 1880–1890 | 84·0 | 74·0 | 75·3 | 66·7 | 60·6 |
| 1890–1900 | 83·1 | 87·5 | 77·5 | 73·0 | 60·2 |
| 1900–1910 | 80·7 | 76·4 | 80·7 | 70·8 | 64·8 |

* Quintiles are numbered in descending order of wealth

For each of the culture groups these rates were applied to the number of households in each quintile and an expected persistence was calculated. The expected persistence was then related to the observed persistence to produce the indices shown in Table 7. A ratio of more than one indicates a greater persistence than expected. The three Swedish regional groups stand in strong contrast to the Norwegians and the Old Americans and Irish, especially during the first two decades.

[1] Rice, *op. cit.* and Ostergren, Cultural homogeneity *op. cit.*
[2] A household is regarded as continuing after the death of its head if ownership of the farm passes to another related household member

TABLE 7

*Decennial persistence indices for selected groups 1880–1910*

|                          | 1880–1890 | 1890–1900 | 1900–1910 |
|--------------------------|-----------|-----------|-----------|
| Old American and Irish   | 0·65      | 0·89      | 1·12      |
| Norwegians               | 0·83      | 0·84      | 0·87      |
| Swedes from:             |           |           |           |
| Gagnef                   | 1·36      | 1·21      | 1·04      |
| Småland                  | 1·23      | 1·17      | 1·14      |
| Skåne                    | 1·07      | 1·09      | 1·01      |
| Other Provinces          | 1·00      | 1·00      | 1·04      |

The indices for the Gagnef group are especially high. Among the Swedes, those from "other provinces", i.e. a group known to have diverse origins, demonstrate the lowest indices.

These findings seem to lend support to the hypothesis that community cohesion promotes persistence. They also suggest that, since persistence promotes the accumulation of wealth, community cohesion may be an important factor in determining economic status. The improvement made by the Gagnef households between 1880 and 1910 is striking (Fig. 10). From a situation in which over forty per cent of the households were in the fifth quintile they moved to one in which thirty-five per cent were in the first quintile. No other group improved so dramatically. Strong persistence in spite of initially low economic status is probably an important reason.

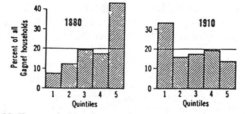

*Figure 10.* Economic betterment of Gagnef households, 1880–1910.

Economic advancement might, however, be related to factors other than length of residence. To eliminate the effect of different persistence rates two Gagnef cohorts were compared with similar cohorts from Småland and Skåne. The cohorts consist of households which persisted to the end of the study period, in one case from 1870, in the other from 1880. Their economic progress can be seen in Fig. 9. Initially both Gagnef cohorts ranked quite low. This group came directly from Sweden to Kandiyohi County and had had no intervening time in North America during which to accumulate some capital as had many of the settlers fron Småland and Skåne. Their rate of economic progress is remarkable, however, especially that of the 1880–1910 cohort. This was a tightly-knit, much interrelated population. It may be that once the community was established its members gained benefit from the mutual aid and support it fostered and were thus able to overtake the less cohesive groups from Småland and Skåne.

If the Gagnef group does represent a community transplanted, functioning to the benefit of all its members, some interesting and important questions arise.

Did the ecomonic status of a person back in Dalarna have any effect on his subsequent status here? Was the "old order" maintained? Did people preserve their status relative to each other, or did they, in Turner's words "destroy the bonds that bound them in their older home"? Finally, were they better off for having made the move, either relatively or absolutely? To try to answer these questions the real estate tax records (*bevillningen*) for Gagnef over the period 1865–85 were examined. For every fifth year all of the households in the parish were ranked by property value and divided into five equal groups just as was done on the American side. Those with no property were placed in a landless category. In this way the position of each emigrant with respect both to each other and to all other residents of the parish could be assessed.

The effect of an immigrant's economic status in Gagnef on the one he achieved in Kandiyohi was measured by using simple correlation regression analysis. The population was divided into two groups, those who arrived before 1880 and those who came during the following decade. These groups correspond fairly well to the first and second "waves" of emigrants who left the parish. For each of the four study years property values in Kandiyohi were compared with the values of the farms people had left in Gagnef. The correlation coefficients (*r* values) are shown in Table 8.

TABLE 8
*Correlations between farm values in Gagnef and Kandiyohi*

|      | 1880–1910 Cohort (N = 25) | 1890–1910 Cohort (N = 28) |
|------|--------------------------|--------------------------|
| 1880 | +0·364                   | —                        |
| 1890 | +0·190                   | +0·148                   |
| 1900 | +0·018                   | +0·058                   |
| 1910 | +0·066                   | +0·045                   |

The first wave settlers seem to have borne some effect of their earlier experience in 1880, but by 1890 this influence had weakened significantly and by 1900 it was gone. In contrast, the second wave people appear to have been freee of their former status almost from the start. The difference may lie in the fact that the first wave of emigrants consisted mainly of already established families, sometimes with as many as eight or ten children. What money they could get for their farms was all they had with them, and with family responsibilities the father was often unable to spend much time during the early years working away from home. The second wave of emigrants was a rather different group. It included many more young single males, and the married couples were younger and had fewer children. Most of them left the farms of their fathers or fathers-in-law and, while they would have received something in payment for their part of the farm, the status of the household they came from would have had only limited influence on their experience in the New World. In addition they were freer, once in Minnesota, to take part-time work in lumber camps and the like.

The question of whether people were better off for having emigrated to America is an especially difficult one to answer. This kind of an appraisal is complex and economic status is but one factor. Nevertheless, if we accept the premise that economic advancement was the prime motivation of most emigrants, it seems reasonable to measure their success in these economic terms. For the Gagnef

settlers on the Kandiyohi prairie there can be little question about absolute betterment. The 1910 tax records reveal that on the average they had 257 acres (104 ha)
of farm property. If the portion cultivated was the same as for the county as a
whole (79·8 per cent) they would have had 205 acres (83 ha) in that category
compared with only 6·5 acres (2·6 ha) for their friends and relatives who stayed
behind. Nor could the alluvial soils of the Dal River valley compare with the rich
black earth of the Kandiyohi prairie, a few dry years and grasshoppers notwithstanding. The photographs which adorn the county history offer further evidence
that they had substantially improved their lot. The entire family is gathered in
front of a large, substantial farmhouse. Everyone is dressed in his Sunday best, the
ladies all with hats. There were pictures taken to be sent home. With them the
emigrant proclaimed his success.

Another way to view economic status is in relation to other members of the
same society. To be on top of the pile in Gagnef was probably a different experience
from being somewhere in the middle in Kandiyohi. A picture of the changes in the
economic status of Gagnef settlers which took place over time is given in Fig. 11.

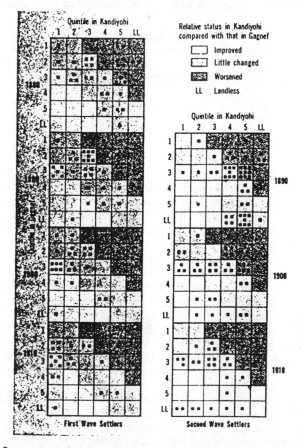

*Figure 11.* Improvement in relative economic status of Gagnef households.

The rows locate each settler in the economic order he left behind. The columns give the position he achieved in his new home. The progress the settlers made may be followed from decade to decade. Of the thirty-five first wave settlers fourteen were relatively worse off in 1880 than they had been before they left while one had improved his position. By 1910 of the twenty-five settlers remaining just three were not as well off, while eight had bettered their lot substantially. The same trend is apparent for the second wave settlers. In economic terms, at least, the move to Minnesota brought positive results, both absolutely and relatively, to most of the Gagnef settlers.

The farming frontier in nineteenth-century America was a more complex place than Frederick Jackson Turner made it out to be. Certainly the opportunity to succeed was there for anyone who wished to seize it. But the settlers did bring their cultural heritage with then and, especially where people from the same district built strong church-centred communities, it could have an effect on the decisions people made. It is hard to find evidence that cultural biases led people to make decisions which did not make sense from an economic point of view. One did not choose to grow oats when wheat was what the market demanded. Perhaps it was not cultural identity so much as the community which grew out of that identity which had an impact on economic behaviour. The frontier experience of the Gagnef settler in his close-knit community transplanted from the valleys of Dalarna certainly seems to have been different from that of his neighbour from New England, or Norway or even Skåne.

*Department of Geography*
*University of Minnesota*

THEODORE SALOUTOS

# THE IMMIGRANT CONTRIBUTION
# TO AMERICAN AGRICULTURE

For various reasons historians have played down the role of the immigrant in our agricultural development. Our provincialism and ineptness with foreign languages may account for part of this, but our attitudes probably have had more to do with it. Our fears and experiences with the foreign-born—real, exaggerated, or imagined—during the early years of the republic and during the 1840s and 1850s haunted us.[1] To complicate matters most immigrants arrived in the half century after the Civil War and before the outbreak of World War I[2] when we were trying to heal the wounds of a conflict that had torn us asunder and were experiencing the painful effects of the shift in our economy from an agricultural to an urban-industrial base,[3] when many doubted our abilities to absorb the millions from foreign shores, and when still others believed our main preoccupation should have been assimilation and Americanization of the foreign born instead of preservation and perpetuation of their ethnic and cultural patterns.[4] Deemphasizing the

THEODORE SALOUTOS is Professor of History at the University of California, Los Angeles. This paper was presented at the Washington Symposium on Two Centuries of American Agriculture in April 1975.

1 The prevalence of such sentiments is implicit, if not stated specifically, in Merle Curti, *The Growth of American Democracy* (New York: Harper and Brothers, 1943), 233–58; Ray Allen Billington, *The Protestant Crusade, 1800–1860: A Study of the Origins of American Nativism* (New York: Macmillan, 1938), and John Higham, *Strangers in the Land: Patterns of American Nativism, 1860–1925* (New Brunswick, N.J.: Rutgers University Press, 1955). On the legislative effort to restrict immigration see Roy L. Garis, *Immigration Restriction* (New York: Macmillan, 1927), 22–28, 59–116.

2 U. S. Department of Justice, Immigration and Naturalization Service, *Annual Report, 1973* (Washington: GPO, 1973), 25.

3 Theodore Saloutos, "The Agricultural Problem and Nineteenth Century Industrialism," *Agricultural History* 22 (July 1948): 156–74.

4 Representative arguments in favor of Americanism and assimilation are to be found in Winthrop Talbott, ed., *Americanization* (New York: H. W. Wilson, 1917); Edward R. Lewis, *America: Nation Or Confusion* (New York: Harper and Brothers, 1928); Julius Drachsler, *Democracy and Assimilation* (New York: Macmillan, 1920); Emory S. Bogardus, *Essentials of Americanization*, 3d ed. (Los Angeles: University of Southern California Press, 1923), 13–33.

45

ethnic factor with the hope of strengthening the bonds of national unity might have been justified under such circumstances, but such a policy also blacked out from our history the constructive role immigrants played in the agricultural development of this country.[5]

The influence of the immigrant farmers, despite our fears or general indifference to them, persisted as an economic and cultural force.[6] It manifested itself in the values, farm techniques, crops, and rural industries introduced; and the languages, dialects, traditions, and life styles brought to the rural communities in which they settled.[7] Even though the ethnic identity of most groups eroded in due time, if it was not obliterated, these immigrants and their children were a positive force in our growth and development as an agricultural nation.[8]

Incomplete data from 1790 to 1860 indicate that many of the approximately 5,300,000 who came to the United States from Europe then were farmers,[9] and that the immigrants who initially contributed the most as agriculturalists and farm laborers came from the more advanced nations of Europe.[10] Of the 5,062,414 arriving from 1819 to 1860 between 3 to 3.25 million came from Great Britain and Ireland, and almost 1.5 million from the German states. The laborers, numbering 872,000 over this same period, many of whom probably were farm workers, ranked first, and the farmers, totaling 765,000, second.[11] The influence of the Homestead Act of 1862 in attracting immigrant farmers from Europe is an unmeasurable quantity,[12] but it must have been substantial, considering the difficulties in acquiring land, the aspirations for ownership in Europe, and the lip service given to it by agents and promoters who anticipated an increased demand for land, farm implements, manufactured articles, and farm products, as well as population increases and a quickened tempo of life.[13]

[5] William S. Bernard, *American Immigration Policy* (New York: Harper and Brothers, 1950), 56.

[6] "Does the Foreign-Born Farmer Make Good?" Edmund de S. Brunner, *Immigrant Farmers and Their Children* (Garden City, N.Y.: Doubleday Doran, 1929), 30–59, esp. 43–59.

[7] William B. Furlong, "Wisconsin: State of Insurgents," *New York Times Magazine,* 3 April 1960, p. 119, cited in Joseph A. Wytrwal, *American Polish Heritage* (Detroit, Mich: Privately Printed, 1961), 246; Brunner, *Immigrant Farmers and Their Children,* "Social Life," 92–115, and "The Church in the Immigrant Community," 116–36. See also John D. Phelan, *Readings in Rural Sociology* (New York: Macmillan, 1920), 75–86.

[8] Alexander E. Cance, "Immigrants and American Agriculture," *Journal of Farm Economics* 7 (January 1925): 113–14.

[9] *Eighth Census of the United States, Population of the United States in 1860* (Washington: GPO, 1864), xviii.

[10] Cance, "Immigrants and American Agriculture," 104–7.

[11] *Population of the United States in 1860,* xxii, xxvi.

[12] Folke Dovring, "European Reaction to the Homestead Act," *Journal of Economic History* 22 (December 1962):461–72.

[13] *Population of the United States in 1860,* xxvi.

The contributions Europeans made as farm operators and laborers, however, should not obscure the role of other ethnic groups such as the Mexicans and other Latin Americans who provided sorely needed labor on the farm, the Chinese, Japanese, Filipinos, and others.[14] Unfortunately statistics on the ethnic identity of our immigrant farmers during the peak years of their involvement with the expansion of agriculture are not as complete as are the statistics of the number of farms and farmers in the country.[15] Fortunately the federal census reports for 1910 and 1920, especially those for 1920 which probably are the most comprehensive of the immigrant in farming, provide us with a wealth of information on the ethnic backgrounds of the farmers, their distribution, tenure status, and related matters. However, they have been marred by racist inclinations that led to listing ethnic groups by the color of their skin.[16]

Of the 6,361,502 farm operators listed in the census reports of 1910, some 669,556 or 10.5 percent were foreign-born whites. If one included

TABLE 1. FOREIGN AND NATIVE-BORN FARM OPERATORS
BY GEOGRAPHIC REGION, 1910 AND 1920

| | All Farm Operators | | Native-Born | | Foreign-Born | |
|---|---|---|---|---|---|---|
| | 1910 | 1920 | 1910 | 1920 | 1910 | 1920 |
| New England | 188,802 | 156,564 | 161,009 | 128,082 | 27,451 | 28,265 |
| Middle Atlantic | 488,379 | 423,147 | 419,342 | 376,701 | 47,089 | 46,919 |
| East No. Central | 1,123,489 | 1,084,744 | 929,619 | 935,492 | 188,157 | 144,778 |
| West No. Central | 1,109,948 | 1,096,951 | 830,642 | 883,809 | 269,465 | 206,287 |
| South Atlantic | 1,111,881 | 1,158,976 | 748,878 | 767,771 | 7,170 | 7,378 |
| East So. Central | 1,042,480 | 1,051,600 | 712,443 | 740,862 | 4,820 | 3,510 |
| West So. Central | 943,186 | 996,068 | 692,624 | 724,301 | 41,556 | 39,979 |
| Mountain | 183,446 | 244,109 | 143,991 | 197,678 | 31,713 | 41,755 |
| Pacific | 189,891 | 234,164 | 132,515 | 162,744 | 55,397 | 69,698 |
| United States | 6,361,502 | 6,448,343 | 5,440,619 | 5,498,454 | 672,818 | 588,569 |

SOURCE: *Fourteenth Census of the United States, 1910*, vol. 5, *Agriculture*, 299, 310. These compilations include the foreign-born Japanese and Chinese farm operators as well as the foreign-born whites.

14 For a general account down to 1945 see Harry Schwartz, *Seasonal Farm Labor in the United States: With Special Reference to Hired Workers in Fruit and Vegetable and Sugar-Beet Production*, Columbia University Studies in the History of American Agriculture, 11 (New York: Columbia University Press, 1945), 29–66, 102–139. See also Paul S. Taylor and Tom Vasey, "Historical Background of California Farm Labor," *Rural Sociology* 1 (September 1936): 281–95; U.S. Congress, Senate, Subcommittee of the Committee on Education and Labor, *Hearings S. Res. 266, A Resolution to Investigate Violation of the Right of Free Speech and Assembly and Interference with the Right of Labor to Organize and Bargain Collectively*, 76 Cong., 3 sess., 25 January 1940, Pt. 59, pp. 21902–03, 21914–19.

15 U. S. Department of Commerce, Bureau of the Census, *Historical Statistics of the United States: Colonial Times To 1957* (Washington: GPO, 1960), 278–79.

16 *Fourteenth Census of the United States, 1920*, vol. 5, *Agriculture* (Washington, GPO, 1922), 299, 302, 310.

the 2,502 Japanese and 760 Chinese farmers listed as colored the grand total of foreign-born farmers in 1910 was 672,818 or roughly 11 percent of all farmers in the country, a figure which does not include the off-spring of immigrants who became farmers. Percentage-wise the foreign-born farmers were a smaller group than the 893,370 Negro and 24,251 Indian farmers who totaled 917,621 or roughly 14 percent of all farmers in the country.[17]

Most immigrant farmers in 1910 were concentrated in the North and constituted 18.4 percent of all farmers in that section of the country. In the West their absolute numbers were smaller, but their proportion higher. On the Pacific Coast almost 28 percent of the farmers in 1910 were foreign-born whites and in the West North Central area nearly 25 percent. In Minnesota and North Dakota the foreign-born whites in 1910 comprised more than one-half the farmers; in Wisconsin, South Dakota, Nevada, and Washington more than 30 percent.[18]

The reluctance of immigrant farmers to settle in large numbers in New England, and in the South Atlantic and East South Central States may be attributed to reasons ranging from the poor infertile soils of the New England states to the presence of slaves in the states of the old Confederacy and the belief that immigrants were unwanted, the absence of relatives and friends with whom immigrants wished to be reunited, and the more favorable reports that circulated on agricultural opportunities in the North.[19]

Prominent among the immigrant farmers were the Germans whose talents were not only recognized early, but persisted through the years in all parts of the country in which they settled, and cut across all phases of farming and industries related to it. Benjamin Rush, who was among the first to note the distinctive qualities of the Germans, wrote in 1789 that "a German farm may be distinguished from the farms of other citizens . . . by the superior size of their barns, the heighth of their inclosures, the extent of their orchards, the fertility of their fields, the luxuriance of their meadows, and the general appearance of plenty and neatness in everything that belongs to them." Crèvecoeur, writing from a different perspective, said, "From whence the difference arises I know not, but of twelve families of emigrants of

[17] *Thirteenth Census of the United States, 1910*, vol. 5, *Agriculture* (Washington: GPO, 1913), 170.
[18] Ibid., 169.
[19] "Immigrant Rural Communities," *Survey* 25 (7 January 1911): 587–95; Rowland T. Berthoff, "Southern Attitudes Toward Immigration 1865–1914," *Journal of Southern History* 17 (August 1951): 328–60; Bert J. Lowenberg, "Efforts of the South to Encourage Immigration, 1865–1900," *South Atlantic Quarterly* 33 (October 1934): 363–89; Robert De C. Ward, "Immigration and the South," *Atlantic Monthly* 96 (November 1905): 611–17.

TABLE 2. IMMIGRANT FARMERS BY NATIONALITY, 1910 AND 1920

|  | 1910 | 1920 |
|---|---|---|
| Germans | 221,800 | 140,667 |
| Swedes | 67,453 | 60,461 |
| Canadians | 61,878 | 48,668 |
| Norwegians | 59,742 | 51,599 |
| English | 39,728 | 26,614 |
| Austrians | 33,338 | 30,172 |
| Irish | 33,480 | 16,562 |
| Danes | 28,375 | 25,565 |
| Russians | 25,788 | 32,388 |
| Swiss | 14,333 | 13,051 |
| Dutch | 13,370 | 15,589 |
| Poles | 7,228 | 17,352 |
| Finns | — | 14,988 |
| Italians | 10,614 | 18,267 |
| French | 5,832 | 6,119 |
| Mexicans | — | 12,142 |
| Hungarians | 3,827 | 7,122 |
| Japanese | 2,215 | 6,075 |
| Portuguese | 5,832 | 6,119 |

SOURCE: *Fourteenth Census of the United States, 1920*, vol. 5, *Agriculture*, 318–21.

each country, generally seven Scotch will succeed, nine Germans, and four Irish. . . ."[20]

The conspicuousness of the Germans on the good lands of southeastern Pennsylvania and of other parts of the country may be attributed to the methods of settlement and farming they used rather than to the fact that they got to these lands first. Like the Scotch-Irish, reputedly the "foremost frontier blazers," the Germans were frontiersmen—with one important difference. The Scotch-Irish in pursuing their frontier activities surrendered some of their good land, while the Germans retained theirs, and formed compact social and economic units to help insure their permanence on the land. Children could rely on their parents and the community to establish them on farms of their own. This tradition, their dedication to agriculture, and the intensive character of the farming they engaged in rooted them to the land to a degree less common among the English-speaking farmers.

Unlike other frontier farmers the Germans tried to become self-sufficient. Wheat was their principal cash crop, but they raised other cereals as well, and gave much attention to their gardens, orchards, vineyards, and meadows. When the distance of their farms from the

20 Walter M. Kollmorgen, "The Pennsylvania German Farmer," in Rudolph Wood, ed., *The Pennsylvania Germans* (Princeton, N.J.: Princeton University Press, 1942), 29–30.

navigable rivers posed transportation problems the Pennsylvania farmers perfected the Conestoga wagon near the river bearing that name to carry their wheat, meat, and other products to market.[21]

Germans prospered on farms purchased from others who nearly starved on them because they cultivated grass, considered one of the best ways of improving the quality of the land before red clover was introduced late in the eighteenth century. George Washington was so impressed with the Palatine Germans that he once considered the importation of some to develop his lands in Ohio.[22]

Walter Kollmorgen, who has stressed the importance of cultural influences on farming more than any other scholar, summarized the contributions of the Pennsylvania Germans as follows: "Not only did the Pennsylvania German adopt new kinds of crops and better stock, he also perfected and popularized certain seeds, crops and foods. He was the first to breed the Conestoga horse; he became known for the variety of vegetables he raised; he played an important part in perfecting several kinds of wheat and apples. Moreover, he pioneered in the rotation and diversification of crops and in providing good shelter for stock. Conservative as the Pennsylvania farmer was in some matters, he was, nevertheless, a progressive farmer."[23]

New German farm settlements emerged in a belt running almost due west of Pennsylvania. Germans who emigrated because of hard times in the homeland and the political strife of the 1830s settled in Ohio, Indiana, Illinois, and Missouri, while others went to New York, Pennsylvania, and Canada. After 1845 Germans settled in Wisconsin and Iowa. They understood the cultivation of wheat, rye, oats, and other crops grown in the north, but they did not understand the products of the south which they believed were grown on land owned by large landowners who rarely sold small plots and degraded free labor by having it compete with slaves.[24]

Germans were attracted to Wisconsin by the opening of the state at an appropriate time, the availability of an abundant supply of low-priced land, the opportunity to use such land for the support of public

[21] Ibid., 31–35.

[22] Ibid., 35–37. See also James Westfall Thompson, *History of Livestock Raising in the United States, 1607–1860*, U.S. Dept. of Agriculture, Agricultural History Series, 5 (Washington, 1942).

[23] Kollmorgen, "The Pennsylvania German Farmer," 53–54. See also Richard H. Shryock, "British Versus German Traditions in Colonial Agriculture," *Mississippi Valley Historical Review* 26 (June 1939): 39–54, Joseph Schafer, "The Yankee and the Teuton in Wisconsin," *Wisconsin Magazine of History* 6 (December 1922): 125–45, and 6 (March 1923): 261–79, and Albert B. Faust, *The German Element in the United States* (Boston: Houghton Mifflin, 1909), 2:28–37.

[24] Kate A. Everst, "How Wisconsin Came By Its Large German Element," *Wisconsin Historical Collections* 12 (Madison, 1892): 311–12.

schools, and the achievements of those Germans who became successful farmers.[25]

German farmers and stock growers in Texas organized agricultural societies early to advance their interests. Among the first of these bodies was an Agricultural and Horticultural Society formed in 1853 to purchase and ship trees and shrubs into New Braunfels. Others encouraged the cooperative herding and grazing of their cattle. Farmers also held a weekly market day to realize greater returns as producers and economize on their purchases, formed a Reform Club to discuss problems of mutual concern, and acquire newspapers, magazines, and books devoted to agriculture. Perhaps the best example of such societies was that formed at Cat Spring, Austin County, in 1856 to advance agriculture in its broadest sense.[26]

A unique group which made its presence felt were the Russian-Germans whose ancestors emigrated to Russia in the days of Catherine the Great.[27] The Russian-Germans came to the United States because of the general unrest in Russia, sheer wanderlust, the quest for a better life, the search for land, and the fact that the Ukase of 4 June 1871 stripped them of the special privileges assured them for "eternal times" by Catherine the Great. Land ownership, which took precedence over all other forms of property, added to the prestige of the family name, and encouraged members to enlarge their holdings, possessed other advantages such as enabling the owners to live on it, till it, and hold it in perpetuity without fear of its being easily destroyed, burned, or stolen.[28]

Russian-Germans, who began arriving as early as 1847–1848, came in increasing numbers after 1873 until World War I, when a decline set in. Their numbers temporarily increased after the restoration of peace. They came seeking living conditions similar to those left behind in Russia. One of the first migrations originating in the Black Sea area in 1873 established itself in Odessa, South Dakota; and another prosperous group, consisting largely of Catholics, later founded the community of Strassburg, North Dakota. These earlier centers of concentration became centers of distribution to other farming communities.[29]

The history of hard winter wheat in the Great Plains is closely linked

25 Ibid., 302–3.

26 Rudolph L. Biesele, *The History of the German Settlements in Texas, 1831–1861* (Austin: Von Boeckmann-Jones, 1930), 208–10.

27 For a comprehensive account of the Russian-Germans see Richard Ballet, *Russian-German Settlements in the United States*, tr. La Vern J. Rippley and Armand Bauer (Fargo: North Dakota Institute for Regional Studies, 1974).

28 Adolph Schock, *In Quest of Free Land* (Asseb, Netherlands: Royal Van Gorcum, 1964), 92–95.

29 Ibid., 99–101.

with the Russian-German immigrants, many of whom settled in Kansas. Each family brought over a bushel or more of Crimean wheat for seed from which came the first crop of Kansas hard winter wheat. The people who knew how to grow this wheat and had migrated together to the Great Plains also were acquainted with deep plowing and thorough surface cultivation that was widely advocated a quarter of a century later in connection with "dry farming."[30] In the Dakotas the Russian-Germans concentrated on grain farming: first flax in the new land and thereafter on hard winter wheat, and helped convert the Dakotas into one of the richest wheat-growing areas of the world. Some of the early trading centers in the Dakotas grew into large villages and towns that channeled wheat grown in the area to commission houses in the East; and the towns, school districts, and townships in which they lived and the churches they worshiped in bore names such as Danzig, Kulm, and Odessa identifying them with their old-world communities.[31] Before World War I the Russian-Germans could be given credit for most of the winter wheat grown successfully in the eastern and southern portions of Russia, the Great Plains, and the western intermountain districts of the United States and Canada.[32] These "earth animals," as someone described them, must occupy a unique place in any account of the immigrant in American agriculture.[33]

Next in terms of quantity at least were the farmers from the Scandinavian countries who had much in common with the Germans. In 1910, the Swedes numbered 67,453, the Norwegians 59,742, and the Danes 28,375.[34]

Swedes had settled in Delaware, New Jersey, and Pennsylvania in colonial times, were reputed to be good farmers and had provided the English with improved livestock when they advanced into this area,[35] but the mass emigration of Swedes began in the 1840s and was directed toward Illinois, Wisconsin, and Iowa. Minnesota Territory attracted them during the 1850s, and Kansas, Nebraska, and Dakota Territory during the 1860s, the 1870s, and 1880s.[36]

[30] Mark Alfred Carleton, "Hard Wheats Winning Their Way," *Yearbook of the Department of Agriculture 1914* (Washington: GPO, 1915), 398–400. See also K. S. Quisenberry and L. P. Reitz, "Turkey Wheat: The Cornerstone of an Empire," *Agricultural History* 48 (January 1974): 101–5.

[31] Schock, *In Quest of Free Land*, 133–34.

[32] *Yearbook of Agriculture 1914*, 420.

[33] Schock, *In Quest of Free Land*, 131.

[34] *Thirteenth Census of the United States 1910*, vol. 5, *Agriculture*, 181.

[35] Lyman Carrier, *The Beginnings of Agriculture in America* (New York: McGraw-Hill, 1923), 172–73.

[36] Florence J. Sherriff, "The Swedish Settlers in North Dakota," *Swedish Pioneer* 4 (January 1953): 17.

Serfdom was unknown in Sweden and the cultivated areas of the nation had been taken up. Land was handed down by the laws of entail and primogeniture: the whole farm passed down to the oldest son or a member of the family who bought out the heirs. The government had not inaugurated a system of homesteading the surplus land in the north; hence the United States held great appeal for the dispossessed sons and daughters of the small free farmers and tenant classes of Sweden. Even farm owners with no genuine economic reasons for emigrating joined the trek to America to obtain land.

The Swedes financed their passage to America and acquired land by various means. Some sold farms in Sweden and received assistance from relatives who preceded them to America; others borrowed or had capital of their own[37]

The Swedes, unlike farmers of other nationalities, often "plunged straight into the wilderness or wandered into the small prairies in small groups," choosing the most inaccessible places instead of land near rivers and lakes that offered easy communication. In due time, however, Swedish-American agricultural communities appeared in almost every part of the Union. "In Minnesota, Iowa, Wisconsin, Illinois, the Dakotas and Ohio whole counties were exclusively Swedish and some settlements dozens of miles in extent. . . . There would be a great void in the Northwest today could a million citizens of Swedish descent be removed from this territory," boasted one proud Swede in 1921, "but for them large tracts would be primeval forests and what is now the most fertile field of this great region would still be waste land."[38]

The Norwegians, who numbered almost 60,000 in 1910 and constituted almost 9 percent of all foreign-born farmers, were the third largest group in agriculture. More than 90 percent lived in the upper Middle West; 70 percent of them in Minnesota, Wisconsin, and North Dakota in climate resembling that of Norway.[39]

The old-world background of the Norwegian helped prepare him to farm in the upper Mississippi Valley. Because of the location and climate of Norway, the Norwegian worked his land from April or May until late October under great pressure instead of on an eight-hour

37 Ibid., 17–19.

38 Amandus Johnson, *Swedish Contributions To American National Life, 1638–1921* (New York: Committee of the Swedish Section of America's Making, 1926), 16–17. See also Eric Englund, "Farmers" in Adolph B. Benson and Naboth Hedin, eds., *Swedes in America 1638–1938* (New Haven, Conn.: Yale University Press, 1938), 75–91.

39 On Norwegian emigration to the United States see Carlton C. Qualey, *Norwegian Settlement in the United States* (Northfield, Minn.: Norwegian-American Historical Association 1938); and *Thirteenth Census of the United States, 1910*, vol. 5, *Agriculture*, 178, 181.

basis. This, with the little soil that nature allowed him to plow and harrow, and the great effort he made to wring out an existence, bred resourcefulness, industry, and thrift. Ownership was the rule, not the exception, in Norway. Rye, wheat, barley, oats, hay, green crops, turnips, and potatoes were grown, and there were ample supplies of vegetables and berries. The farm passed from father to son, usually to the oldest son, who, according to the law of succession, had the right to have it assigned to him against a small payment, and the older people the right to live on the farm and be supported with food and money.[40]

For many years the Norwegians constituted the largest bloc of foreign-born farmers in North Dakota. They settled largely in the eastern tier of counties and westward along the main line of the Great Northern Railroad. The Norwegians were individualists to a greater extent than the other Scandinavians and the Germans; and this, coupled with the fact that the constitution of Norway had given them much power, made them more open and insistent in their behavior.[41]

In Norway the shortage of arable land often forced the peasants to combine work on the farm with work in the forests, fisheries, and mines. They had taken part in labor disputes and strikes, had become acquainted with socialism, demanded a greater voice in government, and formed consumer cooperatives. Much of the radicalism they brought with them from Norway surfaced in the various organized activities and politics they engaged in.[42]

The Norwegian press, especially the *Skandinaven* of Chicago, was a propagandist for farm life and was read by members of the first and second generations. It reminded its readers that the farmer was independent, the bulwark of democracy, and that with the adoption of new machinery, improved means of transportation and communication, consolidated schools, and rural deliveries, farm life was becoming more pleasant. Subscribers of the *Skandinaven* were also urged to read the latest scientific materials on agriculture, raise beef cattle and chickens, maintain cleanliness in their pig pens, go into dairying, organize cooperatives, and encourage the boys to stay on the farm.[43]

The Norwegians were a mighty force in the agricultural develop-

[40] O. T. Bjanes, *Norwegian Agriculture* (Oslo: Landbruksdepartentets Småskrift 29, 1926), 19–25.

[41] T. A. Hoverstad, *The Norwegian Farmers in the United States* (Fargo, N.D.: Hans Jervell, 1915), 8–13.

[42] Elwyn B. Robinson, *History of North Dakota* (Lincoln: University of Nebraska Press, 1966), 282–84, 288.

[43] Agnes Larson, "The Editorial Policy of *Skandinaven*, 1900–1913," *Norwegian-American Studies and Records* 8 (Northfield, Minn.: Norwegian-American Historical Association, 1934), 117, 129–30.

ment of the upper Mississippi Valley, and along with the Swedes, Germans, and other ethnic groups helped replenish the national larder. They employed new methods, tried new machinery, and experimented with new crops as a means of increasing their capacity to produce. Members of the second generation joined the front ranks of livestock breeders, dairymen, and general farmers.[44]

The Danes, the other Scandinavian group, numbered 28,375 in 1910 and constituted slightly more than 4 percent of all foreign-born farmers in the country at the time; about 73 percent of them lived in Iowa, Minnesota, Wisconsin, and Kansas.[45] Like the other Scandinavians the Danes made good pioneers, efficient farmers and livestock producers.[46]

The Swiss were a much smaller group than either the Scandinavians or the Germans, 14,333 in 1910; and like the Scandinavians they, too, settled primarily in the Middle West where they left an indelible mark.[47]

The first Swiss arrived in colonial times but the beginnings of the Swiss cheese industry in the United States is more directly traceable to the Swiss colony that settled in southern Wisconsin in the 1840s and 1850s. The Swiss, unlike most settlers in that part of the state, "betook themselves to dairy farming and the raising of cattle" to which they were fully adapted by training and habit. The lands on which they settled in Green County, Wisconsin, had nutritious grasses and an abundance of good hay and running water—the ingredients for healthy cattle and superior dairy products.[48]

From this modest beginning the production of Swiss cheese spread into areas settled by other ethnic groups and beyond the state. The manufacture of Swiss cheese in northwestern Illinois, for instance, was an overflow of the thriving industry in southern Wisconsin.[49]

The Poles, Czechs, and Finns, although not as numerous and visible as the Germans and Scandinavians, attracted attention because of the

[44] O. P. B. Jacobson, "Contributions To Agriculture," in Harry Sunby-Hansen, ed., *Norwegian Immigrant Contributions To America's Making* (New York: International Press, 1921), 29–42.

[45] *Thirteenth Census of the United States, 1910*, vol. 5, *Agriculture*, 178–79, 181.

[46] U.S. Immigration Commission, *Reports* (Washington: GPO, 1911), 1:549.

[47] *Thirteenth Census of the United States, 1910*, vol. 5, *Agriculture*, 181.

[48] John Luchsinger, "The Swiss Colony at New Glarus, Wisconsin," *Wisconsin Historical Collections* 12 (Madison: State Historical Society of Wisconsin, 1892), 339. See also Richard Egan, *Green County: A History of Agricultural Development* (Oxfordville, Wis., 1929), which is a reprint of a series of articles in the *Monroe Evening Times*, Monroe, Wisconsin.

[49] Loyal Durand, "Cheese Region of Northwestern Illinois," *Economic Geography* 40 (April 1964): 108–9.

special efforts made to attract them to farming, the fact they came from parts of Europe less known to Americans, and employed practices that made for successful farming.[50]

The emigration of the "peasant Pole" to America had been triggered by the Austro-Prussian War of 1866–1867, the Franco-Prussian War of 1870–1871, and later the May laws in Russia that sought to achieve the Russification of the non-Russian peoples. The underrepresentation of the Poles in the federal census (7,228 Polish farmers in 1910)[51] may be accounted for by the practice of our immigration officials of using the country of birth as the basis for establishing the nationality of the entering immigrant. Those who considered themselves Poles but who were born in the Russian, German, and Austrian parts of Poland were counted as Russians, Germans, or Austrians.[52]

While the majority of the Polish immigrants headed for the cities, an important number moved into the timber regions of the Middle West where they could combine farming with work in the lumber camps and sawmills. Their movement onto farms in Wisconsin, Michigan, Indiana, and Illinois assumed significant dimensions in the 1870s.[53]

The Poles hungered for land and were quick to acquire it when available at low prices, but in Illinois, Indiana, and the Connecticut Valley where tenancy and cropping were common many started out as tenants. They also bought large tracts which American, German, and Norwegian farmers thought were impossible to farm because of the time required to bring the land into cultivation. The Pole, much like the Italian, was an untiring laborer who with the help of his wife cleared, ditched, drained, and grubbed the land.[54]

The Polish rural colonies formed in Minnesota, the Dakotas, and the Great Lakes states after 1885 were settled mostly by those who first worked in the mills, mines, quarries, and other industries as day laborers, and had been attracted to the land by advertisements in the Polish-language press of the United States and the efforts of Polish land agents representing real-estate firms and large landowners. Former laborers usually had more savings than the newly arrived, and often were sons of farmers who wanted to become farmers in this country. Land agents usually held up a successful Polish compatriot as an example

[50] U.S. Immigration Commission, *Reports*, 1:581–91; Eugene Van Cleef, "The Finn in America," *Geographical Review* 6 (September 1918): 191–95.
[51] *Thirteenth Census of the United States, 1910*, vol. 5, *Agriculture*, 181.
[52] U.S. Immigration Commission, *Reports*, 1:583–84.
[53] Alexander Cance, "Immigrant Rural Communities," *Annals of the American Academy of Political and Social Science* 40 (March 1912): 76.
[54] U.S. Immigration Commission, *Reports*, 1:585–86.

and persuaded small groups of mill, mine, and industrial workers to visit land awaiting settlement in northern Wisconsin and Minnesota.

In Wisconsin they acquired cutover timberland in the northern part of the state previously owned by speculators or lumbermen. In the Dakotas they often settled on the poorer lands for the same reasons compatriots of theirs bought the less productive lands of Illinois and Indiana—they were cheap; and in the East they bought abandoned farms. The trend in all these areas originated with Poles who came from Europe and worked as farm laborers before they became farm owners, and was sustained by those who came directly from Europe.

The Poles normally followed the established agricultural pattern of the area in which they settled. In the western states they raised livestock and cultivated wheat, flax, barley, dairy products, peas, hay, or some other commercial crop. A cotton farm operated by a Pole in Texas was likely to be self-sustaining. In New England, on the other hand, some Poles took to onion and tobacco farming that required special soils, intensive care, technical skills, and business ability. They familiarized themselves with farming operations unknown to them in the old country by observing their neighbors at work, working as farm hands on onion and tobacco farms, and questioning countrymen who succeeded.[55]

Information on the Czechs who, like the Poles, are frequently listed as nationals of other countries, is limited.[56] Scattered data indicate that in 1910 Czech or Bohemian farmers were settled in Wisconsin, Virginia, Connecticut, Missouri, Nebraska, and Texas;[57] and that the principal Czech farm colonies east of the Mississippi River were in Wisconsin.[58] Farming also was the mainstay of the Czechs in Nebraska.[59] Before World War I an estimated 50,000 Bohemians, mostly in agriculture, were settled in Texas where some had arrived as early as 1835 before Texas became a republic. The Texas Czech farms averaged around 100 acres, but the range was from 40 to 1,000 acres.[60]

Although Czechs came to the United States accustomed to hard work,

55 Ibid., 1:584–87; Albert H. Sanford, "Polish People of Portage County," *Wisconsin Historical Society, Proceedings, 1907, Fifty-Fifth Annual Meeting* (Madison, 1908), 264–66 and 278–81.

56 *Fourteenth Census of the United States, 1920,* vol. 5, *Agriculture,* 519.

57 U.S. Immigration Commission, *Reports,* 1:587–91.

58 Karel D. Bicha, "The Czechs in Wisconsin History," *Wisconsin Magazine of History* 53 (Spring 1970): 194–203; Nan Mashek, "Bohemian Farmers in Wisconsin," *Charities* 13 (3 December 1904), 212.

59 Sarka B. Hrbkova, "Bohemians in Nebraska" *Publications of the Nebraska State Historical Society* 19 (Lincoln 1919): 140–58, esp. 143.

60 U.S. Congress, Senate, LeRoy Hodges, *Slavs on Southern Farms,* Sen. Doc. 595, 63 Cong., 2 sess. (1914), 11–13.

ownership did not come easy to them. Acquiring land, building it up, and erecting buildings required long hours of labor and was a family enterprise as it was with other immigrant groups. Family ties were strong; members of the family worked as a unit instead of as individuals, assuming, of course, that the land, money, and other material goods were family not individual possessions, and that when individual members of the family needed help it would be forthcoming from the other members.

Stability of residence helped solidify these family ties. The farm was a valuable asset to be held, cared for, and built up as a long-term investment, instead of as a speculative venture; hence there was little movement from farm to farm. Anglo-Americans who felt the Czechs abused their wives and children by having them work long hours outdoors simply did not understand this was part of an old-world tradition transplanted to American soil. A study of a small Czech community in Texas shows that in 1948 more than two of every three tenants rented the farms they operated from relatives and almost half of all tenants from parents. In short, a large proportion of the tenants served probationary periods working land they expected to inherit.

Czechs had been conditioned "to a detailed, small-scale, painstaking form of agriculture carried on with a few simple tools" before they reached this country. In the United States they practiced "a live-at-home type of farming" that others often talked about but seldom engaged in. The social status of the rural Czech was determined by the manner with which he treated his soil; if he persisted in the unforgivable practice of allowing grass to grow in his fields his social status suffered. The owner of a well-cared-for farm with the necessary buildings and equipment wore the badge of success.

Czechs who succeeded in farming succeeded in large part because they considered farming a way of life rather than a source of material gain, and this was reflected in the quality of their farming. A study of Czech farmers in selected areas of Virginia, Oklahoma, and Texas on land similar in topography and fertility, who raised the same major crops and contended with the same soil, climatic, and economic conditions as the native white farmers, indicated that the Czechs possessed better land and equipment, had less tenancy, and showed more progress than the native whites. Much of this success may be attributed to the Czechs' traditional values. Their farming methods were a combination of techniques learned abroad and adapted to a new environment, and the application of new techniques developed here through observation and adaptation.[61]

[61] Robert L. Skrabanek, "The Influence of Cultural Backgrounds on Farming Practices in a Czech-American Rural Community," *Southwestern Social Science Quarterly* 31 (March 1951): 258-62.

The Czechs also developed a cooperative spirit. Believing from the beginning that they had little in common with the people they found here and determined to become self-sufficient, they launched programs of mutual assistance. The first two public enterprises normally undertaken in a Czech farming community were the building of a church and a school, but among the Czechs of Snook County, Texas, the establishment of a cooperative general merchandising store came first. This cooperative spirit surfaced in the formation of mutual-benefit associations, a nondenominational Bible school, community-sponsored beef clubs, the sharing of farm machinery and equipment, the exchange of farm work, and the raising of crops for the benefit of the community.[62]

Finnish farmers, as was true with farmers of most other ethnic groups, also settled in the Middle West and in smaller numbers in the Far West and the East.[63] More than 90 percent of all Finnish farmers in 1920 lived in Minnesota, Michigan, Wisconsin, and Washington and many, if not most, were identified with agriculture and lumbering.[64] Agriculture in the cutover region of Wisconsin, where 90 percent of the Finns in the state lived, began near logging camps on poor or submarginal land which should never have been put to agricultural use. Logging furnished seasonal employment that could be combined with farming, but the real development of agriculture in this region began after logging had passed its peak. Agriculture among the Finns was promoted by railroad and land-development companies, colonization, and governmental agencies that stressed the virtues of farming.[65]

The heaviest Finnish immigration into Wisconsin occurred from the 1890s to about 1910, at a time when most Finns were industrial workers or lumberjacks, the majority of whom were deciding to become farmers. During the so-called Golden Age of the Finnish farmer, which continued until about 1925, land was cleared, buildings erected, and neighborhood institutions, cooperatives, and churches established. The depression struck the Finnish farmers as hard as it struck other Wisconsin farmers. Unfortunately, the effects of the mistakes resulting from poor land selection, the misrepresentation of land agencies, and the un-

[62] Robert L. Skrabanek, "Forms of Cooperation and Mutual Aid in a Czech-American Rural Community," *Southwestern Social Science Quarterly* 30 (December 1949): 183–87.

[63] *Fourteenth Census of the United States, 1920*, vol. 5, *Agriculture*, 319, 321.

[64] Eugene Van Cleef, "The Finn in America," *Geographical Review* 6 (September 1918): 185–214; John I. Kolehmainen, "The Finnish Pioneers of Minnesota," *Minnesota History* 25 (December 1944): 317–28; John I. Kolehmainen and George W. Hill, *Haven in the Woods: The Story of the Finns in Wisconsin* (Madison: State Historical Society of Wisconsin, 1951), 70–105; Lew Allen Chase, *Rural Michigan* (New York: Macmillan, 1922), 165–73.

[65] Kolehmainen and Hill, *Haven in the Woods*, 72–74; J. C. McDowell and W. B. Walker, *Farming on the Cut-Over Lands of Michigan, Wisconsin and Minnesota*, U.S. Department of Agriculture, Bulletin 425 (Washington, 1916), 3–4.

sound advice of state and federal land agencies came to a head at once.[66]

However, after World War II second generation Finns with an agricultural education who seem to have profited from the social and economic mistakes of their parents emerged as leaders. This generation of Finns realized that more than land was required to succeed in farming, that the management of the land, buildings, machinery, power, livestock, and labor was extremely important and often spelled the difference between success and failure.[67] The thoughts of the Finns also spread to the formation of cooperatives that started out as consumer enterprises to combat high prices in stores controlled by the local mine or mill operators, and included the processing of milk and the marketing of products in distant markets.

These Finnish immigrant communities of old ceased being the cultural islands they once had been. The first generation derived a sense of security from institutional and community activities rooted in Finnish culture, but the second and third generations became too deeply enmeshed with the culture of the state in which they lived to derive satisfaction from the institutions their parents and grandparents built.

Finnish-sponsored cooperatives served a real purpose and became an element of strength before and immediately after World War I when the Finns were a socially isolated group and held low-status jobs, and cooperative action on an ethnic front helped fulfill certain social, economic, and educational objectives. But social interaction between the Finnish cooperatives and other groups had set in by the 1930s, and the isolation and social differences of the past were eroding. The older immigrant generation had passed from the scene and a new one emerged in a leadership role which saw the need for outside support if commercial expansion was to be had. The cooperative based on nationality might have been appropriate to serve the social and economic needs of a people transplanted into a new world of alien tongues and ways to protect them from exploitation, but it also set them apart from the rest of the community and made it difficult to expand. Participation by all nationalities and creeds, including churches, schools, and government was needed.[68]

On the West Coast, the ethnic stocks that stood out more conspicuously than the more numerous Germans were the Japanese, Italians, Portuguese, and Armenians. The Scandinavians were concentrated in the Pacific Northwest, the Germans in all three states; but the Japan-

[66] Kolehmainen and Hill, *Haven in the Woods*, 101–2.

[67] Ibid., 102–5.

[68] Roland S. Vaile, *Consumers' Cooperatives in the North Central States* (Minneapolis: University of Minnesota Press, 1941), 117–18; Florence E. Parker, *The First 125 Years* (Superior, Wis.: Cooperative Publishing, 1956), 307–21, esp. 321.

ese, Italians, Portuguese and Armenians were more numerous in California as farmers than in any other state in the Union.[69]

The Germans, French, Italians, and Hungarians were prominent in viticulture in the early years of California, especially the Germans, and a Hungarian, Agoston Haraszthy, and later the Italians as producers of commercial wines.[70] Anaheim, California, was founded as a cooperative wine-making colony by Germans years before it became the original site of Disneyland.[71] The Italian-Swiss Colony, originally conceived as a potential site of employment for unemployed Italians from San Francisco, eventually blossomed forth as a highly successful grape-growing and winemaking community, but lost the idealistic overtones under which it originally had been conceived.[72] The Japanese and Italians distinguished themselves as truck farmers, the Portuguese as dairymen, and the Armenians to a lesser extent as fruit and vegetable growers.[73] The Italians in California also stood out remarkably well because one of their compatriots, Amadeo Peter Giannini, and a small group of predominantly Italian farmers founded the Bank of Italy which later was rechristened the Bank of America and all along played an important role in the agricultural development of the state.[74]

The Portuguese began as farmers in the San Francisco Bay area and like the Japanese acquired land at low prices around Sacramento which later became valuable under reclamation. They raised sheep, grew vegetables, and turned into successful dairymen.[75]

The Armenians achieved prominence in Fresno County as growers of grapes, raisins, asparagus, fruits, and vegetables; and at one time one of their numbers owned the largest fig ranch in the world.[76]

Significant as the immigrants were as farmers, their role as farm laborers can hardly be underestimated in late nineteenth- and early twentieth-century rural America when commercial fruit, vegetable, and

[69] *Fourteenth Census of the United States, 1920*, vol. 5, *Agriculture*, 310, 328–29; Charles Mahakian, "History of the Armenians in California" (master's thesis, University of California, Berkeley, 1935), 12–18.

[70] Vincent Carosso, *The California Wine Industry* (Berkeley: University of California Press, 1951), 16–48; Eliot Lord, John J. D. Trenor, and Samuel J. Barrows, *The Italian in America* (New York: B. F. Buck 1906), 135–44; Lanier Bartlett, "An Immigrant in the Land of Opportunity," *World's Work* 17 (March 1909): 11376.

[71] Hallock F. Raup, *The German Colonization of Anaheim, California* (Berkeley: University of California Publications in Geography, 1933), 123–39.

[72] Lord, Trenor, and Barrows, *The Italian in America*, 135–44.

[73] U.S. Immigration Commission, *Reports*, 1:651–53, 670–74.

[74] Marquis James and Bessie R. James, *Biography of a Bank* (New York: Harper and Brothers, 1954), 248–67.

[75] Frederick G. Bohme, "The Portuguese in California," *California Historical Quarterly* 35 (September 1956): 240–43.

[76] Mahakian, "The Armenians in California," 25–34.

beet-sugar production was assuming growing importance.[77] The immigrants provided a large proportion of the casual labor supply until they obtained a more secure footing in our farm society. French Canadians, Poles, and Italians supplanted the Irish and German workers of earlier years in the market gardens of Boston. Bohemians and other Slavs from the nearby centers were used along the Ohio lake-shore fruit and vegetable district even after the immigration curbs of the 1920s went into effect, and when they became too old for this kind of work, their children took their place.

Truck farmers near populous cities with large acreages of closely maturing crops provided work several weeks at a time for workers who were transported to farms. Italians from Philadelphia, for instance, worked on berry and vegetable farms in southern New Jersey and Delaware; Polish families from Baltimore on truck farms just south of the city; and Portuguese Negroes, known as Bravas, from Fall River and New Bedford, Massachusetts, and Providence, Rhode Island, in the cranberry bogs around Cape Cod. If the Italian experience was common, which it probably was, the large farmers secured workers through bosses equivalent to the Italian padrones who lived in the cities.[78]

The fruit and vegetable migrations on the West Coast assumed intricate patterns. There the bulk of the seasonal fruit and vegetable work between 1880 and 1900 was performed by the Chinese who had been released from work on the Union Pacific Railroad. The void left by the Chinese Exclusion Act of 1882 was filled gradually by the Japanese who began arriving by the thousands during the late 1890s and continued arriving until their admission, too, was halted by the Gentlemen's Agreement of 1907. Several thousand Hindus arrived between 1905 and 1910 but they were less satisfactory as workers than either the Chinese or Japanese. Dalmatians, Armenians, Greeks, Spaniards, and other European immigrants were used after 1900 but only in a few crop areas.

The great majority of the Japanese who remained farm workers after the Gentlemen's Agreement went into effect worked for their compatriots and did not become a part of the labor supply for white owners. However, many Japanese farm workers withdrew from farming completely to secure jobs in the city. Still others became farm opera-

---

[77] George K. Holmes, "The Supply of Farm Labor," *Annals of the American Academy* 33 (March 1909): 362–72; *Report of the United States Industrial Commission on Agriculture and Agricultural Labor* (Washington: GPO, 1901), 77–145; George M. Peterson, "Composition and Characteristics of the Agricultural Population in California," University of California, Berkeley, College of Agriculture, Agricultural Experiment Station, Bulletin 630 (June 1939), 17–22, 47.

[78] Schwartz, *Seasonal Farm Labor in the United States*, 38–40.

tors starting out as sharecroppers and worked themselves up to renters and owners until the California Alien Land Laws put obstacles in their path. The law was circumvented in one way or another through the registration of the land in the names of American-born children. Most Japanese farm operators at the time, however, were tenants, not owners.

During World War I the Army and defense industries drained workers off the farms and the Californians were forced to draw upon Mexican-Americans who had been used as seasonal workers for many years in the southern part of the state. In fact, the reliance on the Mexican-Americans had become so great during the 1920s that the large California farmers fought every congressional effort to stop free entry of these workers, claiming that the agriculture of the state would collapse without them. In due time entire Mexican-American families moved about the state with their household goods in old automobiles seeking employment at wages the growers were willing to pay.

Filipino males also entered California from the Philippine Islands and via the Hawaiian Islands where they had worked on labor plantations. They became an important part of the fruit-and-vegetable migratory labor force of the 1920s. Employers naturally encouraged the Filipinos to come. "Stoop" jobs of the most tiring sort, such as lettuce harvesting in the Salinas Valley and asparagus cutting in the Sacramento-San Joaquin Valley, became Filipino monopolies in the 1930s.

The growing competition between the native white workers on the one hand and the Mexicans and Filipinos on the other was responsible for the repatriation of more than 100,000 Mexican farm workers during the depressed 1930s, and the departure of 11,642 Filipinos from 1935 to 1939.

After the outbreak of World War II the expanding defense industries absorbed, gradually at first and then more rapidly, many whites who had crowded Mexicans and Filipinos out of their jobs. This exodus of native whites from farm labor in 1940–1941 revived agitation to import Mexican workers in 1942, a complete turnabout from the repatriation and deportations of the 1930s to the importations of the 1920s.[79]

Apart from the immigrants, Bahama Negroes were brought in to pick vegetables and fruit in Florida, Maryland, Virginia, Delaware, and New York in 1943 and 1944. Jamaicans labored primarily in sugar beets; but many also helped the vegetable and fruit growers in New Jersey and New York, and some even picked potatoes in Aristook County, Maine. Mexican nationals worked in the sugar-beet fields, along the Pacific Coast, and in neighboring states picking fruits and vegetables.

79 Ibid., 54–63; see also Theodore Saloutos, "The Immigrant in Pacific Coast Agriculture, 1880–1900," *Agricultural History* 49 (January 1975): 182–201.

These imported workers shifted as needed from place to place to pick one key crop after another, and became part of a "land army." This planned migration of workers, of course, was in striking contrast to pre–Pearl Harbor days when thousands moved about with little or no information about job opportunities and offered suggestions for the improvement of labor's availability when peace was restored.[80]

A comparable role was performed by immigrant and foreign workers in sugar-beet production. The same ethnic groups were more or less involved in beet-growing work which required much fatiguing labor under pressure and often for fourteen and fifteen hours a day. Much of this had to be done quickly: the blocking and thinning in the spring before the plants became too large and thin, and in the fall when the growers were caught between keeping the beets in the ground as long as possible to obtain the maximum sugar content and harvesting them before the first freeze set in. Employers, anxious to spare themselves the double expense of recruiting workers during the spring and fall, used the written contract so that their workers would know explicitly what was expected in the form of work and compensation before any labor was done.[81]

The first successful sugar-beet factory in California—and in the United States for that matter—used Chinese, Japanese, Mexicans, Hindus, and European immigrants as employees. Beet work paid better than railroad maintenance work or picking fruit and vegetables, but it was less desirable work. Europeans used in Colorado, Nebraska, and adjacent states were primarily Russian-Germans who proved to be excellent workers.

The Russian-Germans worked as families. Since their families were large they had large family incomes which placed them in a position to save money and become independent farmers. Sugar-beet companies wanting resident labor often provided these ambitious Russian-Germans generous terms with which to buy or rent company land. Each year newly arrived Russian-Germans replaced those who climbed the agricultural ladder and provided for the continued expansion of the beet acreage until the outbreak of World War I.

The Japanese in Colorado, Nebraska, and the neighboring states were brought in from California, and they often flocked into beet work from the nearby railroads and mines. The Spanish-Americans used in southern Colorado came from New Mexico, and the Mexican nationals from Mexico. The Japanese, like the Russian-Germans, were anxious to become growers and often paid higher rents to get the lands; while the

80 Schwartz, *Seasonal Farm Labor in the United States*, 66.
81 Ibid., 102–4, 105–6.

overwhelming majority of the Mexicans seemed content with farm labor work.[82]

Recruiting farm laborers in Michigan, Ohio, Indiana, and Wisconsin might have been easier than in the western states, but the Belgians, Bohemians, and Hungarians brought in from Cleveland, Detroit, and other cities in the Middle West to work and live on beet farms formed an unstable labor supply whose availability rose and declined depending on the employment opportunities in industry. Employers were dealt a severe blow by the immigrant quota law of 1924 and the diminished desire of the Russian-Germans, Belgians, and other European workers to labor in the beet fields. This, of course, was welcomed by the Spanish-Americans and the Mexicans, and the employers who showed a preference for these groups because they showed less interest than the Japanese and Russian-Germans in becoming landowners.[83]

Use of Mexican and Spanish-American workers was revived after the gradual recovery of industrial employment in the 1930s, the shrinkage in the availability of labor in the beet fields, and the desire of employers to retain touch with workers in Texas and New Mexico as a means of avoiding becoming unduly dependent on resident labor.[84]

A survey by the Department of Agriculture in 1939 gave a comprehensive picture of the composition of the contract beet labor force in that year. Of the 93,000 workers employed, 57 percent were Mexicans or Spanish Americans; 16.5 percent, native Americans; 7 percent German Russians; 7 percent Filipinos; and the rest, of various nationalities. Fewer than 100 Japanese workers were found. The relatively small number of German Russians among hired workers was due to the rise of this group to farm ownership or tenancy. Colorado had 21,000 workers, two thirds of them Spanish speaking; California had 16,500 workers, two thirds of them Spanish speaking and one fourth Filipinos; Michigan had 12,300 workers, three fourths Mexicans and the rest belonging to miscellaneous groups.[85]

Once World War II broke out and farm workers obtained jobs in the cities on a year-round basis, the California employers asked the federal government for permission to import labor for the beet fields of California. Mexicans in this instance were brought in from areas in Mexico with a surplus of labor so that those sections of the country would not be adversely affected by the departure of these men. This consideration of the possible effect the removal of these men would have on the Mexi-

82 Ibid., 106–9.
83 Ibid., 109–12.
84 Ibid., 117–18.
85 Ibid., 120.

can economy rankled some California employers who thought of the good old days of World War I, but they cooperated to obtain the needed workers.[86]

The immigrants as farm laborers were missed after the quota system went into operation during the 1920s, and especially after World War II began and the need for farm workers was urgent. Our greatest reliance from 1942 to 1972 was on the Mexicans and to a much lesser extent on the British West Indians, Canadians, Japanese, and Filipinos. Our dependence on foreign farm workers was greatest from 1951 to 1964; the peak year was 1960 when almost 460,000 were admitted for temporary employment.[87]

Mention also must be made of the contributions that individual immigrants made to farming, but only in passing and without any degree of finality. Wendelin Grimm, a German, brought with him in 1857 alfalfa seed from his native village in Baden, planted and acclimatized it to the severe winters of Minnesota, until it developed into the outstanding forage crop of the Northwest: ". . . its permanence, enormous yields, high protein content, economy as a crop, and value as a soil builder and weed throttler, is almost without parallel in plant history."[88] David Lubin, a native of Russian Poland, took up the cause of the unprotected American farmer in the export market, founded the International Institute of Agriculture (now the Food and Agriculture Organization of the United Nations) in Rome that still serves as a clearing house of information on crops and other agricultural matters which enables farmers to fight more intelligently in behalf of their interests.[89] Eugene Waldemar Hilgard, a native of Rhenish Bavaria, a professor of agriculture at the University of California and director of the Agricultural Experiment Station in Berkeley, California, was among the very first to recognize the relation of soil analysis to agriculture and to exert great influence in the application of scientific knowledge to practical agriculture.[90] Amadeo P. Giannini exercised a profound influence on the growth and development of agriculture in California through the Bank of Italy which subsequently was renamed the Bank

[86] Ibid., 120–22.
[87] U.S. Department of Labor, MA, USES, Rural Manpower Service, "Foreign Workers Admitted For Temporary Employment in United States Agriculture, By Year and Nationality, 1942–72," mimeographed sheet.
[88] Everett E. Edwards and Horace H. Russell, "Wendelin Grimm and Alfalfa," *Minnesota History* 19 (March 1938): 21–23, 32–33.
[89] "David Lubin," *Dictionary of American Biography* (New York: Charles Scribner's Sons, 1933), 6, Pt. 1:481–82; Olivia R. Agristi, *David Lubin: A Study in Practical Idealism* (Berkeley: University of California Press, 1941), 185–216.
[90] "Eugene Waldemar Hilgard," *DAB*, 5, Pt. 1:22–23; Faust, *The German Element*, 52–54.

of America.[91] Many other immigrants, too numerous to mention individually, made more modest contributions to farming.

Quantifying the impact that the immigrant had on American agriculture is difficult. Those who think in such terms must keep in mind among other things that the immigrant farmers reinforced the often invoked ideal of the family-sized farm in a society that made it difficult for the family farm to survive. Farm techniques, seeds, life styles, and limited quantities of capital brought from the home country and put into American farmlands added to the growth and development of American agriculture. Finally, the immigrants in the cities contributed to our unique agricultural expansion through the increased demand for the products of the farm, the growth of our foreign markets in their native lands as a result of tastes they had developed in the United States. The immigrant farmer may have been ignored by the historians, but the hard evidence is there for those who have the desire to study it.

91 James and James, *Biography of a Bank,* 110–18, 248–67, 393–413.

THEODORE SALOUTOS

# THE IMMIGRANT IN PACIFIC COAST
# AGRICULTURE, 1880–1940

The immigrants who played a significant role in the agriculture of the Pacific Coast states as farm owners and tenants were primarily of northern European origin; to a lesser extent they were of southern European and Asiatic stock. Reaching their numerical strength when xenophobia was at its peak, these immigrants, whom scholars have studied mostly as agricultural laborers, came to the West Coast after they farmed or labored in other parts of the United States. In 1920 they constituted almost 30 percent of all owners, managers, and tenants in the region.[1]

Scholars who study the various ethnic groups in farming face a problem of identifying them.[2] For instance, farmers of English, German, Irish, Norwegian, Swedish, Canadian, and other backgrounds became so much like Americans in their farming operations that they were considered as such, and because they have not received the kind of singular treatment allotted to the Japanese, Chinese, or even those of southern European lineage, one has difficulty in distinguishing them from the native-born.[3]

On the other hand, information on the Japanese, perhaps the most intensively researched immigrant group in American agriculture, is much easier to find, owing to their remarkable achievements in California, the concern and opposition they encountered as a consequence,

THEODORE SALOUTOS is Professor of History at the University of California, Los Angeles. This paper was presented in a session, "Immigrant Groups in Western Agriculture," of the Davis Symposium, 20 June 1974.

[1] U.S. Department of Commerce, Bureau of the Census, *Fourteenth Census of the United States, 1920*, vol. 5, *Agriculture* (Washington: GPO, 1922), 301–2, 322, 328–29.

[2] Kenneth O. Bjork, *West of the Great Divide, 1847–1893* (Northfield, Minn., Norwegian-American Historical Association, 1958); Charles Mahakian, "History of the Armenians in California" (master's thesis, University of California, Berkeley, 1935), 12–18; Hans C. Palmer, "Italian Immigration and the Development of California Agriculture" (Ph.D. diss., University of California, Berkeley, 1965); Levi Varden Fuller, "The Supply of Agricultural Labor as a Factor in the Evolution of Farm Organization in California" (Ph.D. diss., University of California, Berkeley, 1939) and his extensive bibliography.

[3] Donald L. Kieffer, "Your Neighbor, The Foreigner," *Pacific Rural Press*, 1 January 1921, p. 58.

182

and the fact that they were enemy aliens during World War II.[4] Likewise the Italians and Portuguese, who were of southern European origins and presumably of inferior stock (at least according to the conventional wisdom of the day) and also worth watching closely, became conspicuous in some quarters, but not to the same extent as the Japanese, who because of their pigmentation, together with the Negroes, American Indians, and Chinese were designated as "Colored" in the federal census and segregated from the white farmers in the tabulations.[5]

In theory California agriculturalists welcomed European immigrants because they were expected to provide much of the needed agricultural labor, but in the long run the Californians realized that few immigrants left homes thousands of miles away to become permanent agricultural laborers in the United States.[6] Still, the Californians sought to attract newcomers from the states east of the Rocky Mountains as well as from Europe, but there is little evidence to show that immigrants arrived in numbers sufficient to fill the needs.[7] Later many hoped that the completion of the Panama Canal would attract more Europeans, but there is little to show that this happened.[8] Most immigrant traffic from Europe, even though primarily of peasant origin, headed for the cities of the East and Middle West, and the passage of the restrictive measures of the 1920s sealed off hopes of significant future increases.[9]

Most farmers from Europe came to the West Coast after farming or working in other parts of the country. Owing to the long distance, the cost of travel, and the lack of suitable ports of entry (San Francisco being an exception), relatively few came directly by ship to California or the other two Pacific Coast states.

Yet by the opening of the twentieth century the presence of the European immigrant farmer was felt in all three states. Germans, Norwegians, Swedes, Englishmen, Italians, and others were among those who raised grain, fruit, and sugar beets, became dairymen, and engaged in general and stock-farming in Spokane, Clarke, Walla Walla, and a few other counties in the state of Washington.[10] Much of the same pat-

4 See, for instance, Helen E. Hennefrund and Orpha Cummings, *Bibliography on the Japanese in American Agriculture*, U.S. Department of Agriculture, Bibliography Bulletin no. 3 (Washington: USDA, 1943); Floyd W. Matson, "The Anti-Japanese Movement in California, 1890–1942" (master's thesis, University of California, Berkeley, 1950), 47–64.

5 *Fourteenth Census, 1920*, vol. 5, *Agriculture*, 310–13.

6 *Transactions of the California State Agricultural Society During the Years 1864 and 1865* (Sacramento, 1866), 61–63.

7 *Pacific Rural Press*, 28 July 1883, p. 57; 8 September 1883, p. 192; 20 October 1883, p. 329; 3 November 1883, p. 378; 6 October 1883, pp. 290–294.

8 "Forward to the Land," *World's Work* 27 (November 1913): 113.

9 Alexander E. Cance, "Immigrants and American Agriculture," *Journal of Farm Economics* 7 (January 1925): 106–8.

10 Report of the Industrial Commission, *Immigration* (Washington, 1901), 15: 641–42.

tern emerged in Oregon where Germans, Englishmen, Swedes, Swiss, and others farmed in Marion, Washington, Yamhill, Clackamas, Tillamook, and other counties.[11] Immigrants in California went into general farming, fruit growing, truck, alfalfa, poultry, walnut, sugar beet, and other kinds of production. In 1881 Italians from San Francisco formed the Italian-Swiss Agricultural Colony which subsequently gained commercial prominence, and in 1895 Danes in Fresno County organized a cooperative creamery that began taking medals at the State Fair and helped make the butter of Fresno famous throughout the state.[12] The Portuguese were conspicuous in Alameda County, but greater attention was focused on the Germans, Canadians, English, Italians, Swiss, and Scandinavians. No mention, however, was made by the Industrial Commission which conducted this survey of the 777 Chinese and 37 Japanese farm operators in California cited in the federal census in 1900.[13]

Also part of the agricultural landscape of California at the time was a 519-acre experimental farm colony set up by the Salvation Army at Romie, Monterey. Like its larger counterpart in Amity, Colorado, this colony was to provide homes for the "worthy poor" of the cities, but indirectly colonized "foreigners" in rural districts. Built in the vicinity of a sugar beet factory, the colonists reportedly sold to the factory all the sugar beets they could raise at remunerative prices.[14]

The Pacific Coast states, despite their distance from the primary source of European emigration and the time, expense, and energy consumed in reaching the Far West, received a substantial share of the foreign-born farmers. As a geographic region the Pacific Coast states ranked behind the East North Central and the West North Central states in the federal censuses of 1910 and 1920, but continued to attract immigrant farmers after the former two regions began to lose them. While the overall total of foreign-born farmers in the entire county declined from 1910 to 1920 by more than 83,000, the reverse held true in the Pacific Coast states which showed an increase in the same period of more than 14,000—the largest increase of any region in the nation.[15]

A state-by-state study likewise shows that in 1910 slightly more than half of all the 55,397 foreign-born farmers in the Pacific Coast states, or 28,251, lived in California, 17,672 in Washington, and 9,204 in Oregon.

11 Ibid., 643–44.
12 Eliot Lord, John J. D. Trenor, and Samuel J. Barrows, *The Italian in America* (New York: B. F. Buck and Co., 1906), 135–42; French Strother, "Building a Wonderful Community," *World's Work* 9 (February 1905): 5832.
13 *Immigration*, 15: 645–46.
14 Ibid., 578, 581.
15 *Fourteenth Census, 1920*, vol. 5, *Agriculture*, 310.

TABLE 1. FOREIGN-BORN FARM OPERATORS BY GEOGRAPHIC REGION, 1910 AND 1920

|  | 1910 | 1920 |
|---|---|---|
| New England | 27,451 | 28,265 |
| Middle Atlantic | 47,089 | 46,919 |
| East North Central | 188,157 | 144,778 |
| West North Central | 269,465 | 206,287 |
| South Atlantic | 7,170 | 7,378 |
| East South Central | 4,820 | 3,510 |
| West North Central | 41,556 | 39,979 |
| Mountain | 31,713 | 41,755 |
| Pacific | 55,397 | 69,698 |
| Total United States | 672,818 | 588,569 |

SOURCE: *Fourteenth Census of the U.S., 1920*, vol. 5 *Agriculture*, 301, 310. These totals include the "all white" and the Japanese and Chinese.

In each of the three states the Germans constituted the largest ethnic group in 1910, and, except for California, where the Italians and Japanese ranked second and fifth, those of Anglo-Saxon stock dominated the top five groups.[16]

The increase in California in 1920 was due largely to the growth in the number of certain groups, especially among the newer immigrants, and the decrease in the number of those of English, Scotch, Irish, and German stocks. The Census of 1920 further showed that California continued to attract more foreign-born farmers than the other two Pacific Coast states.

Of the 89,698 immigrant farmers in these three states in 1920, 39,407 farmed in California, 20,484 in Washington, and only 9,407 in Oregon. California had 11,286 more foreign-born farmers in 1920 than in 1910; Washington 2,812, and Oregon only 203.[17]

A comparative study of tenure among native- and foreign-born farmers in 1910 and 1920 shows that the percentage of ownership among the foreign-born "All-White Farm Operators" was slightly higher than among the native-born all-white farmers: 83.1 percent among the foreign-born, and 80.1 percent among the native-born whites in 1910, and 81.2 percent among the foreign-born, and 77.9 percent among the native born whites in 1920. However, the percentage of ownership among the "Colored Farm Operators," especially the Japanese and Chinese, was much lower owing to the alien land laws.[18]

Of the 69,698 foreign-born farmers including the Japanese and Chinese in the Pacific Coast states in 1920, 51,877 were owners, 1,351 managers, and 16,470 tenants. Most numerous among the owners were the

16 Ibid., 310, 318–19.
17 Ibid., 312, 318–19.
18 Ibid., 303; Roger Daniels, *The Politics of Prejudice* (Berkeley and Los Angeles: University of California Press, 1962), 79–91.

Germans, followed by the Swedes, Canadians, English, and Italians in the order of their numerical importance. The Japanese, on the other hand, comprised almost one-third of all farm tenants in the Pacific Coast states, with the Italians and Portuguese being distant second and third.[19]

The probable explanation for the higher percentage of ownership among the foreign-born farmers, especially those of older immigrant stock, was their great desire to become landowners, their longer residence in the country compared to the newer arrivals, the less prejudice shown toward them, and perhaps their greater familiarity with American farming methods.[20]

In 1920 the German farmers ranked first in ownership in California as they did throughout the Pacific Coast states, the Italians and Portuguese second and third, the Canadians and Swedes fourth and fifth. The Japanese, however, who constituted the largest foreign group of farmers in the state, ranked first as tenants, third as managers, and thirteenth as owners.[21]

The Germans in Oregon maintained their prime position as owners and managers, and ranked third as tenants, being surpassed in numbers by the Swiss and Japanese. In fact, members of older immigrant stock maintained a firm grip on the top five places as owners and managers, but in the small-tenant class the Japanese and Russians ranked among the top five. Oregon had the same Anglo-Saxon complexion in 1920 that it had in 1910.[22]

Members of older immigrant stock were among the top five as owners and managers in Washington as they were in Oregon, but the Japanese and Russians ranked first and second as tenants. The Swedes headed the list of owners, the Germans were second, the Norwegians third, the Canadians fourth, and the Finns fifth. Italian and Portuguese farmers, although present in the state, were considerably fewer in number than in California.[23]

Among those excluded as an ethnic group from the federal census, because the authorities based the nationality of an immigrant on the country in which he or she was born, were the Armenians who were classified as Turks or Russians by the United States but whose presence as Armenians was felt in Fresno County and wherever else they farmed.[24] Many of the Fresno Armenians came from the shoe factories of New

[19] *Fourteenth Census, 1920*, vol. 5, *Agriculture*, 310–12, 322–23.
[20] Cance, "Immigrants and American Agriculture," 103–4.
[21] *Fourteenth Census, 1920*, vol. 5, *Agriculture*, 328–29.
[22] Ibid., 310–12, 328–9.
[23] Ibid.
[24] Mahakian, "History of the Armenians of California," 12.

England where they found their first gainful employment. Although the center of their farming operations was Fowler in Fresno County, they also expanded northward into the Modesto area where they raised the grapes and fruits with which they had had some familiarity in the old country. However, there is little evidence they had had much farming experience before they reached California.[25]

Meanwhile, the arrival of more foreign-born farmers in California aroused the resentment of those who wanted them to come as agricultural laborers but not as competing land-owning farmers. As one columnist wrote: "When you learn that 20 acres across the road has just been sold or rented . . . you worry for fear some foreigner has taken it. . . . Every native-born American farmer does, and he will continue to worry, for more and more foreigners are arriving and folding their wings on the farms up and down the road."[26] It was these fears that caused scholars, government officials, journalists, and popular writers to focus so much attention on the Japanese, and ignore the Germans, English, Swedes, Canadians, and others considered acceptable.[27]

Although little scholarly material has appeared on the role of the older immigrant groups in agriculture, those fragments that do exist point to their significance. In viticulture, for instance, where a number of early immigrants became famous, they showed that more than good land, climate, and vines native to California were needed for the production of high quality grapes and wine. Those most active in this area were of French, German, and Hungarian extraction.

Among the first to recognize the importance of foreign cuttings in the development of the grape and wine industry was Jean Louis Vignes, a native of Cadillac, France, a small town near the famed wine-producing region of Bordeaux, who established a commercial vineyard in the early 1830s and began importing vine cuttings from France in quantities sufficient to establish vineyards. Vignes is also credited with being the first person to establish a vineyard and raise oranges in Los Angeles.[28]

The success of grape growing and winemaking in the Los Angeles area combined with the discovery of gold and the thirst of the miners in northern California encouraged the planting of vineyards in that part of the state, which was nearer the center of action, and the outplanting of southern California.[29] Unfortunately, much of the wine

25 Kieffer, "Your Neighbor, the Foreigner," 50.
26 Ibid.
27 Irma Borchers, "Legislation Against the Oriental Farmer," *Journal of Land and Public Utility Economics* 1 (October 1925): 509–12.
28 Vincent P. Carosso, *The California Wine Industry* (Berkeley and Los Angeles: University of California Press, 1951), 7–8; William Heath Davis, *Seventy-Five Years in California* (San Francisco: J. Howell, 1929), 121.
29 Carosso, *California Wine Industry*, 14–15.

made by these inexperienced vineyardists was of poor quality. Once the search for gold eased, French and German ex-miners who had some training as vintners turned to grape growing and winemaking, improving and expanding the business.[30]

Most prominent among the immigrants of German origin in the formative stages of the vineyard and winemaking industry were Charles Kohler and John Frohling. Kohler, a native of Grabow, Mecklenberg, Germany, a musician, and Frohling, also a German and a musician, believed they would have greater security from making wine in California than from playing music.[31] Many of the accomplishments these two men scored may be attributed to the success of Kohler in the marketing and distribution of the product.[32] After Frohling's death in 1862, Kohler headed the largest commercial wine house in the state and became the proprietor of the largest vineyards in Los Angeles, Sonoma, and Fresno counties.[33]

Even more influential was Colonel Agoston Haraszthy, "the scion of an old influential Hungarian family." A nationalist and winegrower, he came to the United States in 1840 as a persona non grata and traveled extensively in this country; he also was the first Hungarian to author a book in his native tongue designed to attract immigrants to the United States. A severe asthmatic condition he developed in Wisconsin, where he first settled, and the opportunities California offered drew Haraszthy to San Diego late in 1849 where he purchased 160 acres of land. In 1851 he imported several varieties of Hungarian vine cuttings and in 1852 was elected to the state legislature. Later he purchased large tracts of land near Crystal Springs, thirty miles from San Francisco in what is now San Mateo, and in San Francisco, and continued to import vine cuttings.

Meanwhile, Haraszthy thought seriously about an ideal location for grape growing and winemaking. While in San Francisco he observed that the fog robbed the vines of the sun, thus preventing the fruit from maturing and acquiring the necessary sugar for winemaking purposes. He purchased property in Sonoma County which was ideal for grape growing and winemaking and close to the San Francisco grape market, added to his landholdings, planted newly imported vines, attracted French and German emigrés to the region, and helped correct the impresssion that all vineyards needed irrigation. Sonoma in due time became the center of knowledge in viticulture matters, "the foreign vine

---

[30] Ibid., 16–17; Eugene W. Hilgard, "The Agriculture and Soils of California," *U.S. Department of Agriculture Annual Report, 1878* (Washington, 1879), 504.

[31] Carosso, *California Wine Industry*, 29–33.

[32] Ibid., 33.

[33] Ibid., 35–36.

nursery in the state, and distribution point for some of the finest varieties of California wine."[34]

Haraszthy, despite the failure of other vineyardists in the eastern part of the United States, popularized the idea that the choicest of Europe's vinifera could be grown successfully in California if consideration was given to the adaptability of the soil and climate. He distributed many of these vines to friends and inquirers, and became the most eminent *vigneron* in the state. Haraszthy also pressed for the planting of more foreign varieties despite the continued support by the State Agricultural Society for the growing of the inferior Mission variety. To further the scientific development of viticulture, the Horticultural Society of Sonoma County was founded under his supervision in 1860. An essay and treatise by him remained for years the best guide to practical viticulture and viniculture in print, and won new converts to grape growing and winemaking. He also demonstrated the superiority of hillside culture in the growing of grapes, and used redwood casks to relieve the oak shortage.[35]

Another phase of this same story was the cooperative winemaking experiment in Anaheim, California, in 1857, reputed to be the scene of the first agricultural community in the state. Originally reflecting elements of a pre-1850 utopian orientation, the Anaheim association was incorporated in 1857 as the Los Angeles Vineyard Society with a capital stock of $100,000. Fifty Germans, some of whom were at first described as "practical vineyardists from the Rhine Valley" but who on further inquiry turned out to be an assortment of craftsmen plying various trades, purchased 50 shares at $2,000 each. Although the cooperative features of the association came to an end in 1859 and the problems of making and marketing wine were legion because of floods, the distance to the San Francisco market, and other difficulties, Anaheim soon became the leading viticulture area of California. Within twenty years the frontier qualities of these German pioneers helped give them good incomes, homes, and agricultural investments. Unfortunately the vine disease (probably phylloxera) of the 1880s brought about the complete destruction of the community's grape industry, but the subsequent planting of walnuts and oranges ushered in a new period of prosperity.[36]

The early successes of Vignes, Kohler, Frohling, Haraszthy, and the cooperative experiment at Anaheim aroused an interest in viniculture along the entire California coast.[37] In the twentieth century, however,

34 Ibid., 38–43.

35 Ibid., 43–45.

36 Hallock F. Raup, *The German Colonization of Anaheim, California* (Berkeley: University of California Publications in Geography, 1933), 123–39; Carosso, *California Wine Industry*, 66–67.

37 Carosso, *California Wine Industry*, 33.

the scene changed somewhat. Grape growing and winemaking assumed an even greater commercial importance, but the growing role of the Japanese (instead of the Chinese) as farm laborers, tenants, and owners, the Italians in intensive farming, the Portuguese and other groups in dairying, the Mexicans and Filipinos as agricultural laborers, gave the immigrants in agriculture in a different significance.

Two things worked to the advantage of the Japanese in California agriculture which suffered from an acute labor shortage. They had perfected techniques for extracting the greatest possible sustenance from the smallest piece of land in Japan where farming was held in greater esteem than in the United States and where population pressed hard on resources, and the prevailing labor system here gave them relatively higher earnings and a better opportunity of becoming landowners. Employers hired them as farm workers because of their efficiency and reliability as compared with white migratory workers, and their willingness to accept lower wages and the crudest forms of shelter.[38]

Other practices among the Japanese further tended to make them attractive to employers and to stabilize and rationalize farm employment. As farm laborers, for instance, they formed gangs and placed their labor at the disposal of a boss under whom they agreed to work; such a gang sometimes furnished the nucleus for a club to which the members paid dues for lodgings and cooking during the slack season, and even farm labor camps. The bosses of the Japanese labor camps, because of their contacts with local employers, were able to perform the double function of supplying workers, and intelligently directing these same men elsewhere when jobs were scarce. The larger farmers quickly recognized the advantages of hiring Japanese farm laborers and often had a regular boss in their employment who could mobilize an adequate supply of labor when needed.

However, the very same organizations that helped make the Japanese highly desirable as farm laborers also developed practices that made them undesirable. The bosses, camp managers, and secretaries supplying the labor knew the wage rates in particular areas for particular crops, could speak as a body for the men they represented, and through strikes and boycotts at harvest time could secure increases in wages that equalized or surpassed those of white workers. General factors also

[38] On the role of the Chinese who preceded the Japanese as agricultural laborers, see Ping Chiu, *Chinese Labor in California* (Madison: State Historical Society of Wisconsin, 1967), 79–88. One of the earliest state-sponsored statistical studies of farm labor in California is *Fourteenth Biennial Report, Bureau of Labor Statistics, California, 1909–1910* (Sacramento, 1910), 265–74. See also Sidney M. Gulick, *The American Japanese Problem* (New York: Charles Scribner's Sons, 1914), 316–23.

affected wages in employment. In 1911 the Immigration Commission noted a 50-percent increase in wages for Japanese workers over a fifteen-year period in California.[39]

The chance to work for a boss also helped facilitate the transition of the Japanese from wage earner to tenant and even to landowning farmer. An enterprising Japanese boss with a supply of labor at his disposal, who knew the problems of a given area, often found himself negotiating to lease land. For the ambition of the Japanese to advance beyond mere servility was comparable to that of the Italians, Swiss, Portuguese, and Russian farmers with whom they competed, as well as to that of the American farmers who found it difficult to compete with them.

The California alien land law of 1913 that forbade landownership by Orientals was favored by small white farmers who wanted to eliminate Japanese competition, force the Japanese back into the wage-earning class, and hire them as farm laborers. But instead of reconverting them into farmhands, the alien land act backfired, forced them into city trades and occupations, and enabled them to lease land and become thriving tenant farmers. As a consequence, the large landowners failed to get the Japanese labor they wanted, the white landowners still had to compete with Japanese tenants, and organized labor, perhaps the chief protagonist, had to contend with the unemployed Japanese in the cities.[40]

Meanwhile the large landowners found it more profitable to have Japanese as tenants because they produced larger crops, worked longer hours, used family labor, employed scientific techniques, paid higher rents, and were content with smaller profits. Landowners leasing to a few Japanese bosses also often obtained a monopoly of the most desirable Japanese laborers, while other farmers had difficulties obtaining any.[41]

The Japanese also seemed to have had an easier time obtaining financing. The capital requirements of the tenants in some kinds of production were minimal because most of the equipment was furnished by the landlords, while in sugar-beet production the companies advanced most of the capital; in fruits and vegetables, the commission merchants lent money and supplies and took liens on their crops. Where the competition was keen shippers made large advances to the tenants and in some instances leased and subleased land to other farmers. Part-

39 U.S. Congress, House, *National Defense Migration*, 77 Cong., 2 sess., 1942, pp. 66–67. Hereafter cited as *National Defense Migration*.

40 Matson, "The Anti-Japanese Movement in California, 1890–1942," 49–50.

41 *National Defense Migration*, 69; K. K. Kawakami, *The Real Japanese Question* (New York: Macmillan Co., 1921), 59.

nerships formed by the Japanese were still another way of obtaining financing.[42]

Also as a means of furthering their interests, farmowners and tenants among the Japanese formed organizations to help locate ranches for them to purchase or lease, to reach agreement among themselves on the maximum rents they would pay so as to prevent competitive bidding, to arbitrate disputes between landlords and tenants, to disseminate technical knowledge, and to assist in obtaining supplies and marketing their products.[43]

The success of the Japanese in the rice industry, after the government and some California land companies earlier had abandoned it as "impossible," hardly comes as a surprise. They introduced "superior early-ripening varieties from Japan, [and] devised methods of irrigation and cultivation." Although 85 percent of the varieties of rice grown in California in the early 1920s was from Japanese seed, the Japanese operated no more than 29,000 of the 150,000 acres in rice in the state.[44]

The accomplishments of the Japanese in intensive farming are well known. Through the use of fertilizers and crop rotation a single Japanese family could raise thousands of dollars worth of crops on small pieces of land ranging from 2 to 40 acres.[45] In 1941 the Japanese in California cultivated 205,989 acres of the commercial truck-farming lands, 42 percent of the acreage in this kind of production. The value of all California truck-farm crops for the fresh market and processing at the time was roughly $100,000,000, while the value of the Japanese part was between $30,000,000 and $35,000,000.

When World War II broke out the Japanese operated only 3.9 percent of all farms in California and harvested 2.7 percent of all cropland, yet they produced 90 percent or more of the snap beans for the market, celery, peppers and strawberries; 50 to 90 percent of all the artichokes, snap beans for canning, cauliflower, celery, cucumbers, fall peas, spinach, and tomatoes; 25 to 50 percent of the asparagus, cabbage, cantaloupes, carrots, lettuce, onions and watermelons.

After Pearl Harbor when the order for the evacuation of the Japanese was released, the Bureau of Agricultural Economics reaffirmed the importance of the Japanese to the truck-farming industry and disputed the assertions of those who minimized it. Said the BAE report: "Skill

[42] *National Defense Migration*, 70; Yamato Ichihashi, "Emigration from Japan and Japanese Immigration into the State of California" (Ph.D. diss., Harvard University, 1913), 203–30.

[43] *National Defense Migration*, 70.

[44] Toyoji Chiba, "Truth About Japanese Farming in California," in *California and the Oriental*, Report of the State Board of Control of California (Sacramento, 1922), 240.

[45] Ibid., 246.

and aptitude in farming is far more highly developed among the Japanese population than will be true of any group which may operate the properties from which evacuation will take place, and some loss of efficiency is inevitable."[46] Or as someone else put it, "On a strictly numerical basis it would take more than one okie to replace a Japanese farmer."[47]

The success of the Japanese as farmers may be attributed to the small size of their farms, the intensive nature of the cultivation, and their ability to compete. The average-size California farm in 1920 was roughly 200 acres, that of the average Japanese was only 57 acres. The intensive farming they did required much stooping, squatting, and painstaking labor, as compared with the extensive farming operations engaged in by the white farmers which required expensive machinery and elaborate equipment. The crops raised by the white farmers in California were among the more important ones, while those produced by the Japanese were among the new ones, small in their total value, and limited in the acreage cultivated. However, white farmers engaging in intensive farming, in which the Japanese were experts, found themselves at a competitive disadvantage.[48]

Italians who went into agriculture were unrepresentative of their rank-and-file compatriots who migrated to the cities. Those from northern Italy, as indicated, took a prominent part in the formation of the agricultural colony in Asti, California, which originally was conceived as a means of furnishing jobs for unemployed Italians in San Francisco and which eventually developed into a highly successful enterprise.

Italians entered farming in one of several ways. Construction gang workers who remained in the general area in which they worked bought land at cheap prices and became farmers in this manner, while others who temporarily migrated from the city to the country to pick berries and can fruits and vegetables gradually started to cultivate land of their own near cities.[49] "In 1900, farmers, dairymen, gardeners, etc. of Italian parentage," according to the Immigration Commission, "numbered 2,599 in the West, more than two-thirds of them in California, this num-

[46] National Defense Migration, 117–19. Comparable conditions prevailed in Washington and Oregon. Shotero Frank Miyamoto, "Immigrants and Citizens of Japanese Origins," Annals of the American Academy 223 (September 1942): 108.

[47] Robert Bendiner, "Cool Heads or Martial Law," Nation 154 (14 February 1942): 183–84. See, also, Adon Poli and Warren M. Engstrand, "Japanese Agriculture on the Pacific Coast," Journal of Land and Public Utility Economics 21 (November 1945): 352–64.

[48] T. Iyenaga and Kenoske Sato, Japan and the California Problem (New York: G. P. Putnam's Sons, 1921),133–34.

[49] Philip Rose, The Italians in America (New York: George H. Doran Co., 1921), 53–59.

ber being 8.08 percent of the entire number of Italians gainfully employed in this division. If the agricultural laborers are added, the percentage of the whole is 20.51 ... the number of those ... located upon the land has greatly increased, for the Italians from the northern provinces have exhibited as strong a desire to settle upon the land as any European race, excepting perhaps the German-Russians, immigrating to the West."[50]

Most gardens cultivated by the Italians in the early twentieth century were farmed on a partnership basis; these gardeners usually entered farming after a few years of employment as wage earners and the purchase of a share in a partnership already formed or in the process of being formed. Those who established themselves in truck farming in this manner did so in much less time than farmers of northern European origins who came without capital and worked on an individual basis. This kind of cooperation was less marked among Italians engaged in other kinds of farming.

The Italians, like the Japanese, were as a rule in intensive farming requiring much hand labor instead of diversified or general farming; because of this, the frequency of colony life among them, and the use of the partnership as a form of organization, they, too, differed from the native-born farmers and those of northern and western European origins. They also differed in that their wives and older children did much work in the fields. In Sonoma County, and less so in other California counties, they converted grazing lands and tracts previously used for general farming into productive vineyards and orchards, and greatly contributed to the wealth and development of the community.[51]

The Italians, as mentioned earlier, added to the development of viniculture in California through the formation of the Italian-Swiss Agricultural Colony in 1881. The site of the colony was named after ancient Asti in Piedmont whose wine had been a source of pride for centuries.[52] Once the necessary funds had been accumulated, a committee of three examined forty possible sites before selecting a 1,500-acre tract in the Russian River Valley, near Cloverdale, formerly used as a sheep ranch. Employment, according to the bylaws, was to be given to Italian-Swiss persons who had become citizens of the United States or had declared their intention of doing so. On the surface the provision to pay wages from $30 to $40 per month, plus sleeping quarters, board, and as much wine as one cared to drink appeared attractive, but it was coupled with a proviso that required each laborer to subscribe to at least five shares

[50] *Abstracts of the Immigration Commission* (Washington: GPO, 1911), 1: 651.
[51] Ibid., 651–53; Lord, Trenor, and Barrows, *The Italian in America*, 135–44.
[52] Lord, Trenor, and Barrows, *The Italian in America*, 136.

in the association at $5 per month, the payment to be withheld from the monthly wage. Such payments would give the subscriber a footing of dignity, control over the other shareholders, and, when the land became bountiful, entitle him to receive a number of acres to develop independently. The Italians, however, failed to understand the provisions or else feared being cheated, as many of them probably had been before. Not a single Italian worker accepted the arrangements, and the organizers, as a consequence, disposed of the shares to others, paid their workers in cash, and were defeated in their aim to better the lot of the Italian-Swiss workers.

Meanwhile, the soil at Asti was improved, and choice grape cuttings were imported from Italy, France, Hungary, and the valley of the Rhine through an Italian in Asti, Italy, who became interested in the California experiment. After overcoming numerous obstacles, financial and otherwise, the association began to produce wines similar to the principal Italian wines, and the red and white wines of France and Germany, in addition to sweet wines and extra-dry champagne.[53] Within twenty years the settlers of the colony converted the original 1,500-acre tract into a vineyard of 2,000 acres, built a winery, a community for 100 families, a school attended by many of the children, a railroad station, post office, telephone, and the foundations for a new city. They also established a settlement and built a winery in Madera, and purchased a new winery in Fulton, Sonoma County. By they end of the nineteenth century the land of the colony was worth $2,000,000, a reasonable amount of interest was paid annually to the members, and land improvements made.[54]

A comparable but more individualistic achievement was that of Secondo Guasti, who in 1909 reputedly was responsible for the largest vineyard in the world in what once was known as the "Cucamonga Desert." Guasti came to the United States about 1887 from Piedmont; he, too, remembered that some of the finest wine grapes in Italy were planted in what appeared to be unpromising soil at the base of rugged bare mountains. He thought that, as in the case of Italy, such vineyards "needed no irrigation because of the underlying moist loam, formed of pulverized granite washed down from the range by the freshets of centuries."[55] Convinced that the Cucamonga desert needed money more than water, primarily to overcome the destruction caused by sandstorms and jackrabbits, Guasti succeeded in obtaining the needed initial funds

[53] Ibid., 136–40.

[54] Andrea Sbarboro, "The Vines and Wines of California," Overland Monthly, n. s. 35 (January 1900): 72, 76; Lord, Trenor, and Barrows, The Italian in America, 140–44.

[55] Lanier Bartlett, "An Immigrant in the Land of Opportunity," World's Work 17 (March 1909): 11376.

to set out vineyards, and raise wine grapes and convert them into wine. The 250 workers employed permanently in the vineyards in 1909 came directly from Italy, France, and Spain where some of the best vineyard workers were available; and an additional 250 to 300 "disliked and distrusted" Japanese workers were added to the work force during the crushing season because of the inability to get enough white workers to go out into the hot sun and stay on a temporary job.[56]

The U.S. government recognized the value of the wine ranch and established an experimental vineyard in this previously neglected strip of territory. In 1909 some 492 varieties of vine cuttings, from every part of the world in which grapes were grown, were growing in the station and tested as a means of determining which were best adapted to the region.[57]

The influence of the Italian immigrant was also felt in the field of agricultural finance. The Bank of Italy, founded by Amadeo Peter Giannini with a small number of farmers mostly of Italian descent, became the prime lender in California agriculture by the end of the 1920s. The Bank of Italy at the time held mortgages on 12,147 farms or on one of every 11 farms in the state, totaling $71,296,899 which was slightly less than 9 percent of the farm mortgages in California. These figures, however, did not include the millions of dollars held in mortgages by affiliates, loans to cooperative marketing associations, and seasonal loans to farmers, sometimes secured by crops and sometimes not.[58]

The dominant position of the Bank of Italy in California agriculture was felt in various ways. The bank successfully extended larger loans to farmers and ranchers than the smaller banks of California were able to extend. It inaugurated the popular practice of placing the borrowing farmer on a budget, and contributed to the revival of the raisin industry in the state. It organized the Bankitaly Agricultural Credit Corporation, known as the "Giannini cow bank," to finance (at a rate lower by one-half percent of that specified by the government) stockmen with the "tuberculin milk testing function" and dairymen who appreciated the owning of high-grade cattle, ranchers who owned their ranches, who produced sufficient feed for their herd, and understood the value of better grades of cattle and sheep. It helped finance cotton growing by lending to ginners and brokers who in turn lent to the farmers, instead of the bank itself lending directly to the cotton farmers. It helped save thirty-one small rural banks in California during the depression, and through its valley farms committee diverted much of the foreclosed farm

[56] Ibid., 11379.
[57] Ibid., 11377–79.
[58] Marquis James and Bessie R. James, *Biography of a Bank* (New York: Harper and Brothers, 1954), 248.

land to the growing of cotton, alfalfa, gyp-corn, and grain, and, where the soil warranted, to the planting of more profitable grapes for juice.[59]

The Portuguese, next to the Italians, were the second most important of the southern European groups to enter farming. Whether they came from the Azores or the mainland, they turned to agriculture because of the opportunities it provided them to remain more fully within their own group and occupations than did life in the industrial areas of the East. Reaching the San Leandro area as early as 1854 when the district was just beginning to be developed, they often bought land at exorbitant prices. In 1909 the Immigration Commission found that forty-five of the fifty-six Portuguese farms studied were owned and prosperous; their proprietors relied on hand labor and employed their compatriots almost exclusively.

Meanwhile, the Portuguese began to spread out. During the late 1860s they acquired bottom land around Sacramento which later became valuable under reclamation. During the 1880s Azoreans took up farming and sheep raising in Fresno County, and worked in the vineyards of Santa Clara County; in the San Joaquin Valley men operating in companies of six to fifteen took up leaseholds of from 120 to 600 acres and planted the land with feed and grain crops. Vegetable growing became a prominent part of their farming activities in Alameda and Contra Costa counties, and south of San Francisco some began to specialize in the raising of artichokes. An Azorean, J. B. Avila, who came to California in 1883 and purchased some flood land near Merced, planted sweet potatoes from the Azores that appealed to restaurants and hotels in San Francisco, encouraged the cultivation of the sweet potato in the Sacramento and San Joaquin valleys, and became known as the "Father of the Sweet Potato Industry."

At the start of the twentieth century the Portuguese were found among the fruit pickers of Sonoma County and the neighboring areas, and with the Japanese constituted the most numerous foreign groups doing this kind of work before World War I. However, by the mid-1920s the Portuguese accounted for only 2 percent of the total foreign labor force in the California labor camps.[60]

Since most Portuguese, like members of other ethnic groups, came to the United States with little capital, the presumption is they began as ordinary farm laborers who worked for compatriots, saved their money, and purchased low-priced land which they reclaimed or improved. In

59 Ibid., 249–67.
60 Frederick G. Bohme, "The Portuguese in California," *California Historical Society Quarterly* 35 (September 1956): 240–41; Emily Yates Mowry, "Portuguese Colonies in California," *Out West* 1 (January 1911): 114–15; Kieffer, "Your Neighbor, the Foreigner," 50.

communities in which the land was purchased at low prices, one step in climbing the ladder to ownership, tenant farming, was eliminated. Reputedly excellent farmers who got two or three crops from the same fields in the course of a year, the practice among them was to invest in more land. Unlike the Italians, the Portuguese were highly individualistic and at first were reluctant about renting or owning land in partnership. They made great strides in establishing themselves as independent farmers but the Immigration Commission in 1911 reported they made slower strides than the Italians, Japanese, and German-Russians. However, the farm-tenure statistics in 1920 show that percentage-wise the Portuguese surpassed both the Italians and Japanese as landowners.[61]

The Portuguese also became important in the dairy industry. Truck farmers in the San Leandro area turned to the production of milk, and later they were joined in these efforts by milkers who entered the country before and after World War I. As they accumulated capital they left their Dutch, Swiss, Danish, and other employers and bought land and herds of their own. Around Eureka, California, they produced milk for the manufacture of evaporated milk, butter, cottage cheese, and ice cream. Most of the 150 Portuguese engaged in dairying in the metropolitan area of Los Angeles were of the first generation, many of them illiterate, but they comprised the second largest group in the industry in southern California, being surpassed only by the Dutch.

In the San Joaquin Valley Portuguese owned and operated stores and cattle-feed lots, as well as dairy farms. In the upper valley, around Los Banos, they maintained herds of 25 to 30 cows, but farther south around Tulare the Portuguese were in the majority and owned from 30 to 60 cows per farm. Still lower in the valley, where an estimated 70 to 75 percent of the dairy herds were owned by Portuguese farmers, their herds tended to be larger than those of other ethnic groups. In the mid-1950s a quarter of the 38,000,000 gallons of fluid milk sold in California came from this valley, and two-thirds of the 4,500,000 pounds of milk-fat produced and used each month in this part of the valley was produced by the Portuguese.[62]

The Armenians, whose presence in California agriculture was as conspicuous in certain parts of the state as their absence from the census tabulations, assumed, as we have observed, an important part in the agriculture of Fresno County.[63] Most of them settled in the rural areas because of the lack of factories and became farm laborers, renters, or

[61] *Abstracts of the Immigration Commission*, 1: 653; *Fourteenth Census, 1920*, vol. 5, *Agriculture*, 322–23.

[62] Bohme, "The Portuguese in California," 243.

[63] Mahakian, "History of the Armenians in California," 12.

owners.[64] In 1918 one of them, Henry Markarian, owned 160 acres of figs, the largest fig ranch in the world at the time, controlled 20 percent of all the figs grown in the United States, became the first president of the California Fig Growers Association, and had several varieties of figs named after him.[65] Armenians, among other things, introduced an ancient wheat cereal called boulgour to the market, and took an important part in the grape, raisin, dried fruit, asparagus, melon, and the wholesale fruit and vegetable industries.[66]

The immigrant contribution to agricultural labor is well known. First came the Chinese who, although well-liked by their employers, later were denied entry into the country by the Exclusion Act of 1882 so their importance as farm laborers declined.[67] The opposition of labor to the Chinese is well-known.[68] The vacuum created by the elimination of the Chinese was filled to some extent, we have seen, by the Japanese, immigrants from southern Europe, and a growing number of Americans. But the Americans did not welcome too many Japanese, nor did they wish them "to buy up and lease all the good things of the State and paint the future for Americans on this coast dark brown." They wanted those who were willing to work for fair wages "and fly away with them."[69] Still, members of all these groups and the Mexicans and Filipinos who came in large numbers during the 1920s and 1930s helped fill the labor needs of the landowners.[70]

Statistics on immigrant farm labor are not as complete as they should be, and often one has difficulty in distinguishing between immigrant labor and foreign labor in the country on a temporary basis, but the available figures show rather conclusively that over the years from 1914 to 1916 immigrant aliens comprised more than 50 percent of the farm workers in the inspected labor camps. The farm workers in these camps probably constituted a small percentage of all immigrant laborers, but the most numerous among them were the Italians, Mexicans, and Japanese. Figures for 1917–1921 are unavailable, but those for the 1920s and 1930s show that the "Americans" who were not defined usually constituted almost, but not always, more than half of those in the inspected labor camps. The Italians, who were the most numerous among the

64 Ibid., 15, 19–20.

65 Ibid., 21–25.

66 Ibid., 25–34.

67 Ping, *Chinese Labor in California*, 79–88; Fuller, "The Supply of Agricultural Labor . . . in California," 93–147.

68 Report of the Industrial Commission, *Agriculture and Taxation* (Washington: GPO, 1901), 11: 107.

69 Quoted in Fuller, "The Supply of Agricultural Labor . . . in California," 373.

70 Ibid., 215–18.

ethnic groups in the farm labor camps totaled 4,197 or 12.8 percent of the farm workers in the camps in 1914; 580 or 13.6 percent of those in 1914–1915; and 4,279 or 11.4 percent in 1915–1916.

The Americans in the labor camps during the 1920s retained the levels of 1914–1916 or increased in number; the Italians, however, started to decline, while the Mexicans, as can be seen in table 2, began to increase. The Japanese reached a plateau from 1922 through 1929, ranging from a low of 1,521 in 1923 to a high of 3,408 in 1924 or 2.0 percent in 1923 and 4.2 percent in 1924.

TABLE 2. MEXICAN FARM LABOR IN INSPECTED LABOR CAMPS, 1922–1929

|      | Number | Percent |
|------|--------|---------|
| 1922 | 6,788  | 7.5     |
| 1923 | 11,503 | 15.4    |
| 1924 | 11,752 | 14.5    |
| 1925 | 11,053 | 12.8    |
| 1926 | 16,152 | 25.5    |
| 1927 | 24,287 | 25.9    |
| 1928 | 26,385 | 28.5    |
| 1929 | 26,926 | 31.3    |

SOURCE: U.S. Congress, Senate, Subcommittee of the Committee on Education and Labor, *Hearings* S. Res. 266, *A Resolution to Investigate Violations of the Right of Free Speech and Assembly and Interference With the Right of Labor to Organize and Bargain Collectively*, 76 Cong., 3 sess., 25 January 1940, Pt. 59, pp. 21914–15.

The Scandinavians, Portuguese, Chinese, Slavonians, Spaniards, and Filipinos were also evident in great numbers during the 1920s. Beginning in 1924, however, the Filipinos increased in number and eventually ranked next to the Mexicans in both numbers and percentages.

TABLE 3. FILIPINO FARM LABOR IN INSPECTED LABOR CAMPS, 1922–1929

|      | Number | Percent |
|------|--------|---------|
| 1922 | 315    | 0.3     |
| 1923 | 969    | 1.3     |
| 1924 | 2.148  | 2.7     |
| 1925 | 2,336  | 2.7     |
| 1926 | 3,358  | 5.3     |
| 1927 | 4,645  | 6.9     |
| 1928 | 5,757  | 6.2     |
| 1929 | 6,726  | 7.8     |

SOURCE: U.S. Congress, Senate, Subcommittee of the Committee on Education and Labor, *Hearings* S. Res. 266, *A Resolution to Investigate Violations of the Right of Free Speech and Assembly and Interference With the Right of Labor to Organize. and Bargain Collectively*, 76 Cong., 3 sess., 25 January 1940, Pt. 59, pp. 21916–17.

During the 1930s a sharp decline occurred in the number of all ethnic groups found in these labor camps except for the Mexicans, who, although fewer in number than in the late 1920s, still constituted the largest foreign group furnishing agricultural labor, while the Filipinos equaled or exceeded the numbers they reached during the late 1920s.[71]

TABLE 4. Mexicans and Filipinos in Inspected Farm Labor Camps, 1930–1939

|  | Mexicans | | Filipinos | |
|---|---|---|---|---|
|  | Number | Percent | Number | Percent |
| 1930 | 8,971 | 20.6 | 5,120 | 11.8 |
| 1930–31 | 20,791 | 20.6 | 7,555 | 9.7 |
| 1931–32 | 19,360 | 27.5 | 9,396 | 13.4 |
| 1932–33 | 23,005 | 29.6 | 8,718 | 11.2 |
| 1933–34 | 20,851 | 32.5 | 7,228 | 11.3 |
| 1934–35 | 16,900 | 28.6 | 6,279 | 10.6 |
| 1935–36 | 13,688 | 22.2 | 4,896 | 7.9 |
| 1936–37 | 11,768 | 20.5 | 5,697 | 9.9 |
| 1937–38 | 13,501 | 22.9 | 2,978 | 5.0 |
| 1938–39 | 14,691 | 22.4 | 7,434 | 11.4 |

SOURCE: U.S. Congress, Senate, Subcommittee of the Committee on Education and Labor, *Hearings S. Res. 266, A Resolution to Investigate Violations of the Right of Free Speech and Assembly and Interference With the Right of Labor to Organize and Bargain Collectively*, 76 Cong., 3 sess., 25 January 1940, Pt. 59, pp. 21917–19.

This, in effect, is an account of the immigrant in Pacific Coast agriculture: primarily of European origins in the landowning and tenant classes, and to some extent in agricultural labor. Eventually the European ethnic groups yielded ground to the Mexicans, Asiatics, and native Americans as farm laborers. German and Hungarian immigrants in the nineteenth century, and later the Italians were prominent in grape-growing and winemaking. The Chinese were excellent farm laborers; the Japanese were eminently successful, as were the Italians, in intensive farming; the Portuguese succeeded as dairy farmers, the Armenians as fruit-growers, and the Mexicans and Filipinos as farm laborers. Farmers of European background were prominent and successful in all areas of commercial agriculture, but their achievements along ethnic lines were not as delineated in the earlier years as are those of the Japanese, Italian, Portuguese, and Armenians.

71 See George P. Clements, "Mexican Immigration and Its Bearing on California Agriculture," *California Citrograph* 15 (November 1929): 27–29, 31.

# IMMIGRANTS IN THE NEW SOUTH:
## ITALIANS IN LOUISIANA'S SUGAR PARISHES, 1880-1910*

By JEAN ANN SCARPACI

Louisiana's sugar-cane fields comprise one of that state's leading industries. During the nineteenth century most of the sugar raised in the continental United States grew in the southeast and south central areas of Louisiana. The sugar parishes encircled New Orleans, lined the Mississippi River from its mouth northward to Baton Rouge, and extended westward into the region surrounding Bayou Lafourche and Bayou Teche.[1]

Sugarcane cultivation required a large labor force of skilled and unskilled workers. During the period of culivation, from February through mid July, "hoe gangs" fought the advance of weeds into the rows of cane and kept the drainage ditches clear. During the harvesting or grinding months, from October through January, cane cutters and loaders sent a steady supply of cane to the sugar mill.[2]

Each fall, in the late nineteenth century, the harvest season or *zuccarata,* as they called it, attracted thousands of Italian laborers to Louisiana's sugarcane fields. These immigrants responded to the chronic scarcity of labor on the sugar plantations, but they were only a migratory or temporary element in the state's foreign-born population. The num-

---

* This essay benefitted from the incisive questions and comments offered by my colleagues Perra S. Bell and John G. Van Osdell. The original version was read before the American Historical Association convention in New Orleans, Louisiana, on December 30, 1972.

[1] J. Carlyle Sitterson, *Sugar Country: The Cane Sugar Industry in the South, 1753-1950* (Lexington, 1953), 267; Department of Commerce, Bureau of the Census, *Eleventh Census, 1890: Statistics of Agriculture,* 68, 394-395, 405; Thomas Lynn Smith, "Depopulation of Louisiana's Sugar Bowl," *Journal of Farm Economics,* XX (August 1938), 503-509.

[2] "Facts Concerning Domestic Cane Sugar Production: furnished in a letter to the New York Press by Walter Suthon, a planter of Houma, Louisiana," *Sugar Planters' Journal,* XXXII (April 19, 1902), 428-429, (Hereafter *SPJ.*)

ber of Italians in the labor force of the plantation rose and fell in relation to the cultivating season as well as to the existence of higher paying jobs elsewhere in the United States.

Italians constituted the largest immigrant group in Louisiana around 1900. Census totals recorded an increase in Italian foreign-born from 2,527 in 1880 to 20,233 in 1910. Nor did these official figures reflect the seasonal influx of immigrant labor, which ranged from 30,000 to 80,000. After 1905, the totals sharply decreased. But Italian migration to the sugar parishes (illustrated in Census Chart I) only faintly suggests this pattern of increase in the foreign-born between 1880-1900 and decline in 1910.[8]

## CENSUS CHART I

### Italians and Native Whites of Italian Parentage In Louisiana's Sugar Parishes 1880-1910 (5 or more recorded)

| Parishes | 1880 | 1890* | 1900* | 1910** | 1910*** |
|---|---|---|---|---|---|
| Ascension | 27 | 529 | 1,332 | 578 | 1,206 |
| Assumption | 9 | 270 | 770 | 460 | 926 |
| Iberia | 15 | 41 | 355 | 275 | 549 |
| Iberville | 13 | 645 | 886 | 865 | 1,701 |
| Jefferson | 139 | 380 | 1,012 | 1,209 | 2,455 |
| Lafourche | 6 | 149 | 830 | 343 | 626 |
| Plaquemines | 143 | 324 | 362 | 135 | 265 |
| St. Bernard | 2 | 15 | 123 | 238 | 524 |
| St. Charles | 4 | 323 | 626 | 254 | 615 |
| St. James | 8 | 317 | 1,218 | 699 | 1,225 |
| St. John | 3 | 249 | 450 | 144 | 293 |
| St. Mary | 17 | 207 | 1,639 | 1,246 | 2,363 |
| Terrebonne | 6 | 17 | 550 | 294 | 537 |
| W. Baton Rouge | 5 | 199 | 120 | 210 | 296 |

*Only foreign-born reported in 1880-1900 census
**Foreign-born                ***Native whites of Italian parentage

---

[8] *Tenth Census, 1880: Population*, 511-512 and *Thirteenth Census, 1910: Population*, 778-788. For estimates of floating population see Editorial, "Italian Immigration," *Daily Picayune*, August 12, 1904, 6, and Italy, Ministero Degli Affari Esteri, Commissariato Dell' Emigrazione, *Bollettino Dell' Emigrazione, Anno 1904* (Roma, 1905), A. Ravaiolo, "La Colonizzazione Agricola Negli Stati Uniti," 32. Chart I was compiled from the following: *Tenth Census, 1880: Population*, 511-512; *Eleventh Census, 1890: Population*, I, 630-631; *Twelfth Census, 1900: Statistics of Population*, 757-58; *Thirteenth Census, 1910: Population*, 778-788.

Census Chart II illustrates the overall view of the distributions of the Italian population in the State.[4]

## CENSUS CHART II

### Italians Residing in the Sugar Parishes and in the State of Louisiana 1880-1910

|      | Sugar Parishes Foreign-Born | Total* | Entire State Foreign-Born | Total* |
|------|------------------------------|--------|----------------------------|--------|
| 1880 | 397                          |        | 2,527                      |        |
| 1890 | 3,665                        |        | 7,767                      | 11,076 |
| 1900 | 10,273                       |        | 17,577                     | 26,621 |
| 1910 | 6,940                        | 13,681 | 20,223                     | 42,911 |

*The total indicates the Italian foreign-born and the native whites, one or both of whose parents were born in Italy.

The immigrants, while on the plantation, shared the social status and wage scale of their black co-workers. They adapted to the new work experience, the new environment, and the plantation's work routine, yet they retained their Old World traditions. The continuous link with their native culture provided a group cohesiveness during their time on the plantation, a cohesiveness which remained after they moved from laborer to entrepreneur.

Throughout Reconstruction and well into the 1880s, both cotton and sugar planters complained about the "unreliability" and "inefficiency" of the blacks who comprised their labor force. They failed in their attempts to regiment these workers, who did not respond to their demands and who sought employment in the towns and cities. Furthermore, those agricultural workers remaining in the labor pool on the plantations produced less than the planters expected.[5]

According to many post-bellum plantation accounts, blacks quickly began to demonstrate their desire for economic independence. From 1865 through the 1880s, white planters considered them an unpredictable agricultural labor force. Seemingly dissatisfied with their unchanging existence as plantation labor, for which they received daily or monthly wages, blacks sometimes worked only for a short time and then left. Planters attributed such behavior to their refusal to grant wage advances,

---

[4] Census Chart II was compiled from statistics in Census Chart I, plus *Eleventh Census,* clxvii, 608, 685, 687, 689, *Twelveth Census,* 813-817, and *Thirteenth Census,* 773.

[5] Roger W. Shugg, *Origins of Class Struggle in Louisiana. A Social History of White Farmers and Laborers during Slavery and After, 1840-1875* (Baton Rouge, 1939), 258; Sitterson, *Sugar Country,* 243-245.

or to pay weekly instead of monthly or seasonally. Another cause of discontent involved the wage itself. Black laborers struck for higher wages during periods critical to the cultivation of the sugar crop. Occasionally, they left one plantation for another which offered higher wages. Their search for better work conditions extended over a wide regional and interstate area, with many blacks shuttling between Louisiana and Mississippi. After the Civil War, wages tended to move upward until the 1873 depression, when groups of planters agreed to reduce wages and their black workers refused to contract out on such a basis. These workers were also decidedly unsatisfied with the work schedule imposed upon them.[6]

Planters resented this "Ishmael" or travelling tendency of black workers. Those dependent upon blacks viewed their economic behavior as irresponsible and unreliable. Feeling trapped and fearful of labor trouble, some planters banded together to meet this black challenge. *Ad hoc* associations provided a united front when confronted by demands for higher wages. Their members agreed to pay a standard wage, in order to end the uncertain conditions of sugar cultivation. Some even used extreme measures to thwart migrating blacks, such as having them arrested as "debtors" or for violation of contracts; others effectively controlled the wharf areas and employed river patrols to prevent their field hands from leaving by boat.[7]

This "Negro Exodus" aroused serious concern among those planters who had counted on a permanent black labor force. Benjamin Singleton, a leader of the black movement, likened it to the exodus of Moses and the people of Israel. Many blacks moved to cities, both in the North and the South; others migrated North to work as farm laborers. They might, for instance, go to Kansas, where sugar beets were cultivated, being attracted by the better wage rates there. This veritable "Kansas fever" peaked in 1878. No accurate data is available about those who left the South. The largest migration, however, did occur in 1878-79; and it originated in Mississippi and Louisiana. Estimates ranged from 5,000 to 10,000. Whatever the precise number, it was potentially ruin-

---

[6] Sitterson, *Sugar Country*, 243-245. For more than a decade after the war blacks moved at the end of the year from one plantation to another, and during the first two weeks of each year the roads of the sugar region were lined with carts piled high with all their belongings. Although conditions at their new places were rarely better, many blacks continued to hope, and they also liked to exercise their rights as freedmen to change their employers.

[7] Morgan Dewey Peoples, "Negro Migration From the Lower Mississippi Valley to Kansas, 1879-1880" (unpublished Master's essay, Louisiana State University, 1950), 45.

ous to southern agriculture.[8]

The strikes of black agricultural workers in the early 1880s heightened planter pessimism regarding the possibility of keeping such labor on the plantation or controlling those who worked there. On April 19, 1881, strikes and riots broke out in St. Bernard Parish at cane planting time:

> ... the strike assumed more serious proportions, verging into a riot. It is stated that about three or four hundred negroes banded together under the leadership of some of the Spaniards or "islang," and went from plantation to plantation, compelling the laborers to stop work until the planters consent to pay the wages demanded .... Finding it necessary to quell the turbulent disturbers a committee of planters called at the Governor's office and asked for the authorities of the State to assist them as the parish authorities are powerless.[9]

By April 21, Governor Louis Wiltz had instructed the sheriff in St. Bernard Parish to stop the "rioters" or call upon the militia to help. Instead of questioning their own harsh system, which failed to attract a sufficient and competent labor force, planters condemned the blacks for "deserting" the plantations, for demanding higher wages, and for failing to meet production quotas.[10]

A large supply of labor remained necessary for sugar cultivation, and labor shortages which had haunted the sugar industry in the post-Civil War years continued into the 1880s. Now convinced they could not control a black labor force, planters sought workers from other quarters. One enterprising planter succinctly summed up the situation: "The only draw back I fear is want of reliable labour. Old darkies good but dieing [sic] out. Young ones about good for nothing. Have sent to Portugal for 25 laborers and their families."[11]

Closer at hand was an established colony of Italians in New Orleans. Trade routes long had existed between Louisiana and Sicily, and a colony

[8] Walter L. Fleming, "Pap Singleton, The Moses of the Colored Exodus," *American Journal of Sociology*, XV, no. 1 (1909), 61-78; Peoples, "Negro Migration," 11; Roy Garvin, "Benjamin, or Pap Singleton and His Followers," *Journal of Negro History*, XXXIII (January 1948), 7, 11. Benjamin Singleton was responsible for founding eleven colonies in Kansas between 1873 and 1874, after an unsuccessful effort in 1870 with the Tennessee Real Estate and Homestead Association. By 1879 the movement had become a flood. Singleton wrote pamphlets on Sunny Kansas but "educated" blacks scorned his plans. By the end of 1879 he claimed to have brought 7432 blacks to Kansas.

[9] Riot in St. Bernard," *Daily Picayune*, April 19, 1881, 1.

[10] *Louisiana Capitolian* (Baton Rouge), April 21, 1881, 2. Strikes also occurred in St. John's parish during the spring of 1880 as reported in "Here and There," *Le Louisianais* (Convent, La.), April 17, 1880, 1.

[11] Sitterson, *Sugar Country*, 315. Sitterson cites a letter from Daniel Thompson to Cyrus Woodman, August 1, 1880 in C. L. Marquette (ed.), "Letters of a Yankee Sugar Planter," *Journal of Southern History*, VI (1940), 533.

of Italians, mainly merchants and in related occupations, had resided in
New Orleans by mid-century. In 1850, 915 Italians lived in Louisiana;
in 1870, the number had increased to 1,884. Approximately 97 percent
of them were Sicilians — from north central, central, and western Sicily.
Those emigrating directly had followed the citrus trade routes from
Palermo and Messina to New Orleans.[12]

The connection between trade routes and emigration of people from
the Mediterranean stirred the imagination of many white southerners
after the Civil War. Expanded commercial ties had two advantages:
first, it would increase both profits and economic activity; second, it
might satisfy the need for laborers to develop Southern agricultural and
industrial potential. In 1867, a conference on the problem of Southern
commerce led to a request for government subsidies, through mail contracts, for a steamship line plying between Southern and Mediterranean
ports. Delegates to this commercial convention suggested that there
would be a "natural" balance of trade: ". . . considering that we grow
cereals and they grow fruits — that we can export cotton, tobacco, rice
and petroleum to them, and receive fruits, olive oil, wines, sardines and
works of art in return. . . ."[13]
This trade route also might supply laborers directly to the South.

> We have to glance the eye over the map to see from whence these new sup-
> plies must come. The northern shores of the Mediterranean embracing Spain,
> Italy, Sicily and Sardinia, with Greece, are teeming with a population of fifty
> millions. The climate is the same as that of the Southern States. Their
> farmers, fruit growers and laborers would be at home in the sunny fields of
> the South. The climate which the Northern emigrant shuns they are accus-
> tomed to. While readily acquiring a knowledge of the course of agriculture
> now existing here, they would bring with them, and introduce, the modes of
> producing their various fruits and wines. The waste fields, now deserted,
> would, under their patient labor, become fruitful with the grape, the olive,
> the fig, the orange, the lemon and kindred products. . . .[14]

Other sources also acknowledged a connection between trade routes

---

[12] *Seventh Census*, 1850, *Ninth Census*, 1870, 340-341; Cavalier Guido Rossati and R.
Enotenico, "Gli Italiani nell Agricoltura degli Stati Uniti D'America," in *Gli Italiani
Negli Stati D'America* (New York, 1906), 37; Italy, Ministero Degli Affari Esteri,
Commissariato Generale Dell'Emigrazione, *Emigrazione E Colonie: Raccolta Di Rap-
porti Dell R. R. Agenti Diplomatici E Consolari*, III, *America* (Roma, 1909), 202-
221; interview and letter from Gaetano Mistretta, Donaldsonville, Louisiana, February and November, 1966.
[13] *Remarks on the Importance to the Nation in View of the Condition of the Southern States
and the Prostration of Commerce, of Establishing Steamship Intercourse with the Nations of the Mediterranean Sea* (New York, 1867), 9.
[14] *Ibid.*, 8.

and European immigration. James C. Kathman, Chief of the Bureau of Immigration for the State of Louisiana, compared Sicily's climate and fertility with Louisiana's. Both Kathman and General P. T. Beauregard spoke to this point in *De Bow's Review* in the 1860s. Beauregard also served as president of an Immigration and Homestead Association formed in 1873 to encourage foreigners to come to Louisiana.[15]

Mediterranean ports often appeared as destinations on Louisiana shipping lists. The location of New Orleans along with its position as a center of distribution for the midwest obviously was a factor in the development of such trade. Markets for specific commodities reflected the needs and resources of the trans-Mississippi West. Vessels laden with cotton and wheat sailed to European ports, returning with fresh fruit and other agricultural products for the American market.[16]

The citrus fruit trade was centered in Sicily; hence there was a long tradition of commercial transactions between that island and New Orleans. The ethnic make-up of New Orleans' business community began to reflect such contacts, as may be seen from names in business directories and in newspaper reports. The substantial Italian colony which developed in New Orleans before the Civil War revolved around the citrus fruit trade. Italians not only imported and distributed the fruit, but also unloaded the ships and peddled the fruit throughout New Orleans as well as in the suburbs.[17]

Immigration to Louisiana continued to follow the established citrus trade routes. During the late nineteenth century most of the ships bring-

---

[15] "Department of Immigration and Labor," *De Bow's Review*, IV n.s. (November, 1867), 474; *Address of the People in Behalf of the Louisiana Immigration and Homestead Company*, Louisiana State University Archives, Baton Rouge, P. T. Beauregard Papers.

[16] *Daily Picayune* (New Orleans), December 16, 1880, 1, notes the arrival of the British S. S. *Sciuda* from Palermo with 210 immigrants and a cargo of lemons. The *Daily Picayune*, December 8, 1887, 8, notes the arrival of the British S. S. *Elysia* with 613 Italians and a cargo of lemons and Mediterranean fruits to be shipped north and west by the Illinois Central Railroad. William Harris, State Commissioner of Agriculture and Immigration, in a pamphlet, *Louisiana Products, Resources and Attractions with a Sketch of the Parishes* (New Orleans, 1881), recorded exports of grain from New Orleans to the ports of Leghorn, Venice and Naples and exports of tobacco to Italy. This relationship between trade routes and immigrant traffic across the Atlantic receives attention in Marcus Lee Hansen, *Atlantic Migration*, Chapter VIII, "Commerce Bridges the Atlantic" (Cambridge, Mass., 1951), 172-198.

[17] Alice Fortier, *Louisiana, Comprising Sketches of Parishes, Towns, Events, Institutions and Persons Arranged in Cyclopedic Form* (4 vols. Madison, Wisconsin, 1914), III, 742-743, discusses one of New Orleans' leading Italian businessmen partnerships, the Vaccaro Brothers. Stefano Vaccaro, born in Contessa Entellina, Sicily, came to New Orleans in 1860 and from 1862 engaged in the fruit and produce business until 1893, when his sons, Felix, Luca, and Joseph took over. The Vaccaro Brothers first began at Decatur and North Peters Streets, and were wholesale dealers until 1898, when they began importing bananas and coconuts from Spanish Honduras to New Orleans whence they shipped these products across the country.

ing Italian immigrants and products to New Orleans left from Palermo. For example, in 1880 the British Steamship *Scuida* sailed from Palermo to New Orleans with 210 immigrants and a cargo of lemons from Messina and Palermo. The S. S. *Elysia* in 1887 sailed from Palermo to New Orleans with 613 Italian immigrants and a cargo of lemons as well as Mediterranean fruits. The S. S. *Utopia* with 796 Italians from Piana dei Greci, Sicily, sailed from Palermo to New Orleans in 1888. Sugar planters welcomed this convenient link between commerce, immigration, and a potential labor force for their plantations. In 1881 the Louisiana Sugar Planters' Association created a committee for Italian immigration which, from 1881 through 1908, in concert with the State Bureau of Agriculture and Immigration, supported efforts to recruit such immigrants.[18]

The majority of Italians still clustered around the city, but some individuals sought economic opportunities outside New Orleans itself. John Dymond of Plaquemines Parish, located south of New Orleans, was in 1870, the first sugar planter to hire an Italian laborer. During the next decade, Dymond and his neighbors offered jobs to other Italian immigrants. The census figures for Plaquemines Parish record the scattering of Italians in the sugar parishes as being 143 by 1880.[19]

This influx of Italian laborers was largely seasonal. They came directly from Italy to the cane fields at grinding time (October through December), and returned to their homeland immediately after the harvest, thereby following a nomadic pattern that had long been a way of life for Italian peasants. Augusto Miceli, a New Orleans attorney who arrived in America in the 1920s, reported that tramp steamers between New Orleans and Palermo would carry Italian "birds of passage" to Louisiana expressly for the grinding season. Charles Cangelosi of Baton Rouge noted that ships carrying immigrants for the plantations sometimes came directly up river to his community.[20]

---

[18] *Daily Picayune*, December 16, 1880, 1, December 8, 1887, 8 (this article notes that most of the passengers originated from Sicily and Southern Italy); *Weekly Times Democrat* (New Orleans), October 20, 1888, 3; "Cane and Corn," *Daily Picayune*, June 11, 1881, 1 and Minutes, May 12 and June 9, 1881, Louisiana State University Archives, Louisiana Sugar Planters' Association Papers. William Harris, State Commissioner of Agriculture and Immigration, in a pamphlet, *Louisiana: Products, Resources and Attractions with a Sketch of the Parishes* (New Orleans, 1881), recorded exports of grain from New Orleans to Leghorn, Venice, and Naples and exports of tobacco to Italy.

[19] "Italian Immigration." *Louisiana Planter and Sugar Manufacturer* (New Orleans), XXXVIII (September 22, 1906), 179-180 (hereafter LPSM); *Tenth Census, 1880: Population*, 511-512.

[20] Grazia Dore, "Some Social and Historical Aspects of Italian Emigration to America," trans., by Andrea Martonetty, *Journal of Social History*, II, no. 2 (1968), 110; Au-

Similarly, on a seasonal basis, during the 1890s and early 1900s, other Italian laborers began to migrate down into the sugar region from Chicago and New York, and Italians residing in New Orleans and in other Louisiana towns outside the sugar region often temporarily supplemented the labor force. This annual journey of Italian immigrants usually began in October and tapered off by March. For those from Chicago and New York there was the added attraction of being able to avoid the cold northern winters. One sugar planter observed:

> You see, our Dagoes have a way of going to Chicago for the summer months. They work in the sugar fields until May 1 or May 10, and then put out for Chicago where they work in shops, in mines and on railroads until winter sets in when they pack up and come to the sugar belt. Their fuel bills would be more than the railroad fares, and they make money on the deal.

It is clear, then, that much of the annual migration of Italians to Louisiana was internal as well as seasonal.[21]

Italian laborers on the plantation had to adjust to the firmly established work routine. Planters continued to welcome them as replacements for black labor, although the immigrant at best supplemented the native work force. Most Italians filled the unskilled, low-paying jobs that were essential to the cultivation and harvesting of sugar cane, for the planters did not change wages or work functions as the ethnic composition of the labor force changed.

Pay rolls and time books indicate that ordinary labor received 75 cents a day during the growing season. For grinding, teamsters and cane loaders received $1.40 per day, and cane cutters $1.25. Only the best workers held positions as teamsters and loaders. And only first-rate cane cutters received $1.25. The others workers — old men, women, and boys—were paid less, from 75 cents to $1.20 per day, depending upon the amount of work they could do. Their wages for cultivating the crops ranged from 25 to 60 cents. Whatever the labor, the work day lasted from sun up to sun down.[22]

In addition to his wages, the plantation laborer was given a house and a

gusto Miceli, interview in New Orleans, Louisiana, November 10, 1965; Mr. Luigi Scala, former Italian Consul at Independence, Louisiana, noted that steamship companies encouraged "birds of passage." (interview in Providence, Rhode Island, October 1966); letter from Mr. Charles Cangelosi, Baton Rouge, Louisiana, September 26, 1965.

21 "Importation of Porto [sic] Rican Sugar and Exportation of Italians: Interview with Hon. W. E. Howell of Lafourche Parish," *SPJ*, XXXI (August 31, 1901), 722-723.
22 Payroll for Dunboyne Plantation, January to December, 1897, Louisiana State University Archives, Edward J. Gay and Family Papers: Time Books 1898-1901 and 1905-1908; Facts Concerning Domestic Can Sugar," 428-429.

garden patch of about one-quarter acre; there he grew corn, peas, and sweet potatoes, aided by the plantation mules and plows furnished free of charge. He also received free fuel, which he hauled to his house by using the plantation team provided for this purpose.[23]

Vincent Brocato, who came from Cefalu, Sicily, to Raceland, Louisiana, in 1895 at age 22, described the housing for families as tenement-like buildings of one story divided into apartments. The single men lived in dormitories. All the houses were crudely built and, like most rural dwellings of that period, lacked indoor plumbing. Wood stoves and open fireplaces provided both heating and cooking facilities. Kerosene lamps provided the light.[24]

The plantation tasks requiring little skill, such as hoeing and ditching, were assigned to the Italians. When Donelson Caffery of St. Mary's Parish wrote to his son from Washington, D. C., in 1897, he noted: "Some few hundred Dagoes will be required to ditch the swamp land." This kind of work was necessary to keep the land dry. As hoe men and briar-hook handlers, Italians were considered "superior" to other laborers; at least so the planters believed and they preferred them for this work in the cane fields.[25]

Some Italian immigrants believed that plantation work meant "plenty money" compared with economic rewards in Sicily, where poverty and misery had surrounded them. The habits of years of impoverishment at home helped ambitious and frugal laborers to survive in Louisiana and, in some cases, to get ahead. A. Piaggio, an Italian who visited Donaldsonville, Louisiana, in 1895, a time of depression in the sugar industry, explained how an immigrant family could achieve subsistence or better in the plantation setting:

> A family of five Italians, the father, the mother and three children, arriving on a cane plantation from Italy all set to work. Even in a depressed labor market, the father by working three watches of six hours each, at 50 cents a watch, could earn $1.50 a day. The mother could earn $1, and the children, even if only 5 years old manage as a rule to earn 10 cents a day. So that the aggregate of such an average family's work per day was about $3. . . .[26]

[23] Ibid.
[24] Interview with Mrs. Vincent Brocato, Raceland, Louisiana, November 14, 1965. Mrs. Brocato came to Raceland with her family in 1895. There they joined her father who had emigrated in 1894. Mrs. Brocato conveyed information from her own life and from her husband's experiences. Mr. Brocato was alive in 1965, but unable to provide an interview. See also interview with Mistretta.
[25] Letter dated March 3, 1897, Letter Book 1866-1906, Louisiana State University Archives, Donelson Caffery and Family Papers; Hall Clipper, "Special Correspondent, LPSM, XXIV (June 9, 1900), 359.
[26] Letter from John V. Baiamonti, Jr., Tickfaw, Louisiana, December 8, 1970. (Mr. Baia-

It is difficult to understand how these laborers could *save* money on wages ranging from 50 to 75 cents per day, even with the whole family working and even though, during the depression years, the wages did not compare unfavorably with those received by industrial workers. One old Sicilian said he saved money because he "ate nothing but *pane e cutadro* [bread and knife]." Ridley Le Blanc, who worked at Raceland Plantation in Louisiana, expanded on this account, describing Italian laborers as:

> very good workers in the fields. . . . They were good gardeners, raised goats, made and baked their own bread, made and formed their spaghetti, made cheese and made their clothes. They were self supporting and saved nearly all of their small earnings and quickly went into their own successful business.

Gaetano Mistretta, the son of an Italian merchant in Assumption Parish, supports these observations. His father's store accounts, Mistretta recalled, indicated that the immigrant laborers purchased very little. They either made or grew the necessities of life; they were accustomed to subsist on bread and cheese for an entire working day. The Italians, then, adjusted to the long-established work routine on the plantation and the kinds of work available, and so the wages and living conditions did not vary with the ethnic composition of the labor force.[27]

Although contemporaries predicted that Italians would soon replace black labor in the sugar region, blacks continued to dominate the work force between 1880 and 1910. For the Italian, direct contact with blacks as co-workers was a new experience. He faced a double adjustment, then; the first was to the work routine, the second to the indigenous socioeconomic structure. Since Italians and black laborers shared the same positions in the plantation system, they also shared the low occupational status of agricultural labor.

The particular composition of the work force prompted comparisons between the two groups. Most of the studies, conducted by native whites, concluded that immigrant labor was more productive than black

---

monte interviewed Sicilian immigrants and their children in Tangipahoa Parish during the course of his research on the Italians in Tangipahoa Parish); "Italians Returning to their Fatherland," *Daily Picayune,* December 21, 1895, 9.

27 Henry Marshall Booker notes in his study "Efforts of the South to Attract Immigrants, 1860-1900" (unpublished Ph.D. diss., University of Virginia, 1965), 54, that the Southern States paying the highest wages for farm labor with board for the period 1866-1899 were Texas, Florida, and Louisiana. Letter from Mr. George Piazza, a New Orleans attorney, September 29, 1965; letter from Mr. Ridley Le Blanc, December 1965, formerly connected with the Godchaux Company in Raceland, Louisiana; Mistretta letter and interview.

labor. In this competitive setting, hostility might conceivably have developed between black and Italian wage earners, but the immigrants seemed unperturbed. As one observer concluded, the Italians "have no rooted prejudice to competition with negro labor. Intermixture with negro labor can usually be obviated by the division of employment on plantations and any necessary association of the Italian whites with the blacks is not precluded by any race animosity." When blacks and Italians comprised the work force, Walter Fleming observed, as they did at Sunnyside Plantation in Arkansas, "there is no friction . . . between Italian and black; but there is no race mixture." One Louisiana planter affirmed that the forty families of Italian laborers on his plantation did not quarrel among themselves or with the other workers. The Italians, he stated, kept separate from the blacks in social relations and, in fact, the immigrants tended to keep their own counsel in all matters.[28]

Some individuals reported that all plantation workers, Italians, blacks, and those of French ancestry ate and lived together without any hostility. One informant claimed that it was not unusual to have a black family living next door to an Italian family. In the fields, work squads had both immigrant and black laborers, and when a black served as hoe gang boss, he did not encounter resentment from Italian crew members. Blacks, one might conjecture, served as on-the-job trainers for the newcomers.[29]

Although both conflict and violence did trouble some Italian-black relationships, newspapers did not report persistent hostility. Immediate events precipitated what instances there were of conflict rather than "racial" or national confrontation. Significantly, the press did not evaluate the fights, shootings, and thefts which occurred from 1880 to 1910 between Italians and Southern blacks as "racial" provocations. Certainly, Louisiana's Anglo-American society considered both these groups as violence prone, and Southerners were very sensitive to any evidence of "race" incompatibility. In fact, much of the crime committed by Italian and black workers occurred within their own ethnic communities. Southerners only became alarmed when they were personally affected.[30]

Consquently, Italians and blacks appear to have reacted with tolerance in their associations. Neutrality was the keynote. Immigrant acceptance of persons so unlike themselves in appearance, religion, language, and

---

[28] Eliot Lord, *The Italian in America* (New York, 1905), 184; Walter Fleming, "Immigration to the Southern States," *Political Science Quarterly*, XX (June 1905), 297; Lee J. Langely, "To Build Up Louisiana: Needed Outside Capital and Labor will be Welcomed," *Manufacturers' Record* (Baltimore), XLV (April 14, 1904), 276-277.
[29] Brocato interview and letter from Le Blanc.
[30] *L'Italia* (Chicago), August 15-16, 1896.

specific customs may be largely explained by the Sicilians' general indifference to the world outside their town. *Campanilismo,* or provincialism, characterized the South Italians. They identified with their village existence, as Charlotte Chapman's study of Milocca, a Sicilian community indicates. Those who came from other Sicilian towns always retained their *furasteri,* or refugee, quality; and their offspring, though born in Milocca, were *furasteri* children. And such identities followed the Miloccese emigrants to Pittston, Pennsylvania, and Birmingham, Alabama. Chapman also observes that the individual's willingness to interact with groups or entities *within* the village varied according to his sense of identification. To the Sicilian, his family and town were his prime interests. All else for him was secondary. In Louisiana, the indifference with which the Sicilian regarded black labor reflected this scale of priorities and led to a minimum of interaction.[31]

When describing intergroup relations between immigrants and blacks, Mistretta and others claimed that Italian wage earners initially bore n ɔ ill-will toward their black co-workers. They had no reason to dislike the blacks and regarded them with curiosity, But once aware that they shared the same socio-economic position, at the lowest level of Southern society, they decided to avoid further association with blacks. Indeed, this decision was one factor in their resolve to leave the cane fields.[32]

An interview with Italians who had moved from sugar plantations to farming in Independence, Louisiana provided a detailed explanation:

> One Italian informant... said he and his family had been badly mistreated by a French plantation owner near New Roads. When asked how he had been mistreated, he stated that he and his family were made to live among the Negroes and were treated in the same manner. At first he did not mind because he did not know any difference, but when he learned the position that Negroes occupied in this country, he demanded that his family be moved to a different house and be given better treatment.

In fact, much of the criticism of plantation conditions derived from the observation that blacks occupied an inferior position in the South's social hierarchy. Representatives of the Italian government repeatedly stated their wish that Italians settle in the South on a par with the native Anglo-Saxon, and not compete with the native black for his title of agricultural proletariat.[33]

---

[31] Charlotte Gower Chapman, *Milocca: A Sicilian Village* (Cambridge, Mass., 1971), 151-157. Chapman collected her data on Milocca in 1928.
[32] Mistretta interview.
[33] Luther Williams, "The People of Tangipahoa Parish: A Sociological Comparison of

Thus, the exposure of the Italian immigrant to white prejudices ultimately influenced his attitude toward Southern blacks. He realized that treatment equal to that accorded the blacks was inferior treatment. And much of the conflict that developed between the groups reflected the upward mobility of Italians from laborer to tenant to farmer or businessman.

Economic competition had always threatened to create an environment of hostility between Italians and blacks on the plantation. The conclusions drawn from the studies of Alfred Holt Stone and others prompted some of the planters to continue to seek Italian workers. Stone, for example, emphasized that Italians worked harder, produced larger yields per acre, labored in all weather, and made greater sacrifices in order to accumulate savings, and implied that the blacks did not match these characteristics. Conceivably, the combination of an increasing number of Italian workers on the plantations and their reputation for high productivity would arouse hostility among the blacks. This increase, all evidence indicates, had been in direct response to an endemic labor scarcity and did not necessarily sharpen job competition. But blacks might well have regarded the immigrant as responsible for lowering wages because of his high rate of productivity.[84]

When depression hit the sugar industry, many Italians, rather than accepting lower wages, left the cane fields altogether. Repeal of the McKinley Tariff, which removed protection for domestic industry, also encouraged their departure. Perhaps the proximity of New Orleans and the relative ease of movement in and out of the sugar parishes and into industrial centers, acted as a "safety valve" for these Italian laborers. In any case, many of them viewed plantation work as merely temporary. It provided a means to accumulate savings in order to embark on a career as agricultural or business entrepreneur.[85]

Although the exodus of blacks from the South declined during the 1880s, planters also continued to record a decrease in their annual migration within the south, from a region where cotton was baled to the plantation which was grinding sugar. But this movement of blacks from staple farming to the lumber mill regions, and to southern towns and cities, did not remove them entirely from the plantation work force. Indeed, plant-

Two Ethnic Groups" (Unpublished Masters' essay, Louisiana State University, 1951), 85; Baron Des Planches and Italian Immigration," *LPSM*, XXXIV (April 21, 1906), 246.

[84] Alfred Holt Stone, "Italian Cotton Growers in Arkansas," *American Monthly Review of Reviews*, XXXV (February 1907), 209-213.

[85] "The Plantation Labor Problem," *LPSM*, XVII (December 5, 1896), 362.

ers still depended primarily upon black labor throughout the nineteenth century.[36]

Later, as the rate of immigration to Louisiana decreased, and as Italian sugar workers already there responded to better economic conditions elsewhere in the United States, planters again began to recruit blacks and whites from the cotton region. Obviously, the flow of Italians to Louisiana had not forced black laborers from the plantations as the literature of the period had predicted. A growing number of immigrants worked on the plantations until 1900 and planters always seemed anxious to employ more each year, but there apparently never was a sufficient number of Italians to meet the needs of the sugar industry. When blacks left the fields, Italians were recruited to fill their places; when Italian migration slackened, blacks were again courted. However the general pool of plantation labor remained insufficient.[37]

Louisiana's sugar plantations, as indicated, exposed the Italian immigrant to many new conditions and experiences, Nothing in his past had prepared him for the cycle of cane cultivation, the process of sugar refining, the English-speaking population, and the presence of black wage earners. He had to adapt these experiences to his own frame of reference, which was the strong cohesive group identity that had been brought over almost undiluted from Italy. Although gradually redefined in America, the basic pattern of values involving close ties with family, fellow villagers (paesani), and co-nationals, remained. It provided a familiar setting which more than counterbalanced the unfamiliar aspects of American life.

Rather than these day-to-day patterns within the Italian-American community, the press mainly documented "sensational" or "colorful" events. It focused on incidents of conflict or violence, celebrations, and participation in local events. On the plantations much of the reported violence stemmed from disagreements over money or work assignments, where the conflicts were generally among family members and friends. In most cases of violence among Italians, the press assumed that the motives had been personal and that all the witnesses would remain

---

[36] Sitterson, *Sugar Country*, 315-317. David Hellwig's study of the blacks' response to immigration also considered their reaction to the South's attempt to recruit Italian labor. He noted that blacks displayed their displeasure against the recruiters, not their proteges. Hellwig found no massive conflict between the two groups. The blacks contrasted the virtues of a traditional labor source against the potential threat of "the Italian as corrupt, violent, anarchistic, prone to join unions and in general a threat to both the American and Southern way of life." Letter, September 30, 1973, St. Cloud, Minnesota.
[37] *Ibid.*

silent. (In such newspaper accounts, the stereotyping of Italians as violence prone was typical.) When an Italian fruit peddler, Luca Rizzo, shot his brother-in-law, Vito Corenno, on the Glenn Orange Plantation near Morgan City, the *Thibodaux Sentinel* noted ". . . these same parties had a cutting affair about two years ago and the usual dense ignorance of the shooting is shown by those who presumably know all about it, including the wounded man." This code of silence and determination to remain apart was also a direct legacy from the Old World, as Danilo Dolci has documented. Dolci, who has worked among the inhabitants of western and central Sicily, acknowledged these attitudes by referring to two proverbs: "The man who goes his own road can never go wrong," and " the man who plays alone never loses." As one Sicilian emigrant explained:

> If a man goes alone, he needn't get involved in any trouble. He goes his own way. He does whatever he pleases, he goes his own road. With other people as one says one thing, another says something else, and they can't agree.

This self-imposed isolation implies not the isolation of the individual but of his extended family group.[38]

Identification with the family group typical of life in Sicily and brought over intact to America, encouraged laborers to save money in order to send for their wives, Ship arrivals in New Orleans set the stage for family reunions. This tradition of close family ties included reprisals for family dishonor. An Italian laborer in Lafourche Parish carried out this private code when he shot and killed the prospective husband of his sixteen-year old sister. He had learned, observers hypothesized, that her fiance was already married to a woman in Italy. At any rate, it seems clear that the Old World code of honor which touched the family, making each member of a family responsible for the other's behavior, also functioned in Louisiana.[39]

The persistence of group cohesiveness impressed Count Gerolamo Moroni, Italian consul at New Orleans. In 1912, he observed that Italians preferred to work on the sugar plantations because these were situated near villages and cities in which Italian merchants resided. The merchant offered sociability as well as familiar commodities. Workers, further-

---

[38] "Italian Killed," *Thibodaux Sentinel*, May 29, 1909, 1; Danilo Dolci, *The Man who Plays Alone*, trans. by Antonia Cowan (Garden City, N. Y., 1970), 4.
[39] Chapman, *Milocca*, 73 "Southern States Items," *Daily Picayune*, August 30, 1894, 11; "Italian Murdered," Weekly *Thibodaux Sentinel*, October 13, 1900, 1.

more, lived in close proximity on plantations, and in effect formed small villages of their own. This retention of group cohesiveness, though thousands of miles from the Old World, probably played an important role in attracting Sicilians to Louisiana. Most of the newcomers had once lived in towns, more aptly termed "rural cities," with populations ranging from 2,000 upward to the tens of thousands. Life in America's isolated rural communities would not readily appeal to peasants who were accustomed to residential clusters. Certainly the proximity of a large Italian colony in New Orleans easily reached by train and boat helped the immigrant to feel that the environment was familiar.[40]

Mutual benefit or benevolent societies which were common in Sicily and had reinforced *campanilismo* in the Old World, served similarly in the United States. Including fraternal as well as welfare functions, they provided health benefits and burial costs, and they sponsored such social functions as anniversary celebrations, religious observances, and commemorations of American holidays, like Columbus Day. Many of these societies reflected the Old World emphasis upon town and regional loyalties. Six mutual benefit societies were listed for the sugar parishes in the Italian consul's report of 1910. Two other societies were recorded in the press. Indeed, the very names of some societies demonstrated their regional orientation. In addition to town and regional identities, Sicilian saints such as Santa Lucia and Santa Rosalia, as well as the Immaculate Conception, particularly revered by Sicilians, also provided names for societies. Whenever these societies staged a celebration, dignitaries representing the native American community participated. In 1907, when the Duca D'Aosta Association of Franklin sponsored a celebration, both Senator Murphy J. Foster and Lieutenant Governor J. Y. Sanders addressed the gathering. Such official attention to the Italian Americans who had become citizens encouraged them to support these politicians.[41]

We have seen that those Italians who remained in Louisiana as entrepreneurs continued to maintain that group cohesiveness which preserved

---

[40] *Bolletino Dell' Emigrazione, Anno 1913,* Gerolamo Moroni, "La Louisiana e L'immigrazione Italiana," 51-53; Rudolph Vecoli, "Contadini in Chicago: A Critique of *The Uprooted," Journal of American History,* LIV (December 1964), 404-405.
[41] *Ibid.,* 413; Chapman, *Milocca,* 172-73; *Bollettino Dell' Emigrazione, Anno 1910,* Moroni, "Societa Italiane Nel Distretto Consolate di New Orleans," 1118-1193; "Over the State—Pattterson," *Kentwood Commercial,* June 18, 1895, 4; "Latest News in Louisiana," *Daily Picayune,* October 16, 1906, 16; "Latest News in Louisiana," *Ibid,* July 27, 1910, 14; *Bolletino Dell' Emigrazione, 1910;* Latest News in All Louisiana—Kenner," *Daily Picayune,* August 30, 1903, 14; "A Gala Day in Franklin," *St. Mary Banner* (Franklin), May 11, 1907, 3-4.

their ethnic identity. And as the immigrant moved out of the agricultural laborer class, he placed a wider distance between himself and his former black co-worker. He even acquired the race prejudice of Southerners — which was the price paid in exchange for social acceptance.

From available statistical data, it is difficult to determine precisely how many Italians actually worked on sugar plantations. Neither United States Census figures nor the yearly reports of the arrivals of immigrants in Louisiana reflect the volume and impact of this migration. Indeed, the temporary nature of work in the *zuccarata,* which caused a rapid turnover in the labor force, led to an internal migratory pattern. Workers from Chicago, Kansas City, St. Louis, New Orleans, and New York, as well as from Sicily, flooded the sugar regions each year seeking employment.

Even before 1910, a decreasing number of Italians came to work in the cane fields. Instead, some of them climbed out of the wage earner category and became economically self-sufficient. They achieved their goal through frugality and a singleminded concentration upon saving. Wages on the sugar plantations permitted ambitious immigrants to move into tenantry, share cropping, and eventually land ownership.

Yet, as we have seen, most of the temporary or seasonal migrants did not remain in Louisiana. They had originally followed the call of the annual *zuccarata* because wages and work conditions had seemed more favorable than elsewhere. Conditions soon changed, however, and by 1908 an Italian government official noted than an immigrant laborer could save one-fifth more over eight months of construction work than he could save in a year of farm labor.[42]

In addition, Louisiana's social climate caused some immigrants to leave. Italians shared with black workers the low status assigned to agricultural wage earners. Southerners considered such work dirty and undesirable, and placed the stamp of inferiority upon those who did it. The attitude was partly social in origin, a contempt for manual labor; and partly racial, the undesirable jobs were only for groups rated inferior by the native white community.

Italians might have been willing to tolerate these attitudes if good salaries were at stake, but not when they could obtain higher wages elsewhere. There were additional considerations: peonage, yellow fever,

---

[42] Robert Foerster, *The Italian Emigration of Our Times* (New York, 1969. Originally published by Harvard University Press in 1919), 369. Foerster cites "Memorandum degl' instituti italiani di patronate per gli emigranti in sulle cause che ostacolano L'avviamento all' agricoltura degl' immigranti italiani negli Stati Uniti" in the *Bollettino Dell' Emigrazione, Anno 1909,* 9. The factors contributing to the decline of

the lynching of Italians, and Southern expressions of intolerance toward some immigrant customs, and these prompted many immigrants to leave Louisiana altogether. With the original attraction of high agricultural wages canceled by better economic opportunities elsewhere, Italian migrants no longer responded to the annual call of labor in the *zuccarata*.

immigration to Louisiana are discussed in Chapters V and VI of Jean Ann Scarpaci, "Italian Immigrants in Louisiana's Sugar Parishes: Recruitment, Conditions of Labor, and Community Relations, 1880-1910" (unpublished Ph.D. diss., Rutgers University, 1972).

ROBERT P. SWIERENGA

# Ethnicity and American Agriculture

## *Ethnic Patterns in Land Settlement*

Rural America was never as ethnic as urban America. The vastness of the agricultural hinterland and the traditional family farm both worked against the formation and survival of ethnic communities. Nevertheless, ever since Americans populated the land, every national and denominational group, in greater or lesser degree, is represented in the farming population. Rural America, especially the Upper Middle West during the nineteenth century, had a remarkable cultural diversity, traces of which still exist today in the countryside. Agricultural historian Allan Bogue has aptly described the midwestern frontier: "Farm operators might be native-born or foreign-born, born to the English tongue or highly inept in its use. If continental-born, they might have been raised among the Rhineland vineyards or trained to a mixed life of farming and fishing in Scandinavia, been emigrants from the grain fields of eastern Europe or come from many other backgrounds. If native-born, they might be Yankee or Yorker, Kentuckian or Buckeye, Pennsylvanian or Sucker."[1]

There were three major ethnic settlement streams in rural America—New Englanders, Scotch-Irish, and Germans—and several minor concentrations of Scandinavians, Canadians, Dutch, Italians, Czechs, Japanese, and Mexicans.[2] The New England ex-

Robert P. Swierenga is Professor of History at Kent State University

1. Allan G. Bogue, *From Prairie to Cornbelt: Farming on the Illinois and Iowa Prairies in the Nineteenth Century* (Chicago, 1963), 194-95.

2. Excellent descriptions of these major settlement patterns are: John L. Shover, *First Majority—Last Minority: The Transformation of Rural Life in America* (DeKalb, Ill., 1976), 38-50; Frederick C. Luebke, "Ethnic Group Settlement on the Great Plains," *Agricultural History*, 8 (Oct., 1977), 405-30; Randall M. Miller, "Immigrants in the Old South," *Immigration History Newsletter*, X (Nov., 1978), 8-14; Hilldegard Binder Johnson, "The Location of German Immigrants in the Middle West," *Annals of the Association of American Geographers*, 41 (1951), 1-41; Frederick Jackson Turner, *The United States, 1830-1850, The Nation and Its Sections* (New York, 1935).

odus, which began in the early nineteenth century, carried Yankees across much of the northern United States. The New Englanders migrated in stages, first to upper New York and northwestern Pennsylvania (1800s), then to the "Burned-Over District" of western New York and northeast Ohio (1820s), next to southern Michigan or northern Illinois, southern Wisconsin, and Iowa (1840s and 1850s), and finally to Kansas and westward to Oregon (1870s). The Yankee frontiersmen usually arrived first, chose the richest glaciated soils, and transplanted intact their culture, churches, and schools.

While the Yankees moved across the northern tier of the frontier, the Scotch-Irish in Pennsylvania and the Carolinas, half a million strong by the end of the colonial era, crossed the mountains into Tennessee and Kentucky.[3] From the Appalachian valley they fanned out southward across the Gulf Plains and northward along the Ohio valley and eventually west of the Mississippi River into the hilly, unglaciated regions of eastern Missouri and southern Iowa. Typically, the Scotch-Irish spied out the "loose-dirt" bottom lands and sandy uplands with which they were familiar. Unfortunately, such hilly terrain often contained inferior soils. The Scotch-Irish dominated the interior South and Ohio Valley and stamped this region with a common ethnic and cultural identity that was unique in the nation. In 1850, 98 percent of the people in the South Central states were native-born, a higher proportion than any other region.

The third major ethnic contingent in rural America was the Germans, the largest non-English speaking immigrant group. Fed by a continuous stream of immigrants from the colonial period to World War I, Germans first settled in the lowland limestone soils of Pennsylvania and then after the Revolution they moved into the fertile glaciated oak openings and prairies of the Midwest from northern Ohio to Kansas and the Dakotas. Texas also attracted a large contingent, so that by 1900 almost a third of the Texans were either German or of Germanic ancestry.

Nationally, according to the 1910 census report, Germans were "over-represented" in agriculture by 51.8 percent. (See Table.) They comprised 2.7 percent of the total population, but 4.1 percent of the nation's farmers. Among the 670,000 immigrant farm operators they were the overwhelming nationality, with 33 percent. In 1880, Germans had made up 36 percent of all farmers, but in proportion to their total numbers, they were under-represented in farming by 2.6 percent. Thus, the German presence in agriculture, as with the

3. James G. Leyburn, *The Scotch-Irish, A Social History* (Chapel Hill, N.C., 1962).

Table. Percent Distribution of Population and Agricultural Workforce, by Nativity, 1880 and 1912

| NATIVITY | 1880 | | | 1910 | | |
|---|---|---|---|---|---|---|
| | Population (1) | Agricultural Workforce¹ (2) | Over-(Under-)Representation Col 2−1/1+100 | Population (1) | Agricultural Workforce² (2) | Over-(Under-)Representation Col 2−1/1 |
| United States | 86.7 | 89.4 | 3.1 | 85.3 | 87.6 | 7.7 |
| Germany | 3.9 | 3.8 | (-2.6) | 2.7 | 4.1 | 51.8 |
| Ireland | 3.7 | 1.8 | (-51.3) | 1.5 | .6 | (-60.0) |
| Great Britain | 1.8 | 1.4 | (-22.2) | 1.4 | 1.0 | (-28.6) |
| British/N. Amer. | 1.4 | 1.0 | (-28.6) | 1.3 | 1.1 | (-15.4) |
| Scandinavia | .9 | 1.2 | 33.3 | 1.3 | 2.9 | 123.1 |
| Other Countries | 1.6 | 1.4 | (-12.5) | 6.5 | 2.6 | (-60.0) |
| N (in 1000s) | 50,155 | 7,670 | | 91,972 | 5,441 | |

¹The 1880 census provides statistics by nativity for all workers in agriculture.

²The 1910 census provides statistics by nativity only for white farm operators.

Source: Compendium of the Tenth Census, June 1, 1880 (2 vols., Washington D.C., 1883), I, 482-87, II, 1368-69; Thirteenth Census of the United States, 1910, Vol. I, Population, 795, Vol. 5, Agriculture, 178.

Scandinavians, increased greatly at the end of the nineteenth century.

The Germans preferred to buy partially-improved farms rather than open new lands. There were many exceptions to this generalization, however. Carl Wittke reported that Germans developed 672,000 American farms, totaling one hundred million acres. Some of these farms were in colonial Pennsylvania, where Germans went to the frontier as frequently as the Scotch-Irish.[4] Wherever they settled, Germans established the reputation of developing excellent farms. The German farmer's regard for his barn and animals at the expense of his home and family is proverbial in frontier America. Nevertheless, in the Mennonite county of Lancaster, stone houses outnumbered stone barns among Germans, and small log barns were still the norm as late as the 1780s. The large "Swisser" stone barns in Pennsylvania "Dutch" country appeared only after the farmers had prospered greatly during the Revolution.[5]

The Germans in America comprised three diverse groups in language and religion.[6] There were the Anabaptist sects (Volga or Russo-Germans, Mennonites, Dunkers, and Amish), Lutherans and Reformed from northern Germany, and Catholics from Bavaria and the south. Each group maintained its cultural distance and distinctiveness and some, such as the Russians, spoke languages other than German. By 1900, the German immigrant population had swelled to three million, half of whom lived in the North Central states. Many others, such as the Russo-Germans, clustered throughout the great plains on land resembling their native steppes, where they uniformly introduced hard winter wheat. Prominent German areas were Lancaster County, Pennsylvania; Holmes and Madison counties, Ohio; Ellis County, Kansas; Franklin County, Missouri; and Jefferson County, Wisconsin. The latter two were 80 percent German in 1900.

Scandinavians numbered more than 1.2 million in 1910 and were concentrated in the heavily wooded, forest and lake country of the Upper Mississippi Valley, which resembled their homeland. Minnesota and Wisconsin were the primary areas, but scattered

4. Carl Wittke, *We Who Built America: The Saga of the Immigrant* (New York, 1946), 208. Wittke describes the settlement patterns of all of the major immigrant groups which are described in this and succeeding paragraphs.
5. James T. Lemon, *The Poor Man's Country: A Geographical Study of Early Southeastern Pennsylvania* (Baltimore and London, 1976), 177.
6. This and the following paragraphs rely heavily on Wittke, *We Who Built America*.

Swedish, Norwegians, Danish, and Finnish settlements also sprang up in Iowa, Nebraska, and the Dakotas. The Norwegians were the most rural and clannish of the Scandinavians. As late as 1940, over half of all midwestern Norwegians lived on farms or in small villages. Indeed, they were the only immigrant group with a lower proportion of city-dwellers than the native Americans. Swedes also led in the conquest of the rolling prairies. By 1925, they had cleared and opened an estimated twleve million acres. The 1910 census counted 156,000 Scandinavian farm operators, the second largest immigrant nationality. Indeed, the Scandinavians were over-represented in agriculture by 123 percent in 1918 (Table), which was more than twice the proportion among Germans. In 1880, the Scandinavians were the only major foreign-born group over-represented in agriculture. The Scandinavians truly sought after the land.

Other sizeable immigrant groups in the midwestern farm population were Canadians, English, Irish, Swiss, Dutch, Czechs (Bohemians), and Poles, but no group was over-represented in proportion to its total numbers. The Canadians, English, Irish, and Swiss were widely scattered in the Upper Great Lakes, but were especially strong in Michigan. The Swiss in northern Wisconsin laid the basis for the Swiss cheese industry in the 1840s and 1850s. The Dutch were concentrated particularly in the lake and woodland regions of southwestern Michigan, northern Illinois, and southern Wisconsin, but several thousand also settled on the prairies of Iowa and neighboring states. The Czechs preferred prairie land; the major colonies were in Wisconsin, Nebraska, and Texas. The latter state had 50,000 Czechs in 1910, mainly farmers. By that date one-third of all first generation Czechs in America followed agricultural pursuits. Among the southern and eastern European immigrants, the Czechs considered farming an ideal way of life.[7] Poles were more inclined to head for the cities, but some managed to acquire low-priced "cutover" timber land in northern Wisconsin and Minnesota or abandoned farms in the East. Many began as farm tenants or worked in the sawmills, mines, and quarries as day laborers before they became land owners. Polish farmers were less familiar with modern farming techniques than other immigrants, and therefore imitated their neighbors more than most.

7. In addition to Wittke, *We Who Built America*, 409-16, sociological analyses of specific Czech farming communities are: Robert L. Skrabanek, "The Influence of Cultural Backgrounds on Farming Practices in a Czech-American Rural Community," *Southwestern Social Science Quarterly*, 31 (1951), 258-62 and Russell Wilford Lynch, *Czech Farmers in Oklahoma: A Comparative Study of the Stability of a Czech Farm Group in Lincoln County, Oklahoma* ... (Oklahoma Agricultural and Mechanical College *Bulletin*, 39 [June, 1942]), 107.

The high proportion of northern European immigrants in rural midwestern communities was a result of several factors: the coincidence of their arrival and the opening of the frontier, the influence of the Homestead Act of 1862, the promotional efforts of railroad agents and immigration bureaus, their relative prosperity that enabled them to become farm owners, and the geographical similarity of the Midwest to their native lands.

Later immigrant groups had neither the opportunity and capital to obtain farm land nor the experience and temperament to confront a lonely and often hostile environment. But some southern and eastern Europeans could be found in the countryside, especially as truck farmers near coastal metropolises. Jewish farmers were prominent in the borscht belt of New York's Catskills, and among chicken ranchers in Petaluma, California and Vineland, New Jersey. Italians raised fruit and vegetables in the East, and in the Pacific Northwest they engaged in dairying, fruit raising, and built wineries in California (notably the Italian Swiss-Colony). California's Italians competed for prime farm land with Yugoslavs, Japanese, Portuguese, Armenians, Basques, and various northern European groups. The Portuguese distinguished themselves as dairymen in the San Francisco Bay and Sacramento areas. The Armenians were prominent in Fresno County as market gardeners. One developed the largest fig ranch in the world.[8]

The role as seasonal farm laborers of Orientals, Eastern Europeans, and Spanish-Americans, was also crucial to agricultural growth. The Chinese and Japanese provided the initial pool of "stoop" labor in the far west until the Oriental exclusion acts shut the door between 1882 and 1907. Filipinos and especially Mexicans had a near monopoly thereafter, except during the depression of the 1930s when tens of thousands were repatriated. The quota law of 1921 did not apply to Mexico and during the 1920s more than a million and a half Mexicans crossed the border. Most settled in the Southwest, but many moved into the large midwestern cities of Chicago, Kansas City, Minneapolis, and St. Paul. These migrants on the fruit and vegetable farms of the sunbelt and the midwest generally moved northward following the harvest in three main streams: from Florida to New Jersey, Texas to Michigan and Minnesota, and up California's Salinas and Sacramento-San Joaquin Valleys. The peak year of dependency on foreign farm workers was

8. Theodore Saloutos, "The Immigrant Contribution to American Agriculture," *Agricultural History*, 50 (Jan., 1976), 60-62.

1960 when the federal government admitted 460,000 for harvest labor.[9]

The Immigration Commission Reports give the rural concentration of the major immigrant groups in 1900. In descending order, the percentage of foreign-born, male bread-winners following agriculture pursuits was Norwegians fifty, Czechs thirty-two, Swedes thirty, Germans twenty-seven, British-Canadians twenty-two, English eighteen, Irish and French Canadians fourteen, Poles ten, Italians six, and Hungarians three. These percentages would increase an average of five points if sons of the foreign-born were included. Thus, most ethnic groups were more than half urban at a time when the national percentage was 45 percent. The census of 1910 further indicates the low incidence of immigrant farmers: only 12 percent of the nation's farm operators were foreign-born.[10]

The geographical distribution of immigrant farmers was strikingly uneven. In 1910, nearly seven out of ten lived in the Midwest, where they comprised 20.5 percent of all farm operators. However, in Minnesota and North Dakota more than half of the farmers were foreign-born, and in Wisconsin and South Dakota over 30 percent. The remaining three-tenths were nearly evenly divided between the Northeast and Far West regions, but their small absolute members were noticed more in the West where they comprised 23 percent of all farmers, compared to 11 percent in the East. A mere 12,000 immigrant farmers (.06 percent) settled in the South because of its reputedly inferior soils, slavery or its legacy, and the absence of friends and relatives. The immigrants, in short, chose the cities rather than the countryside, and those who opted for farming headed for the midwestern and plains states.

To what extent climate, ethnic idiosyncracy, and the pull of already-established communities accounted for the distribution of the immigrant groups is unknown. In general, however, immigrants first gathered in and near the large seaport cities of the Atlantic Coast, especially in the Middle Atlantic states, and to a lesser measure, near the Pacific harbor cities. They gradually spread out over the northern, central, and western sections of the country wherever transportation and job opportunities in agricultural and industry beckoned. Usually the immigrants clustered around communities of their compatriots. Some sought certain climates or soil

9. Louis Adamic, *A Nation of Nations* (New York and London, 1944), 62-65; Saloutos, "Immigrant Contribution," 63-65.

10. U.S. Immigration Commission, *Reports* (Washington, GPO, 1911), Vol. 28, 60-62. U.S. Bureau of the Census, 13th Census, *1910,* Vol. 5, Agriculture, 178.

areas that resembled their homelands, while others preferred urban life. Many who joined the frontier movement to the cornbelt and prairies eventually were swept back into the cities by the strong urban tide of the Industrial Revolution.

## Cultural Patterns in Farming

Throughout the history of settlement in the American wilderness, European immigrant farmers had to deal with a variety of unfamiliar soils, weather conditions, vegetation, and terrains. The fields of Europe had been cleared or drained for generations, if not centuries, and land was farmed intensively and with great variety of grains, fruits, vegetables, and livestock. The American frontier, whether forests or prairies, was strikingly different. It required that immigrant farmers adapt themselves to an alien land.

The degree to which the varying cultural backgrounds of the immigrants influenced their choice of settlement areas and affected their farming practices and success rate has long intrigued Americans. The literature of rural history is replete with contemporary comments and observations about the relationship between cultural background and farming behavior. Bogue identifies two key propositions in accounts of midwestern agriculture.[11] The first is that various ethnic groups, when learning to farm in America, initially drew upon their particular Old World skills and modes of husbandry, thereby introducing specific crops and farming techniques into American agriculture. The second hypothesis is that certain ethnic groups in the same geographical region farmed for generations in ways significantly different from their neighbors, within the limits of the common constraints imposed by climate and soils in each region. He finds the first proposition more plausible than the second, but neither has been sufficiently tested by systematic research. Only recently have scholars attempted comparative studies of ethnic cropping patterns, animal husbandry, technological skills, tenure differences, and mobility and persistence rates, based upon census records, tax lists, and estate inventories.[12]

11. Bogue, *Prairie to Cornbelt,* 237-38.
12. See, for example, Bogue, *Prairie to Cornbelt,* 25, 237-40; John G. Gagliardo, "Germans and Agriculture in Colonial Pennsylvania," *Pennsylvania Magazine of History and Biography,* 83 (1959), 192-218; James T. Lemon, "The Agricultural Practices of National Groups in Eighteenth-Century Southeastern Pennsylvania," *The Geographical Review,* 56 (Oct. 1966), 467-96; David Aidan McQuillan, "Adaptation of Three Immigrant Groups to Farming in Central Kansas, 1875-1925" (Ph.D.

Many of the traditional generalizations about ethnic behavior in agriculture have been tainted by stereotypes of "national character" or frontier mythologies. Benjamin Rush, Benjamin Franklin, and other scientists of the Revolutionary era, for example, believed that agricultural traditions of national groups were distinct. They cited as evidence the supposed superior farming practices in the eighteenth century of the Germans, as compared to their English and Scotch-Irish neighbors.[13] German farmers were literally described as "earth animals," superior to all other nationality groups in land selection, agricultural skills, animal husbandry, barn construction, product specialization, soil conversion, consumption habits, and labor-intensive family work teams.[14]

The classic statement of this "national character" genre is from the pen of Benjamin Rush, the renowned Philadelphia physician and one of the early advocates of German agricultural practices. German farms, said Rush in 1789, "may be distinguished from farms of other citizens . . . by the superior size of their farms, the height of their inclosures, the extent of their orchards, the fertility of their fields, the luxuriance of their meadows, and a general appearance of plenty and neatness in everything that belongs to them."[15] The Frenchman J. Hector St. John de Crevecoeur agreed with Rush. "Whence the difference arises I know not, but out of twelve families of emigrants of each country, generally seven Scotch will succeed,

diss., University of Wisconsin, 1975); John G. Rice, *Patterns of Ethnicity in a Minnesota County, 1880-1905* (Geographical Reports, 4, Norway, University of Umea, 1973); Rice, "The Role of Culture and Community in Frontier Prairie Farming," *Journal of Historical Geography*, 3 (1977), 155-75; Terry D. Jordan, *German Seed in Texas Soil: Immigrant Farmers in Nineteenth Century Texas* (Austin, 1966); Robert Ostergren, "Rättvik to Isanti: A Community Transplanted" (Ph.D. diss., University of Minnesota, 1976); E.D. Ball, "The Process of Settlement in 18th Century Chester County, Pa.: A Social and Economic History" (Ph.D. diss., University of Pennsylvania, 1973).

13. Lemon, "Agricultural Practices," 467-68, 495-96; Lemon, *Best Poor Man's Country,* xiv.

14. The "earth animals" quote is from Adolph Schock, *In Quest of Free Land* (Assen, Netherlands, 1964), 131. Major traditional stereotypical studies are: Walter M. Kollmorgan, "The Pennsylvania German Farmer," in Rudolph Wood (ed.), *The Pennsylvania Germans* (Princeton, 1942), 27-55; Stevenson Whitcomb Fletcher, *Pennsylvania Agriculture and Country Life, 1640-1840* (Harrisburg, 1950); Richard H. Shryock, "British Versus German Traditions in Colonial Agriculture," *Mississippi Valley Historical Review, 26 (1939),* 39-54. Similar perspectives regarding nineteenth-century German farmers are Joseph Schafer, "The Yankee and Teuton in Wisconsin," *Wisconsin Magazine of History,* 6 (1922), 125-45, 261-79, 386-402; *Ibid.,* 7 (1923), 3-19, 148-71; William H. Gehrke, "The Ante-Bellum Agriculture of the Germans in North Carolina," *Agricultural History,* 9 (July, 1935), 143-60; Marcus Lee Hansen, *The Immigrant in American History* (Cambridge, Mass., 1940), 61-63; Saloutos, "Immigrant Contribution," 45-67.

15. Quoted in Saloutos, "Immigrant Contribution," 48.

nine Germans, and four Irish. . . . ''[16] Methodical, frugal, and industrious, German farmers rapidly achieved self-sufficiency, according to these accounts. They raised other cereals to supplement their principal cash crop, wheat, and perfected the Conestoga wagon and bred the Conestoga horse to carry their products to market. Scotch-Irish farmers, on the other hand, were said to mine their land and leave livestock and machinery to weather the winter elements unprotected. James Lemon is correct in viewing the origins of such attitudes as an English colonial import, stemming from a set of stereotypes held by Englishmen about the superiority of German peasants and the inferiority of Celtic peoples in agricultural practices.[17] Once fixed, the beliefs were reinforced by late-nineteenth century ethnic societies and filiopietistic historians.

In marked contrast to the ethnic apologists, frontier historian Frederick Jackson Turner, the most respected scholar in the early twentieth century, completely rejected the nationalist views of Rush, Franklin, and other European-oriented historians. The frontier, for Turner, was a democratic melting pot, the great economic leveller, a place that destroyed the European "cultural baggage" of the immigrant pioneers. The land and not the culture of the immigrant was the significant factor in acculturation. After a very short period of settlement, immigrant farmers became indistinguishable from American-born neighbors in the operation of their farming businesses.[18]

Several modern studies, based upon the manuscript population and agricultural census lists, seem to confirm Turner's thesis of rapid assimilation and cultural conformity among immigrant farmers. In a study of early settlement in a Wisconsin county (Trempealeau), Merle Curti compared the socioconomic structure and relative economic success of all major nativity groups, for the census years 1850, 1860, 1870, and 1880. Initially, Americans and English-speaking foreign-born farmers owned better land, had more implements and livestock, obtained higher crop yields, and were less transient than the Continental-born farmers. This was largely due to their lateness of settlement and inadequate financial resources.

16. J. Hector St. John de Crevecoeur, *Letters from an American Farmer and Sketches of Eighteenth-Century America* (New York, 1963), 79. This is quoted in Crevecouer's famous essay, "What is an American?"

17. Lemon, "Agricultural Practices," 493-94; Lemon, *Poor Man's Country*, 17-18.

18. Frederick Jackson Turner, "The Significance of the Frontier in American History," American Historical Association, *Annual Report for the Year 1893* (Washington, G.P.O., 1894), 199-227. Turner elaborated his thesis in *The Frontier in American History* (New York, 1920).

Continental-born farmers arrived after the Anglo-Americans had picked the choice prairie lands. Gradually, however, the poorer immigrant groups—Irish, Poles, and Germans—made steady gains and within a generation their farm valuations approached the level of the Americans. The only group to lag behind was the Norwegians, who arrived last and selected hilly, wooded slopes resembling their homeland. Even this difference was only in degree, not in kind; and Curti stressed the essential similarity of all ethnic groups in frontier Wisconsin.[19]

In his study of pioneer farming in Illinois and Iowa, Bogue specifically addressed the issue of whether ethnic groups in the same region farmed differently over a considerable period of time. The conventional wisdom was that Germans and Swedes raised more pigs than did Yankees. Charles Towne and Edward Wentworth, in their history of the pig, state that these two nationality groups pulled themselves "out of the red" with a "combination of pluck, perspicacity, and pigs. . . . Less skilled in the management of horses, sheep, and beef cattle than the English and native Americans, they concentrated with dogged tenacity on their hogs."[20] In his statistical analysis of hog production in Hamilton and Bremer counties in northcentral Iowa in 1880, Bogue found that foreign-born farmers actually owned *fewer* swine than native farmers, a direct contradiction of the prevailing wisdom. In their crop production, however, immigrant farmers conformed to the general observation. Immigrants raised more wheat and less corn than natives and they hired more farm hands, an indication that they practiced a more intensive type of agriculture.[21] Thus, the native-born farmers in Iowa anticipated the future corn-hog symbiosis more than did immigrant farmers, but neither group differed substantially.

Additional midwestern studies bear out this conclusion of semblance. Seddie Cogswell compared livestock valuation and the number of farm animals in six eastern Iowa counties (1850-1880) and concluded that "for the most part there was essential similarity between the farms of native-and foreign-born. . . . [They] did not differ very much, either in the numbers of the various farm animals or in their mix."[22] The immigrant farmers had a slightly lower in-

19. Merle Curti, *The Making of an American Community: A Case Study of Democracy in a Frontier County* (Stanford, Cal., 1959), 80-83, 91-97, 179-97.
20. Quoted in Bogue, *Prairie to Cornbelt*, 237.
21. *Ibid.*, 238.
22. Seddie Cogswell, Jr., *Tenure, Nativity and Age as Factors in Iowa Agriculture, 1850-1880* (Ames, Iowa, 1975), 75, 78.

vestment in livestock, but this was more than offset by a greater amount of machinery. Donald Winters likewise found that native or foreign-born tenants in Iowa were not distinguishable in terms of rental arrangements, farm practices, or success rates.[23]

In a pathbreaking study, Robert Ostergren compared cropping patterns and livestock enterprises among Old Americans, Germans, and Scandinavian farmers in Isanti County, Minnesota, in 1880. He concluded that cultural factors had a minimal impact on crop decisions compared to the overrriding effects of geographic and environmental conditions in the community. Only in the case of secondary crops such as oats and livestock such as sheep did cultural traditions have an impact.[24] The economic status of the various ethnic groups in Isanti measured by land and wealth data likewise revealed few striking differences not explained by length of occupance.[25] Ostergren traced one group of Isanti Swedes back to their Old Country parish of Rättvik and compared their farming practices before and after migration. This thoroughly innovative technique revealed that in Rättvik barley had been the primary crop, with oats a secondary crop. In Minnesota, by contrast, wheat (which had never been raised in Sweden) was the primary crop and oats a secondary one. The Rättvik colonists transplanted their institutions, Ostergren concluded, but not their farming practices. "When it came to making a living it seems that the immigrants were faced with little choice but to adapt as quickly as possible to the American system." "In fact," said Ostergren, "there is little evidence that there ever was much resistance to the dictates of the new environment and the local market economy. The situation was so different from home, that one probably did not even seriously contemplate farming in the same manner."[26]

David McQuillan used a different technique to assess the adaptation process among immigrant groups in the more arid region of central Kansas. He selected three ethnic groups—Swedes, Mennonites, and French-Canadians—and compared farming practices not only between the groups but *within* the groups by selecting one township in which the group was clearly dominant and one township in which the particular immigrant group was a minority among native-born farmers. Rural segregation of the ethnic groups had no significant impact on farming practices, McQuillan concluded. Only the Men-

23. Donald L. Winters, *Farmers Without Farms: Agricultural Tenancy in Nineteenth-Century Iowa* (Westport, Conn., 1978), 77, 88, 135.
24. Ostergren, *Rättvik to Isanti,* 107-21.
25. *Ibid.,* 121-28.
26. *Ibid.,* 140.

"Wood Self-Rake Reaper." A typical illustration from 19th century farming catalogues. (SOCIETY COLLECTION)

nonites diverged from the American norm by operating smaller farms of higher value, by diversifying their crop and livestock enterprises, and by owning debt-free farms rather than rentals.[27] Religious values may have been the determining factor in the case of the Mennonites, although McQuillan does not pursue this intriguing lead.

In brief, the immigrant farmers of frontier Wisconsin, Illinois, Iowa, and Minnesota adjusted rapidly and without apparent difficulty. From the earliest period of settlement, they made greater gains than the native-born, obtaining a proportionate share of the land and developing unsurpassed commercial farming businesses. Instead of the common picture of the relatively "poor" and traditional-bound immigrant farmer, the census research indicates that measured by farm size, livestock, crops, and machinery, European immigrants quickly adopted the best practices of the region and they had the financial resources to do so. At least at the broad level of the nationality group, economic differentials did not mark immigrant farmers from natives.

This midwestern picture is repeated in Terry Jordan's detailed comparison of German and Anglo-American farmers in Texas (1850-1880). Although the Germans clung to Old World cultural traits that made them distinctive for generations among Texas

27. McQuillan, "Adaptation of Three Immigrant Groups to Farming."

farmers, in other important ways they "became Southerners almost from the first." The Germans were more attracted to the soil and committed to commercial agriculture. They farmed with greater intensity and productivity, were less mobile, and had a higher rate of landownership. They diversified more by actively pursuing market gardening near the major Texas towns, by producing wine and white potatoes (in a sweet potato region), by cultivating small grains, and by using mules instead of horses as draft animals. But the similarities between Germans and southern-born farmers were "even more striking than the differences." The Germans were imitators rather than innovators. They introduced no new major crops or livestock practices, but rather began cultivating the three southern staples—corn, cotton, and sweet potatoes. They adopted the southern farmstead architecture and open range system, with no barns for wintering stock. They neither dunged their fields nor stall-fed their livestock.[28]

In a German settlement in the Missouri Ozarks dating from the 1890s, Russell Gerlach compared agricultural land use and crop production in 1972 in four sample counties that contained clearly defined German and non-German farming regions.[29] As in Texas, more Germans were full-time farmers and they worked their land more intensively, but their crops, farm size, yield per acre, and tenancy rates did not appreciably differ from that of the Old Stock Americans who had emigrated from Appalachia to the Ozarks in the last century. The major difference is cultural. Germans are more traditional and share a deeper commitment to an agrarian way of life than the native Americans, but their farming behavior is barely distinguishable.

Jordan suggests a four-class typology of the "survival tendencies" of imported agricultural systems by immigrant groups.[30] (1) Old Country traits never introduced, such as the Texas Germans' failure to dung fields and winter livestock in barns. (2) European traits introduced but not successfully implemented. For Texan Germans these included viticulture, European fruit trees, the farm village plan and communal herding on the West Texan plains, and small grain production in the east Texas cotton belt. (3) European traits that survived only the first generation. These included

28. Jordan, *German Seed in Texas Soil*, chaps. 4-6. The quotes are on p. 195.
29. Russell L. Gerlach, *Immigrants in the Ozarks: A Study in Ethnic Geography* (Columbia and London, 1976).
30. This paragraph and the four following are summarized from Jordan, *German Soil in Texas Soil*, 194-203.

small-scale farm operations, German farmstead structures, and the free-labor system in east Texas. By the 1850s, some Germans in East Texas were purchasing slaves. (4) Long-lived traits. Texas German farmers were distinguishable for generations by their labor-intensive, highly productive, stable, diversified agriculture.

The determinant factors in these various outcomes were the physical and cultural-economic environments. The mild Texas climate, for example, obviated the need for large barns and winter quartering of livestock. Without barns, manure was lost. The economic milieu likewise encouraged immigrants to adapt farming practices of the region because those of the native Southerners were proven superior. For example, Germans shifted from small family farms to large-scale commercial agriculture common to the region. Moreover, those traits that did survive, either intact or modified, such as intensive farming methods, cheese-making, and cultivating white potatoes, were those that did not interfere with or undermine the economic viability of Texas agriculture.

Many of these surviving traits were curiously absent in the earliest years of settlement but emerged later in what Jordan calls a "cultural rebound." The initial shock of adjustment to a new environment apparently inclined immigrants to ape indigeneous American practices. But gradually this initial "artificial" assimilation was reversed and unique dormant traits reappeared. The Germans were an alien group in Texas confronting an agricultural society that had evolved over two hundred years. The uniqueness almost guaranteed the survival of their "Europeanness."

Whether the "built-in" traits of agricultural immigrants from northwestern and central Europe suvived in American farm communities depended largely on the disimilarity to their Old Country environment. The more alien the cultural environment, the more defensive and persistent the group. Since the southern United States was not as congenial to European-born farmers as the northern regions, immigrants in the South retained their distinctiveness more than did their compatriots in the North. On the other hand, German wheat farmers in Kansas, Rhine winegrowers in California, and Norwegian dairymen in Wisconsin risked losing their ethnic identity quickly because they blended in with their neighbors from the beginning.

The rapid assimilation of immigrant farmers was due to more than a familiar cultural environment. Before leaving Europe, immigrants often purchased crude farming manuals and guide books to ease their introduction to America. They also sought direct contacts with American neighbors to learn proven farm methods in the area. Many unmarried young men and women "hired out" to Americans as field hands and domestics. If fellow-ethnics had previously settled the region, newcomers naturally sought their aid and served "apprenticeships" under them. Despite the rapid acculturation, foreign-born farmers, of course, always faced a greater adjustment than natives.

The Texan farmers of German ancestry today still retain some distinctive social-cultural traits, but Jordan concluded that differences in agricultural practices are largely "invisible," if they persist at all. As farmers and ranchers, the Germans in Texas are businessmen first and foremost; they are ethnics only in the farmhouse, in church, and in social clubs.[31] This finding agrees with Bogue's assessment of midwestern ethnic farmers: Cultural differences "were more apparent than real—most obvious in food ways, dress, and lingual traits, and less important when the farmer decided on his combination of major enterprises."[32]

The census research summarized here is seminal. It provides the first solid evidence regarding ethnic patterns in agriculture. But all of these studies suffer from two limitations, which are inherent in the census sources. The first is that all farmers of a given nationality are lumped together, without taking account of local and regional differences in the motherland. The censuses only record the country of birth, of course, and it would be a herculean task to link the census with foreign records at the local level. Yet in nineteenth century Europe, farming practices, life styles, and even languages often differed widely between two adjacent provinces in the same country, or even between two parishes in the same province. Secondly, the early studies slight the importance of religious group differences, again because the censuses do not report religious or denominational affiliation. Thousands of close-knit, church-centered, ethnic communities dotted the landscape of rural America a century ago. These homogeneous clusters of people often had common origins in the Old Country and they deliberately sought to create isolated settlements in hopes of preserving their cultural identity and retaining the mother tongue for generations to come. Such cohesive sectarian communities differed greatly from settlements composed of a mixture of main-line "church" groups, even if all were Protestant.[33]

31. *Ibid.*, 203.
32. Bogue, *Prairie to Cornbelt*, 238.
33. This is the perceptive approach of Marianne Wokeck in her dissertation in progress at Temple University. See Marianne Wokeck, "Cultural Persistence and Adaptation: The Germans of Lancaster County, Pennsylvania, 1729-76," in Paul

There are several recent micro-studies that take into account the parish background of American immigrant farmers. These are highly rewarding and suggestive of the direction of future research in agricultural history. John Rice studied farming patterns in a six-township area of frontier Minnesota (Kandiyohi County), which was settled by Swedes, Norwegians, Irish, and Americans from the East.[34] Each of the nationality groups was diverse in origin, except for one group of Swedes who came from the same parish—Gagnef in Dalarna Province. Two other Swedish settlements were more diverse, comprising people from many parishes, yet all from the same provinces. Moreover, each of the three subnational Swedish culture groups was affiliated with the three major church communities in the sample townships. Thus, Rice was able to compare agricultural practices of Swedish cultural groups defined at the national, provincial, and parish levels.

Rice's findings, based on both Swedish and American sources, reveal that farmers from all the nationality groups, except the Swedes of Gagnef parish, were similar in their cropping patterns, livestock holdings, persistence rates, and economic status. All the groups concentrated on wheat. The Scandinavians (including the Norwegians) raised more livestock, especially sheep, than the Irish and Americans, and the Swedes were more persistent. But the Gagnef parishioners stand out as unique. They retained their oxen as draught animals into the 1880s, long after the other farmers in the area had switched to horses. The Gagnef community was the most stable by far, and it prospered economically, advancing from the poorest of the Swedish settlements to the wealthiest. In sum, the agricultural experience of the church-centered Gagnef group, transplanted en masse from Dalarna, differed markedly from the neighboring immigrant settlements, including those of Swedes and Norwegians. Religion and its cultural trappings, not nationality per se, determined farming behavior among Minnesota Swedes.

The impact of religion on immigrant farmers was not unique to Swedes. A century early in southeastern Pennsylvania, sectarian "plain folk," Mennonites from the Rhine Valley and Switzerland, Friends (Quakers) from England and Wales, and German Baptist "Dunkers" and Moravian Brethren similarly occupied and used the land differently than immigrants from mainline European chur-

Uselding, ed., *Business and Economic History Papers Presented at the Twenty-Fourth Annual Meeting of the Business History Conference* (Urbana, Ill., 1978), n.p.
34. The findings of this paragraph and the next are from Rice, "The Role of Culture" and "Community in Frontier Prairie Farming," 166-75.

ches—Lutheran, Reformed, Anglican, and Presbyterian. The sect groups valued discipline and cooperation. The Moravians lived communally in agricultural villages, following the European "open-field" system, but the Mennonites and Quakers lived on family farms. The sects were tightly clustered geographically, owned the most valuable farms, and were least transient. Although most farmers in Lancaster and Chester counties were involved in general mixed agriculture with an emphasis on wheat, the Mennonites and Quakers farmed more intensively, sowed more wheat acreage, and possessed more livestock than other national and denominational groups.[35] Thus, in a relatively homogeneous agricultural region, the only significant differences in farming behavior derived from religious, rather than ethnic origins. The seven Amana villages in Iowa and numerous Spanish-American peasant villages in New Mexico, the latter antedating the Mexican war of independence from Spain in the 1820s, provide additional examples of religiously-based communities that to this day use the open-field system of agricultural settlement. In all of these communities, behavioral distinctions in farming can be determined only through microscopic local studies.

## Contributions

Not only did immigrant farmers bring to America a willingness to confront an alien land, they also made specific contributions to agriculture.[36] The most general contribution of farmers from the advanced nations of northern Europe was simply their dedication to farming as a way of life and their skill in farm techniques, animal husbandry, and cropping practices. The extent to which the idealized family-sized farm has survived the forces of modernization is largely due to the determination of third and fourth generation immigrants to maintain their traditional life style and values.

In animal husbandry, immigrant farmers throughout the northern part of the country consistently set the standard for livestock winter care, utilization of manure, and selective breeding. The Pennsylvania Germans by the late eighteenth century had demonstrated the necessity of huge, functional barns, but native-born farmers were exceedingly slow to emulate them.[37] As late as 1849, a Dutch

35. Lemon, *Poor Man's Country*, 63-64, 81-85, 174, and *passim*; Lemon, "Agricultural Practices," 467-96.
36. The best survey is Saloutos, "Immigrant Contribution," 45-67. The 91 notes also provide an extensive bibliography.
37. Perry Wells Bidwell and John I. Falconer, *History of Agriculture in the Northern United States, 1620-1860* (Washington, D.C., 1925), 107-08, 122-23.

immigrant in central Iowa reported to relatives in the Province of Friesland: "Americans do not have barns. . . . As a rule the cattle here are not as heavy as in Friesland, and as far as I can see, this is caused by the fact that they are left on their own during the winter. Calves are not placed in the stable and no colts are taken inside, so livestock suffers terribly."[38] From their firsthand knowledge, immigrants, especially those from the British Isles, introduced in the half century after Independence the improved varieties of animals developed in Europe, such as the Spanish Marino sheep and English cattle and hogs—the Herefords, Shorthorns, Durhams, and Devons. Indeed, as with the Industrial Revolution of the nineteenth century, English agricultural reforms of the eighteenth century came a generation or two earlier than in America and provided the impetus for change, especially in livestock.[39]

Immigrant farmers also contributed to the introduction of new or improved varieties of plants and crops that were so important in the development of American agriculture. In the Carolina and Georgia tidewater region in the eighteenth century, French settlers led in the introduction of the more esoteric agricultural products such as grapes, silk-worm and mulberry trees, olives, and indigo.[40] The Frenchmen, Lewis Gervais, Lewis St. Pierre and Pierre Legaux, successfully transplanted native French grapevines and established the vineyard industry in North America. Similarly, Andrew Deveaux was the provincial indigo expert whose efforts raised the quality of American indigo to that of the best French product. Farmers of English-stock in New England and the Middle Colonies, meanwhile, introduced the cultivation of grasses and legumes for animal forage and hay. The fact that early clovers were simply called "English grass" testifies to their origin.

Notable nineteenth century plant imports were Grimm alfalfa and Turkey Red wheat. A German immigrant to Carver County, Minnesota in 1857, Wendelin Grimm, brought a twenty-pound bag of alfalfa seed from his homeland. Over a number of years the alfalfa acclimatized to withstand winterkill until it became the prime

38. Robert P. Swierenga, ed., "A Dutch Immigrant's View of Frontier Iowa" (Sjoerd Aukes Sipma, *Belangryke Berigten uit Pella, in de Vereenigde Staten van Noord-Amerika* [Important Reports from Pella, in the United States of North America], 1849), *Annals of Iowa*, 3rd Series, 38 (Fall, 1965), 95, 89.

39. Rodney C. Loehr, "The Influence of English Agriculture on American Agriculture," *Agricultural History*, 11 (Jan. 1937), 3-15.

40. Arthur H. Hirsch, "French Influence on American Agriculture in the Colonial Period With Special Reference to Southern Provinces," *Ibid.*, 4 (Jan., 1930), 1-9. See also Arthur P. Whitaker, "The Spanish Contribution to American Agriculture," *Ibid.*, 3 (Jan., 1929), 1-14.

forage crop of the Northwest. Agricultural historians have stated that "its permanence, enormous yields, high protein content, economy as a crop, and value as a soil builder and weed throttler is almost without parallel in plant history."[41] No wonder that farmers called it the "everlasting clover seed!" Mennonite settlers from the Crimea introduced Turkey Red wheat in south-central Kansas in 1873, and this hardy winter wheat and other durum varieties became within a generation the great cash crop of the semi-arid regions of the northwestern plains. Ten years earlier, Russian immigrants had brought durum wheat to the Dakotas. In the 1890s, other Russian peasants brought to the United States from their native steppes the seeds of kabanka and arnautska wheat and also special rye and sunflower seeds, all of which became widely cultivated on the plains.[42] The white potato is another plant that added variety to the American diet because of the persistent efforts of German and Irish farmers to cultivate it.

Farmland reclamation was another immigrant specialty, especially among those groups who arrived penniless after the great homesteading era had ceased. "The foreign-born take the marginal land," Edmund de S. Brunner declared, "hoping that their energy and muscle will overcome other handicaps."[43] The Poles, Russians, and Finns were notable examples. Between 1870 and 1920, three million Polish peasants migrated to the United States. They were unskilled and poor but willing to work hard and accumulate savings. With these meager savings some 750,000 Poles purchased farms abandoned by New Englanders in Massachusetts, the Connecticut Valley, and upstate New York. Others acquired lower quality lands in the Midwest and Texas. By dint of toil and thrifty management, Poles restored numerous farms to a productive state. By 1940, some 30,000 Russian immigrants were also in the land, many in the East on abandoned farms.[44] The Polish and Russian story is repeated among the Finns, who were too poor to buy choice farms.[45] By working first as the lowest-paid laborers in the mills,

41. Saloutos, "Immigrant Contribution," 66; Peter C. Marzio, ed., *A Nation of Nations: The People Who Came to America as Seen Through Objects and Documents Exhibited at the Smithsonian Institution* (New York, 1976), 148.

42. Adamic, *Nation of Nation,* 155.

43. Edmund de S. Brunner, *Immigrant Farmers and Their Children* (Garden City, N.Y., 1929), 44.

44. Wittke, *We Who Built America,* 421, 428-29; Saloutos, "Immigrant Contribution," 56-57.

45. A. William Hogland, "Finnish Immigrant Farmers in New York, 1910-1960," in O. Fritrof Ander, ed., *In the Trek of the Immigrants: Essays Presented to Carl Wittke* (Rock Island, Ill., 1964), 141-55.

mines, and forests of the East coast or Midwest, they slowly accumulated enough capital to buy the "cutover" lumber lands of northern Wisconsin, Michigan, and Minnesota. These areas had thin, rocky soil and required much back-breaking labor to root out the stumps before the land could be farmed. In 1920, 90 percent of the Finns in Wisconsin agriculture were in the cutover area. Other Finns purchased abandoned farms in the old agricultural regions of New England and New York. The Finnish historian, A. William Hogland, has described one such group of several hundred Finns who in 1910, at the behest of local real estate agents, began settling on abandoned land in New York's hill country. The farms sold for $500 to $3,000. The Finns eventually by 1950 numbered over five hundred and dominated the agriculture of three townships. Most had little farming experience; yet they developed profitable dairy farms and during the 1930s turned to large-scale poultry raising. The Finns played a major part in the agricultural revival in New York after World War I.

Although most immigrant farmers brought less capital with them to the frontier than the native-born farmers, at least one group of Italian farmers in California, led by Amadeo Peter Giannini, founded the Bank of Italy which subsequently became the Bank of America. The credit operation of the Bank of America had a profound impact on the agricultural development of the state. An immigrant from Russian Poland, David Lukin, likewise strengthened the marketing mechanism of American farmers by protecting their export markets in Europe through the creation of the International Institute of Agriculture (now the United Nations Food and Agriculture Organization). This organization served as a clearing house of information on European crop production and prices, which enabled American farmers to compete in the world market.[46]

## Conclusion

The forces of change in modern life are breaking down the local ethnic and cultural distinctions in American agriculture; they are tending to "homogenize rural society." But in the past local conditions varied greatly and the process of acculturation was uneven. Unfortunately, the ethnic variety in rural America remains an enigma because the subject of ethnicity and agriculture is virtually unexplored. Marcus Lee Hansen's 1940 list of "suggestive subjects for investigation" remains intact. Hansen urged the study of "the

46. Saloutos, "Immigrant Contribution," 66-67.

immigrant as an outright [land] purchaser, the rise of the hired land to ownership; the immigrant as renter or mortgaged debtor; occupation of abandoned farms by any race; the different racial customs in providing for the second generation; the immigrant as a market gardener, cotton planter or tobacco grower, as a fruitman, rancher or ordinary prairie mixed-farmer; the employment of farm hands and older sons in lumbering, ice cutting and other seasonal labor; the attitude toward improvements and scientific farming.''[47] Comparative local studies of specific ethnic groups, considering topics such as these, would greatly enlarge our understanding of rural America and the impact on ethnic groups of the forces of modernization since the early days of settlement.

47. Hansen, *Immigrant in American History*, n200.

RICHARD H. ZEITLIN


# WHITE EAGLES IN THE NORTH WOODS:
# POLISH IMMIGRATION TO RURAL WISCONSIN
# 1857-1900


During the century following 1820, nearly 28 million people crossed the
Atlantic Ocean to settle in the United States.[1] These individuals, and those
who preceded them, participated in the largest population movement in the
history of mankind. Emigration from Europe to America altered the
course of world events, first, by populating the sparsely-settled North
American continent, second, by fostering the development of the dynamic
society of the United States, and third, by alleviating some of the distur-
bances caused by overcrowding and industrialization on the resources of
the Old World.[2]

The population of America is composed of very heterogeneous elements
as the result of the phenomenon of immigration. Indeed, the single common experience shared by all people of the United States is the fact that, at
one time or another, all migrated from someplace else. President Franklin
D. Roosevelt, for this very reason, correctly addressed the Daughters of the
American Revolution in 1938 as "my fellow immigrants."[3]

Responding at different times to political, religious, and most importantly, to economic conditions, immigrants from different areas of Europe
were drawn to America. Upon arriving in the United States, immigrants
frequently located themselves among people from the same areas in
Europe. Friends, relatives, and neighbors from the homeland had often
been in communication with one another by letter. Potential migrants
learned of job opportunities through this channel of information and were
also provided with temporary living quarters until they could establish
themselves in the New World. In other words, migrants chose specific locations in the United States because of the information provided for them by

---

[1] *U.S. Senate Executive Document* No. 747, 61st Congress 2nd session, *Reports of the U.S.
Immigration Commission,* 42 vols. (Washington, D.C., 1911), Vol. 1, *Abstracts,* p. 23. Cited
hereafter as *Sen. Doc.* with appropriate number, title of volume, and *Rpt. Imig. Com.*

[2] Franklin D. Scott, *The Peopling of America: Perspectives on Immigration,* American
Historical Association Pamphlet No. 241 (Washington, D.C., 1963), pp. 5-6.

[3] Speech delivered by President Franklin D. Roosevelt to Daughters of the American
Revolution, April 21, 1938, *New York Times,* April 22, 1938.


69

previous settlers who were their countrymen. This process has been called "chain migration."[4]

Because of the process of chain migration, communities of immigrants from particular locations in Europe arose in both urban and rural areas in the United States. Language and cultural adjustments were thereby minimized as the new settlers began operating within the context of the American economy. These clusterings formed the basis for what are known as ethnic groups.

Andrew Greeley provides a useful and streamlined definition of ethnic groups. According to Greeley, ethnic groups are "human collectivities based on an assumption of common origin, real or imaginary."[5] Recent commentators have emphasized the fact that ethnic consciousness became important after members of a group began interacting in the new environment of the United States.

Frequently, European peasants had but little understanding of their common backgrounds. They identified themselves as citizens of certain towns or provinces of the homeland. Only after arriving in the social setting of America did they begin to realize that commonality of language, religion, and social custom made them distinctive. "Ethnicization" took place, in other words, after arrival in the United States. Intergroup experience and internal conflicts gave rise to ethnic awareness.[6]

One of the largest human waves of migrants to the United States came from east-central Europe, especially from Poland. Reliable statistics on total Polish immigration are not readily available, but it is estimated that between two and three million Poles journeyed to the United States in the period between 1865 and 1920.[7]

---

[4] John MacDonald and Leatrice MacDonald, "Urbanization, Ethnic Groups and Social Segmentation," *Social Research,* Vol. 29 (Winter, 1962), 435; *Rpt. Imig. Com., Sen. Doc.* No. 747, Vol. 1, *Abstracts,* p. 187.

[5] Andrew M. Greeley, "Ethnicity as an Influence on Behavior," in Otto Feintein (ed.) *Ethnic Groups in the City* (Toronto, London, Lexington, Massachusetts, 1971), p. 4.

[6] Victor L. Greene, *For God and Country: The Rise of Polish and Lithuanian Consciousness in America 1860–1910* (Madison, Wisconsin, 1975), p. 3, p. 10; S. R. Charsley, "Theory of Ethnic Group Formation," in Abner Cohen (ed.) *Urban Ethnicity* (London, New York, Toronto, 1974), p. 363.

[7] Helena Z. Lopata, "The Formation of Voluntary Associations in an Ethnic Community: Polonia" unpublished Ph.D., University of Chicago, 1954, p. 15; also see Helena Z. Lopata, *Polish Americans: Status Competition in an Ethnic Community* (Englewood Cliffs, N.J., 1976), *passim.*; Anthony Kuzniewski, Jr., "Faith and Fatherland: An Intellectual History of the Polish Immigrant Community in Wisconsin 1838–1918," unpublished Ph.D., Harvard University, 1973, p. 30. Recently, scholars have been systematically exploring manuscript archival data for biographic and demographic information concerning Polish immigrants. See Maria J. E. Copson-Niecko, "The Poles in America From the 1830s to 1870s, Some Reflections on the Possibilities of Research," in Frank Mocha (ed.) *Poles in America* (Stevens Point, Wisconsin, 1978), 45–302.

Polish emigration to the United States has been divided into three time periods. The first, and smallest, group came during the Colonial period, between 1608 and 1778. These people came as individual adventurers and participated in a wide range of activities in the New World. Political exiles made up the second wave. Because of their revolutionary activities in Europe, these individuals sought refuge and freedom in America between 1778 and 1865. The third wave was composed of masses of peasants seeking to better themselves. It is this last wave, which began about 1860 and lasted until the 1920s, which is the most relevant for our purposes. This emigration will be mainly dealt with hereafter.[8]

Like other immigrants, Poles availed themselves of the opportunities for employment in industrial pursuits. Almost 90 percent of the total Polish immigration settled in industrial and urban areas in the United States. Like their fellow new immigrants, Poles were directed into industry because of the functioning of the expanding American economy in these fields, even though 64.5 percent of them had been engaged in agricultural activities in Europe.[9]

Many Polish immigrants settling in the Midwest, however, were able to secure farmlands. In Wisconsin, for instance, over 30 percent of the total engaged in agricultural pursuits.[10] In comparative terms, Poles in agriculture proved to be the leading group of new immigrants in the rural areas of the United States and concentrated themselves overwhelmingly in the North-Central and Prairie states.[11]

Many factors influenced Poles to leave their native lands and emigrate to the United States. Small agricultural holdings, rising birth rates, high taxes, lack of adequate machinery, falling world grain prices, military service, political tensions all played a role in creating the social climate contributing to emigration. But, individual motivations may not have been based totally on an analysis of these conditions. Some people had a spirit of adventure, heard of the opportunities in the United States, and decided to leave Europe and see for themselves what was going on across the Atlantic.

"My father was a great dancer," explained Peter Mlynek:

He liked to dance. He had heard of the U.S.A. from somebody . . . and he just

---

[8] Neil C. Sandberg, *Ethnic Identity and Assimilation: Polish-American Community* (New York, London, Washington, 1974), p. 10.

[9] *Rpt. Imig. Com., Sen. Doc.* No. 282, *Occupations of Immigrants,* p. 14; *Ibid. Sen. Doc.* No. 338, Vol. 1, *Immigrants in Cities,* p. 125.

[10] *Ibid. Sen. Doc.* No. 633, Vol. 22, *Immigrants in Industries,* pt. 24, *Recent Immigrants in Agriculture,* p. 153.

[11] *Ibid.,* p. 8.

picked up one day when he had accumulated enough passage money. He was headed for no particular place in the U.S.A., he knew no one anywhere in this country; he travelled with no friends or relatives. He did strike up some friendships on board ship, however, and since these people were headed for Wisconsin, he followed, and found himself in Trempealeau County.[12]

For whatever their reasons, millions of Poles emigrated to the United States. Pushed and pulled by circumstances often beyond their control, individuals and groups responded by making the arduous voyage across the Atlantic in search of opportunity and the chance to begin life again in a new social and economic setting. This was not a movement of the "huddled masses" or only of the "tired and poor yearning to breathe free" as Emma Lazarus' poem inscribed on the base of the Statue of Liberty would have it, but rather a movement of the young, the energetic, the confident, and the adventurous.[13]

Trying to determine the total number of Poles who emigrated to Wisconsin is difficult because Poland had been partitioned by its more powerful neighbors and existed only in spirit during the nineteenth century. Poles, therefore, were enumerated by U.S. Census-takers according to their partition of origin in Europe. Thus, Poles were classified as Austrians, Russians, or Prussians. Only after 1910 did the Census Bureau begin using language for determining nationality.[14] Because of this confusion, official statistics on the Polish immigration are erroneous. In 1900, the U.S. Census Bureau calculated that a mere 31,103 Poles resided in Wisconsin. An historian of Polish settlement in Wisconsin, on the other hand, has recently estimated this figure to be about 200,000 — thereby making Poles close to the second largest group in the Badger State.[15]

The foreign-born population of Wisconsin in the last decade of the nineteenth century was very high. Indeed, over half the population of the Badger State in 1890 had been born in Europe.[16] Between 1890 and 1900 the foreign-born male population of Racine, Oshkosh, and Superior rose to about 50 percent. Milwaukee, one of the least American cities in the

---

[12] Peter Mlynek file, Zawacki Papers, 6 boxes of unprocessed papers of Professor Edmund Zawacki in Manuscripts Division, State Historical Society of Wisconsin, Madison, Wisconsin, cited hereafter as Zawacki Papers.

[13] Emma Lazarus, "The New Colosus," poem on base of Statue of Liberty, *American Museum of Immigration* (New York, 1973), last page; Joseph Wytrwal, *America's Polish Heritage* (Detroit, 1969), p. 10.

[14] Kuzniewski, Ph.D., p. 87.

[15] *Ibid.*, p. 88; Rev. Constantine Klukowski, O.F.M., "History of St. Mary of the Angels Church, Green Bay, Wisconsin," unabridged manuscript copy in Provincial Archives, Pulaski, Wisconsin, p. 32.

[16] *Rpt. Imig. Com., Sen. Doc.* No. 747, *Abstracts*, Vol. 1, p. 149.

entire nation, had a foreign-born male population of nearly 65 percent.[17] Investigators for the U.S. Immigration Commission, under the leadership of William P. Dillingham, wrote in 1910 that "Milwaukee can scarcely be said to have any native sections, so generally are its citizens either foreign born or of foreign parentage."[18] It is in the context of massive waves of various groups of immigrant settlers that Polish settlement in Wisconsin must be viewed.

The first Pole who settled in Wisconsin, and about whom anything is known, was Count Vincent Dziewanowski. Dziewanowski came from Russian Poland where he had participated in the abortive revolution of 1830. Forced to flee from the repressive judicial system of the Czars, Dziewanowski settled in the Wisconsin lead mining region. After running a smelter, the Count eventually established himself on a farm near Avoca in Grant County. He married an American woman and became an important and wealthy member of the community before his death in the 1880s.[19] Count Dziewanowski represented the second, political wave of Polish immigration. His importance rests with the fact that he was among the earliest settlers of Wisconsin Territory. But, he in no way typifies the wave of individual Poles who began settling in Wisconsin several decades later. For this story we will look at the three largest rural Polish settlements in the state. These are in Portage County, Trempealeau County, and the Pulaski-Sobieski area of Brown, Shawano, and Oconto counties. These three communities will be examined separately, and their similarities and differences pointed out.

The earliest and largest Polish rural settlement in Wisconsin is located in Portage County. In fact, the Portage County settlement is the second oldest Polish rural settlement in the United States. Starting in 1857, the Portage County group — concentrated mainly in the Stevens Point-Polonia area — grew to be one of the leading cultural centers of rural Polish life in Wisconsin.

Portage County is composed largely of sandy soils. The surface of the land is undulating and contains many bluffs and uneven ridges. Vegetation consisted of large forested areas with white pine predominating along the rivers and water courses and hardwoods in the interiors. "Beautiful

[17] *Ibid.*, p. 151.

[18] *Ibid., Sen. Doc.* No. 338, Vol. 1, *Immigrants in Cities,* p. 681.

[19] Margaret L. Allen, "A Polish Pioneer's Story," *Wisconsin Magazine of History,* Vol. VI (June, 1923), 373–385; also see George Lerski, *A Polish Chapter in Jacksonian America: The United States and the Polish Exiles of 1831* (Madison, 1958) for background and other information of Polish political exiles in the ante-bellum United States.

openings of prairie" land extend throughout the whole length of the county.[20]

The city of Stevens Point was, and is, the major town in the county. Its location, on a bend of the Wisconsin River, made it a natural site for locating the town and sawmills which could make use of the fine stands of pine which grew in the region. By the middle of the 1850s, several large lumber companies had established themselves in the Stevens Point area. These included the Wisconsin Lumber Company and the Hugh McGrear Company. Millions of board feet of pine were turned out of these mills.[21]

Along with the lumbermen came the area's first settlers. Securing work at lumber camps supplemented the meager cash incomes which pioneer farms provided. Irish and German farmers came to the area first, but in 1857 Michael von Koziczkowski arrived in the Town of Sharon not far from Stevens Point. Koziczkowski had been a petty noble in Prussian Poland from the province of Danzig. He spoke fluent German as well as Polish, and four other languages. His contact with Germans in Milwaukee, where he lived for about a year after moving to Wisconsin from Chicago, led him to Portage County. He arrived in Stevens Point with $50 and a desire to settle himself and, hopefully, more of his countrymen on the land.[22]

Koziczkowski and his family of nine were the first emissaries from his native district to Wisconsin. Before leaving, the townspeople had gathered to see him off. The well-educated Koziczkowski remained in contact with home through letters, and within a year after arriving in Portage County, three more citizens from his home district with their families made the trip across the Atlantic to obtain farms in Wisconsin. In 1858, Adam Klesmit, John Zynda, and Joseph Platta arrived in the Town of Sharon.[23]

These early Polish settlers, and the ones that followed, purchased farm lands from various agencies. Some preempted government land which they obtained at $1.25 an acre. Others purchased 40, 80, or 120 acres from the Fox and Wisconsin River Improvement Company. Koziczkowski pur-

---

[20] Lewis Publishing Company, *A Standard History of Portage County Wisconsin: An Authentic Narrative of the Past, with Particular Attention to the Era in the Commercial, Industrial, Educational, Civil, and Social Development,* 2 volumes (Chicago and New York, 1919), Vol. 1, pp. 40–41, cited hereafter as *Standard History of Portage County.*

[21] A. G. Ellis, *Handbook of Stevens Point and the Upper Wisconsin: Its Character, Early Settlement, Villages, Population and General Advantages for Settlers* (Stevens Point, 1857), p. 40.

[22] *Standard History of Portage County,* Vol. 1, p. 64; Malcolm Rosholt, *Our County, Our Story: Portage County, Wisconsin* (Stevens Point, Wisconsin, 1959), p. 123.

[23] *Ibid.*; Albert Hart Sanford, "The Polish People of Portage County," Wisconsin State Historical Society *Proceedings* (1907), pp. 259–260.

chased his lands — which grew to about 480 acres at the time of his death in 1882 — from Joseph Osterle, a German immigrant who owned 1,000 acres in the Town of Sharon.[24] Through the medium of correspondence, additional Polish families learned about Wisconsin and continued flowing into the Town of Sharon and soon thereafter into the neighboring Town of Hull. Census figures reflect this growth. In 1870 the population of the Town of Sharon amounted to 948 with all but 50 families being of Polish descent. In 1880 all but 28 families were Polish, and the population had reached 1,640.[25] In 1900 Sharon's population had grown to 2,225, and it remained at that level a decade later.[26]

The neighboring Town of Hull's population statistics also demonstrate the growth of the Polish element. In 1870 less than half of the 108 families residing in Hull were of Polish descent. By the next decade, over two-thirds of the town populace was Polish, and by 1900 Poles dominated the census figures to an even greater extent with the total population reaching about 1,500.[27]

Trying to determine the exact points of origin in Europe of Sharon and Hull's Polish settlers proved to be difficult. Marriage records assisted greatly. Of the 528 marriages that occurred in the Polish communities of Hull and Sharon between 1874 and 1896, over 98 percent reported Prussian or German Poland to be their native homeland. One hundred fifty couples recorded specific towns and provinces in Prussian Poland. In this category, Posen, Danzig, and Pomerania, all in northwestern Poland, were most frequently reported as the provinces of origin. The towns of Kościerzyna, Lipusz, Brusy Chojnickie, Sulęczyn, Lesno (Leszno), and Gowidlińskie Jezioro contributed the overwhelming majority of Poles from Prussia settling in both Hull and Sharon.[28]

Many of the settlers from northwestern Poland belong to a Polish subgroup known as *Kashube*. Kashubes speak a dialect which is Slavic with certain Germanic words and constructions frequently used.[29] Originally

---

[24] Rosholt, *Our County*, pp. 115–116; *Standard History of Portage County*, Vol. 1, pp. 64–65.

[25] Federal Manuscript Census 1870 and 1880, Population Schedule, in Manuscript Division, State Historical Society of Wisconsin, Madison, Wisconsin, cited hereafter as Federal Manuscript Census, schedule, and year.

[26] *Standard History of Portage County*, Vol. 1, pp. 80–81.

[27] Federal Manuscript Census, Population Schedule, 1870–1880.

[28] Portage County Records, Register of Deeds, Registration of Marriages 1844–1896, in Archives of State Historical Society of Wisconsin, Madison, Wisconsin.

[29] Tape-recorded interview: Rev. Joseph Schulist, April 10, 1975; tape-recorded interview: Mrs. Matt Skupniewich, November 27, 1974; all tapes in possession of State Historical Society of Wisconsin, Archives and Manuscripts Division, Madison, Wisconsin.

fishermen and small farmers, the independent Kashubes occupied the lands between the Vistula and Oder Rivers in Poland.[30] Once in the United States, Kashubes settled among other German Poles.

The creation of a Polish community in Portage County, with its own institutional structure, did not arise without difficulties. The single most important institution for Poles was, and is, their church. When the early pioneers from Poland began their settlement of Portage County, they attended church with their Irish and German co-religionists. As in other rural areas of the United States, tension developed between Poles and Germans. The Germans often wanted the Poles to sit in special areas of the church.[31] Considering the wide range of functions that the church and parish played in the lives of European immigrants — it was the center of religious, social, and communal life — it was hardly surprising that the growing Polish element in Portage County desired their own priests and language to be used in church services.[32] St. Martin's Church at Ellis became the center of a long controversy. "Differences in language and customs brought about mounting tension and it became apparent that separate places of worship would bring about a happier situation."[33] With the permission of Bishop John Martin Henni of Milwaukee, Poles established St. Joseph's Church in 1864, one block away from St. Martin's. This did not solve the problem, however.

The three saloons operating across the road, called Poland Corner, refused to close during Sunday. "The unlimited sale of liquor led to brawls, assaults, and petty riots."[34] After five pastors and "bitter intergroup tension," Father Joseph Dabrowski successfully moved St. Joseph's two miles east, to the Town of Polonia, and renamed it Sacred Heart of Jesus in 1872. In 1875, a fire of mysterious origin gutted the Sacred Heart, and Dabrowski and his parishioners built another edifice.

The energetic Dabrowski, born in Russian Poland, in 1842, led the fight to encourage a Polish speaking clergy for immigrant communities, and also

---

[30] Stanislaw Gorzuchowski, "Some Aspects of Rural Poland," in Louise P. Boyd, *Polish Countrysides,* American Geographical Society Special Publication, #20 (N.Y., 1937), p. 91.

[31] Lopata, Ph.D., p. 139; Peter A. Ostafin, "The Polish Peasant in Transition: A Study of Group Integration as a Function of Symbiosis and Common Definitions," unpublished Ph.D., University of Chicago, 1954, p. 74; Thaddeus Radzialowski, "The View from a Polish Ghetto, Some Observations on the First One Hundred Years in Detroit," *Ethnicity,* Vol. 1, No. 2 (July, 1974), 126-127; Benjamin C. Stancyzk, Anthony Rathnaw (eds.) *Poles in Michigan* (Detroit, 1953), p. 37 — all attest to the significant interaction between Poles from the Prussian partition and other German immigrants.

[32] Felician Sisters, *Centennial Memoir* (Polonia, Wisconsin, 1974), n.p.

[33] *Ibid.*

[34] *Ibid.*

figured prominently in the creation of a Polish parochial school system in Portage County. In 1874 Dabrowski helped establish the Felician Sisters — a teaching order — at Sacred Heart parish. Five sisters, under the leadership of Mother Mary Monica Sybliska, came to Polonia.[35]

Driven out of Russia by Czarist opposition, the Felicians quickly organized a parochial school system and an orphanage in Portage County. Polonia became the U.S. headquarters for the Felicians until the middle of the 1880s. For these reasons Reverend Dabrowski became known as the "father of the Polish-American parochial schools."[36]

As the population of Sharon grew, so did the size of the Sacred Heart Church. By 1902 another church had been erected on this site. By all accounts, the new church, standing until 1934, was the largest rural Catholic church in the entire nation.[37] The Felician convent also grew, and the grateful parishioners assisted the sisters in building an immense fence made of small stones which remains an impressive display of masonry skill and represents untold hours of hand labor.[38]

Aside from the church, the basic institution of the Polish community of Portage County was the agricultural unit, or family farm. Settling on "cutover" sandy and rocky soil, the Poles showed themselves to be tireless workers and efficient husbandmen. The many stone fences in the Polonia area reminds observers of the hard work necessary to clear and farm in the region.

The family unit functioned as the basic work force. With large numbers of children and the significant role allowed women, the Polish family utilized hand labor, instead of machinery, to clear the farms and to improve their acreage. In every description of Polish rural life, the role of women figured prominently. Indeed, Polish women often shared in the decision-making process. Women worked in the fields, harvested grain, cut trees, pulled stumps, all in addition to caring for the children and farm animals, keeping house, and cooking. Representatives of Senator William P. Dillingham's Commission charged with investigating the phenomenon of immigration visited Portage County in 1910 and observed:

The European custom of field work by women . . . prevails. Polish women and children may be seen working side by side with the men of the family in the . . . fields every working day of the week.[39]

---

[35] *Ibid.*

[36] Rosholt, *Our Country,* p. 140; *Poles in Michigan.* pp. 32–35.

[37] Rosholt, *Ibid.*

[38] Still standing at Felician Convent, Polonia, Wisconsin.

[39] *Rpt. Imig. Com., Sen. Doc.* No. 633, Vol. 2, *Recent Immigrants in Agriculture,* p. 175.

With the European experience only recently behind them, Portage County's Poles organized their farms to provide economic self-sufficiency. Diversified cropping characterized this Polish rural settlement. A statistical analysis of the Town of Hull and the Town of Sharon farmers was undertaken. Based on the agricultural schedules of the Federal Manuscript Censuses of 1870 and 1880, several features of a Polish farm community — as compared with non-Polish groups in the same area — became clear.

Poles hired few agricultural laborers on their farms. The Polish stem family, as previously explained, provided the muscle to clear, break, and till the sandy, rocky soils of the county.[40] The "typical" Polish farm ranged from 90 to 120 acres. Polish farmers utilized rye to a greater extent than other groups. This grain was found on nearly 90 percent of all Polish farms, with 63 percent of the tillable land sown to rye.[41] The neighboring Irish and Yankee farmers relied on wheat and corn to a higher degree than Poles. Potatoes, however, were the main staple for all groups in the area.[42] Other crops grown by Poles and non-Poles included (in this order) corn (maize), oats, wheat, buckwheat, and barley. In the Town of Sharon the cultivation of hops was a minor, although significant, attempt at experimenting with a cash crop. The important consideration about the Polish grain crop and livestock picture is that it was primarily aimed at providing self-sufficiency.

Livestock included cattle, swine, and chickens but none in large enough numbers to indicate a specialization in any of these forms of husbandry. Another indication of the distinctiveness of the Polish agriculture in both Sharon and Hull is in the horse/ox ratio. Poles utilized oxen more often than their non-Polish neighbors. That animal's cheapness and ease of feeding — as well as its utility for breaking soil and pulling stumps — was appreciated by the Poles. Fifty percent of the non-Poles in the Town of Hull in 1870 and 1880 kept horses, whereas the number was very low for Poles in 1870 and rose to only two out of five a decade later.[43] Even in the more established Polish community of Sharon, the horse/ox ratio among the Poles was significantly different than among the non-Polish element in the same area.

Horses represented considerable investment. "Bad luck with horses and illness," reported Mrs. Matt Skupniewich, spelled the ruin of many immigrant farmers.[44] Another reason Poles did not utilize horses until a later

---

[40] Peter D. Frank, "Agricultural Profile of Hull and Sharon Townships Portage County 1870–1880," p. 2, in possession of Ethnic Heritage Studies Collections of the State Historical Society of Wisconsin (1976), Madison, Wisconsin.

[41] *Ibid.*, p. 5.

[42] *Ibid.*

[43] *Ibid.*, p. 3.

[44] Tape-recorded interview with Mrs. Matt Skupniewich, November 27, 1974.

date rests with the labor system which prevailed on Polish farms. Hand labor provided the bulk of the farmer's needs. As the Dillingham Commission investigators explained:

> . . . whereas Americans and Irish are using horse machinery and keeping more horses, the Polish farmers are still depending on hand labor, notably that of their wives and children, to raise and harvest their crops. . . . The fact remains that the Polish farmer gets out of debt by employing hand labor. . . .[45]

Summing up the differences between Portage County's Polish farmers and their more American neighbors, the Dillingham Commissioners emphasized the Poles' reliance on hand labor:

> The principal differences . . . between the American farmers and the Poles in the same neighborhood lie in the latter's reliance on hard work and the substitution of muscular and family labor for capital and equipment. . . .[46]

The cultivation of the potato as a cash crop became important by the turn of the century. Polish farmers still continued to utilize hand labor to a greater extent than non-Polish groups in the area, however. State agricultural agents assisted in the development of the potato industry by printing literature on new types of fertilizers and insecticides in Polish.[47]

By 1910 the average Polish farmer of Portage County owned 134 acres with the median about 120 acres. Net value of farm units and all property averaged out to be $4,825.[48] By that time, one-third of the entire population of Portage County was Polish and two-thirds of the Poles resided on farms.[49] Even the racially oriented Dillingham Commissioners had to admit that Polish farmers had become highly successful by 1910. In "clearing the land, ditching, draining, and grubbing, he (the Polish farmer) has succeeded as have few others . . . , even north Europeans. . . ."[50]

The market square at Stevens Point was another interesting feature of Polish farm life. As in Europe, Polish farmers brought their products to the central square.[51] There, they bought or exchanged goods and socialized with their neighbors. Taverns abounded in the area as well as other service-oriented facilities.

---

[45] *Rpt. Imig. Com., Sen. Doc.* No. 633, Vol. 2, *Recent Immigrants in Agriculture,* p. 181.
[46] *Ibid.,* p. 192.
[47] *Standard History of Portage County,* Vol. 1, p. 46.
[48] *Rpt. Imig. Com., Sen. Doc.* No. 633, Vol. 2, *Recent Immigrants in Agriculture,* pp. 176–177.
[49] Sanford, "Polish People of Portage County," p. 259.
[50] *Rpt. Imig. Com., Sen. Doc.* No. 633, Vol. 2, *Recent Immigrants in Agriculture,* p. 160.
[51] Tape-recorded interview with Michael Liss, November 29, 1974.

Marriage customs made up another feature in the area's social life. Poles enjoyed big wedding celebrations which often lasted through the night. Bands, dancing, and singing, accompanied by vast quantities of food, were other distinctive attributes of Polish weddings.

Poles also understood marriage to be a serious business which involved other considerations besides romance. The potential husband might be asked by the bride's family to demonstrate his conscientiousness by revealing his bank account to the inlaws-to-be. This custom of showing money to the bride's family is called *dobramaz* in the *Kashube* language.[52] The display of cash was an important consideration because Poles were interested in maintaining debt-free farm units. The transfer of farm property, like the extensive use of hand labor, the maintenance of diversified farms, and the *dobramaz* all added to the securing and continuance of keeping the agricultural unit intact. Usually one of the sons would be given title to the family farms by a "life lease" or a "bill of maintenance." This obligated the new owner, however, to maintain the original owner and his family until death. It also gave the father and mother an important say in any decision affecting the farm. This method of land transfer was a common practice in other Polish rural communities as well.[53] As one rural sociologist explained:

The indigenous culture of the Polish farm people emphasizes security. The family was the security giving institution. In the new environment, the mortgage free owner/operator farm became the means through which the objective security could be obtained.[54]

The growth of the Polish element in Portage County necessitated other ethnic institutions besides the church and the family. An ethnic press, designed to appeal to farmers, also arose. In 1881 Sigmund Hutter, born in 1856 in Suwalki, Russian Poland, established himself in Stevens Point. Hutter began publishing the Polish farm newspaper *Rolnik* (*Farmer*). In 1902 *Rolnik* was taken over by the Worzalla brothers, who continued publishing the journal until the 1960s.[55] Today, the *Gwiazda Polarna* (*North Star*) provides some of the same functions as its predecessor.

Politically, the Polish settlers of Portage County have been allied with the Democratic Party. Even in early periods, it seems that the Democrats

[52] Tape-recorded interview with Mrs. Matt Skupniewich, November 27, 1974.
[53] Harold A. Pedersen, "Acculturation Among Danish and Polish Ethnic Groups in Wisconsin," unpublished Ph.D., University of Wisconsin, 1949, p. 157.
[54] *Ibid.*, p. 176.
[55] *Standard History of Portage County*, Vol. 2, p. 511.

provided a more comfortable atmosphere which attracted and kept the Poles within that Party's ranks. Stories of the Democratic Party's band-wagon — called *Demokrat* — moving through the rural areas near Stevens Point are often heard.[56] In recent years, Poles have become well represented in local political offices and have generally remained faithful to the Democratic Party.

The growth of the Polish community in Portage County demonstrates a steady maturation process. From the early period with its high turnover rates of over 80 percent — as indicated by the survey of the 1870 and 1880 Manuscript Censuses — to the establishment of a more permanent settlement and the development of specialized agricultural production, Polish farmers steadily increased the total value and total output of their holdings.[57] From diversified farming to the specialization in potatoes, the Polish element progressed. The earliest settlement of *Prusaks* (Prussian Poles) and *Kashube* was enlarged by migration of *Galicijaks* (Austrian Poles) who began arriving after the turn of the century.[58] Clique rivalries within the parishes, based upon the regional and linguistic differences in Polish subgroups, disappeared after the First World War as the Polish ethnic group became a more uniform collectivity, not only locally, but nationally as well.[59] The ethnic press; the growing power of the Poles establishing their own parishes complete with their own schools and Polish speaking priests within the Catholic hierarchy; and the rise of a number of national organizations such as the Polish Roman Catholic Union (1880), the Polish National Alliance (1883), the Polish Falcon Society (1887), and the Polish Women's Alliance (1898) helped overcome the regionalism and lack of Polish national awareness which characterized the early period.[60]

The neighboring towns of Independence and Arcadia in Trempealeau County are the site of another Polish rural settlement. The Polish element in Trempealeau County, like those of Portage County, began migrating to the area early in the 1860s. Unlike those of Portage County, these Polish settlers came originally as part of a group movement of two villages in Upper Silesia — Popielow and Siałkowice.[61]

Andrew and Lawrence Bautch, Peter Sura, and their respective families

---

[56] Tape-recorded interviews with Mrs. Matt Skupniewich, Mr. Michael Liss, and Frank Beck, October 3, 1974.

[57] Frank, "Agricultural Profile," p. 5.

[58] Rosholt, *Our County,* p. 129.

[59] Radzialowski, "View from a Polish Ghetto," p. 127; Ostafin, Ph.D., p. 205; Pedersen, Ph.D., pp. 113-114; Lopata, Ph.D., pp. 58-59.

[60] Lopata, Ph.D., p. 125; Sandberg, *Ethnic Identity,* pp. 15-16.

[61] H. Pawlowska to Edmund Zawacki, August 29, 1946, Zawacki Papers, box I.

were among early Silesians to investigate the Trempealeau County area for themselves and their neighbors in Europe.

The men heard of the United States while serving in the Prussian Army. All were afraid that their tours of duty would be increased after the three-year term which they had already served. They departed for the United States in 1853 and arrived in Chicago after first landing in Quebec.[62]

The voyage experience was much like that of other immigrants — long, dangerous, and arduous. After departing from Hamburg their vessel became lost at sea for three days. The voyage lasted for nearly a month.[63] Mrs. Rose Libowski described her family's experience on board the vessel which brought them from Europe:

She remembers a storm at sea which so frightened the passengers that her mother woke all the members of the . . . family during the night, dressed the children and waited for the worst. There was much praying among the men and women that night to their patron . . . , and hymns were sung.[64]

The Bautch brothers and Sura worked in Milwaukee between 1855 and 1857 to obtain cash in order to continue in their search for farmlands. In 1862 the Bautches moved to the Pine Creek area of Trempealeau County after working on a cranberry farm near New Lisbon in Juneau County. They made the trip from Milwaukee to western Wisconsin by oxcart.[65]

Trempealeau County is a nonglaciated area, rolling hills with limestone ridges dominate the region, and early transportation routes centered around the towns along the Mississippi River. County soils are generally good and not sandy. In 1870 Trempealeau City was a major wheat shipping area.[66] The early Silesians obtained homesteads and built sod houses to provide temporary living quarters. Sod houses, called *szopa,* were dug into a hillside and then covered with a straw roof. No floors existed.[67] Log houses were the next step in the home building process, and these often had floors covered with sand.[68]

The decade of the 1870s witnessed the influx of many Silesian families to the Arcadia and Independence region. These Silesians had been primarily

---

[62] Sura file, *Ibid.*

[63] Bautch file, *Ibid.*

[64] Libowski file, *Ibid.*

[65] Sura file, *Ibid.*

[66] *Soil Survey of Trempealeau County Wisconsin,* Bureau of Chemistry and Soils USDA. Series 1927, No. 35; Merle Curti, *The Making of an American Community: A Case Study of Democracy in a Frontier Community* (Stanford, California, 1959), p. 9.

[67] Bautch file, Zawacki Papers.

[68] Lyga file, *Ibid.*

small landowners in Europe, and most belonged to the *halupnicy* class.[69] Although by no means wealthy, Silesians, nevertheless, secured large farm holdings. In 1870 the median land holding for Polish farmers in the area was 150 acres. In comparative terms, the Silesians had some of the highest land holdings in the county, ahead of both their Norwegian and German neighbors.[70]

Like the Portage County Poles, Silesians geared their lives to obtain debt-free farms. They lived a frugal existence in order to save cash. Men sometimes spent the winter in lumber camps near Black River Falls or went on log drives on the Mississippi. "Much was the suffering during the earliest days," reported Michael Lyga whose family settled in Trempealeau County in 1872, "meat was often not eaten for months, sometimes several years except on rare occasions."[71]

Women worked in the fields along with their husbands. As in other rural Polish settlements, women assisted the men. "My mother had been used to working hard on her husband's farm," reported Mrs. Kate Mlynek:

. . . doing the field work side by side with her husband. One of the tasks which she had done for years was to tie by hand the grain that had been cut.[72]

Silesian women hauled grain and other farm products in European style carrying bags called *rozsiewka*. Mrs. Mary U. Skroch observed:

One of the things which these people brought with them in their two Silesian trunks was a *rozsiewka*, a large linen square (two yards square) which was used by the women field workers . . . for carrying large burdens on their backs. Each corner of this square was turned back . . . and over this reinforcement was tied a strong . . . rope, long enough and strong enough for tying the burden over the arms and shoulders as well as chest and waistline. . . . When filled, the woman sat down with her back to it, crossed the corner of the *rozsiewka*, and brought this crisscrossed (rope) forward over her shoulders and chest where she crossed the ropes again and tied them around her waist.[73]

Silesian women also wore European-style dress during the pioneer days in Trempealeau County. Mrs. Eliza Cripps, a Yankee, described the costumes of Silesian women:

Their dress was strange . . . ; the women wore wide heavy skirts closely pleated.

---

[69] *Ibid.*
[70] Curti, *American Community*, pp. 182–183.
[71] Lyga file, Zawacki Papers.
[72] Kate Mlynek file, *Ibid.*
[73] Mary Urban Skroch file, *Ibid.*

Their blouses were made of white linen, with round low necklines, short puff sleeves. Over these they wore a waist length close fitting jacket with a high neckline and long tightly fitted sleeves. The jackets were buttoned down the center front. When the women came inside, they removed these jackets. Their aprons were long and full, tied around the waist and made of white home spun linen. The colors were usually somber in these costumes, either brown or navy.[74]

Trempealeau County was a wheat frontier between 1860 and 1880. When the Silesians arrived they adopted the same farm crops as their non-Polish neighbors.[75] Oats, barley, corn (maize), and buckwheat — in that order — were the next most important grains. Potatoes provided the staple food for all groups in Trempealeau.[76] Rye was a minor crop in Trempealeau. Poles, however, utilized this grain to a greater extent than their non-Silesian neighbors. By glancing at the agricultural schedules in the census, one could almost identify Polish farmers by locating the existence of a rye crop — however small. Rye was a Polish crop in this area by a two-to-one majority.[77]

The chinch bug ended the primacy of wheat in Trempealeau County during the 1880s. Thereafter, diversified cropping became the pattern — with corn becoming the important grain. By the turn of the century, the Silesians began specializing in dairy production.[78] Comparing Polish and non-Polish farmers shows that the Poles more than held their own. Indeed, Poles were the most successful European group in the region in terms of farm value and total production. By 1880 Polish mean holdings nearly equalled those of U.S.-born farmers.[79]

Another indication of the relative success of the Independence-Arcadia Polish community is evidenced by the horse ox ratio. Unlike the Portage County group, oxen were not a highly important farm animal among the Silesians. In comparative terms, Silesians utilized horses to a much greater extent than the German Poles of Portage County. Of the 165 Silesian families living in Independence-Arcadia in 1880, only 30 owned oxen. Norwegians, on the other hand, utilized oxen to a significantly greater extent.[80]

The Silesians enjoyed a reputation for keeping high-quality horses. Even the Dillingham Commissioners, who visited the area in 1910, commented

---

[74] Eliza Cripps file, *Ibid.*
[75] Zuzanna Kulig file, *Ibid.*
[76] Survey of 1870 and 1880, Federal Manuscript Census, Agricultural Schedules, Trempealeau County.
[77] *Ibid.*
[78] *Rpt. Imig. Com., Sen. Doc.* No. 633, Vol. 2, *Recent Immigrants in Agriculture,* p. 219.
[79] Curti, *American Community,* pp. 172, 186, 190–192, 202.
[80] 1880 Federal Manuscript Census, Agricultural Schedule, Trempealeau County.

about the "good horses" of the Silesian farmers.[81] This fact is yet another indication of the relative prosperity of the Polish community in Arcadia and Independence.

Between 1860 and 1870 the turnover rate of Polish farmers was high. Nearly 85 percent left the area between these census decades. But, the large increase in the population between 1870 and 1880 made up for initial population instability. By 1875 the Polish community was large enough and stable enough to create their own parish. St. Peter's and St. Paul's Church in Independence was completed in the middle of the 1870s and enlarged 20 years later.[82]

Marriage made up an important part of the Polish community life. As in Portage County, weddings were festive occasions involving large numbers of people. Mrs. Frances Bautch described a wedding party:

> Friends and neighbors . . . baked, cooked, several days before the wedding. At the feast, there were homemade sausages, roast beef and pork, cabbage, potatoes, dill pickles, coffee cake (*holoce*) and bread baked in the outside ovens (*wieloki*). There was much singing by the cooks as they baked . . . ; songs which were reminiscent of other weddings or told of events to come. There was also singing during the serving of food and drinks.[83]

As in Europe, marriages were often arranged and involved negotiations between the families.[84] Again, material considerations were an important feature of any prospective marriage. The stabilizing function of the family farm unit, as in other Polish rural settlements, also operated in Trempealeau County.

The life lease, or *wysyp*, had a stabilizing influence on Trempealeau's Silesian farmers. The desirability of keeping the family farm unit intact helped the Silesian pioneers to maintain their land holdings through succeeding generations. In addition, the *wysyp* provided a pension for the older generation and had a conservative influence since the father and/or mother had an important say in any decision affecting the farm unit through their control of the mortgage. The *wysyp*, in effect, was a "pension mortgage."[85]

The Silesians of Trempealeau County were joined, in later years, by

---

[81] *Rpt. Imig. Com., Sen. Doc.* No. 633, Vol. 2, *Recent Immigrants in Agriculture,* p. 217.

[82] *Pamietnik Zlotego Jubileuszu Parafji S. S. Piotra: Pawlaw Independence, Wisconsin 1875–1925,* in Zawacki Papers.

[83] Bautch file, *Ibid.*

[84] Grutzik file, *Ibid.*

[85] "Brief Description and Impression of Independence, Wisconsin," *Ibid.*; Pedersen, Ph.D., pp. 170–172.

other Polish settlers. Regional and subgroup differences between Poles from different areas in Europe were often commented about. Dialect and linguistic variations between Silesians and other Poles from the German partition were only one of these differences. Christmas customs and the Silesians' non-interest in formal education were other distinctions.[86] Relations with priests were apparently different, as well. Peter Mlynek, a Silesian, observed:

The *Slonzaki* (Silesians) are known for being good to their priests and obeying the priests. What a priest says, goes with them. They do not believe in causing trouble, objecting, forcing their will upon the priest. They are not like the *Poznioniaki* (Poles from Posen Province in Germany) who insist upon having their way with the priest.[87]

Social interaction between Poles and non-Poles was confined to community dances. "There wasn't much mixing between the Poles," observed Mrs. Frances Bautch. "Catholic parents made great efforts to keep their children away from non-Catholics."[88] Even at these social functions, there was a certain amount of tension which led eventually, however, to accommodation between groups:

In the early days, the chief community recreation was the dance. Circle dances such as the *polka, mazur, krakowak* were danced. When the Yankees intercepted these dances or took part in them to the dissatisfaction of the Poles, fighting and arguments often took place. After a while, through mutual agreement, it was decided to have so many Polish dances, and so many quadrilles. The Poles danced the quadrilles — learning them from the Yankees. Many Poles brought with them German folk dances which called for clapping of hands and stamping of feet to the rhythm of a German folk song.[89]

Another example of intergroup rivalry was described by Mrs. Rose Libowski. She commented about an experience that her father, Peter Tomala, had while working as an agricultural laborer on a farm belonging to a German:

It was just before Thanksgiving and the Pole worked with all that there was in him. He became thirsty but hesitated to ask for a drink. The farmer was a German; he was a Pole. It wouldn't do for Peter Tomala to give the German an opportunity to think that the immigrant was shirking for even a short while.[90]

---

[86] Szczepanski file, Zawacki Papers; Jaszewski file, *Ibid.*
[87] Mlynek file, *Ibid.*
[88] Bautch file, *Ibid.*
[89] Lyga file, *Ibid.*
[90] Libowski file, *Ibid.*

As in Portage County the Silesians of Arcadia and Independence witnessed the steady maturation of their communities. The wheat economy of the frontier period passed into a more enduring stage of diversified agriculture and eventually specialized dairy production. Because of the function of the *wysyp*, the Silesians' agricultural units remained large and stable. As the community matured, the differences and subgroup variations among the Poles from one region and another became less important.

Another Polish settlement arose in the Pulaski-Sobieski area of Brown, Oconto, and Shawano counties. These communities — Pulaski, Sobieski, Krakow, and Hofa Park — represent yet another type of settlement pattern. Unlike either the Portage County group, which emigrated in an informal fashion, or the Silesians of Trempealeau County, who had sent emissaries from Popielow and Siałkowice to "scout" for farmlands in America, the Pulaski-Sobieski group arose as the result of a highly organized effort on the part of an energetic churchman and an enterprising land company agent.

There is an old Polish proverb which says that if one would build a bridge across the ocean and place a loaf of bread on the far side, no Pole would cross. If, on the other hand, one would build a church on the other side of the bridge, then Poles would rush over.[91] However true this saying is, the experience of the Pulaski-Sobieski settlement does demonstrate that a relationship exists between a strong religious and parish organization and the attractiveness of a community to Polish farmers.

The lands upon which this Polish settlement grew were partially cutover. Devoid of pine, many hardwoods and cedars still remained after an initial exploitation by the Milwaukee Lumber Company. Sandy soils and swampy areas predominated in a glaciated region.[92]

Over 160,000 acres in the tri-county area had been in the possession of the General Land Office of Milwaukee. Members of the company then organized the Northern Colonization Society and attempted to locate Norwegian immigrants upon their lands. The company employed John J. Hof as one of its agents.[93]

---

[91] Tape-recorded interview with Rev. Constantine Klukowski, O.F.M., April 30, 1975, Tape No. 1, in possession of State Historical Society of Wisconsin in Ethnic Heritage Collection.

[92] Land descriptions appear on the numerous plat maps which are contained in the J. J. Hof Land Company Records, five reels of microfilm obtained from the Provincial Archives at Pulaski, Wisconsin; also see Cyril Piontek, O.F.M. manuscript "History of Krakow" in Provincial Archives, Pulaski, Wisconsin, pp. 2–4, cited hereafter as Provincial Archives.

[93] Rev. Constantine Klukowski. O.F.M., *Diamond Jubilee, St. Stanislaus Church, Hofa Park, Wisconsin* (Pulaski, Wisconsin, 1958). p. 14.

Hof was born John J. Hofhaug in Domaas, Norway, in 1842.[94] In 1875 Hof began working for the General Land Office which William, John, and Ephriam Mariner headed. Unable to attract Norwegians, the company then turned to the Poles.

In 1877 Valentine Peplinski, Valentine Zygmanski, Michael and Frank Lepak moved to the area from Milwaukee. All came originally from the German Partition — specifically from the provinces of Poznan and West Prussia.[95] All had been engaged in industrial pursuits in Milwaukee.

These were merely the first. By 1880 the Polish settlers had grown numerous enough to desire their own church. Previous to this time, Polish Catholics had attended church with their German co-religionists in the Town of Seymour. In 1883 the Poles erected a small log chapel which served the community until 1885.[96]

Hof, meanwhile, had opened his own land company in Sobieski. Although Hof's name appeared on the land company's title, the principal stockholders remained the Mariner brothers of Milwaukee.[97] In 1886 Hof donated a 120-acre parcel of land and nearly $400 for the construction of a Franciscan Monastery at Pulaski.[98]

Brother Augustine Zeytz assisted Hof in organizing and starting the Franciscan Monastery at Pulaski. Born in the Lithuanian region of Russian Poland, Zeytz fled to the United States to escape Czarist oppression. The Franciscan order had run into difficulties with the Czar between 1864 and 1873. Zeytz came to Wisconsin in 1886 after spending some time in Pennsylvania and, in cooperation with Hof, helped establish the Franciscans at Pulaski. In 1888 the Novitiate of the Assumption began operating on the lands donated by the J. J. Hof Land Company.

After the establishment of the Franciscans, Hof turned to advertising his "Polish colonies," as he called them, in the ethnic presses of virtually every city in the country which had a sizeable Polish element. Hof went to great length to extol the land's fertility, easy accessibility, good marketing loca-

---

[94] Mathias J. Hofhaug to Serumgard, June 20, 1910; J. J. Hof Land Company, Special Correspondence, reel 2, Provincial Archives.

[95] Piontek manuscript, "History of Krakow," pp. 2–4; Advertising Circular, J. J. Hof Land Company, 1891, (trans.) Rev. Fulgence Masiak, Provincial Archives; Klukowski, *Hofa Park*, p. 37.

[96] Piontek manuscript, "History of Krakow," pp. 2–4, Provincial Archives.

[97] J. J. Hof Land Company Records, Stock Certificates, reel 2, Provincial Archives.

[98] Piontek manuscript, "History of Krakow," p. 1; Rev. Leo Adasiewicz manuscript, "History of the Assumption Province," Provincial Archives, Pulaski, Wisconsin, p. 1; Rev. Fulgence Masiak manuscript, "History of the Province," Provincial Archives, pp. 2–3; J. J. Hof to F. W. Katzer, November 11, 1886, J. J. Hof Land Company Correspondence, reel No. 3, Provincial Archives.

tion, and the existence of trees for lumber. Another of his main selling points was the presence of the Polish Franciscans which assured potential settlers that their religious needs would be serviced during the pioneer era in rural Wisconsin.[99]

Hof's extensive advertising campaign took several forms. In addition to the advertisements in the Polish-language press of major industrial centers, Hof sent calendars and brochures and maps which depicted the Franciscan Monastery and scenes of farm life to individuals who wrote asking for additional information. In return, querists were asked to send J. J. Hof advertising circulars to their neighbors and friends. Postage was provided by Hof. Hof sent lists which contained the names of Polish settlers already owning farms in his colonies to thousands of individuals in an attempt to reassure them of the area's Polishness. Hof's yearly advertising costs ran between $1,100 and $3,000 throughout the period 1887 to 1895.[100]

In addition to extolling his colonies' fertility and the existence of the Franciscans, Hof's literature explained how an interested party could secure a farm unit of 40 or 80 acres for $10 to $15 an acre. Information as to crops, equipment, and the complete range of J. J. Hof's service — such as his home building service, his sawmill, and his field plowing service — were also advertised. Down payments of $50 or $100 would begin the settlement process. Or, for $25, an interested party could obtain an option to buy a farm.[101] The Hof Land Company advertising campaign proved to be successful. Poles from many areas in the United States came to the Hof colonies. Very few came directly from Europe; rather, they relocated to rural Wisconsin from industrial centers within the United States. Because of this fact, the Hof colonies have a mixture of Polish subgroups. Galician and Russian Poles are well represented in the area, even though the majority of rural land seekers came from the German Partition. Many Lithuanians also settled in the area.[102]

Poles from Chicago, Milwaukee, Buffalo, Detroit, various mining and industrial centers in Pennsylvania, Cleveland, and even Greeley, Colorado, and San Francisco, California, relocated themselves in Hof's colonies.[103] As the Dillingham Commissioners who visited Pulaski explained, there was:

---

[99] J. J. Hof, "Our Experience in Hofa Park and Pulaski, Wisconsin," Rev. Fulgence Masiak (trans.), Provincial Archives; "Hofa Park, Krakow and Poland," Masiak (trans.), *Ibid.*

[100] J. J. Hof Land Company, Land Ledger, Vol. II, reel 1, Provincial Archives.

[101] *Ibid.*, Land Ledger, Vol. 1, reel 1, Provincial Archives.

[102] "Hofa Park, Pulaski, Krakow, and Poland," Advertising Circular, J. J. Hof Land Company, 1891, Rev. Fulgence Masiak (trans.) Provincial Archives.

[103] *Gazeta Katolica*, April 10, 1891, J. J. Hof Land Company, Advertisement List, Rev. Fulgence Masiak (trans.), Provincial Archives, Pulaski, Wisconsin.

. . . no immigration of Poles directly to these localities from Europe, the settlement being composed almost exclusively of persons who had been employed as industrial laborers in various parts of the United States before entering agriculture.[104]

Hof also worked in improving the accessibility of his Polish colonies. In 1894 Hof convinced the operators of the Chicago, Milwaukee, St. Paul Railroad Company to have their trains stop at Sobieski. This facilitated the movement of settlers who up to this point had to walk or ride by horse to the area from Green Bay. In 1906 the Chicago and Northwestern Railroad Company also began stopping at Pulaski.[105]

Between 1877 and 1905 the population of Hof's "Polish colonies" grew from four families to 650.[106] Poles owned nearly 60,000 acres of farmlands.[107] Hay, oats, wheat, barley, and corn (maize) (in that order) were the main crops.[108] Rye remained, as in Portage and Trempealeau counties, a distinctively Polish crop.

The sugar beet was another crop grown in the Pulaski-Sobieski area. That cultigen's distinction of being a "Russian" crop surely came from its prominence in Russian Poland. The settlement of numbers of Poles from the Russian Partition in Hof's colonies perhaps accounts for the presence, however minor, of the sugar beet.

Although it is not possible to find the exact statistics, features of the early Polish agricultural setup of Hof's colonies are well remembered by local informants and historians of the region. In the beginning of the period, Poles, as in Portage County, utilized oxen to a greater extent than the more expensive horses.[109] Again, the oxen's ease of feeding and utility in the initial breaking of the soil and stump pulling made them attractive for farmers without the economic means of acquiring farm machinery. Only after Polish farmers established themselves, had control of their lands, and had paid off some of their debts to Hof could they then become more ven-

---

[104] *Rpt. Imig. Com., Sen. Doc.* No. 633, Vol. 2, *Recent Immigrants in Agriculture,* p. 347. John Gallienski, a Green Bay businessman and well-respected member of the Polish community of that city — he was often called "The Polish King of Green Bay" — probably was employed by various steamship companies in advertising Wisconsin to Polish emigrants. Gallienski also knew J. J. Hof, as Hof often stayed in Green Bay, and might also have helped in the advertising campaign for Hof's Polish colonies. See Klukowski, "St. Mary of the Angels Church, Green Bay, Wisconsin," unabridged typed manuscript, Provincial Archives.

[105] Klukowski, *Hofa Park,* p. 16.

[106] 1905 Wisconsin State Census, agricultural statistics (Madison, 1905).

[107] *Ibid.*

[108] *Ibid.*

[109] Klukowski, conversation, July 7, 1975 — notes on file, Ethnic History Collection of Old World Wisconsin, State Historical Society of Wisconsin, Madison, Wisconsin.

turesome with their agricultural establishment and invest in horses and expensive equipment.

Marriage and land transfer methods in Hof's colonies were similar to those in both Trempealeau and Portage counties. Polish farmers primarily concerned themselves with passing on their agricultural establishments intact with provisions for the care of the older generation built into the terms of the transfer. Whether this method of land transfer was called a pension mortgage, bill of maintenance, *wysyp*, life lease, or as in the Pulaski area, successorship (*nastepstwo*) the intent and results were the same.[110] Indeed, land transfer methods are one of the most distinctive features of farm life in a Polish rural community. Stability and conservatism are among the aims, and the European experience of steadily shrinking farm units probably accounts for the motivation behind this type of behavior.

In summation, there does seem to be a Polish farm type. Polish farmers first of all utilized muscular and hand labor to a large extent. The structure and size of a family unit, along with the important role of women, contributed to the functioning of a disciplined work force necessary to turn cutover areas, or prairies, into prosperous farms. The desire for land, perhaps the European carry-over, also played an important role. Whether a Pole came originally from Silesia, Poznan, or Chicago, he brought with him a desire to obtain a self-sufficient rural unit which could be passed on to succeeding generations debt free.

Poles seemed to have utilized rye to a larger extent than other groups. That grain's ability to flourish on sandy and poor soils is a partial explanation of its prominence in Polish communities. Rye was used to make bread and in various soups as well. It can be used as a fertilizer, or "green manure." It had also been an important crop in Poland. The rye straw was used as a roofing material on sheds and even barns during early settlement days.

In all Polish rural settlements, the church played a major role. Indeed, that religious institution was the focus of much of the social, educational, and community life in an area. Poles quickly organized their own parishes and shortly had priests of their own nationality ministering to the congregation in their native language. This achievement, it must be noted, took place within a hierarchy dominated by Irish and German prelates who, at the time, desired to "Americanize" the Poles by attempting to encourage the use of English.

Another interesting, although conjectural, feature related to church

---

[110] *Ibid.*

affairs is the impression that many of the priests who came to rural Wisconsin emigrated from either the Russian or Austrian sectors of Poland. Perhaps the first step in the awakening of Polish national consciousness in Wisconsin came through the efforts of these early churchmen, who found themselves among flocks of German Poles.

# ACKNOWLEDGMENTS

Robert L. Brandfon, "The End of Immigration to the Cotton Fields," *The Mississippi Valley Historical Review*, 50:4 (March 1964), 591–611. Reprinted with the permission of the *Mississippi Valley Historical Review*. Courtesy of Yale University Library.

Sucheng Chan, "Chinese Livelihood in Rural California: The Impact of Economic Change, 1860–1880," *Pacific Historical Review*, 53:3 (August 1984), 273–307. Reprinted with the permission of the *Pacific Historical Review*. Courtesy of Yale University Library.

Robert Higgs, "Landless by Law: Japanese Immigrants in California Agriculture to 1941," *Journal of Economic History*, 38:1 (March 1978), 205–225. Reprinted with the permission of the *Journal of Economic History*. Courtesy of Yale University Library.

John C. Hudson, "Migration to an American Frontier," *Annals of the Association of American Geographers*, 66 (1976), 242–265. Reprinted with the permission of the Association of American Geographers. Courtesy of the Library of Congress.

Terry G. Jordan, "A Century and a Half of Ethnic Change in Texas, 1836–1986," *Southwestern Historical Quarterly*, 89:4 (April 1986), 385–422. Reprinted with the permission of the *Southerstern Historical Quarterly*. Courtesy of Yale University.

Ann M. Legreid and David Ward, "Religious Schism and the Development of Rural Immigrant Communities: Norwegian Lutherans in Western Wisconsin, 1880–1905," *Upper Midwest History*, 2 (1982), 13–29. Reprinted with the permission of *Upper Midwest History*. Courtesy of *Upper Midwest History*.

Frederick C. Luebke, "Ethnic Group Settlement on the Great Plains," *Western Historical Quarterly*, 8:4 (October 1977), 405–430. Reprinted with the permission of the *Western Historical Quarterly*. Courtesy of Yale University Library.

Murray W. Nicolson, "The Irish Experience in Ontario: Rural or Urban?" *Urban History Review*, 14 (June 1985), 37–45. Courtesy of the New York Public Library.

Robert C. Ostergren, "European Settlement and Ethnicity Patterns on the Agricultural Frontiers of South Dakota," *South Dakota History*, 13:1 & 2 (Spring/Summer 1983), 49–82. Reprinted with the permission of *South Dakota History*. Courtesy of George E. Pozzetta.

Robert C. Ostergren, "Land and Family in Rural Immigrant Communities," *Annals of the Association of American Geographers*, 71:3 (September 1981), 400–411. Reprinted with the permission of the Association of American Geographers. Courtesy of Yale University Library.

George E. Pozzetta, "Foreigners in Florida: A Study of Immigration Promotion, 1865–1910," *Florida Historical Quarterly*, LIII, no. 2 (October 1974), 164–180. Reprinted with the permission of *Florida Historical Quarterly*. Courtesy of Yale University Library.

John G. Rice, "The Role of Culture and Community in Frontier Prairie Farming," *Journal of Historical Geography*, 3:2 (1977), 155–175. Reprinted with the permission of the *Journal of Historical Geography*. Courtesy of Yale University Library.

Theodore Saloutos, "The Immigrant Contribution to American Agriculture," *Agricultural History*, 50:1 (January 1976), 45–67. Reprinted with the permission of *Agricultural History*. Courtesy of Yale University Library.

Theodore Saloutos, "The Immigrant in Pacific Coast Agriculture, 1880–1940," *Agricultural History*, 49:1 (January 1975), 182–201. Reprinted with the permission of *Agricultural History*. Courtesy of Yale University Library.

Jean Ann Scarpaci, "Immigrants in the New South: Italians in Louisiana's Sugar Parishes, 1880–1910," *Labor History*, 16:2 (Spring 1975), 165–183. Reprinted with the permission of *Labor History*. Courtesy of Yale University Library.

Robert P. Swierenga, "Ethnicity and American Agriculture," *Ohio History*, 89:3 (Summer 1980), 323–344. Reprinted with the permission of *Ohio History*. Courtesy of Georte E. Pozzetta.

Richard H. Zeitlin, "White Eagles in the North Woods: Polish Immigration to Rural Wisconsin 1857–1900," *Polish Review*, 25:1 (1980) 69–92. Reprinted with the permission of *Polish Review*. Courtesy of George E. Pozzetta.